THE ∞ INFINITY CRUSADE

THE ∞ INFINITY CRUSADE

Writer: Jim Starlin
Pencilers: Ron Lim, Tom Raney, Angel Medina and Tom Grindberg
Inkers: Al Milgrom, Keith Williams and Bob Almond
Colorists: Ian Laughlin, Gina Going and Reneé Witterstaetter
Letterer: Jack Morelli
Editors: Craig Anderson & Terry Kavanagh

Cover Art: Ron Lim
Front Cover Colors: Tom Smith
Back Cover Colors: Jerron Quality Color

Collection Editor: Mark D. Beazley
Assistant Editors: John Denning & Cory Levine
Editor, Special Projects: Jennifer Grünwald
Senior Editor, Special Projects: Jeff Youngquist
Senior Vice President of Sales: David Gabriel
Production: Jerron Quality Color
Research: Stuart Vandal

Editor in Chief: Joe Quesada
Publisher: Dan Buckley

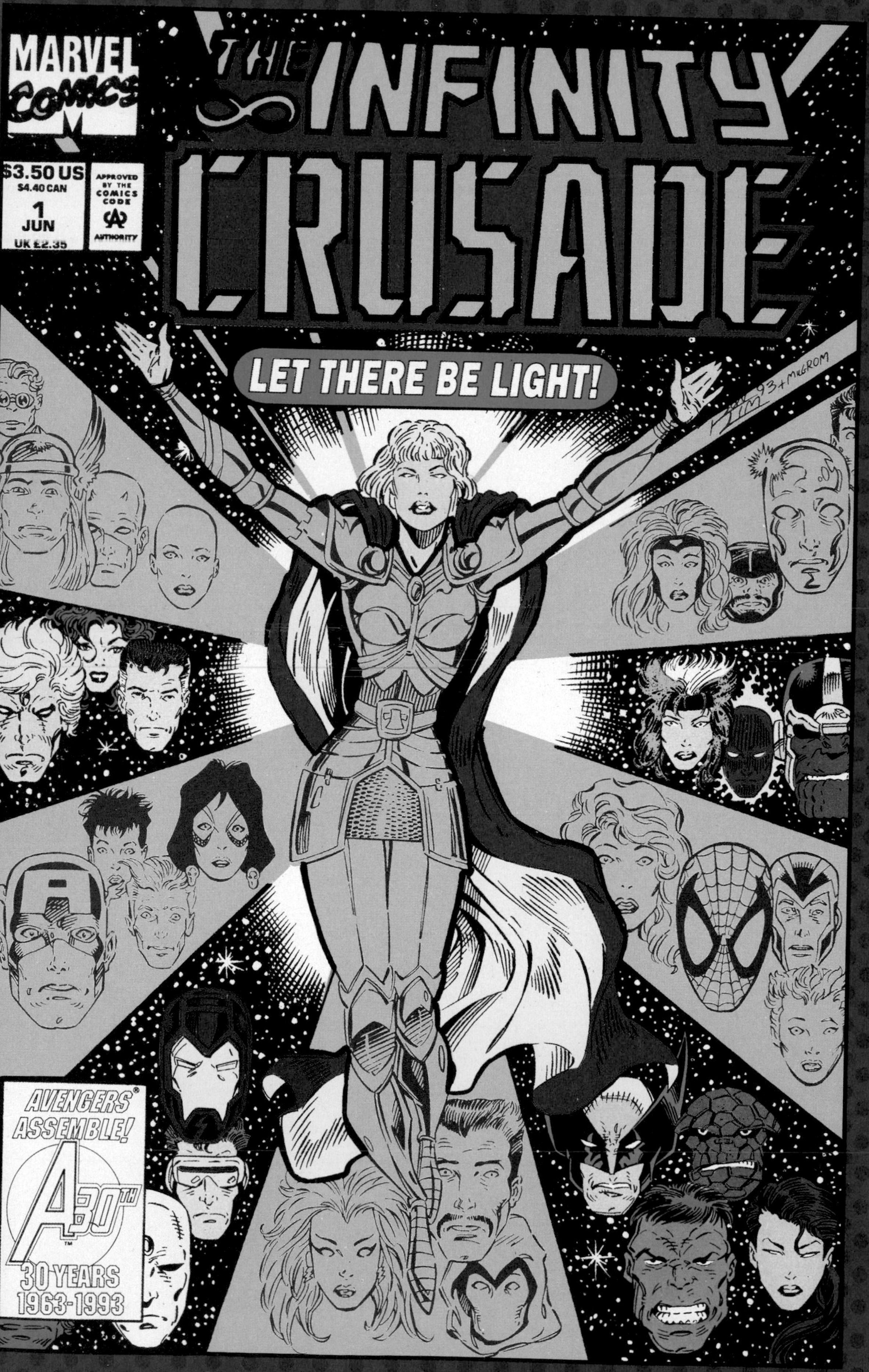
MARVEL COMICS
THE INFINITY CRUSADE
$3.50 US
$4.40 CAN
1
JUN
UK £2.35
APPROVED BY THE COMICS CODE AUTHORITY
LET THERE BE LIGHT!
AVENGERS ASSEMBLE!
30TH
30 YEARS
1963-1993

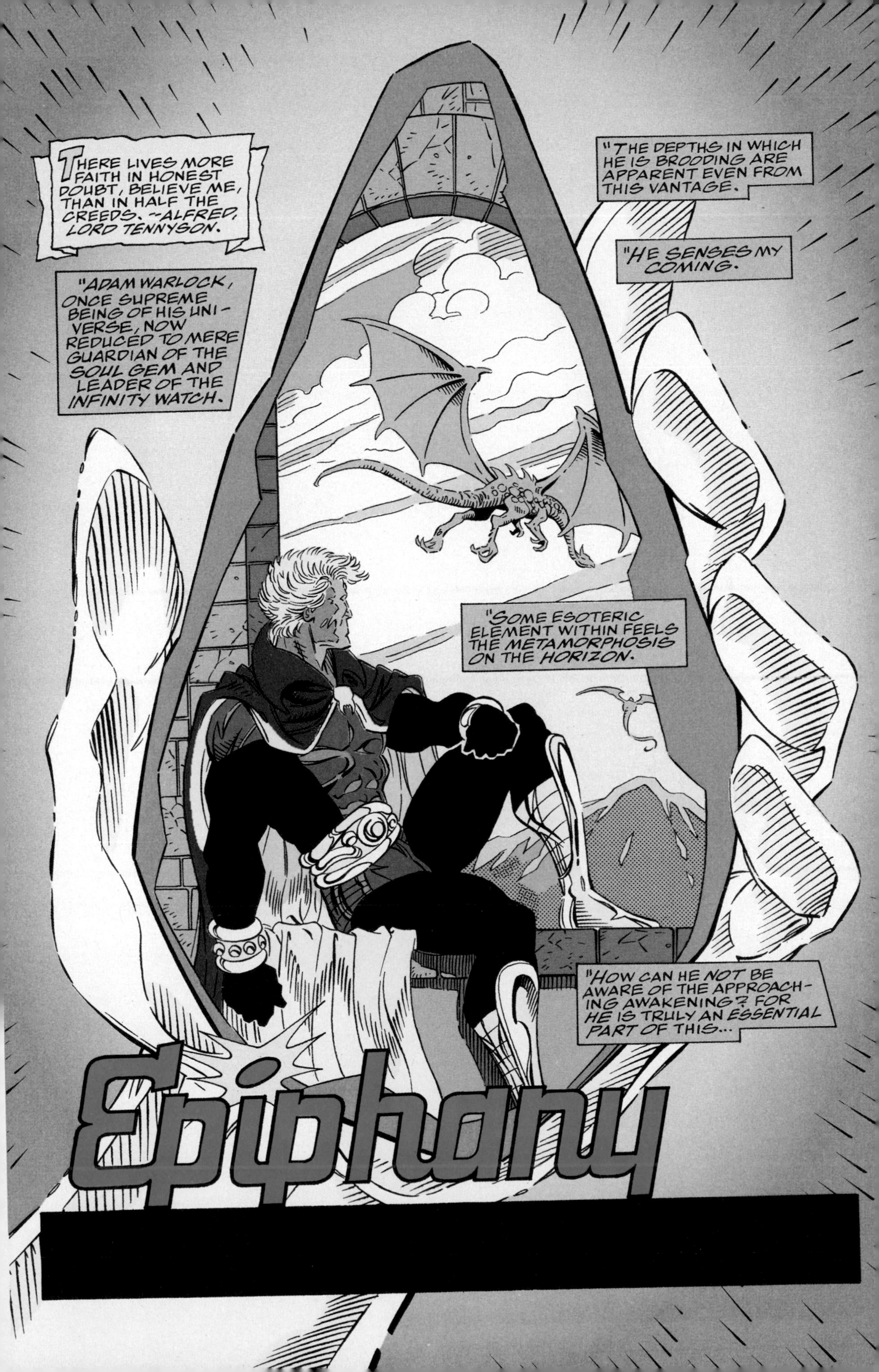
THERE LIVES MORE FAITH IN HONEST DOUBT, BELIEVE ME, THAN IN HALF THE CREEDS. --ALFRED, LORD TENNYSON.
"ADAM WARLOCK, ONCE SUPREME BEING OF HIS UNI-VERSE, NOW REDUCED TO MERE GUARDIAN OF THE SOUL GEM AND LEADER OF THE INFINITY WATCH.
"THE DEPTHS IN WHICH HE IS BROODING ARE APPARENT EVEN FROM THIS VANTAGE.
"HE SENSES MY COMING.
"SOME ESOTERIC ELEMENT WITHIN FEELS THE METAMORPHOSIS ON THE HORIZON.
"HOW CAN HE NOT BE AWARE OF THE APPROACH-ING AWAKENING? FOR HE IS TRULY AN ESSENTIAL PART OF THIS...
Epiphany
[redacted]

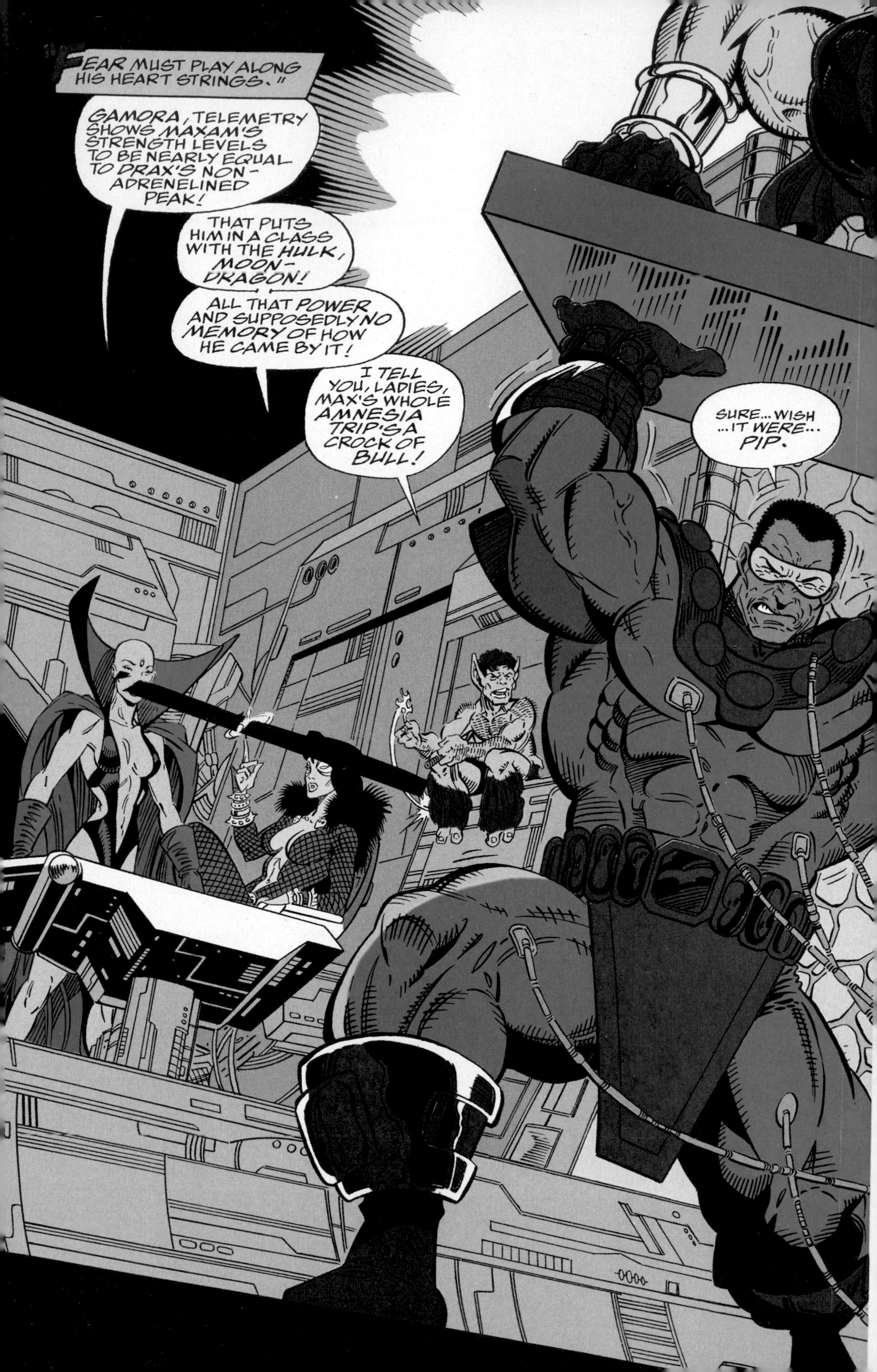
"FEAR MUST PLAY ALONG HIS HEART STRINGS."
GAMORA, TELEMETRY SHOWS MAXAM'S STRENGTH LEVELS TO BE NEARLY EQUAL TO DRAX'S NON-ADRENELINED PEAK!
THAT PUTS HIM IN A CLASS WITH THE HULK, MOON-DRAGON!
ALL THAT POWER AND SUPPOSEDLY NO MEMORY OF HOW HE CAME BY IT!
I TELL YOU, LADIES, MAX'S WHOLE AMNESIA TRIP'S A CROCK OF BULL!
SURE... WISH ...IT WERE... PIP.

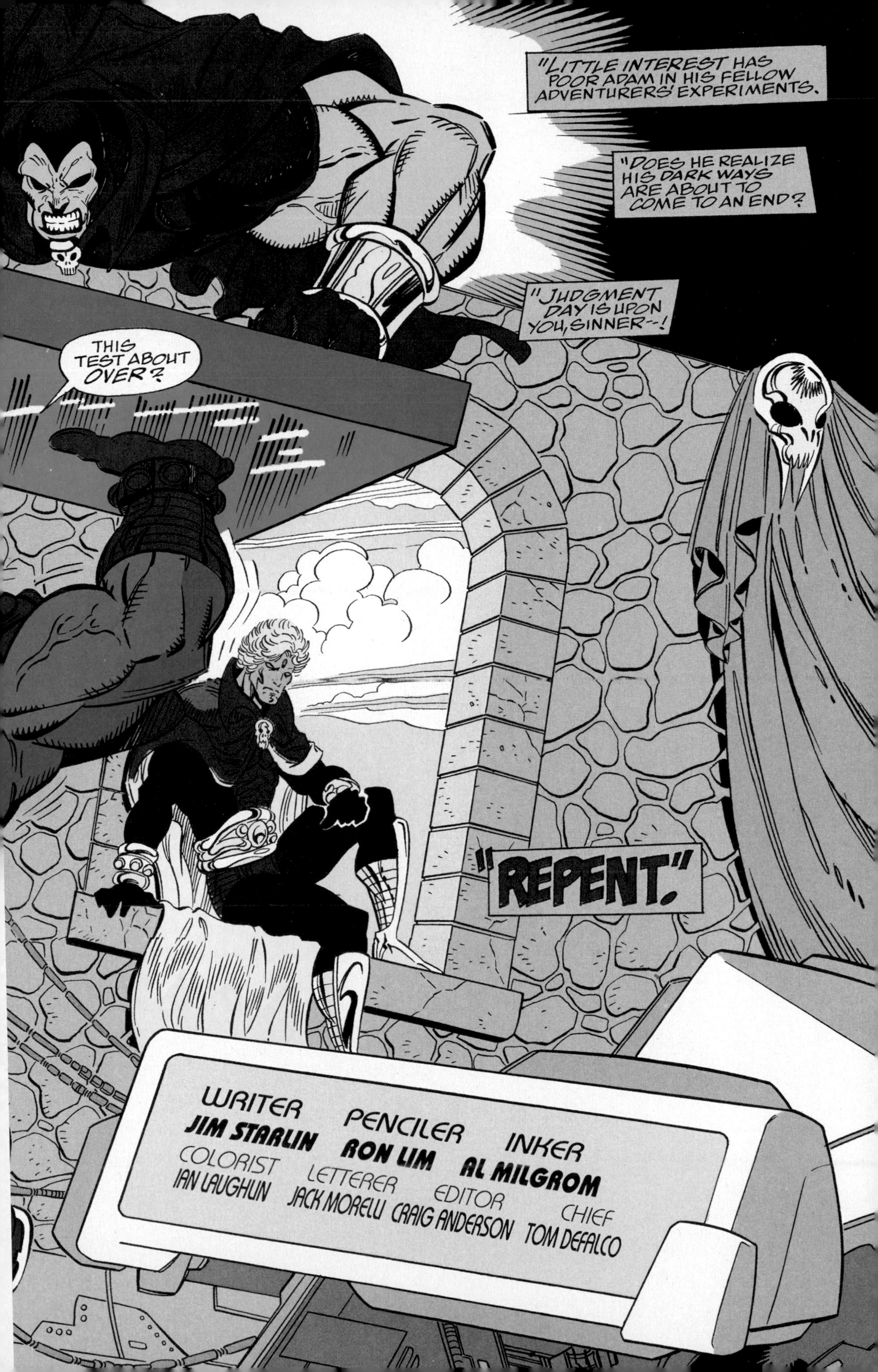
"LITTLE INTEREST HAS POOR ADAM IN HIS FELLOW ADVENTURERS' EXPERIMENTS.
"DOES HE REALIZE HIS DARK WAYS ARE ABOUT TO COME TO AN END?
"JUDGMENT DAY IS UPON YOU, SINNER--!
THIS TEST ABOUT OVER?
"REPENT."
WRITER JIM STARLIN
PENCILER RON LIM
INKER AL MILGROM
COLORIST IAN LAUGHLIN
LETTERER JACK MORELLI
EDITOR CRAIG ANDERSON
CHIEF TOM DEFALCO

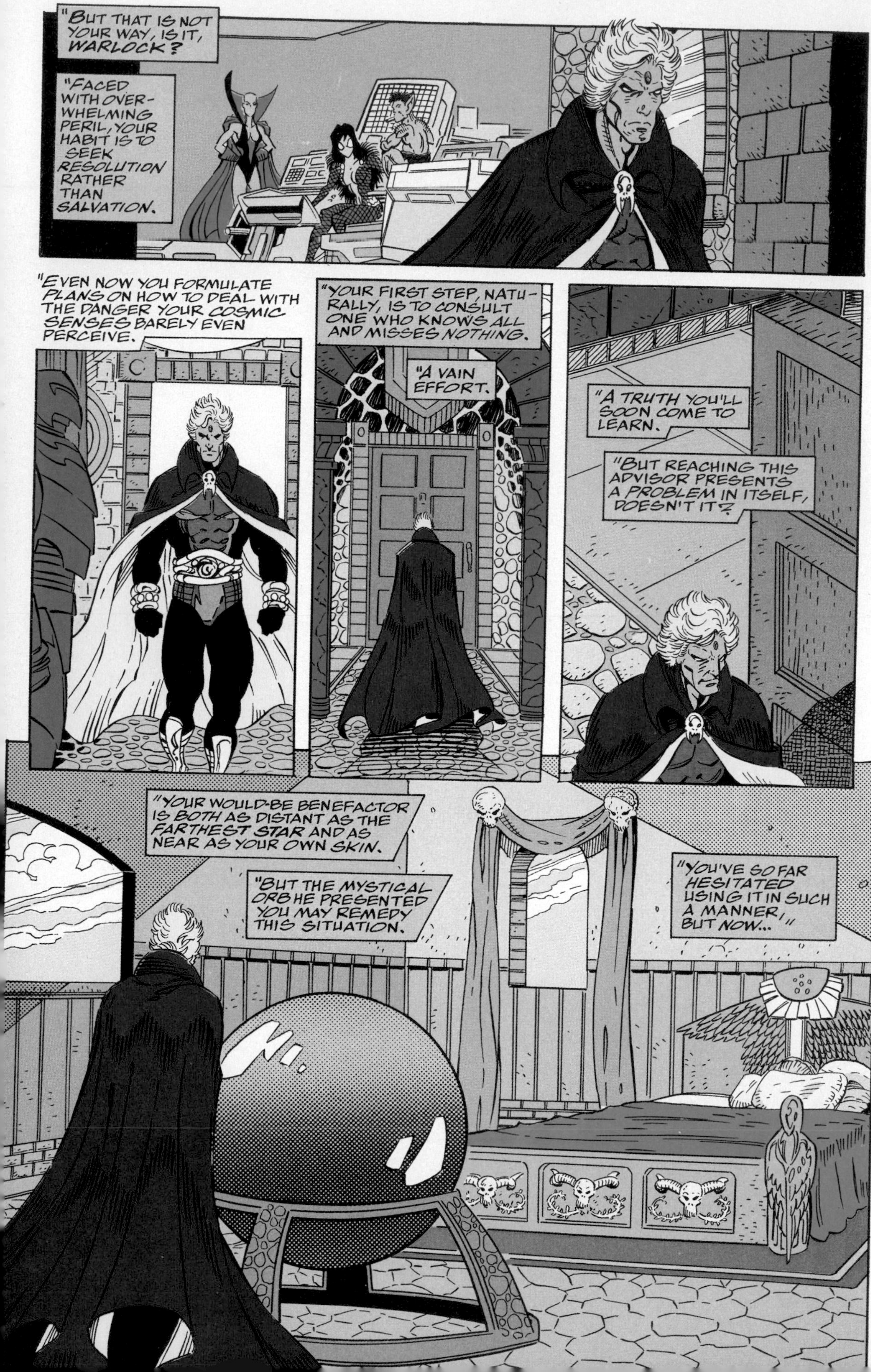
"BUT THAT IS NOT YOUR WAY, IS IT, WARLOCK?
"FACED WITH OVER-WHELMING PERIL, YOUR HABIT IS TO SEEK RESOLUTION RATHER THAN SALVATION.
"EVEN NOW YOU FORMULATE PLANS ON HOW TO DEAL WITH THE DANGER YOUR COSMIC SENSES BARELY EVEN PERCEIVE.
"YOUR FIRST STEP, NATU-RALLY, IS TO CONSULT ONE WHO KNOWS ALL AND MISSES NOTHING.
"A VAIN EFFORT.
"A TRUTH YOU'LL SOON COME TO LEARN.
"BUT REACHING THIS ADVISOR PRESENTS A PROBLEM IN ITSELF, DOESN'T IT?
"YOUR WOULD-BE BENEFACTOR IS BOTH AS DISTANT AS THE FARTHEST STAR AND AS NEAR AS YOUR OWN SKIN.
"BUT THE MYSTICAL ORB HE PRESENTED YOU MAY REMEDY THIS SITUATION.
"YOU'VE SO FAR HESITATED USING IT IN SUCH A MANNER, BUT NOW..."

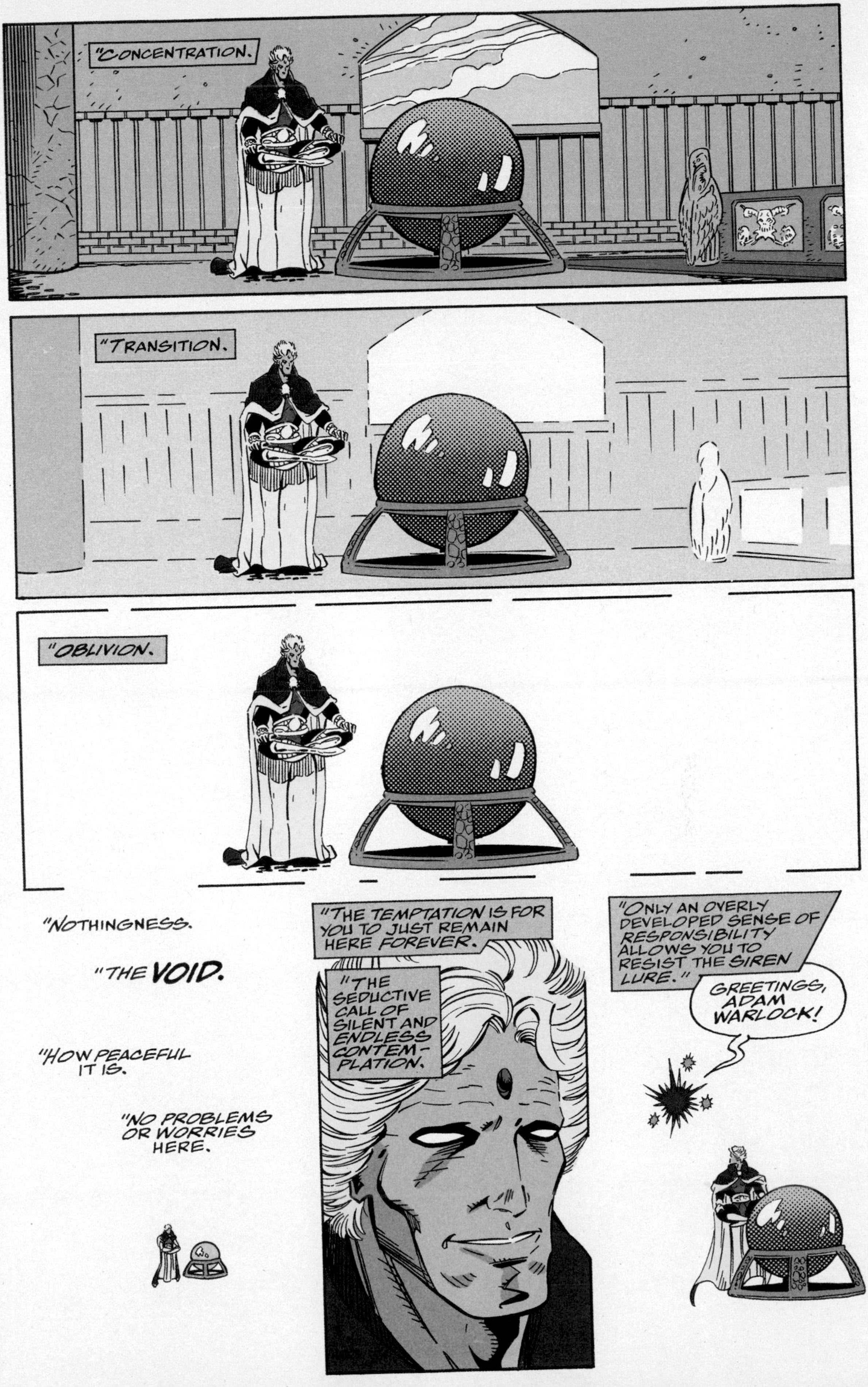
"CONCENTRATION.
"TRANSITION.
"OBLIVION.
"NOTHINGNESS.
"THE VOID.
"HOW PEACEFUL IT IS.
"NO PROBLEMS OR WORRIES HERE.
"THE TEMPTATION IS FOR YOU TO JUST REMAIN HERE FOREVER.
"THE SEDUCTIVE CALL OF SILENT AND ENDLESS CONTEM-PLATION.
"ONLY AN OVERLY DEVELOPED SENSE OF RESPONSIBILITY ALLOWS YOU TO RESIST THE SIREN LURE."
GREETINGS, ADAM WARLOCK!

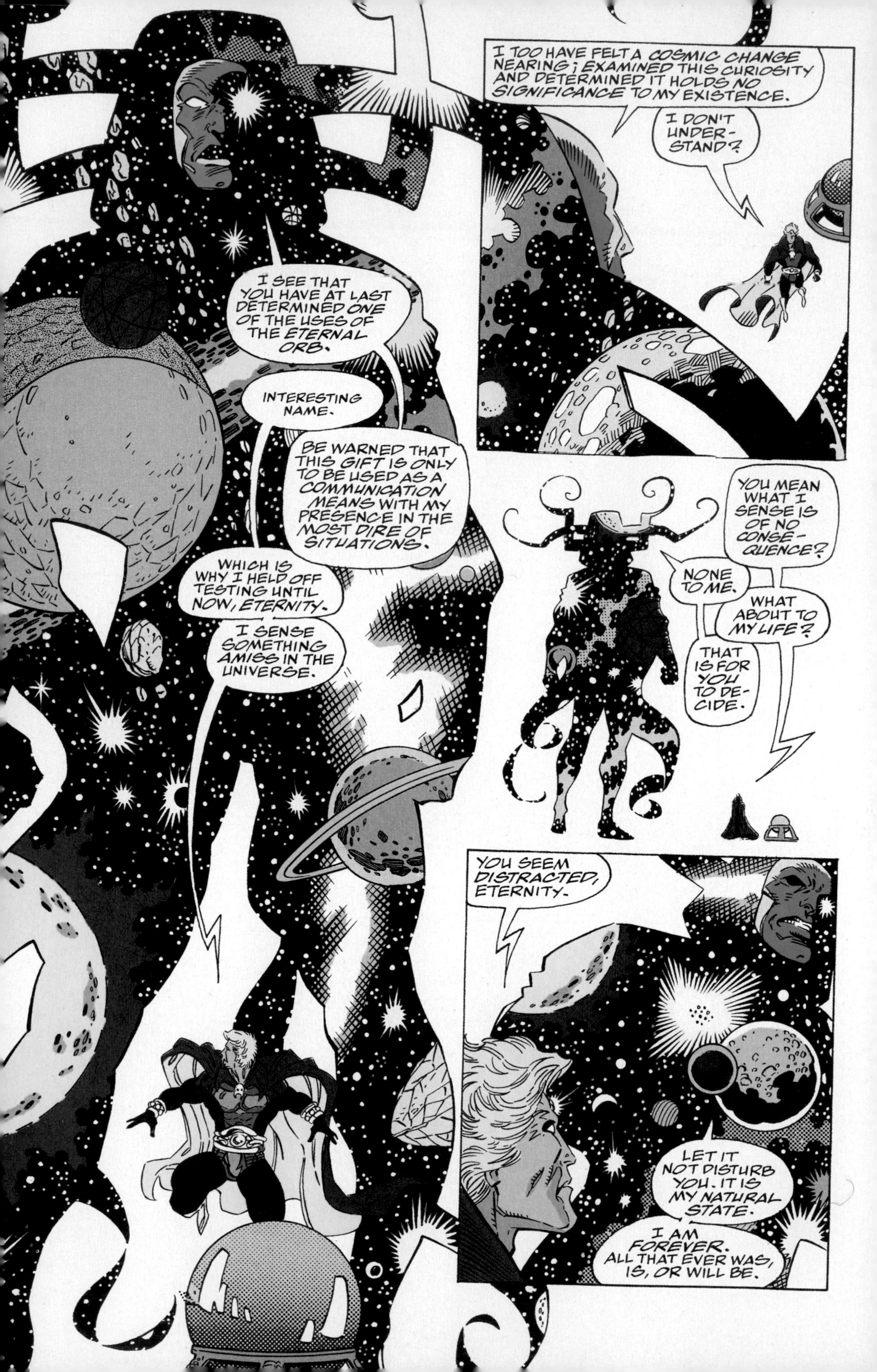
I SEE THAT YOU HAVE AT LAST DETERMINED ONE OF THE USES OF THE ETERNAL ORB.
INTERESTING NAME.
BE WARNED THAT THIS GIFT IS ONLY TO BE USED AS A COMMUNICATION MEANS WITH MY PRESENCE IN THE MOST DIRE OF SITUATIONS.
WHICH IS WHY I HELD OFF TESTING UNTIL NOW, ETERNITY.
I SENSE SOMETHING AMISS IN THE UNIVERSE.
I TOO HAVE FELT A COSMIC CHANGE NEARING; EXAMINED THIS CURIOSITY AND DETERMINED IT HOLDS NO SIGNIFICANCE TO MY EXISTENCE.
I DON'T UNDER-STAND?
YOU MEAN WHAT I SENSE IS OF NO CONSE-QUENCE?
NONE TO ME.
WHAT ABOUT TO MY LIFE?
THAT IS FOR YOU TO DE-CIDE.
YOU SEEM DISTRACTED, ETERNITY.
LET IT NOT DISTURB YOU. IT IS MY NATURAL STATE.
I AM FOREVER. ALL THAT EVER WAS, IS, OR WILL BE.

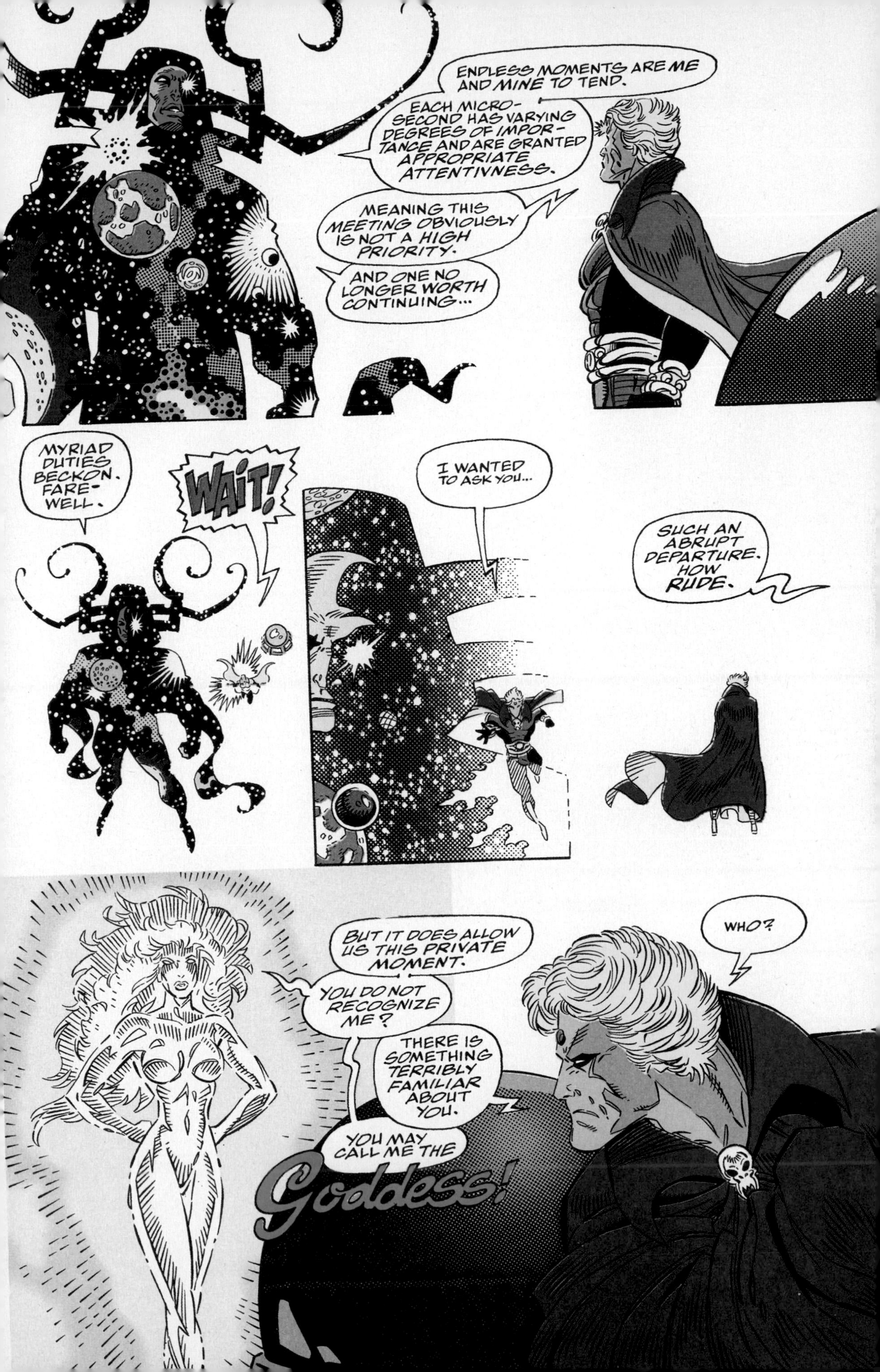
ENDLESS MOMENTS ARE ME AND MINE TO TEND.
EACH MICRO-SECOND HAS VARYING DEGREES OF IMPOR-TANCE AND ARE GRANTED APPROPRIATE ATTENTIVNESS.
MEANING THIS MEETING OBVIOUSLY IS NOT A HIGH PRIORITY.
AND ONE NO LONGER WORTH CONTINUING...
MYRIAD DUTIES BECKON. FARE-WELL.
WAIT!
I WANTED TO ASK YOU...
SUCH AN ABRUPT DEPARTURE. HOW RUDE.
BUT IT DOES ALLOW US THIS PRIVATE MOMENT.
WHO?
YOU DO NOT RECOGNIZE ME?
THERE IS SOMETHING TERRIBLY FAMILIAR ABOUT YOU.
YOU MAY CALL ME THE
Goddess!

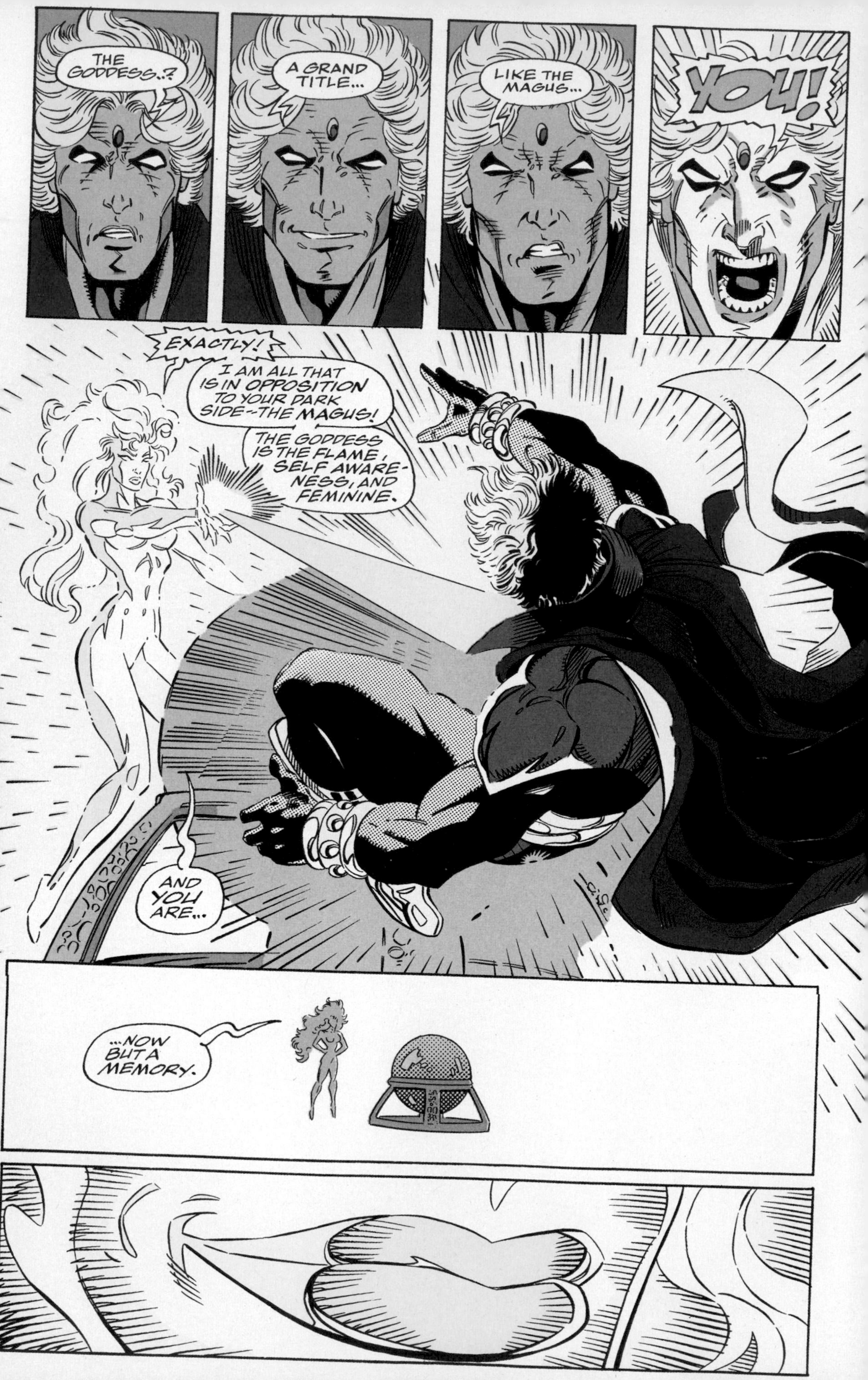
THE GODDESS..?
A GRAND TITLE...
LIKE THE MAGUS...
YOU!
EXACTLY!
I AM ALL THAT IS IN OPPOSITION TO YOUR DARK SIDE--THE MAGUS!
THE GODDESS IS THE FLAME, SELF AWARENESS, AND FEMININE.
AND YOU ARE...
...NOW BUT A MEMORY.

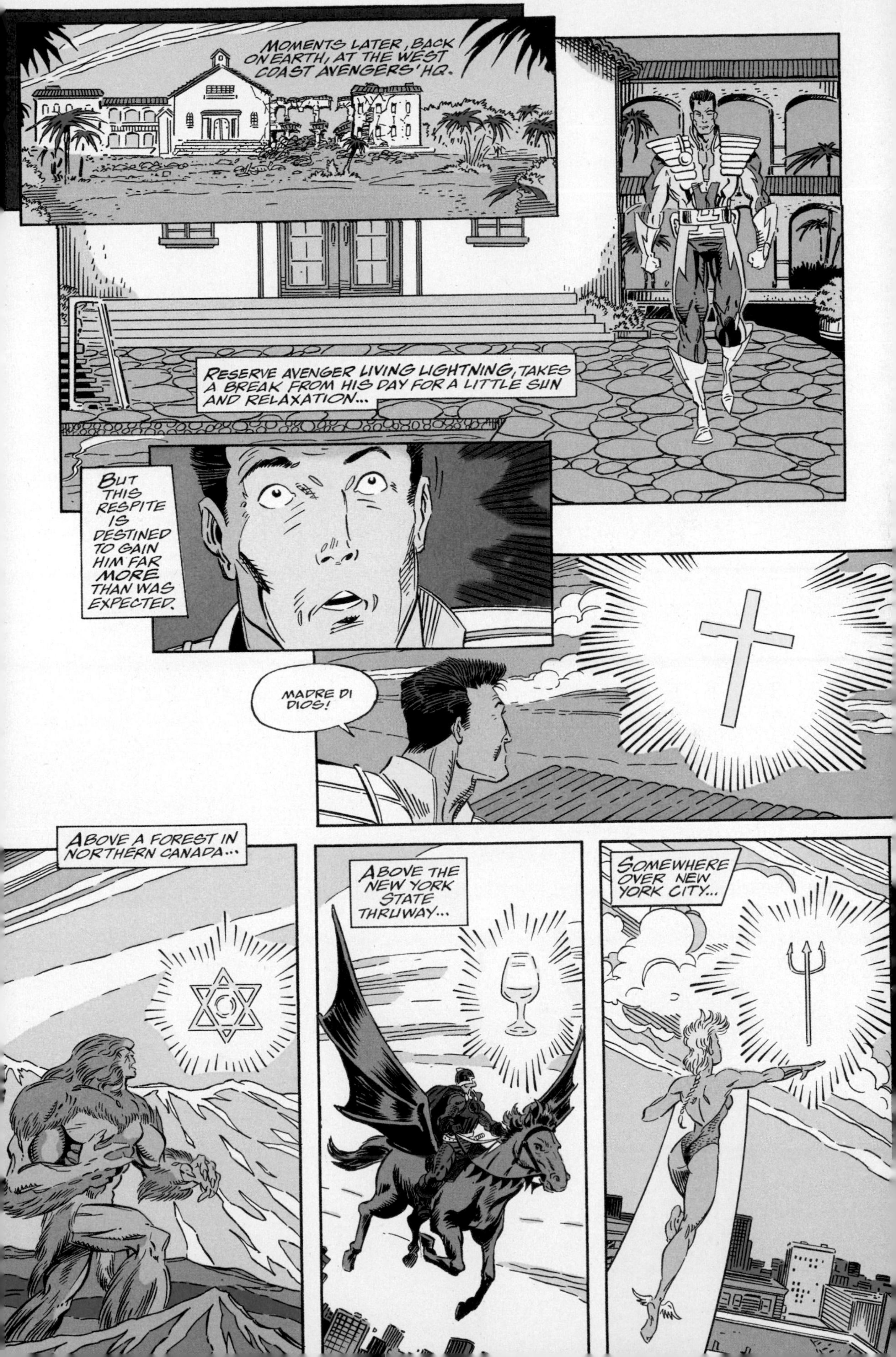
MOMENTS LATER, BACK ON EARTH, AT THE WEST COAST AVENGERS' HQ.
RESERVE AVENGER LIVING LIGHTNING, TAKES A BREAK FROM HIS DAY FOR A LITTLE SUN AND RELAXATION...
BUT THIS RESPITE IS DESTINED TO GAIN HIM FAR MORE THAN WAS EXPECTED.
MADRE DI DIOS!
ABOVE A FOREST IN NORTHERN CANADA...
ABOVE THE NEW YORK STATE THRUWAY...
SOMEWHERE OVER NEW YORK CITY...

ATOP THE ROOF OF AVENGERS HEADQUARTERS IN NEW YORK...

ON THE GROUNDS OF A WEST-CHESTER ESTATE...

AND OUT THE WINDSHIELD OF AN AVENGERS QUINJET...

THIS CANNOT BE!

HUH?

GONE!

IF IT WAS EVER TRULY THERE.

A VISION?

IMAGINATION?

TOO MUCH WORK?

WHO IS TO SAY?

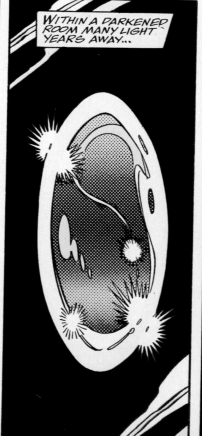

WITHIN A DARKENED ROOM MANY LIGHT YEARS AWAY...

A DARING TRANSGRESSION.

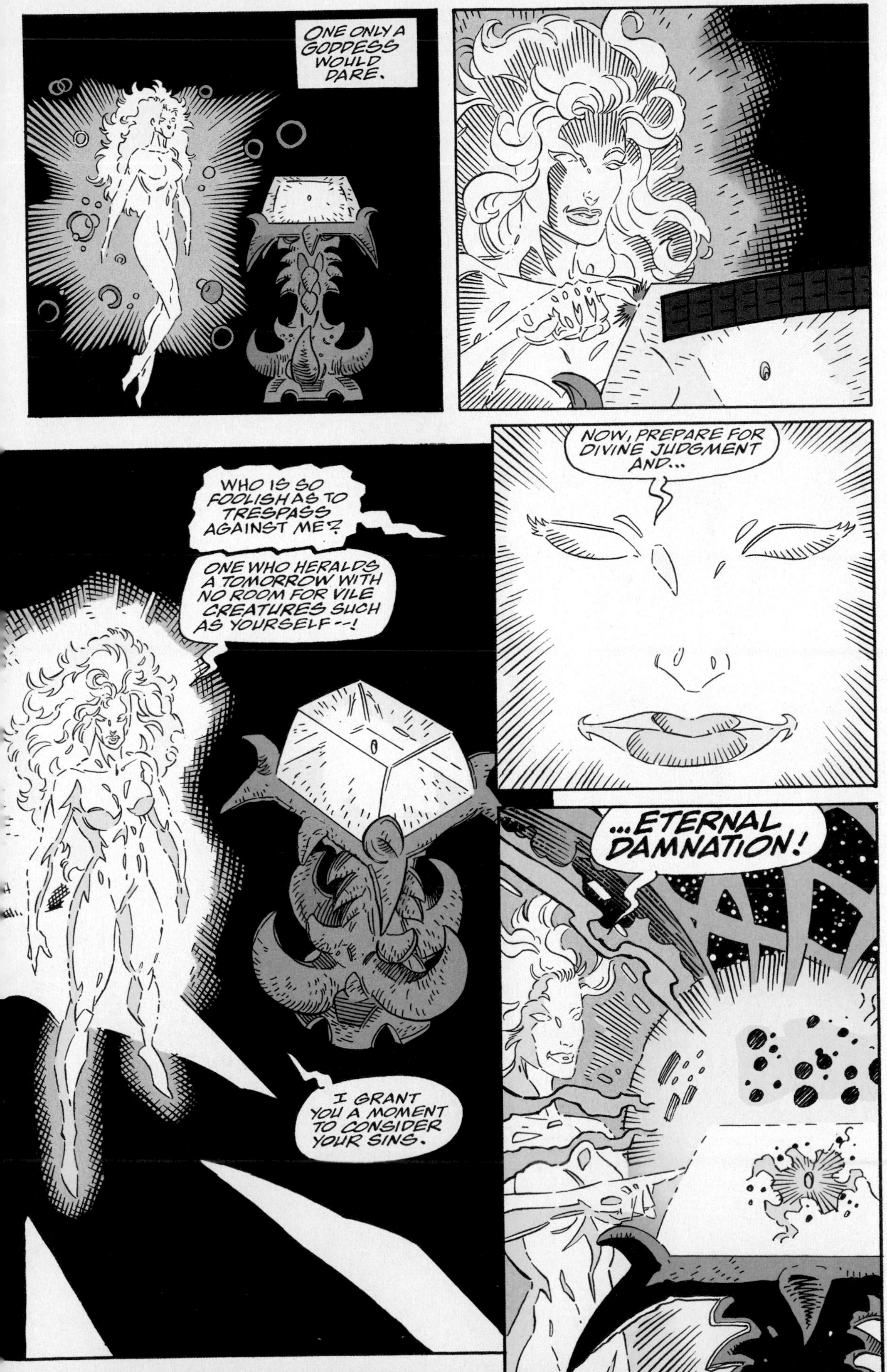
ONE ONLY A GODDESS WOULD DARE.
WHO IS SO FOOLISH AS TO TRESPASS AGAINST ME?
ONE WHO HERALDS A TOMORROW WITH NO ROOM FOR VILE CREATURES SUCH AS YOURSELF--!
I GRANT YOU A MOMENT TO CONSIDER YOUR SINS.
NOW, PREPARE FOR DIVINE JUDGMENT AND...
...ETERNAL DAMNATION!

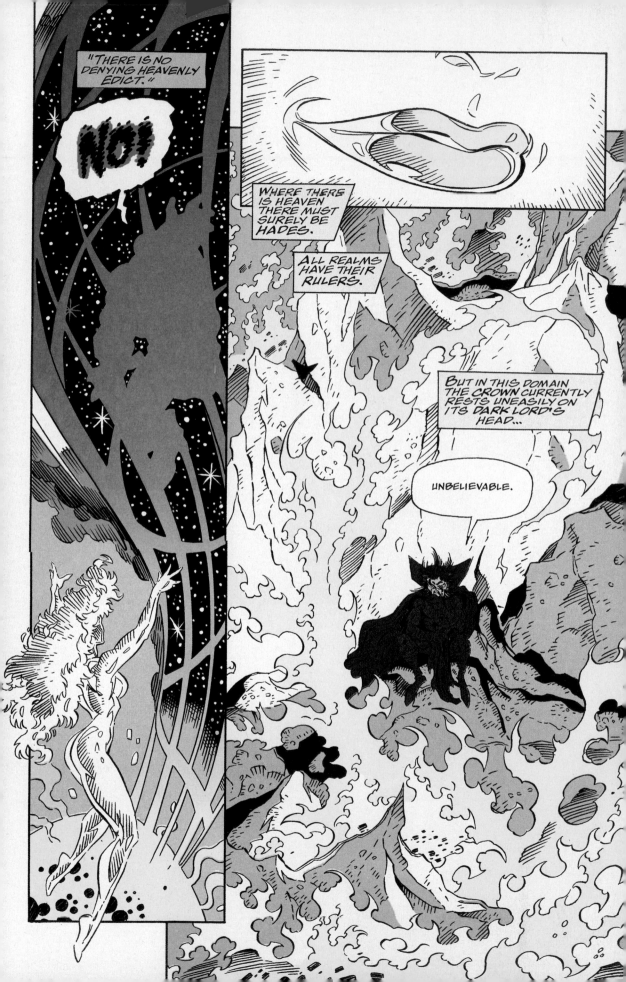

"THERE IS NO DENYING HEAVENLY EDICT."

NO!

WHERE THERE IS HEAVEN THERE MUST SURELY BE HADES.

ALL REALMS HAVE THEIR RULERS.

BUT IN THIS DOMAIN THE CROWN CURRENTLY RESTS UNEASILY ON ITS DARK LORD'S HEAD...

UNBELIEVABLE.

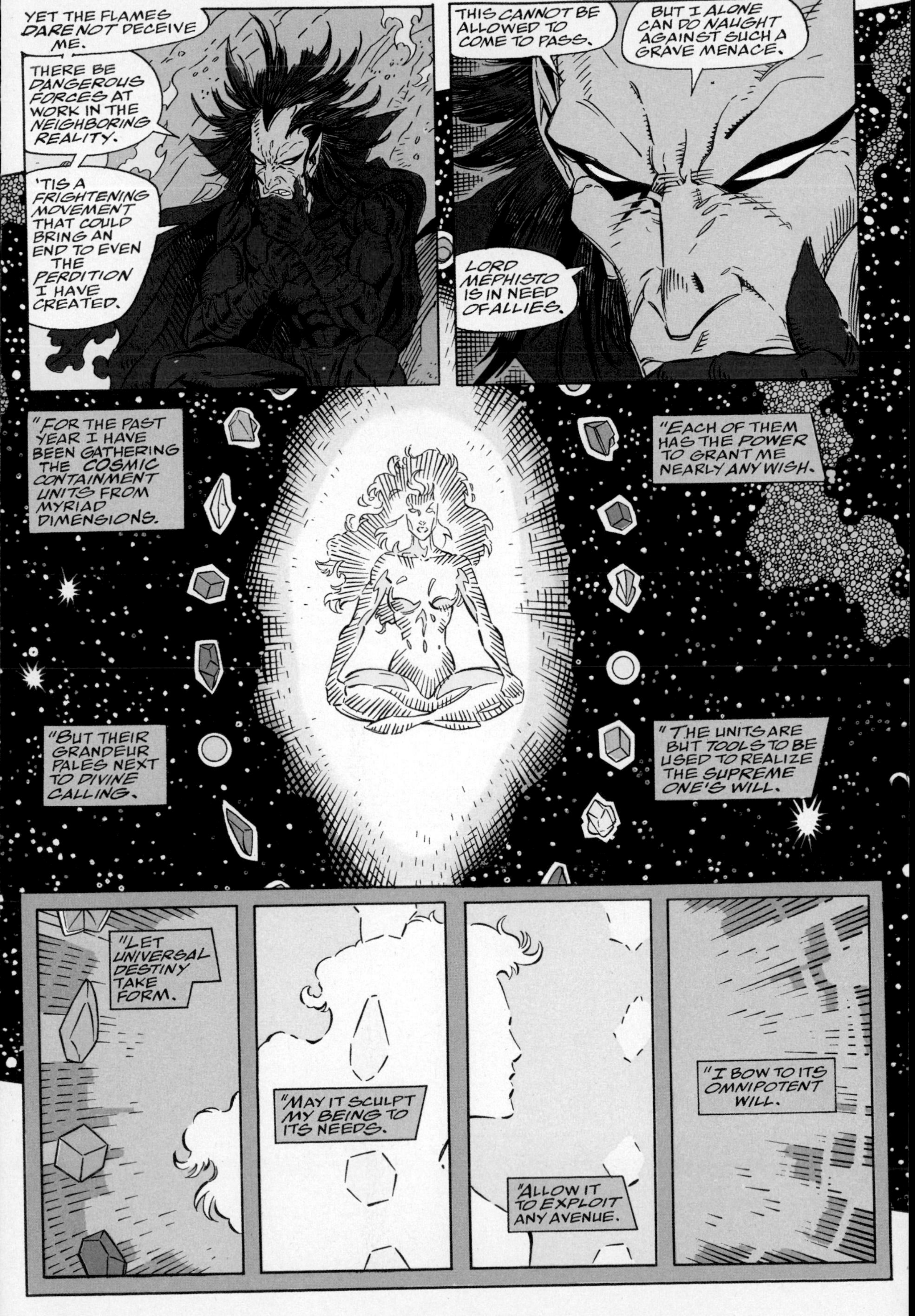
YET THE FLAMES DARE NOT DECEIVE ME.
THERE BE DANGEROUS FORCES AT WORK IN THE NEIGHBORING REALITY.
'TIS A FRIGHTENING MOVEMENT THAT COULD BRING AN END TO EVEN THE PERDITION I HAVE CREATED.
THIS CANNOT BE ALLOWED TO COME TO PASS.
BUT I ALONE CAN DO NAUGHT AGAINST SUCH A GRAVE MENACE.
LORD MEPHISTO IS IN NEED OF ALLIES.
"FOR THE PAST YEAR I HAVE BEEN GATHERING THE COSMIC CONTAINMENT UNITS FROM MYRIAD DIMENSIONS.
"EACH OF THEM HAS THE POWER TO GRANT ME NEARLY ANY WISH.
"BUT THEIR GRANDEUR PALES NEXT TO DIVINE CALLING.
"THE UNITS ARE BUT TOOLS TO BE USED TO REALIZE THE SUPREME ONE'S WILL.
"LET UNIVERSAL DESTINY TAKE FORM.
"MAY IT SCULPT MY BEING TO ITS NEEDS.
"ALLOW IT TO EXPLOIT ANY AVENUE.
"I BOW TO ITS OMNIPOTENT WILL.

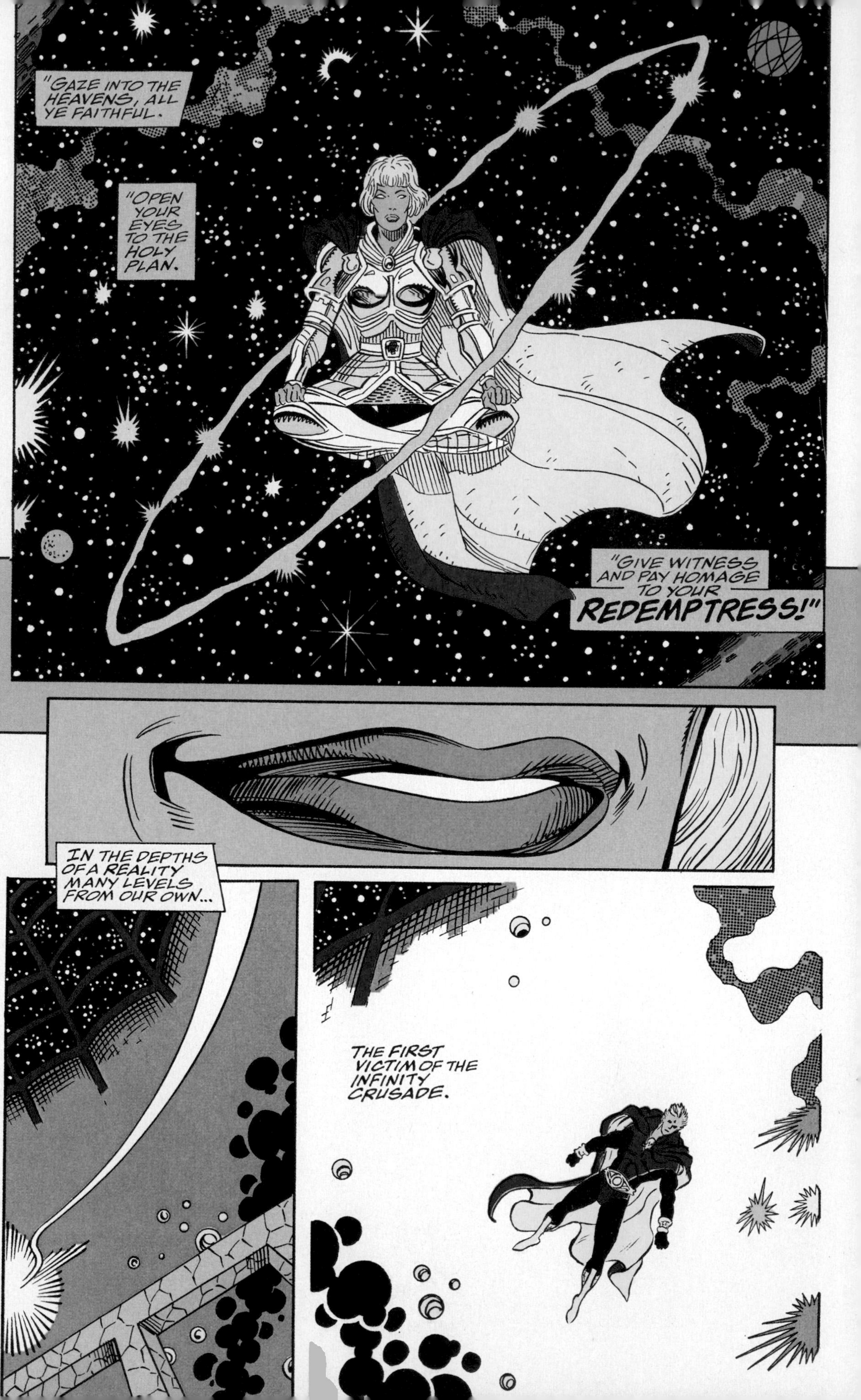
"GAZE INTO THE HEAVENS, ALL YE FAITHFUL.
"OPEN YOUR EYES TO THE HOLY PLAN.
"GIVE WITNESS AND PAY HOMAGE TO YOUR REDEMPTRESS!"
IN THE DEPTHS OF A REALITY MANY LEVELS FROM OUR OWN...
THE FIRST VICTIM OF THE INFINITY CRUSADE.

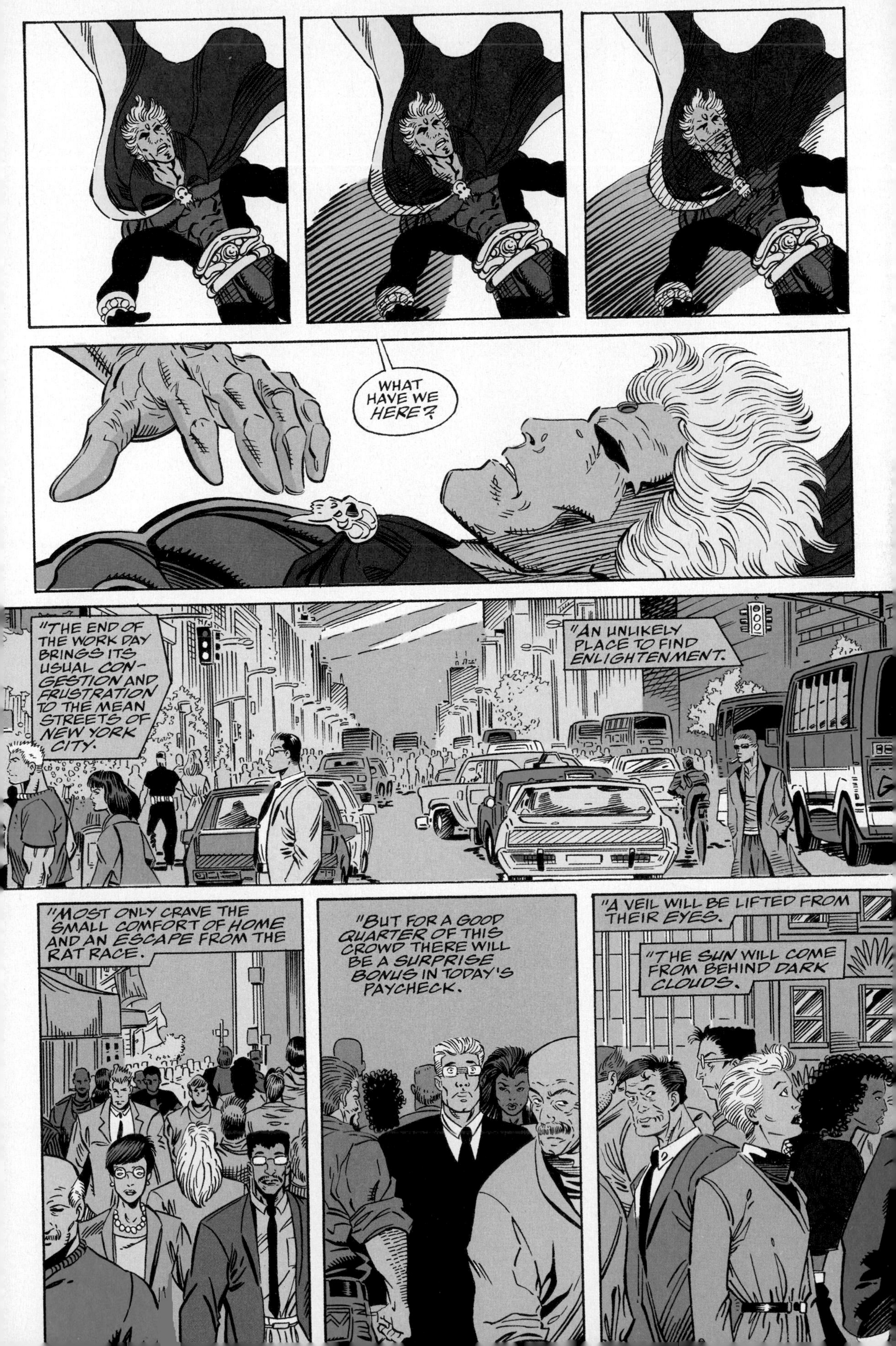
WHAT HAVE WE HERE?
"THE END OF THE WORK DAY BRINGS ITS USUAL CON- GESTION AND FRUSTRATION TO THE MEAN STREETS OF NEW YORK CITY.
"AN UNLIKELY PLACE TO FIND ENLIGHTENMENT.
"MOST ONLY CRAVE THE SMALL COMFORT OF HOME AND AN ESCAPE FROM THE RAT RACE.
"BUT FOR A GOOD QUARTER OF THIS CROWD THERE WILL BE A SURPRISE BONUS IN TODAY'S PAYCHECK.
"A VEIL WILL BE LIFTED FROM THEIR EYES.
"THE SUN WILL COME FROM BEHIND DARK CLOUDS.

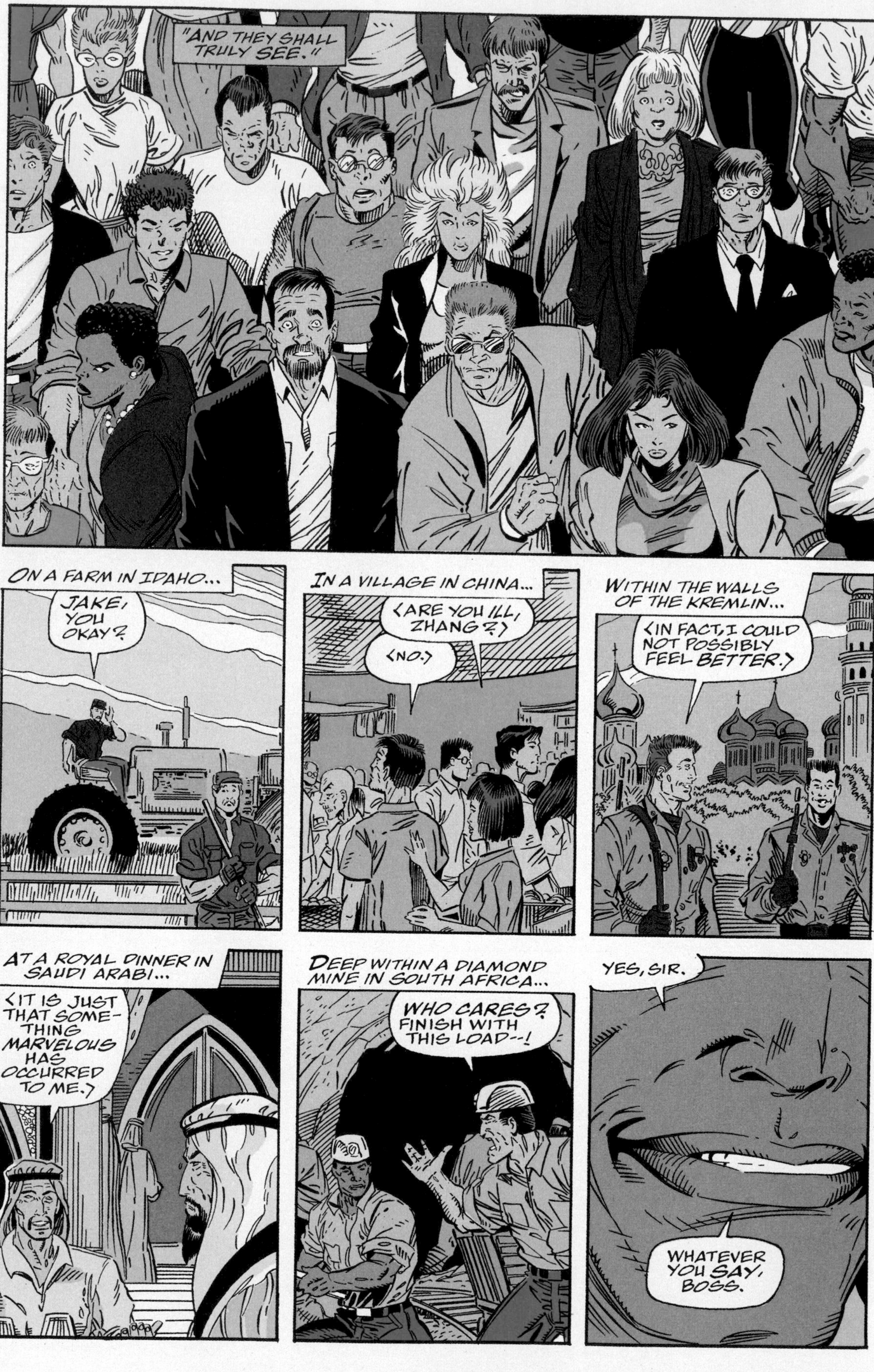
"AND THEY SHALL TRULY SEE."
ON A FARM IN IDAHO...
JAKE, YOU OKAY?
IN A VILLAGE IN CHINA...
<ARE YOU ILL, ZHANG?>
<NO.>
WITHIN THE WALLS OF THE KREMLIN...
<IN FACT, I COULD NOT POSSIBLY FEEL BETTER.>
AT A ROYAL DINNER IN SAUDI ARABI...
<IT IS JUST THAT SOME-THING MARVELOUS HAS OCCURRED TO ME.>
DEEP WITHIN A DIAMOND MINE IN SOUTH AFRICA...
WHO CARES? FINISH WITH THIS LOAD--!
YES, SIR.
WHATEVER YOU SAY, BOSS.

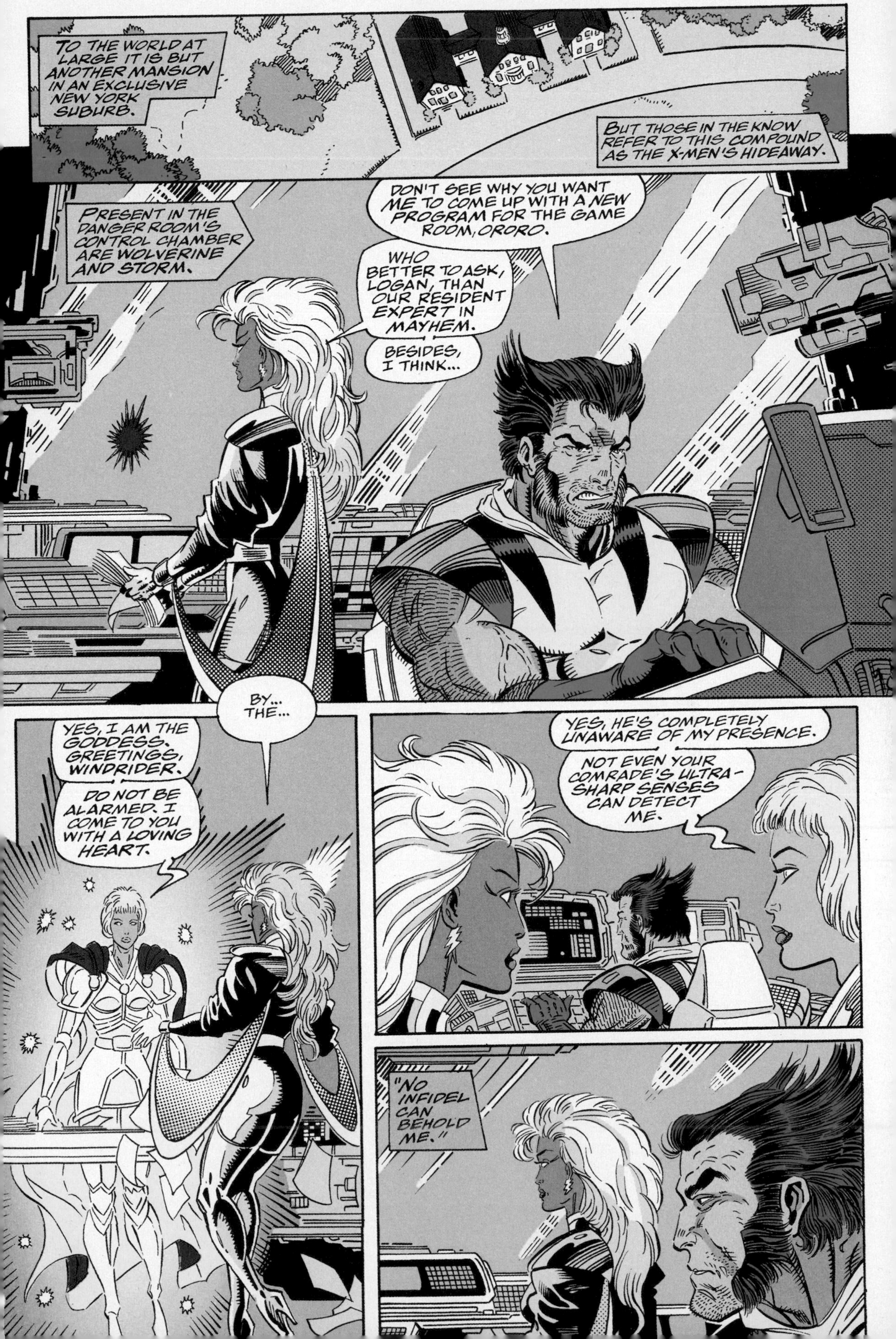
TO THE WORLD AT LARGE IT IS BUT ANOTHER MANSION IN AN EXCLUSIVE NEW YORK SUBURB.
BUT THOSE IN THE KNOW REFER TO THIS COMPOUND AS THE X-MEN'S HIDEAWAY.
PRESENT IN THE DANGER ROOM'S CONTROL CHAMBER ARE WOLVERINE AND STORM.
DON'T SEE WHY YOU WANT ME TO COME UP WITH A NEW PROGRAM FOR THE GAME ROOM, ORORO.
WHO BETTER TO ASK, LOGAN, THAN OUR RESIDENT EXPERT IN MAYHEM.
BESIDES, I THINK...
BY... THE...
YES, I AM THE GODDESS. GREETINGS, WINDRIDER.
DO NOT BE ALARMED. I COME TO YOU WITH A LOVING HEART.
YES, HE'S COMPLETELY UNAWARE OF MY PRESENCE.
NOT EVEN YOUR COMRADE'S ULTRA-SHARP SENSES CAN DETECT ME.
"NO INFIDEL CAN BEHOLD ME."

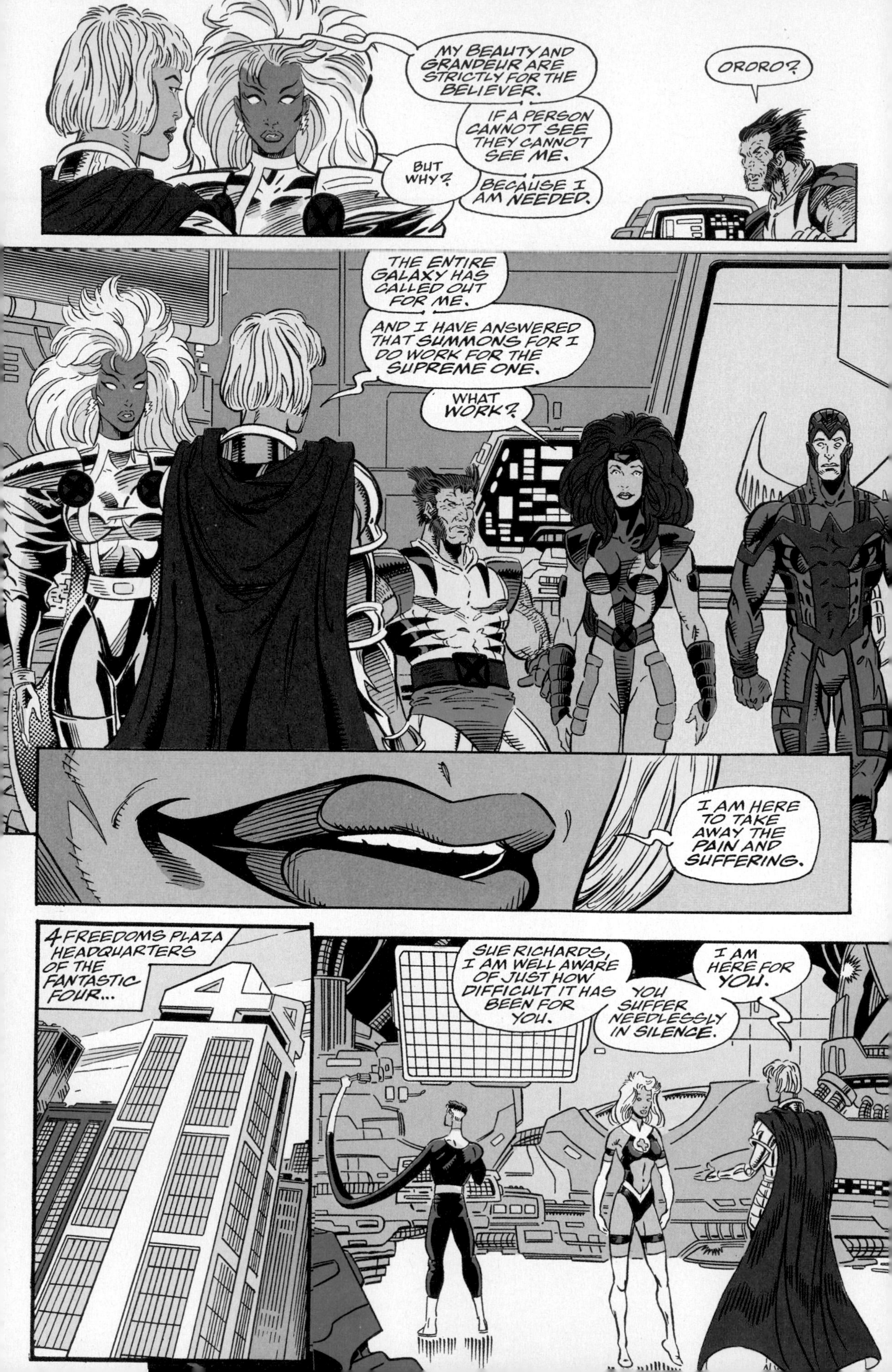

MY BEAUTY AND GRANDEUR ARE STRICTLY FOR THE BELIEVER.
IF A PERSON CANNOT SEE THEY CANNOT SEE ME.
BUT WHY?
BECAUSE I AM NEEDED.
ORORO?
THE ENTIRE GALAXY HAS CALLED OUT FOR ME.
AND I HAVE ANSWERED THAT SUMMONS FOR I DO WORK FOR THE SUPREME ONE.
WHAT WORK?
I AM HERE TO TAKE AWAY THE PAIN AND SUFFERING.
4 FREEDOMS PLAZA HEADQUARTERS OF THE FANTASTIC FOUR...
SUE RICHARDS, I AM WELL AWARE OF JUST HOW DIFFICULT IT HAS BEEN FOR YOU.
YOU SUFFER NEEDLESSLY IN SILENCE.
I AM HERE FOR YOU.

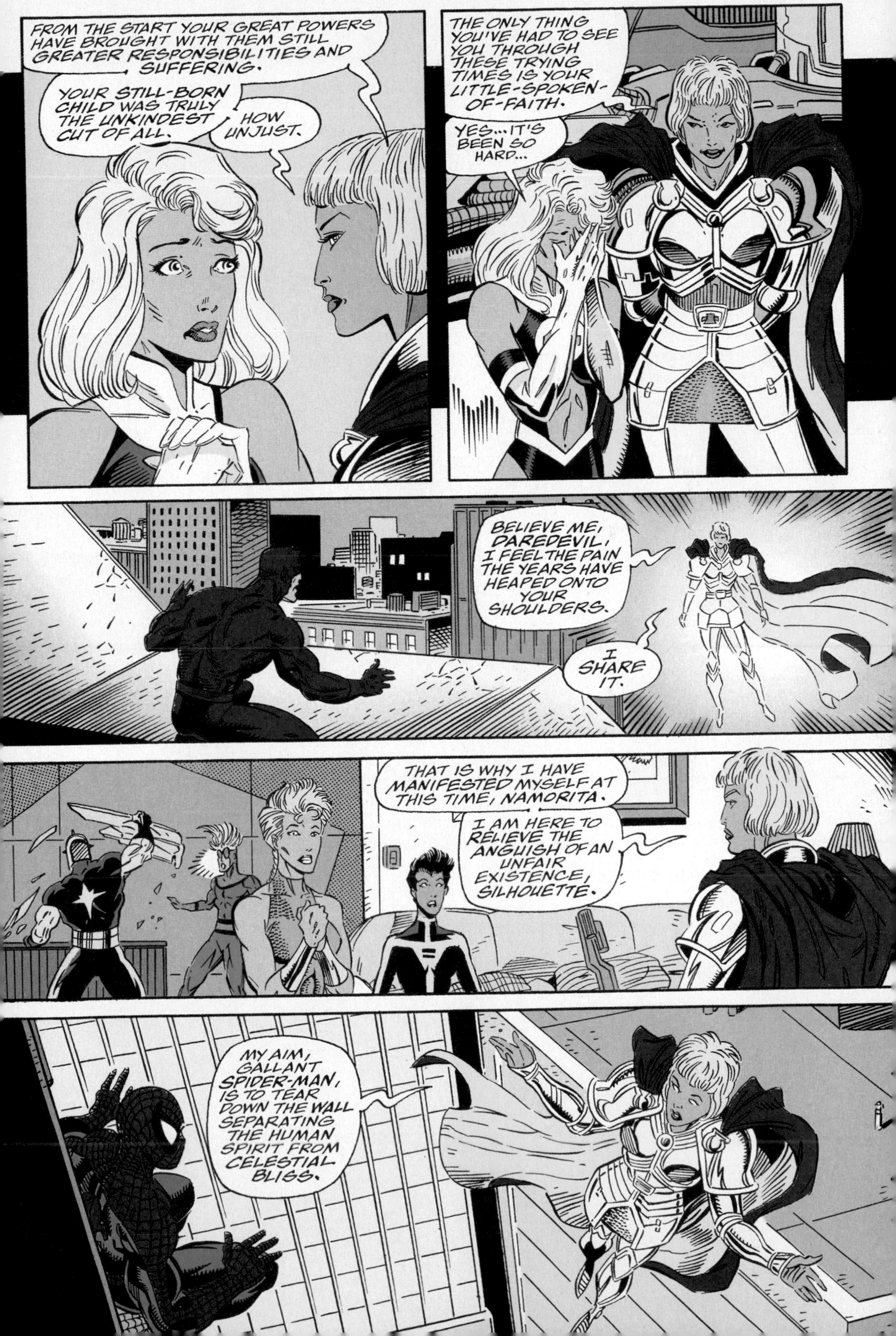
FROM THE START YOUR GREAT POWERS HAVE BROUGHT WITH THEM STILL GREATER RESPONSIBILITIES AND SUFFERING.
YOUR STILL-BORN CHILD WAS TRULY THE UNKINDEST CUT OF ALL.
HOW UNJUST.
THE ONLY THING YOU'VE HAD TO SEE YOU THROUGH THESE TRYING TIMES IS YOUR LITTLE-SPOKEN-OF-FAITH.
YES... IT'S BEEN SO HARD...
BELIEVE ME, DAREDEVIL, I FEEL THE PAIN THE YEARS HAVE HEAPED ONTO YOUR SHOULDERS.
I SHARE IT.
THAT IS WHY I HAVE MANIFESTED MYSELF AT THIS TIME, NAMORITA.
I AM HERE TO RELIEVE THE ANGUISH OF AN UNFAIR EXISTENCE, SILHOUETTE.
MY AIM, GALLANT SPIDER-MAN, IS TO TEAR DOWN THE WALL SEPARATING THE HUMAN SPIRIT FROM CELESTIAL BLISS.

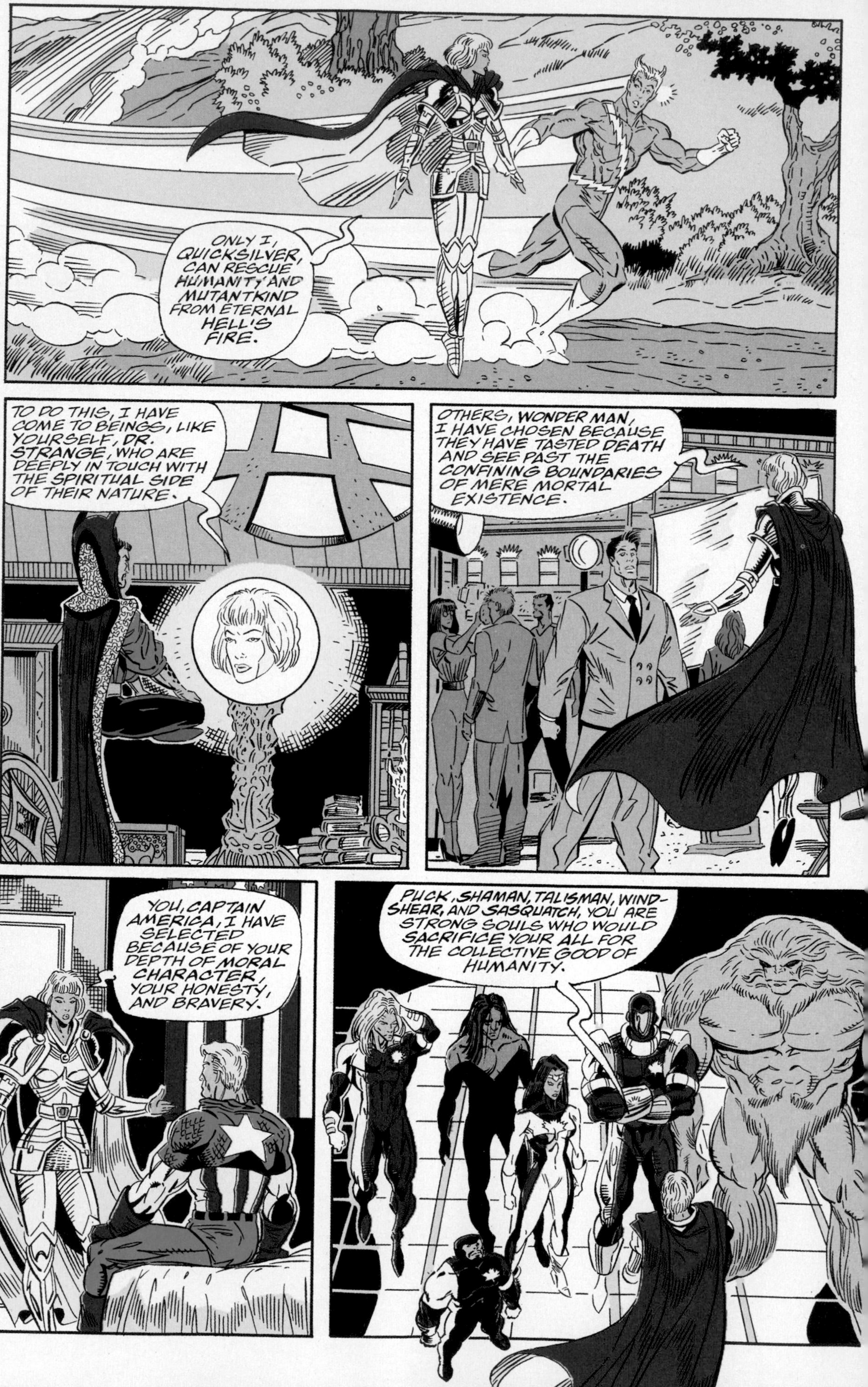
ONLY I, QUICKSILVER, CAN RESCUE HUMANITY AND MUTANTKIND FROM ETERNAL HELL'S FIRE.
TO DO THIS, I HAVE COME TO BEINGS, LIKE YOURSELF, DR. STRANGE, WHO ARE DEEPLY IN TOUCH WITH THE SPIRITUAL SIDE OF THEIR NATURE.
OTHERS, WONDER MAN, I HAVE CHOSEN BECAUSE THEY HAVE TASTED DEATH AND SEE PAST THE CONFINING BOUNDARIES OF MERE MORTAL EXISTENCE.
YOU, CAPTAIN AMERICA, I HAVE SELECTED BECAUSE OF YOUR DEPTH OF MORAL CHARACTER, YOUR HONESTY, AND BRAVERY.
PUCK, SHAMAN, TALISMAN, WINDSHEAR, AND SASQUATCH, YOU ARE STRONG SOULS WHO WOULD SACRIFICE YOUR ALL FOR THE COLLECTIVE GOOD OF HUMANITY.

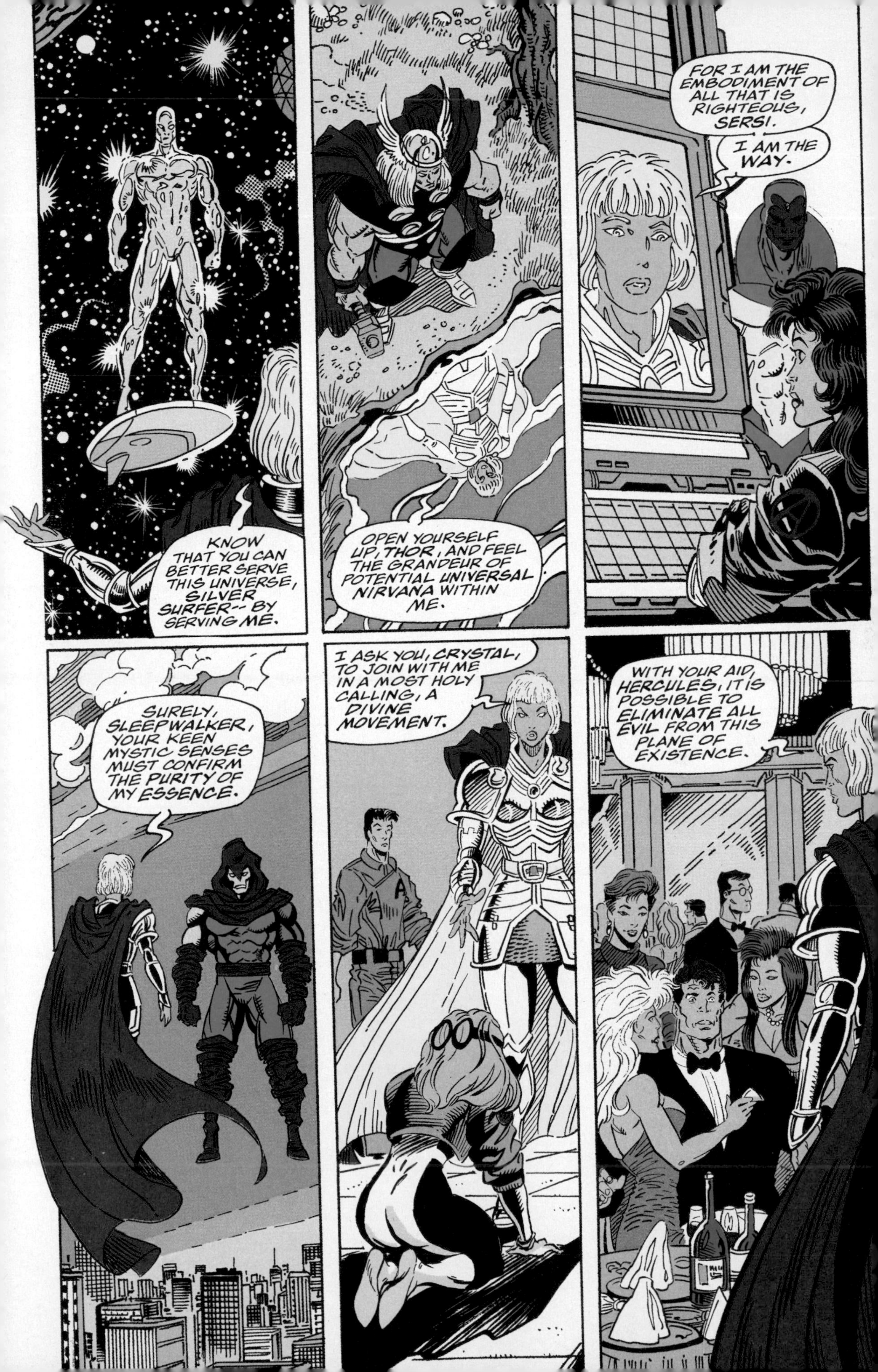
KNOW THAT YOU CAN BETTER SERVE THIS UNIVERSE, SILVER SURFER-- BY SERVING ME.
OPEN YOURSELF UP, THOR, AND FEEL THE GRANDEUR OF POTENTIAL UNIVERSAL NIRVANA WITHIN ME.
FOR I AM THE EMBODIMENT OF ALL THAT IS RIGHTEOUS, SERSI.
I AM THE WAY.
SURELY, SLEEPWALKER, YOUR KEEN MYSTIC SENSES MUST CONFIRM THE PURITY OF MY ESSENCE.
I ASK YOU, CRYSTAL, TO JOIN WITH ME IN A MOST HOLY CALLING, A DIVINE MOVEMENT.
WITH YOUR AID, HERCULES, IT IS POSSIBLE TO ELIMINATE ALL EVIL FROM THIS PLANE OF EXISTENCE.

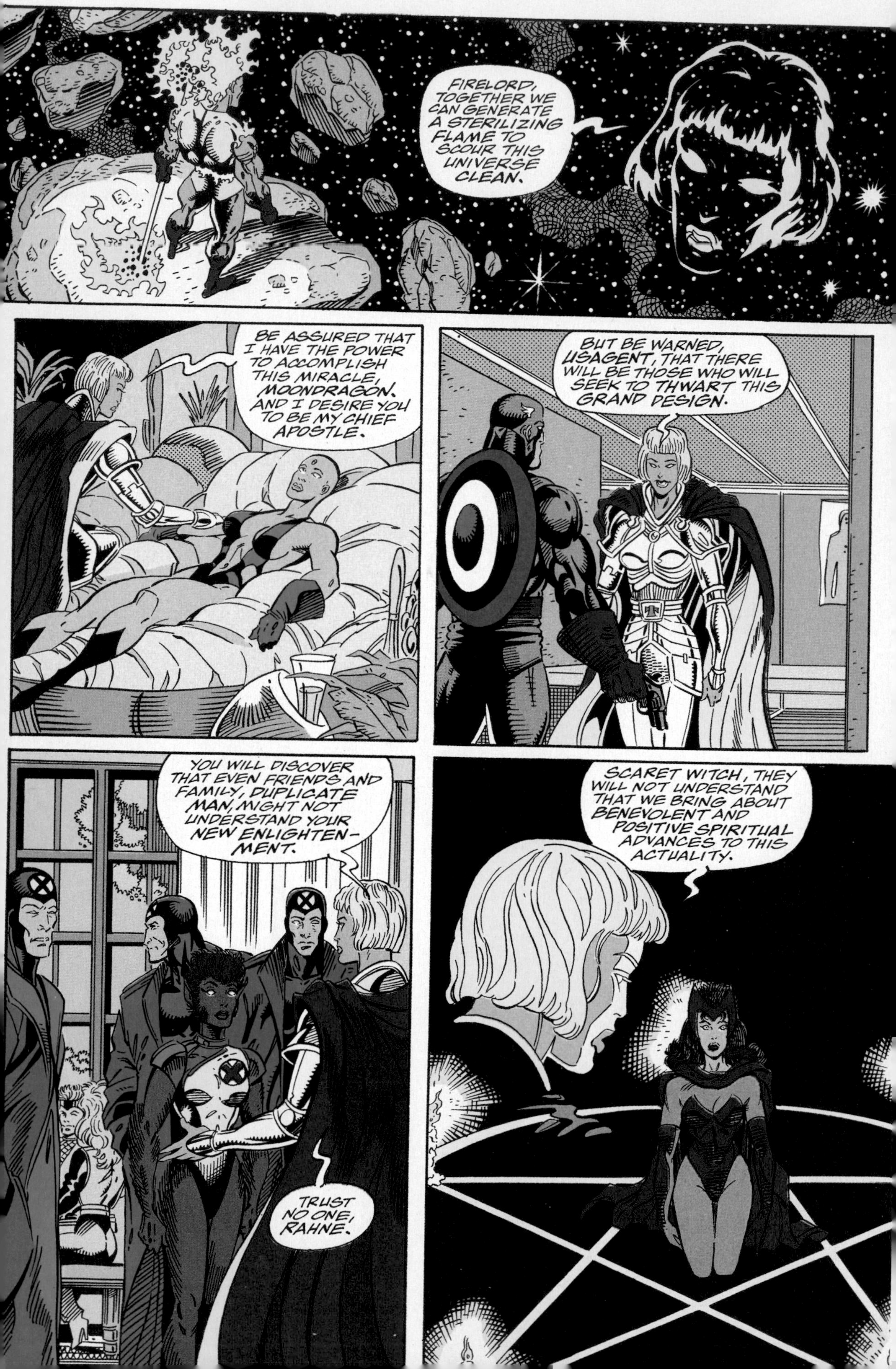
FIRELORD, TOGETHER WE CAN GENERATE A STERILIZING FLAME TO SCOUR THIS UNIVERSE CLEAN.
BE ASSURED THAT I HAVE THE POWER TO ACCOMPLISH THIS MIRACLE, MOONDRAGON. AND I DESIRE YOU TO BE MY CHIEF APOSTLE.
BUT BE WARNED, USAGENT, THAT THERE WILL BE THOSE WHO WILL SEEK TO THWART THIS GRAND DESIGN.
YOU WILL DISCOVER THAT EVEN FRIENDS AND FAMILY, DUPLICATE MAN, MIGHT NOT UNDERSTAND YOUR NEW ENLIGHTEN-MENT.
TRUST NO ONE, RAHNE.
SCARET WITCH, THEY WILL NOT UNDERSTAND THAT WE BRING ABOUT BENEVOLENT AND POSITIVE SPIRITUAL ADVANCES TO THIS ACTUALITY.

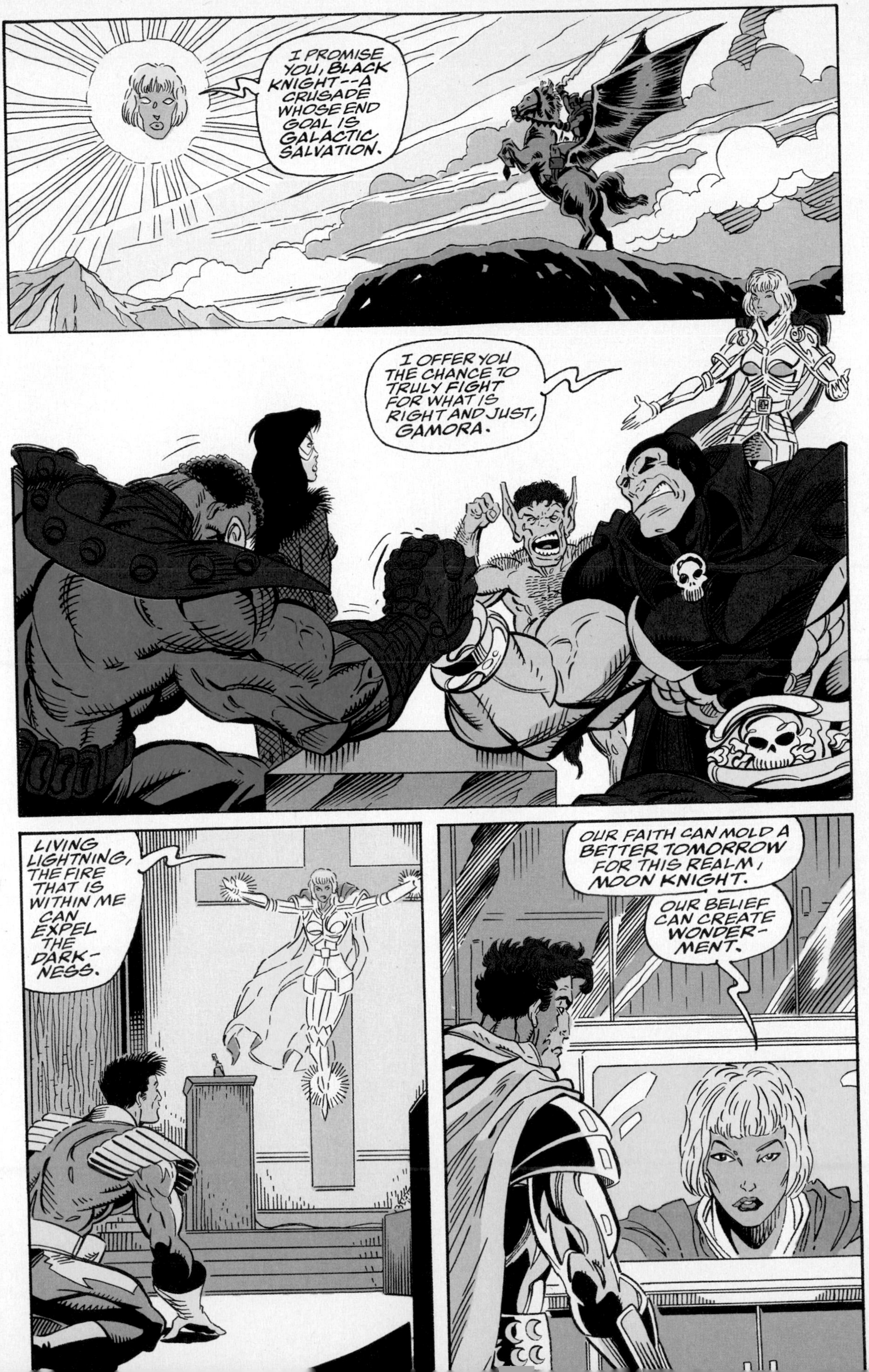
I PROMISE YOU, BLACK KNIGHT--A CRUSADE WHOSE END GOAL IS GALACTIC SALVATION.
I OFFER YOU THE CHANCE TO TRULY FIGHT FOR WHAT IS RIGHT AND JUST, GAMORA.
LIVING LIGHTNING, THE FIRE THAT IS WITHIN ME CAN EXPEL THE DARK-NESS.
OUR FAITH CAN MOLD A BETTER TOMORROW FOR THIS REALM, MOON KNIGHT.
OUR BELIEF CAN CREATE WONDER-MENT.

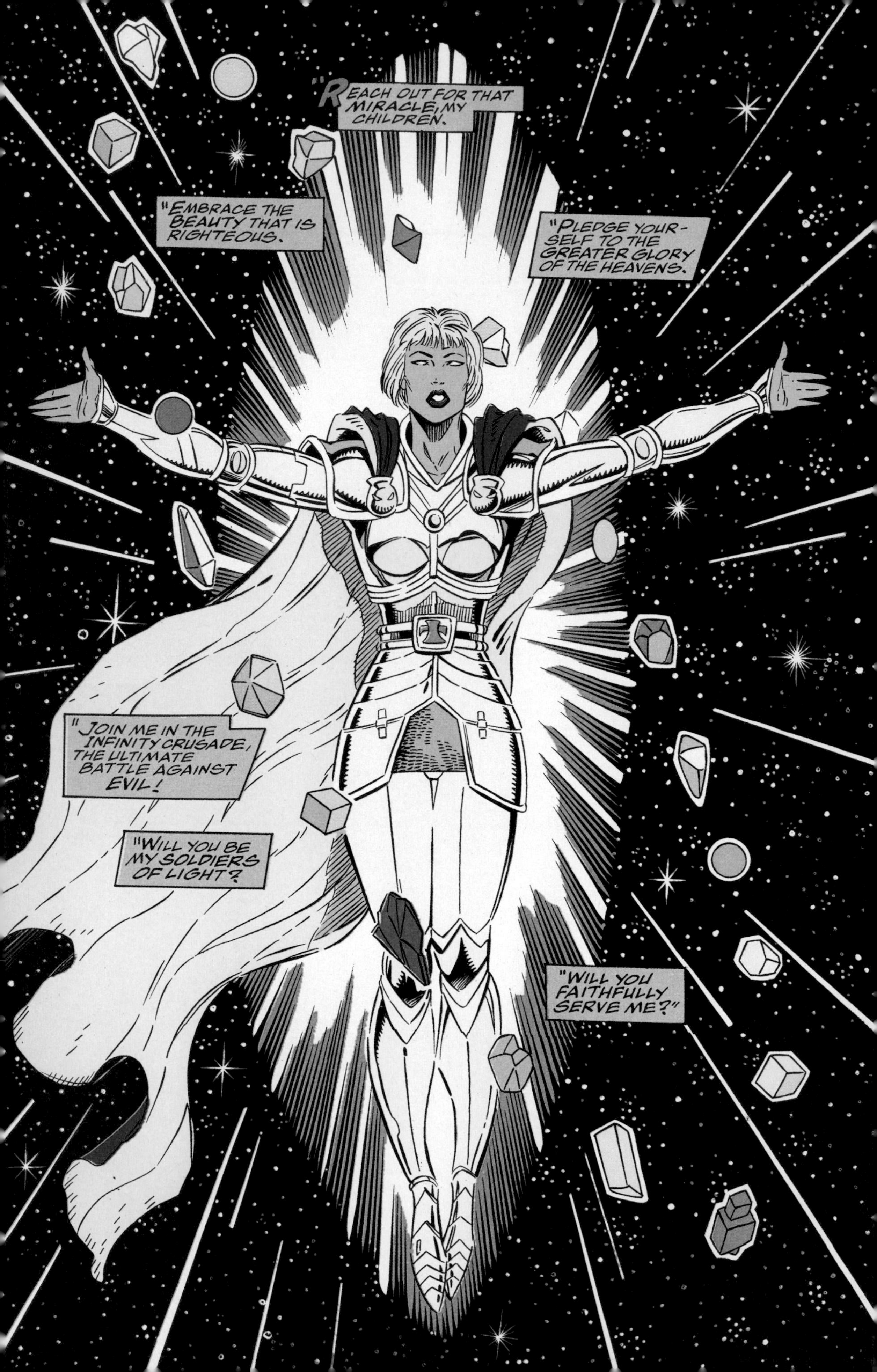
"REACH OUT FOR THAT MIRACLE, MY CHILDREN.
"EMBRACE THE BEAUTY THAT IS RIGHTEOUS.
"PLEDGE YOURSELF TO THE GREATER GLORY OF THE HEAVENS.
"JOIN ME IN THE INFINITY CRUSADE, THE ULTIMATE BATTLE AGAINST EVIL!
"WILL YOU BE MY SOLDIERS OF LIGHT?
"WILL YOU FAITHFULLY SERVE ME?"

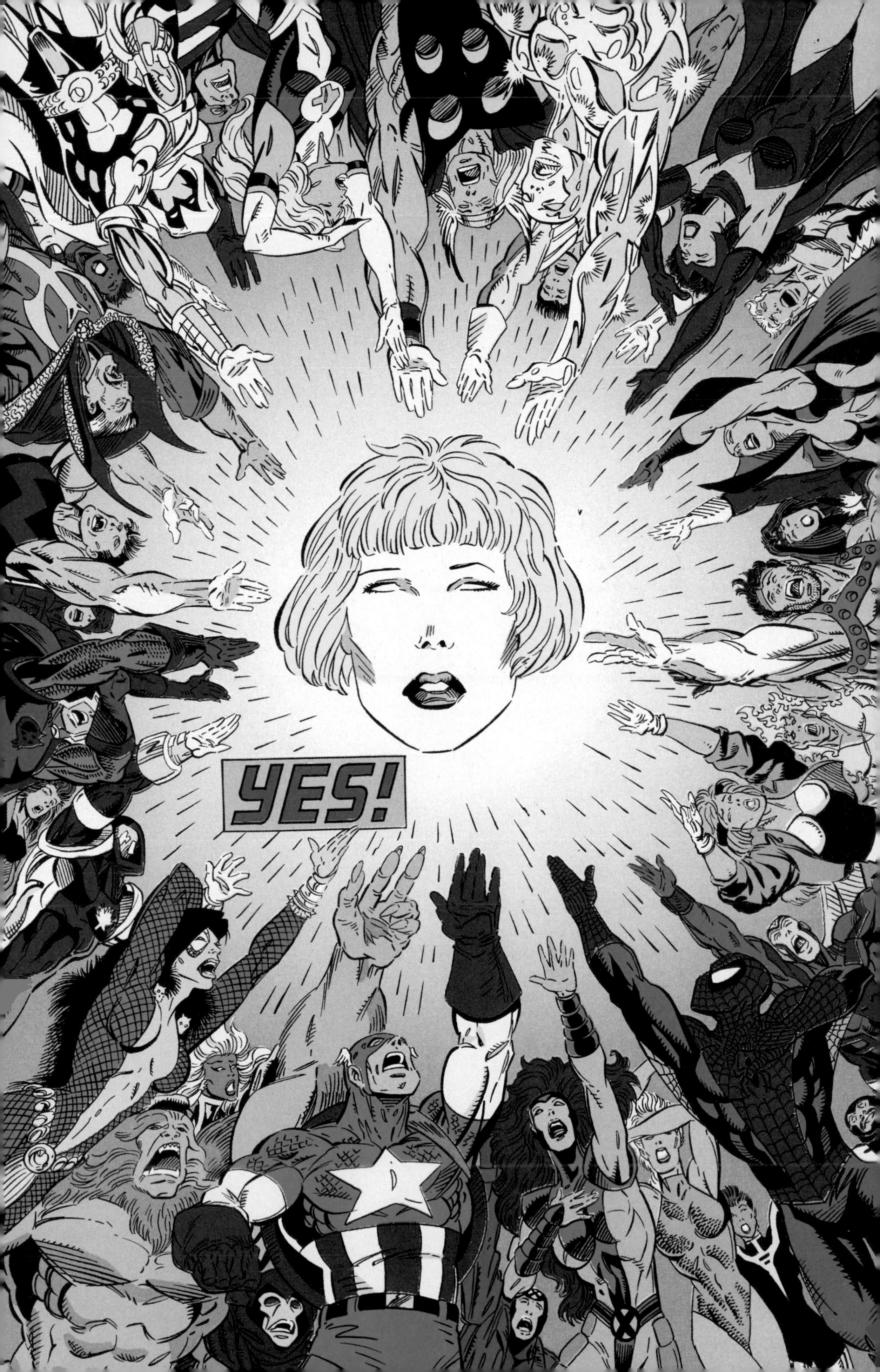
YES!

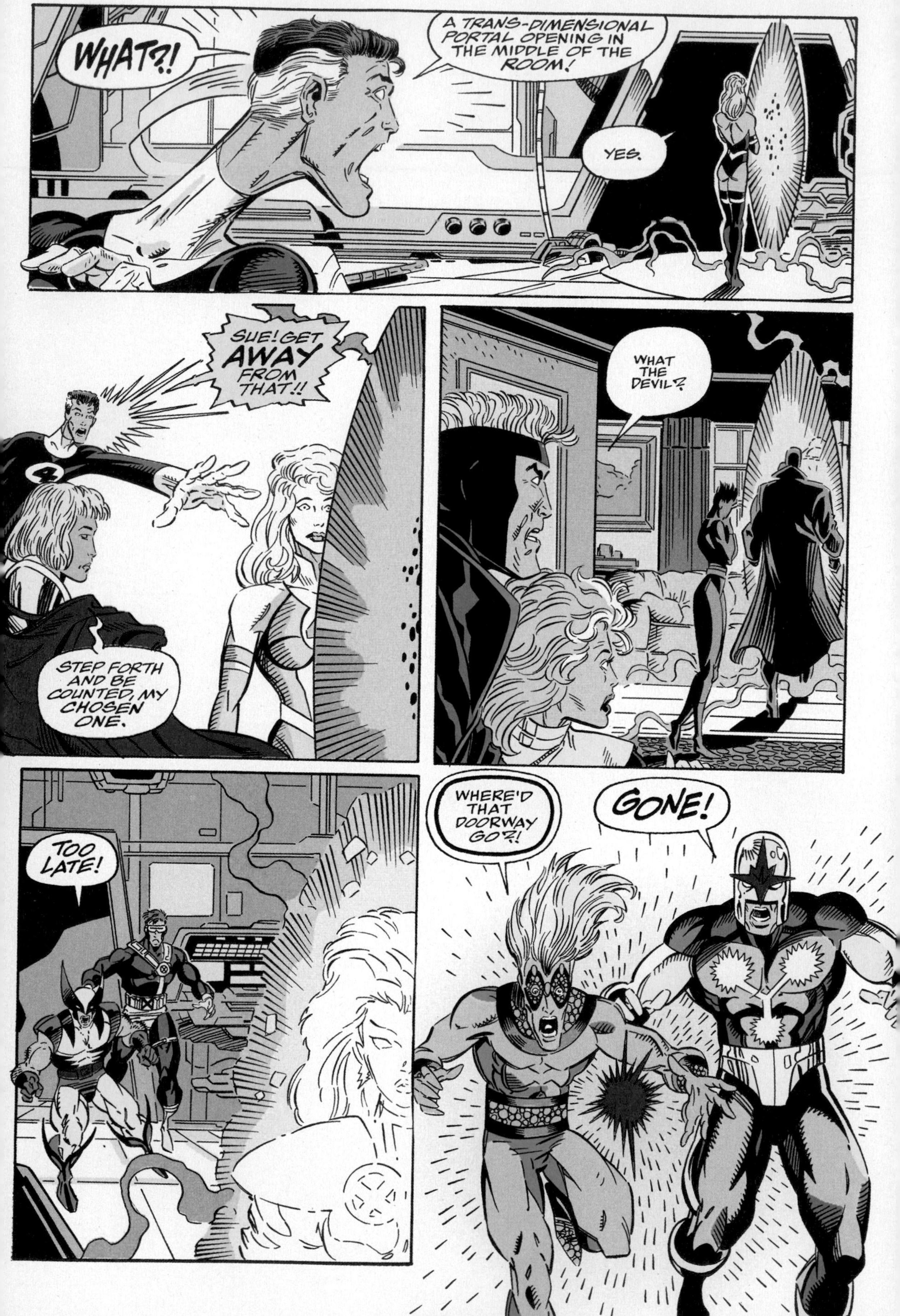
WHAT?!
A TRANS-DIMENSIONAL PORTAL OPENING IN THE MIDDLE OF THE ROOM!
YES.
SUE! GET AWAY FROM THAT!!
STEP FORTH AND BE COUNTED, MY CHOSEN ONE.
WHAT THE DEVIL?!
TOO LATE!
WHERE'D THAT DOORWAY GO?!
GONE!

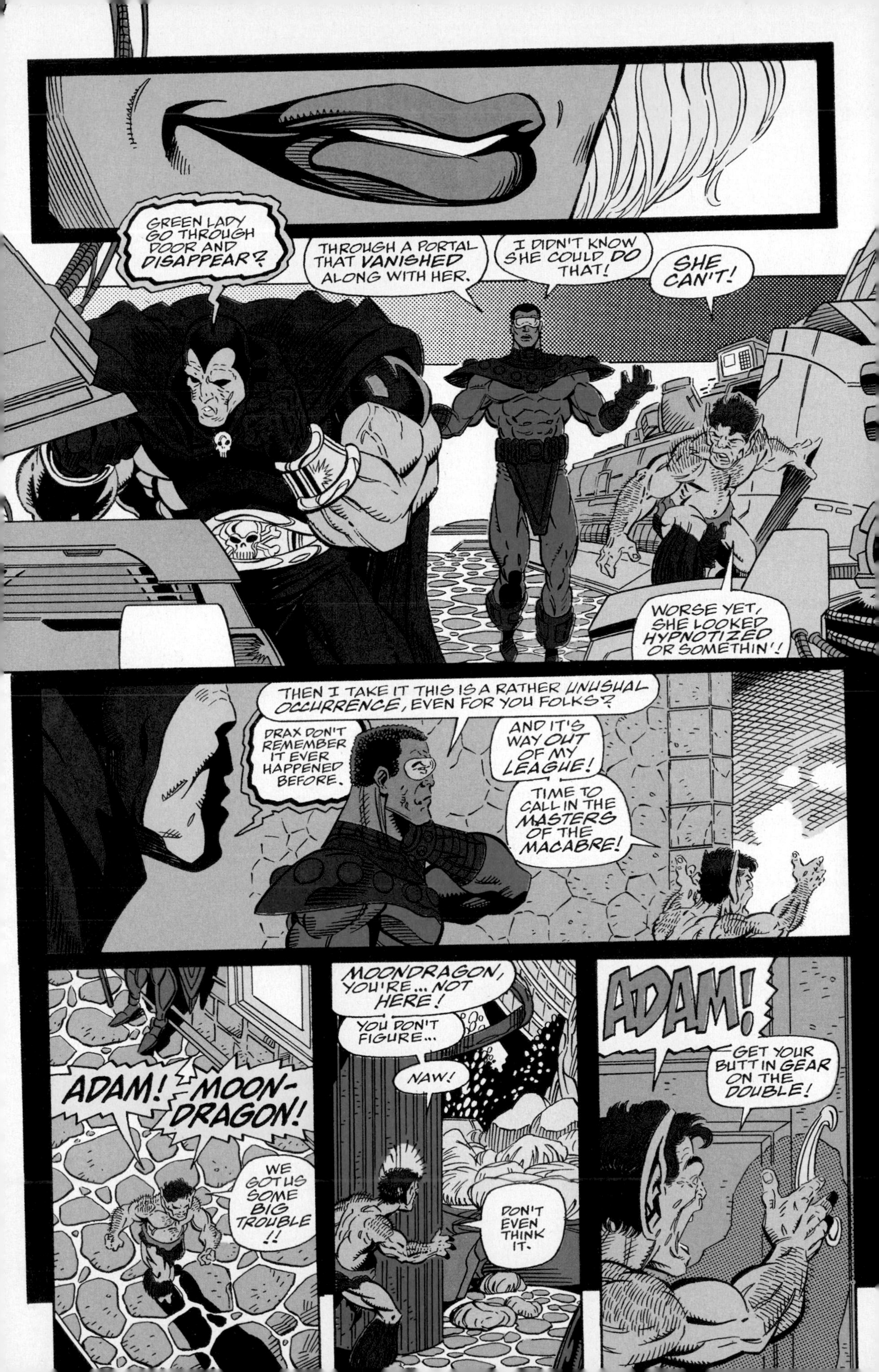
GREEN LADY GO THROUGH DOOR AND DISAPPEAR?
THROUGH A PORTAL THAT VANISHED ALONG WITH HER.
I DIDN'T KNOW SHE COULD DO THAT!
SHE CAN'T!
WORSE YET, SHE LOOKED HYPNOTIZED OR SOMETHIN'!
THEN I TAKE IT THIS IS A RATHER UNUSUAL OCCURRENCE, EVEN FOR YOU FOLKS?
DRAX DON'T REMEMBER IT EVER HAPPENED BEFORE.
AND IT'S WAY OUT OF MY LEAGUE!
TIME TO CALL IN THE MASTERS OF THE MACABRE!
ADAM!
MOON-DRAGON!
WE GOT US SOME BIG TROUBLE!!
MOONDRAGON, YOU'RE... NOT HERE!
YOU DON'T FIGURE...
NAW!
DON'T EVEN THINK IT.
ADAM!
GET YOUR BUTT IN GEAR ON THE DOUBLE!

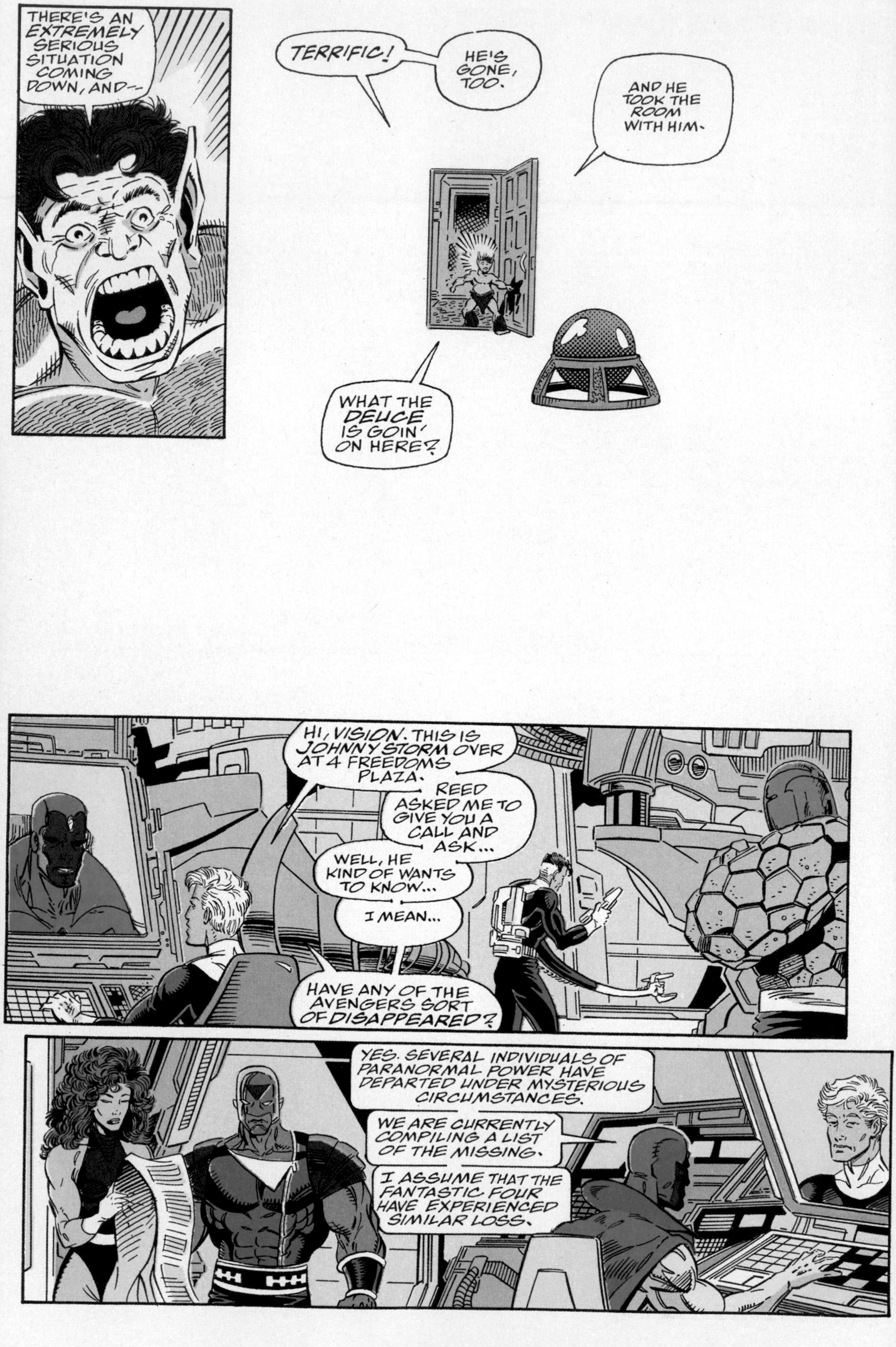
THERE'S AN EXTREMELY SERIOUS SITUATION COMING DOWN, AND--
TERRIFIC!
HE'S GONE, TOO.
AND HE TOOK THE ROOM WITH HIM.
WHAT THE DEUCE IS GOIN' ON HERE?
HI, VISION. THIS IS JOHNNY STORM OVER AT 4 FREEDOMS PLAZA.
REED ASKED ME TO GIVE YOU A CALL AND ASK...
WELL, HE KIND OF WANTS TO KNOW...
I MEAN...
HAVE ANY OF THE AVENGERS SORT OF DISAPPEARED?
YES. SEVERAL INDIVIDUALS OF PARANORMAL POWER HAVE DEPARTED UNDER MYSTERIOUS CIRCUMSTANCES.
WE ARE CURRENTLY COMPILING A LIST OF THE MISSING.
I ASSUME THAT THE FANTASTIC FOUR HAVE EXPERIENCED SIMILAR LOSS.

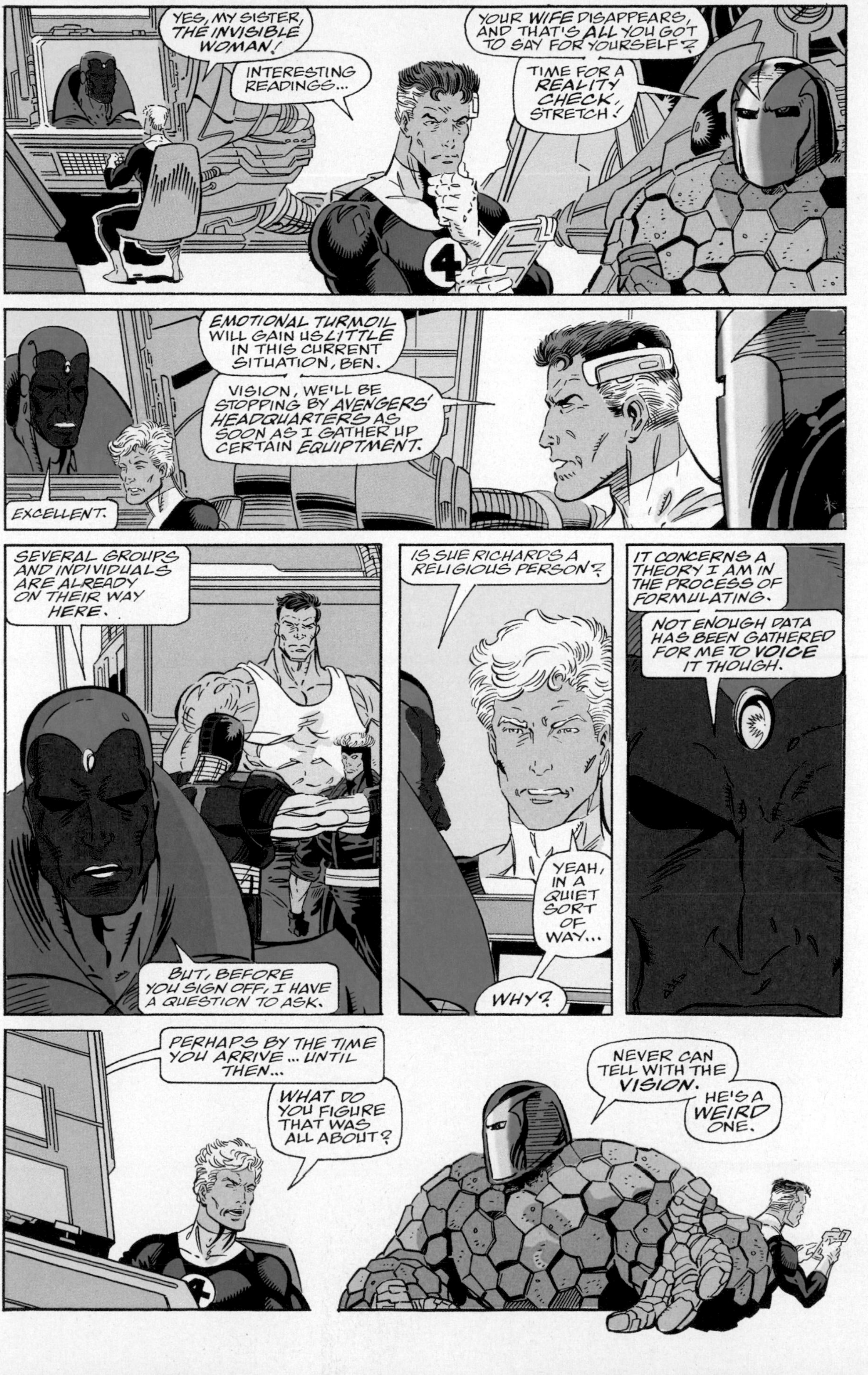
YES, MY SISTER, THE INVISIBLE WOMAN!
INTERESTING READINGS...
YOUR WIFE DISAPPEARS, AND THAT'S ALL YOU GOT TO SAY FOR YOURSELF?
TIME FOR A REALITY CHECK, STRETCH!
EMOTIONAL TURMOIL WILL GAIN US LITTLE IN THIS CURRENT SITUATION, BEN.
VISION, WE'LL BE STOPPING BY AVENGERS' HEADQUARTERS AS SOON AS I GATHER UP CERTAIN EQUIPTMENT.
EXCELLENT.
SEVERAL GROUPS AND INDIVIDUALS ARE ALREADY ON THEIR WAY HERE.
BUT, BEFORE YOU SIGN OFF, I HAVE A QUESTION TO ASK.
IS SUE RICHARDS A RELIGIOUS PERSON?
YEAH, IN A QUIET SORT OF WAY...
WHY?
IT CONCERNS A THEORY I AM IN THE PROCESS OF FORMULATING.
NOT ENOUGH DATA HAS BEEN GATHERED FOR ME TO VOICE IT THOUGH.
PERHAPS BY THE TIME YOU ARRIVE ... UNTIL THEN...
WHAT DO YOU FIGURE THAT WAS ALL ABOUT?
NEVER CAN TELL WITH THE VISION.
HE'S A WEIRD ONE.

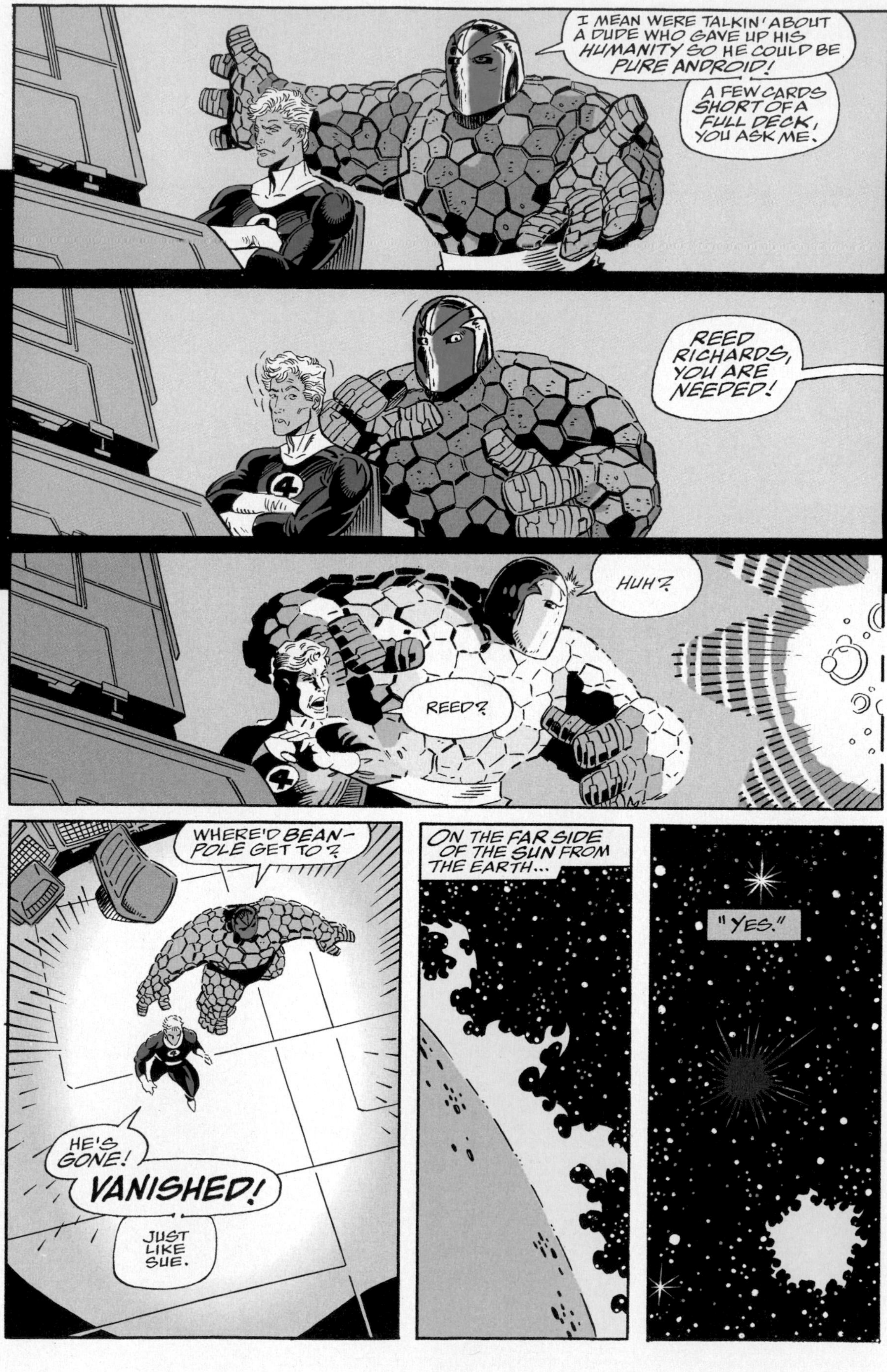
I MEAN WERE TALKIN' ABOUT A DUDE WHO GAVE UP HIS HUMANITY SO HE COULD BE PURE ANDROID!
A FEW CARDS SHORT OF A FULL DECK, YOU ASK ME.
REED RICHARDS, YOU ARE NEEDED!
HUH?
REED?
WHERE'D BEAN-POLE GET TO?
HE'S GONE! VANISHED!
JUST LIKE SUE.
ON THE FAR SIDE OF THE SUN FROM THE EARTH...
"YES."

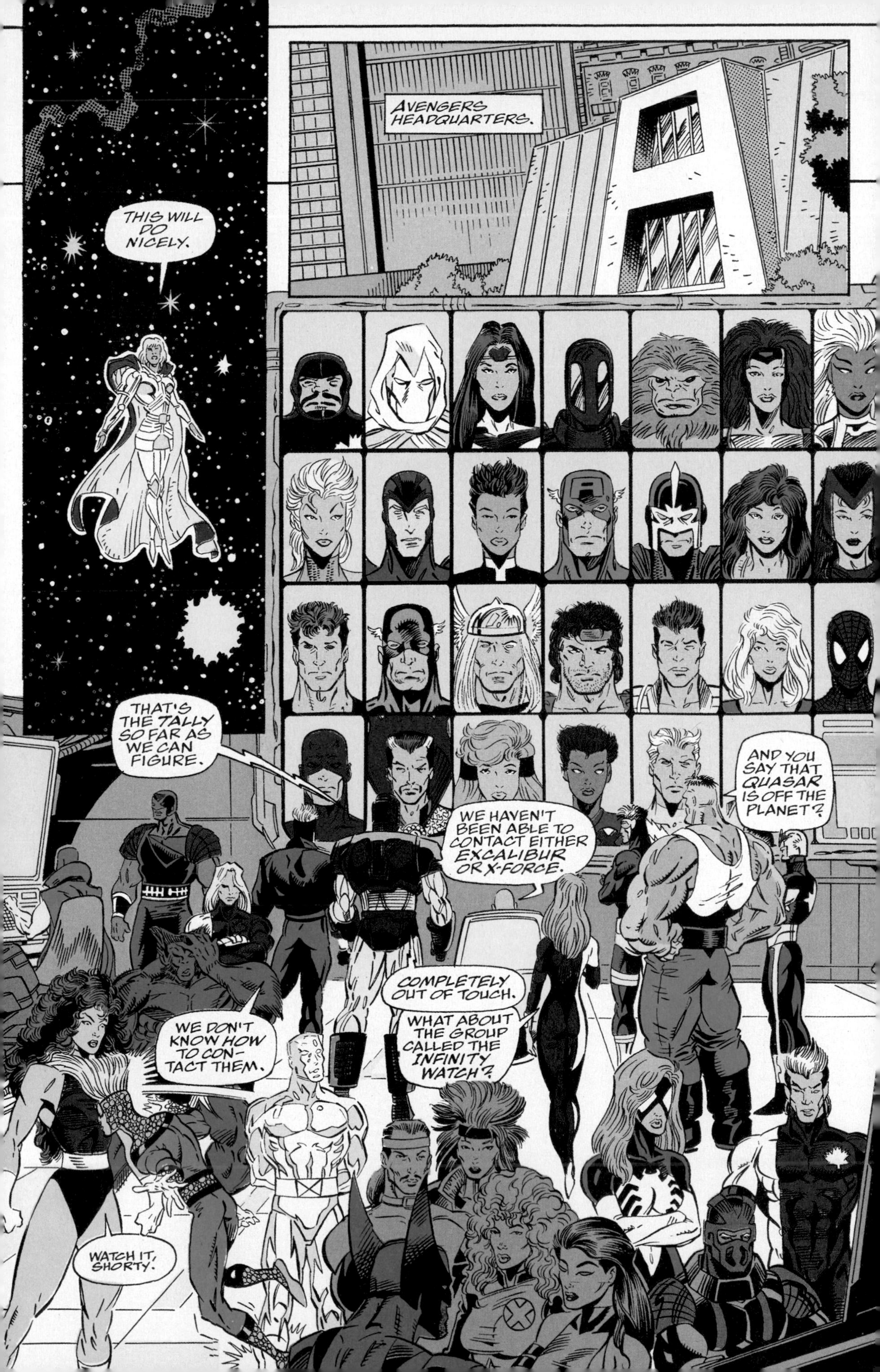

THIS WILL DO NICELY.
AVENGERS HEADQUARTERS.
THAT'S THE TALLY SO FAR AS WE CAN FIGURE.
AND YOU SAY THAT QUASAR IS OFF THE PLANET?
WE HAVEN'T BEEN ABLE TO CONTACT EITHER EXCALIBUR OR X-FORCE.
COMPLETELY OUT OF TOUCH.
WHAT ABOUT THE GROUP CALLED THE INFINITY WATCH?
WE DON'T KNOW HOW TO CON-TACT THEM.
WATCH IT, SHORTY.

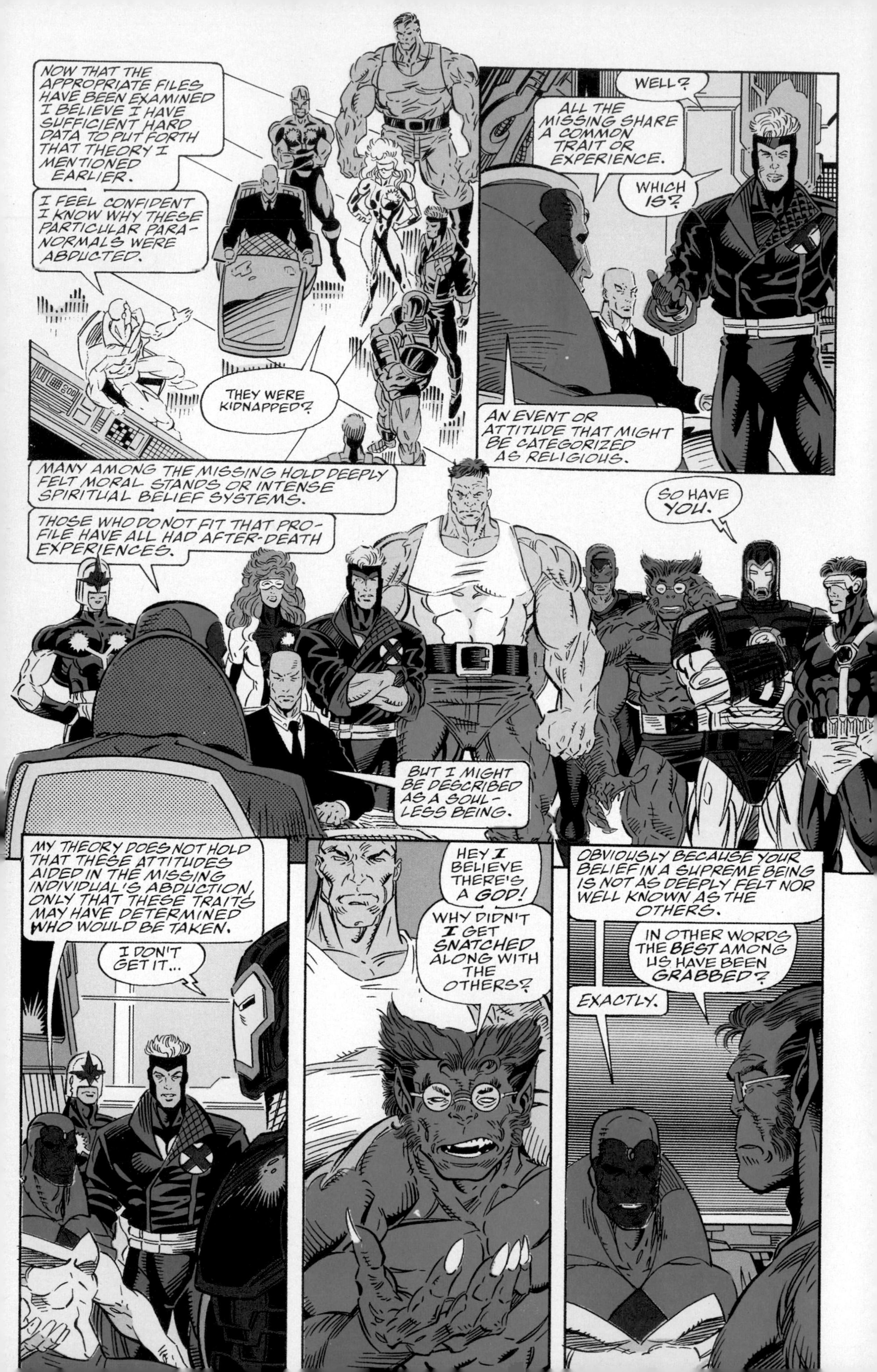
NOW THAT THE APPROPRIATE FILES HAVE BEEN EXAMINED I BELIEVE I HAVE SUFFICIENT HARD DATA TO PUT FORTH THAT THEORY I MENTIONED EARLIER.
I FEEL CONFIDENT I KNOW WHY THESE PARTICULAR PARA-NORMALS WERE ABDUCTED.
THEY WERE KIDNAPPED?
WELL?
ALL THE MISSING SHARE A COMMON TRAIT OR EXPERIENCE.
WHICH IS?
AN EVENT OR ATTITUDE THAT MIGHT BE CATEGORIZED AS RELIGIOUS.
MANY AMONG THE MISSING HOLD DEEPLY FELT MORAL STANDS OR INTENSE SPIRITUAL BELIEF SYSTEMS.
THOSE WHO DO NOT FIT THAT PRO-FILE HAVE ALL HAD AFTER-DEATH EXPERIENCES.
SO HAVE YOU.
BUT I MIGHT BE DESCRIBED AS A SOUL-LESS BEING.
MY THEORY DOES NOT HOLD THAT THESE ATTITUDES AIDED IN THE MISSING INDIVIDUAL'S ABDUCTION, ONLY THAT THESE TRAITS MAY HAVE DETERMINED WHO WOULD BE TAKEN.
I DON'T GET IT...
HEY I BELIEVE THERE'S A GOD!
WHY DIDN'T I GET SNATCHED ALONG WITH THE OTHERS?
OBVIOUSLY BECAUSE YOUR BELIEF IN A SUPREME BEING IS NOT AS DEEPLY FELT NOR WELL KNOWN AS THE OTHERS.
IN OTHER WORDS THE BEST AMONG US HAVE BEEN GRABBED?
EXACTLY.

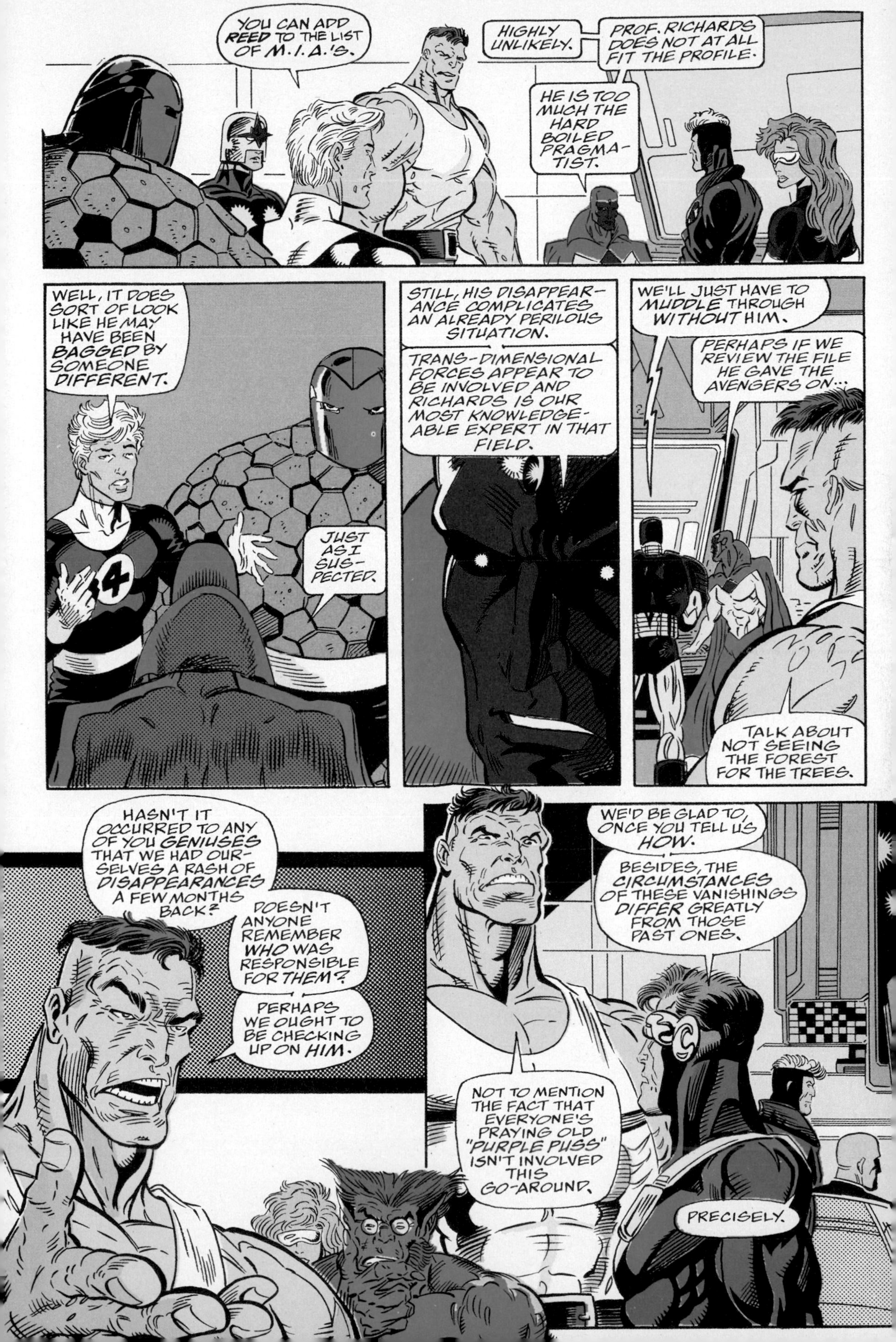
YOU CAN ADD REED TO THE LIST OF M.I.A.'S.
HIGHLY UNLIKELY.
PROF. RICHARDS DOES NOT AT ALL FIT THE PROFILE.
HE IS TOO MUCH THE HARD BOILED PRAGMATIST.
WELL, IT DOES SORT OF LOOK LIKE HE MAY HAVE BEEN BAGGED BY SOMEONE DIFFERENT.
JUST AS I SUSPECTED.
STILL, HIS DISAPPEARANCE COMPLICATES AN ALREADY PERILOUS SITUATION.
TRANS-DIMENSIONAL FORCES APPEAR TO BE INVOLVED AND RICHARDS IS OUR MOST KNOWLEDGEABLE EXPERT IN THAT FIELD.
WE'LL JUST HAVE TO MUDDLE THROUGH WITHOUT HIM.
PERHAPS IF WE REVIEW THE FILE HE GAVE THE AVENGERS ON...
TALK ABOUT NOT SEEING THE FOREST FOR THE TREES.
HASN'T IT OCCURRED TO ANY OF YOU GENIUSES THAT WE HAD OURSELVES A RASH OF DISAPPEARANCES A FEW MONTHS BACK?
DOESN'T ANYONE REMEMBER WHO WAS RESPONSIBLE FOR THEM?
PERHAPS WE OUGHT TO BE CHECKING UP ON HIM.
WE'D BE GLAD TO, ONCE YOU TELL US HOW.
BESIDES, THE CIRCUMSTANCES OF THESE VANISHINGS DIFFER GREATLY FROM THOSE PAST ONES.
NOT TO MENTION THE FACT THAT EVERYONE'S PRAYING OLD "PURPLE PUSS" ISN'T INVOLVED THIS GO-AROUND.
PRECISELY.

NOBODY IN HIS RIGHT MIND SHOULD WANT TO CONFRONT THANOS AGAIN, IF IT CAN BE AVOIDED.

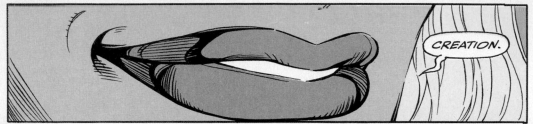

CREATION.

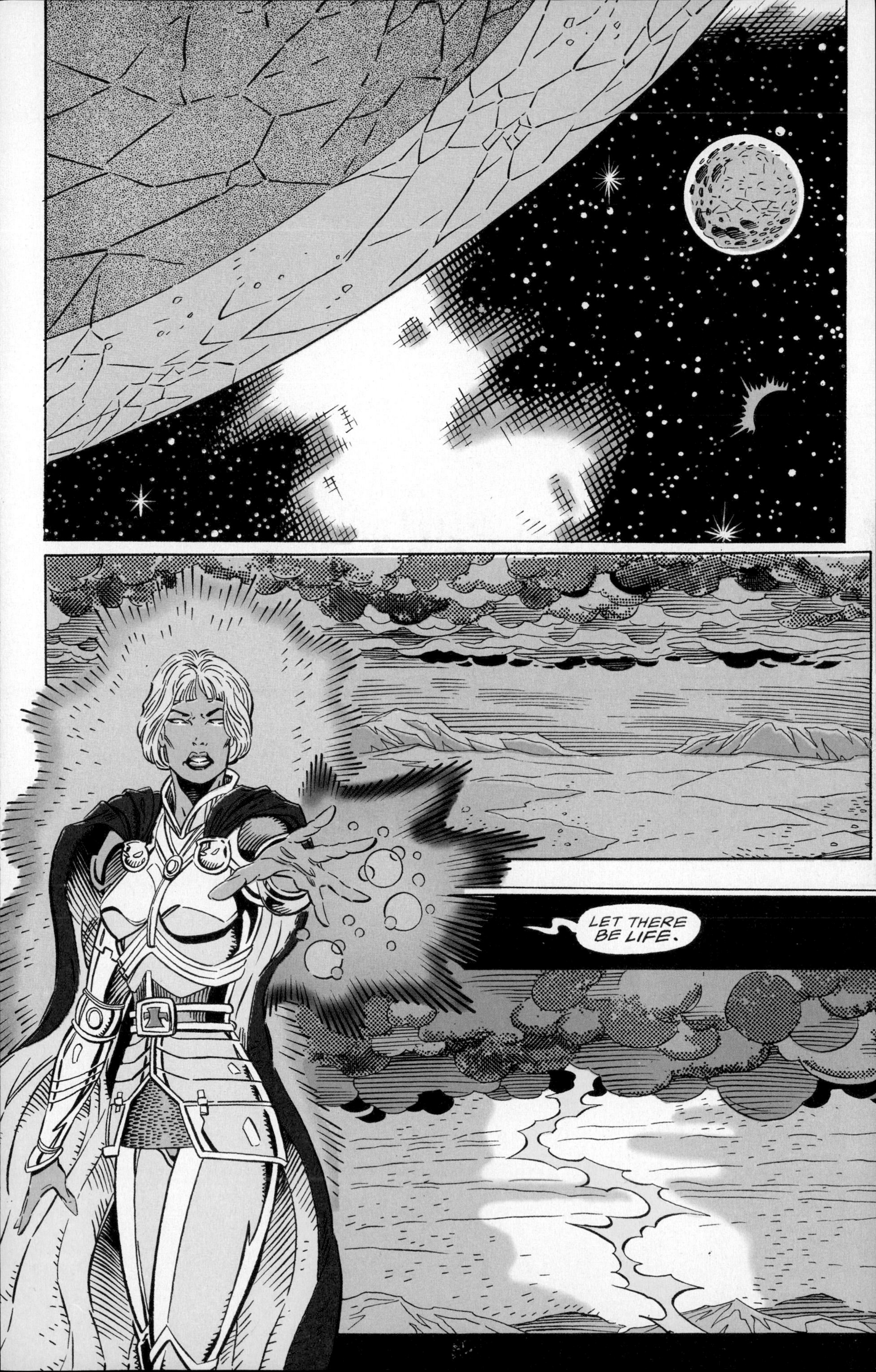
LET THERE BE LIFE.

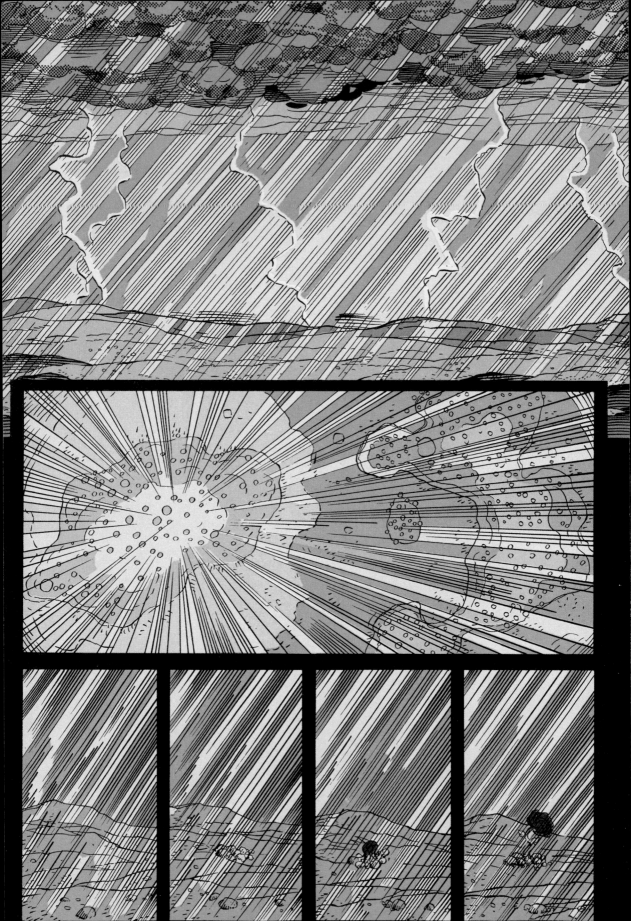

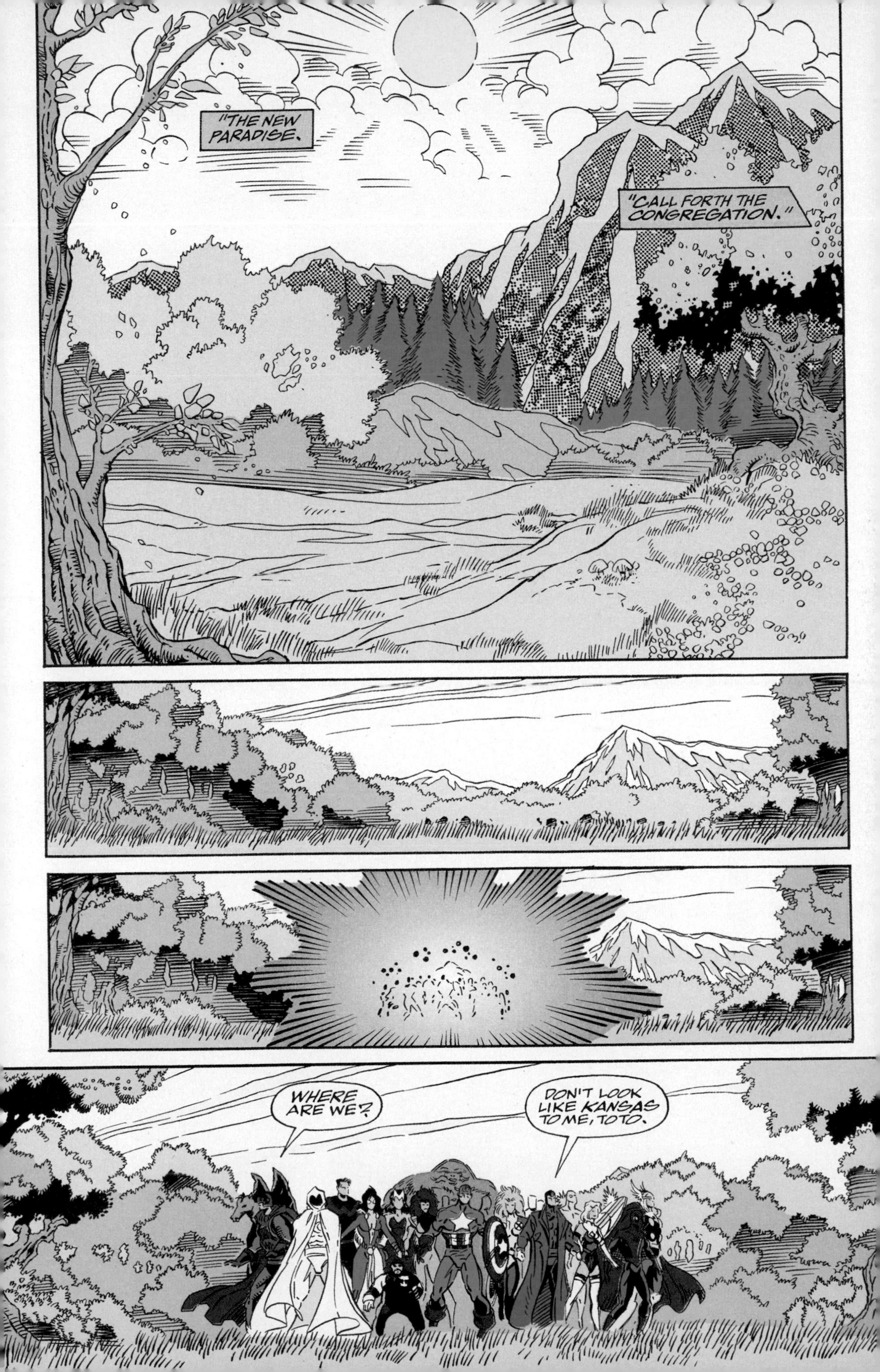
"THE NEW PARADISE.
"CALL FORTH THE CONGREGATION."
WHERE ARE WE?
DON'T LOOK LIKE KANSAS TO ME, TOTO.

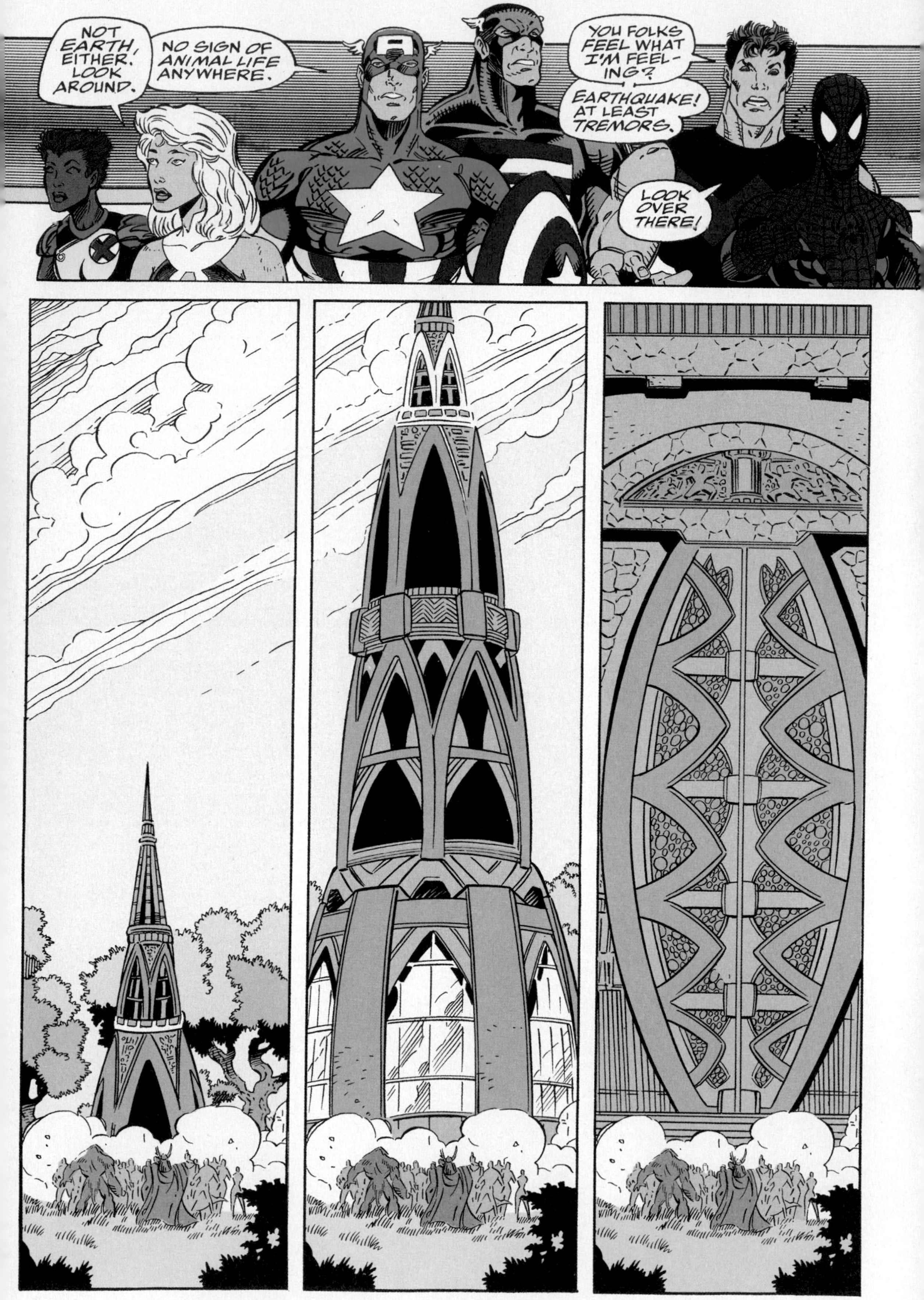
NOT EARTH, EITHER. LOOK AROUND.
NO SIGN OF ANIMAL LIFE ANYWHERE.
YOU FOLKS FEEL WHAT I'M FEEL-ING?
EARTHQUAKE! AT LEAST TREMORS.
LOOK OVER THERE!

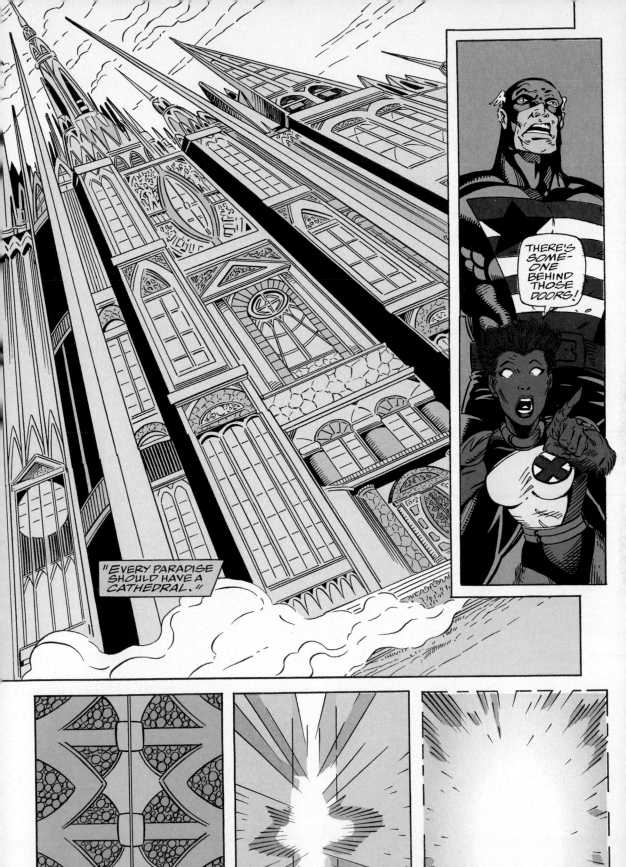

THERE'S SOMEONE BEHIND THOSE DOORS!

"EVERY PARADISE SHOULD HAVE A CATHEDRAL."

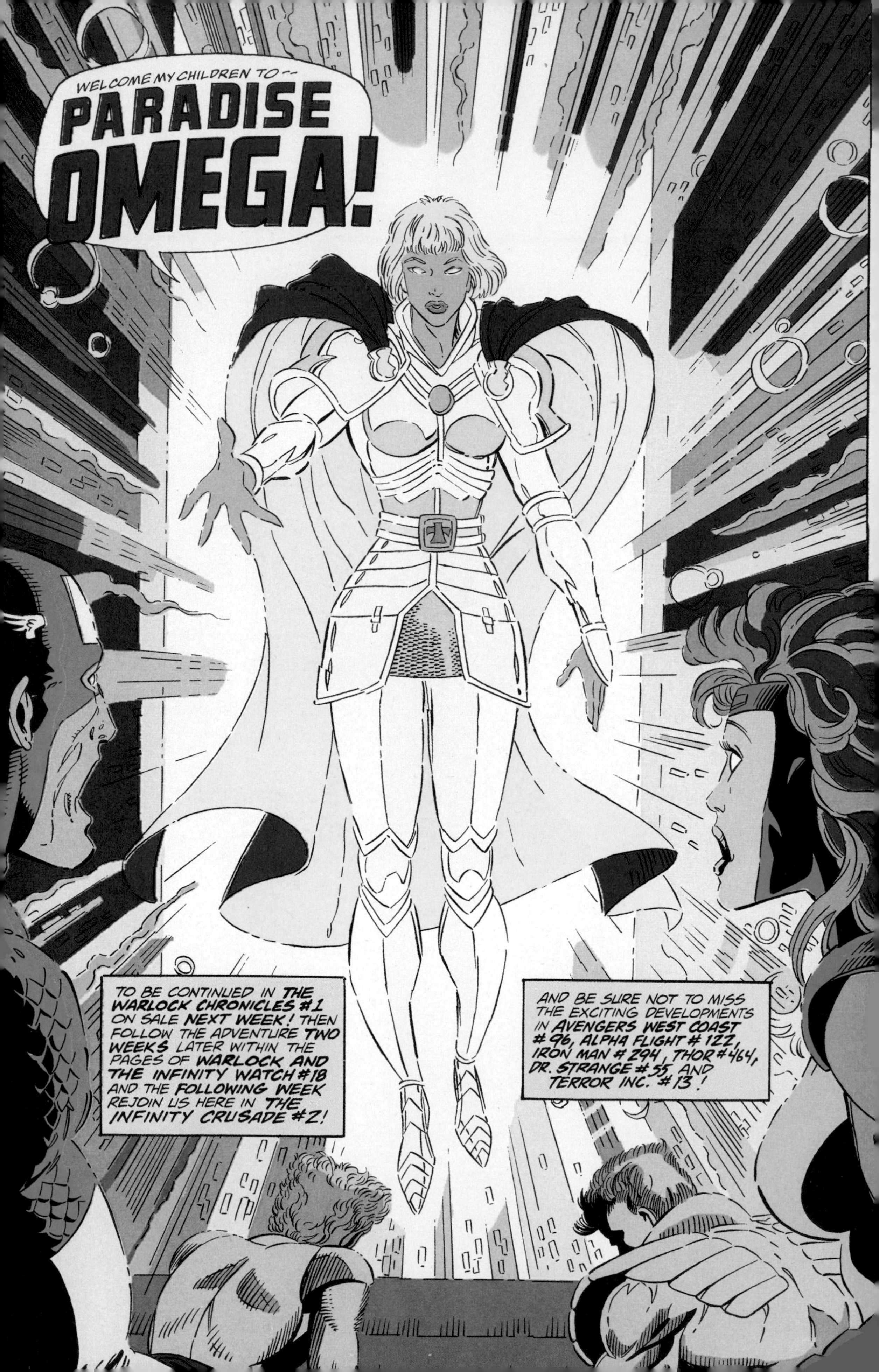
WELCOME MY CHILDREN TO-- PARADISE OMEGA!
TO BE CONTINUED IN THE WARLOCK CHRONICLES #1 ON SALE NEXT WEEK! THEN FOLLOW THE ADVENTURE TWO WEEKS LATER WITHIN THE PAGES OF WARLOCK AND THE INFINITY WATCH #18 AND THE FOLLOWING WEEK REJOIN US HERE IN THE INFINITY CRUSADE #2!
AND BE SURE NOT TO MISS THE EXCITING DEVELOPMENTS IN AVENGERS WEST COAST #96, ALPHA FLIGHT #122, IRON MAN #294, THOR #464, DR. STRANGE #55 AND TERROR INC. #13!

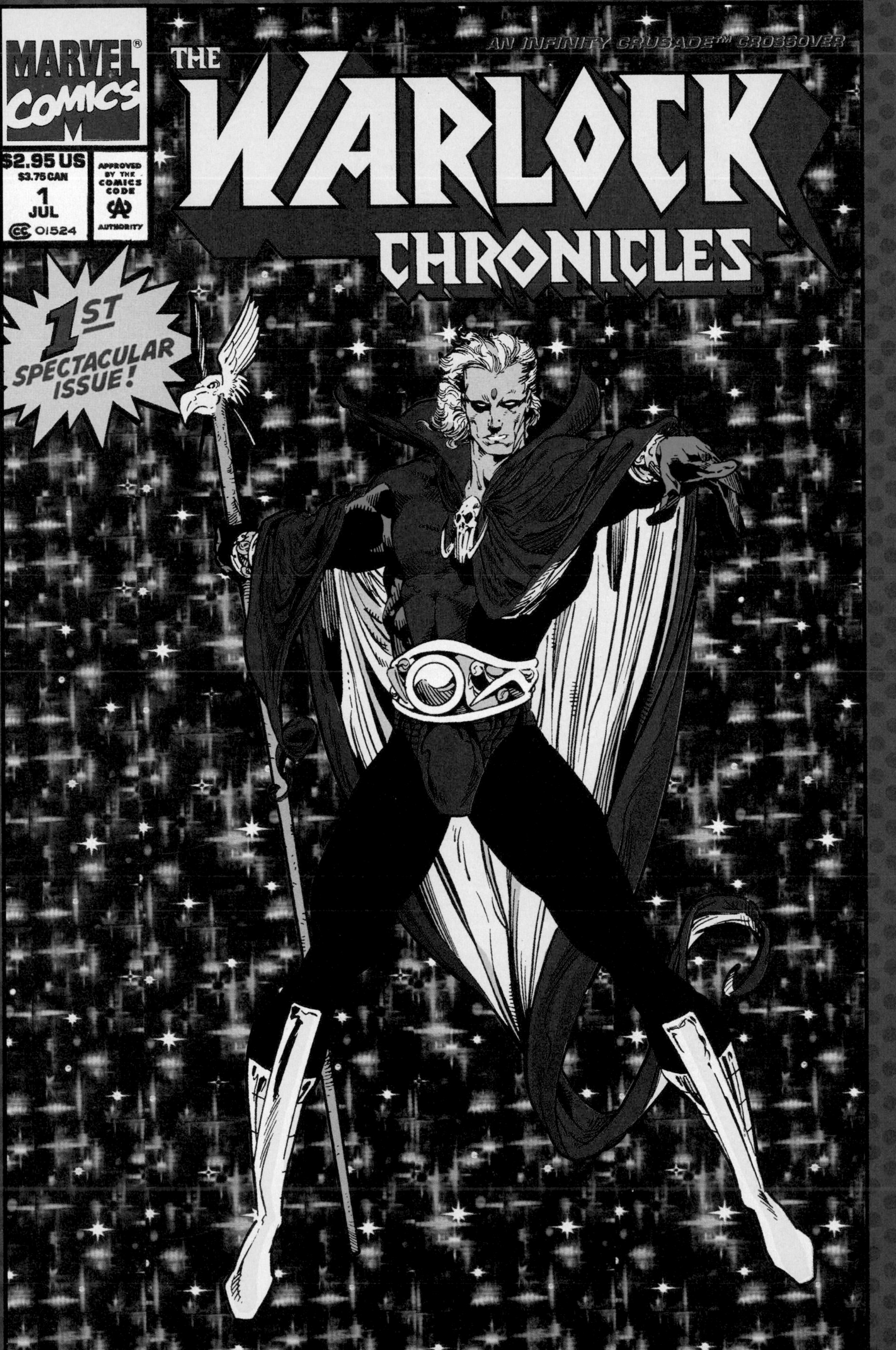
MARVEL® COMICS
$2.95 US
$3.75 CAN
1
JUL
APPROVED BY THE COMICS CODE AUTHORITY
AN INFINITY CRUSADE™ CROSSOVER
THE WARLOCK CHRONICLES
1ST SPECTACULAR ISSUE!

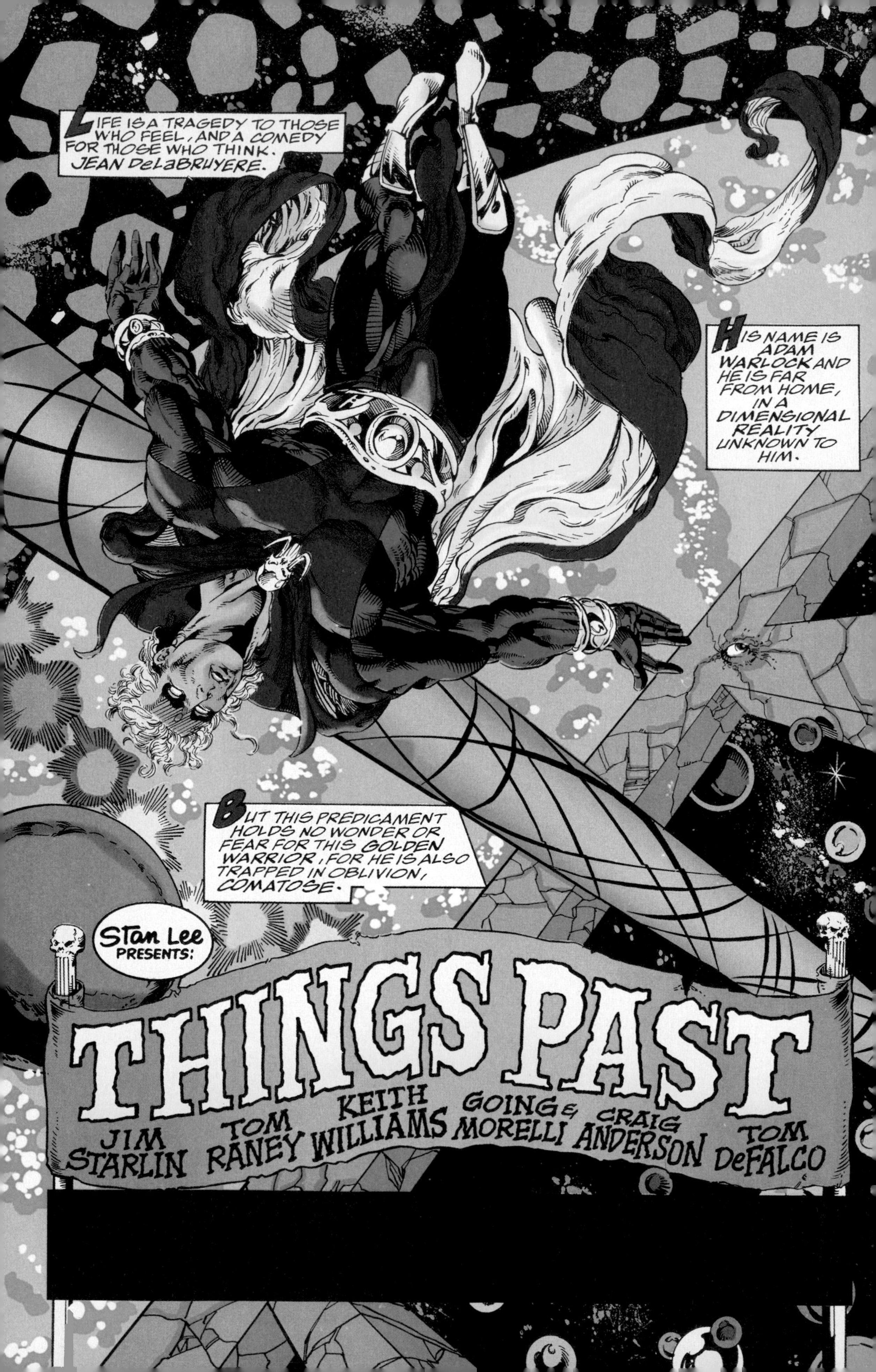
LIFE IS A TRAGEDY TO THOSE WHO FEEL, AND A COMEDY FOR THOSE WHO THINK. JEAN DeLABRUYERE.
HIS NAME IS ADAM WARLOCK AND HE IS FAR FROM HOME, IN A DIMENSIONAL REALITY UNKNOWN TO HIM.
BUT THIS PREDICAMENT HOLDS NO WONDER OR FEAR FOR THIS GOLDEN WARRIOR, FOR HE IS ALSO TRAPPED IN OBLIVION, COMATOSE.
STAN LEE PRESENTS:
THINGS PAST
JIM STARLIN
TOM RANEY
KEITH WILLIAMS
GOING & MORELLI
CRAIG ANDERSON
TOM DeFALCO
[redacted]

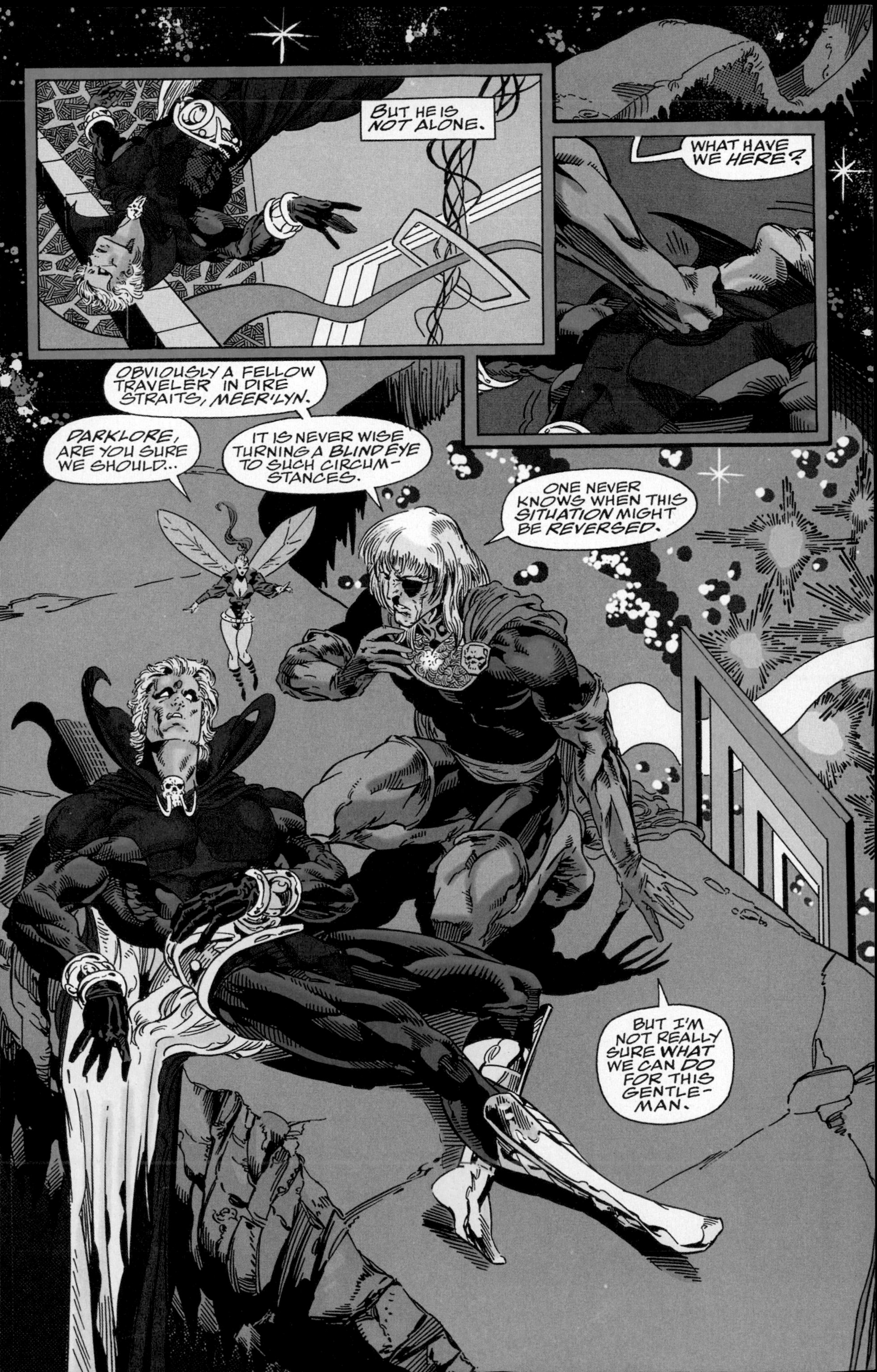

BUT HE IS NOT ALONE.
WHAT HAVE WE HERE?
OBVIOUSLY A FELLOW TRAVELER IN DIRE STRAITS, MEER'LYN.
DARKLORE, ARE YOU SURE WE SHOULD...
IT IS NEVER WISE TURNING A BLIND EYE TO SUCH CIRCUM-STANCES.
ONE NEVER KNOWS WHEN THIS SITUATION MIGHT BE REVERSED.
BUT I'M NOT REALLY SURE WHAT WE CAN DO FOR THIS GENTLE-MAN.

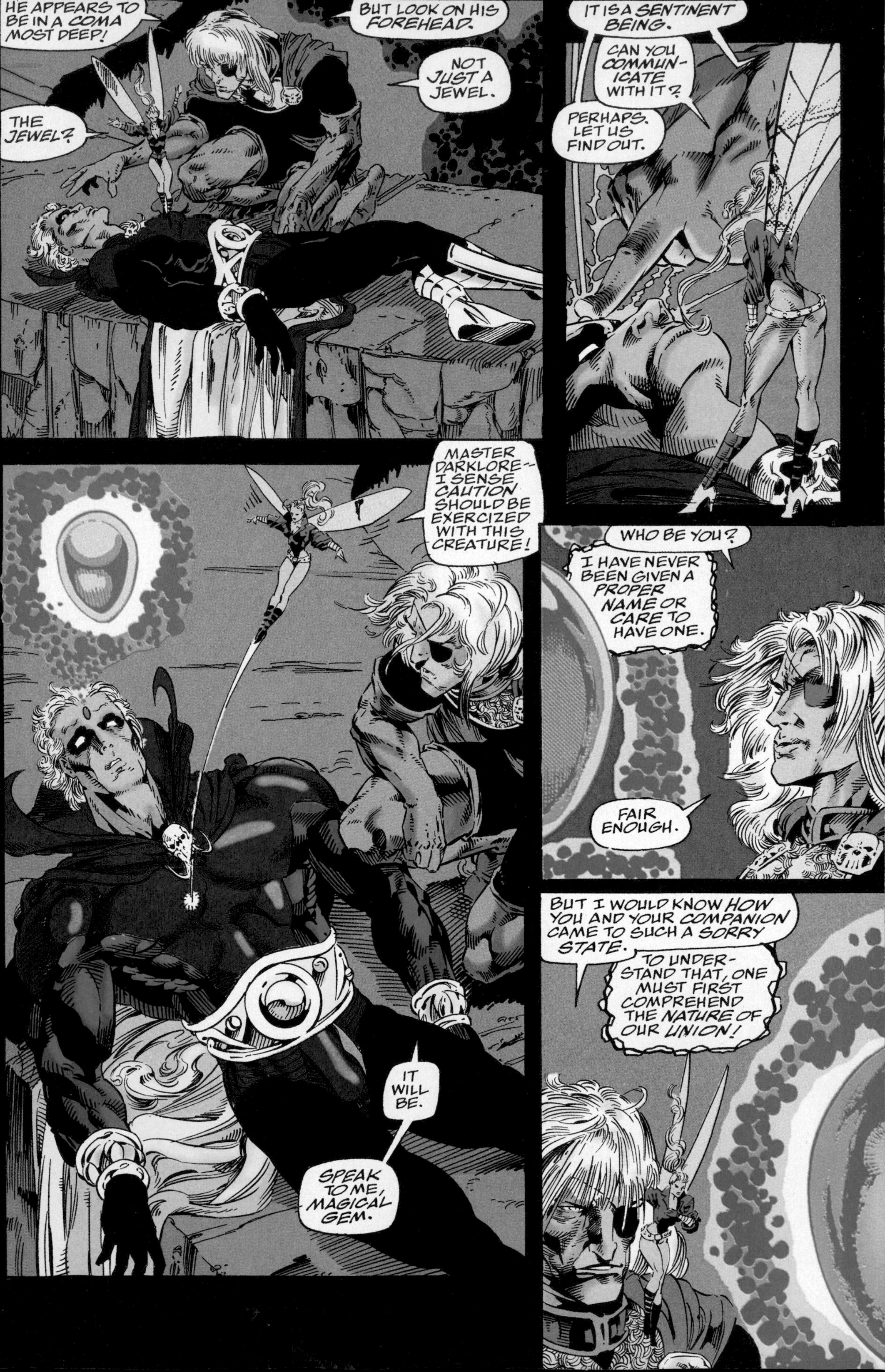
HE APPEARS TO BE IN A COMA MOST DEEP!
BUT LOOK ON HIS FOREHEAD.
NOT JUST A JEWEL.
THE JEWEL?
IT IS A SENTINENT BEING.
CAN YOU COMMUNICATE WITH IT?
PERHAPS. LET US FIND OUT.
MASTER DARKLORE-- I SENSE CAUTION SHOULD BE EXERCIZED WITH THIS CREATURE!
IT WILL BE.
SPEAK TO ME, MAGICAL GEM.
WHO BE YOU?
I HAVE NEVER BEEN GIVEN A PROPER NAME OR CARE TO HAVE ONE.
FAIR ENOUGH.
BUT I WOULD KNOW HOW YOU AND YOUR COMPANION CAME TO SUCH A SORRY STATE.
TO UNDERSTAND THAT, ONE MUST FIRST COMPREHEND THE NATURE OF OUR UNION!

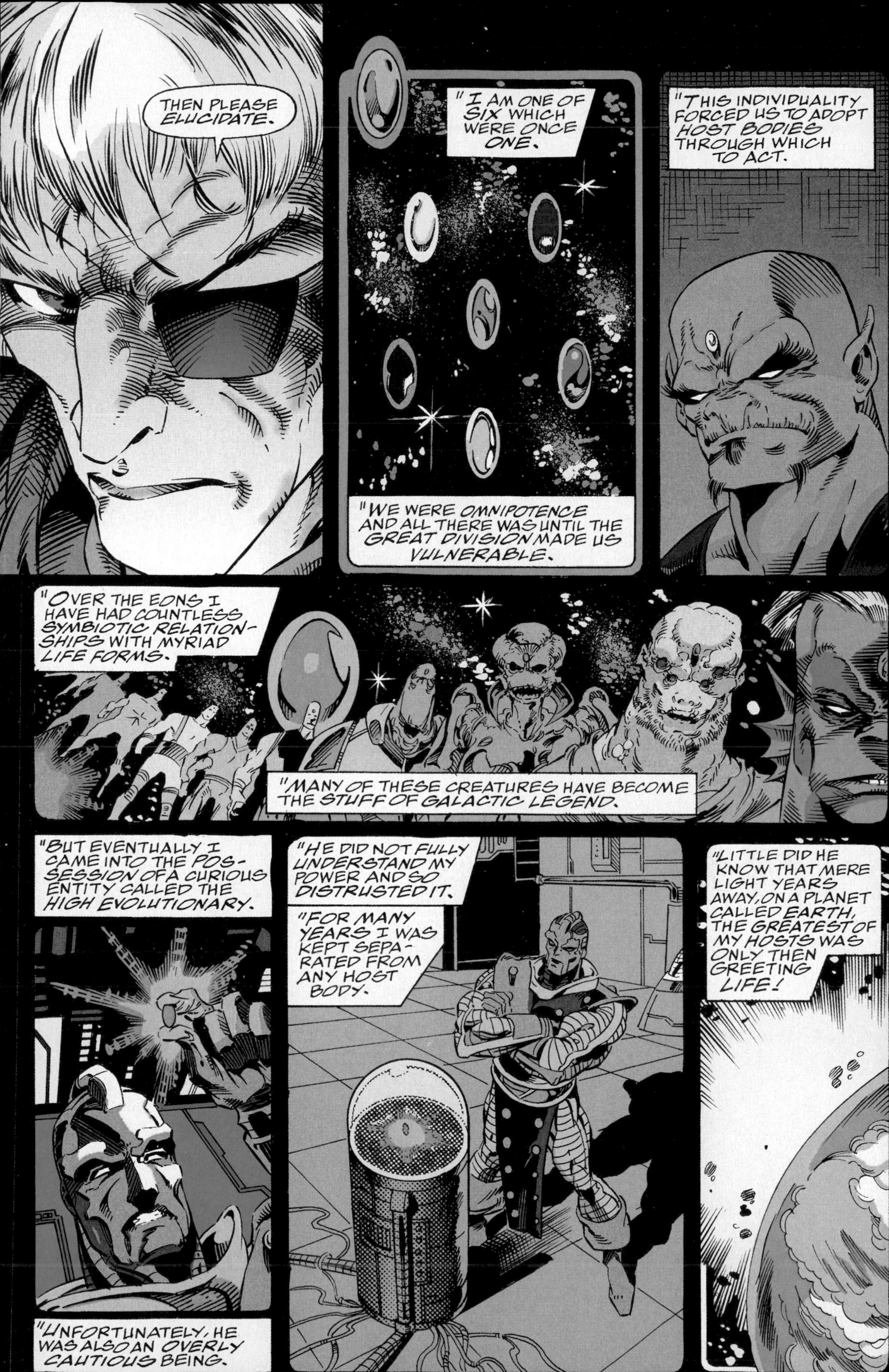

THEN PLEASE ELUCIDATE.
"I AM ONE OF SIX WHICH WERE ONCE ONE.
"WE WERE OMNIPOTENCE AND ALL THERE WAS UNTIL THE GREAT DIVISION MADE US VULNERABLE.
"THIS INDIVIDUALITY FORCED US TO ADOPT HOST BODIES THROUGH WHICH TO ACT.
"OVER THE EONS I HAVE HAD COUNTLESS SYMBIOTIC RELATIONSHIPS WITH MYRIAD LIFE FORMS.
"MANY OF THESE CREATURES HAVE BECOME THE STUFF OF GALACTIC LEGEND.
"BUT EVENTUALLY I CAME INTO THE POSSESSION OF A CURIOUS ENTITY CALLED THE HIGH EVOLUTIONARY.
"UNFORTUNATELY, HE WAS ALSO AN OVERLY CAUTIOUS BEING.
"HE DID NOT FULLY UNDERSTAND MY POWER AND SO DISTRUSTED IT.
"FOR MANY YEARS I WAS KEPT SEPARATED FROM ANY HOST BODY.
"LITTLE DID HE KNOW THAT MERE LIGHT YEARS AWAY, ON A PLANET CALLED EARTH, THE GREATEST OF MY HOSTS WAS ONLY THEN GREETING LIFE!

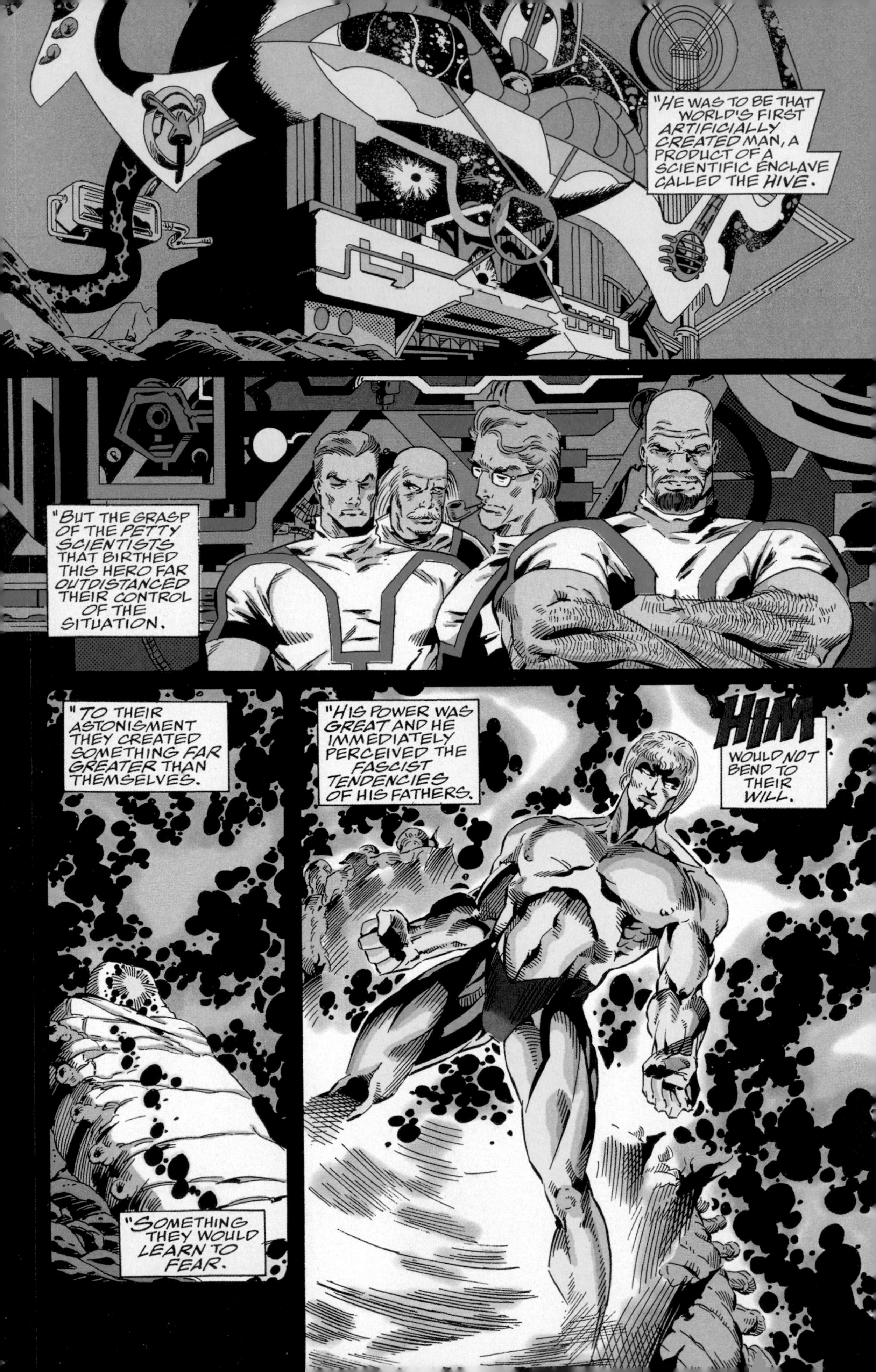
"HE WAS TO BE THAT WORLD'S FIRST ARTIFICIALLY CREATED MAN, A PRODUCT OF A SCIENTIFIC ENCLAVE CALLED THE HIVE.
"BUT THE GRASP OF THE PETTY SCIENTISTS THAT BIRTHED THIS HERO FAR OUTDISTANCED THEIR CONTROL OF THE SITUATION.
"TO THEIR ASTONISHMENT THEY CREATED SOMETHING FAR GREATER THAN THEMSELVES.
"SOMETHING THEY WOULD LEARN TO FEAR.
"HIS POWER WAS GREAT AND HE IMMEDIATELY PERCEIVED THE FASCIST TENDENCIES OF HIS FATHERS.
HIM WOULD NOT BEND TO THEIR WILL.

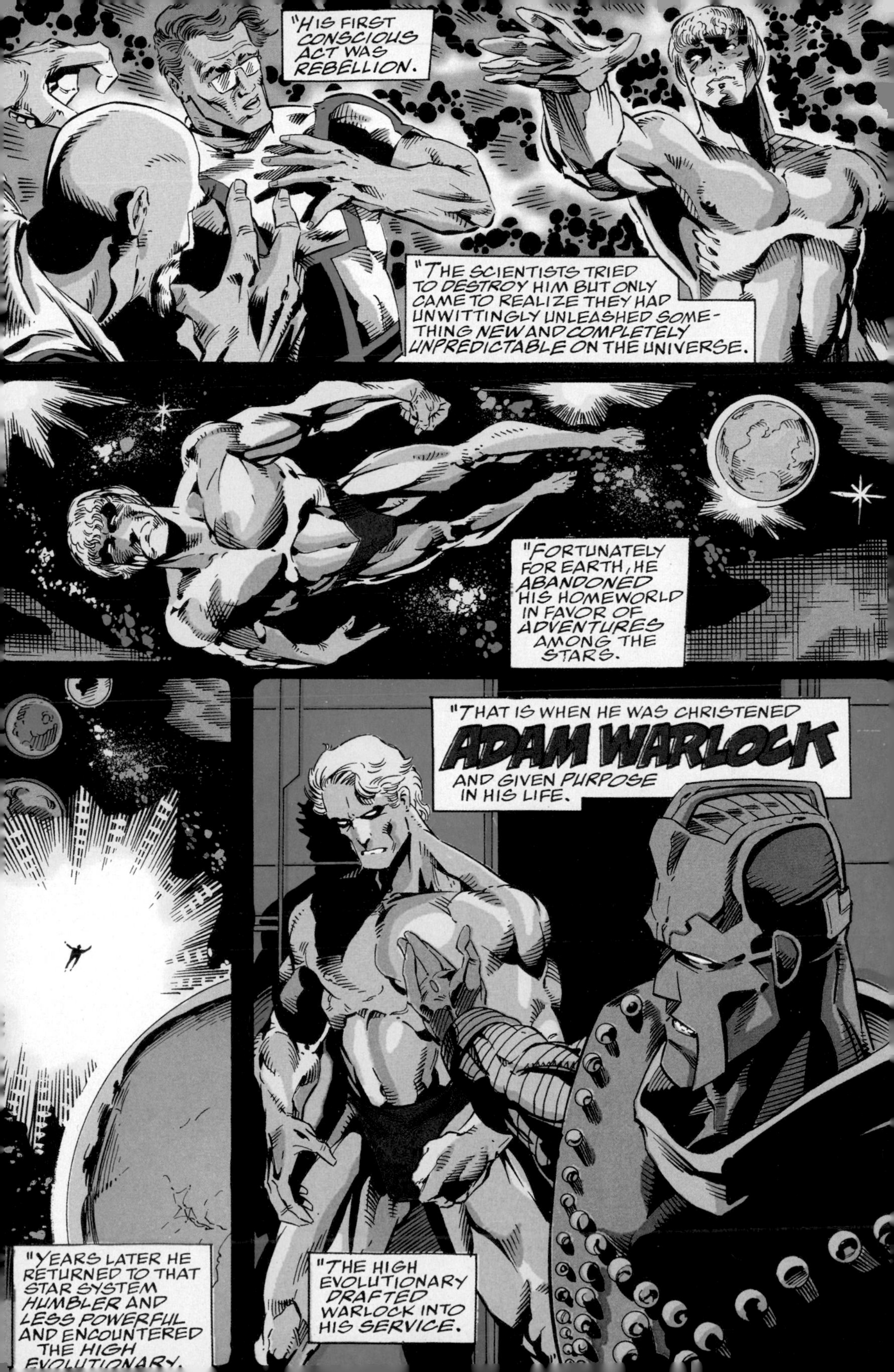
"HIS FIRST CONSCIOUS ACT WAS REBELLION.
"THE SCIENTISTS TRIED TO DESTROY HIM BUT ONLY CAME TO REALIZE THEY HAD UNWITTINGLY UNLEASHED SOMETHING NEW AND COMPLETELY UNPREDICTABLE ON THE UNIVERSE.
"FORTUNATELY FOR EARTH, HE ABANDONED HIS HOMEWORLD IN FAVOR OF ADVENTURES AMONG THE STARS.
"THAT IS WHEN HE WAS CHRISTENED
ADAM WARLOCK
AND GIVEN PURPOSE IN HIS LIFE.
"YEARS LATER HE RETURNED TO THAT STAR SYSTEM HUMBLER AND LESS POWERFUL AND ENCOUNTERED THE HIGH EVOLUTIONARY.
"THE HIGH EVOLUTIONARY DRAFTED WARLOCK INTO HIS SERVICE.

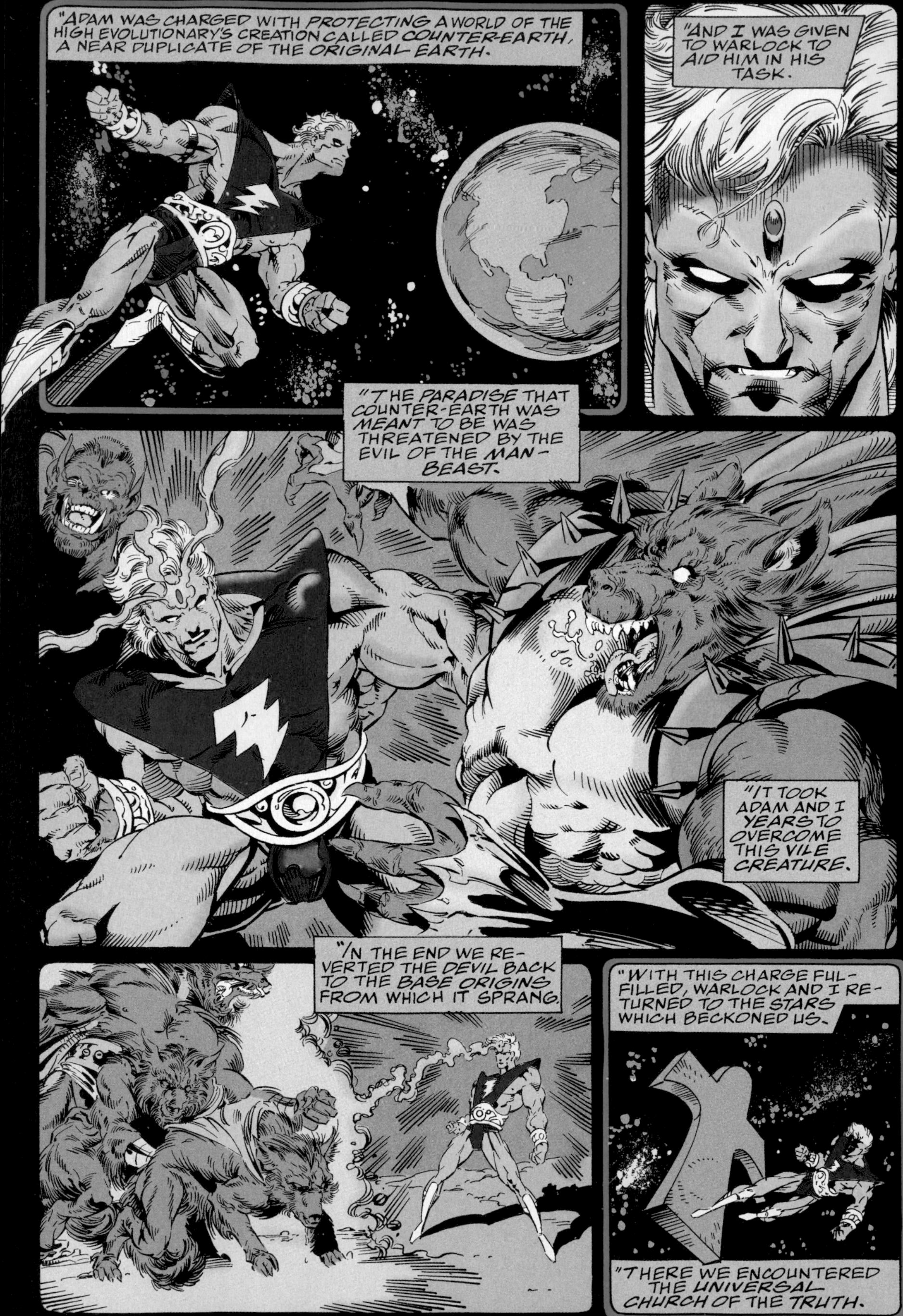
"ADAM WAS CHARGED WITH PROTECTING A WORLD OF THE HIGH EVOLUTIONARY'S CREATION CALLED COUNTER-EARTH, A NEAR DUPLICATE OF THE ORIGINAL EARTH.
"AND I WAS GIVEN TO WARLOCK TO AID HIM IN HIS TASK.
"THE PARADISE THAT COUNTER-EARTH WAS MEANT TO BE WAS THREATENED BY THE EVIL OF THE MAN-BEAST.
"IT TOOK ADAM AND I YEARS TO OVERCOME THIS VILE CREATURE.
"IN THE END WE REVERTED THE DEVIL BACK TO THE BASE ORIGINS FROM WHICH IT SPRANG.
"WITH THIS CHARGE FULFILLED, WARLOCK AND I RETURNED TO THE STARS WHICH BECKONED US.
"THERE WE ENCOUNTERED THE UNIVERSAL CHURCH OF THE TRUTH.

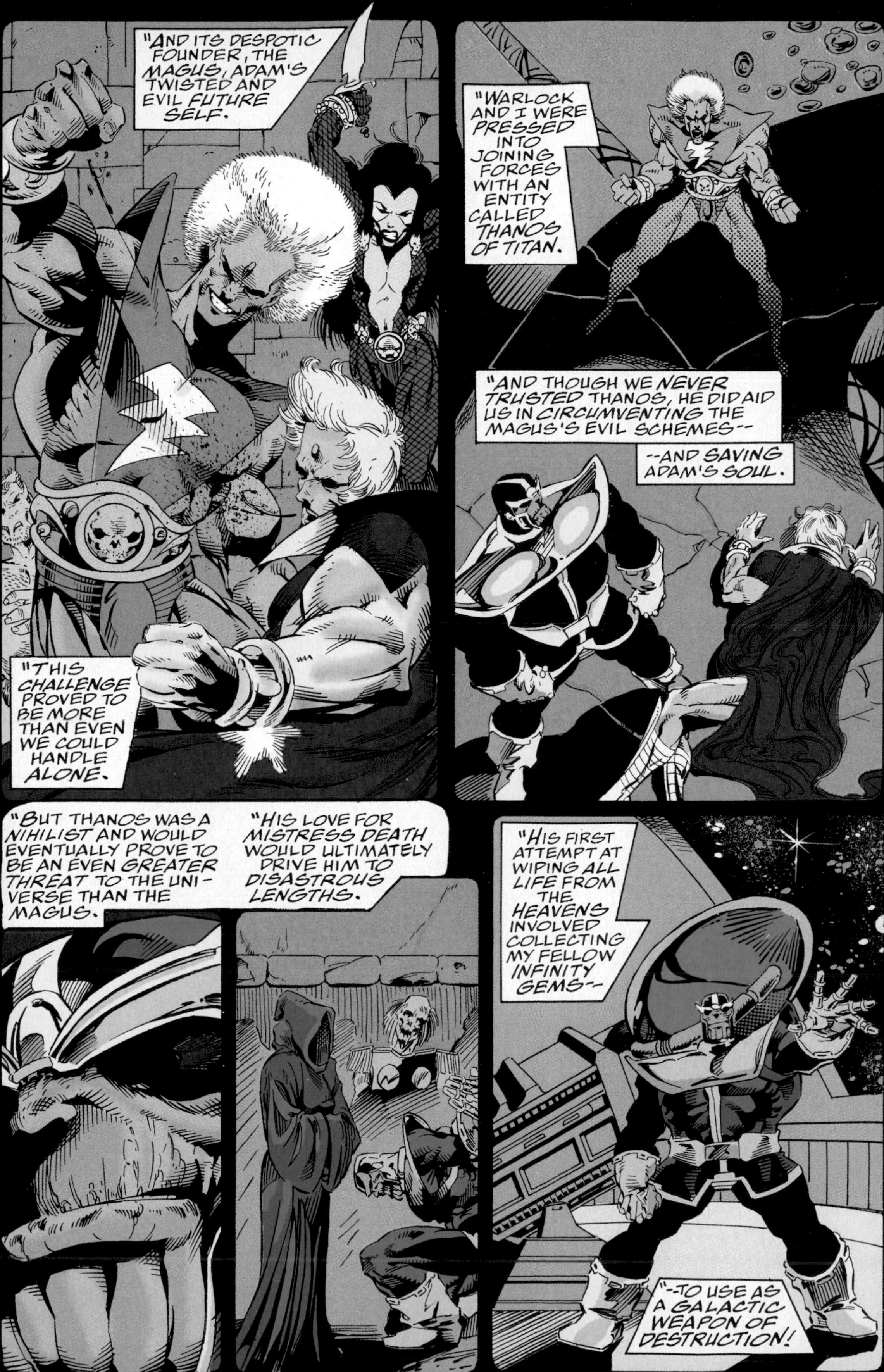
"AND ITS DESPOTIC FOUNDER, THE MAGUS, ADAM'S TWISTED AND EVIL FUTURE SELF.
"THIS CHALLENGE PROVED TO BE MORE THAN EVEN WE COULD HANDLE ALONE.
"WARLOCK AND I WERE PRESSED INTO JOINING FORCES WITH AN ENTITY CALLED THANOS OF TITAN.
"AND THOUGH WE NEVER TRUSTED THANOS, HE DID AID US IN CIRCUMVENTING THE MAGUS'S EVIL SCHEMES--
--AND SAVING ADAM'S SOUL.
"BUT THANOS WAS A NIHILIST AND WOULD EVENTUALLY PROVE TO BE AN EVEN GREATER THREAT TO THE UNI-VERSE THAN THE MAGUS.
"HIS LOVE FOR MISTRESS DEATH WOULD ULTIMATELY DRIVE HIM TO DISASTROUS LENGTHS.
"HIS FIRST ATTEMPT AT WIPING ALL LIFE FROM THE HEAVENS INVOLVED COLLECTING MY FELLOW INFINITY GEMS--
"--TO USE AS A GALACTIC WEAPON OF DESTRUCTION!

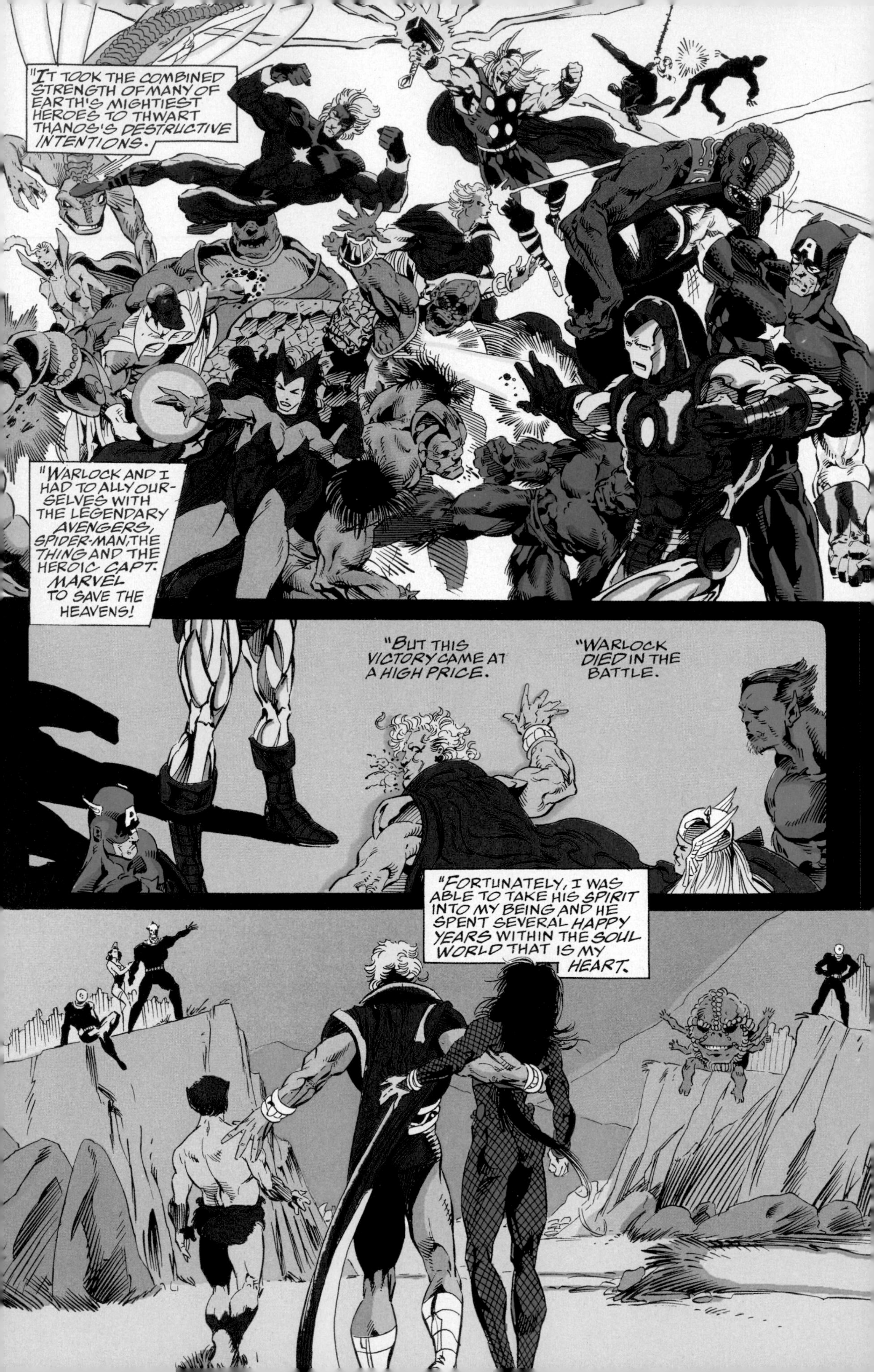
"IT TOOK THE COMBINED STRENGTH OF MANY OF EARTH'S MIGHTIEST HEROES TO THWART THANOS'S DESTRUCTIVE INTENTIONS.
"WARLOCK AND I HAD TO ALLY OURSELVES WITH THE LEGENDARY AVENGERS, SPIDER-MAN, THE THING AND THE HEROIC CAPT. MARVEL TO SAVE THE HEAVENS!
"BUT THIS VICTORY CAME AT A HIGH PRICE.
"WARLOCK DIED IN THE BATTLE.
"FORTUNATELY, I WAS ABLE TO TAKE HIS SPIRIT INTO MY BEING AND HE SPENT SEVERAL HAPPY YEARS WITHIN THE SOUL WORLD THAT IS MY HEART.

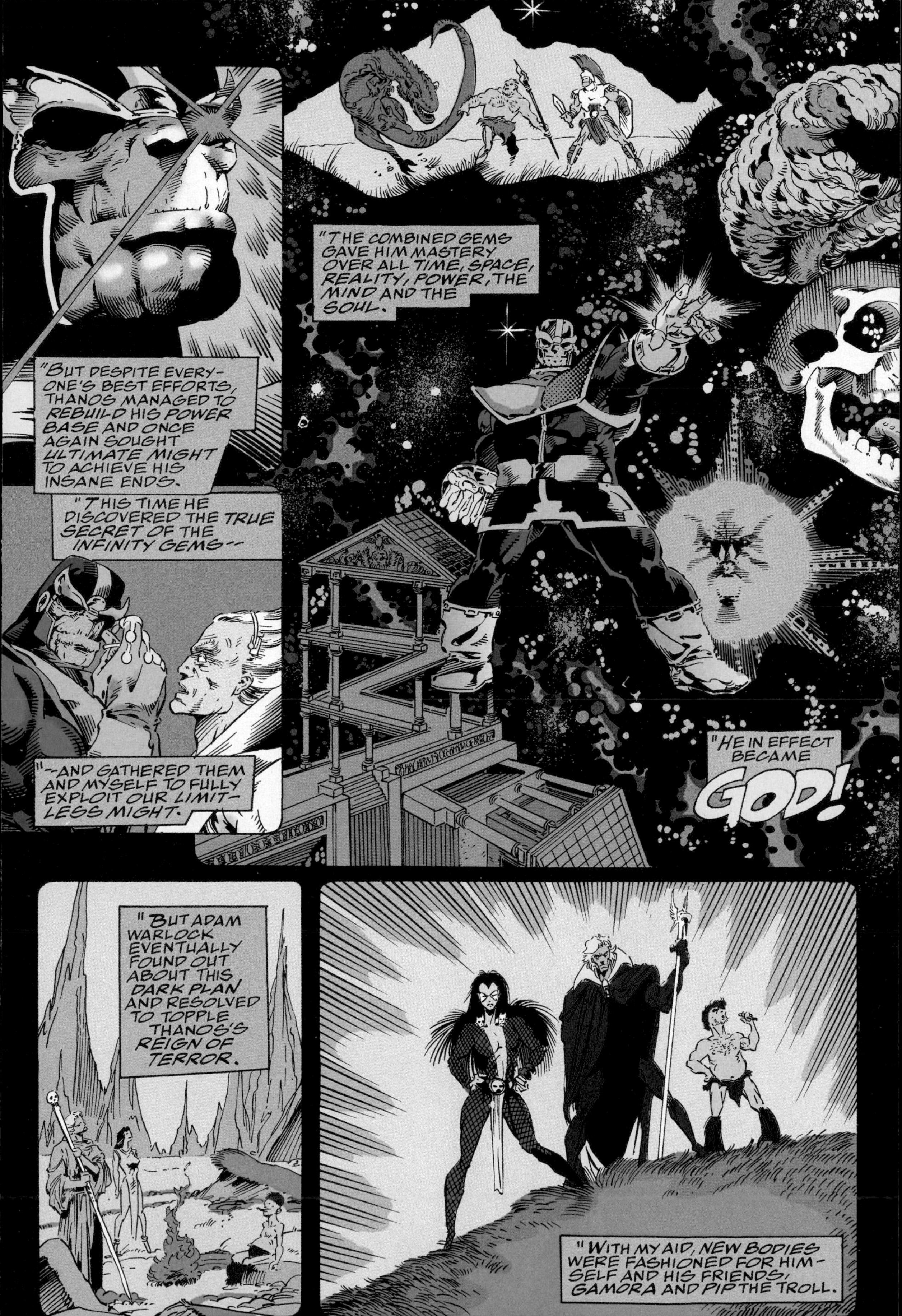
"BUT DESPITE EVERY-ONE'S BEST EFFORTS, THANOS MANAGED TO REBUILD HIS POWER BASE AND ONCE AGAIN SOUGHT ULTIMATE MIGHT TO ACHIEVE HIS INSANE ENDS.
"THIS TIME HE DISCOVERED THE TRUE SECRET OF THE INFINITY GEMS--
"--AND GATHERED THEM AND MYSELF TO FULLY EXPLOIT OUR LIMIT-LESS MIGHT.
"THE COMBINED GEMS GAVE HIM MASTERY OVER ALL TIME, SPACE, REALITY, POWER, THE MIND AND THE SOUL.
"HE IN EFFECT BECAME
GOD!
"BUT ADAM WARLOCK EVENTUALLY FOUND OUT ABOUT THIS DARK PLAN AND RESOLVED TO TOPPLE THANOS'S REIGN OF TERROR.
"WITH MY AID, NEW BODIES WERE FASHIONED FOR HIM-SELF AND HIS FRIENDS, GAMORA AND PIP THE TROLL.

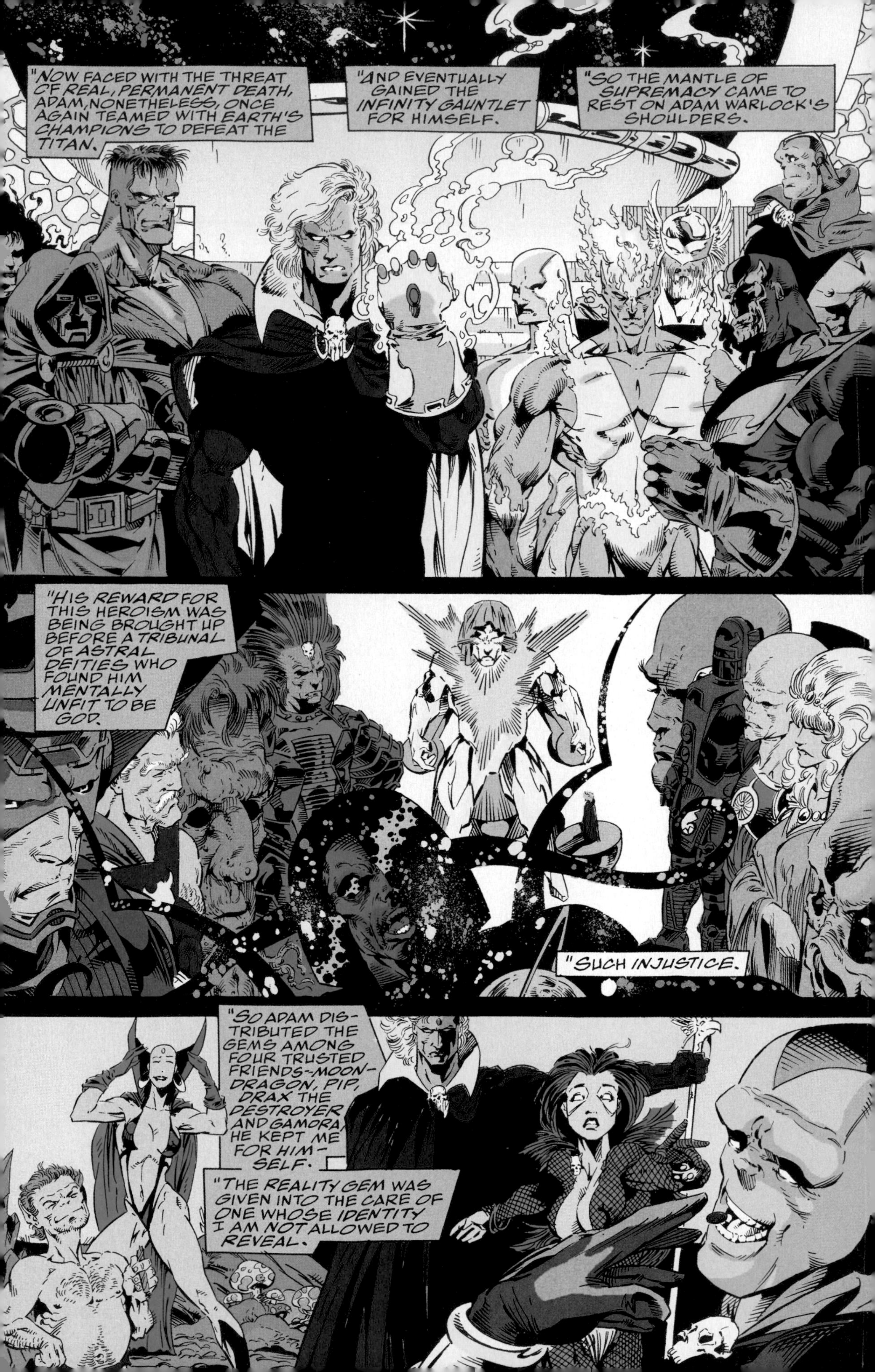
"NOW FACED WITH THE THREAT OF REAL, PERMANENT DEATH, ADAM, NONETHELESS, ONCE AGAIN TEAMED WITH EARTH'S CHAMPIONS TO DEFEAT THE TITAN.
"AND EVENTUALLY GAINED THE INFINITY GAUNTLET FOR HIMSELF.
"SO THE MANTLE OF SUPREMACY CAME TO REST ON ADAM WARLOCK'S SHOULDERS.
"HIS REWARD FOR THIS HEROISM WAS BEING BROUGHT UP BEFORE A TRIBUNAL OF ASTRAL DEITIES WHO FOUND HIM MENTALLY UNFIT TO BE GOD.
"SUCH INJUSTICE.
"SO ADAM DISTRIBUTED THE GEMS AMONG FOUR TRUSTED FRIENDS-MOONDRAGON, PIP, DRAX THE DESTROYER AND GAMORA; HE KEPT ME FOR HIMSELF.
"THE REALITY GEM WAS GIVEN INTO THE CARE OF ONE WHOSE IDENTITY I AM NOT ALLOWED TO REVEAL.

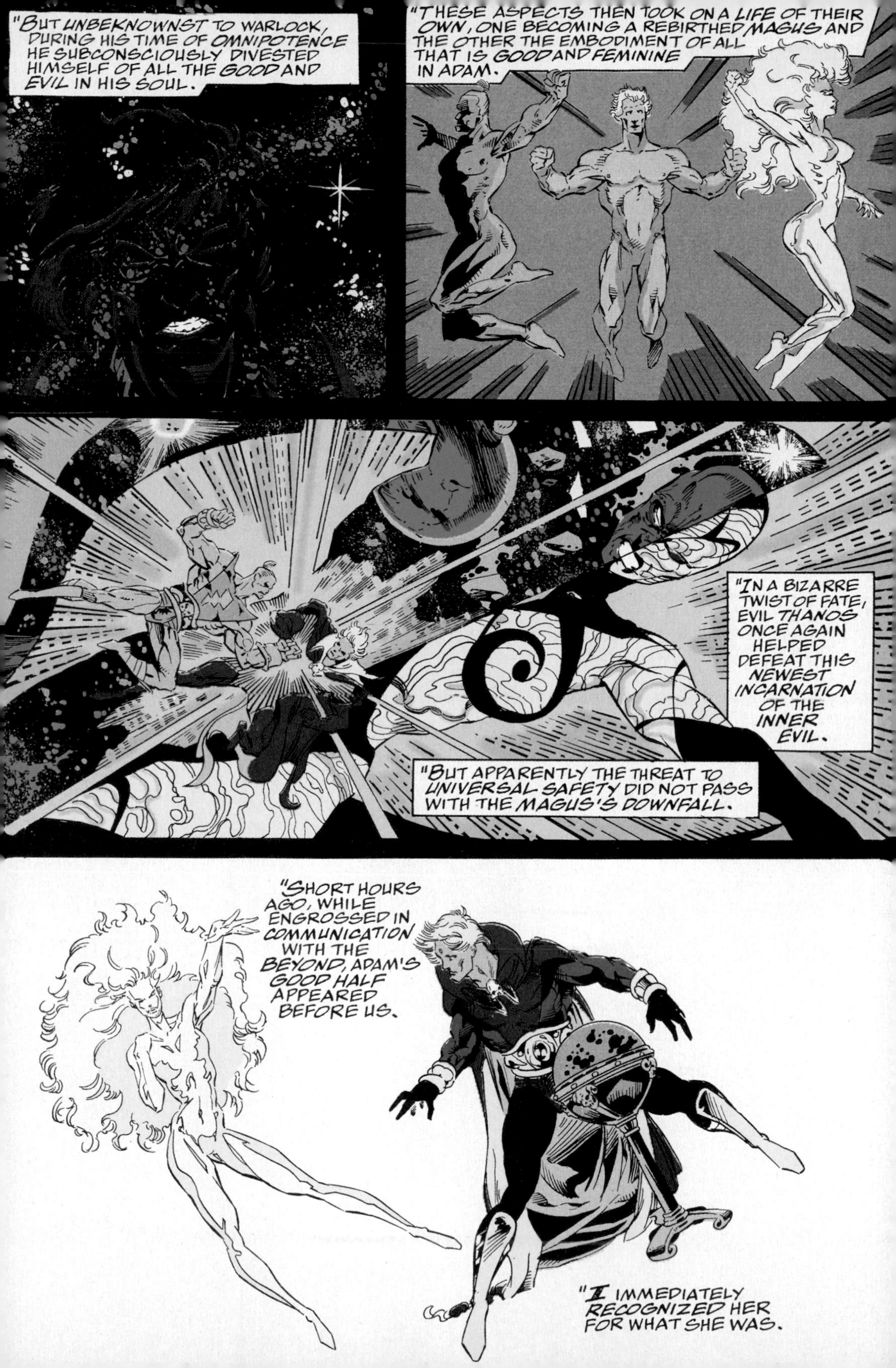
"BUT UNBEKNOWNST TO WARLOCK, DURING HIS TIME OF OMNIPOTENCE HE SUBCONSCIOUSLY DIVESTED HIMSELF OF ALL THE GOOD AND EVIL IN HIS SOUL.
"THESE ASPECTS THEN TOOK ON A LIFE OF THEIR OWN, ONE BECOMING A REBIRTHED MAGUS AND THE OTHER THE EMBODIMENT OF ALL THAT IS GOOD AND FEMININE IN ADAM.
"IN A BIZARRE TWIST OF FATE, EVIL THANOS ONCE AGAIN HELPED DEFEAT THIS NEWEST INCARNATION OF THE INNER EVIL.
"BUT APPARENTLY THE THREAT TO UNIVERSAL SAFETY DID NOT PASS WITH THE MAGUS'S DOWNFALL.
"SHORT HOURS AGO, WHILE ENGROSSED IN COMMUNICATION WITH THE BEYOND, ADAM'S GOOD HALF APPEARED BEFORE US.
"I IMMEDIATELY RECOGNIZED HER FOR WHAT SHE WAS.

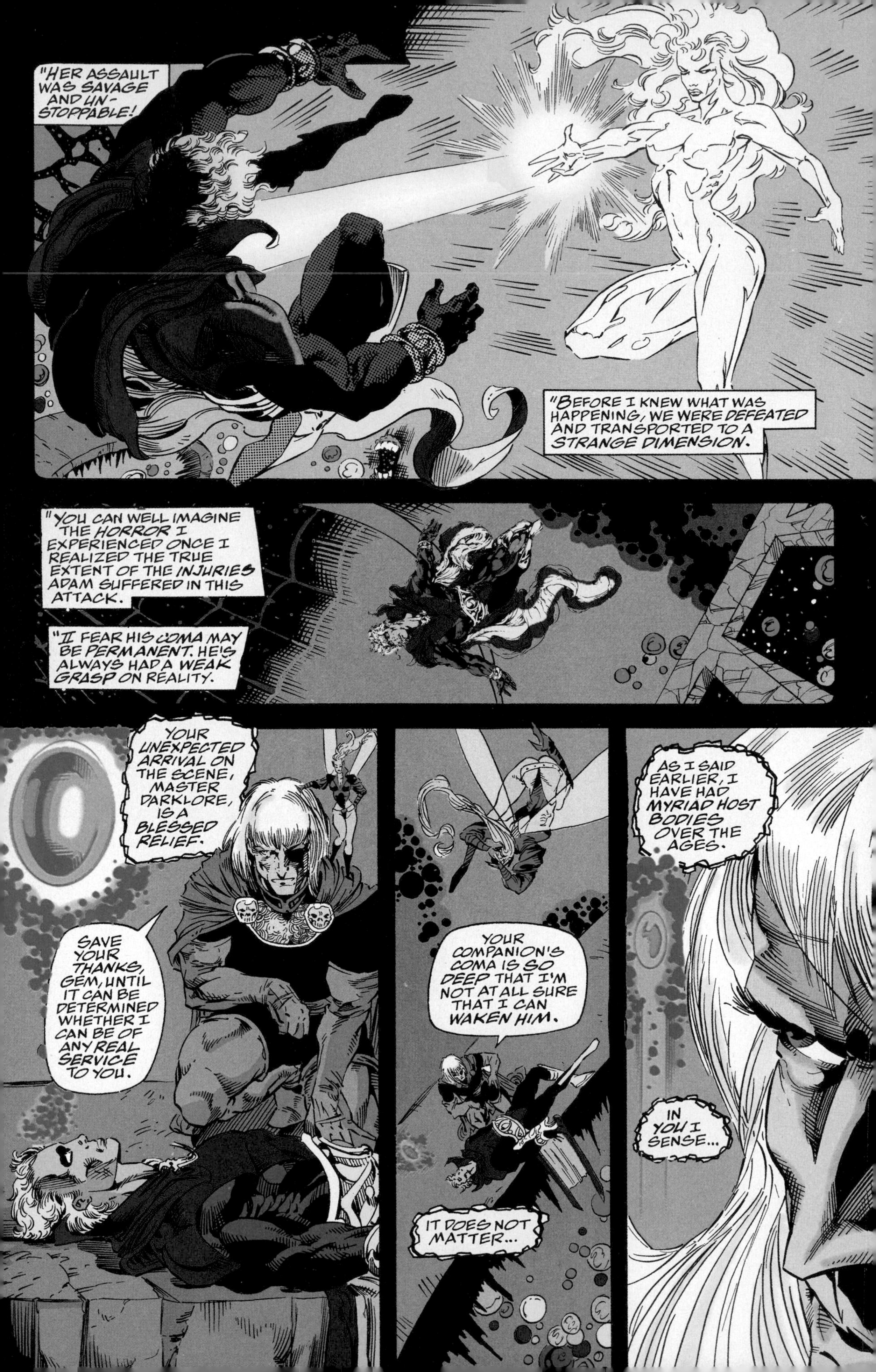
"HER ASSAULT WAS SAVAGE AND UN-STOPPABLE!
"BEFORE I KNEW WHAT WAS HAPPENING, WE WERE DEFEATED AND TRANSPORTED TO A STRANGE DIMENSION.
"YOU CAN WELL IMAGINE THE HORROR I EXPERIENCED ONCE I REALIZED THE TRUE EXTENT OF THE INJURIES ADAM SUFFERED IN THIS ATTACK.
"I FEAR HIS COMA MAY BE PERMANENT. HE'S ALWAYS HAD A WEAK GRASP ON REALITY.
YOUR UNEXPECTED ARRIVAL ON THE SCENE, MASTER DARKLORE, IS A BLESSED RELIEF.
SAVE YOUR THANKS, GEM, UNTIL IT CAN BE DETERMINED WHETHER I CAN BE OF ANY REAL SERVICE TO YOU.
YOUR COMPANION'S COMA IS SO DEEP THAT I'M NOT AT ALL SURE THAT I CAN WAKEN HIM.
IT DOES NOT MATTER...
AS I SAID EARLIER, I HAVE HAD MYRIAD HOST BODIES OVER THE AGES.
IN YOU I SENSE...

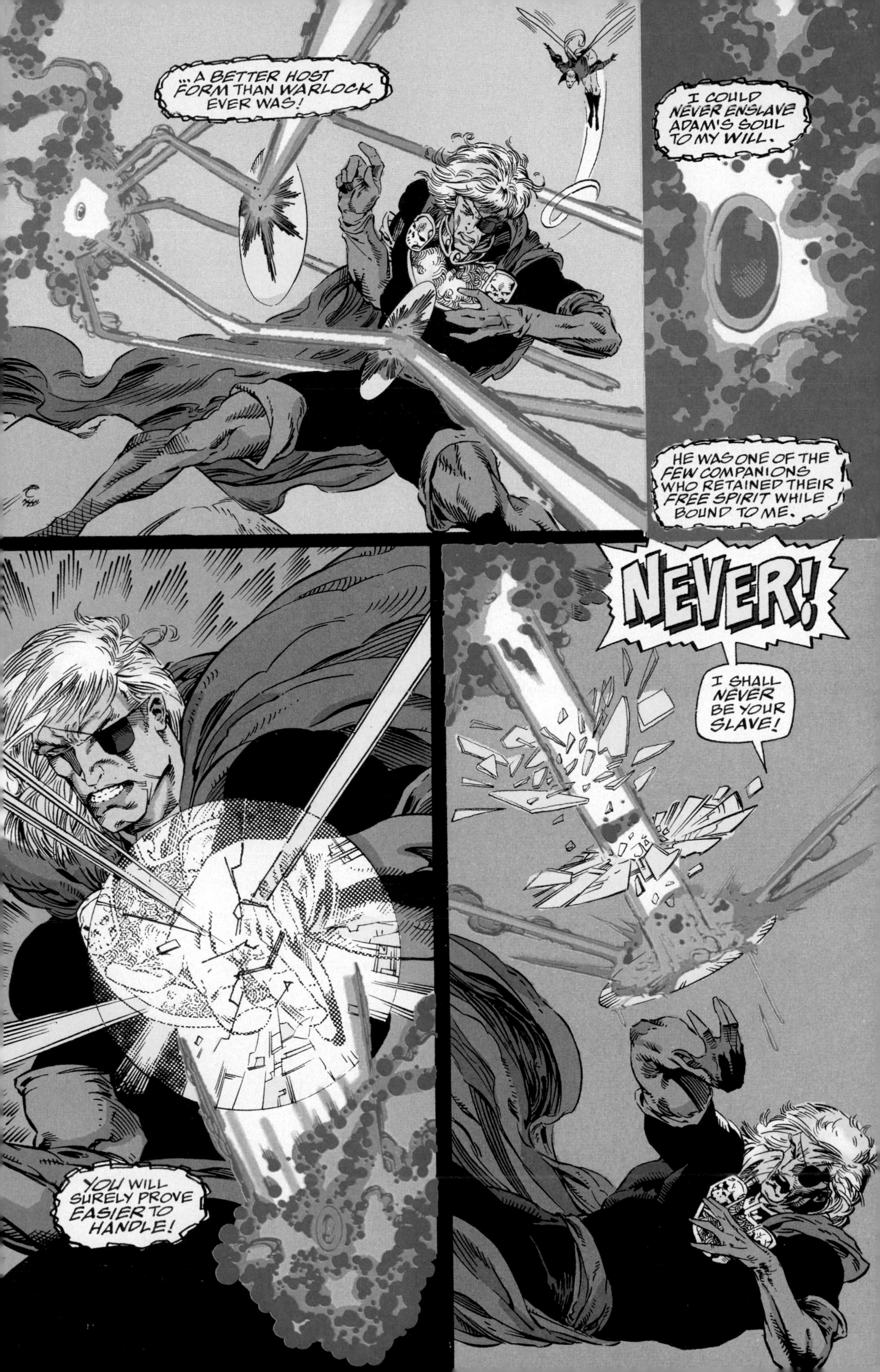
...A BETTER HOST FORM THAN WARLOCK EVER WAS!
I COULD NEVER ENSLAVE ADAM'S SOUL TO MY WILL.
HE WAS ONE OF THE FEW COMPANIONS WHO RETAINED THEIR FREE SPIRIT WHILE BOUND TO ME.
YOU WILL SURELY PROVE EASIER TO HANDLE!
NEVER!
I SHALL NEVER BE YOUR SLAVE!

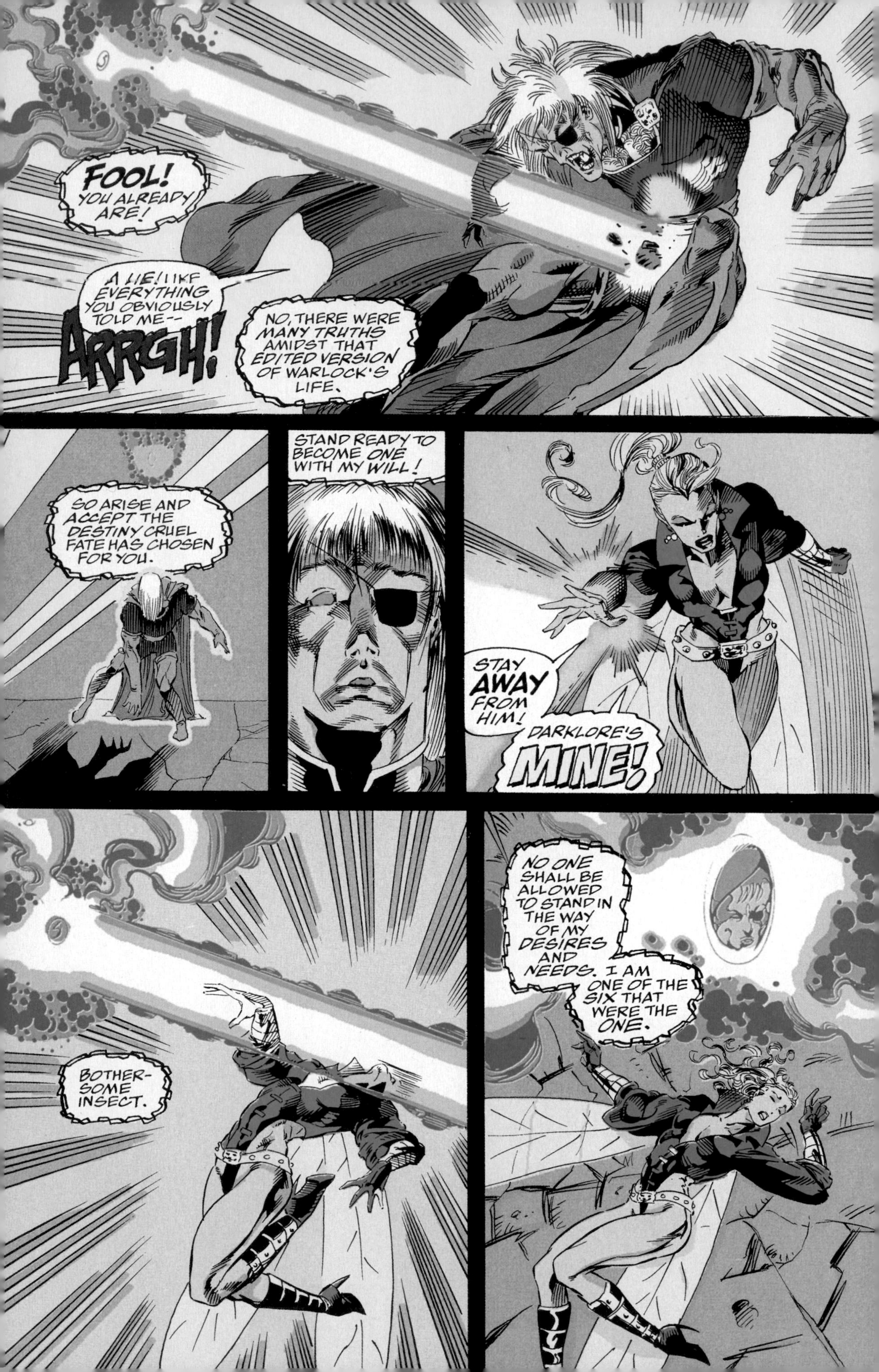
FOOL! YOU ALREADY ARE!
A LIE! LIKE EVERYTHING YOU OBVIOUSLY TOLD ME--
ARRGH!
NO, THERE WERE MANY TRUTHS AMIDST THAT EDITED VERSION OF WARLOCK'S LIFE.
SO ARISE AND ACCEPT THE DESTINY CRUEL FATE HAS CHOSEN FOR YOU.
STAND READY TO BECOME ONE WITH MY WILL!
STAY AWAY FROM HIM!
DARKLORE'S MINE!
BOTHER-SOME INSECT.
NO ONE SHALL BE ALLOWED TO STAND IN THE WAY OF MY DESIRES AND NEEDS. I AM ONE OF THE SIX THAT WERE THE ONE.

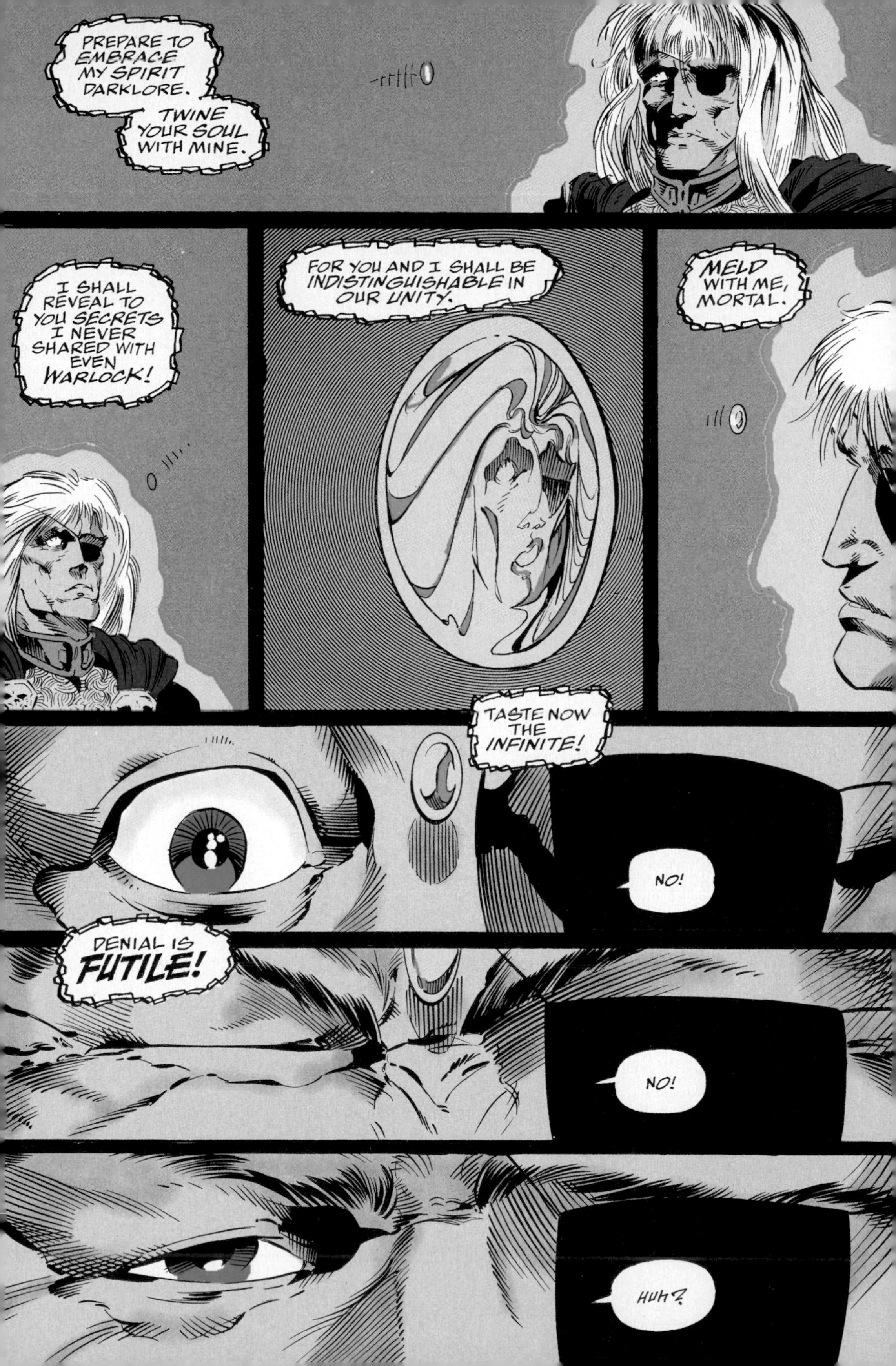
PREPARE TO EMBRACE MY SPIRIT DARKLORE.
TWINE YOUR SOUL WITH MINE.
I SHALL REVEAL TO YOU SECRETS I NEVER SHARED WITH EVEN WARLOCK!
FOR YOU AND I SHALL BE INDISTINGUISHABLE IN OUR UNITY.
MELD WITH ME, MORTAL.
TASTE NOW THE INFINITE!
NO!
DENIAL IS FUTILE!
NO!
HUH?

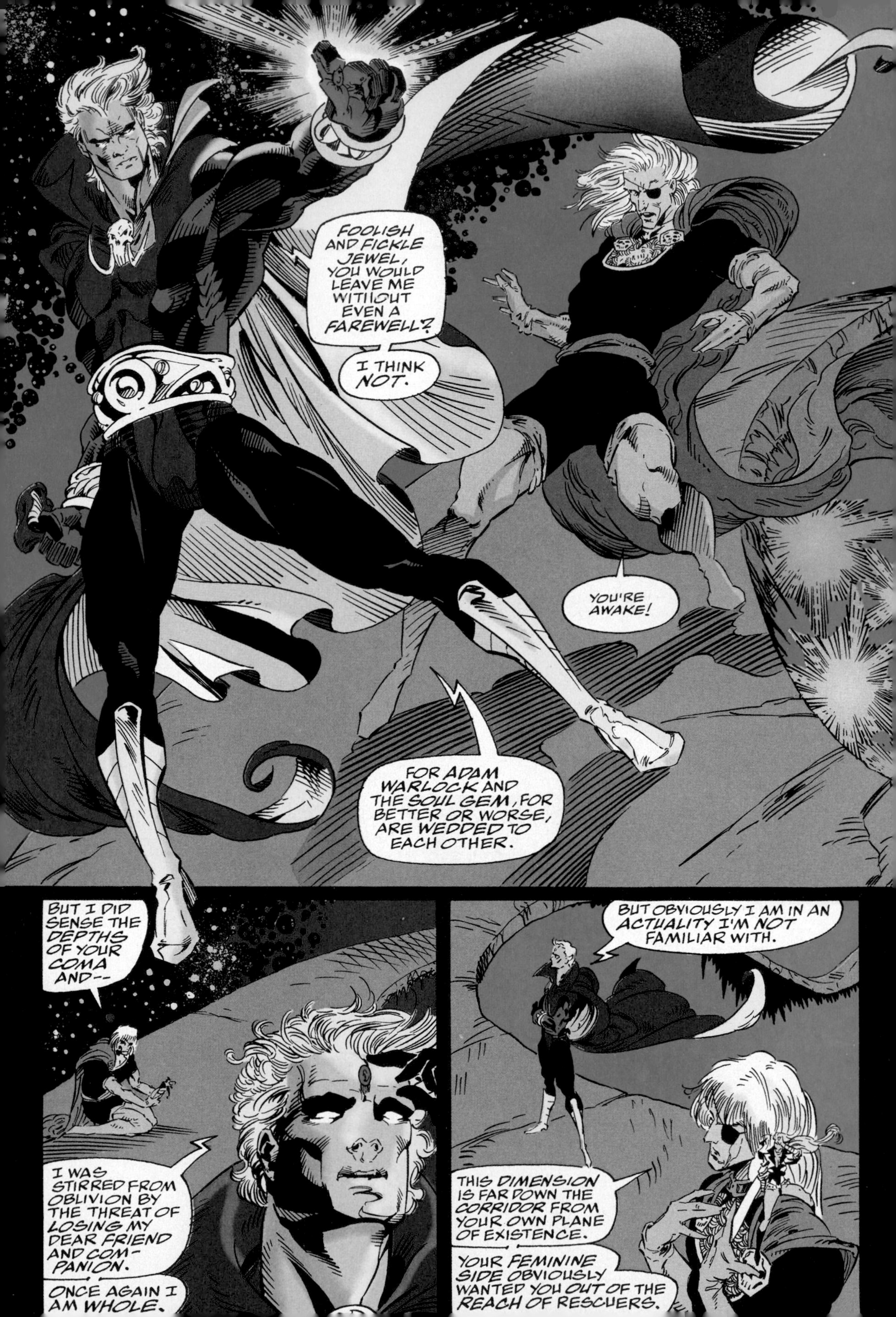

FOOLISH AND FICKLE JEWEL, YOU WOULD LEAVE ME WITHOUT EVEN A FAREWELL?
I THINK NOT.
YOU'RE AWAKE!
FOR ADAM WARLOCK AND THE SOUL GEM, FOR BETTER OR WORSE, ARE WEDDED TO EACH OTHER.
BUT I DID SENSE THE DEPTHS OF YOUR COMA AND--
I WAS STIRRED FROM OBLIVION BY THE THREAT OF LOSING MY DEAR FRIEND AND COMPANION.
ONCE AGAIN I AM WHOLE.
BUT OBVIOUSLY I AM IN AN ACTUALITY I'M NOT FAMILIAR WITH.
THIS DIMENSION IS FAR DOWN THE CORRIDOR FROM YOUR OWN PLANE OF EXISTENCE.
YOUR FEMININE SIDE OBVIOUSLY WANTED YOU OUT OF THE REACH OF RESCUERS.

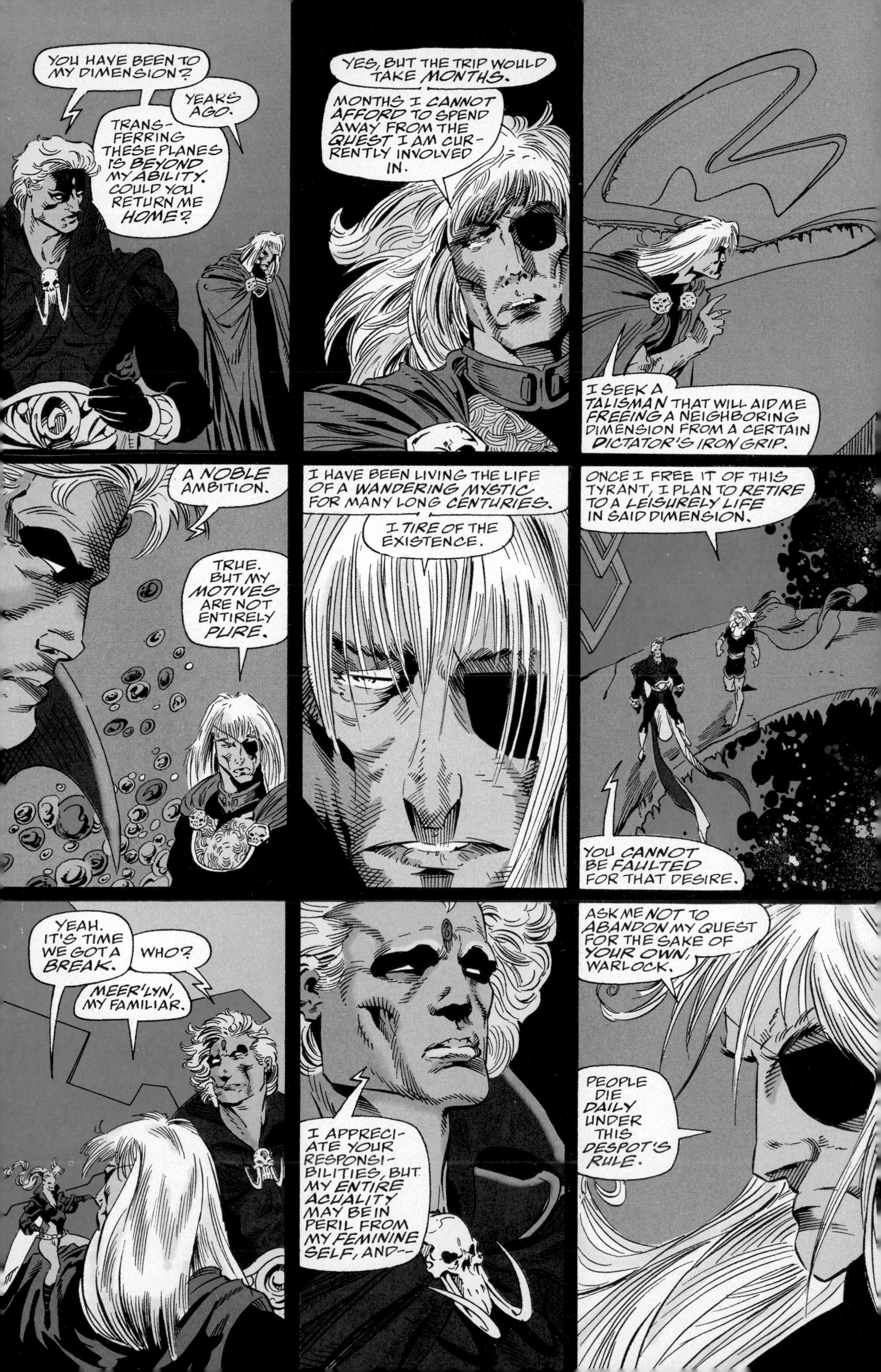
YOU HAVE BEEN TO MY DIMENSION?
YEARS AGO.
TRANSFERRING THESE PLANES IS BEYOND MY ABILITY. COULD YOU RETURN ME HOME?
YES, BUT THE TRIP WOULD TAKE MONTHS.
MONTHS I CANNOT AFFORD TO SPEND AWAY FROM THE QUEST I AM CURRENTLY INVOLVED IN.
I SEEK A TALISMAN THAT WILL AID ME FREEING A NEIGHBORING DIMENSION FROM A CERTAIN DICTATOR'S IRON GRIP.
A NOBLE AMBITION.
TRUE. BUT MY MOTIVES ARE NOT ENTIRELY PURE.
I HAVE BEEN LIVING THE LIFE OF A WANDERING MYSTIC FOR MANY LONG CENTURIES.
I TIRE OF THE EXISTENCE.
ONCE I FREE IT OF THIS TYRANT, I PLAN TO RETIRE TO A LEISURELY LIFE IN SAID DIMENSION.
YOU CANNOT BE FAULTED FOR THAT DESIRE.
YEAH. IT'S TIME WE GOT A BREAK.
WHO?
MEER'LYN, MY FAMILIAR.
I APPRECIATE YOUR RESPONSIBILITIES, BUT MY ENTIRE ACUALITY MAY BE IN PERIL FROM MY FEMININE SELF, AND--
ASK ME NOT TO ABANDON MY QUEST FOR THE SAKE OF YOUR OWN, WARLOCK.
PEOPLE DIE DAILY UNDER THIS DESPOT'S RULE.

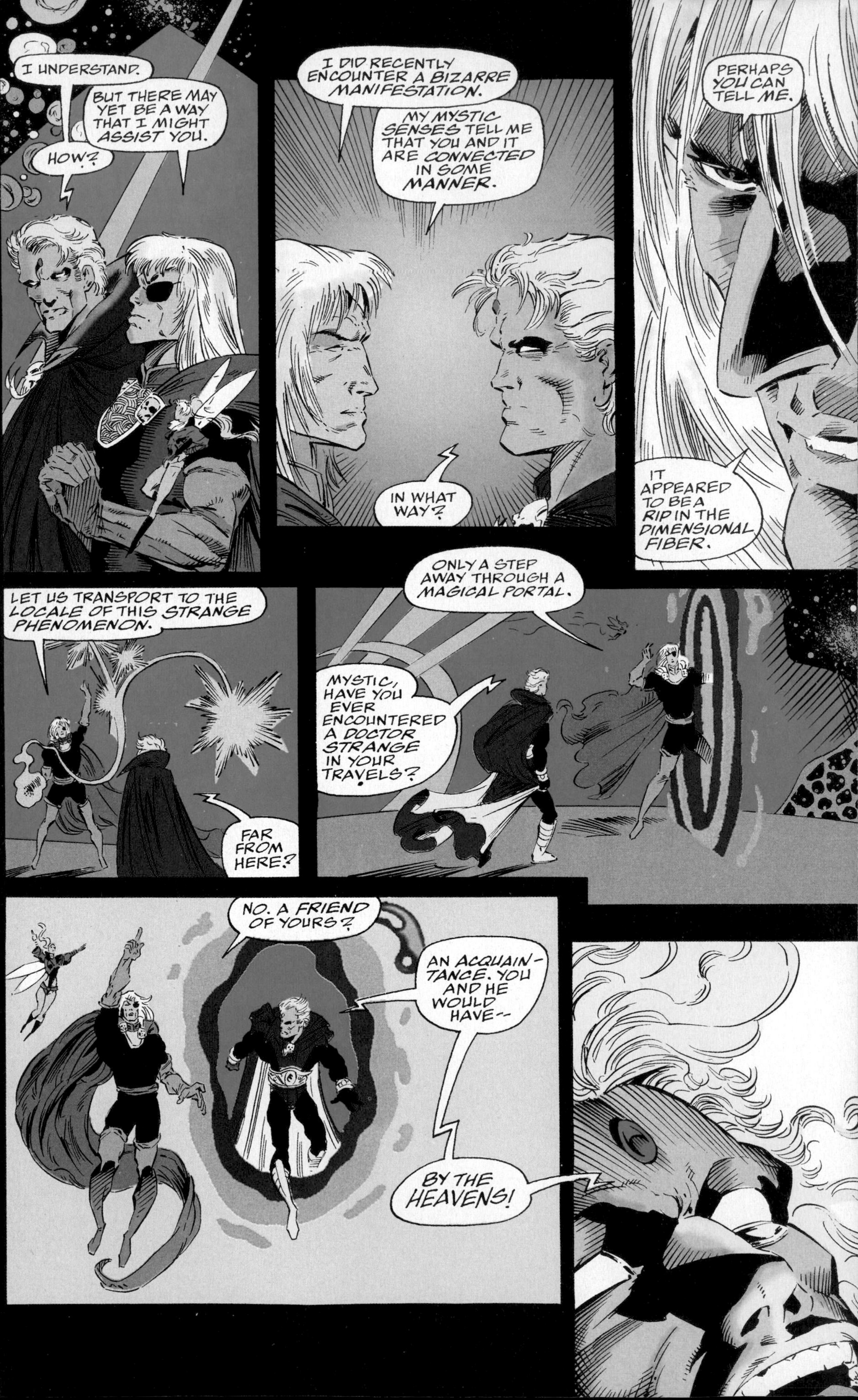
I UNDERSTAND.
BUT THERE MAY YET BE A WAY THAT I MIGHT ASSIST YOU.
HOW?
I DID RECENTLY ENCOUNTER A BIZARRE MANIFESTATION.
MY MYSTIC SENSES TELL ME THAT YOU AND IT ARE CONNECTED IN SOME MANNER.
IN WHAT WAY?
PERHAPS YOU CAN TELL ME.
IT APPEARED TO BE A RIP IN THE DIMENSIONAL FIBER.
LET US TRANSPORT TO THE LOCALE OF THIS STRANGE PHENOMENON.
FAR FROM HERE?
ONLY A STEP AWAY THROUGH A MAGICAL PORTAL.
MYSTIC, HAVE YOU EVER ENCOUNTERED A DOCTOR STRANGE IN YOUR TRAVELS?
NO. A FRIEND OF YOURS?
AN ACQUAIN-TANCE. YOU AND HE WOULD HAVE--
BY THE HEAVENS!

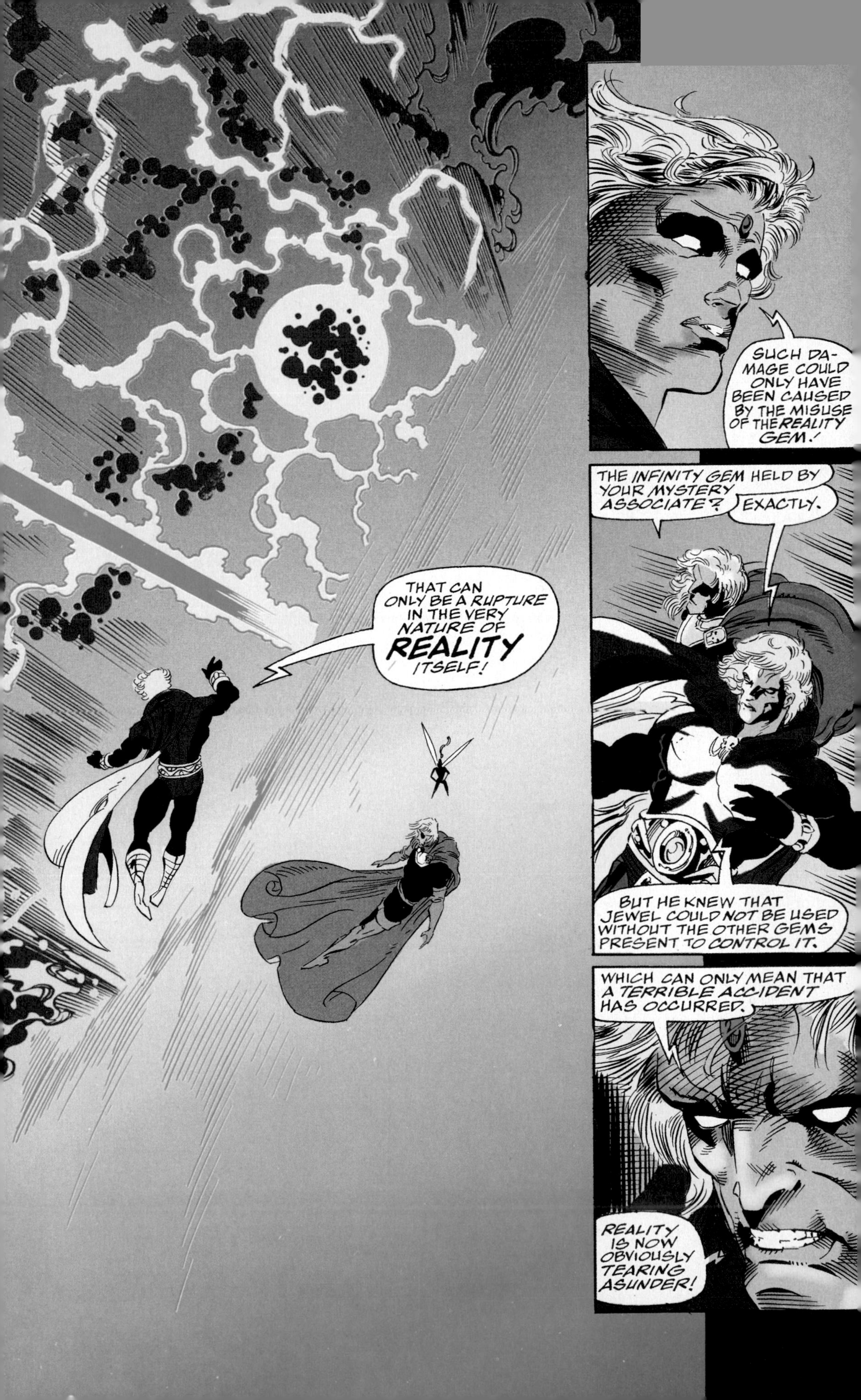
THAT CAN ONLY BE A RUPTURE IN THE VERY NATURE OF REALITY ITSELF!
SUCH DAMAGE COULD ONLY HAVE BEEN CAUSED BY THE MISUSE OF THE REALITY GEM!
THE INFINITY GEM HELD BY YOUR MYSTERY ASSOCIATE?
EXACTLY.
BUT HE KNEW THAT JEWEL COULD NOT BE USED WITHOUT THE OTHER GEMS PRESENT TO CONTROL IT.
WHICH CAN ONLY MEAN THAT A TERRIBLE ACCIDENT HAS OCCURRED.
REALITY IS NOW OBVIOUSLY TEARING ASUNDER!

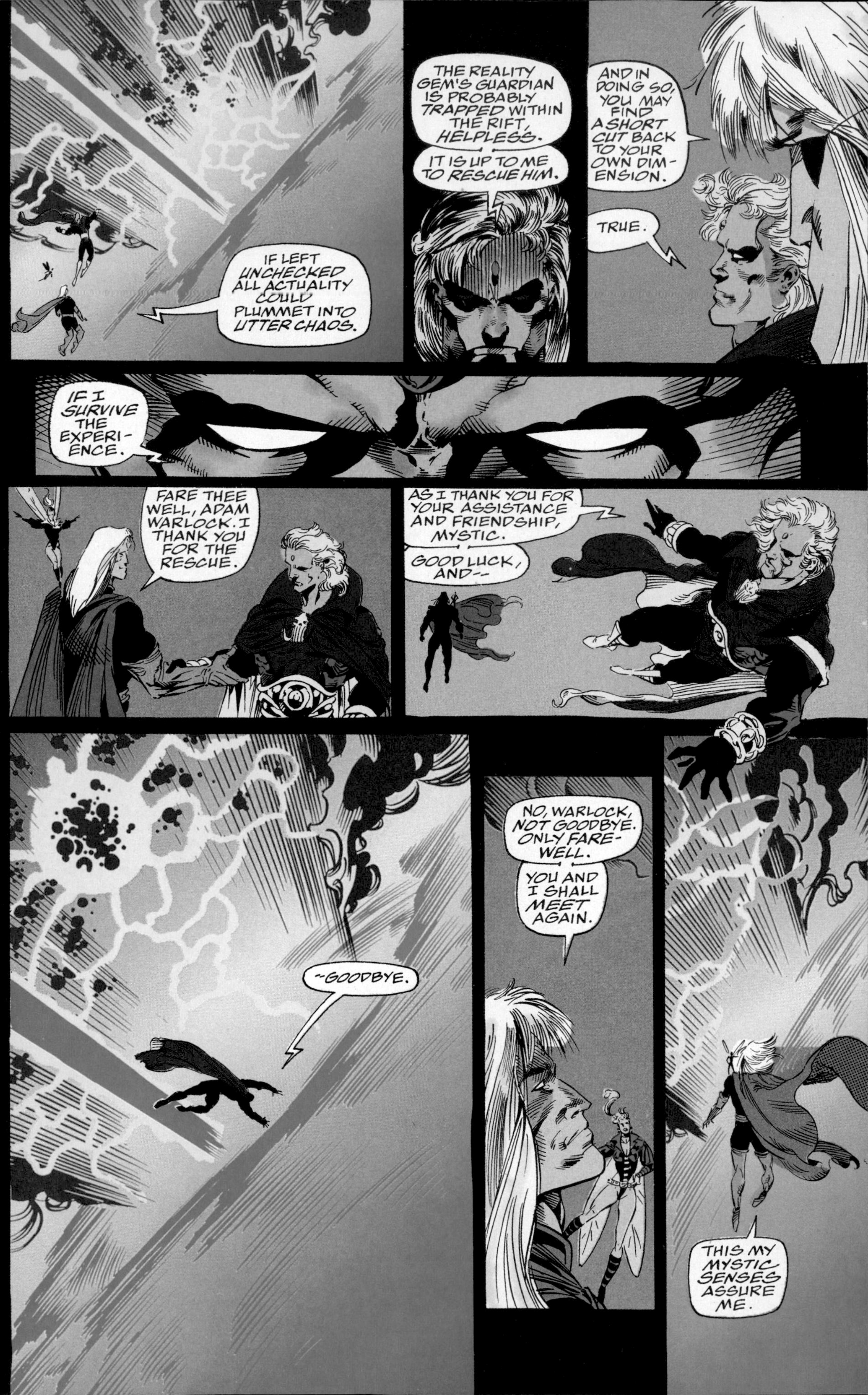

IF LEFT UNCHECKED ALL ACTUALITY COULD PLUMMET INTO UTTER CHAOS.
THE REALITY GEM'S GUARDIAN IS PROBABLY TRAPPED WITHIN THE RIFT, HELPLESS.
IT IS UP TO ME TO RESCUE HIM.
AND IN DOING SO, YOU MAY FIND A SHORT CUT BACK TO YOUR OWN DIMENSION.
TRUE.
IF I SURVIVE THE EXPERIENCE.
FARE THEE WELL, ADAM WARLOCK. I THANK YOU FOR THE RESCUE.
AS I THANK YOU FOR YOUR ASSISTANCE AND FRIENDSHIP, MYSTIC.
GOOD LUCK, AND--
--GOODBYE.
NO, WARLOCK, NOT GOODBYE. ONLY FAREWELL.
YOU AND I SHALL MEET AGAIN.
THIS MY MYSTIC SENSES ASSURE ME.

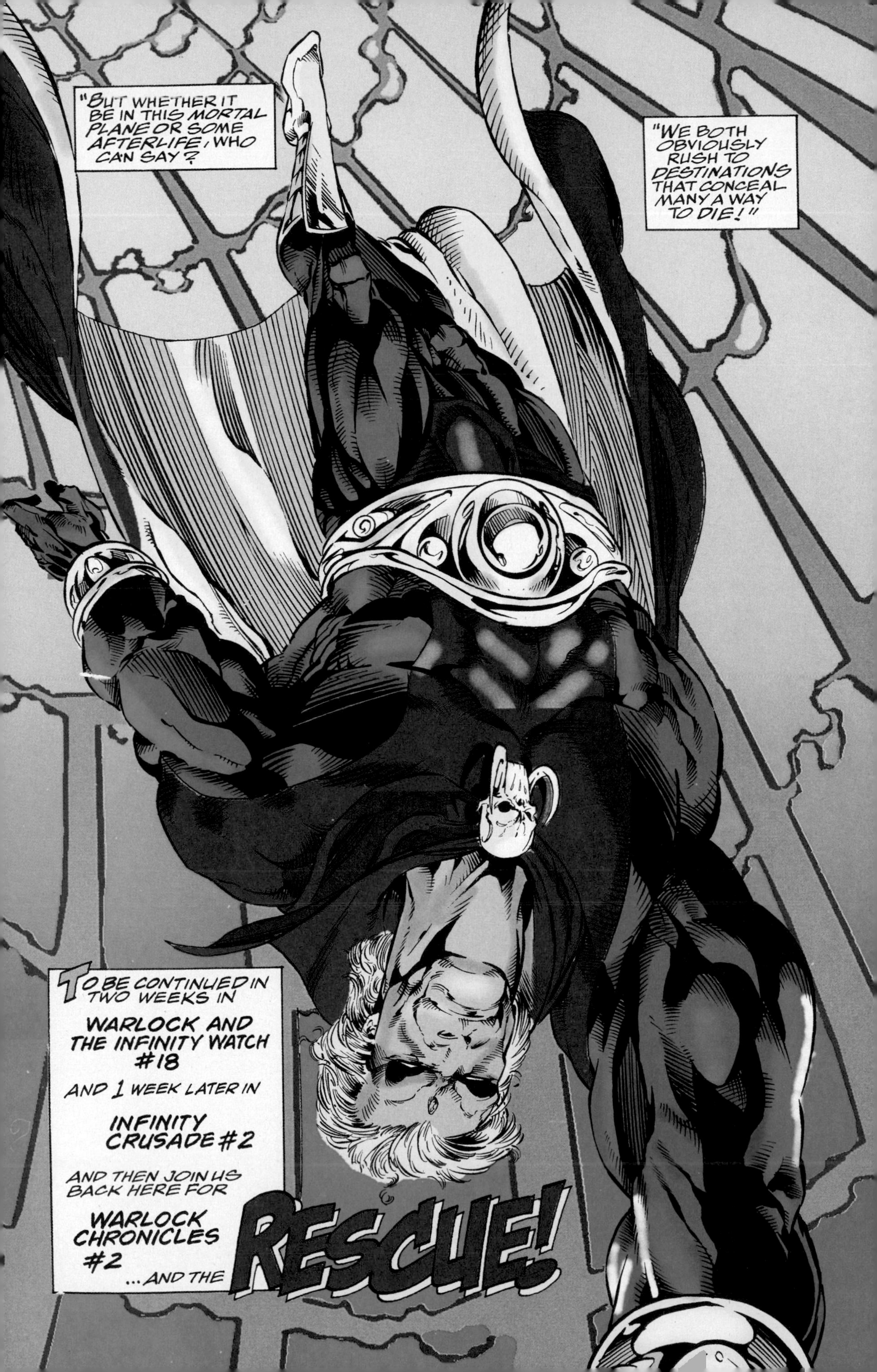
"BUT WHETHER IT BE IN THIS MORTAL PLANE OR SOME AFTERLIFE, WHO CAN SAY?
"WE BOTH OBVIOUSLY RUSH TO DESTINATIONS THAT CONCEAL MANY A WAY TO DIE!"
TO BE CONTINUED IN TWO WEEKS IN
WARLOCK AND THE INFINITY WATCH #18
AND 1 WEEK LATER IN
INFINITY CRUSADE #2
AND THEN JOIN US BACK HERE FOR
WARLOCK CHRONICLES #2
...AND THE
RESCUE!

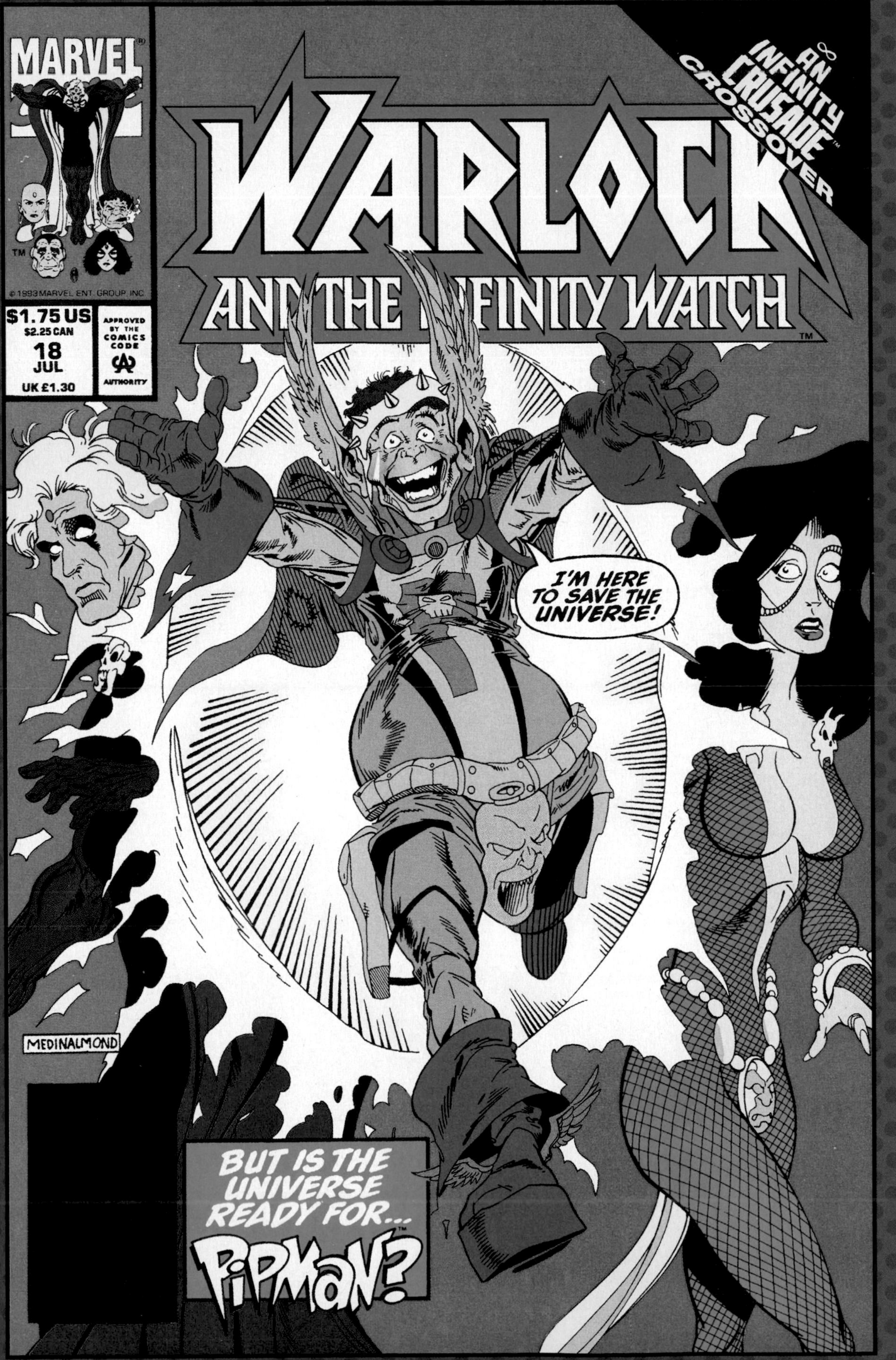
MARVEL
© 1993 MARVEL ENT. GROUP, INC.
$1.75 US
$2.25 CAN
18
JUL
UK £1.30
APPROVED BY THE COMICS CODE AUTHORITY
AN INFINITY CRUSADE CROSSOVER
WARLOCK
AND THE INFINITY WATCH
I'M HERE TO SAVE THE UNIVERSE!
MEDINA/ALMOND
BUT IS THE UNIVERSE READY FOR...
PIPMAN?

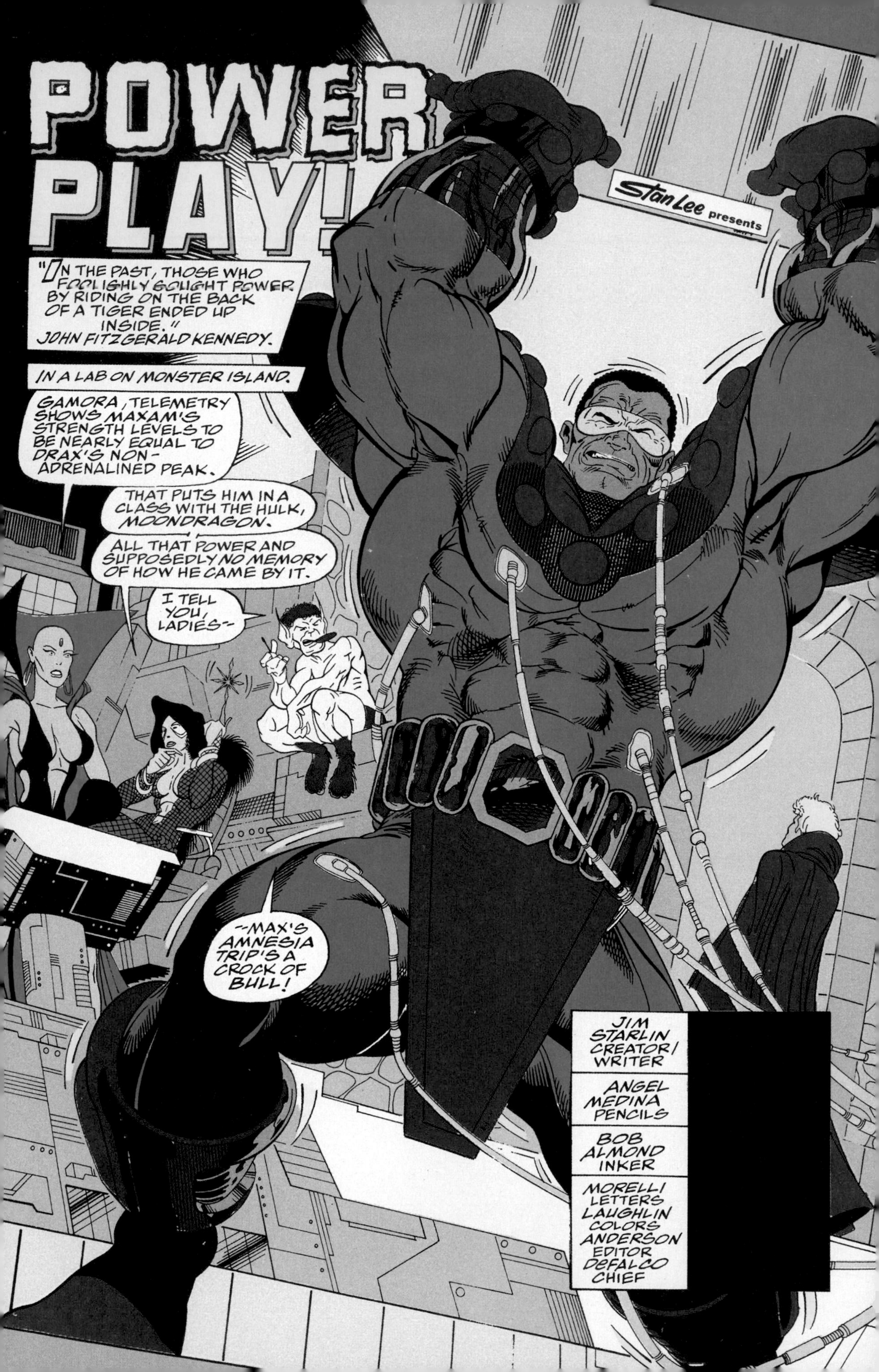
POWER PLAY!
Stan Lee presents
"In the past, those who foolishly sought power by riding on the back of a tiger ended up inside." John Fitzgerald Kennedy.
In a lab on Monster Island.
Gamora, telemetry shows Maxam's strength levels to be nearly equal to Drax's non-adrenalined peak.
That puts him in a class with the Hulk, Moondragon.
All that power and supposedly no memory of how he came by it.
I tell you, ladies--
--Max's amnesia trip's a crock of bull!
Jim Starlin creator/writer
Angel Medina pencils
Bob Almond inker
Morelli letters
Laughlin colors
Anderson editor
DeFalco chief

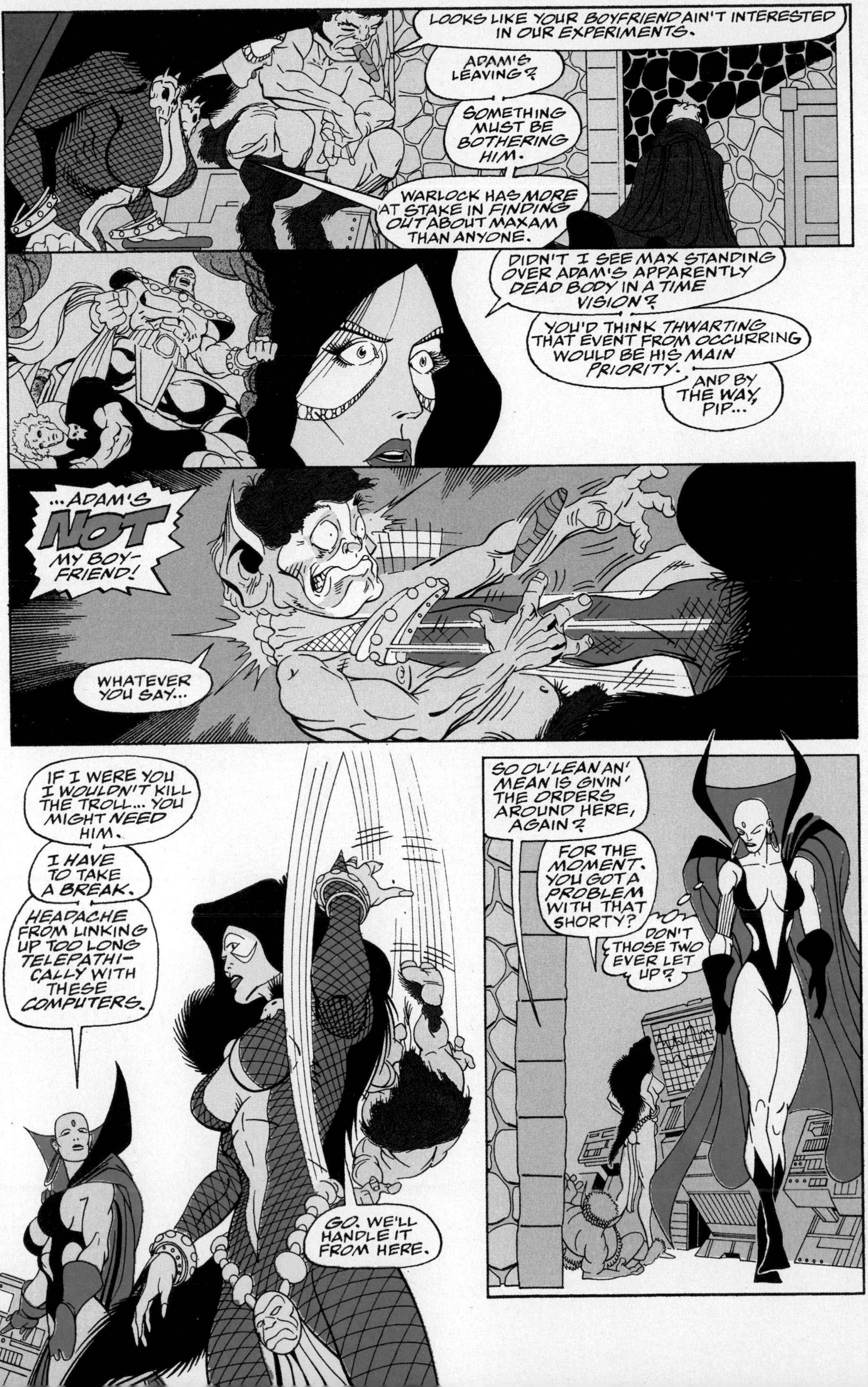
LOOKS LIKE YOUR BOYFRIEND AIN'T INTERESTED IN OUR EXPERIMENTS.
ADAM'S LEAVING?
SOMETHING MUST BE BOTHERING HIM.
WARLOCK HAS MORE AT STAKE IN FINDING OUT ABOUT MAXAM THAN ANYONE.
DIDN'T I SEE MAX STANDING OVER ADAM'S APPARENTLY DEAD BODY IN A TIME VISION?
YOU'D THINK THWARTING THAT EVENT FROM OCCURRING WOULD BE HIS MAIN PRIORITY.
AND BY THE WAY, PIP...
...ADAM'S NOT MY BOY-FRIEND!
WHATEVER YOU SAY...
IF I WERE YOU I WOULDN'T KILL THE TROLL... YOU MIGHT NEED HIM.
I HAVE TO TAKE A BREAK.
HEADACHE FROM LINKING UP TOO LONG TELEPATHI-CALLY WITH THESE COMPUTERS.
GO. WE'LL HANDLE IT FROM HERE.
SO OL' LEAN AN' MEAN IS GIVIN' THE ORDERS AROUND HERE, AGAIN?
FOR THE MOMENT. YOU GOT A PROBLEM WITH THAT SHORTY?
DON'T THOSE TWO EVER LET UP?

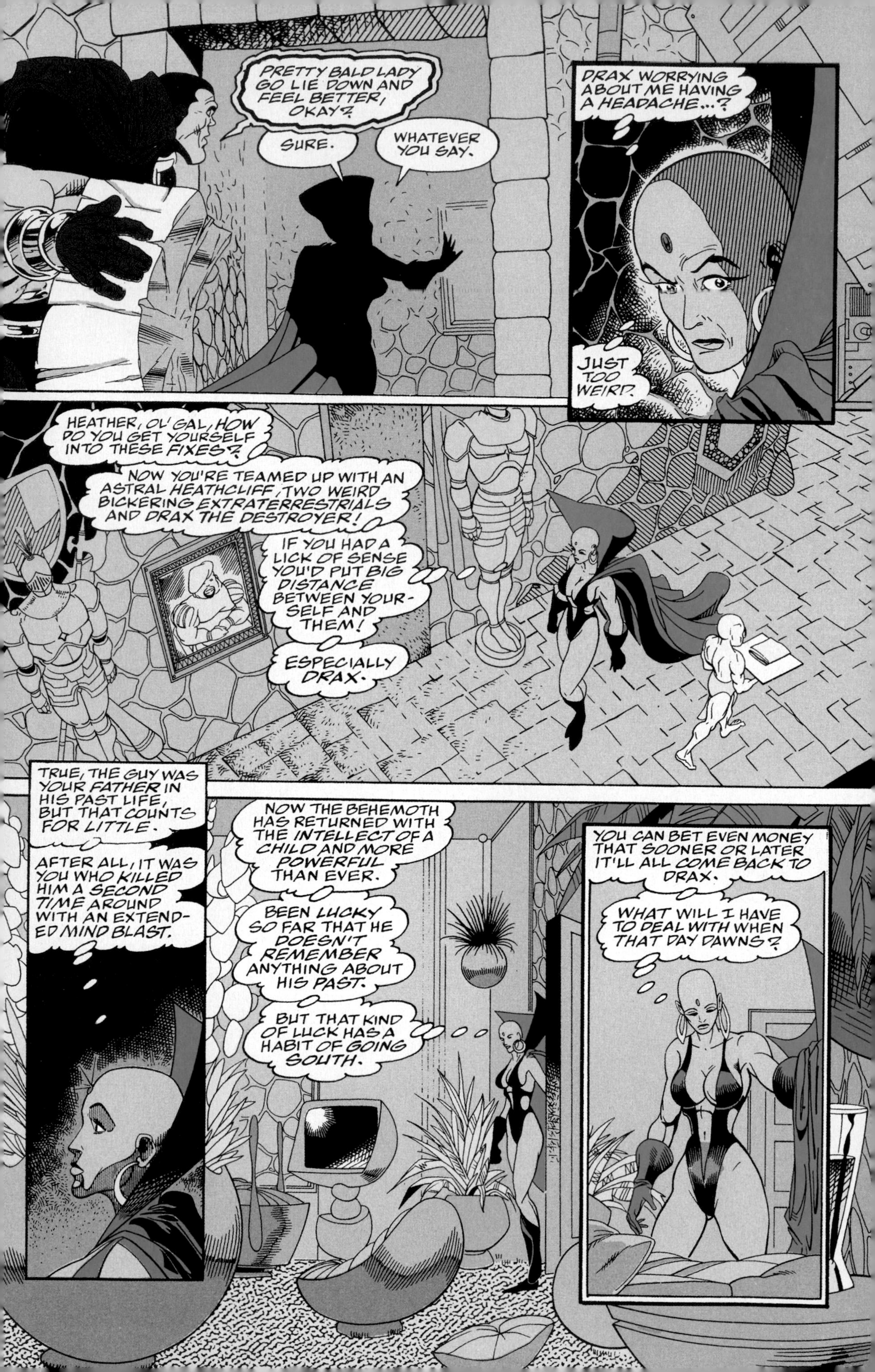
PRETTY BALD LADY GO LIE DOWN AND FEEL BETTER, OKAY?
SURE.
WHATEVER YOU SAY.
DRAX WORRYING ABOUT ME HAVING A HEADACHE...?
JUST TOO WEIRD.
HEATHER, OL' GAL, HOW DO YOU GET YOURSELF INTO THESE FIXES?
NOW YOU'RE TEAMED UP WITH AN ASTRAL HEATHCLIFF, TWO WEIRD BICKERING EXTRATERRESTRIALS AND DRAX THE DESTROYER!
IF YOU HAD A LICK OF SENSE YOU'D PUT BIG DISTANCE BETWEEN YOURSELF AND THEM!
ESPECIALLY DRAX.
TRUE, THE GUY WAS YOUR FATHER IN HIS PAST LIFE, BUT THAT COUNTS FOR LITTLE.
AFTER ALL, IT WAS YOU WHO KILLED HIM A SECOND TIME AROUND WITH AN EXTENDED MIND BLAST.
NOW THE BEHEMOTH HAS RETURNED WITH THE INTELLECT OF A CHILD AND MORE POWERFUL THAN EVER.
BEEN LUCKY SO FAR THAT HE DOESN'T REMEMBER ANYTHING ABOUT HIS PAST.
BUT THAT KIND OF LUCK HAS A HABIT OF GOING SOUTH.
YOU CAN BET EVEN MONEY THAT SOONER OR LATER IT'LL ALL COME BACK TO DRAX.
WHAT WILL I HAVE TO DEAL WITH WHEN THAT DAY DAWNS?

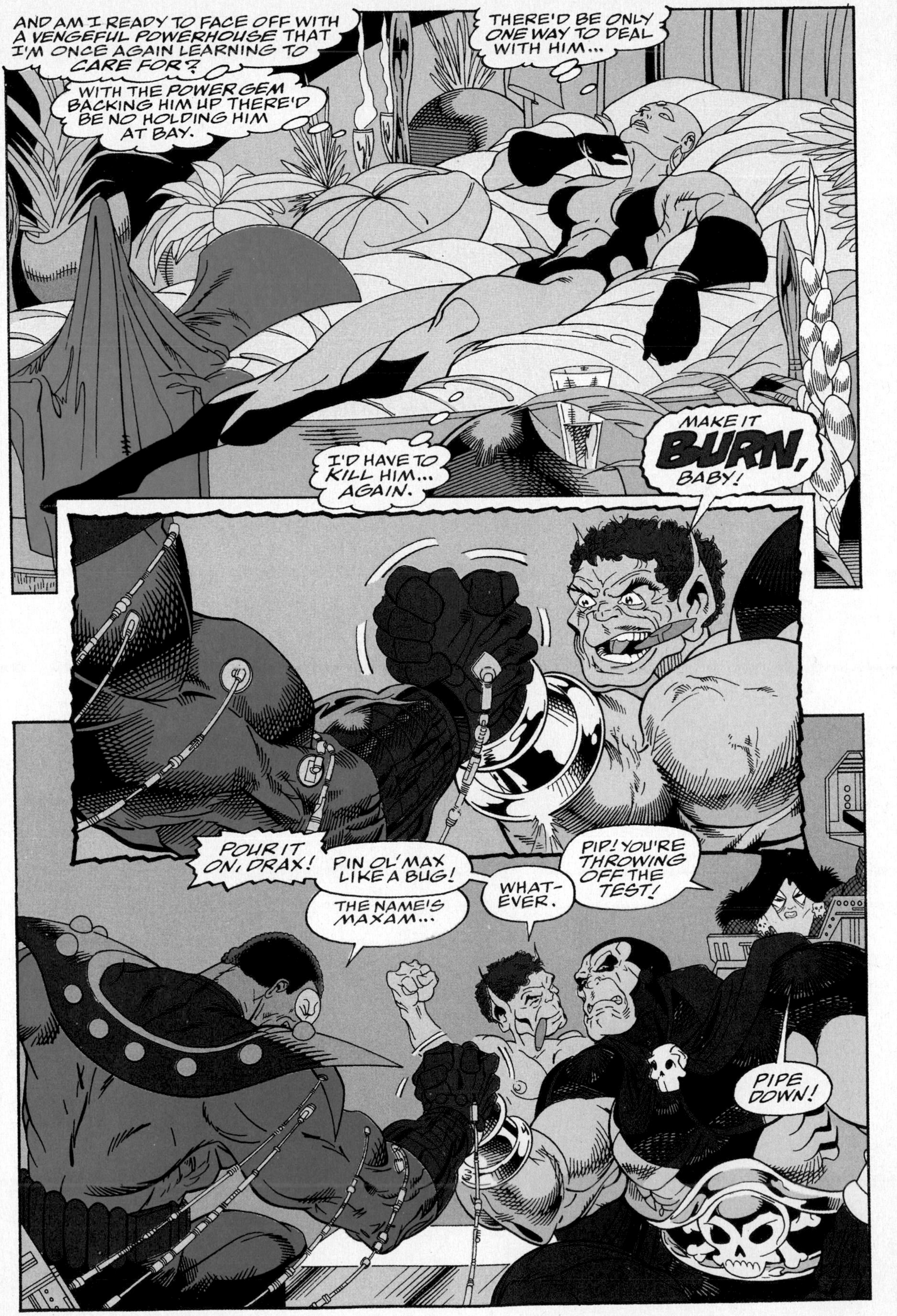
AND AM I READY TO FACE OFF WITH A VENGEFUL POWERHOUSE THAT I'M ONCE AGAIN LEARNING TO CARE FOR?
WITH THE POWER GEM BACKING HIM UP THERE'D BE NO HOLDING HIM AT BAY.
THERE'D BE ONLY ONE WAY TO DEAL WITH HIM...
I'D HAVE TO KILL HIM... AGAIN.
MAKE IT BURN, BABY!
POUR IT ON, DRAX!
PIN OL' MAX LIKE A BUG!
THE NAME'S MAXAM...
WHAT-EVER.
PIP! YOU'RE THROWING OFF THE TEST!
PIPE DOWN!

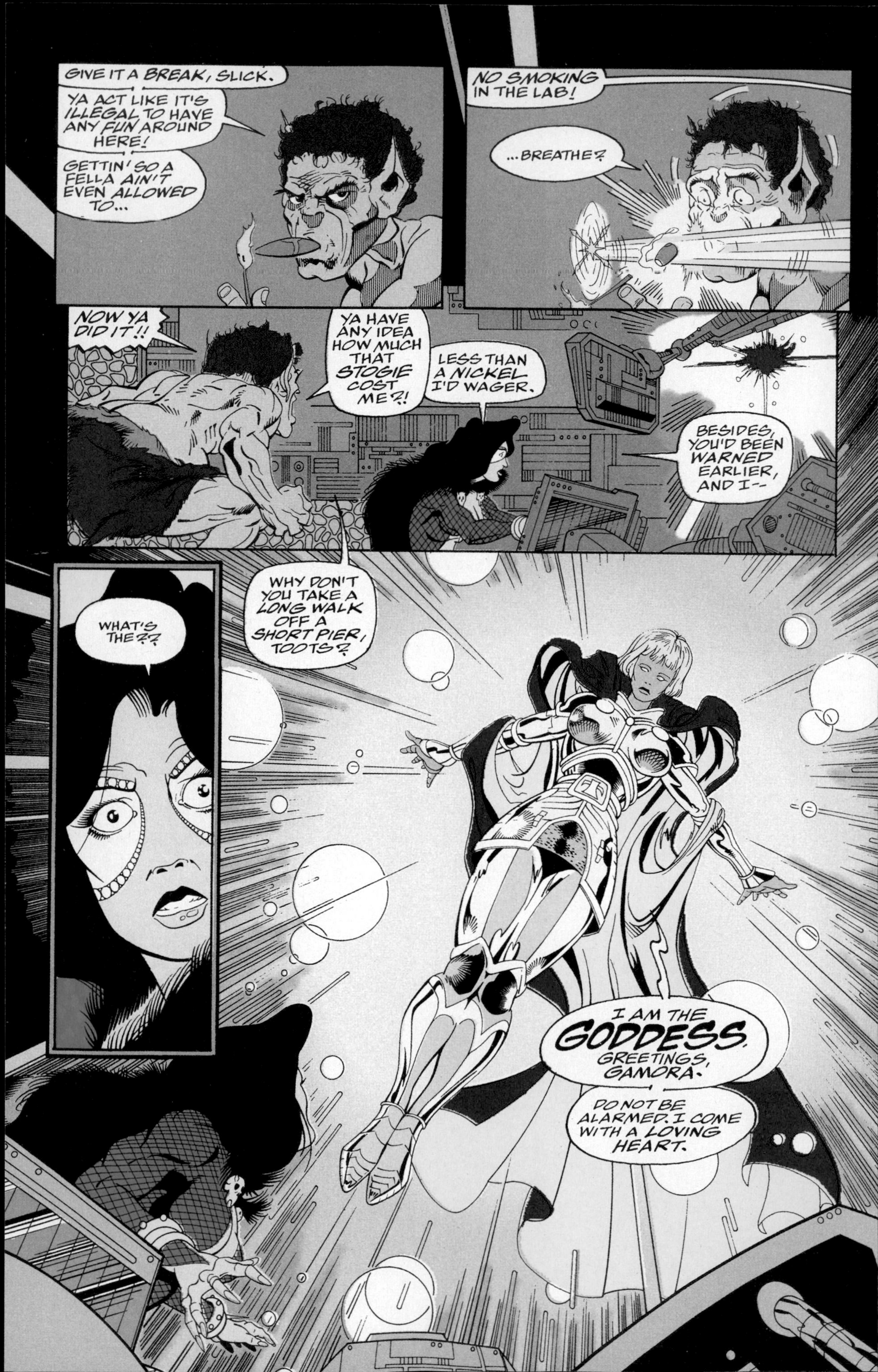
GIVE IT A BREAK, SLICK.
YA ACT LIKE IT'S ILLEGAL TO HAVE ANY FUN AROUND HERE!
GETTIN' SO A FELLA AIN'T EVEN ALLOWED TO...
NO SMOKING IN THE LAB!
...BREATHE?
NOW YA DID IT!!
YA HAVE ANY IDEA HOW MUCH THAT STOGIE COST ME?!
LESS THAN A NICKEL I'D WAGER.
BESIDES, YOU'D BEEN WARNED EARLIER, AND I--
WHY DON'T YOU TAKE A LONG WALK OFF A SHORT PIER, TOOTS?
WHAT'S THE??
I AM THE GODDESS. GREETINGS, GAMORA.
DO NOT BE ALARMED. I COME WITH A LOVING HEART.

C'MON, DRAX! YOU CAN TAKE THIS CREEP!

YOU'RE GETTING ON MY NERVES LITTLE MAN...

IF GAMORA DOESN'T CALL YOU OFF, I MIGHT HAVE TO...

OOOPS! I FORGOT!

HUH?

LOOKS LIKE GREENIE'S SPACING OUT!

MAYBE SHE'S HAVIN' ANOTHER OF THOSE TIME VISIONS.

I WANT A REMATCH!

I WAS DISTRACTED.

GREAT GOIN' DRAX OL' BOY!

SURE WISH I HAD SOME DOUGH ON THAT LITTLE MATCH!

GOTCHA!

MAX, HOW 'BOUT A LITTLE WAGER ON THE NEXT BOUT?

SURE, I BET YOU CAN'T GET TO THE DOOR BEFORE I WRING YOUR SCRAWNY LITTLE NECK!

AND DON'T TRY TO-- HUH?

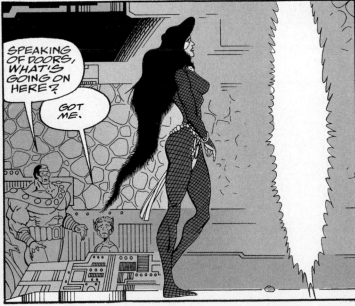

SPEAKING OF DOORS, WHAT'S GOING ON HERE?

GOT ME.

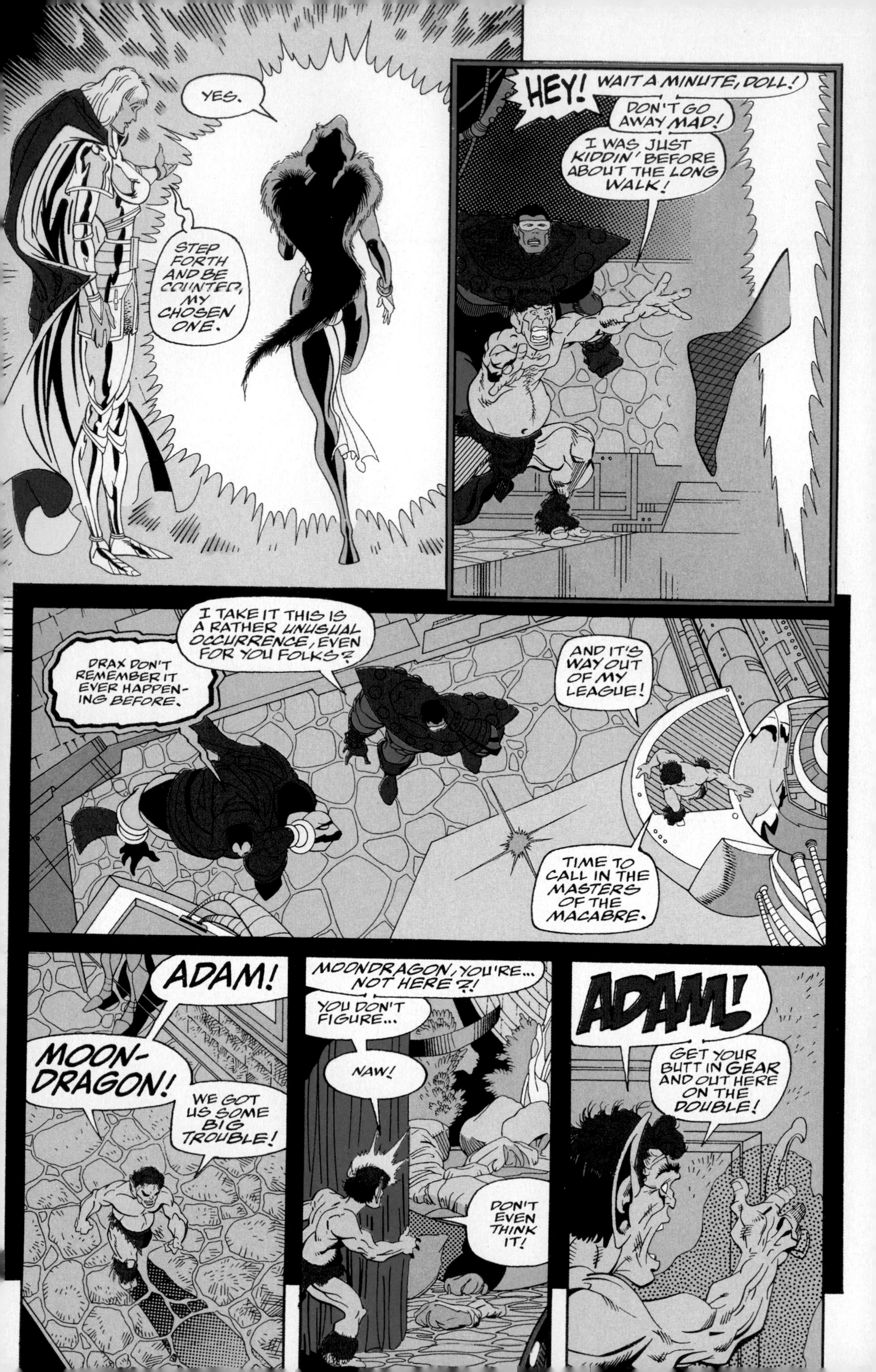
YES.
STEP FORTH AND BE COUNTED, MY CHOSEN ONE.
HEY! WAIT A MINUTE, DOLL!
DON'T GO AWAY MAD!
I WAS JUST KIDDIN' BEFORE ABOUT THE LONG WALK!
I TAKE IT THIS IS A RATHER UNUSUAL OCCURRENCE, EVEN FOR YOU FOLKS?
DRAX DON'T REMEMBER IT EVER HAPPENING BEFORE.
AND IT'S WAY OUT OF MY LEAGUE!
TIME TO CALL IN THE MASTERS OF THE MACABRE.
ADAM!
MOON-DRAGON!
WE GOT US SOME BIG TROUBLE!
MOONDRAGON, YOU'RE... NOT HERE?!
YOU DON'T FIGURE...
NAW!
DON'T EVEN THINK IT!
ADAM!
GET YOUR BUTT IN GEAR AND OUT HERE ON THE DOUBLE!

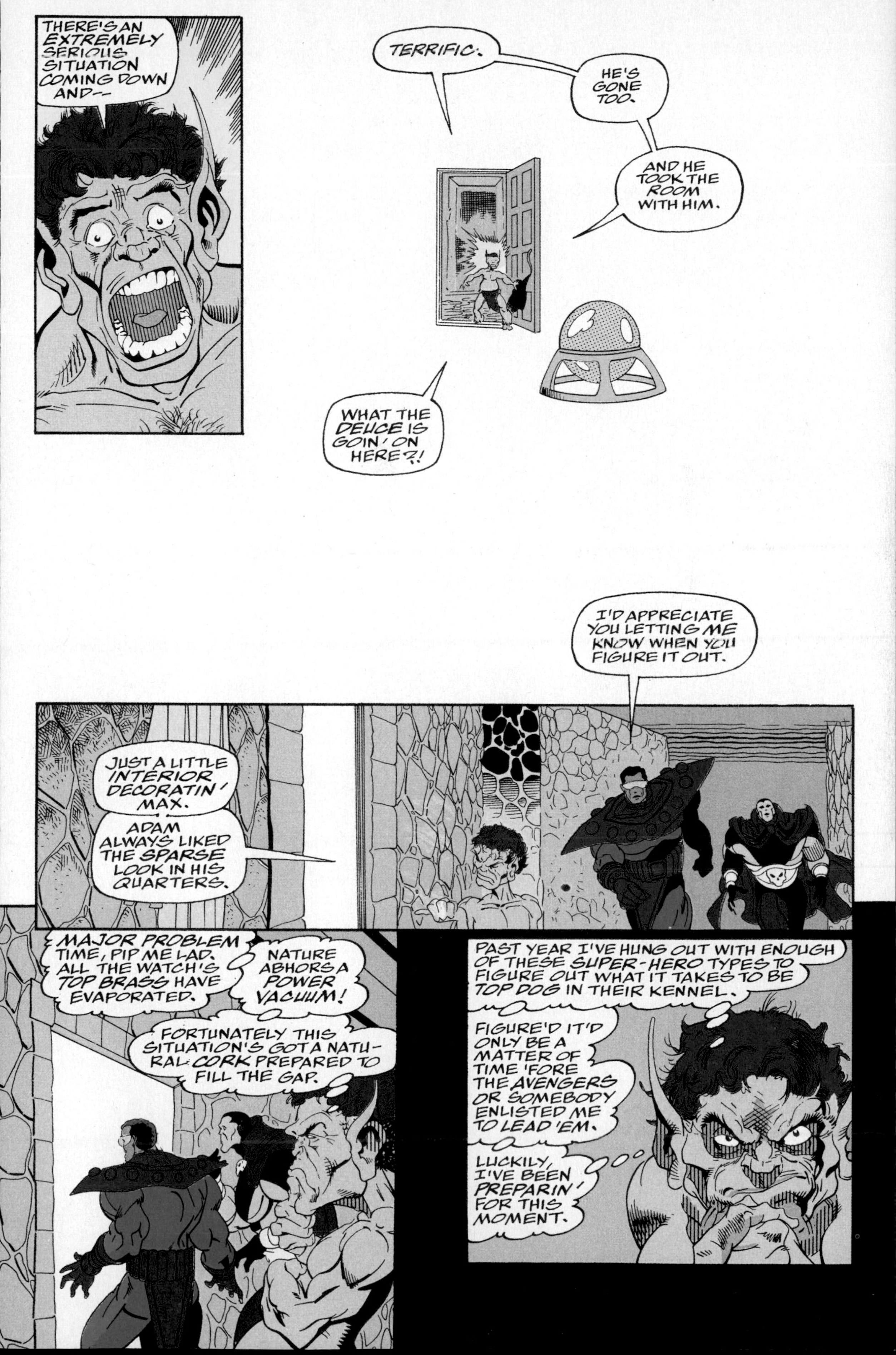
THERE'S AN EXTREMELY SERIOUS SITUATION COMING DOWN AND--
TERRIFIC.
HE'S GONE TOO.
AND HE TOOK THE ROOM WITH HIM.
WHAT THE DEUCE IS GOIN' ON HERE?!
I'D APPRECIATE YOU LETTING ME KNOW WHEN YOU FIGURE IT OUT.
JUST A LITTLE INTERIOR DECORATIN' MAX.
ADAM ALWAYS LIKED THE SPARSE LOOK IN HIS QUARTERS.
MAJOR PROBLEM TIME, PIP ME LAD. ALL THE WATCH'S TOP BRASS HAVE EVAPORATED.
NATURE ABHORS A POWER VACUUM!
FORTUNATELY THIS SITUATION'S GOT A NATURAL CORK PREPARED TO FILL THE GAP.
PAST YEAR I'VE HUNG OUT WITH ENOUGH OF THESE SUPER-HERO TYPES TO FIGURE OUT WHAT IT TAKES TO BE TOP DOG IN THEIR KENNEL.
FIGURE'D IT'D ONLY BE A MATTER OF TIME 'FORE THE AVENGERS OR SOMEBODY ENLISTED ME TO LEAD 'EM.
LUCKILY, I'VE BEEN PREPARIN' FOR THIS MOMENT.

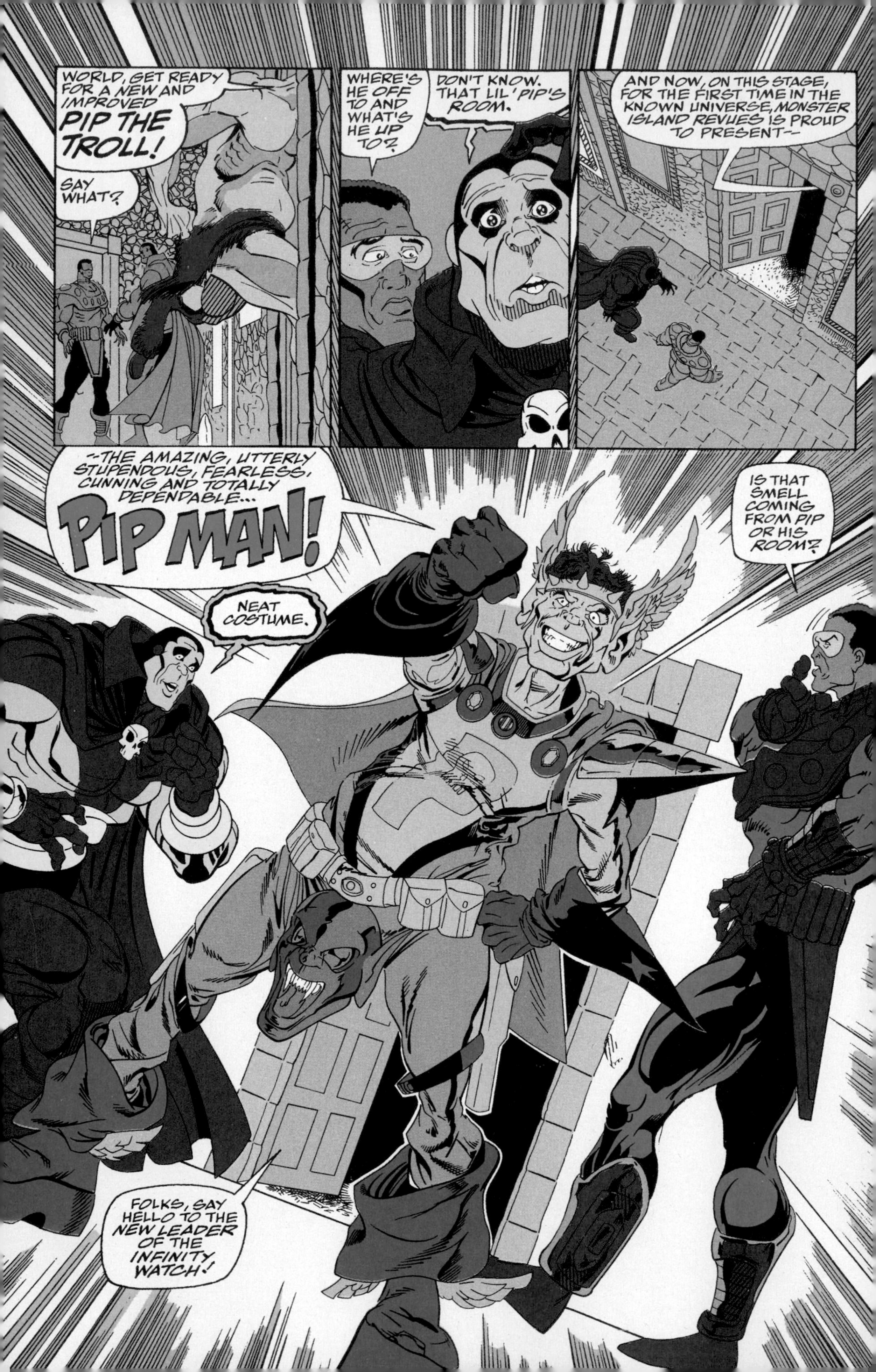
WORLD, GET READY FOR A NEW AND IMPROVED PIP THE TROLL!
SAY WHAT?
WHERE'S HE OFF TO AND WHAT'S HE UP TO?
DON'T KNOW. THAT LIL' PIP'S ROOM.
AND NOW, ON THIS STAGE, FOR THE FIRST TIME IN THE KNOWN UNIVERSE, MONSTER ISLAND REVUES IS PROUD TO PRESENT--
--THE AMAZING, UTTERLY STUPENDOUS, FEARLESS, CUNNING AND TOTALLY DEPENDABLE... PIP MAN!
IS THAT SMELL COMING FROM PIP OR HIS ROOM?
NEAT COSTUME.
FOLKS, SAY HELLO TO THE NEW LEADER OF THE INFINITY WATCH!

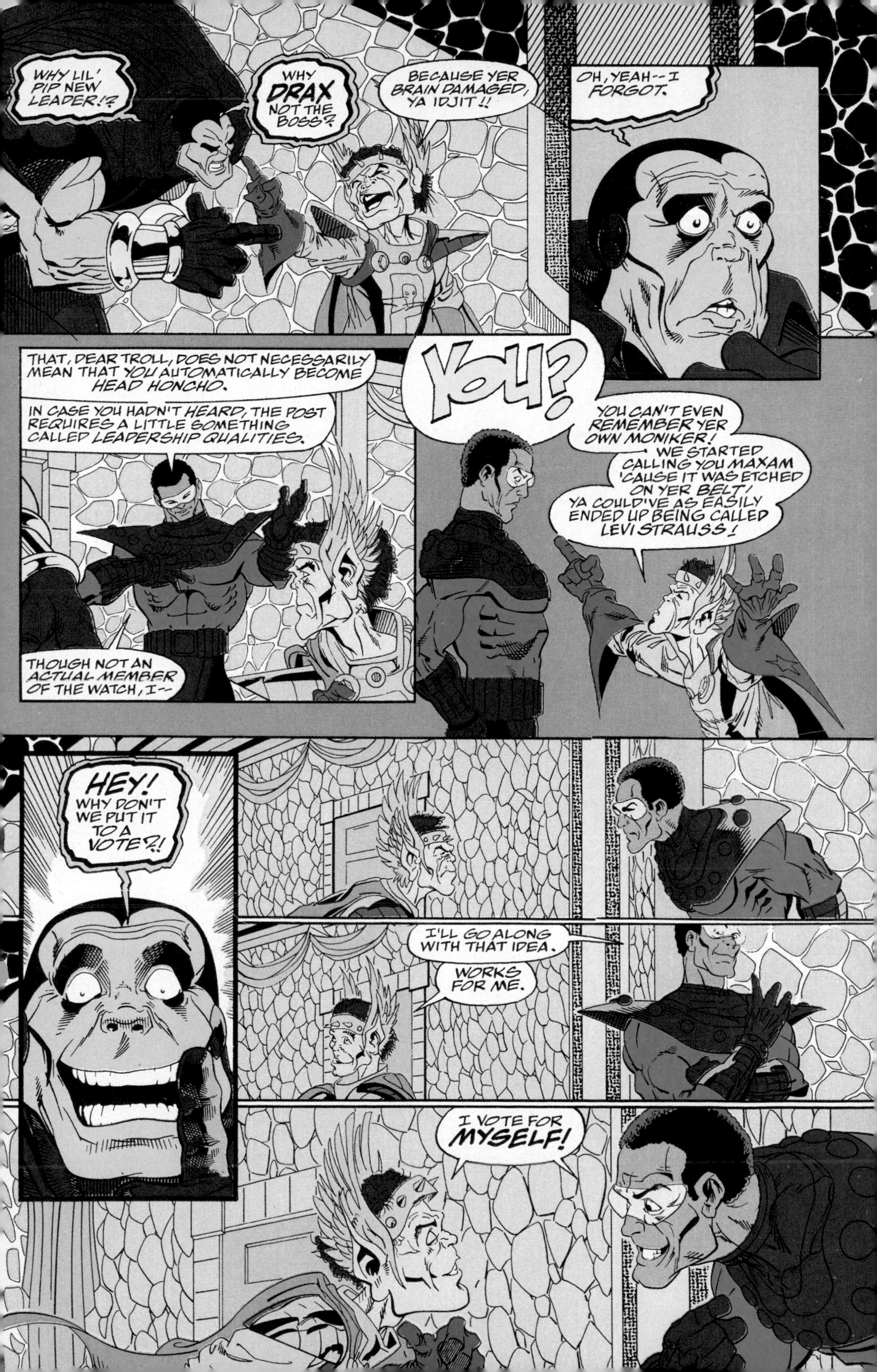
WHY LIL' PIP NEW LEADER!?
WHY DRAX NOT THE BOSS?
BECAUSE YER BRAIN DAMAGED, YA IDJIT!!
OH, YEAH--I FORGOT.
THAT, DEAR TROLL, DOES NOT NECESSARILY MEAN THAT YOU AUTOMATICALLY BECOME HEAD HONCHO.
IN CASE YOU HADN'T HEARD, THE POST REQUIRES A LITTLE SOMETHING CALLED LEADERSHIP QUALITIES.
THOUGH NOT AN ACTUAL MEMBER OF THE WATCH, I--
YOU?
YOU CAN'T EVEN REMEMBER YER OWN MONIKER!
WE STARTED CALLING YOU MAXAM 'CAUSE IT WAS ETCHED ON YER BELT!
YA COULD'VE AS EASILY ENDED UP BEING CALLED LEVI STRAUSS!
HEY! WHY DON'T WE PUT IT TO A VOTE?!
I'LL GO ALONG WITH THAT IDEA.
WORKS FOR ME.
I VOTE FOR MYSELF!

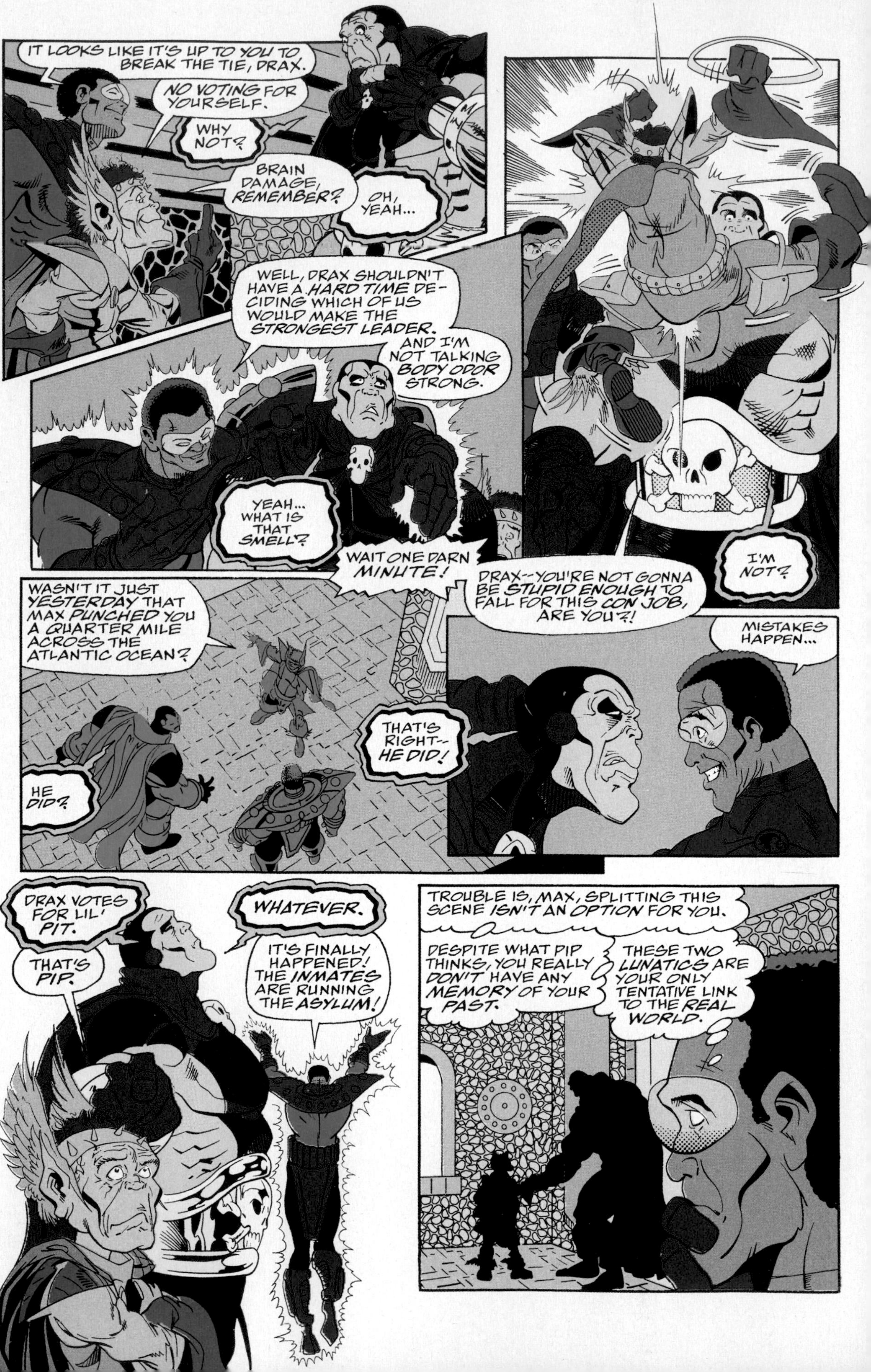
IT LOOKS LIKE IT'S UP TO YOU TO BREAK THE TIE, DRAX.
NO VOTING FOR YOURSELF.
WHY NOT?
BRAIN DAMAGE, REMEMBER?
OH, YEAH...
WELL, DRAX SHOULDN'T HAVE A HARD TIME DECIDING WHICH OF US WOULD MAKE THE STRONGEST LEADER.
AND I'M NOT TALKING BODY ODOR STRONG.
YEAH... WHAT IS THAT SMELL?
I'M NOT?
WAIT ONE DARN MINUTE!
DRAX--YOU'RE NOT GONNA BE STUPID ENOUGH TO FALL FOR THIS CON JOB, ARE YOU?!
WASN'T IT JUST YESTERDAY THAT MAX PUNCHED YOU A QUARTER MILE ACROSS THE ATLANTIC OCEAN?
THAT'S RIGHT-- HE DID!
HE DID?
MISTAKES HAPPEN...
DRAX VOTES FOR LIL' PIT.
THAT'S PIP.
WHATEVER.
IT'S FINALLY HAPPENED! THE INMATES ARE RUNNING THE ASYLUM!
TROUBLE IS, MAX, SPLITTING THIS SCENE ISN'T AN OPTION FOR YOU.
DESPITE WHAT PIP THINKS, YOU REALLY DON'T HAVE ANY MEMORY OF YOUR PAST.
THESE TWO LUNATICS ARE YOUR ONLY TENTATIVE LINK TO THE REAL WORLD.

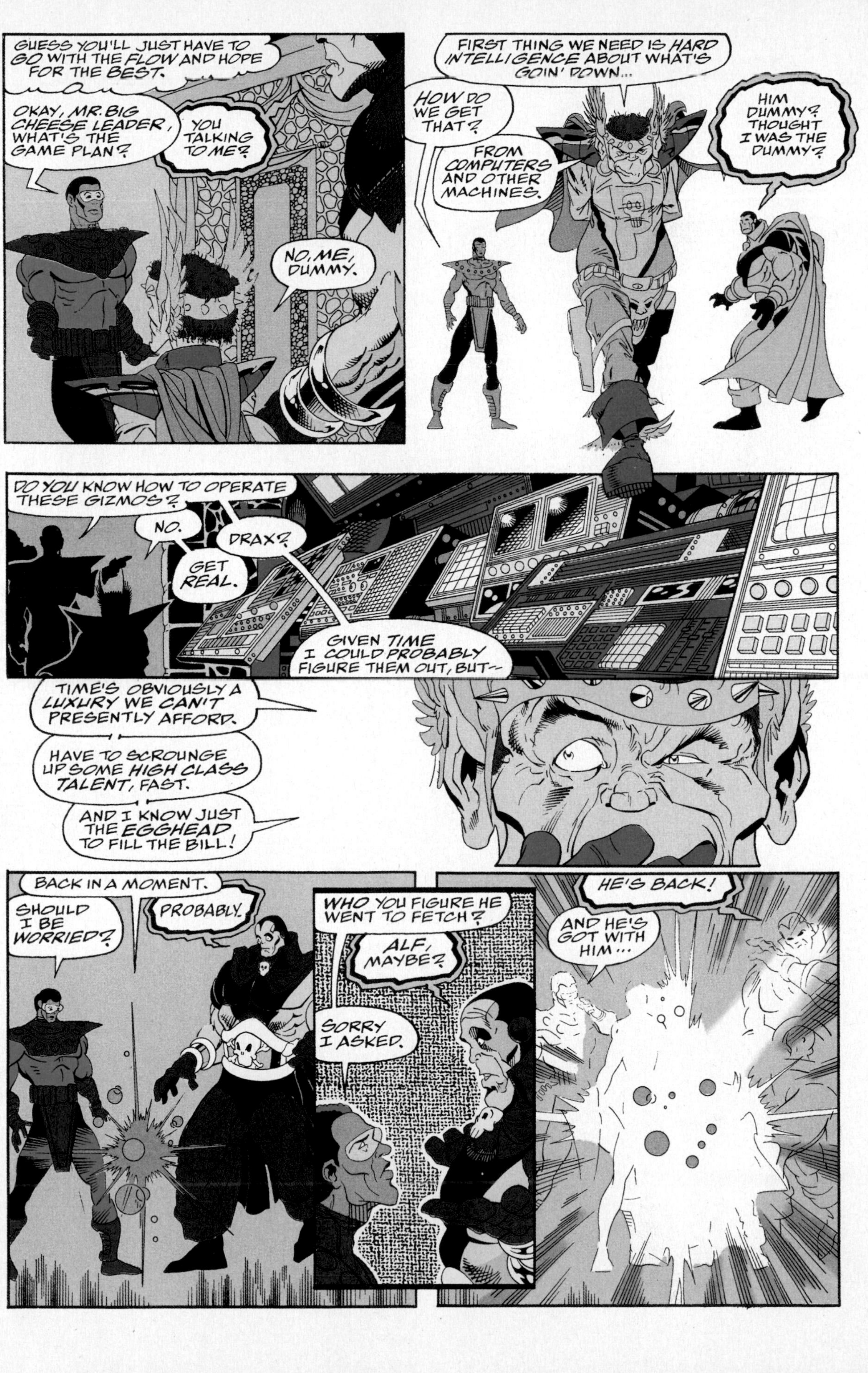
GUESS YOU'LL JUST HAVE TO GO WITH THE FLOW AND HOPE FOR THE BEST.
OKAY, MR. BIG CHEESE LEADER, WHAT'S THE GAME PLAN?
YOU TALKING TO ME?
NO, ME, DUMMY.
FIRST THING WE NEED IS HARD INTELLIGENCE ABOUT WHAT'S GOIN' DOWN...
HOW DO WE GET THAT?
FROM COMPUTERS AND OTHER MACHINES.
HIM DUMMY? THOUGHT I WAS THE DUMMY?
DO YOU KNOW HOW TO OPERATE THESE GIZMOS?
NO.
DRAX?
GET REAL.
GIVEN TIME I COULD PROBABLY FIGURE THEM OUT, BUT--
TIME'S OBVIOUSLY A LUXURY WE CAN'T PRESENTLY AFFORD.
HAVE TO SCROUNGE UP SOME HIGH CLASS TALENT, FAST.
AND I KNOW JUST THE EGGHEAD TO FILL THE BILL!
BACK IN A MOMENT.
SHOULD I BE WORRIED?
PROBABLY.
WHO YOU FIGURE HE WENT TO FETCH?
ALF, MAYBE?
SORRY I ASKED.
HE'S BACK!
AND HE'S GOT WITH HIM...

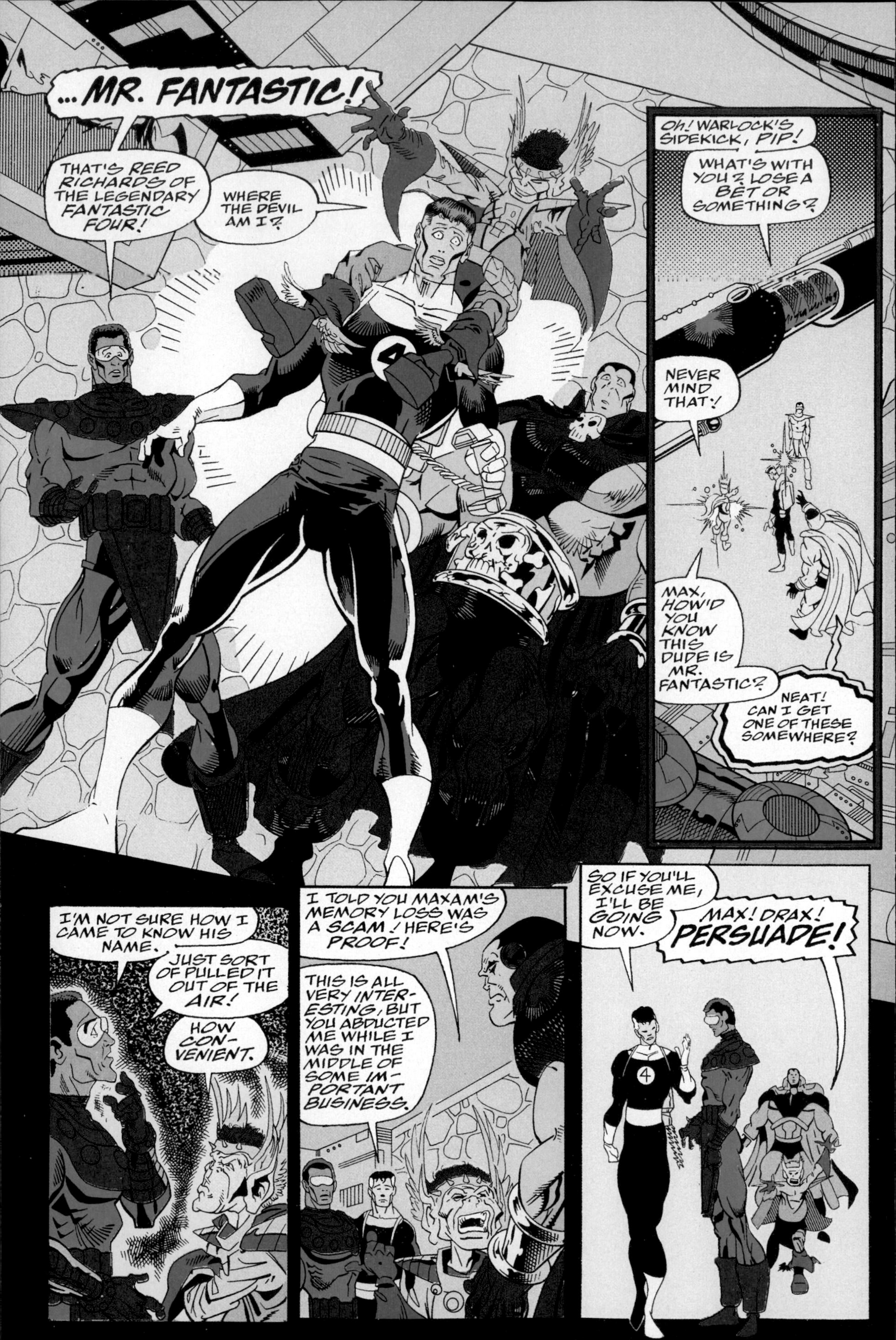
...MR. FANTASTIC!
THAT'S REED RICHARDS OF THE LEGENDARY FANTASTIC FOUR!
WHERE THE DEVIL AM I?!
OH! WARLOCK'S SIDEKICK, PIP!
WHAT'S WITH YOU? LOSE A BET OR SOMETHING?
NEVER MIND THAT!
MAX, HOW'D YOU KNOW THIS DUDE IS MR. FANTASTIC?
NEAT! CAN I GET ONE OF THESE SOMEWHERE?
I'M NOT SURE HOW I CAME TO KNOW HIS NAME.
JUST SORT OF PULLED IT OUT OF THE AIR!
HOW CON-VENIENT.
I TOLD YOU MAXAM'S MEMORY LOSS WAS A SCAM! HERE'S PROOF!
THIS IS ALL VERY INTER-ESTING, BUT YOU ABDUCTED ME WHILE I WAS IN THE MIDDLE OF SOME IM-PORTANT BUSINESS.
SO IF YOU'LL EXCUSE ME, I'LL BE GOING NOW.
MAX! DRAX! PERSUADE!

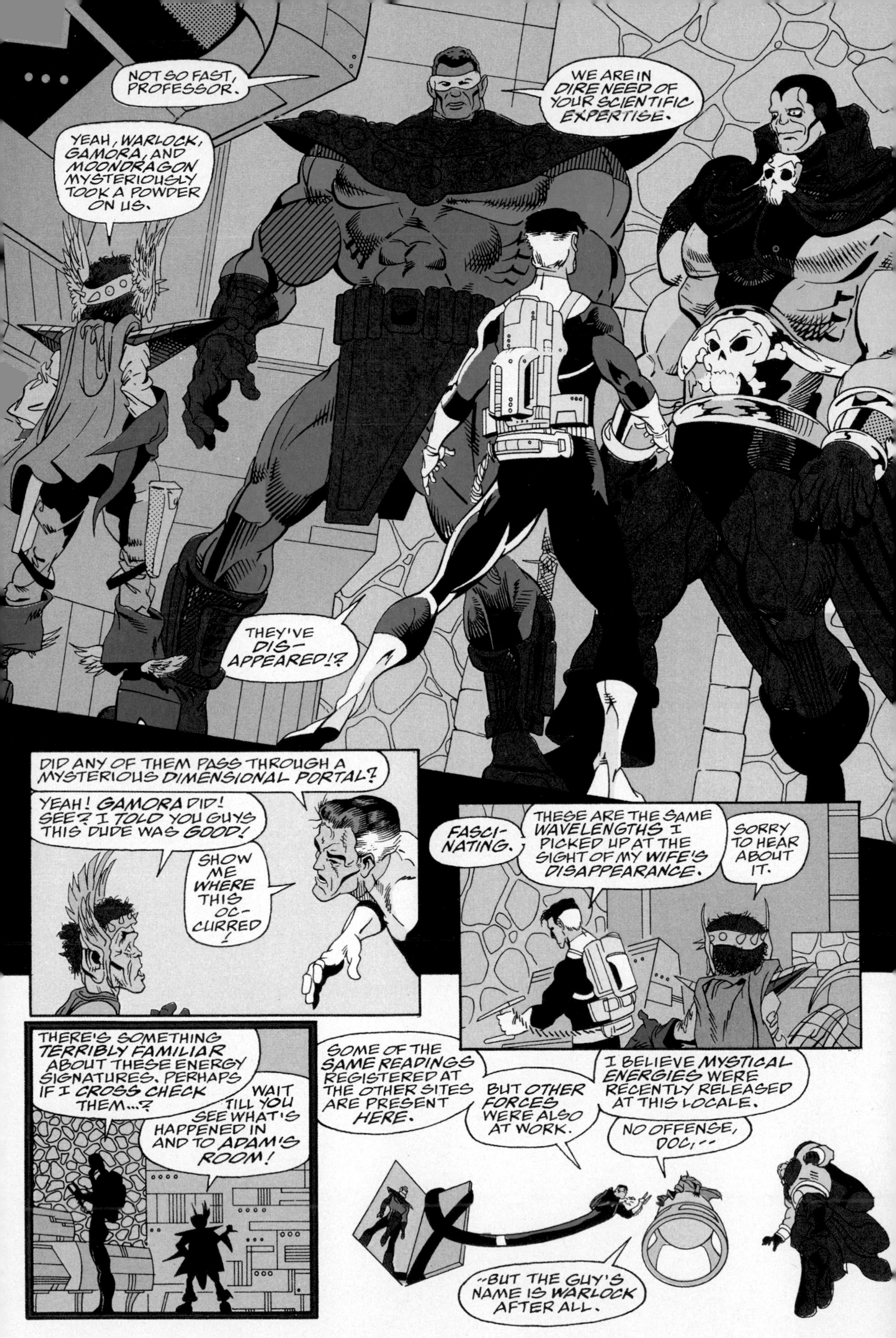
NOT SO FAST, PROFESSOR.
WE ARE IN DIRE NEED OF YOUR SCIENTIFIC EXPERTISE.
YEAH, WARLOCK, GAMORA, AND MOONDRAGON MYSTERIOUSLY TOOK A POWDER ON US.
THEY'VE DIS-APPEARED!?
DID ANY OF THEM PASS THROUGH A MYSTERIOUS DIMENSIONAL PORTAL?
YEAH! GAMORA DID! SEE? I TOLD YOU GUYS THIS DUDE WAS GOOD!
SHOW ME WHERE THIS OC-CURRED!
FASCI-NATING.
THESE ARE THE SAME WAVELENGTHS I PICKED UP AT THE SIGHT OF MY WIFE'S DISAPPEARANCE.
SORRY TO HEAR ABOUT IT.
THERE'S SOMETHING TERRIBLY FAMILIAR ABOUT THESE ENERGY SIGNATURES. PERHAPS IF I CROSS CHECK THEM...?
WAIT TILL YOU SEE WHAT'S HAPPENED IN AND TO ADAM'S ROOM!
SOME OF THE SAME READINGS REGISTERED AT THE OTHER SITES ARE PRESENT HERE.
BUT OTHER FORCES WERE ALSO AT WORK.
I BELIEVE MYSTICAL ENERGIES WERE RECENTLY RELEASED AT THIS LOCALE.
NO OFFENSE, DOC,--
--BUT THE GUY'S NAME IS WARLOCK AFTER ALL.

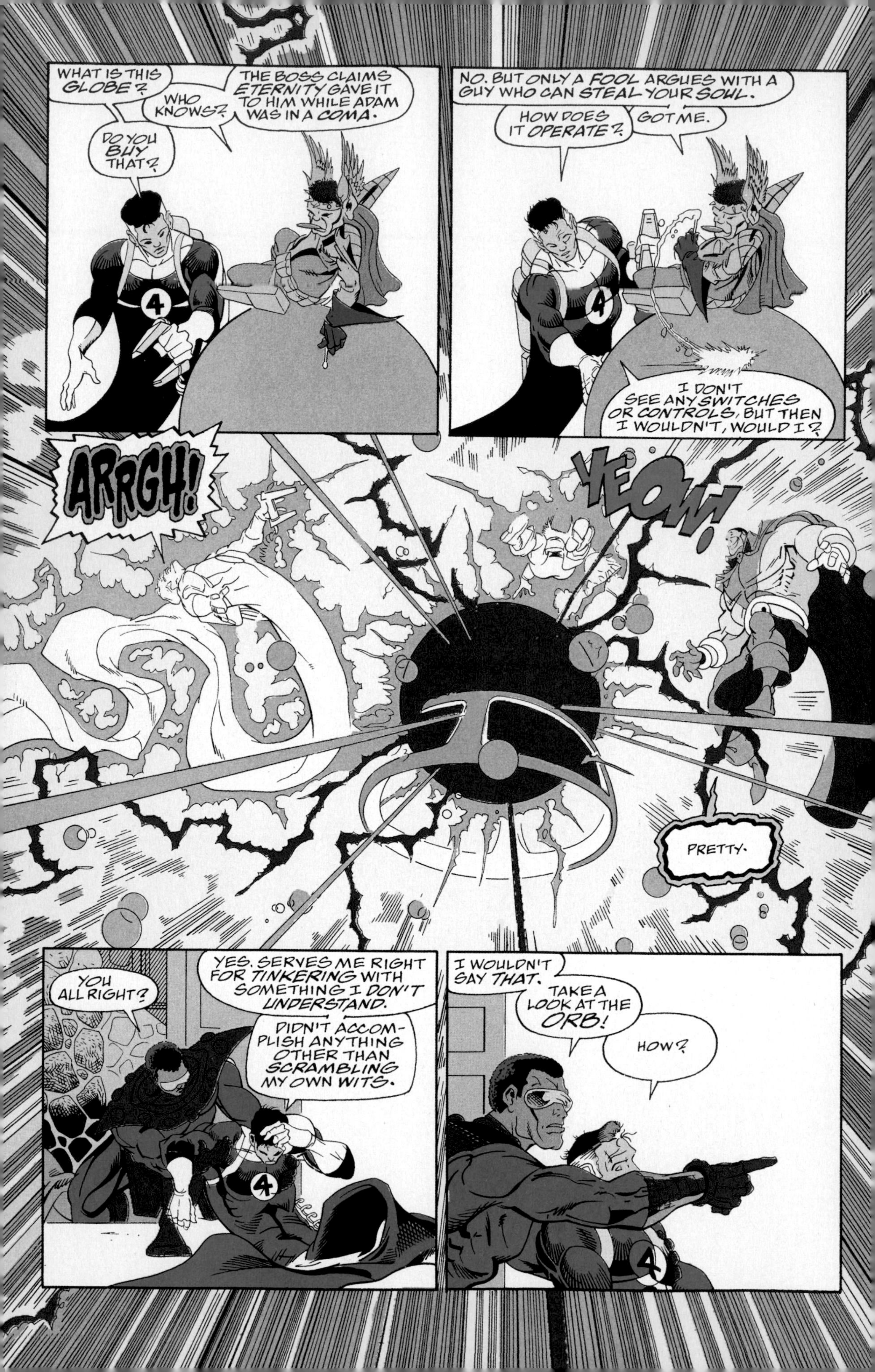
WHAT IS THIS GLOBE?
WHO KNOWS?
THE BOSS CLAIMS ETERNITY GAVE IT TO HIM WHILE ADAM WAS IN A COMA.
DO YOU BUY THAT?
NO. BUT ONLY A FOOL ARGUES WITH A GUY WHO CAN STEAL YOUR SOUL.
HOW DOES IT OPERATE?
GOT ME.
I DON'T SEE ANY SWITCHES OR CONTROLS, BUT THEN I WOULDN'T, WOULD I?
ARRGH!
YEOW!
PRETTY.
YOU ALL RIGHT?
YES. SERVES ME RIGHT FOR TINKERING WITH SOMETHING I DON'T UNDERSTAND.
DIDN'T ACCOMPLISH ANYTHING OTHER THAN SCRAMBLING MY OWN WITS.
I WOULDN'T SAY THAT.
TAKE A LOOK AT THE ORB!
HOW?

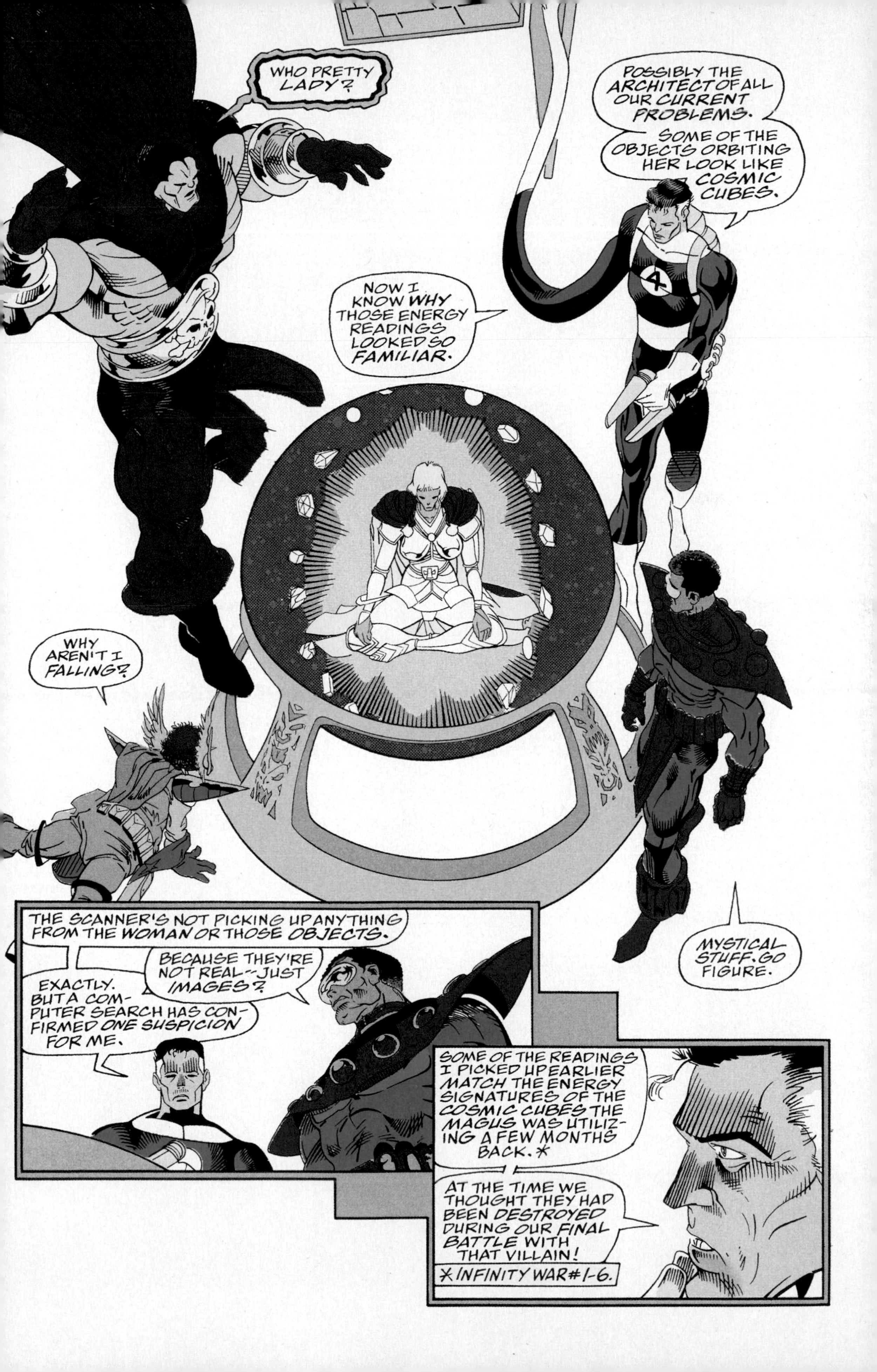
WHO PRETTY LADY?
POSSIBLY THE ARCHITECT OF ALL OUR CURRENT PROBLEMS.
SOME OF THE OBJECTS ORBITING HER LOOK LIKE COSMIC CUBES.
NOW I KNOW WHY THOSE ENERGY READINGS LOOKED SO FAMILIAR.
WHY AREN'T I FALLING?
MYSTICAL STUFF. GO FIGURE.
THE SCANNER'S NOT PICKING UP ANYTHING FROM THE WOMAN OR THOSE OBJECTS.
BECAUSE THEY'RE NOT REAL--JUST IMAGES?
EXACTLY. BUT A COMPUTER SEARCH HAS CONFIRMED ONE SUSPICION FOR ME.
SOME OF THE READINGS I PICKED UP EARLIER MATCH THE ENERGY SIGNATURES OF THE COSMIC CUBES THE MAGUS WAS UTILIZING A FEW MONTHS BACK. *
AT THE TIME WE THOUGHT THEY HAD BEEN DESTROYED DURING OUR FINAL BATTLE WITH THAT VILLAIN!
* INFINITY WAR #1-6.

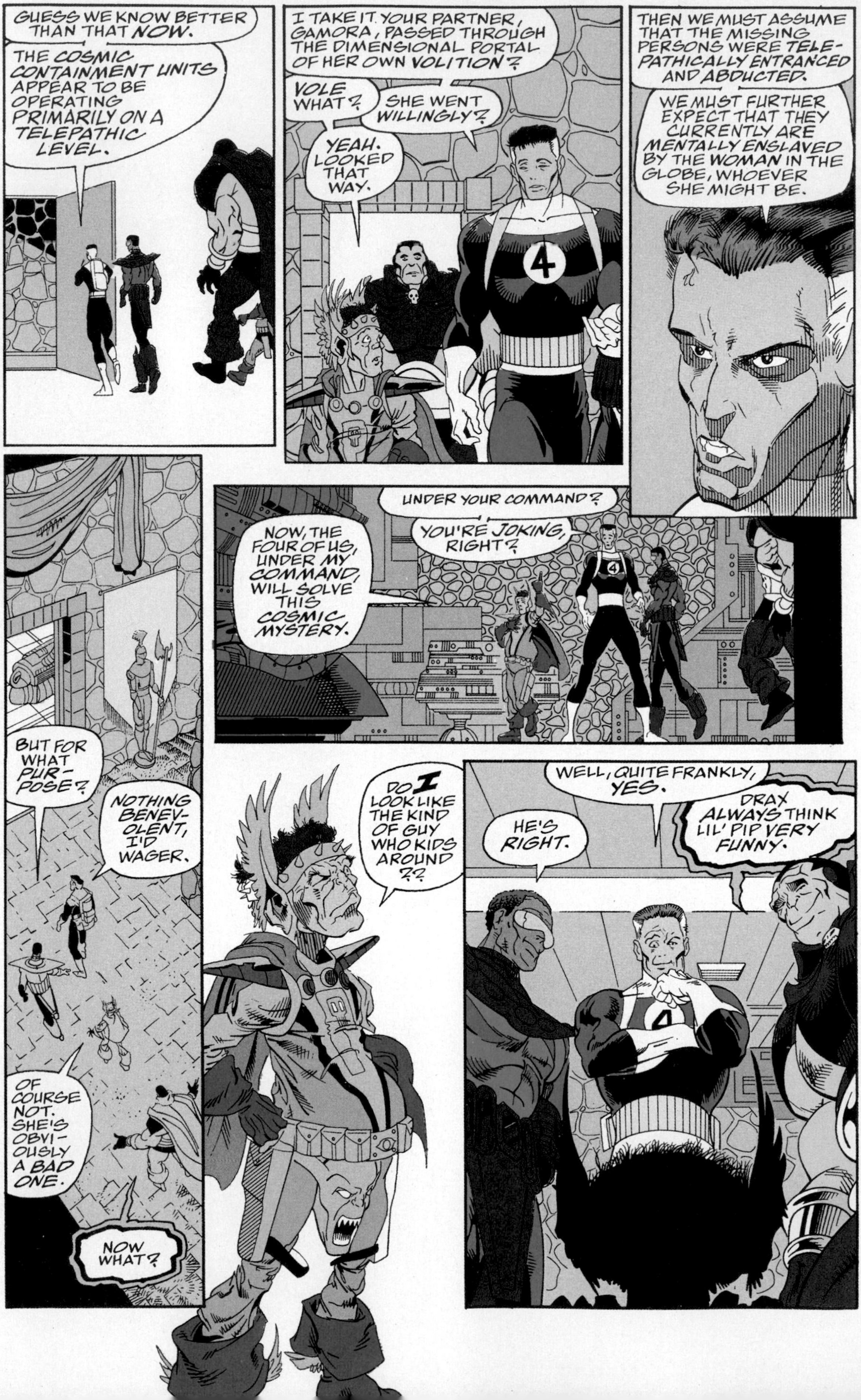
GUESS WE KNOW BETTER THAN THAT NOW.
THE COSMIC CONTAINMENT UNITS APPEAR TO BE OPERATING PRIMARILY ON A TELEPATHIC LEVEL.
I TAKE IT, YOUR PARTNER, GAMORA, PASSED THROUGH THE DIMENSIONAL PORTAL OF HER OWN VOLITION?
VOLE WHAT?
SHE WENT WILLINGLY?
YEAH. LOOKED THAT WAY.
THEN WE MUST ASSUME THAT THE MISSING PERSONS WERE TELEPATHICALLY ENTRANCED AND ABDUCTED.
WE MUST FURTHER EXPECT THAT THEY CURRENTLY ARE MENTALLY ENSLAVED BY THE WOMAN IN THE GLOBE, WHOEVER SHE MIGHT BE.
NOW, THE FOUR OF US, UNDER MY COMMAND, WILL SOLVE THIS COSMIC MYSTERY.
UNDER YOUR COMMAND?
YOU'RE JOKING, RIGHT?
BUT FOR WHAT PURPOSE?
NOTHING BENEVOLENT, I'D WAGER.
OF COURSE NOT. SHE'S OBVIOUSLY A BAD ONE.
NOW WHAT?
DO I LOOK LIKE THE KIND OF GUY WHO KIDS AROUND??
WELL, QUITE FRANKLY, YES.
HE'S RIGHT.
DRAX ALWAYS THINK LIL' PIP VERY FUNNY.

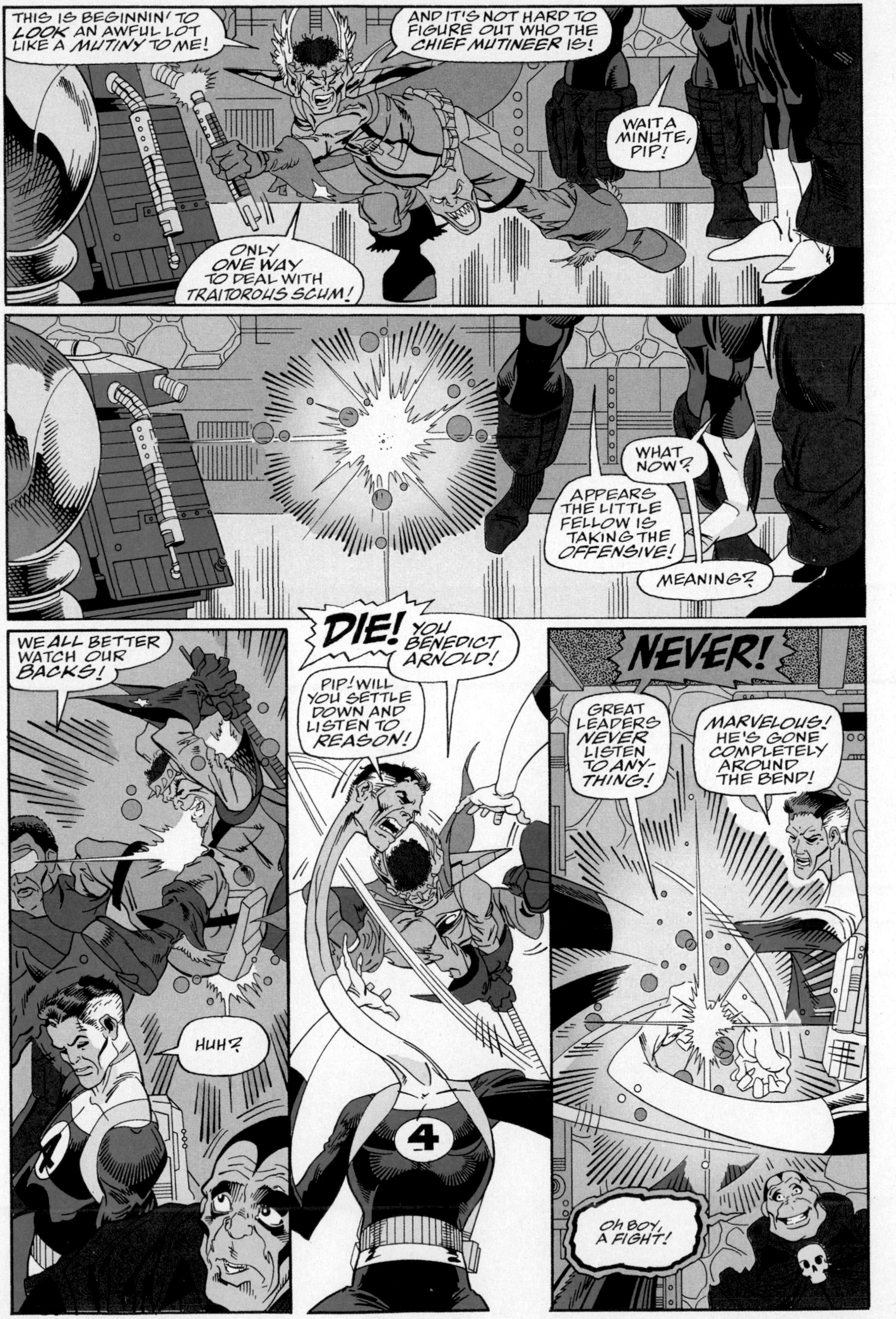

THIS IS BEGINNIN' TO LOOK AN AWFUL LOT LIKE A MUTINY TO ME!
AND IT'S NOT HARD TO FIGURE OUT WHO THE CHIEF MUTINEER IS!
WAIT A MINUTE, PIP!
ONLY ONE WAY TO DEAL WITH TRAITOROUS SCUM!
WHAT NOW?
APPEARS THE LITTLE FELLOW IS TAKING THE OFFENSIVE!
MEANING?
WE ALL BETTER WATCH OUR BACKS!
HUH?
DIE! YOU BENEDICT ARNOLD!
PIP! WILL YOU SETTLE DOWN AND LISTEN TO REASON!
NEVER!
GREAT LEADERS NEVER LISTEN TO ANYTHING!
MARVELOUS! HE'S GONE COMPLETELY AROUND THE BEND!
Oh BOY, A FIGHT!

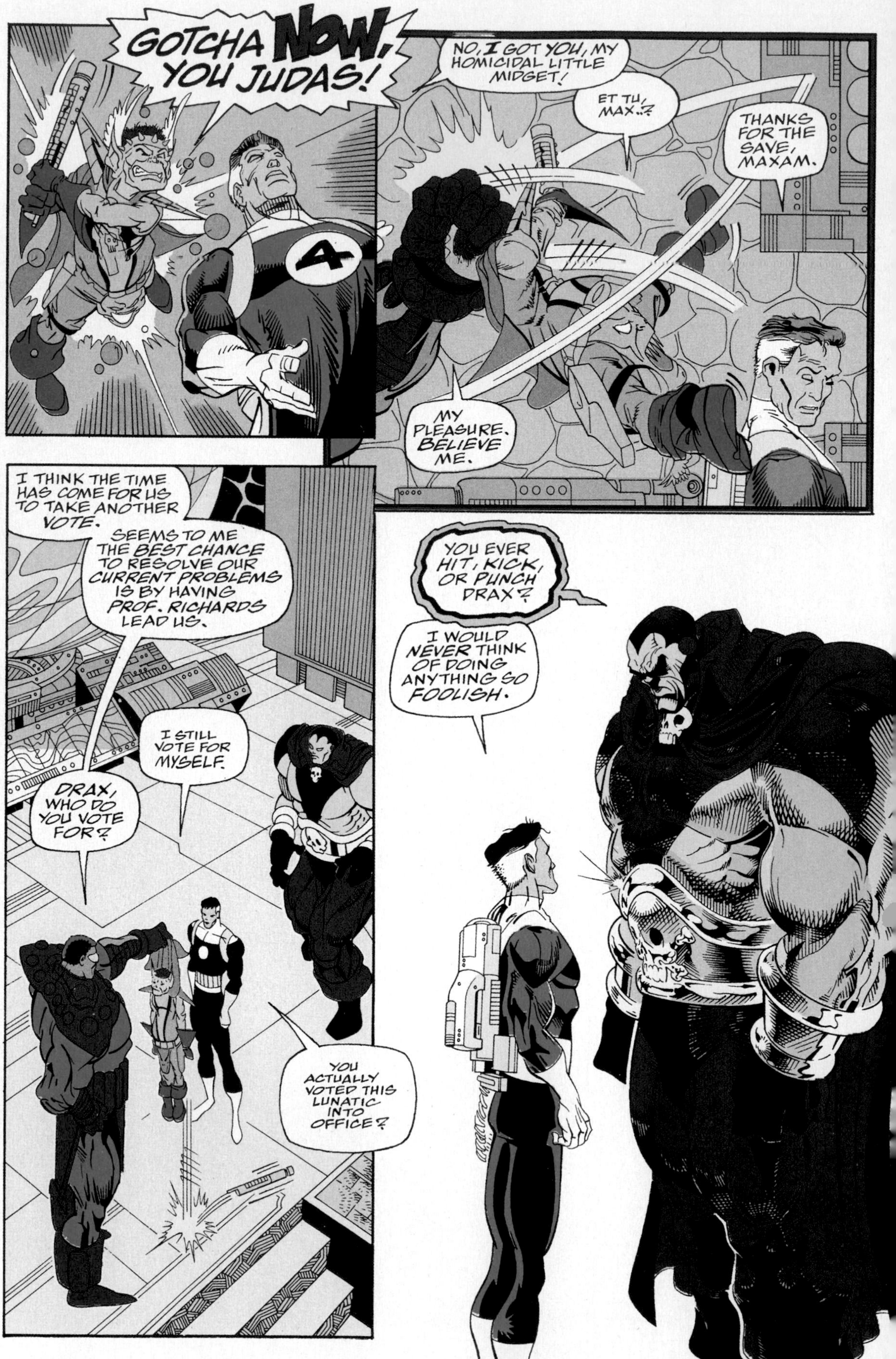
GOTCHA NOW, YOU JUDAS!
NO, I GOT YOU, MY HOMICIDAL LITTLE MIDGET!
ET TU, MAX..?
THANKS FOR THE SAVE, MAXAM.
MY PLEASURE. BELIEVE ME.
I THINK THE TIME HAS COME FOR US TO TAKE ANOTHER VOTE.
SEEMS TO ME THE BEST CHANCE TO RESOLVE OUR CURRENT PROBLEMS IS BY HAVING PROF. RICHARDS LEAD US.
I STILL VOTE FOR MYSELF.
DRAX, WHO DO YOU VOTE FOR?
YOU ACTUALLY VOTED THIS LUNATIC INTO OFFICE?
YOU EVER HIT, KICK, OR PUNCH DRAX?
I WOULD NEVER THINK OF DOING ANYTHING SO FOOLISH.

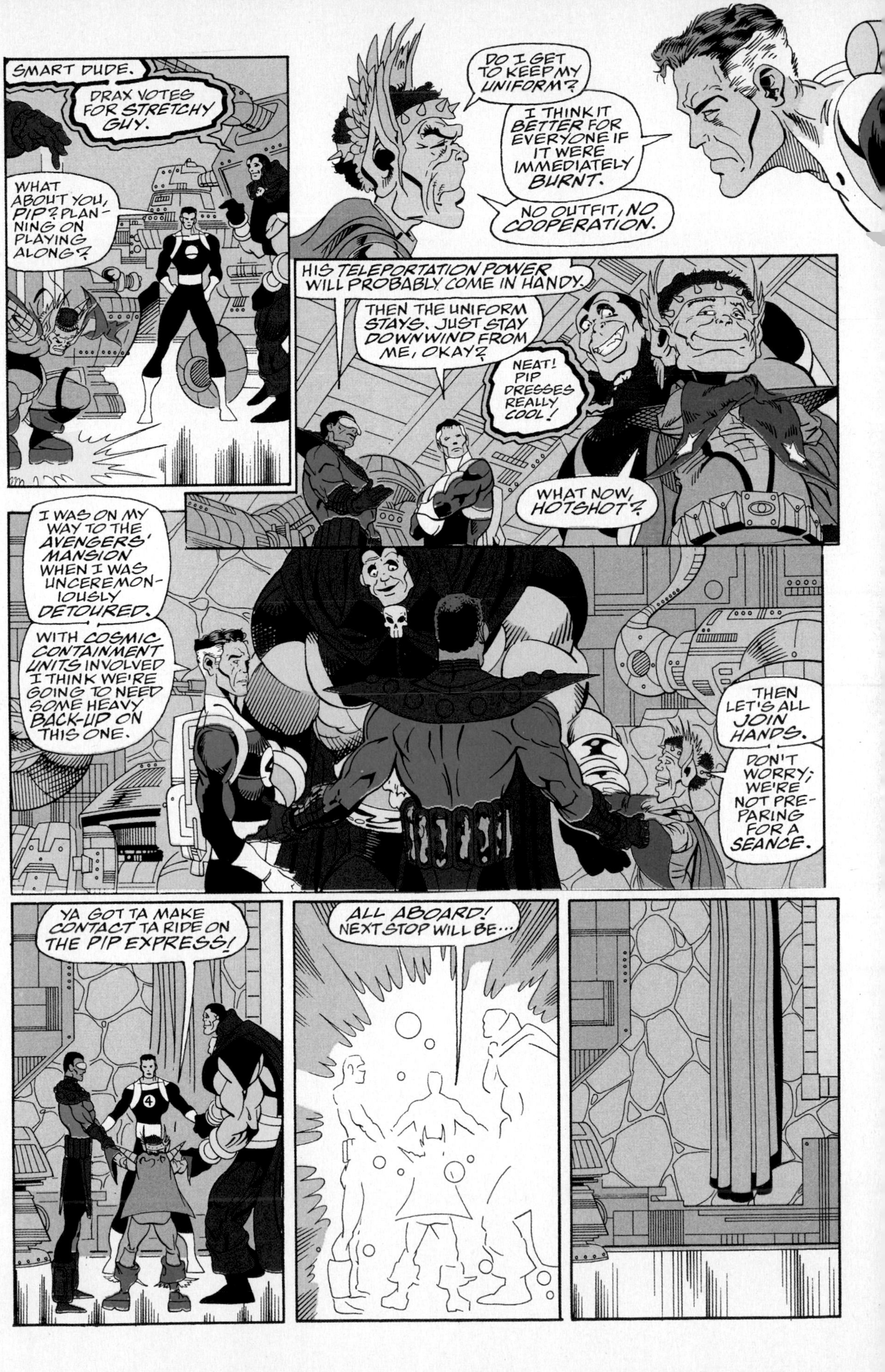
SMART DUDE.
DRAX VOTES FOR STRETCHY GUY.
WHAT ABOUT YOU, PIP? PLANNING ON PLAYING ALONG?
DO I GET TO KEEP MY UNIFORM?
I THINK IT BETTER FOR EVERYONE IF IT WERE IMMEDIATELY BURNT.
NO OUTFIT, NO COOPERATION.
HIS TELEPORTATION POWER WILL PROBABLY COME IN HANDY.
THEN THE UNIFORM STAYS. JUST STAY DOWNWIND FROM ME, OKAY?
NEAT! PIP DRESSES REALLY COOL!
WHAT NOW, HOTSHOT?
I WAS ON MY WAY TO THE AVENGERS' MANSION WHEN I WAS UNCEREMONIOUSLY DETOURED.
WITH COSMIC CONTAINMENT UNITS INVOLVED I THINK WE'RE GOING TO NEED SOME HEAVY BACK-UP ON THIS ONE.
THEN LET'S ALL JOIN HANDS.
DON'T WORRY; WE'RE NOT PREPARING FOR A SEANCE.
YA GOTTA MAKE CONTACT TA RIDE ON THE PIP EXPRESS!
ALL ABOARD! NEXT STOP WILL BE...

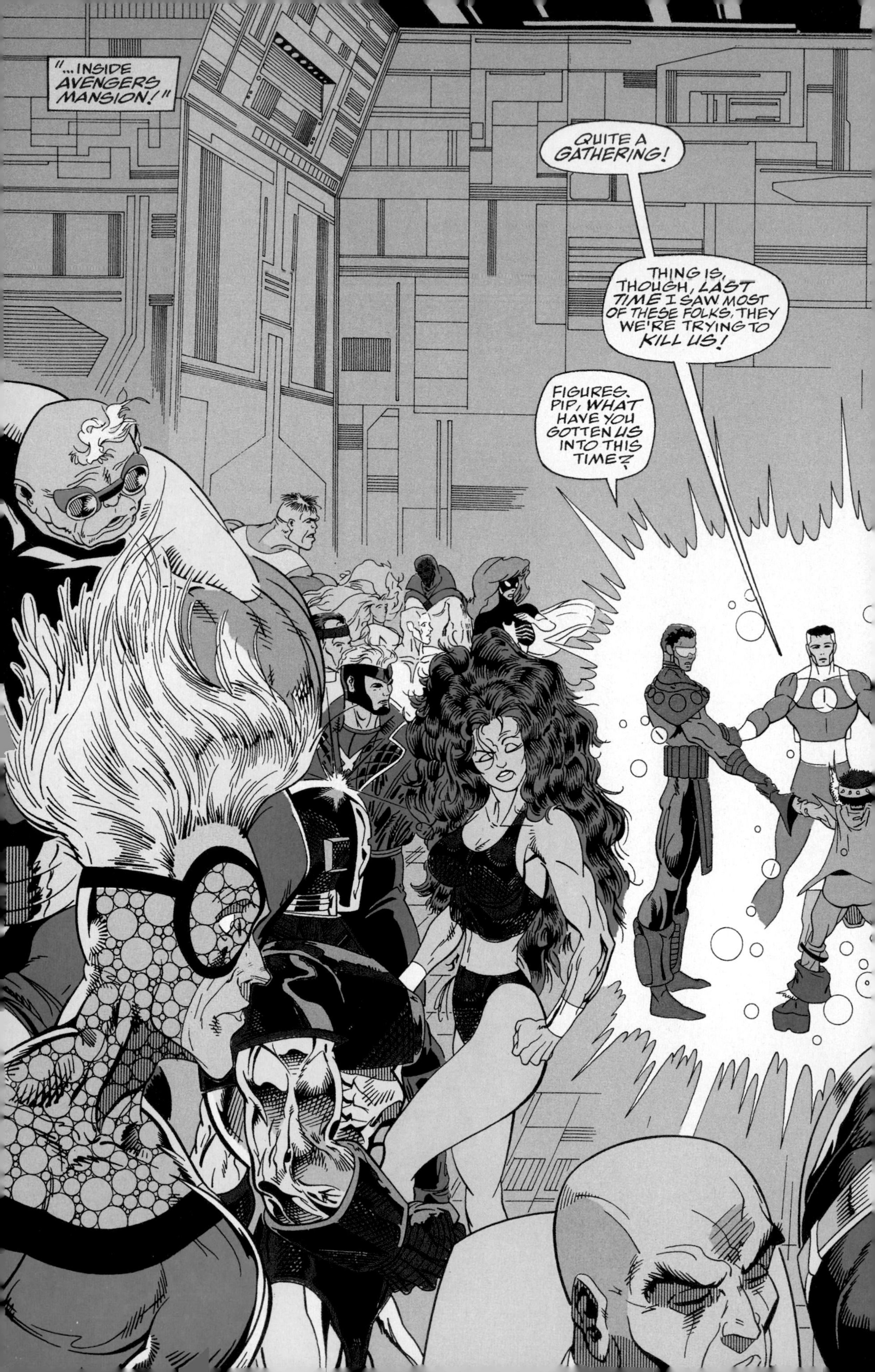
"...INSIDE AVENGERS MANSION!"
QUITE A GATHERING!
THING IS, THOUGH, LAST TIME I SAW MOST OF THESE FOLKS, THEY WE'RE TRYING TO KILL US!
FIGURES. PIP, WHAT HAVE YOU GOTTEN US INTO THIS TIME?

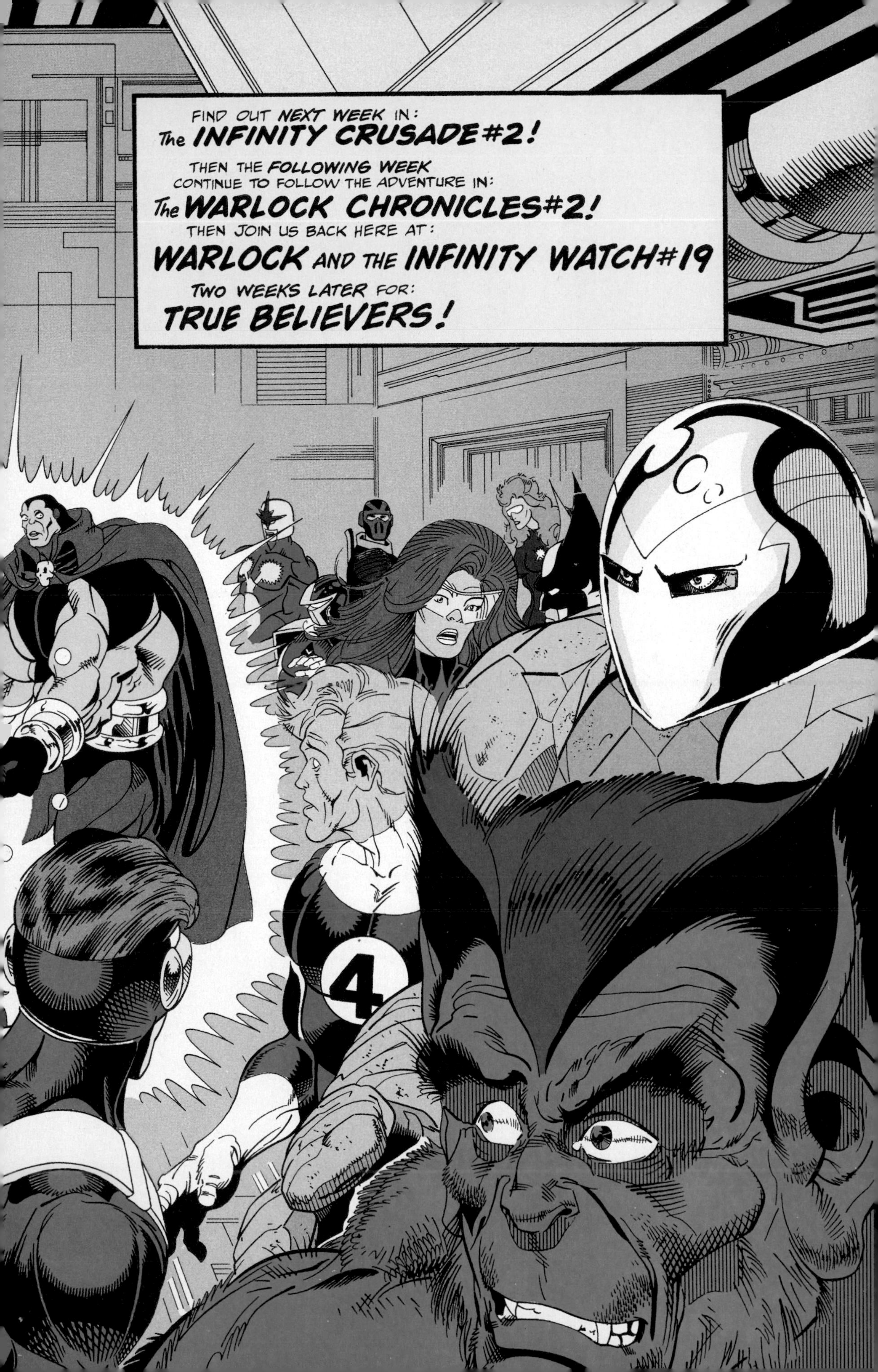
FIND OUT NEXT WEEK IN:
The INFINITY CRUSADE #2!
THEN THE FOLLOWING WEEK
CONTINUE TO FOLLOW THE ADVENTURE IN:
The WARLOCK CHRONICLES #2!
THEN JOIN US BACK HERE AT:
WARLOCK AND THE INFINITY WATCH #19
TWO WEEKS LATER FOR:
TRUE BELIEVERS!

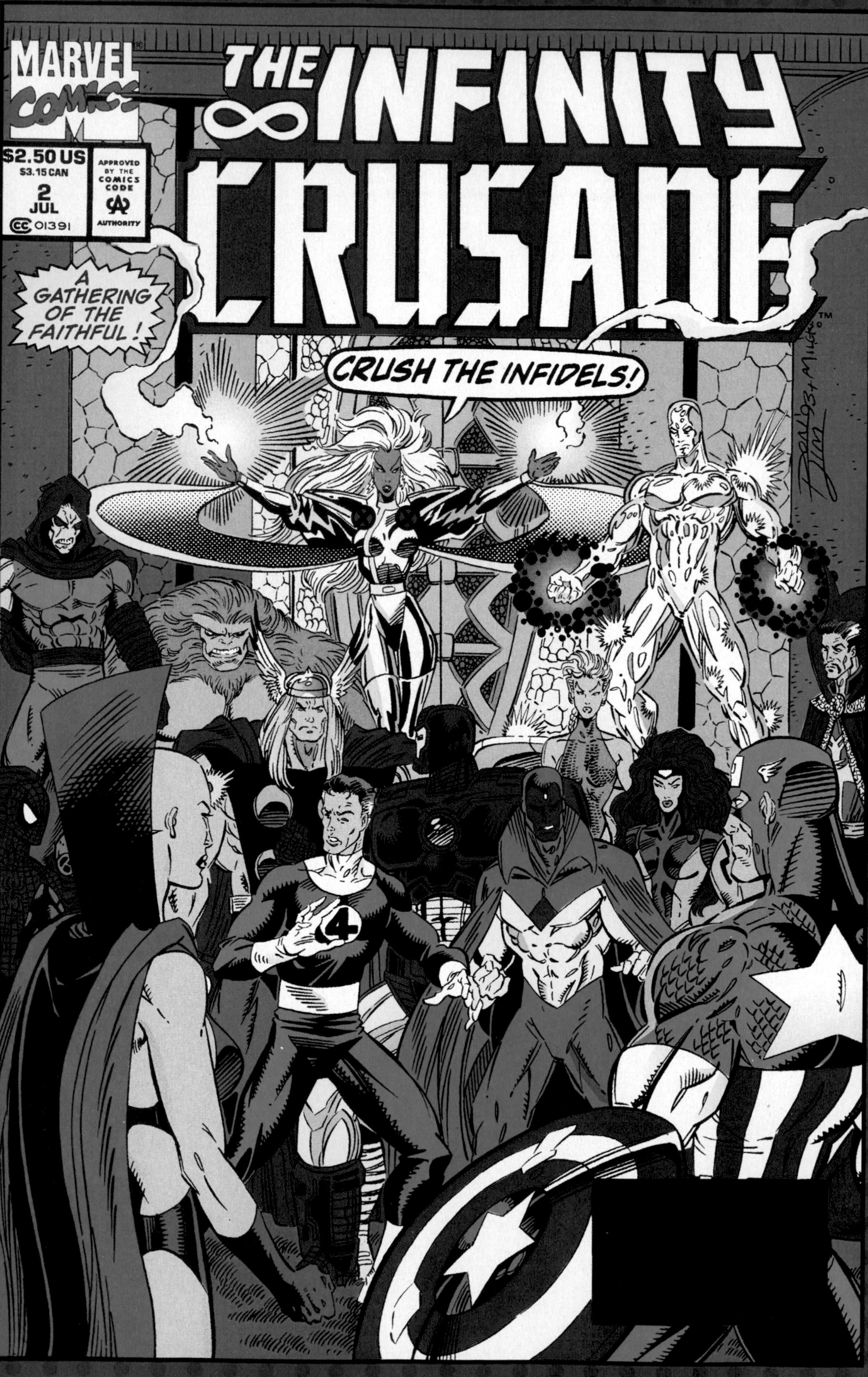
MARVEL COMICS
THE INFINITY CRUSADE
$2.50 US
$3.15 CAN
2
JUL
01391
APPROVED BY THE COMICS CODE AUTHORITY
A GATHERING OF THE FAITHFUL!
CRUSH THE INFIDELS!

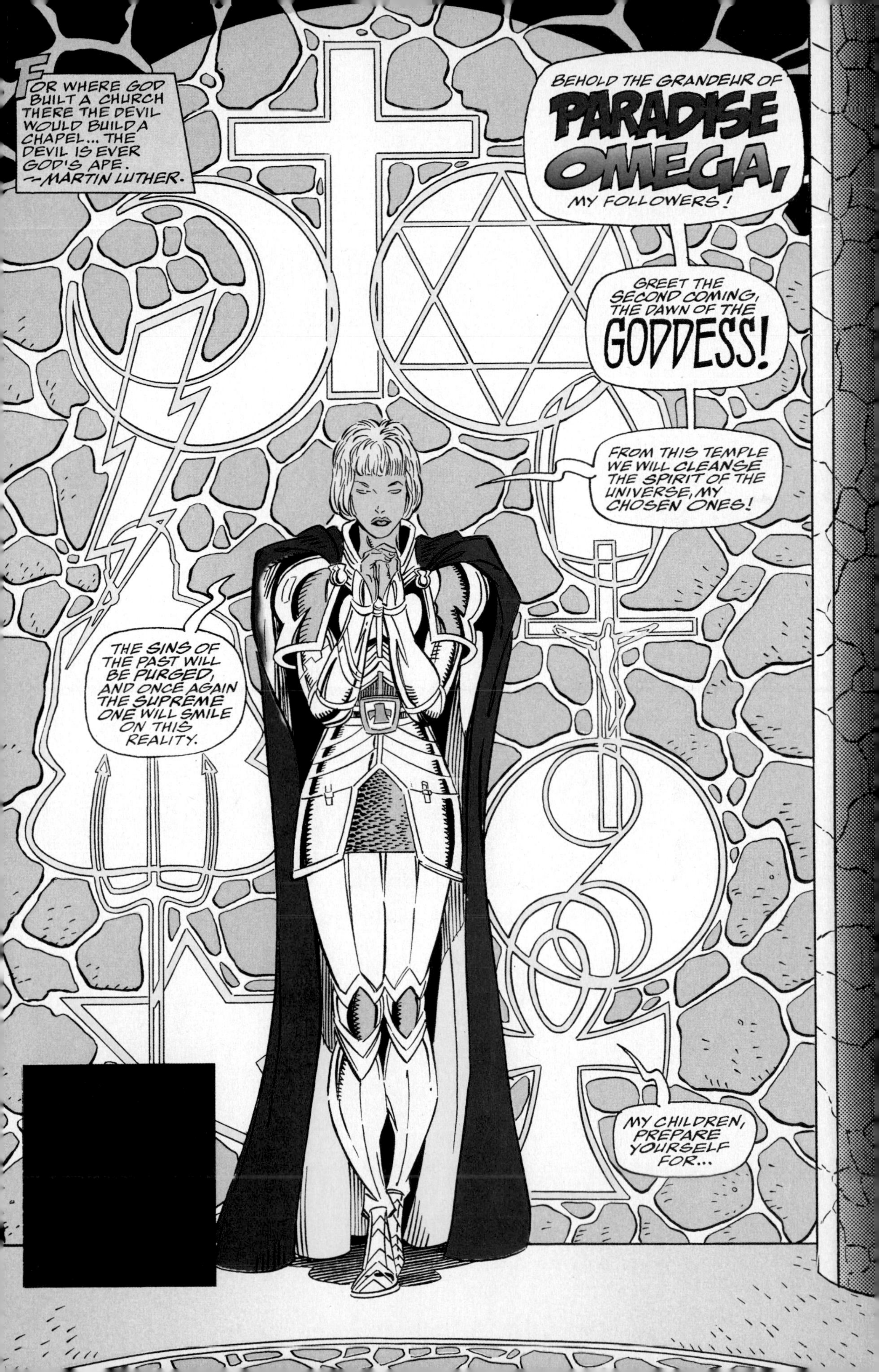
FOR WHERE GOD BUILT A CHURCH THERE THE DEVIL WOULD BUILD A CHAPEL... THE DEVIL IS EVER GOD'S APE. —MARTIN LUTHER.
BEHOLD THE GRANDEUR OF PARADISE OMEGA, MY FOLLOWERS!
GREET THE SECOND COMING, THE DAWN OF THE GODDESS!
FROM THIS TEMPLE WE WILL CLEANSE THE SPIRIT OF THE UNIVERSE, MY CHOSEN ONES!
THE SINS OF THE PAST WILL BE PURGED, AND ONCE AGAIN THE SUPREME ONE WILL SMILE ON THIS REALITY.
MY CHILDREN, PREPARE YOURSELF FOR...
[redacted]

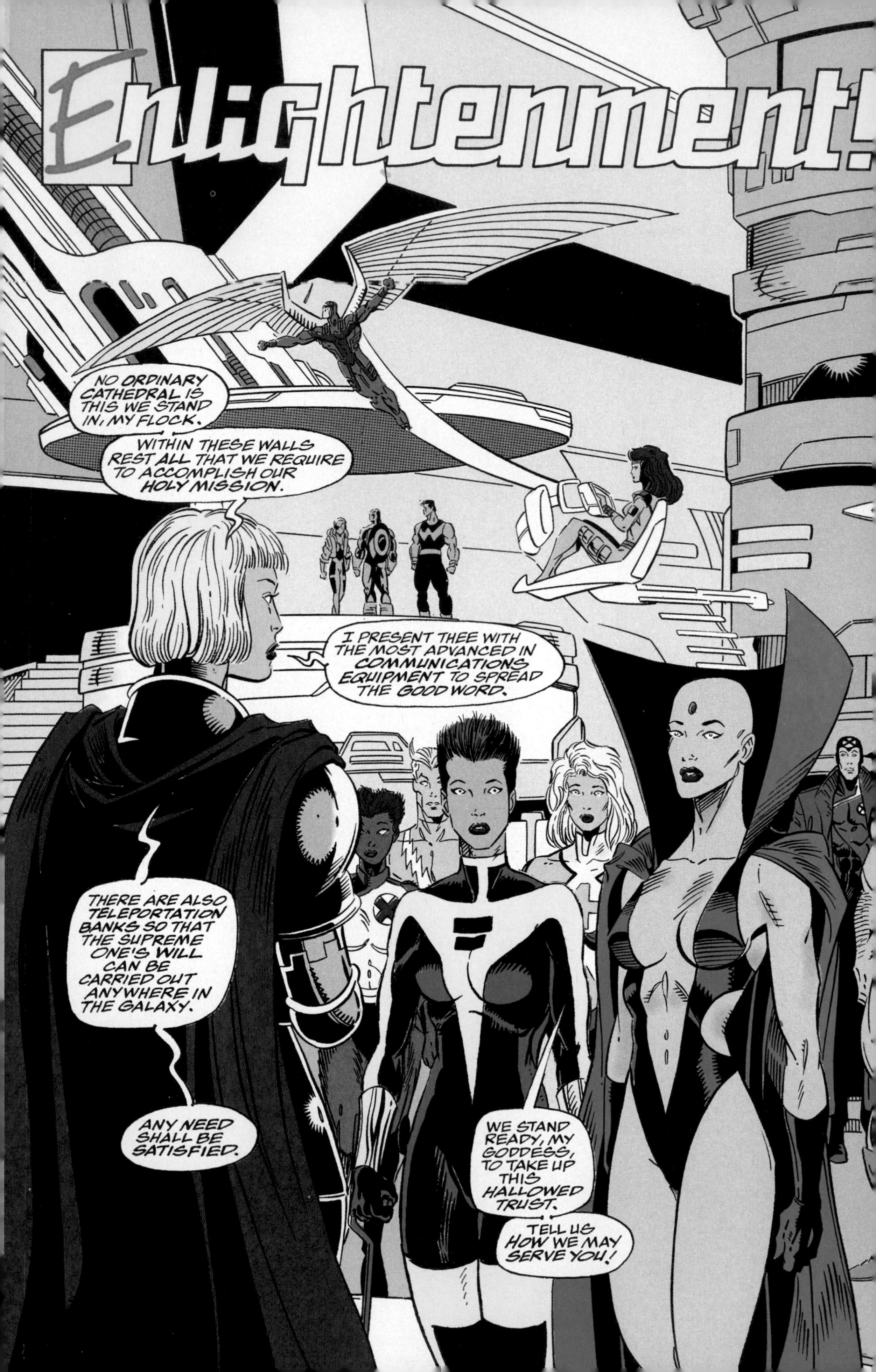
Enlightenment!
NO ORDINARY CATHEDRAL IS THIS WE STAND IN, MY FLOCK.
WITHIN THESE WALLS REST ALL THAT WE REQUIRE TO ACCOMPLISH OUR HOLY MISSION.
I PRESENT THEE WITH THE MOST ADVANCED IN COMMUNICATIONS EQUIPMENT TO SPREAD THE GOOD WORD.
THERE ARE ALSO TELEPORTATION BANKS SO THAT THE SUPREME ONE'S WILL CAN BE CARRIED OUT ANYWHERE IN THE GALAXY.
ANY NEED SHALL BE SATISFIED.
WE STAND READY, MY GODDESS, TO TAKE UP THIS HALLOWED TRUST.
TELL US HOW WE MAY SERVE YOU!

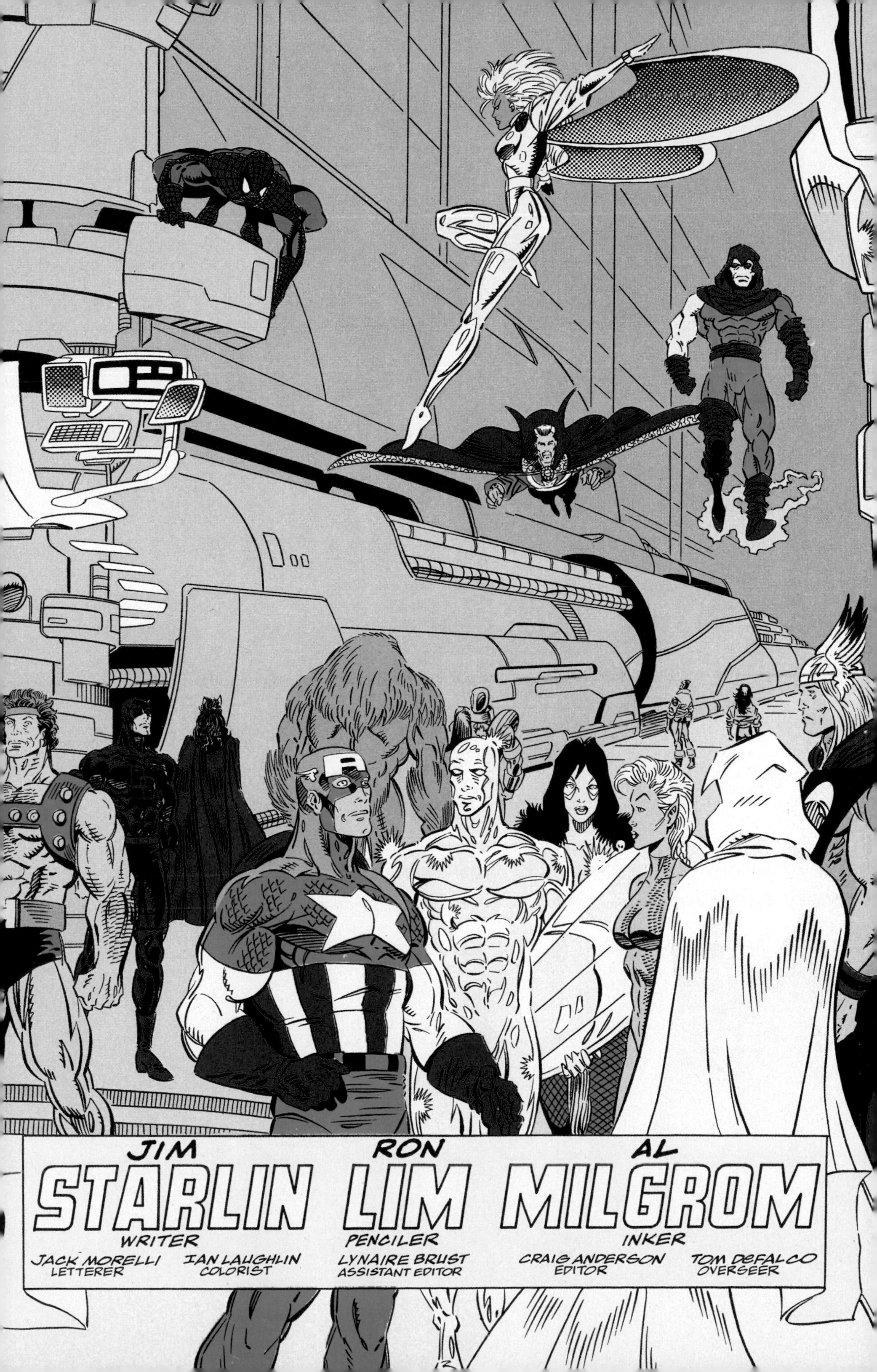
JIM STARLIN WRITER
RON LIM PENCILER
AL MILGROM INKER
JACK MORELLI LETTERER
IAN LAUGHLIN COLORIST
LYNAIRE BRUST ASSISTANT EDITOR
CRAIG ANDERSON EDITOR
TOM DEFALCO OVERSEER

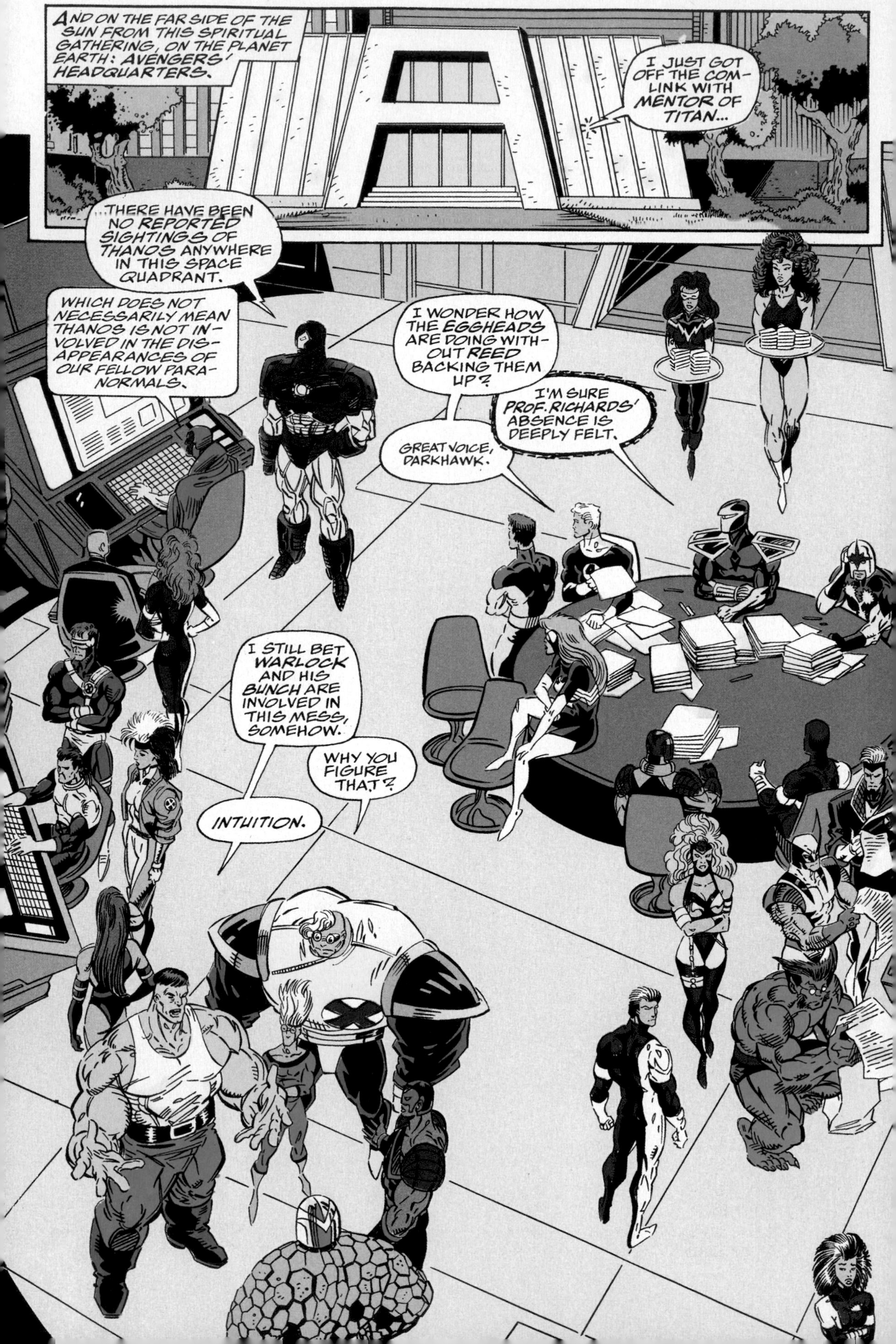
AND ON THE FAR SIDE OF THE SUN FROM THIS SPIRITUAL GATHERING, ON THE PLANET EARTH: AVENGERS' HEADQUARTERS.
I JUST GOT OFF THE COM-LINK WITH MENTOR OF TITAN...
...THERE HAVE BEEN NO REPORTED SIGHTINGS OF THANOS ANYWHERE IN THIS SPACE QUADRANT.
WHICH DOES NOT NECESSARILY MEAN THANOS IS NOT IN-VOLVED IN THE DIS-APPEARANCES OF OUR FELLOW PARA-NORMALS.
I WONDER HOW THE EGGHEADS ARE DOING WITH-OUT REED BACKING THEM UP?
I'M SURE PROF. RICHARDS' ABSENCE IS DEEPLY FELT.
GREAT VOICE, DARKHAWK.
I STILL BET WARLOCK AND HIS BUNCH ARE INVOLVED IN THIS MESS, SOMEHOW.
WHY YOU FIGURE THAT?
INTUITION.

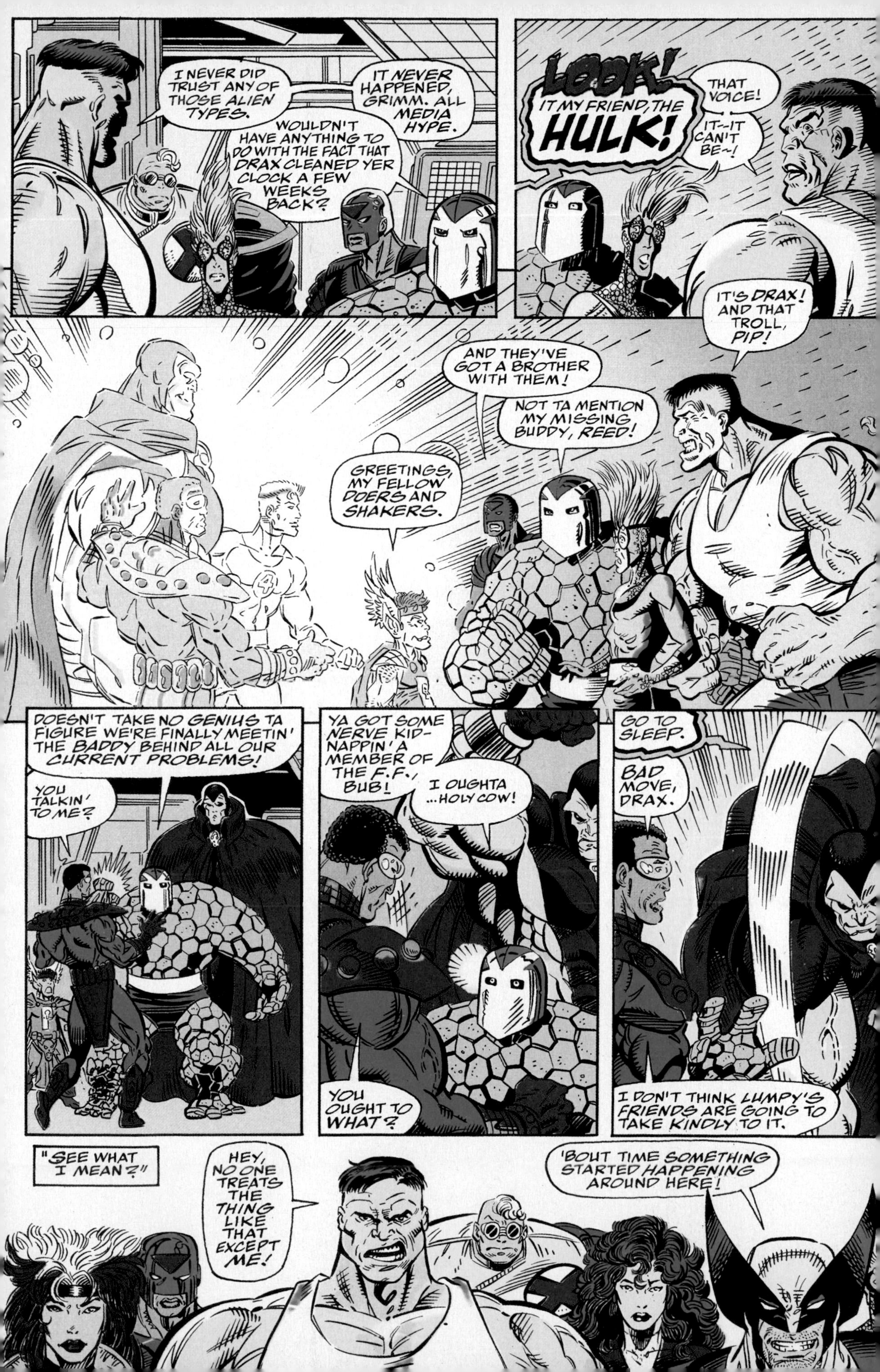
I NEVER DID TRUST ANY OF THOSE ALIEN TYPES.
IT NEVER HAPPENED, GRIMM. ALL MEDIA HYPE.
WOULDN'T HAVE ANYTHING TO DO WITH THE FACT THAT DRAX CLEANED YER CLOCK A FEW WEEKS BACK?
LOOK!
IT MY FRIEND, THE HULK!
THAT VOICE!
IT--IT CAN'T BE--!
IT'S DRAX! AND THAT TROLL, PIP!
AND THEY'VE GOT A BROTHER WITH THEM!
NOT TA MENTION MY MISSING BUDDY, REED!
GREETINGS, MY FELLOW DOERS AND SHAKERS.
DOESN'T TAKE NO GENIUS TA FIGURE WE'RE FINALLY MEETIN' THE BADDY BEHIND ALL OUR CURRENT PROBLEMS!
YOU TALKIN' TO ME?
YA GOT SOME NERVE KID-NAPPIN' A MEMBER OF THE F.F., BUB!
I OUGHTA ...HOLY COW!
YOU OUGHT TO WHAT?
GO TO SLEEP.
BAD MOVE, DRAX.
I DON'T THINK LUMPY'S FRIENDS ARE GOING TO TAKE KINDLY TO IT.
"SEE WHAT I MEAN?"
HEY, NO ONE TREATS THE THING LIKE THAT EXCEPT ME!
'BOUT TIME SOMETHING STARTED HAPPENING AROUND HERE!

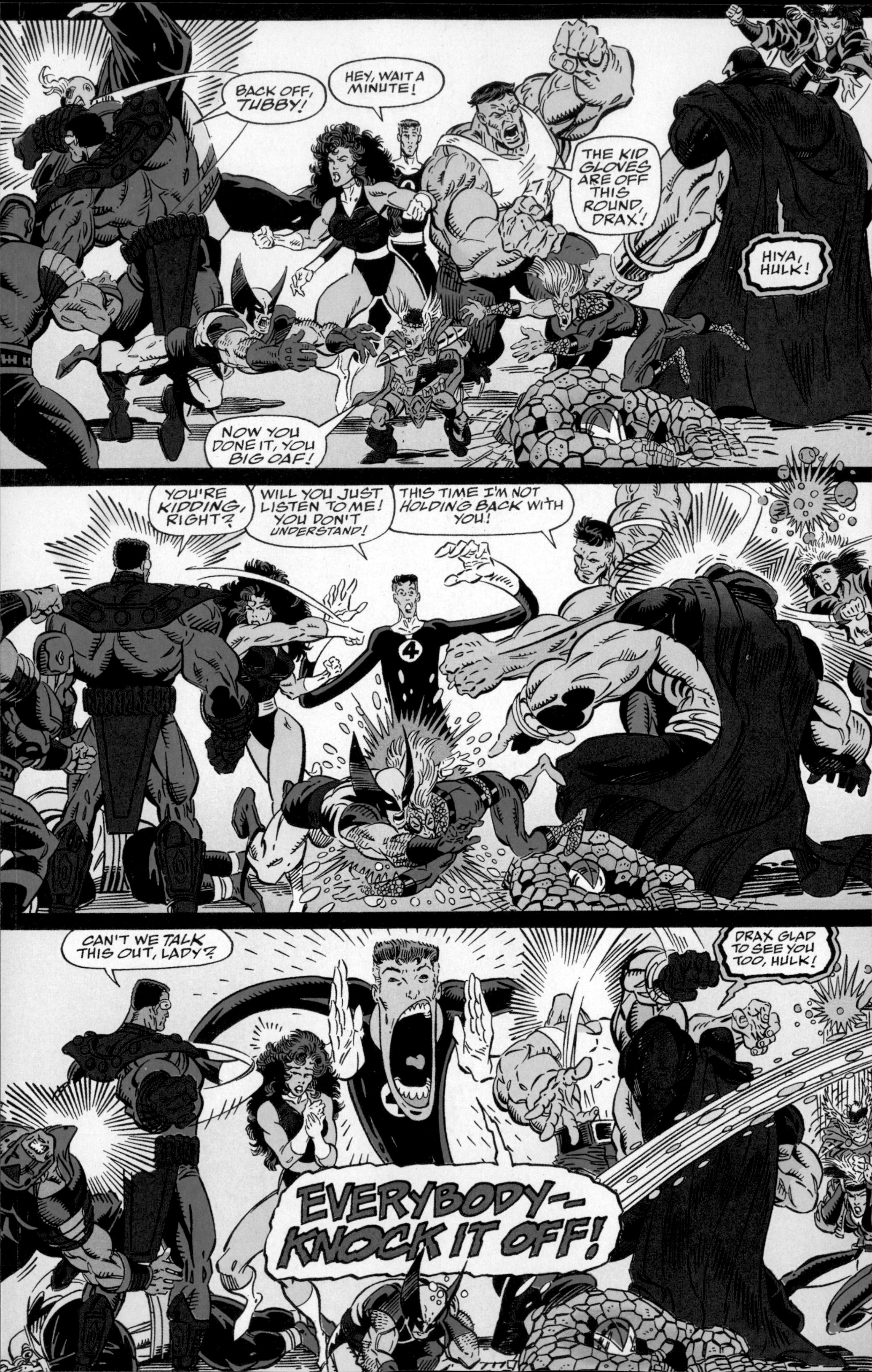
BACK OFF, TUBBY!
HEY, WAIT A MINUTE!
THE KID GLOVES ARE OFF THIS ROUND, DRAX!
HIYA, HULK!
NOW YOU DONE IT, YOU BIG OAF!
YOU'RE KIDDING, RIGHT?
WILL YOU JUST LISTEN TO ME! YOU DON'T UNDERSTAND!
THIS TIME I'M NOT HOLDING BACK WITH YOU!
CAN'T WE TALK THIS OUT, LADY?
DRAX GLAD TO SEE YOU TOO, HULK!
EVERYBODY-- KNOCK IT OFF!

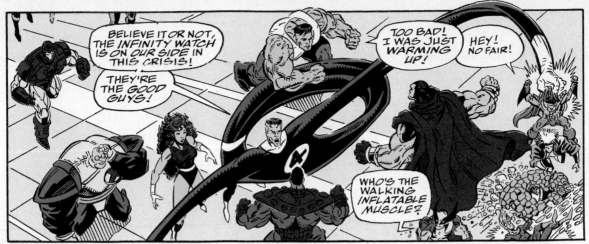

BELIEVE IT OR NOT, THE INFINITY WATCH IS ON OUR SIDE IN THIS CRISIS!

THEY'RE THE GOOD GUYS!

TOO BAD! I WAS JUST WARMING UP!

HEY! NO FAIR!

WHO'S THE WALKING INFLATABLE MUSCLE?

HIS NAME IS MAXAM, APPARENTLY AN UNOFFICIAL NEW MEMBER OF THE WATCH, AND HE SUFFERS FROM AMNESIA.

AND HE'S MY PAL.

FIGURES.

LET DRAX INTRODUCE YOU TO HIS OTHER PALS...

THIS IS MY BUDDY, THE BULK.

THAT'S THE HULK.

WHAT-EVER.

THIS IS IRON PAN.

IRON MAN.

CHAOS.

HAVOK.

THE BADGER.

WOLVERINE.

AND THIS IS--

YOU!

YOU'RE THE VISION!

HUH?

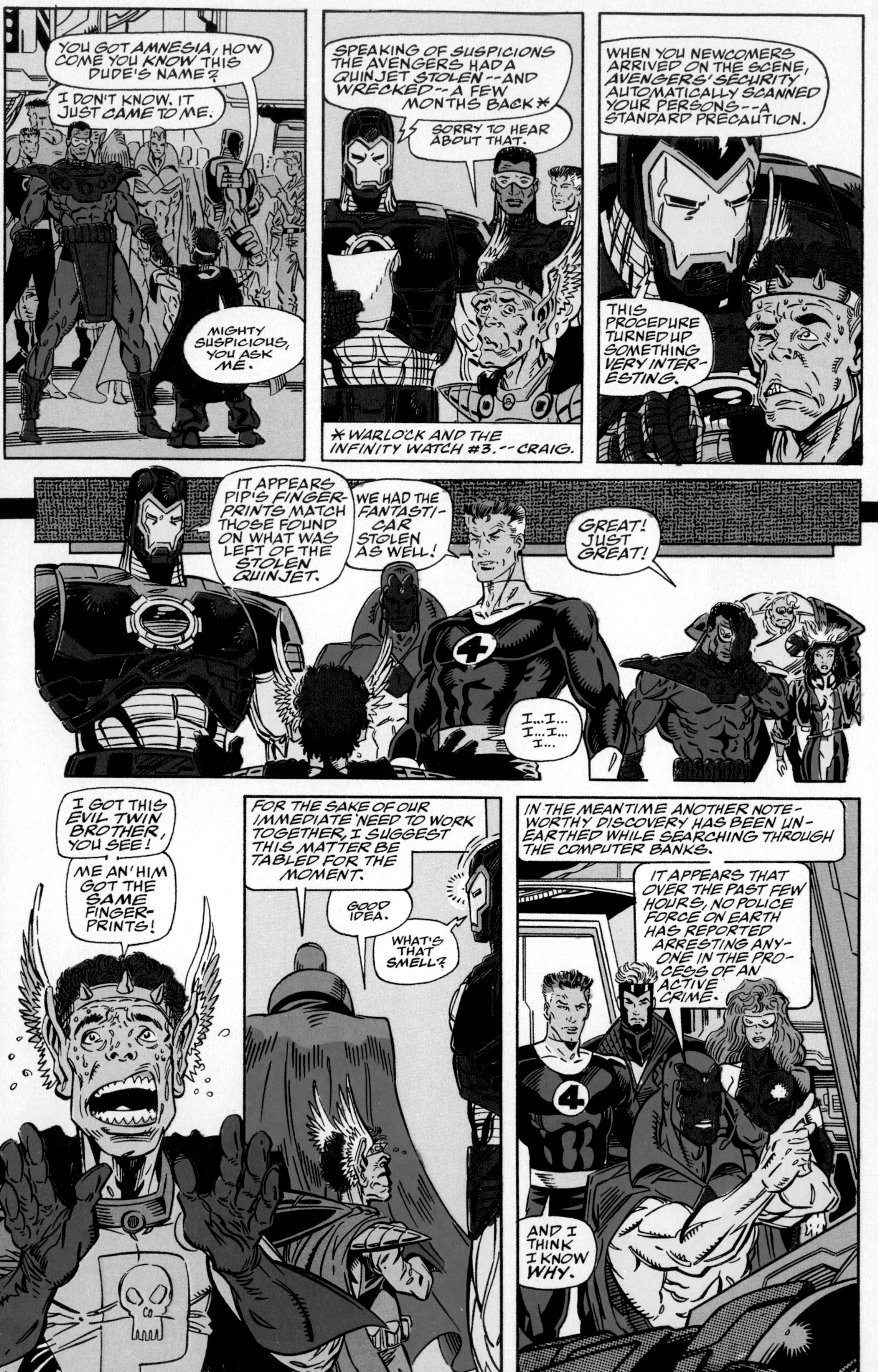
YOU GOT AMNESIA, HOW COME YOU KNOW THIS DUDE'S NAME?
I DON'T KNOW. IT JUST CAME TO ME.
MIGHTY SUSPICIOUS, YOU ASK ME.
SPEAKING OF SUSPICIONS THE AVENGERS HAD A QUINJET STOLEN--AND WRECKED--A FEW MONTHS BACK*
SORRY TO HEAR ABOUT THAT.
*WARLOCK AND THE INFINITY WATCH #3.--CRAIG.
WHEN YOU NEWCOMERS ARRIVED ON THE SCENE, AVENGERS' SECURITY AUTOMATICALLY SCANNED YOUR PERSONS--A STANDARD PRECAUTION.
THIS PROCEDURE TURNED UP SOMETHING VERY INTERESTING.
IT APPEARS PIP'S FINGERPRINTS MATCH THOSE FOUND ON WHAT WAS LEFT OF THE STOLEN QUINJET.
WE HAD THE FANTASTI-CAR STOLEN AS WELL!
GREAT! JUST GREAT!
I...I... I...I... I...
I GOT THIS EVIL TWIN BROTHER, YOU SEE!
ME AN' HIM GOT THE SAME FINGER-PRINTS!
FOR THE SAKE OF OUR IMMEDIATE NEED TO WORK TOGETHER, I SUGGEST THIS MATTER BE TABLED FOR THE MOMENT.
GOOD IDEA.
WHAT'S THAT SMELL?
IN THE MEANTIME ANOTHER NOTE-WORTHY DISCOVERY HAS BEEN UN-EARTHED WHILE SEARCHING THROUGH THE COMPUTER BANKS.
IT APPEARS THAT OVER THE PAST FEW HOURS, NO POLICE FORCE ON EARTH HAS REPORTED ARRESTING ANY-ONE IN THE PRO-CESS OF AN ACTIVE CRIME.
AND I THINK I KNOW WHY.

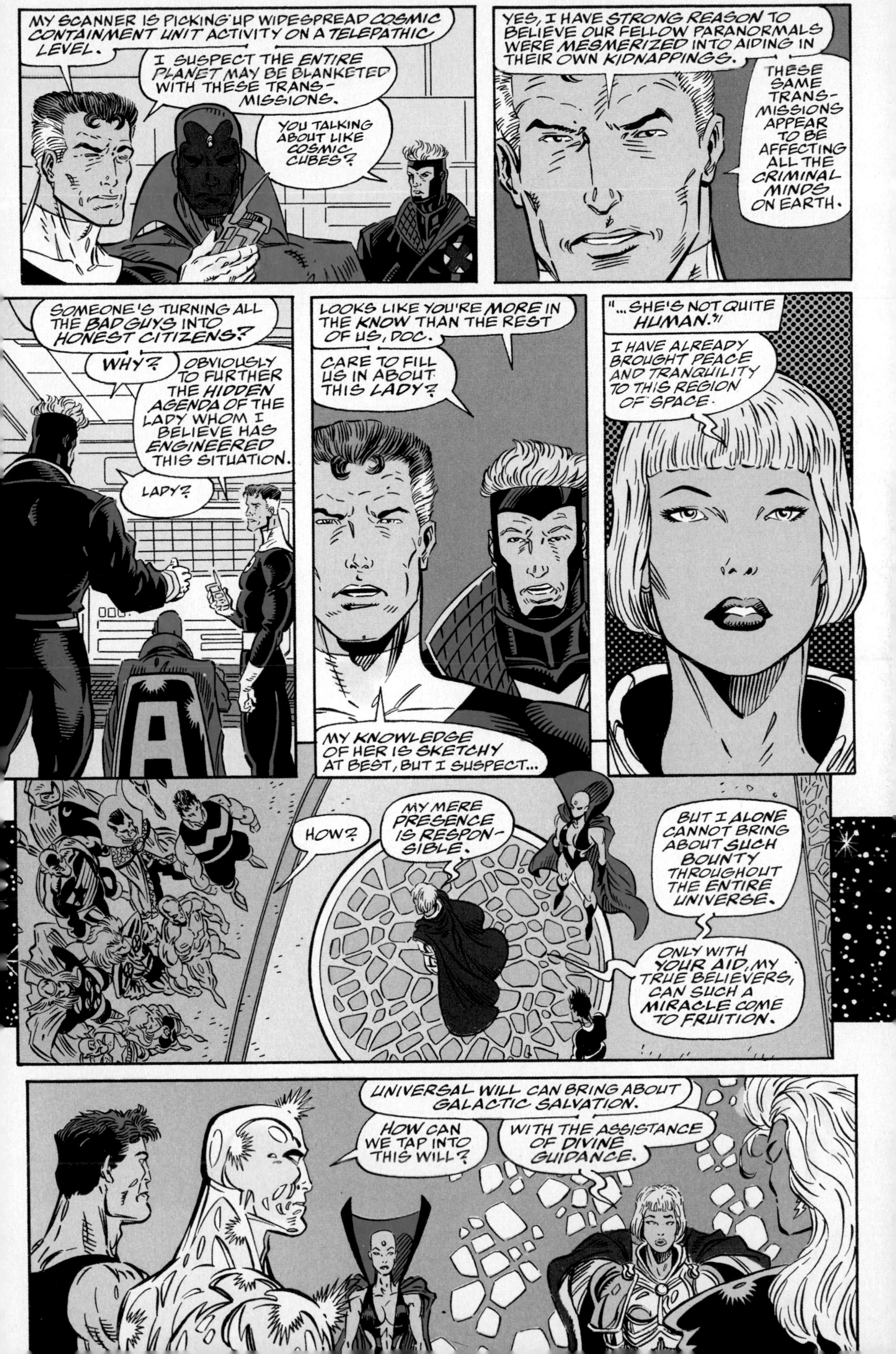

MY SCANNER IS PICKING UP WIDESPREAD COSMIC CONTAINMENT UNIT ACTIVITY ON A TELEPATHIC LEVEL.
I SUSPECT THE ENTIRE PLANET MAY BE BLANKETED WITH THESE TRANS-MISSIONS.
YOU TALKING ABOUT LIKE COSMIC CUBES?
YES, I HAVE STRONG REASON TO BELIEVE OUR FELLOW PARANORMALS WERE MESMERIZED INTO AIDING IN THEIR OWN KIDNAPPINGS.
THESE SAME TRANS-MISSIONS APPEAR TO BE AFFECTING ALL THE CRIMINAL MINDS ON EARTH.
SOMEONE'S TURNING ALL THE BAD GUYS INTO HONEST CITIZENS?
WHY?
OBVIOUSLY TO FURTHER THE HIDDEN AGENDA OF THE LADY WHOM I BELIEVE HAS ENGINEERED THIS SITUATION.
LADY?
LOOKS LIKE YOU'RE MORE IN THE KNOW THAN THE REST OF US, DOC.
CARE TO FILL US IN ABOUT THIS LADY?
MY KNOWLEDGE OF HER IS SKETCHY AT BEST, BUT I SUSPECT...
"...SHE'S NOT QUITE HUMAN."
I HAVE ALREADY BROUGHT PEACE AND TRANQUILITY TO THIS REGION OF SPACE.
HOW?
MY MERE PRESENCE IS RESPON-SIBLE.
BUT I ALONE CANNOT BRING ABOUT SUCH BOUNTY THROUGHOUT THE ENTIRE UNIVERSE.
ONLY WITH YOUR AID, MY TRUE BELIEVERS, CAN SUCH A MIRACLE COME TO FRUITION.
HOW CAN WE TAP INTO THIS WILL?
UNIVERSAL WILL CAN BRING ABOUT GALACTIC SALVATION.
WITH THE ASSISTANCE OF DIVINE GUIDANCE.

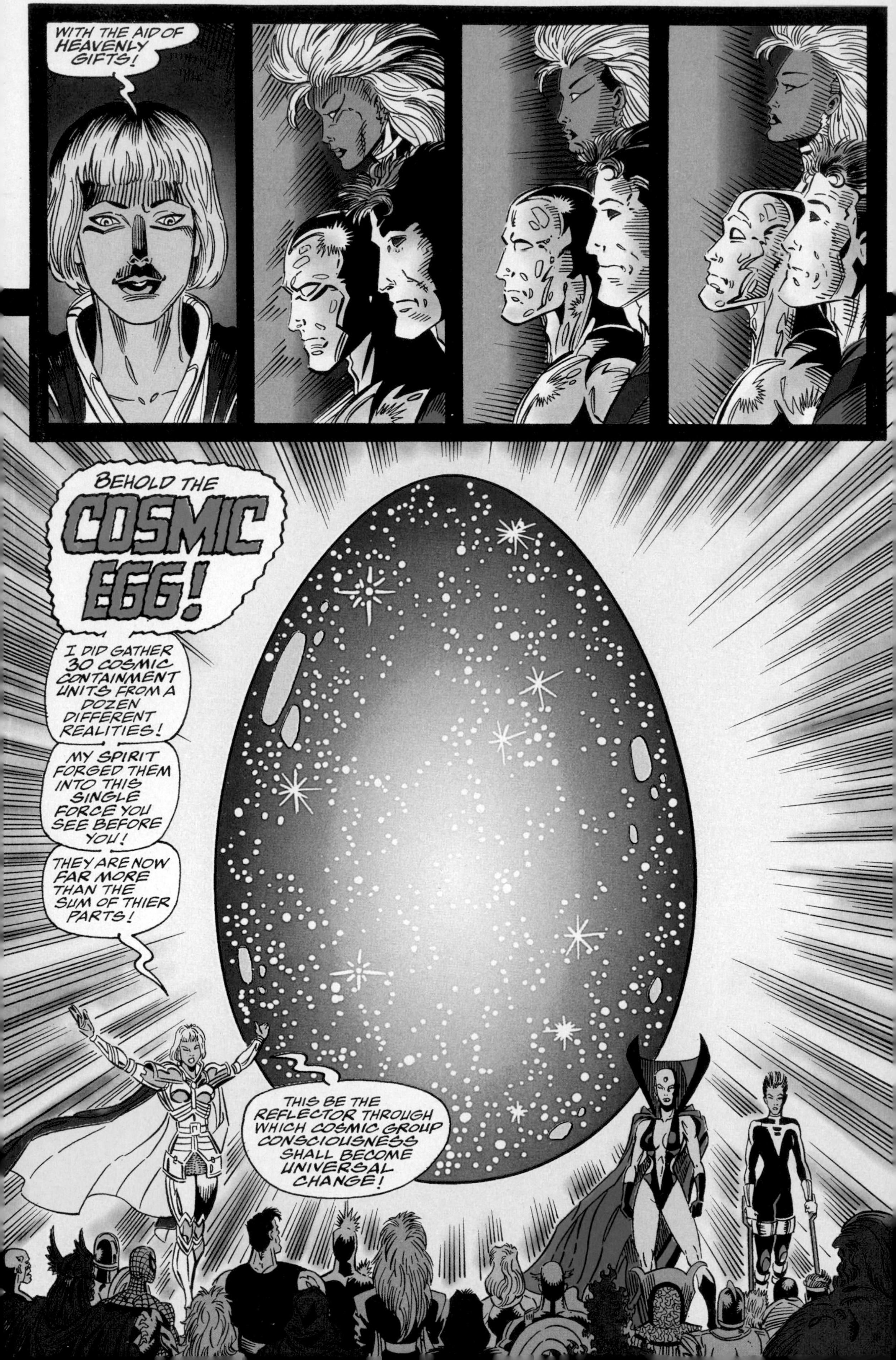
WITH THE AID OF HEAVENLY GIFTS!
BEHOLD THE COSMIC EGG!
I DID GATHER 30 COSMIC CONTAINMENT UNITS FROM A DOZEN DIFFERENT REALITIES!
MY SPIRIT FORGED THEM INTO THIS SINGLE FORCE YOU SEE BEFORE YOU!
THEY ARE NOW FAR MORE THAN THE SUM OF THIER PARTS!
THIS BE THE REFLECTOR THROUGH WHICH COSMIC GROUP CONSCIOUSNESS SHALL BECOME UNIVERSAL CHANGE!

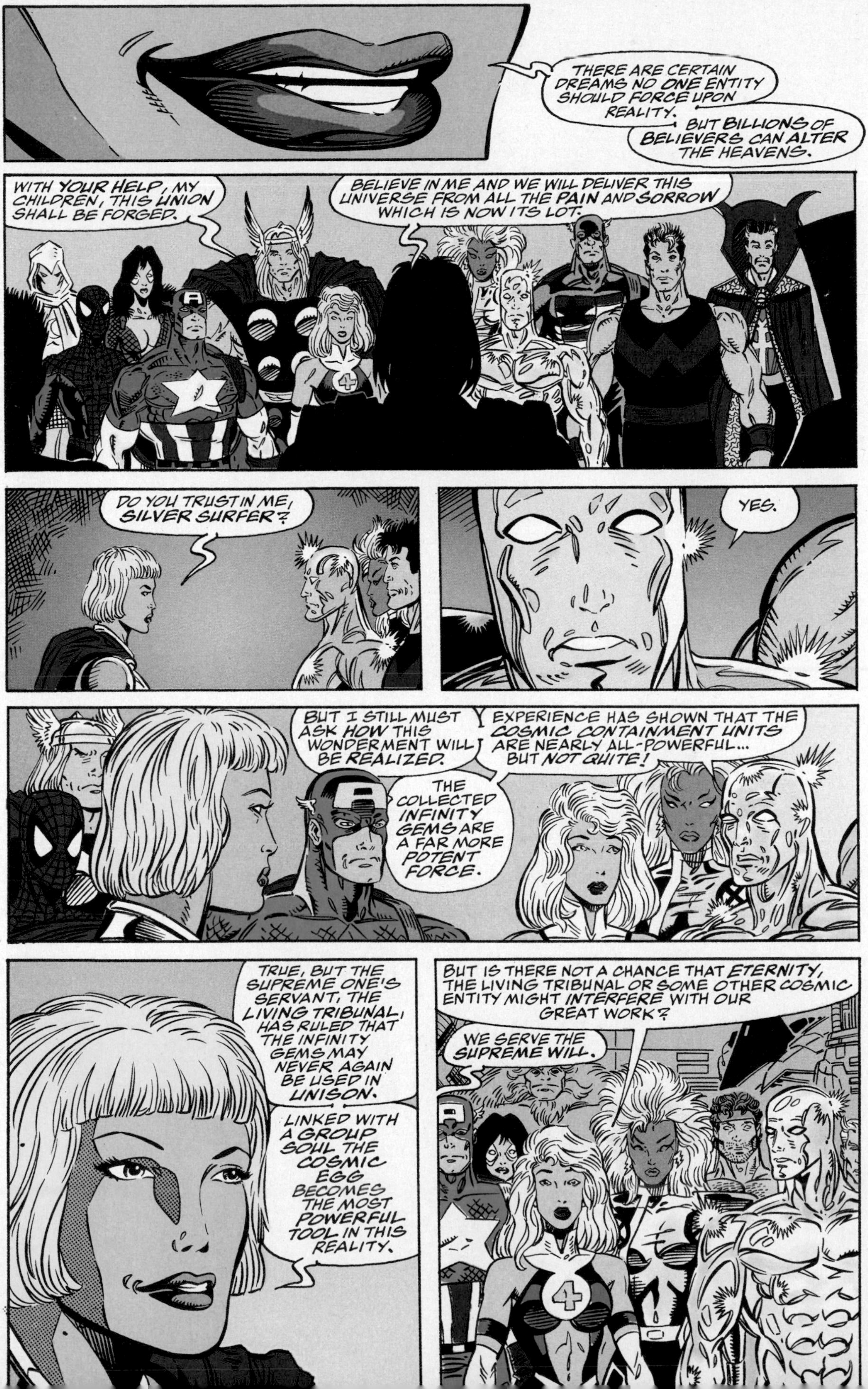
THERE ARE CERTAIN DREAMS NO ONE ENTITY SHOULD FORCE UPON REALITY.
BUT BILLIONS OF BELIEVERS CAN ALTER THE HEAVENS.
WITH YOUR HELP, MY CHILDREN, THIS UNION SHALL BE FORGED.
BELIEVE IN ME AND WE WILL DELIVER THIS UNIVERSE FROM ALL THE PAIN AND SORROW WHICH IS NOW ITS LOT.
DO YOU TRUST IN ME, SILVER SURFER?
YES.
BUT I STILL MUST ASK HOW THIS WONDERMENT WILL BE REALIZED.
EXPERIENCE HAS SHOWN THAT THE COSMIC CONTAINMENT UNITS ARE NEARLY ALL-POWERFUL... BUT NOT QUITE!
THE COLLECTED INFINITY GEMS ARE A FAR MORE POTENT FORCE.
TRUE, BUT THE SUPREME ONE'S SERVANT, THE LIVING TRIBUNAL, HAS RULED THAT THE INFINITY GEMS MAY NEVER AGAIN BE USED IN UNISON.
LINKED WITH A GROUP SOUL THE COSMIC EGG BECOMES THE MOST POWERFUL TOOL IN THIS REALITY.
BUT IS THERE NOT A CHANCE THAT ETERNITY, THE LIVING TRIBUNAL OR SOME OTHER COSMIC ENTITY MIGHT INTERFERE WITH OUR GREAT WORK?
WE SERVE THE SUPREME WILL.

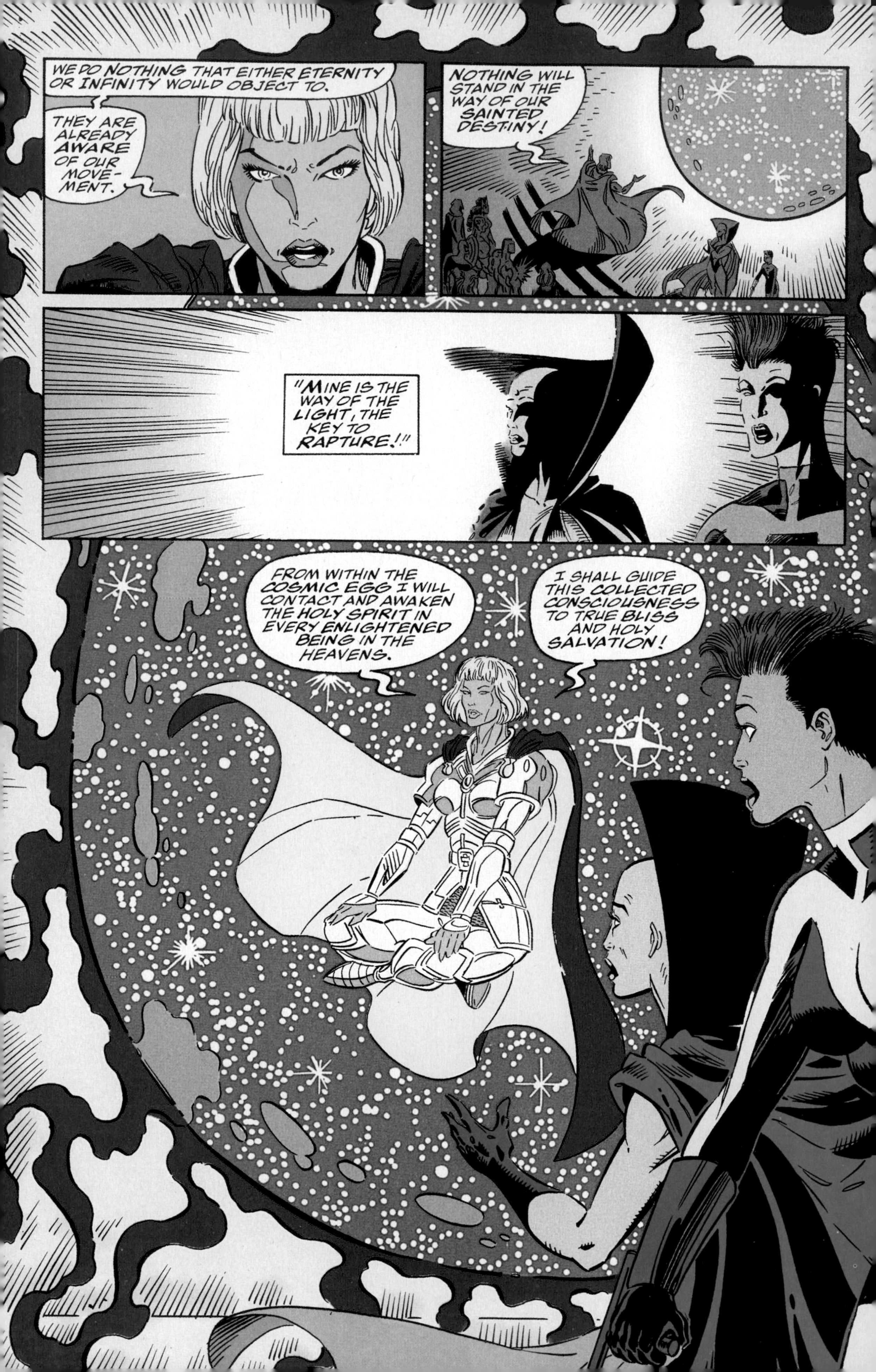
WE DO NOTHING THAT EITHER ETERNITY OR INFINITY WOULD OBJECT TO.
THEY ARE ALREADY AWARE OF OUR MOVEMENT.
NOTHING WILL STAND IN THE WAY OF OUR SAINTED DESTINY!
"MINE IS THE WAY OF THE LIGHT, THE KEY TO RAPTURE!"
FROM WITHIN THE COSMIC EGG I WILL CONTACT AND AWAKEN THE HOLY SPIRIT IN EVERY ENLIGHTENED BEING IN THE HEAVENS.
I SHALL GUIDE THIS COLLECTED CONSCIOUSNESS TO TRUE BLISS AND HOLY SALVATION!

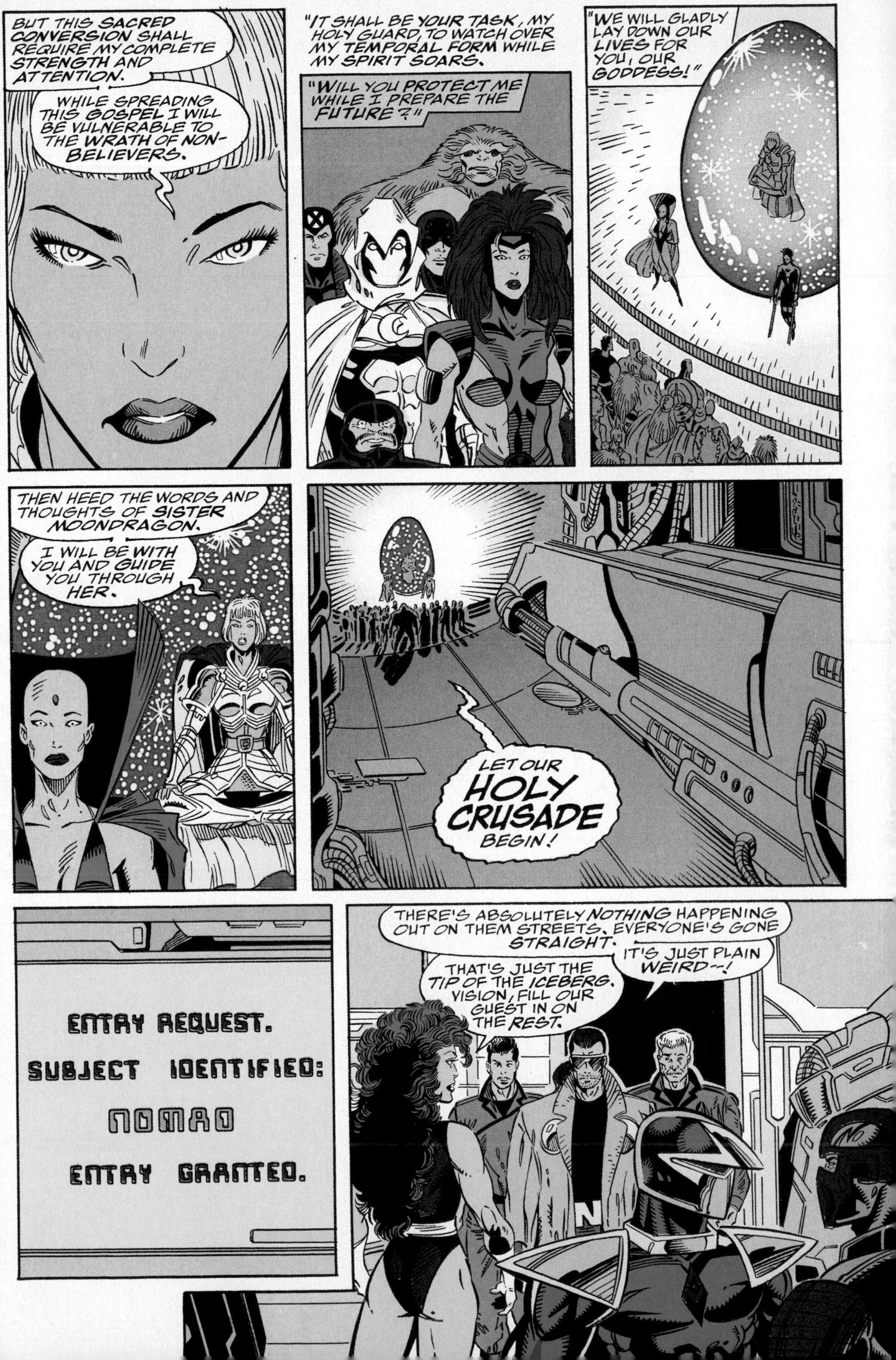
BUT THIS SACRED CONVERSION SHALL REQUIRE MY COMPLETE STRENGTH AND ATTENTION.
WHILE SPREADING THIS GOSPEL I WILL BE VULNERABLE TO THE WRATH OF NON-BELIEVERS.
"IT SHALL BE YOUR TASK, MY HOLY GUARD, TO WATCH OVER MY TEMPORAL FORM WHILE MY SPIRIT SOARS.
"WILL YOU PROTECT ME WHILE I PREPARE THE FUTURE?"
"WE WILL GLADLY LAY DOWN OUR LIVES FOR YOU, OUR GODDESS!"
THEN HEED THE WORDS AND THOUGHTS OF SISTER MOONDRAGON.
I WILL BE WITH YOU AND GUIDE YOU THROUGH HER.
LET OUR HOLY CRUSADE BEGIN!
ENTRY REQUEST.
SUBJECT IDENTIFIED:
NOMAD
ENTRY GRANTED.
THERE'S ABSOLUTELY NOTHING HAPPENING OUT ON THEM STREETS. EVERYONE'S GONE STRAIGHT.
IT'S JUST PLAIN WEIRD--!
THAT'S JUST THE TIP OF THE ICEBERG. VISION, FILL OUR GUEST IN ON THE REST.

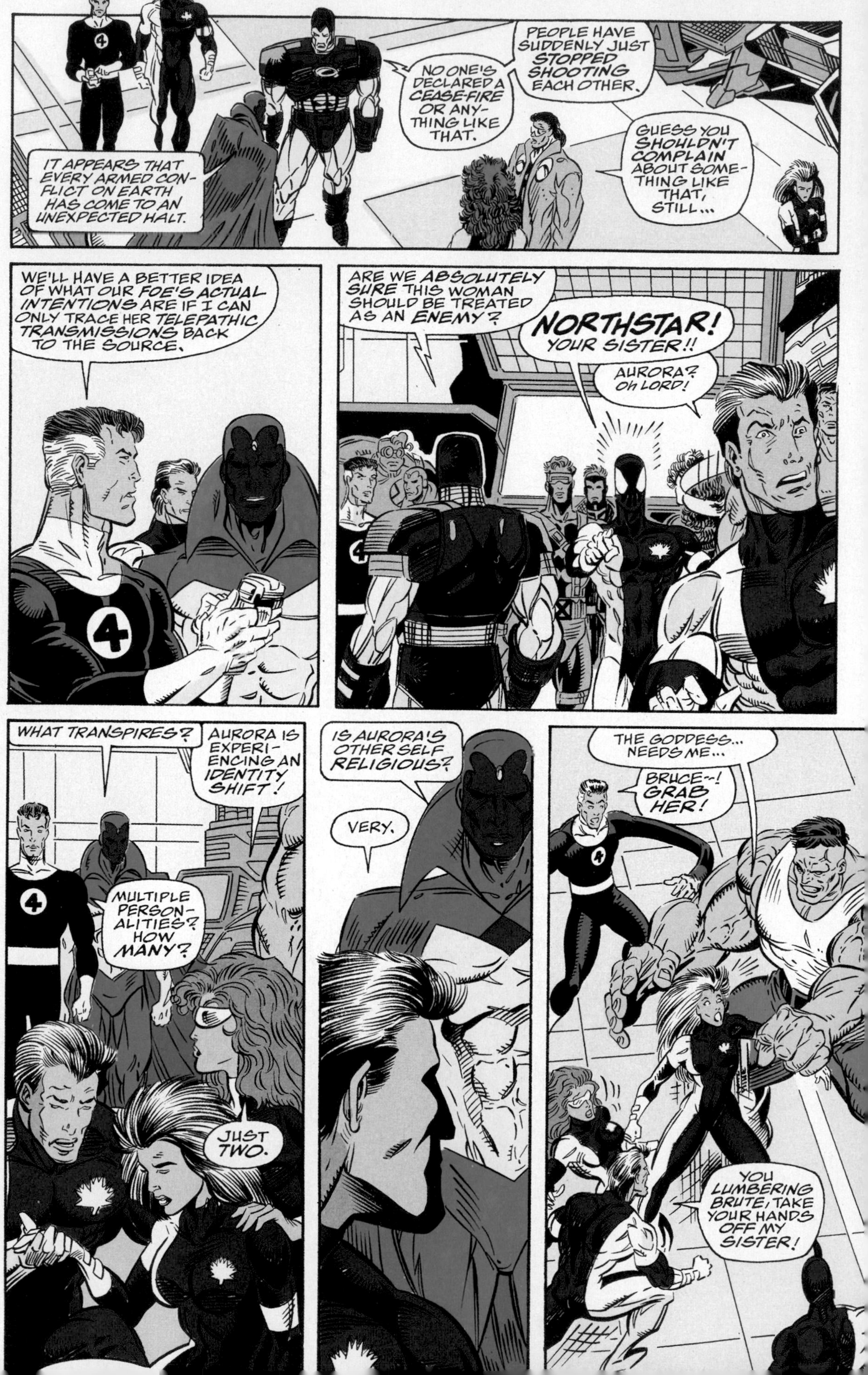
IT APPEARS THAT EVERY ARMED CONFLICT ON EARTH HAS COME TO AN UNEXPECTED HALT.
NO ONE'S DECLARED A CEASE-FIRE OR ANYTHING LIKE THAT.
PEOPLE HAVE SUDDENLY JUST STOPPED SHOOTING EACH OTHER.
GUESS YOU SHOULDN'T COMPLAIN ABOUT SOMETHING LIKE THAT, STILL...
WE'LL HAVE A BETTER IDEA OF WHAT OUR FOE'S ACTUAL INTENTIONS ARE IF I CAN ONLY TRACE HER TELEPATHIC TRANSMISSIONS BACK TO THE SOURCE.
ARE WE ABSOLUTELY SURE THIS WOMAN SHOULD BE TREATED AS AN ENEMY?
NORTHSTAR! YOUR SISTER!!
AURORA? Oh LORD!
WHAT TRANSPIRES?
AURORA IS EXPERIENCING AN IDENTITY SHIFT!
MULTIPLE PERSONALITIES? HOW MANY?
JUST TWO.
IS AURORA'S OTHER SELF RELIGIOUS?
VERY.
THE GODDESS... NEEDS ME...
BRUCE--! GRAB HER!
YOU LUMBERING BRUTE, TAKE YOUR HANDS OFF MY SISTER!

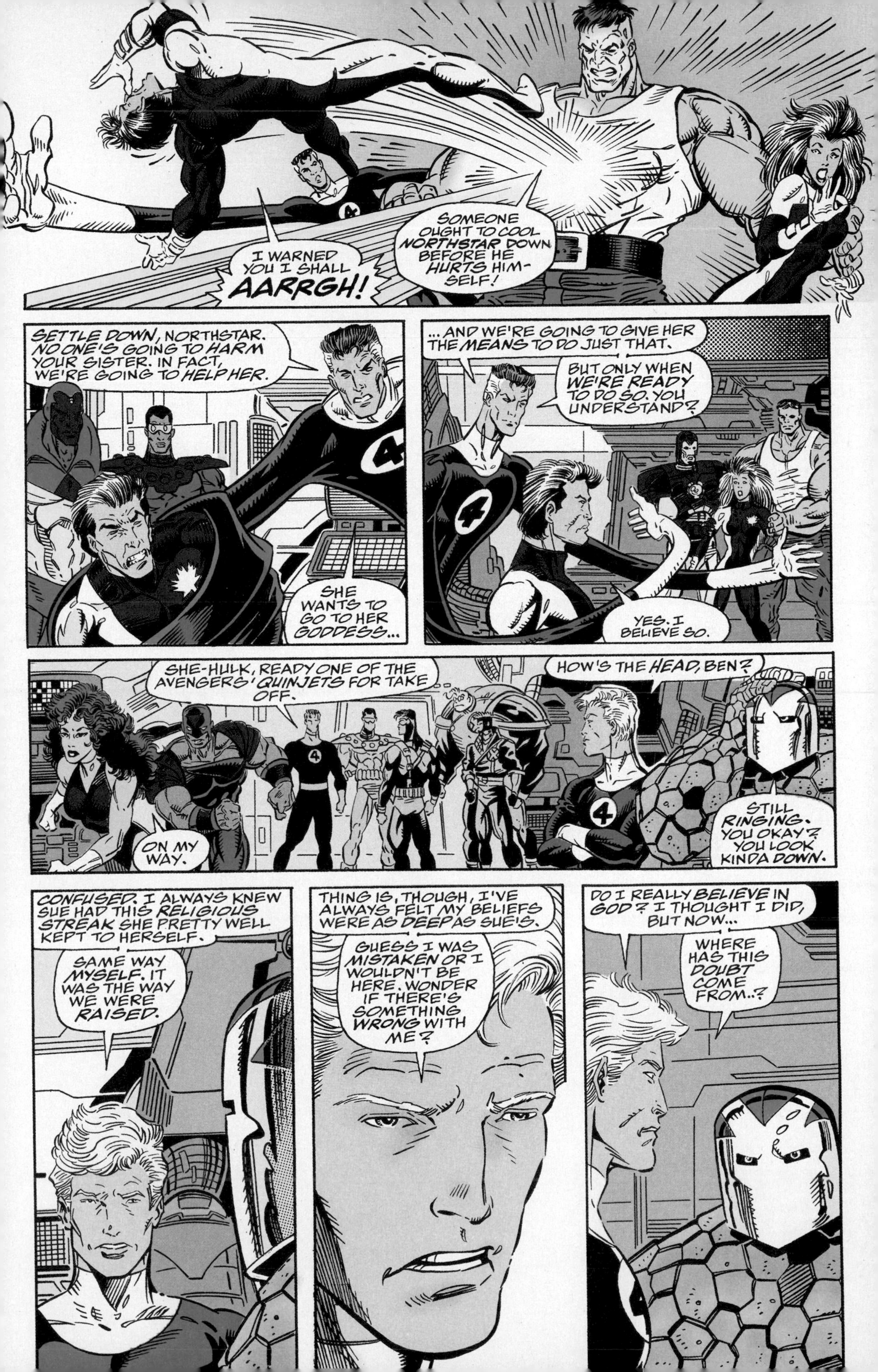
I WARNED YOU I SHALL AARRGH!
SOMEONE OUGHT TO COOL NORTHSTAR DOWN BEFORE HE HURTS HIMSELF!
SETTLE DOWN, NORTHSTAR. NO ONE'S GOING TO HARM YOUR SISTER. IN FACT, WE'RE GOING TO HELP HER.
SHE WANTS TO GO TO HER GODDESS...
...AND WE'RE GOING TO GIVE HER THE MEANS TO DO JUST THAT.
BUT ONLY WHEN WE'RE READY TO DO SO. YOU UNDERSTAND?
YES. I BELIEVE SO.
SHE-HULK, READY ONE OF THE AVENGERS' QUINJETS FOR TAKE OFF.
ON MY WAY.
HOW'S THE HEAD, BEN?
STILL RINGING. YOU OKAY? YOU LOOK KINDA DOWN.
CONFUSED. I ALWAYS KNEW SUE HAD THIS RELIGIOUS STREAK SHE PRETTY WELL KEPT TO HERSELF.
SAME WAY MYSELF. IT WAS THE WAY WE WERE RAISED.
THING IS, THOUGH, I'VE ALWAYS FELT MY BELIEFS WERE AS DEEP AS SUE'S.
GUESS I WAS MISTAKEN OR I WOULDN'T BE HERE. WONDER IF THERE'S SOMETHING WRONG WITH ME?
DO I REALLY BELIEVE IN GOD? I THOUGHT I DID, BUT NOW...
WHERE HAS THIS DOUBT COME FROM..?

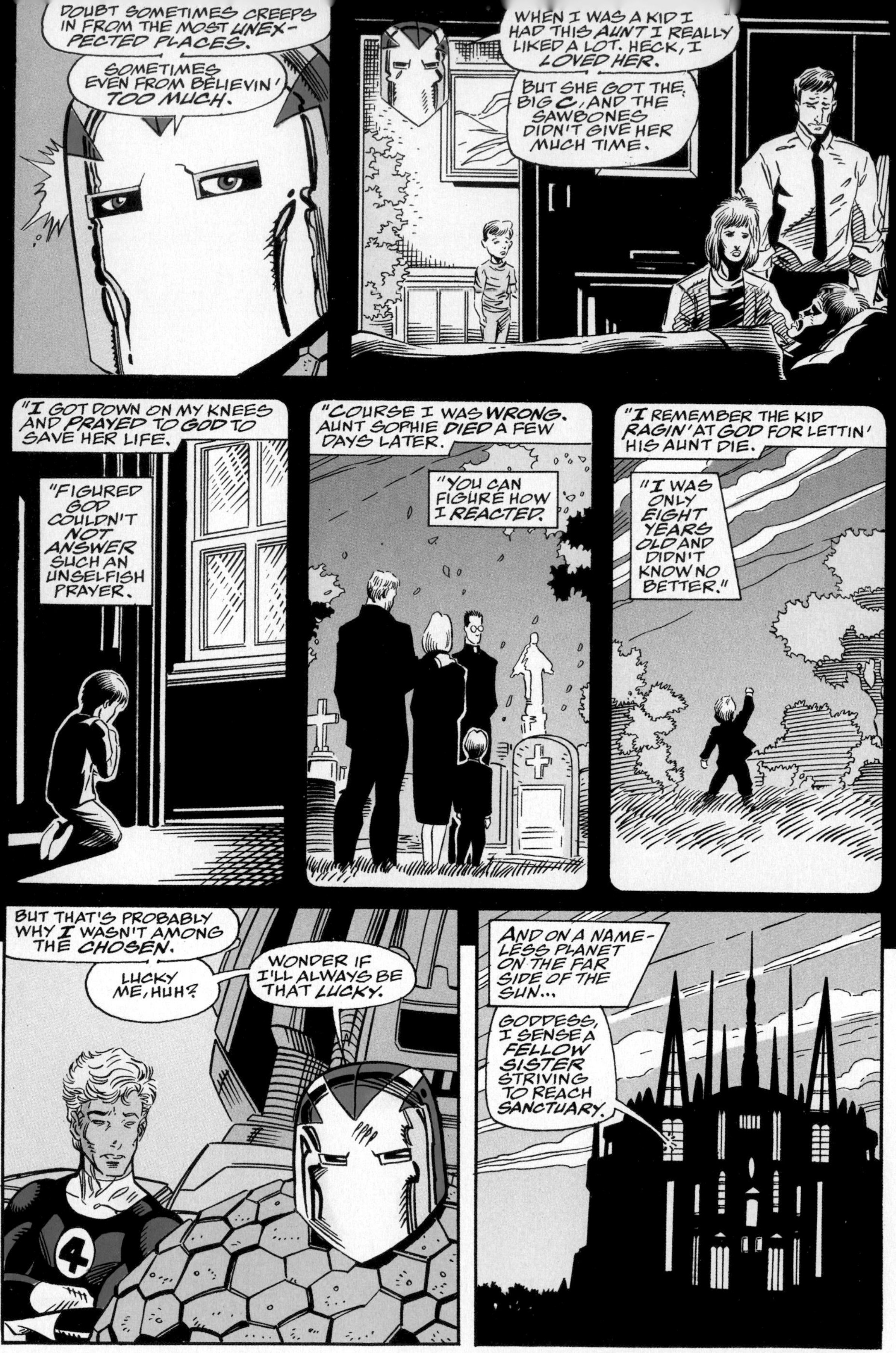
DOUBT SOMETIMES CREEPS IN FROM THE MOST UNEXPECTED PLACES.
SOMETIMES EVEN FROM BELIEVIN' TOO MUCH.
WHEN I WAS A KID I HAD THIS AUNT I REALLY LIKED A LOT. HECK, I LOVED HER.
BUT SHE GOT THE BIG C, AND THE SAWBONES DIDN'T GIVE HER MUCH TIME.
"I GOT DOWN ON MY KNEES AND PRAYED TO GOD TO SAVE HER LIFE.
"FIGURED GOD COULDN'T NOT ANSWER SUCH AN UNSELFISH PRAYER.
"COURSE I WAS WRONG. AUNT SOPHIE DIED A FEW DAYS LATER.
"YOU CAN FIGURE HOW I REACTED.
"I REMEMBER THE KID RAGIN' AT GOD FOR LETTIN' HIS AUNT DIE.
"I WAS ONLY EIGHT YEARS OLD AND DIDN'T KNOW NO BETTER."
BUT THAT'S PROBABLY WHY I WASN'T AMONG THE CHOSEN.
LUCKY ME, HUH?
WONDER IF I'LL ALWAYS BE THAT LUCKY.
AND ON A NAMELESS PLANET ON THE FAR SIDE OF THE SUN...
GODDESS, I SENSE A FELLOW SISTER STRIVING TO REACH SANCTUARY.

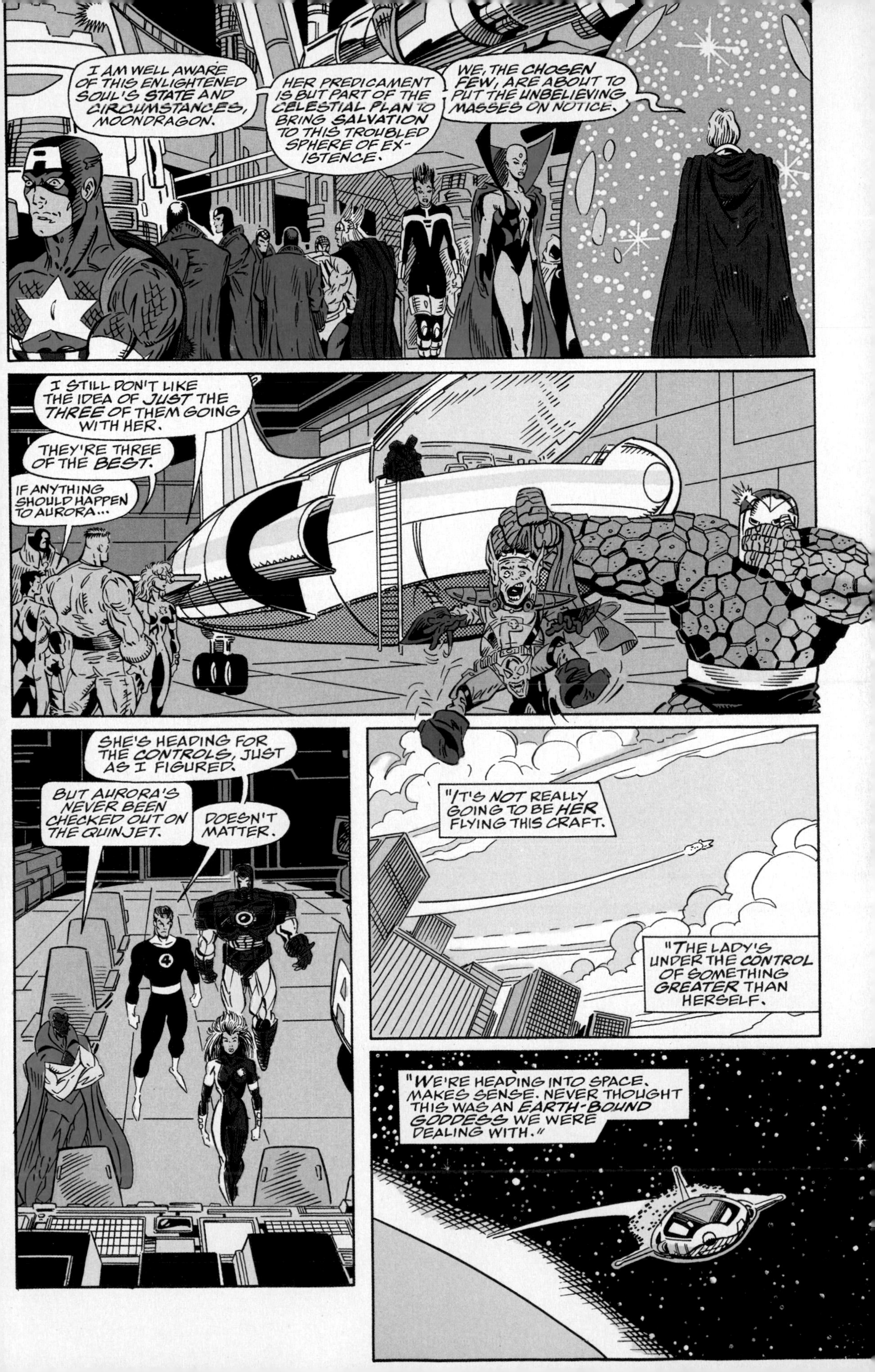
I AM WELL AWARE OF THIS ENLIGHTENED SOUL'S STATE AND CIRCUMSTANCES, MOONDRAGON.
HER PREDICAMENT IS BUT PART OF THE CELESTIAL PLAN TO BRING SALVATION TO THIS TROUBLED SPHERE OF EX-ISTENCE.
WE, THE CHOSEN FEW, ARE ABOUT TO PUT THE UNBELIEVING MASSES ON NOTICE.
I STILL DON'T LIKE THE IDEA OF JUST THE THREE OF THEM GOING WITH HER.
THEY'RE THREE OF THE BEST.
IF ANYTHING SHOULD HAPPEN TO AURORA...
SHE'S HEADING FOR THE CONTROLS, JUST AS I FIGURED.
BUT AURORA'S NEVER BEEN CHECKED OUT ON THE QUINJET.
DOESN'T MATTER.
"IT'S NOT REALLY GOING TO BE HER FLYING THIS CRAFT.
"THE LADY'S UNDER THE CONTROL OF SOMETHING GREATER THAN HERSELF.
"WE'RE HEADING INTO SPACE. MAKES SENSE. NEVER THOUGHT THIS WAS AN EARTH-BOUND GODDESS WE WERE DEALING WITH."

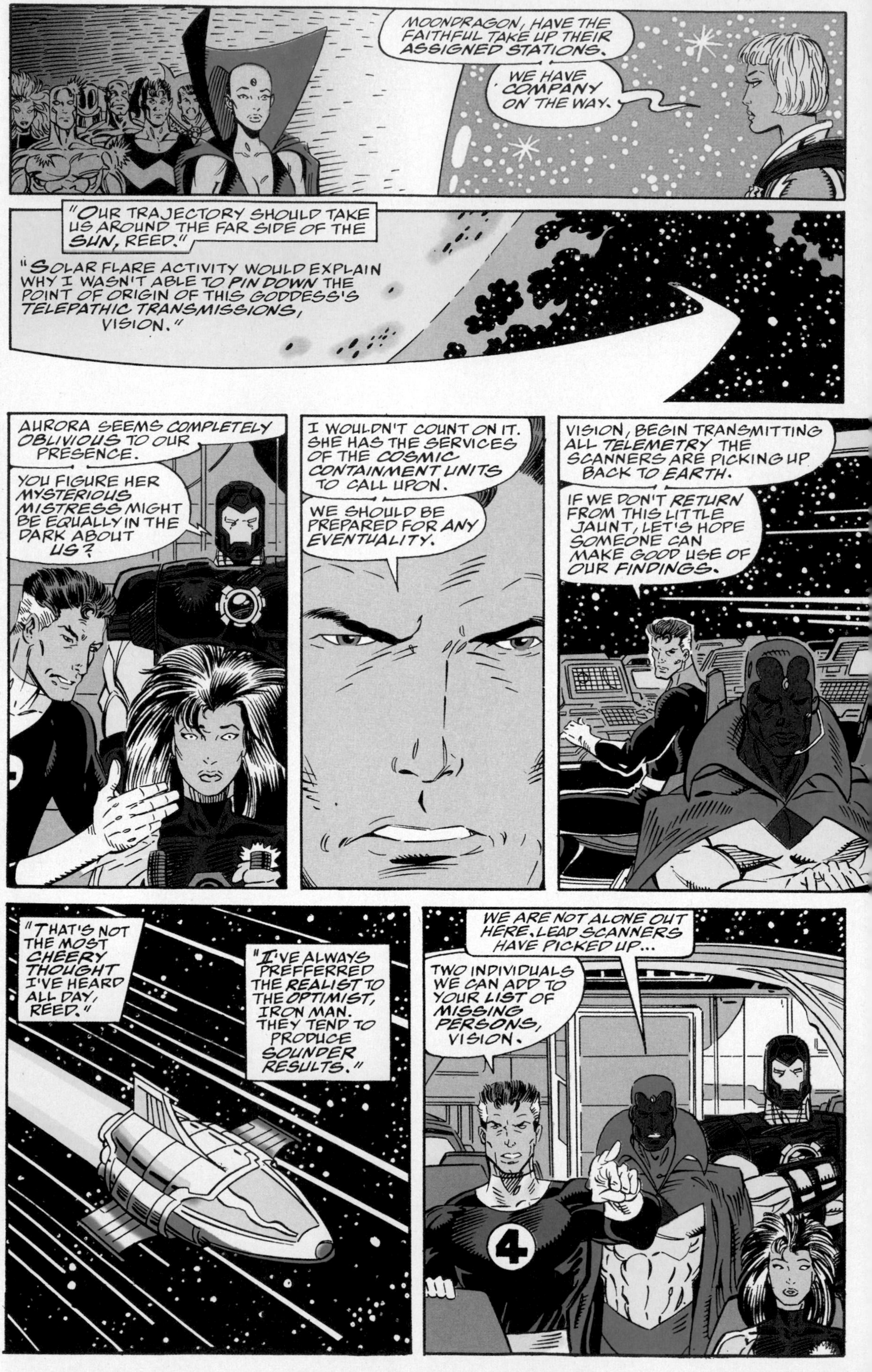
MOONDRAGON, HAVE THE FAITHFUL TAKE UP THEIR ASSIGNED STATIONS.
WE HAVE COMPANY ON THE WAY.
"OUR TRAJECTORY SHOULD TAKE US AROUND THE FAR SIDE OF THE SUN, REED."
"SOLAR FLARE ACTIVITY WOULD EXPLAIN WHY I WASN'T ABLE TO PIN DOWN THE POINT OF ORIGIN OF THIS GODDESS'S TELEPATHIC TRANSMISSIONS, VISION."
AURORA SEEMS COMPLETELY OBLIVIOUS TO OUR PRESENCE.
YOU FIGURE HER MYSTERIOUS MISTRESS MIGHT BE EQUALLY IN THE DARK ABOUT US?
I WOULDN'T COUNT ON IT. SHE HAS THE SERVICES OF THE COSMIC CONTAINMENT UNITS TO CALL UPON.
WE SHOULD BE PREPARED FOR ANY EVENTUALITY.
VISION, BEGIN TRANSMITTING ALL TELEMETRY THE SCANNERS ARE PICKING UP BACK TO EARTH.
IF WE DON'T RETURN FROM THIS LITTLE JAUNT, LET'S HOPE SOMEONE CAN MAKE GOOD USE OF OUR FINDINGS.
"THAT'S NOT THE MOST CHEERY THOUGHT I'VE HEARD ALL DAY, REED."
"I'VE ALWAYS PREFFERRED THE REALIST TO THE OPTIMIST, IRON MAN. THEY TEND TO PRODUCE SOUNDER RESULTS."
WE ARE NOT ALONE OUT HERE. LEAD SCANNERS HAVE PICKED UP...
TWO INDIVIDUALS WE CAN ADD TO YOUR LIST OF MISSING PERSONS, VISION.

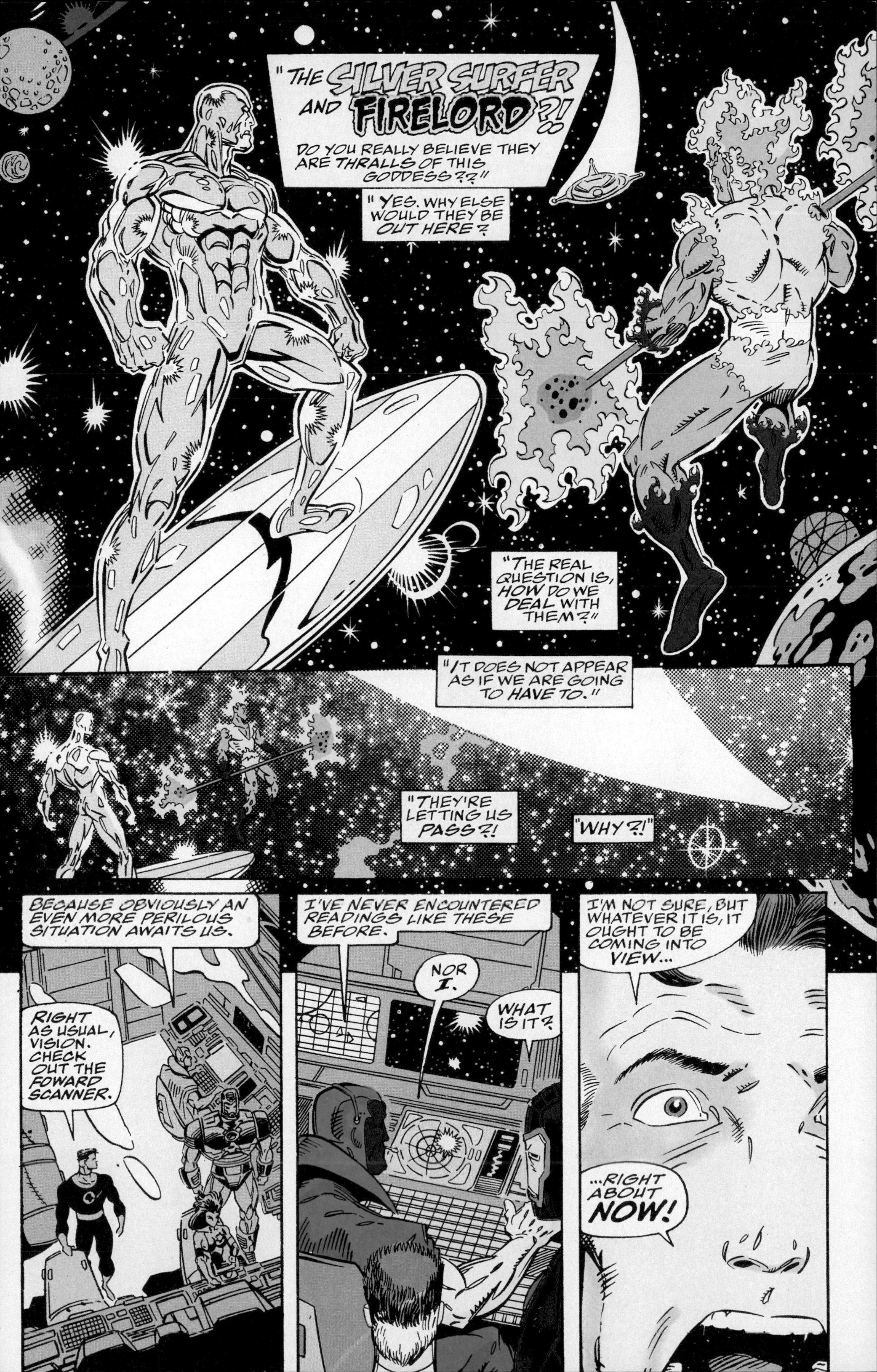
"THE SILVER SURFER AND FIRELORD?! DO YOU REALLY BELIEVE THEY ARE THRALLS OF THIS GODDESS??"
"YES. WHY ELSE WOULD THEY BE OUT HERE?
"THE REAL QUESTION IS, HOW DO WE DEAL WITH THEM?"
"IT DOES NOT APPEAR AS IF WE ARE GOING TO HAVE TO."
"THEY'RE LETTING US PASS?!
"WHY?!"
BECAUSE OBVIOUSLY AN EVEN MORE PERILOUS SITUATION AWAITS US.
RIGHT AS USUAL, VISION. CHECK OUT THE FOWARD SCANNER.
I'VE NEVER ENCOUNTERED READINGS LIKE THESE BEFORE.
NOR I.
WHAT IS IT?
I'M NOT SURE, BUT WHATEVER IT IS, IT OUGHT TO BE COMING INTO VIEW...
...RIGHT ABOUT NOW!

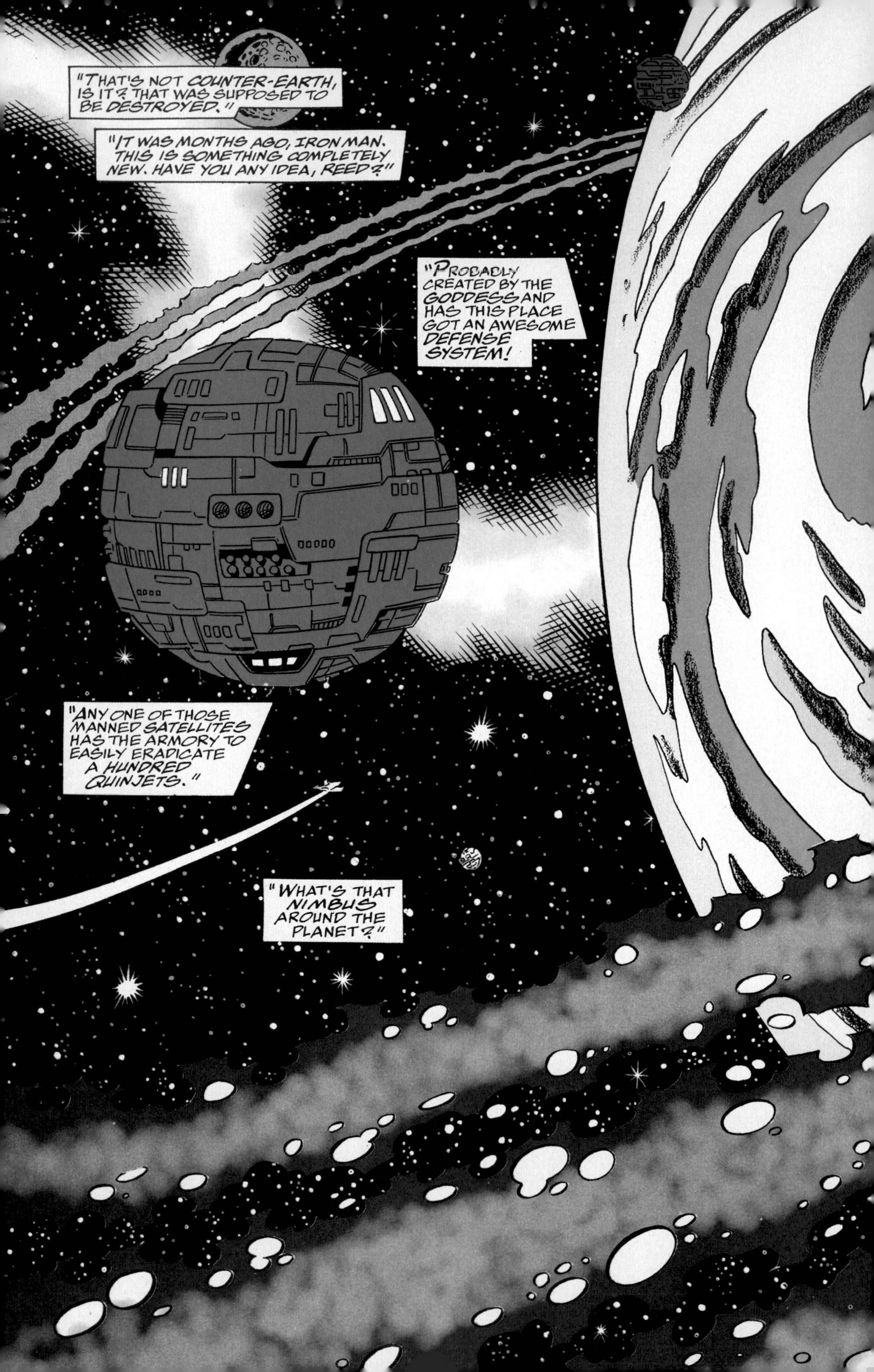
"THAT'S NOT COUNTER-EARTH, IS IT? THAT WAS SUPPOSED TO BE DESTROYED."
"IT WAS MONTHS AGO, IRON MAN. THIS IS SOMETHING COMPLETELY NEW. HAVE YOU ANY IDEA, REED?"
"PROBABLY CREATED BY THE GODDESS AND HAS THIS PLACE GOT AN AWESOME DEFENSE SYSTEM!
"ANY ONE OF THOSE MANNED SATELLITES HAS THE ARMORY TO EASILY ERADICATE A HUNDRED QUINJETS."
"WHAT'S THAT NIMBUS AROUND THE PLANET?"

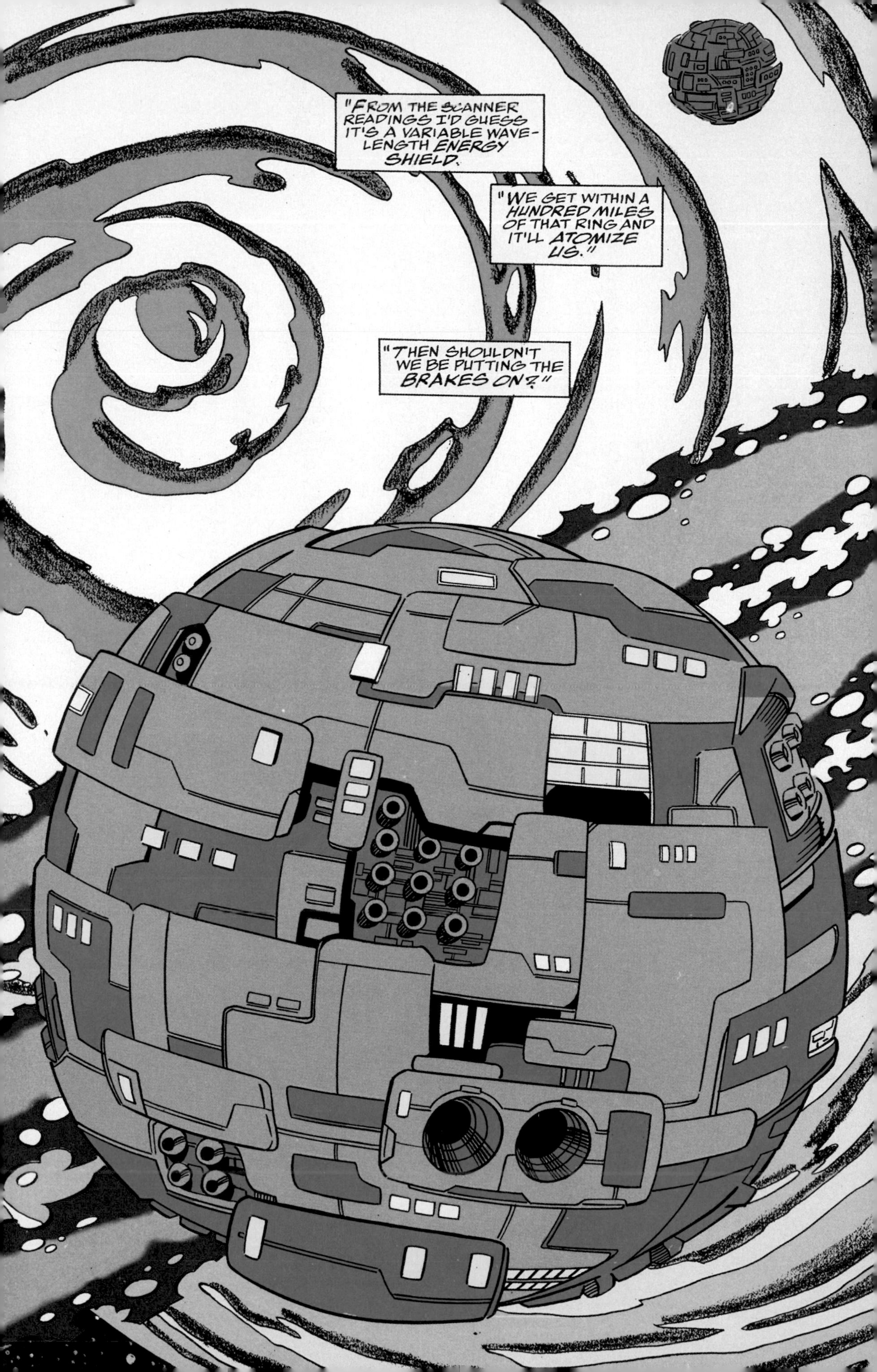
"FROM THE SCANNER READINGS I'D GUESS IT'S A VARIABLE WAVE-LENGTH ENERGY SHIELD.
"WE GET WITHIN A HUNDRED MILES OF THAT RING AND IT'LL ATOMIZE US."
"THEN SHOULDN'T WE BE PUTTING THE BRAKES ON?"

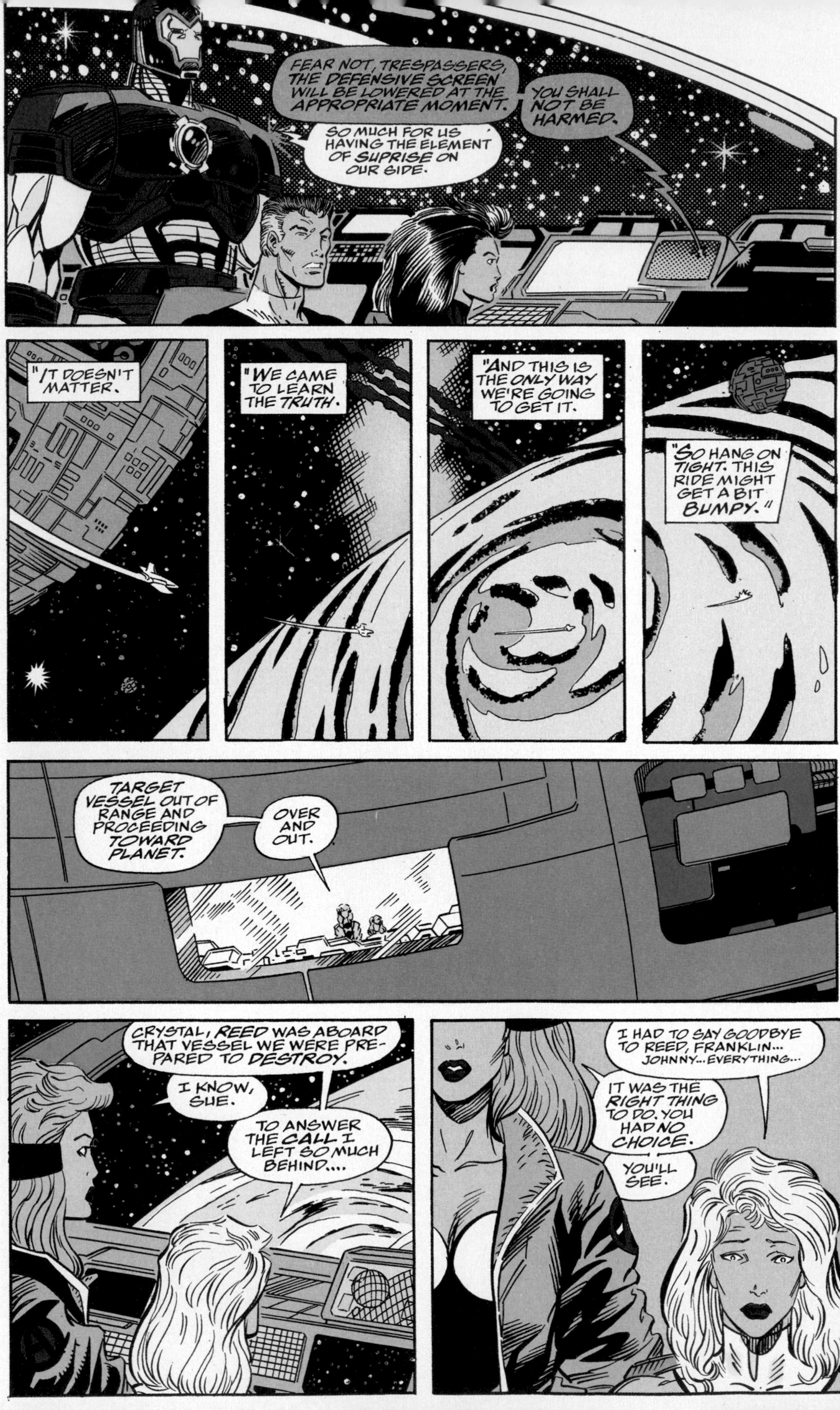
FEAR NOT, TRESPASSERS, THE DEFENSIVE SCREEN WILL BE LOWERED AT THE APPROPRIATE MOMENT.
YOU SHALL NOT BE HARMED.
SO MUCH FOR US HAVING THE ELEMENT OF SUPRISE ON OUR SIDE.
"IT DOESN'T MATTER.
"WE CAME TO LEARN THE TRUTH.
"AND THIS IS THE ONLY WAY WE'RE GOING TO GET IT.
"SO HANG ON TIGHT. THIS RIDE MIGHT GET A BIT BUMPY."
TARGET VESSEL OUT OF RANGE AND PROCEEDING TOWARD PLANET.
OVER AND OUT.
CRYSTAL, REED WAS ABOARD THAT VESSEL WE WERE PREPARED TO DESTROY.
I KNOW, SUE.
TO ANSWER THE CALL I LEFT SO MUCH BEHIND....
I HAD TO SAY GOODBYE TO REED, FRANKLIN... JOHNNY... EVERYTHING...
IT WAS THE RIGHT THING TO DO. YOU HAD NO CHOICE.
YOU'LL SEE.

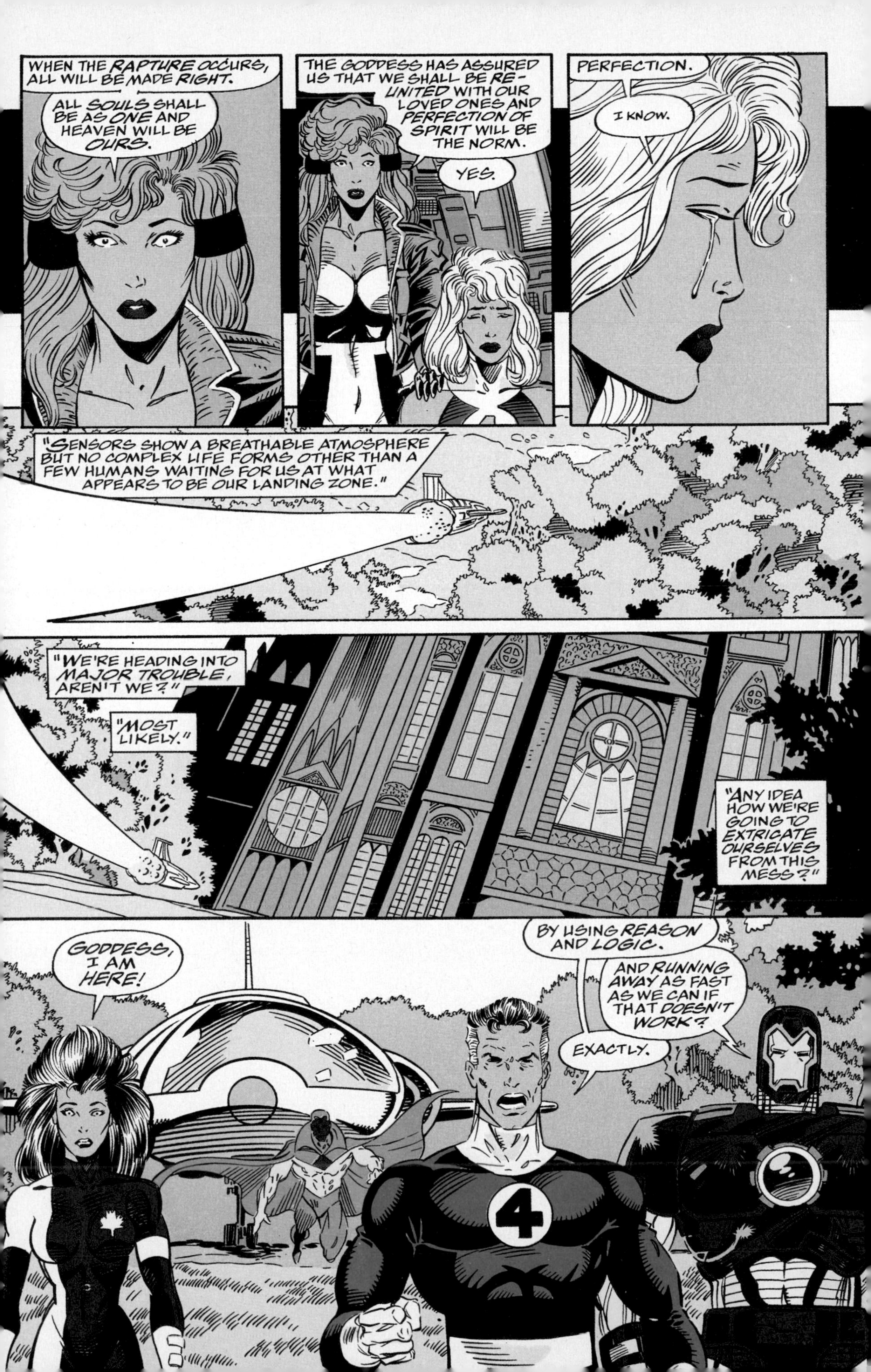

WHEN THE RAPTURE OCCURS, ALL WILL BE MADE RIGHT.
ALL SOULS SHALL BE AS ONE AND HEAVEN WILL BE OURS.
THE GODDESS HAS ASSURED US THAT WE SHALL BE RE-UNITED WITH OUR LOVED ONES AND PERFECTION OF SPIRIT WILL BE THE NORM.
YES.
PERFECTION.
I KNOW.
"SENSORS SHOW A BREATHABLE ATMOSPHERE BUT NO COMPLEX LIFE FORMS OTHER THAN A FEW HUMANS WAITING FOR US AT WHAT APPEARS TO BE OUR LANDING ZONE."
"WE'RE HEADING INTO MAJOR TROUBLE, AREN'T WE?"
"MOST LIKELY."
"ANY IDEA HOW WE'RE GOING TO EXTRICATE OURSELVES FROM THIS MESS?"
GODDESS, I AM HERE!
BY USING REASON AND LOGIC.
AND RUNNING AWAY AS FAST AS WE CAN IF THAT DOESN'T WORK?
EXACTLY.

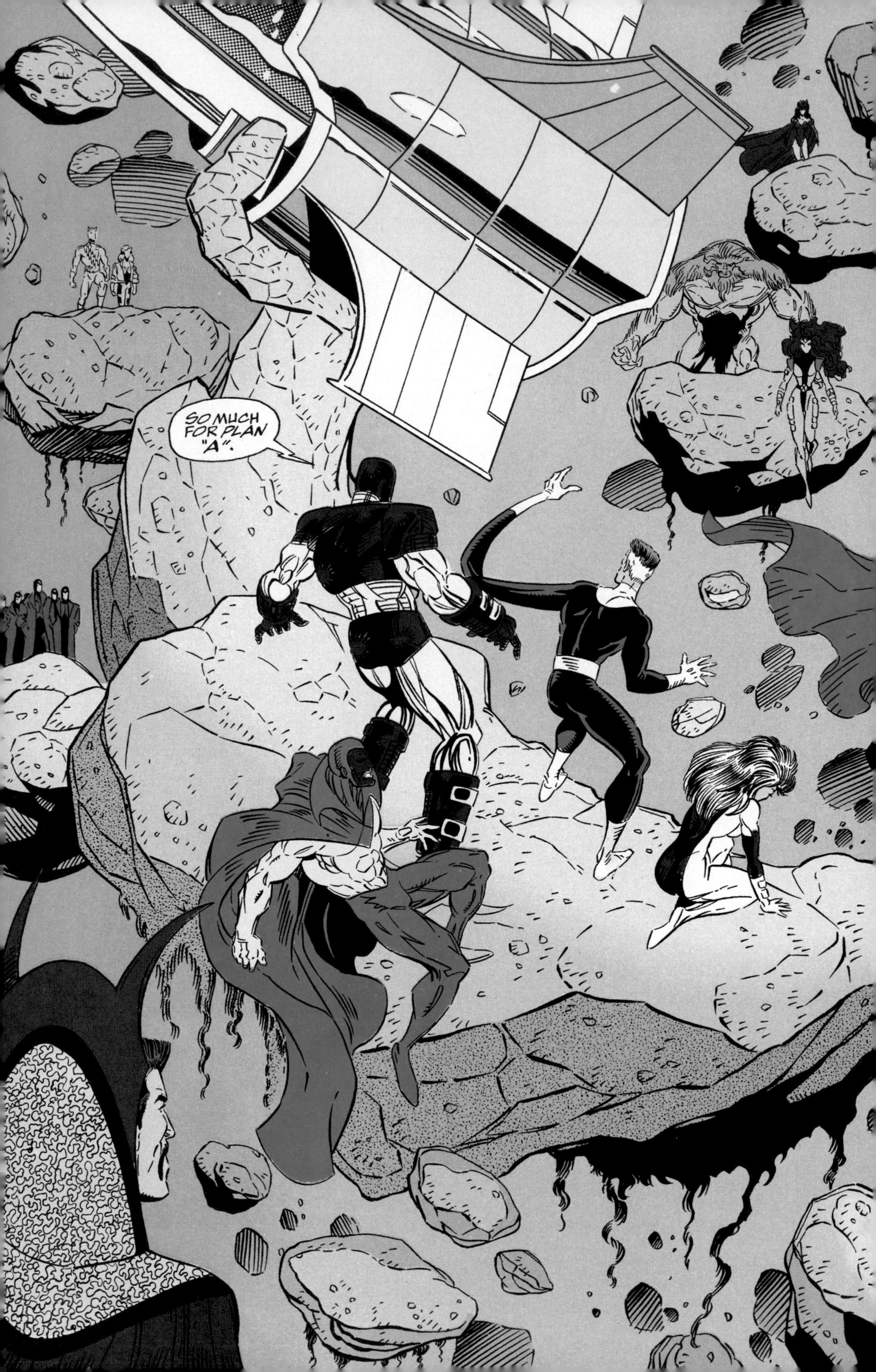
SO MUCH FOR PLAN "A".

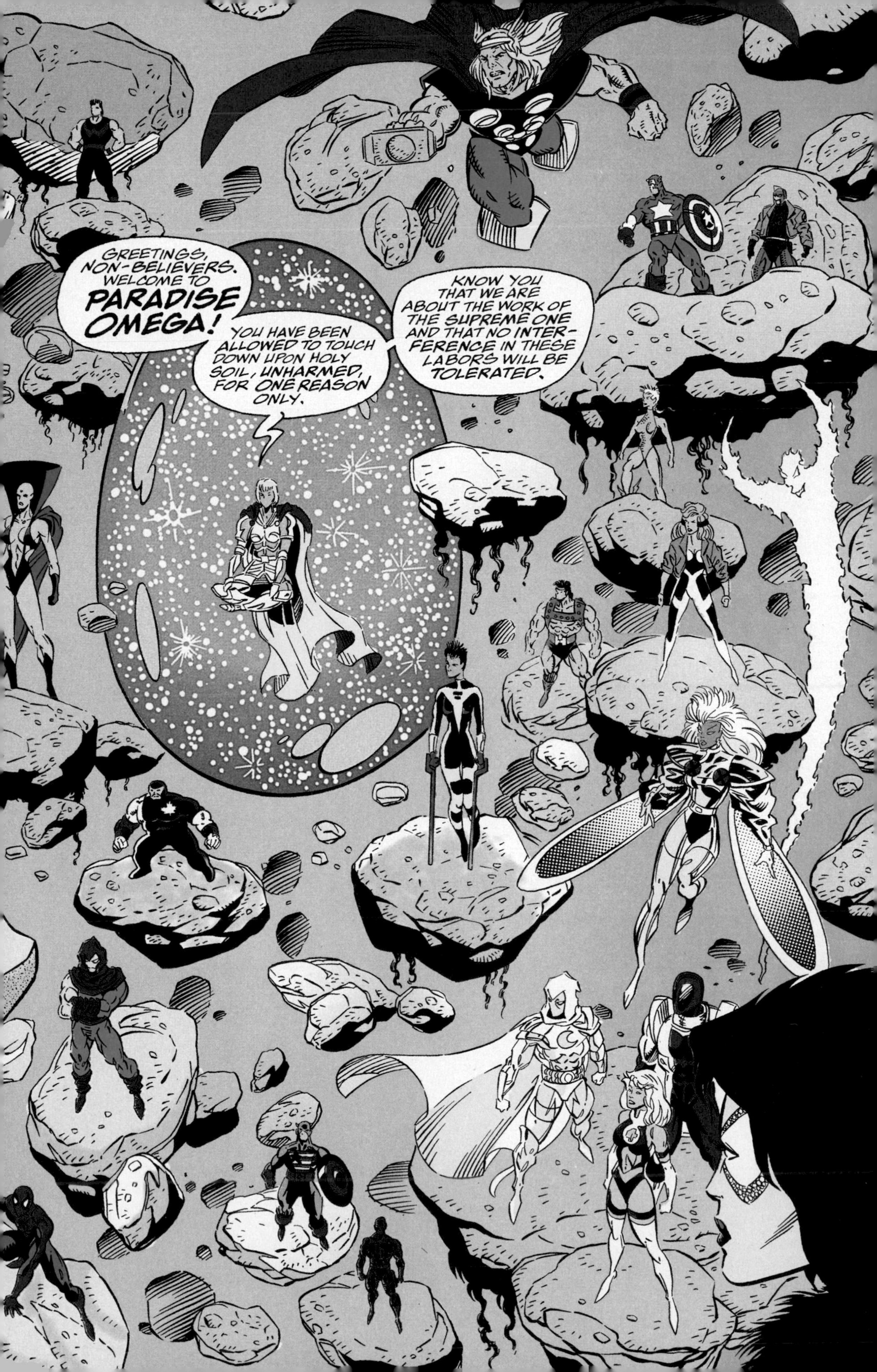
GREETINGS, NON-BELIEVERS. WELCOME TO PARADISE OMEGA!
YOU HAVE BEEN ALLOWED TO TOUCH DOWN UPON HOLY SOIL, UNHARMED, FOR ONE REASON ONLY.
KNOW YOU THAT WE ARE ABOUT THE WORK OF THE SUPREME ONE AND THAT NO INTERFERENCE IN THESE LABORS WILL BE TOLERATED.

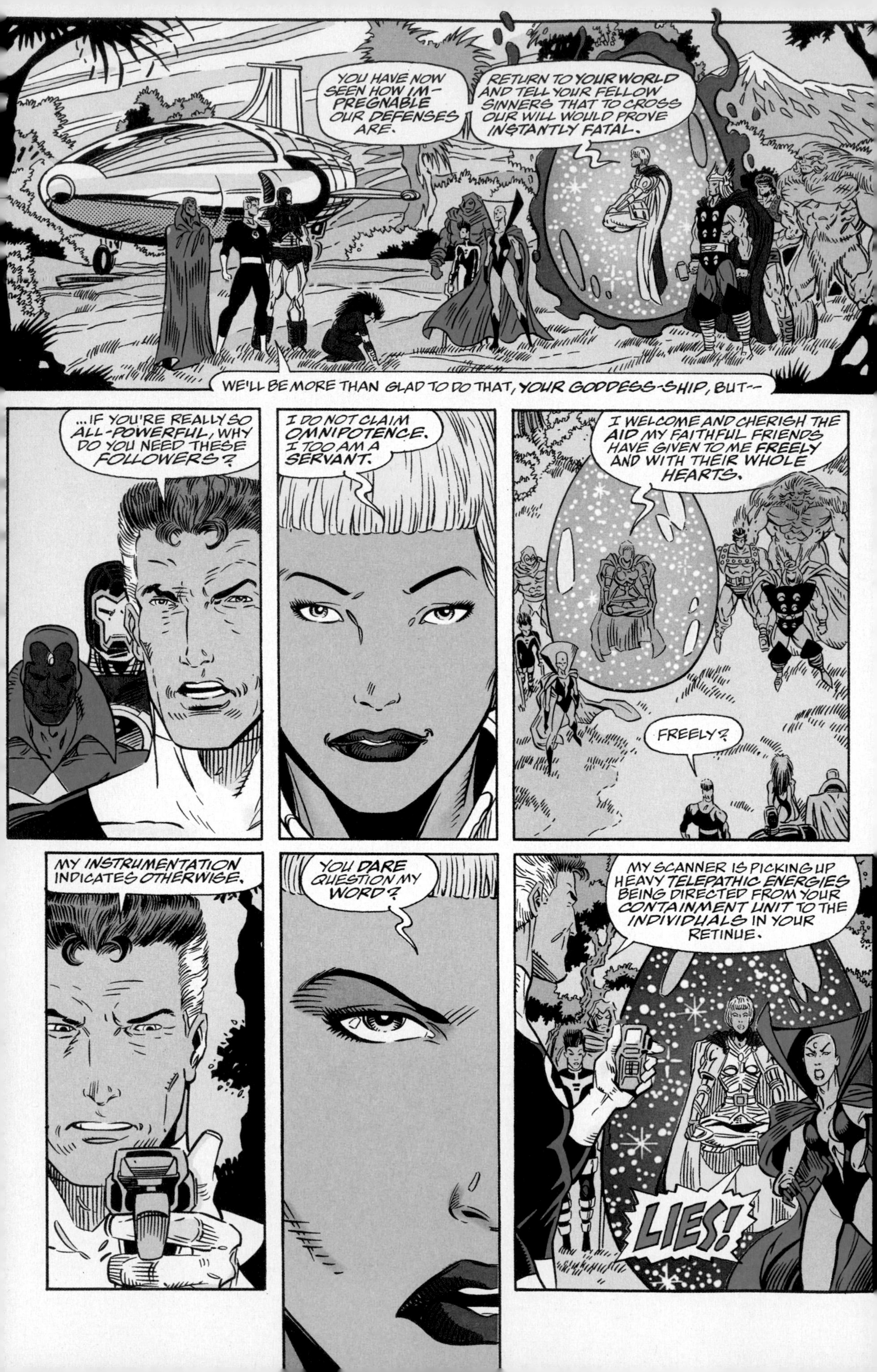
YOU HAVE NOW SEEN HOW IM-PREGNABLE OUR DEFENSES ARE.
RETURN TO YOUR WORLD AND TELL YOUR FELLOW SINNERS THAT TO CROSS OUR WILL WOULD PROVE INSTANTLY FATAL.
WE'LL BE MORE THAN GLAD TO DO THAT, YOUR GODDESS-SHIP, BUT--
...IF YOU'RE REALLY SO ALL-POWERFUL, WHY DO YOU NEED THESE FOLLOWERS?
I DO NOT CLAIM OMNIPOTENCE. I TOO AM A SERVANT.
I WELCOME AND CHERISH THE AID MY FAITHFUL FRIENDS HAVE GIVEN TO ME FREELY AND WITH THEIR WHOLE HEARTS.
FREELY?
MY INSTRUMENTATION INDICATES OTHERWISE.
YOU DARE QUESTION MY WORD?
MY SCANNER IS PICKING UP HEAVY TELEPATHIC ENERGIES BEING DIRECTED FROM YOUR CONTAINMENT UNIT TO THE INDIVIDUALS IN YOUR RETINUE.
LIES!

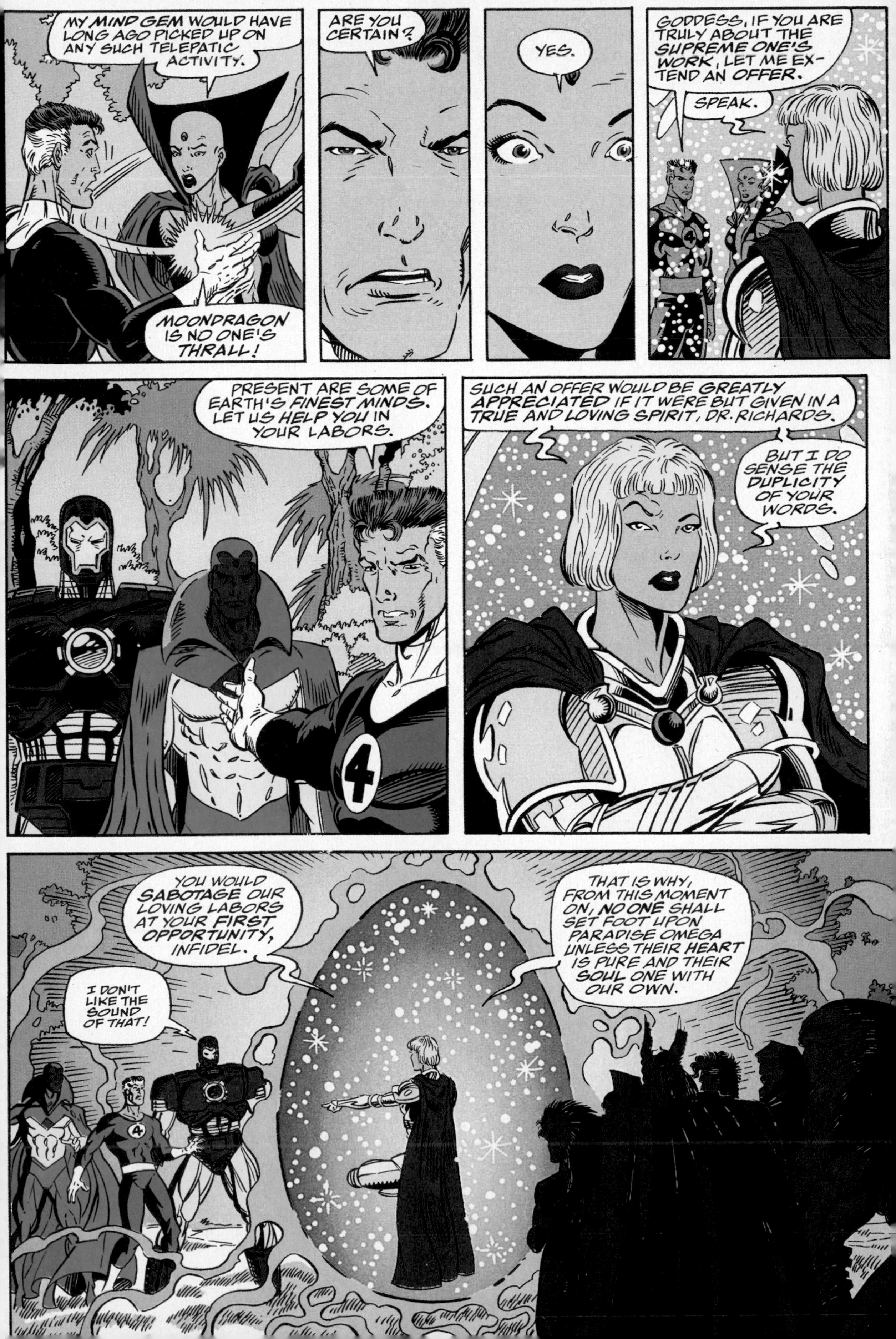
MY MIND GEM WOULD HAVE LONG AGO PICKED UP ON ANY SUCH TELEPATIC ACTIVITY.
MOONDRAGON IS NO ONE'S THRALL!
ARE YOU CERTAIN?
YES.
GODDESS, IF YOU ARE TRULY ABOUT THE SUPREME ONE'S WORK, LET ME EXTEND AN OFFER.
SPEAK.
PRESENT ARE SOME OF EARTH'S FINEST MINDS. LET US HELP YOU IN YOUR LABORS.
SUCH AN OFFER WOULD BE GREATLY APPRECIATED IF IT WERE BUT GIVEN IN A TRUE AND LOVING SPIRIT, DR. RICHARDS.
BUT I DO SENSE THE DUPLICITY OF YOUR WORDS.
YOU WOULD SABOTAGE OUR LOVING LABORS AT YOUR FIRST OPPORTUNITY, INFIDEL.
THAT IS WHY, FROM THIS MOMENT ON, NO ONE SHALL SET FOOT UPON PARADISE OMEGA UNLESS THEIR HEART IS PURE AND THEIR SOUL ONE WITH OUR OWN.
I DON'T LIKE THE SOUND OF THAT!

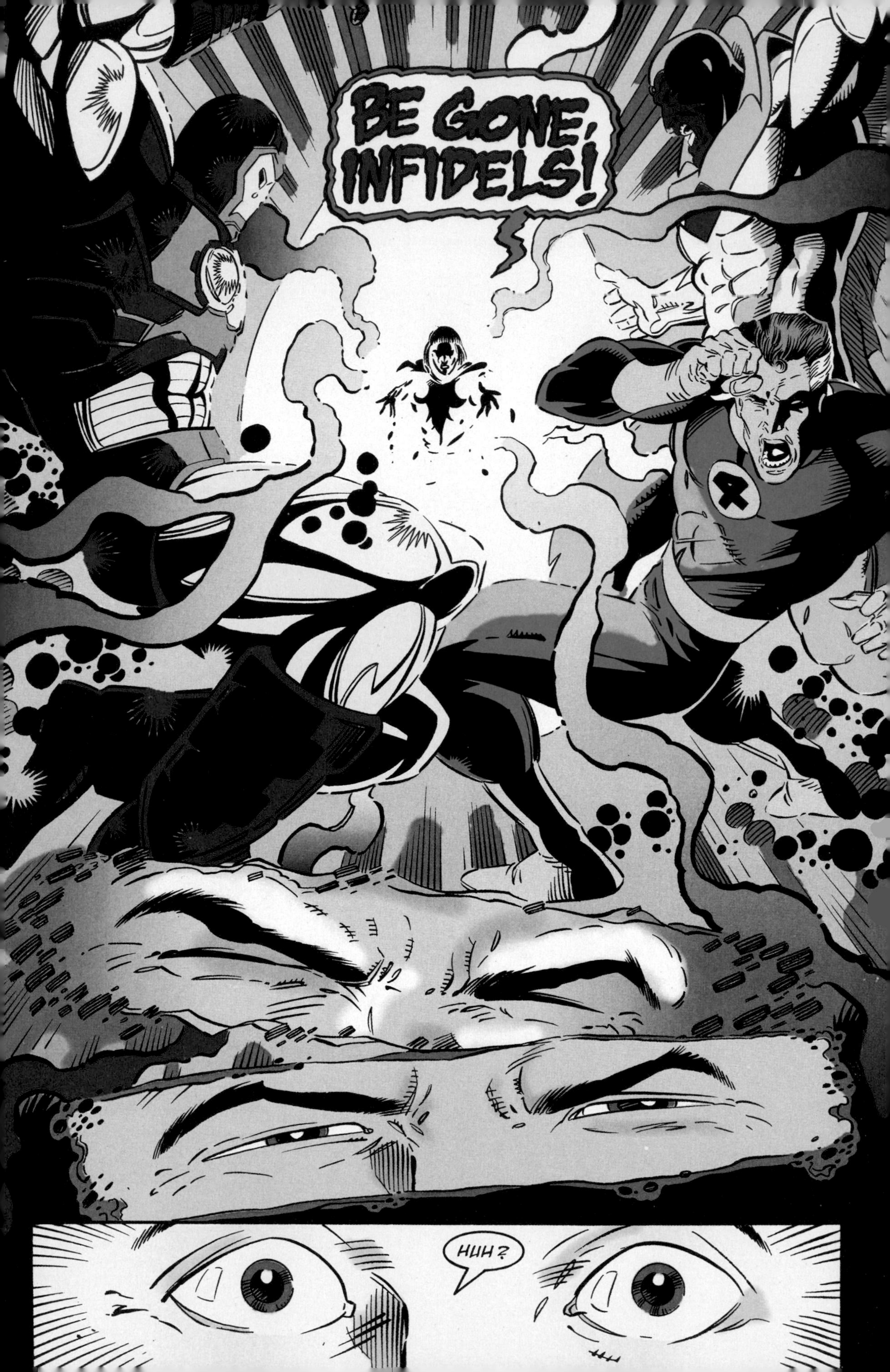
BE GONE, INFIDELS!
HUH?

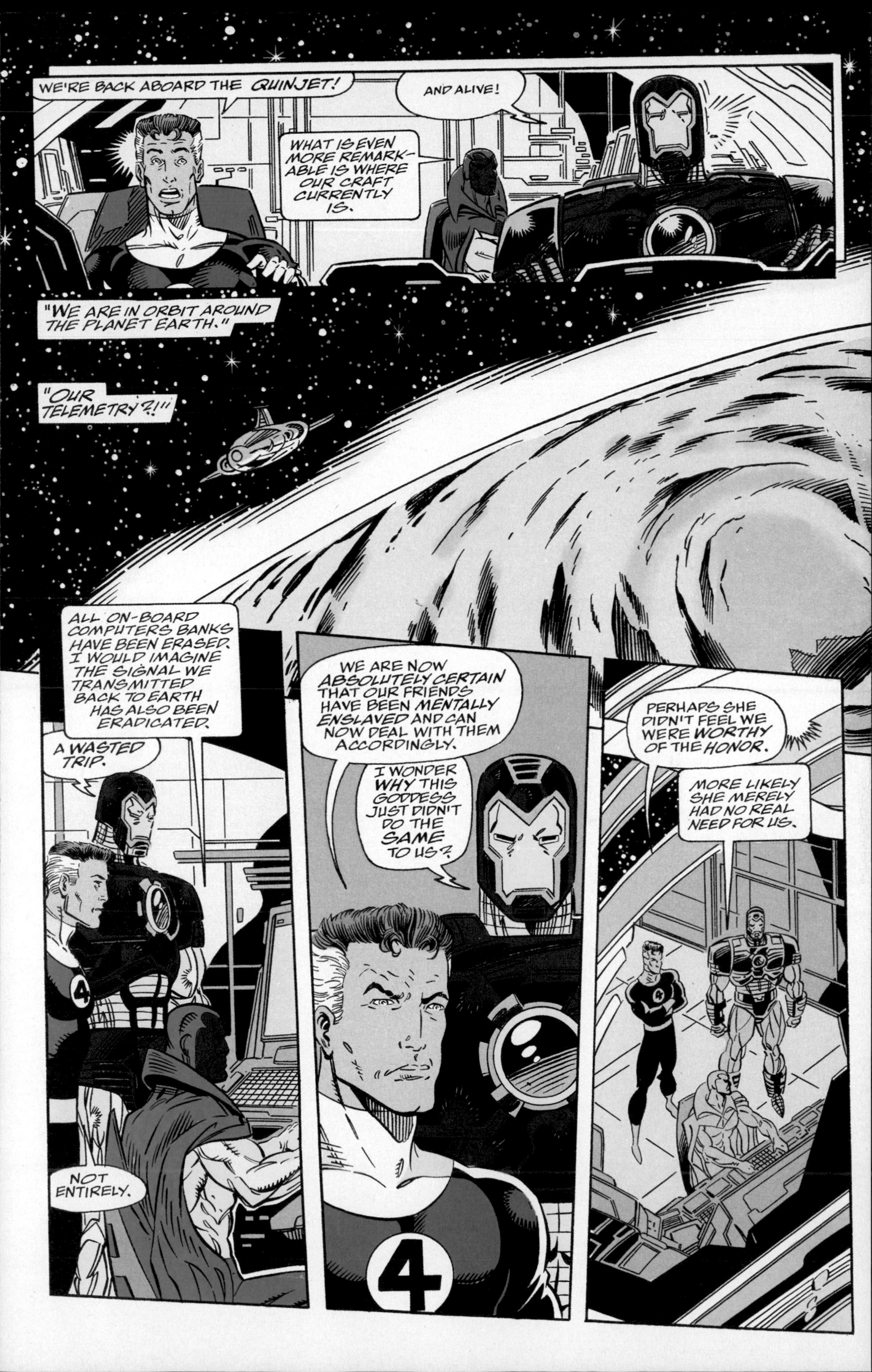

WE'RE BACK ABOARD THE QUINJET!
AND ALIVE!
WHAT IS EVEN MORE REMARKABLE IS WHERE OUR CRAFT CURRENTLY IS.
"WE ARE IN ORBIT AROUND THE PLANET EARTH."
"OUR TELEMETRY?!"
ALL ON-BOARD COMPUTERS BANKS HAVE BEEN ERASED. I WOULD IMAGINE THE SIGNAL WE TRANSMITTED BACK TO EARTH HAS ALSO BEEN ERADICATED.
A WASTED TRIP.
NOT ENTIRELY.
WE ARE NOW ABSOLUTELY CERTAIN THAT OUR FRIENDS HAVE BEEN MENTALLY ENSLAVED AND CAN NOW DEAL WITH THEM ACCORDINGLY.
I WONDER WHY THIS GODDESS JUST DIDN'T DO THE SAME TO US?
PERHAPS SHE DIDN'T FEEL WE WERE WORTHY OF THE HONOR.
MORE LIKELY SHE MERELY HAD NO REAL NEED FOR US.

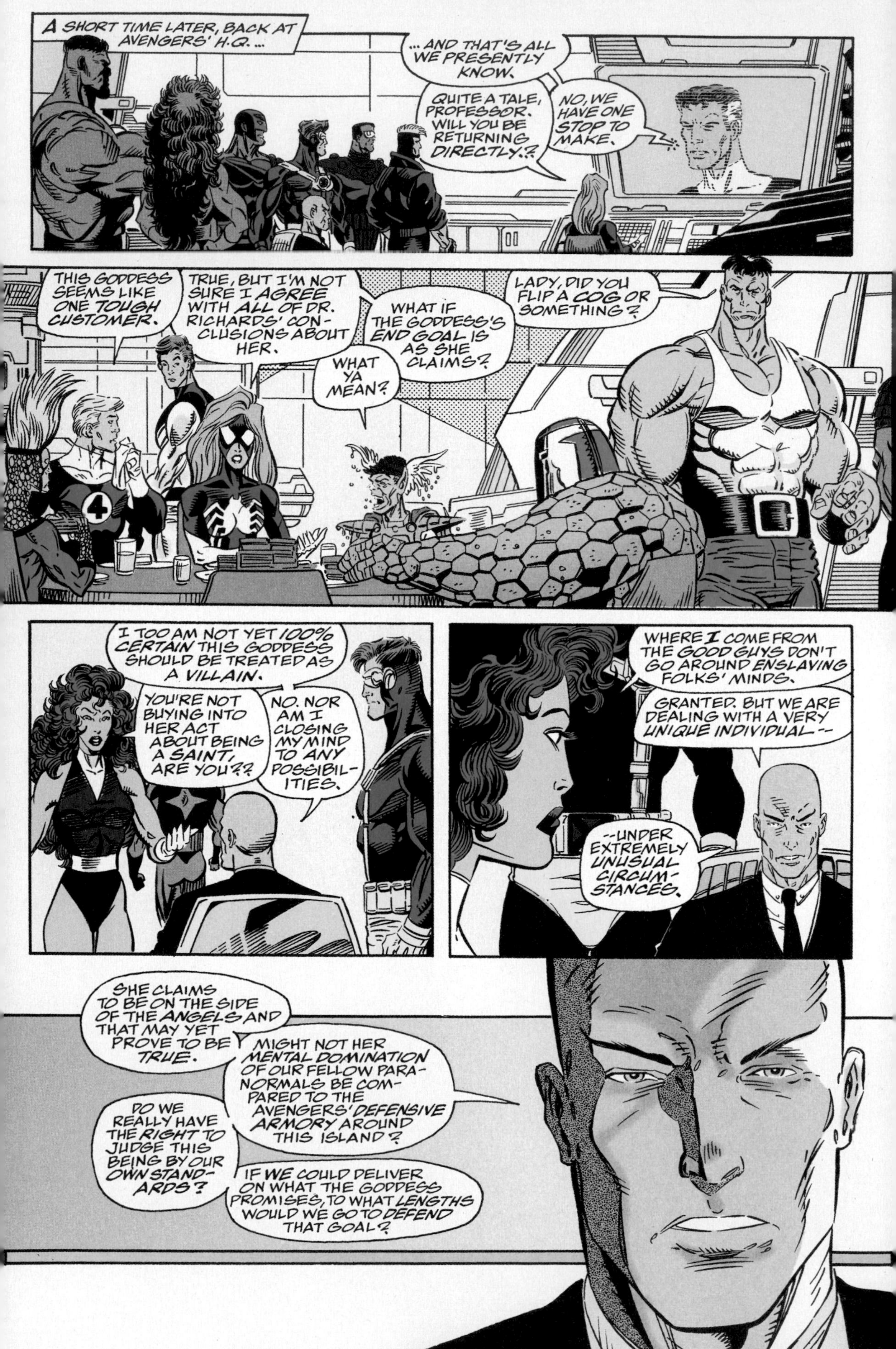
A SHORT TIME LATER, BACK AT AVENGERS' H.Q. ...
... AND THAT'S ALL WE PRESENTLY KNOW.
QUITE A TALE, PROFESSOR. WILL YOU BE RETURNING DIRECTLY..?
NO, WE HAVE ONE STOP TO MAKE.
THIS GODDESS SEEMS LIKE ONE TOUGH CUSTOMER.
TRUE, BUT I'M NOT SURE I AGREE WITH ALL OF DR. RICHARDS' CONCLUSIONS ABOUT HER.
WHAT YA MEAN?
WHAT IF THE GODDESS'S END GOAL IS AS SHE CLAIMS?
LADY, DID YOU FLIP A COG OR SOMETHING?
I TOO AM NOT YET 100% CERTAIN THIS GODDESS SHOULD BE TREATED AS A VILLAIN.
YOU'RE NOT BUYING INTO HER ACT ABOUT BEING A SAINT, ARE YOU??
NO. NOR AM I CLOSING MY MIND TO ANY POSSIBILITIES.
WHERE I COME FROM THE GOOD GUYS DON'T GO AROUND ENSLAVING FOLKS' MINDS.
GRANTED. BUT WE ARE DEALING WITH A VERY UNIQUE INDIVIDUAL--
--UNDER EXTREMELY UNUSUAL CIRCUMSTANCES.
SHE CLAIMS TO BE ON THE SIDE OF THE ANGELS AND THAT MAY YET PROVE TO BE TRUE.
MIGHT NOT HER MENTAL DOMINATION OF OUR FELLOW PARANORMALS BE COMPARED TO THE AVENGERS' DEFENSIVE ARMORY AROUND THIS ISLAND?
DO WE REALLY HAVE THE RIGHT TO JUDGE THIS BEING BY OUR OWN STANDARDS?
IF WE COULD DELIVER ON WHAT THE GODDESS PROMISES, TO WHAT LENGTHS WOULD WE GO TO DEFEND THAT GOAL?

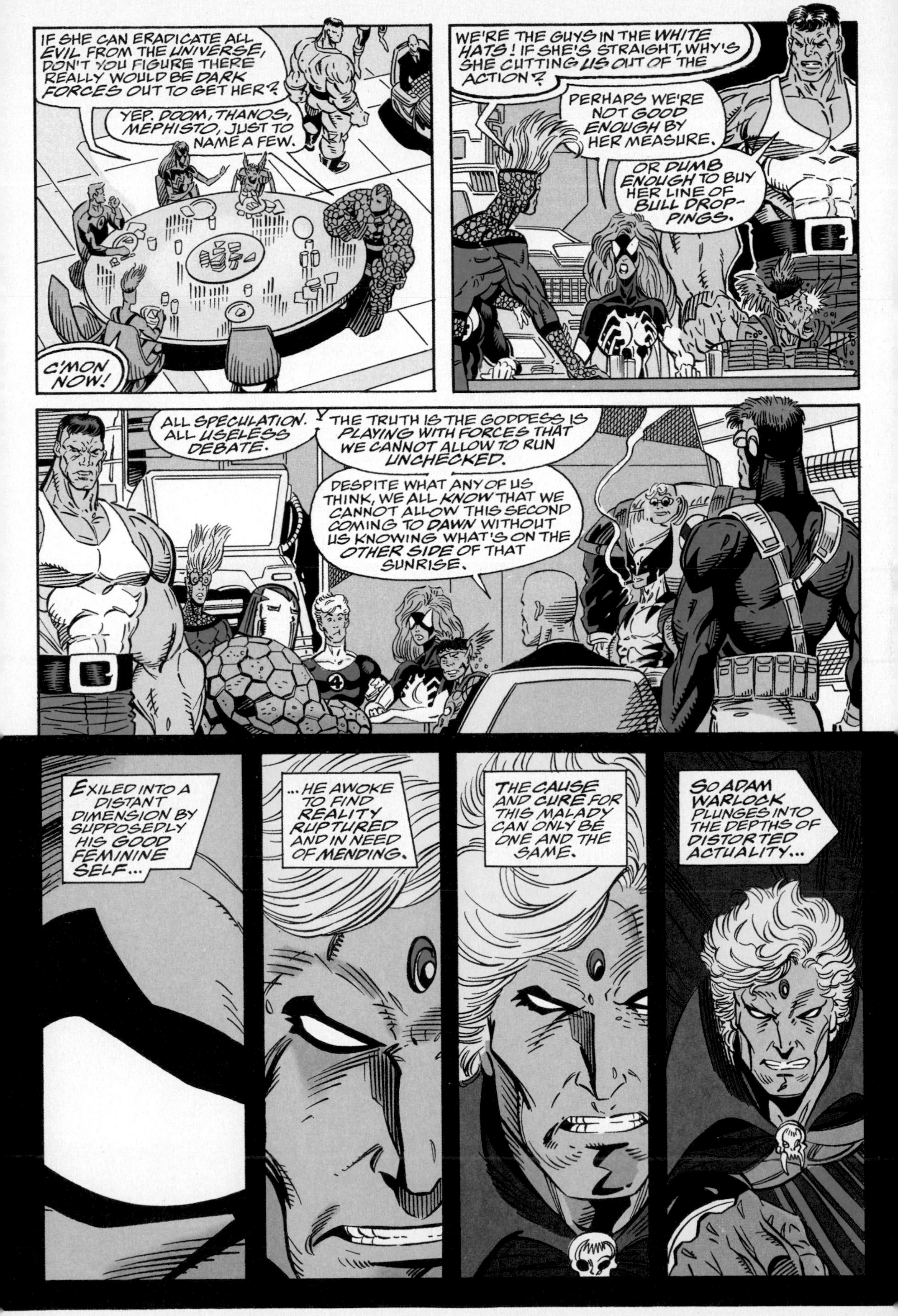
IF SHE CAN ERADICATE ALL EVIL FROM THE UNIVERSE, DON'T YOU FIGURE THERE REALLY WOULD BE DARK FORCES OUT TO GET HER?
YEP. DOOM, THANOS, MEPHISTO, JUST TO NAME A FEW.
C'MON NOW!
WE'RE THE GUYS IN THE WHITE HATS! IF SHE'S STRAIGHT, WHY'S SHE CUTTING US OUT OF THE ACTION?
PERHAPS WE'RE NOT GOOD ENOUGH BY HER MEASURE.
OR DUMB ENOUGH TO BUY HER LINE OF BULL DROP-PINGS.
ALL SPECULATION. ALL USELESS DEBATE.
THE TRUTH IS THE GODDESS IS PLAYING WITH FORCES THAT WE CANNOT ALLOW TO RUN UNCHECKED.
DESPITE WHAT ANY OF US THINK, WE ALL KNOW THAT WE CANNOT ALLOW THIS SECOND COMING TO DAWN WITHOUT US KNOWING WHAT'S ON THE OTHER SIDE OF THAT SUNRISE.
EXILED INTO A DISTANT DIMENSION BY SUPPOSEDLY HIS GOOD FEMININE SELF...
...HE AWOKE TO FIND REALITY RUPTURED AND IN NEED OF MENDING.
THE CAUSE AND CURE FOR THIS MALADY CAN ONLY BE ONE AND THE SAME.
SO ADAM WARLOCK PLUNGES INTO THE DEPTHS OF DISTORTED ACTUALITY...

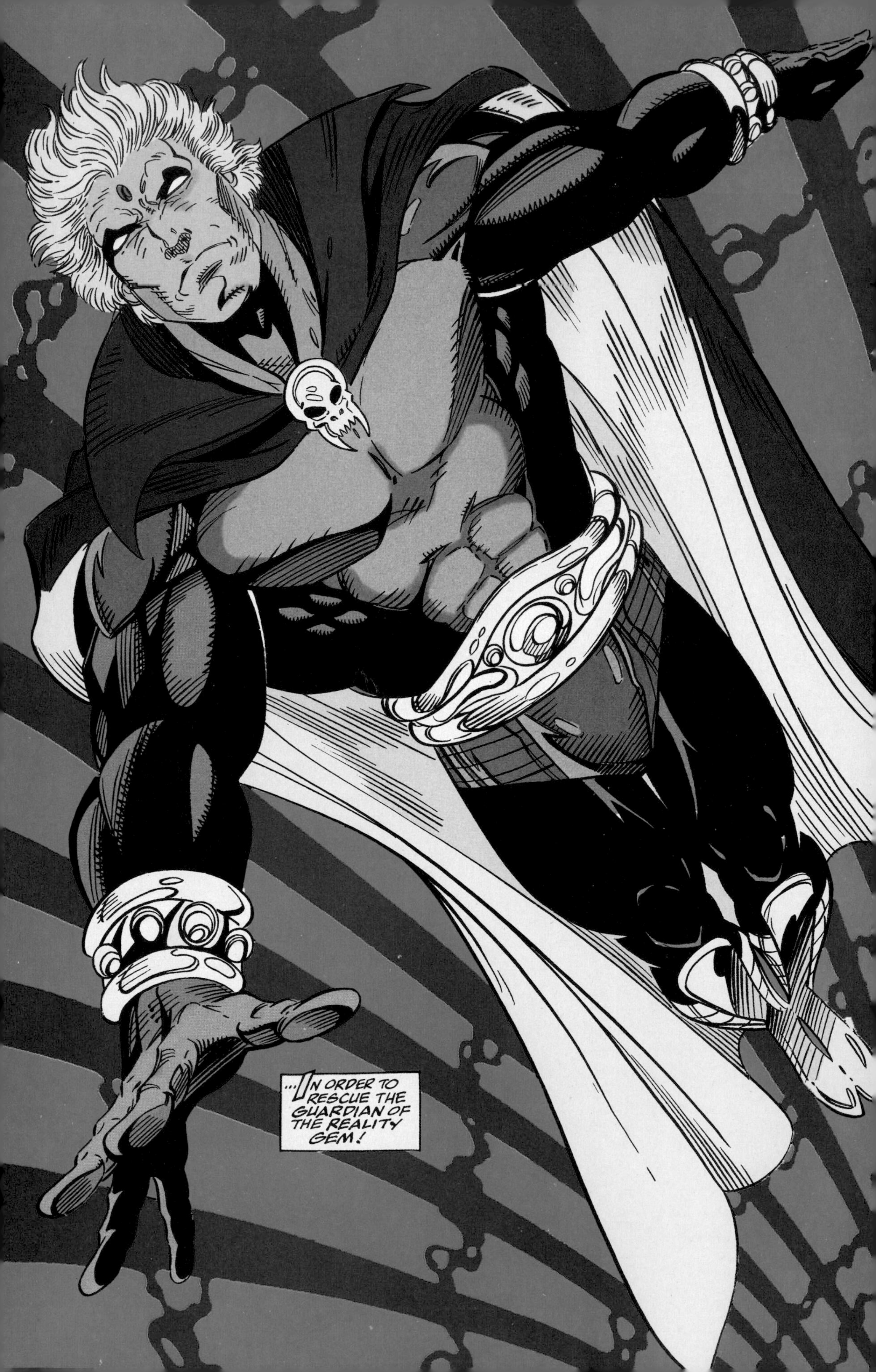
...IN ORDER TO RESCUE THE GUARDIAN OF THE REALITY GEM!

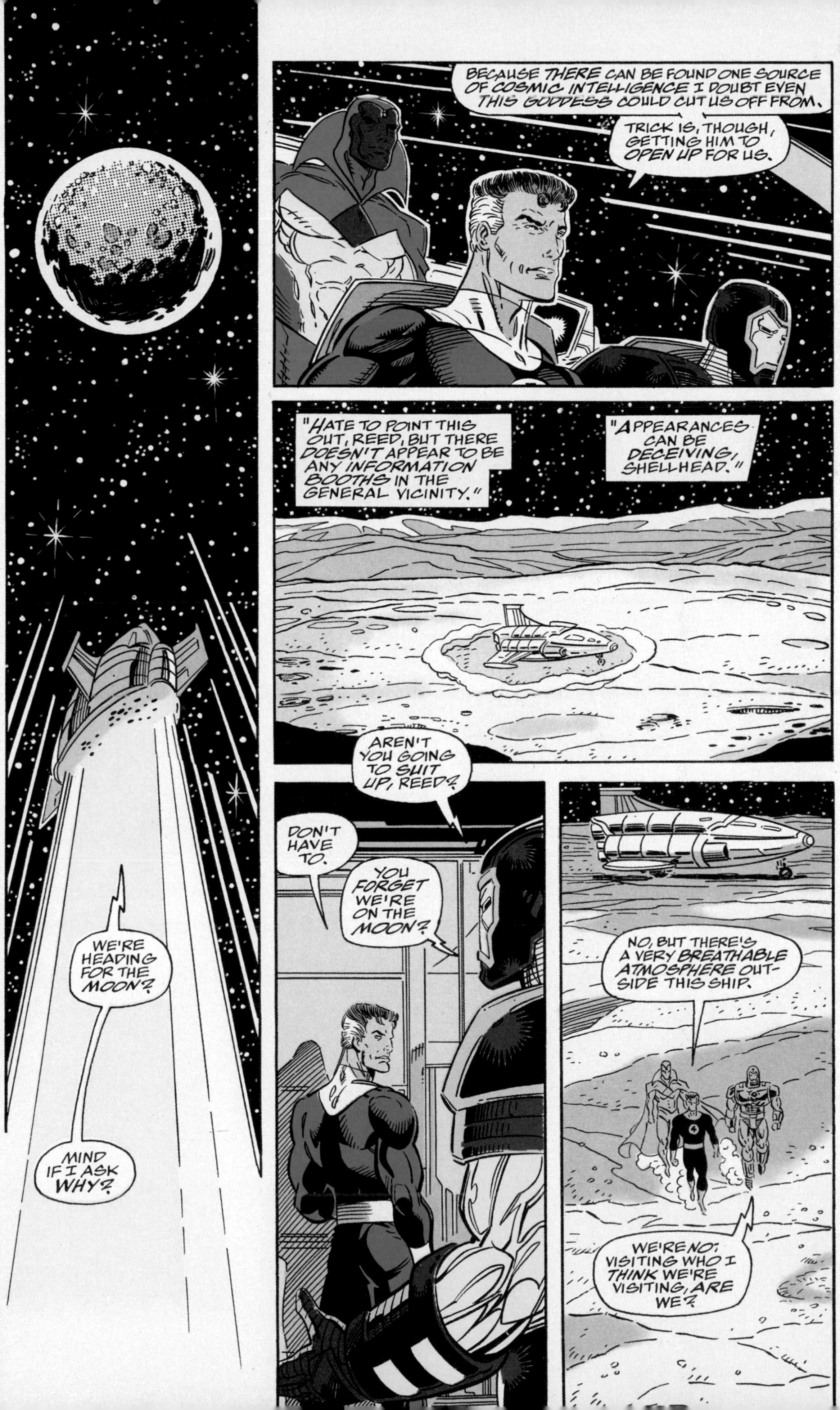
BECAUSE THERE CAN BE FOUND ONE SOURCE OF COSMIC INTELLIGENCE I DOUBT EVEN THIS GODDESS COULD CUT US OFF FROM.
TRICK IS, THOUGH, GETTING HIM TO OPEN UP FOR US.
WE'RE HEADING FOR THE MOON?
MIND IF I ASK WHY?
"HATE TO POINT THIS OUT, REED, BUT THERE DOESN'T APPEAR TO BE ANY INFORMATION BOOTHS IN THE GENERAL VICINITY."
"APPEARANCES CAN BE DECEIVING, SHELLHEAD."
AREN'T YOU GOING TO SUIT UP, REED?
DON'T HAVE TO.
YOU FORGET WE'RE ON THE MOON?
NO, BUT THERE'S A VERY BREATHABLE ATMOSPHERE OUT-SIDE THIS SHIP.
WE'RE NOT VISITING WHO I THINK WE'RE VISITING, ARE WE?

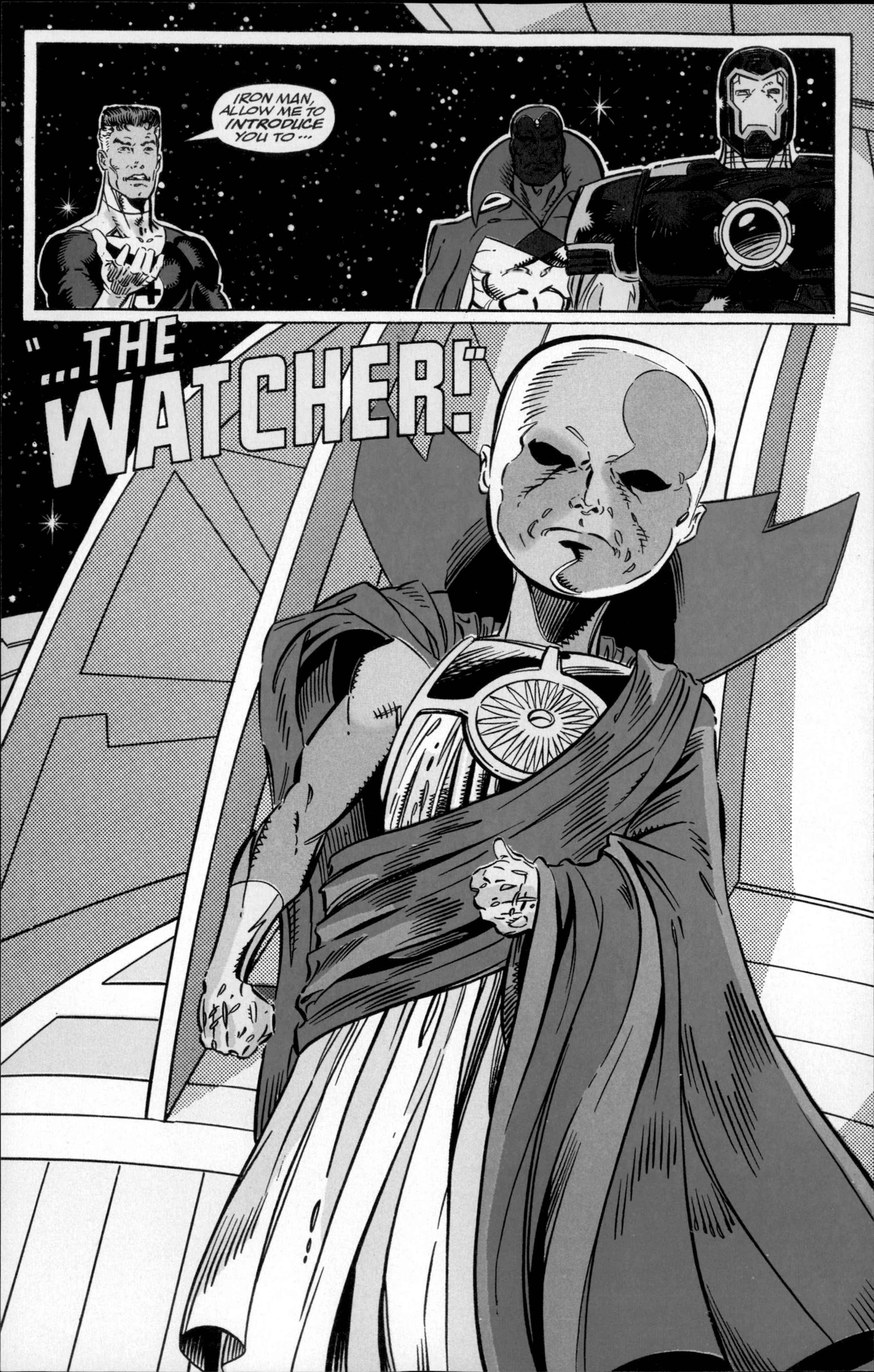
IRON MAN, ALLOW ME TO INTRODUCE YOU TO...
"...THE WATCHER!"

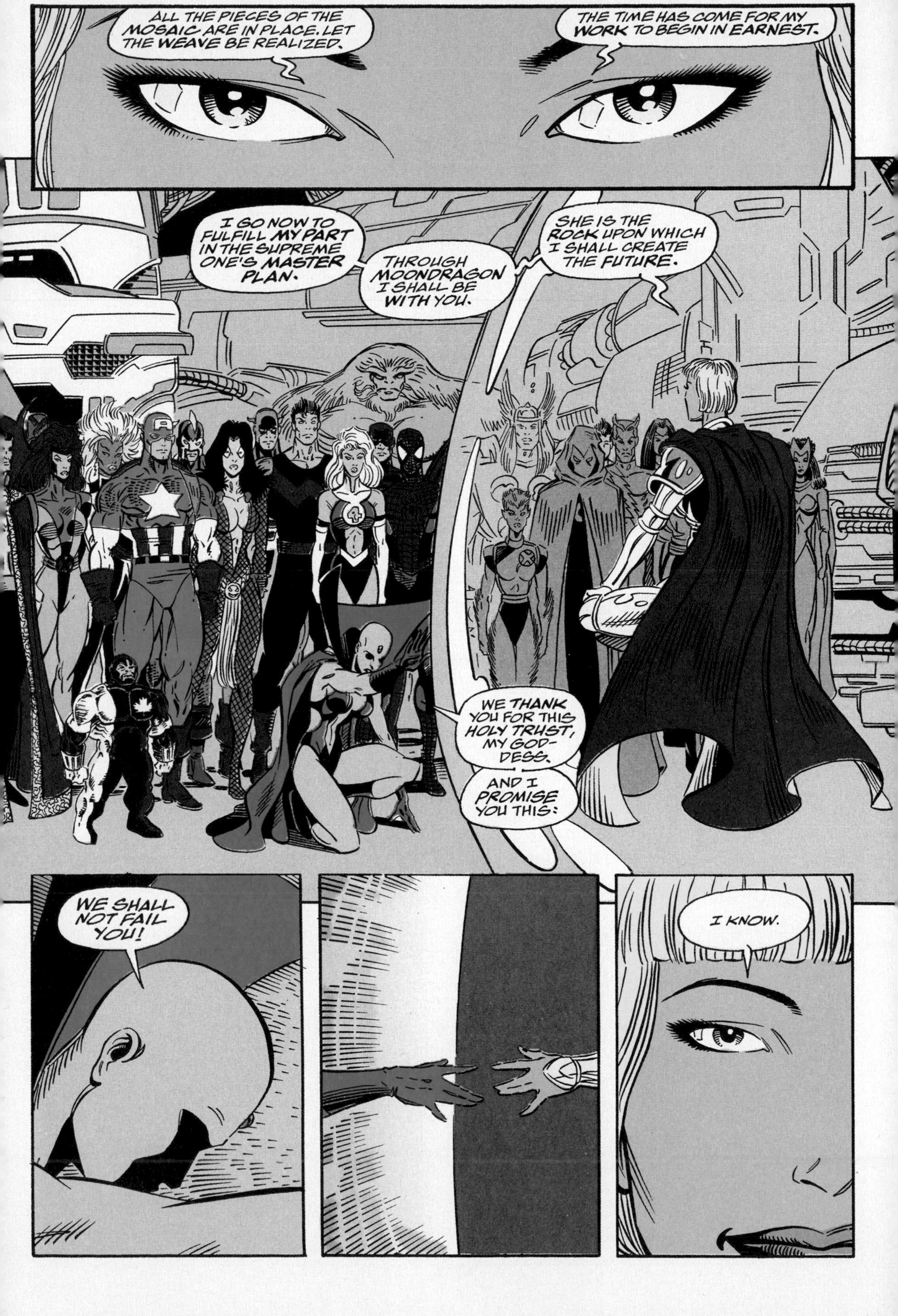
ALL THE PIECES OF THE MOSAIC ARE IN PLACE. LET THE WEAVE BE REALIZED.
THE TIME HAS COME FOR MY WORK TO BEGIN IN EARNEST.
I GO NOW TO FULFILL MY PART IN THE SUPREME ONE'S MASTER PLAN.
THROUGH MOONDRAGON I SHALL BE WITH YOU.
SHE IS THE ROCK UPON WHICH I SHALL CREATE THE FUTURE.
WE THANK YOU FOR THIS HOLY TRUST, MY GOD-DESS.
AND I PROMISE YOU THIS:
WE SHALL NOT FAIL YOU!
I KNOW.

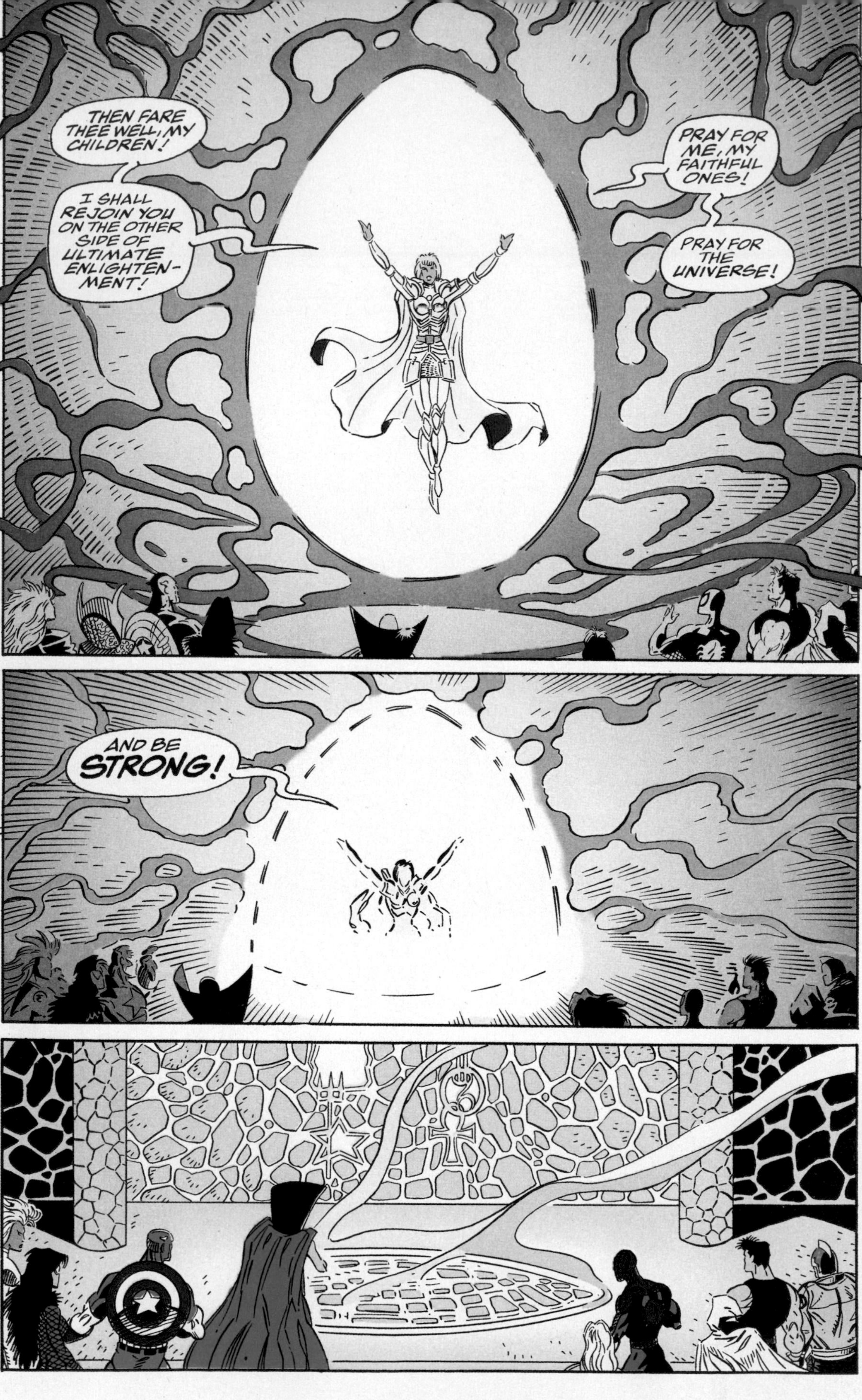
THEN FARE THEE WELL, MY CHILDREN!
I SHALL REJOIN YOU ON THE OTHER SIDE OF ULTIMATE ENLIGHTEN-MENT!
PRAY FOR ME, MY FAITHFUL ONES!
PRAY FOR THE UNIVERSE!
AND BE STRONG!

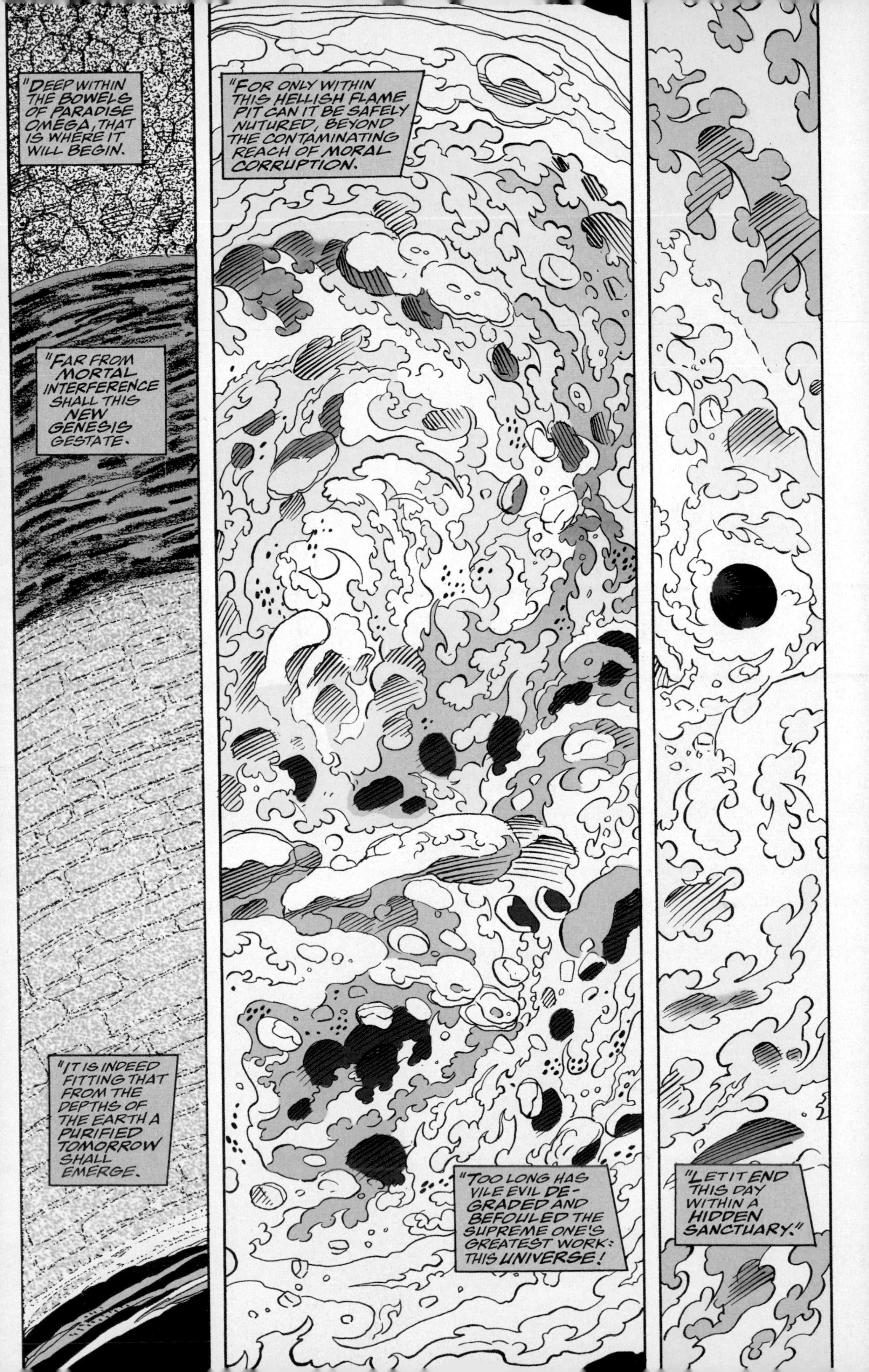
"DEEP WITHIN THE BOWELS OF PARADISE OMEGA, THAT IS WHERE IT WILL BEGIN.
"FAR FROM MORTAL INTERFERENCE SHALL THIS NEW GENESIS GESTATE.
"IT IS INDEED FITTING THAT FROM THE DEPTHS OF THE EARTH A PURIFIED TOMORROW SHALL EMERGE.
"FOR ONLY WITHIN THIS HELLISH FLAME PIT CAN IT BE SAFELY NUTURED, BEYOND THE CONTAMINATING REACH OF MORAL CORRUPTION.
"TOO LONG HAS VILE EVIL DE-GRADED AND BEFOULED THE SUPREME ONE'S GREATEST WORK: THIS UNIVERSE!
"LET IT END THIS DAY WITHIN A HIDDEN SANCTUARY."

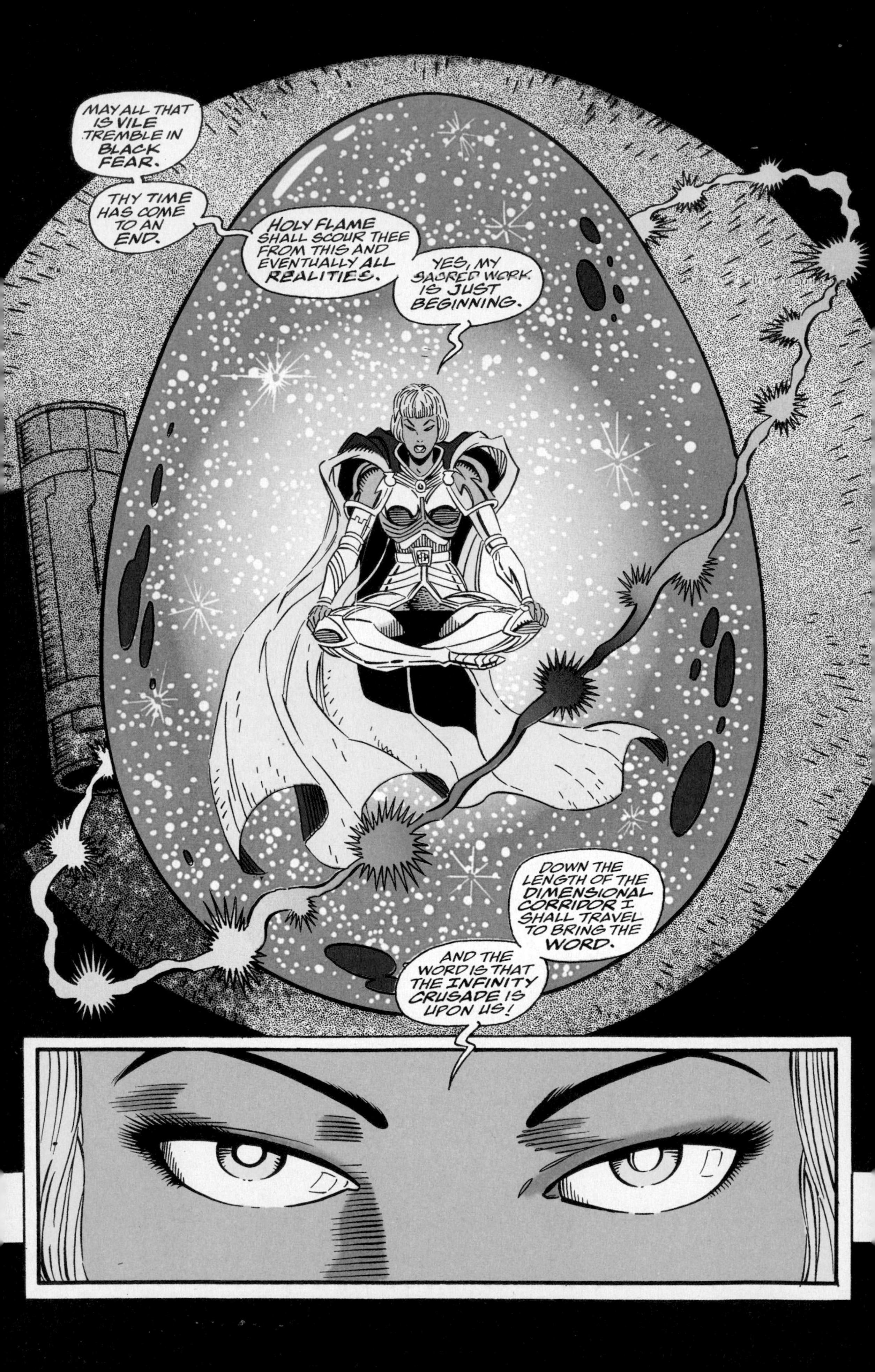
MAY ALL THAT IS VILE TREMBLE IN BLACK FEAR.
THY TIME HAS COME TO AN END.
HOLY FLAME SHALL SCOUR THEE FROM THIS AND EVENTUALLY ALL REALITIES.
YES, MY SACRED WORK IS JUST BEGINNING.
DOWN THE LENGTH OF THE DIMENSIONAL CORRIDOR I SHALL TRAVEL TO BRING THE WORD.
AND THE WORD IS THAT THE INFINITY CRUSADE IS UPON US!

"IT BEGINS HUMBLY ENOUGH ON A BARREN PLANET WITHOUT PAST OR FUTURE.

"A VIRGIN BIRTH SET IN A COSMIC BACKWATER.

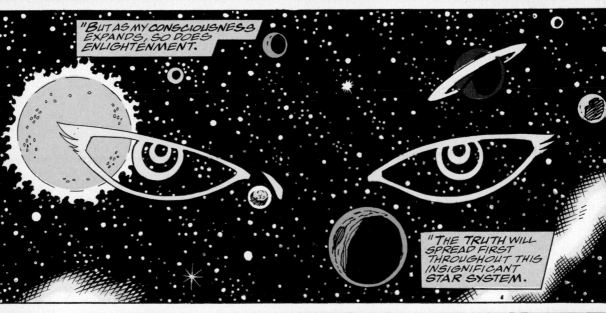

"BUT AS MY CONSCIOUSNESS EXPANDS, SO DOES ENLIGHTENMENT.

"THE TRUTH WILL SPREAD FIRST THROUGHOUT THIS INSIGNIFICANT STAR SYSTEM.

"THEN THE ENTIRE GALAXY WILL JOIN WITHIN THE COMFORTING FOLDS OF COLLECTIVE CONSCIOUSNESS.

"AND THE GOSPEL WILL SPREAD EVEN BEYOND THESE VAST REACHES, THROUGHOUT ALL REALITIES!

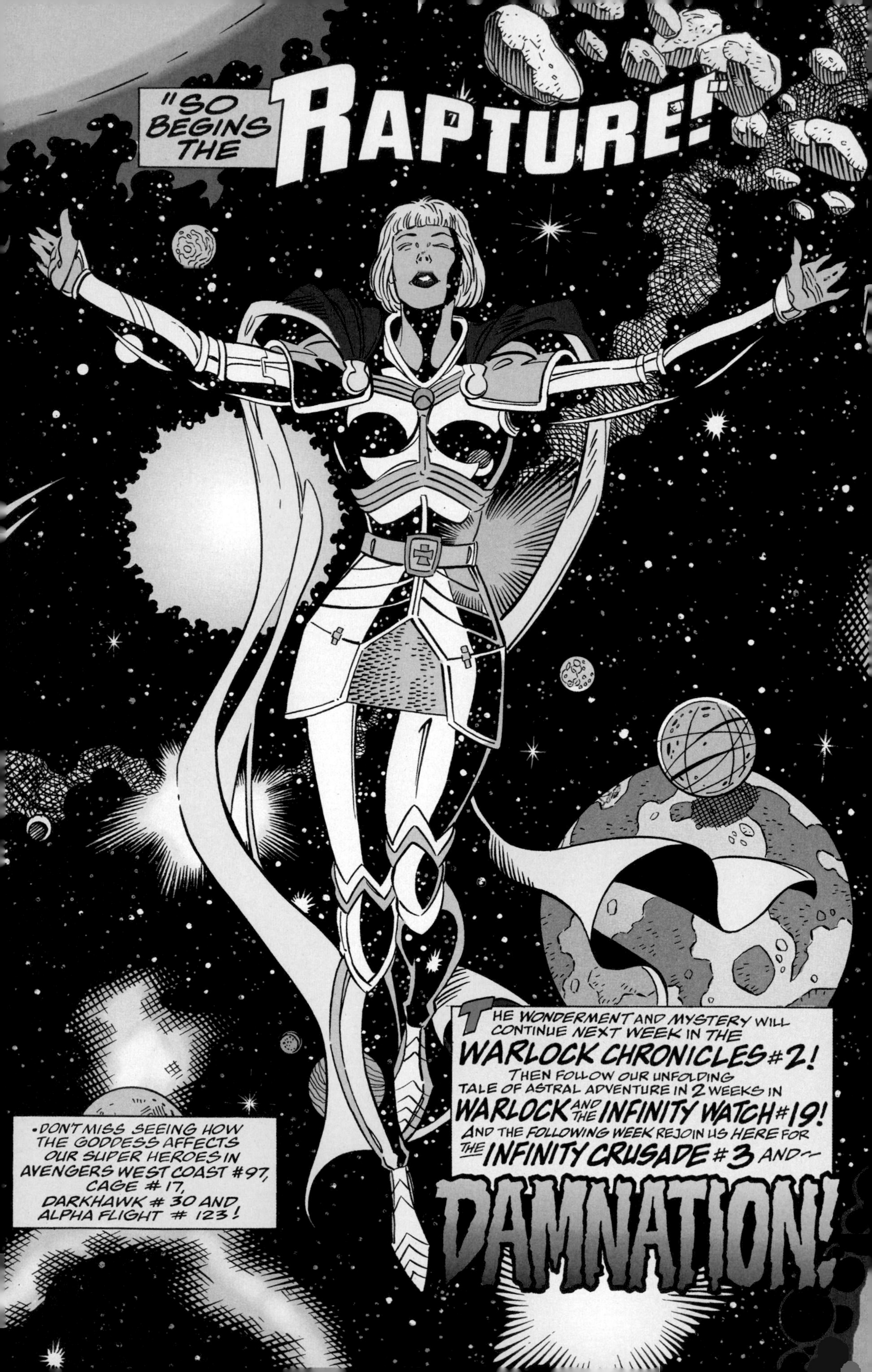
"SO BEGINS THE RAPTURE!"
THE WONDERMENT AND MYSTERY WILL CONTINUE NEXT WEEK IN THE WARLOCK CHRONICLES #2! THEN FOLLOW OUR UNFOLDING TALE OF ASTRAL ADVENTURE IN 2 WEEKS IN WARLOCK AND THE INFINITY WATCH #19! AND THE FOLLOWING WEEK REJOIN US HERE FOR THE INFINITY CRUSADE #3 AND--
DAMNATION!
•DON'T MISS SEEING HOW THE GODDESS AFFECTS OUR SUPER HEROES IN AVENGERS WEST COAST #97, CAGE #17, DARKHAWK #30 AND ALPHA FLIGHT #123!

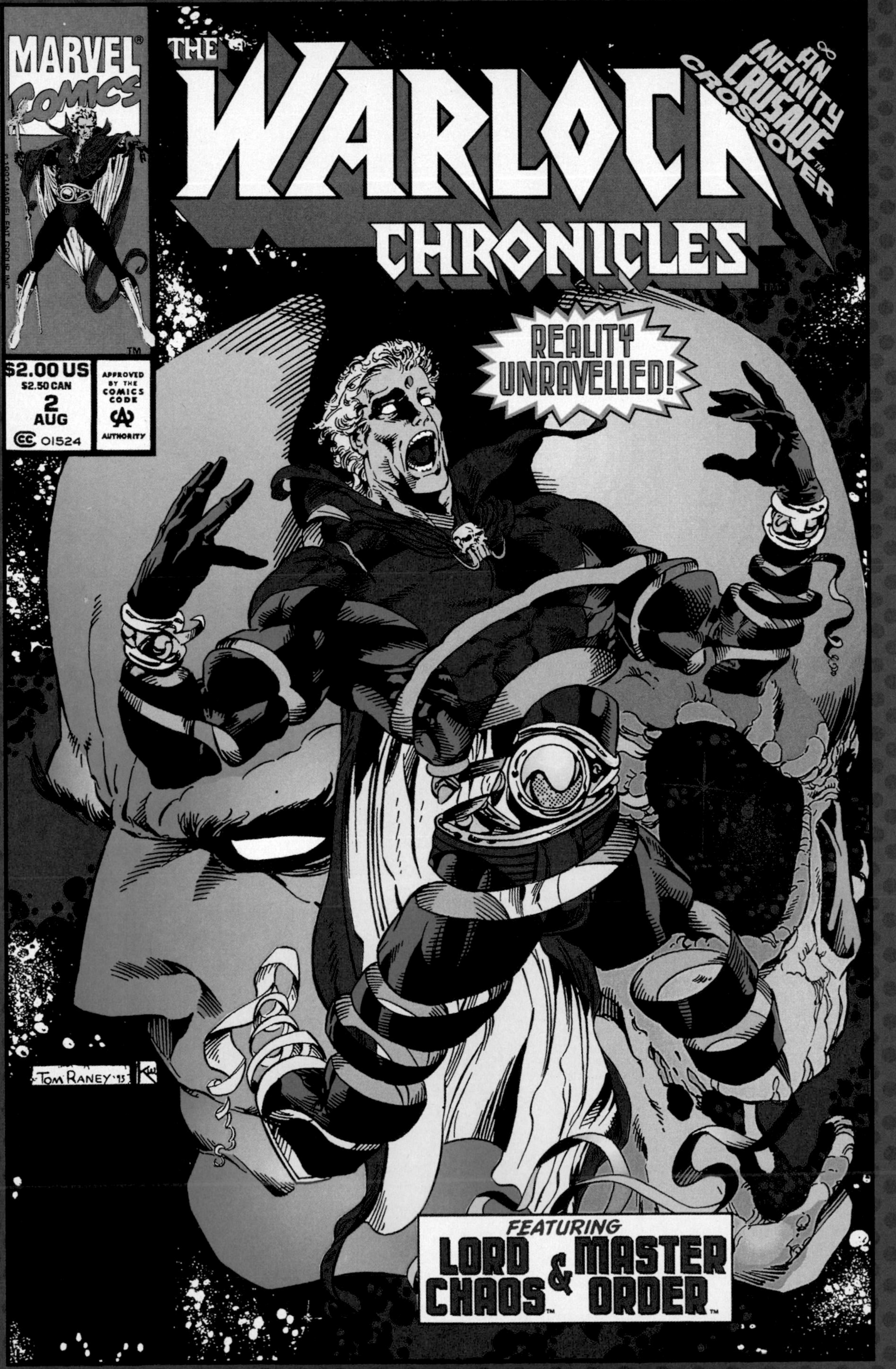
MARVEL COMICS
THE WARLOCK CHRONICLES
AN INFINITY CRUSADE CROSSOVER
$2.00 US
$2.50 CAN
2
AUG
01524
APPROVED BY THE COMICS CODE AUTHORITY
REALITY UNRAVELLED!
TOM RANEY '93
FEATURING
LORD CHAOS & MASTER ORDER

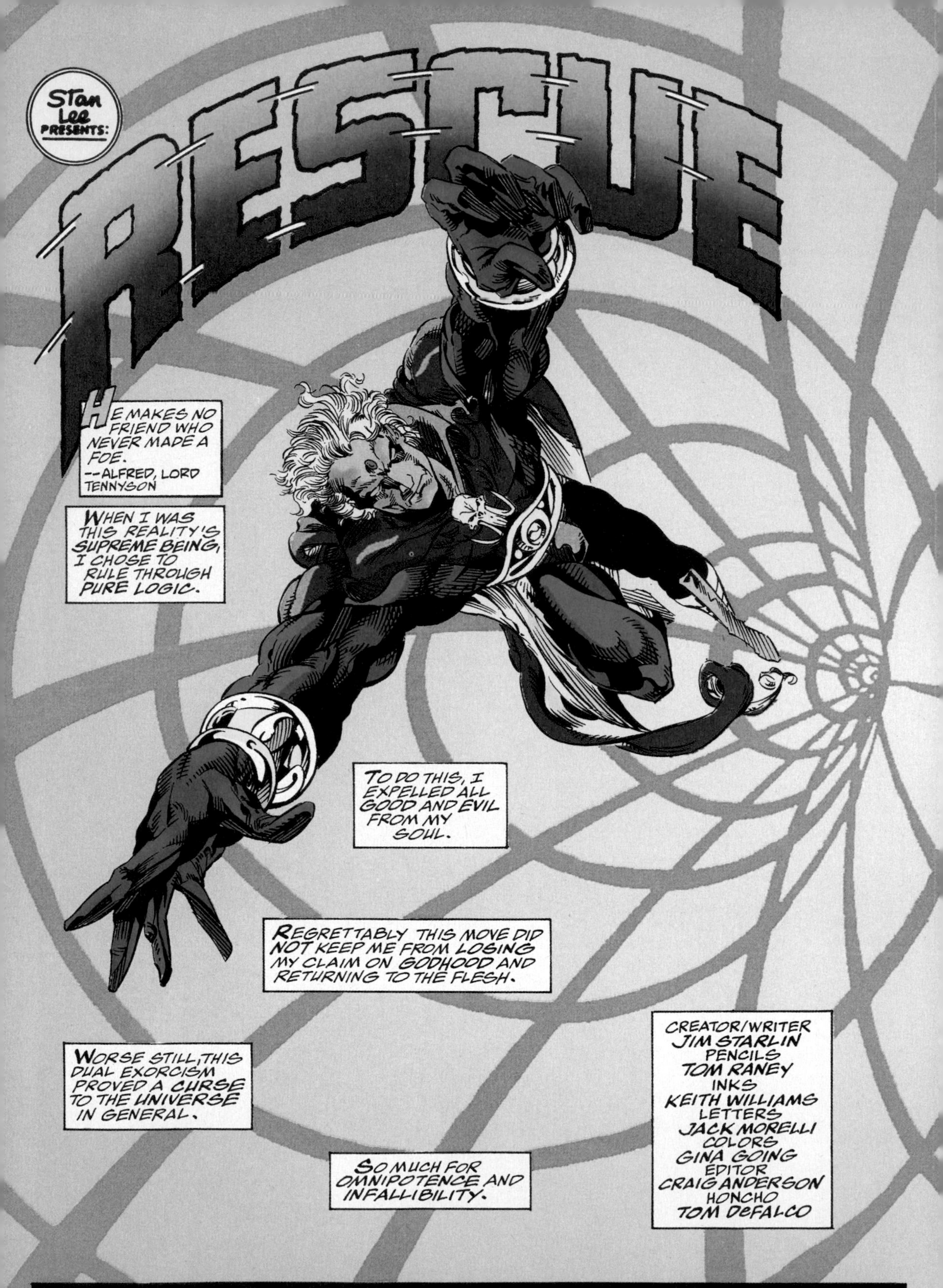
STAN LEE PRESENTS:
RESCUE
HE MAKES NO FRIEND WHO NEVER MADE A FOE.
--ALFRED, LORD TENNYSON
WHEN I WAS THIS REALITY'S SUPREME BEING, I CHOSE TO RULE THROUGH PURE LOGIC.
TO DO THIS, I EXPELLED ALL GOOD AND EVIL FROM MY SOUL.
REGRETTABLY THIS MOVE DID NOT KEEP ME FROM LOSING MY CLAIM ON GODHOOD AND RETURNING TO THE FLESH.
WORSE STILL, THIS DUAL EXORCISM PROVED A CURSE TO THE UNIVERSE IN GENERAL.
SO MUCH FOR OMNIPOTENCE AND INFALLIBILITY.
CREATOR/WRITER JIM STARLIN
PENCILS TOM RANEY
INKS KEITH WILLIAMS
LETTERS JACK MORELLI
COLORS GINA GOING
EDITOR CRAIG ANDERSON
HONCHO TOM DEFALCO

[redacted]

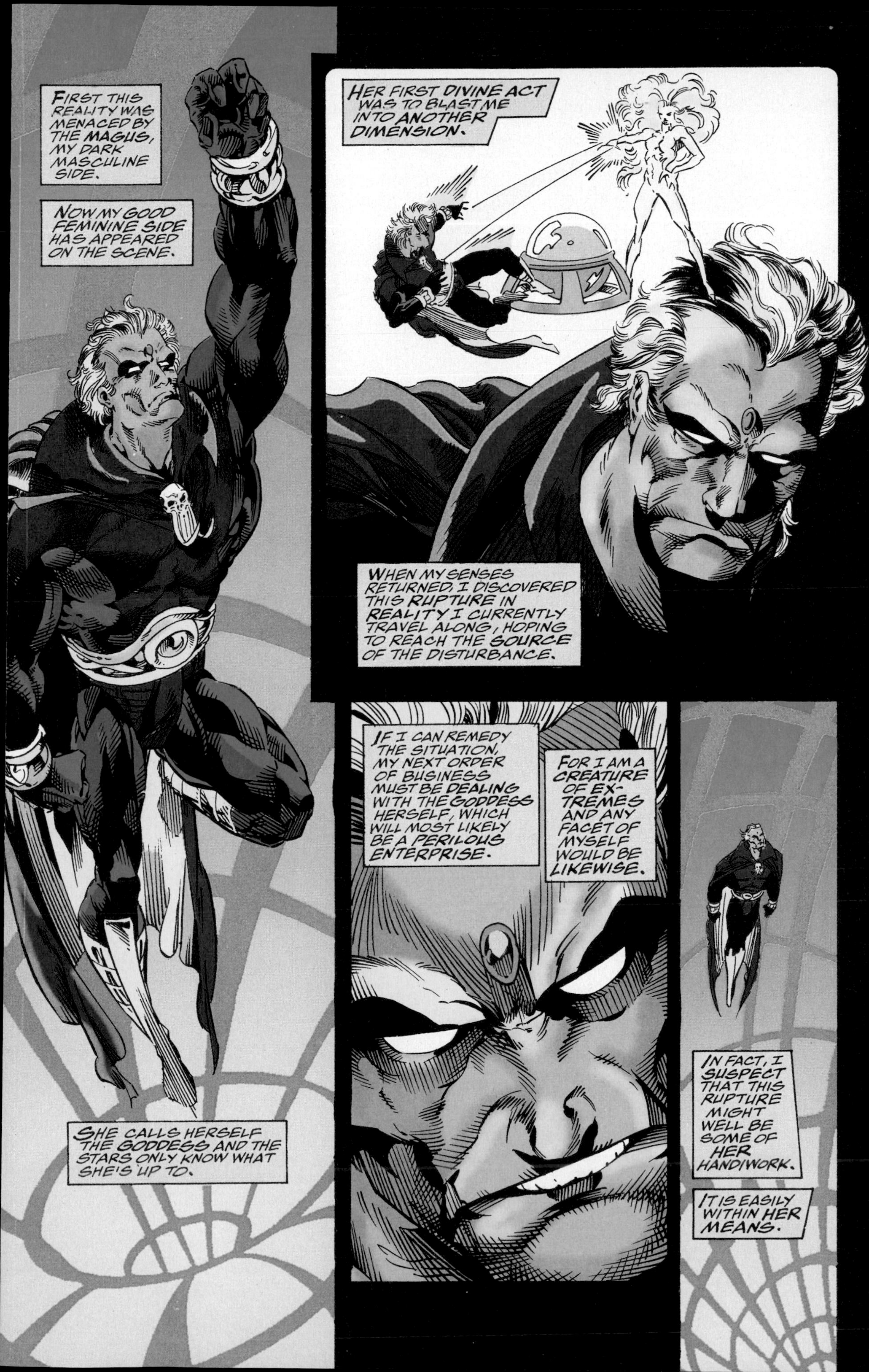

FIRST THIS REALITY WAS MENACED BY THE MAGUS, MY DARK MASCULINE SIDE.
NOW MY GOOD FEMININE SIDE HAS APPEARED ON THE SCENE.
SHE CALLS HERSELF THE GODDESS AND THE STARS ONLY KNOW WHAT SHE'S UP TO.
HER FIRST DIVINE ACT WAS TO BLAST ME INTO ANOTHER DIMENSION.
WHEN MY SENSES RETURNED, I DISCOVERED THIS RUPTURE IN REALITY I CURRENTLY TRAVEL ALONG, HOPING TO REACH THE SOURCE OF THE DISTURBANCE.
IF I CAN REMEDY THE SITUATION, MY NEXT ORDER OF BUSINESS MUST BE DEALING WITH THE GODDESS HERSELF, WHICH WILL MOST LIKELY BE A PERILOUS ENTERPRISE.
FOR I AM A CREATURE OF EX-TREMES AND ANY FACET OF MYSELF WOULD BE LIKEWISE.
IN FACT, I SUSPECT THAT THIS RUPTURE MIGHT WELL BE SOME OF HER HANDIWORK.
IT IS EASILY WITHIN HER MEANS.

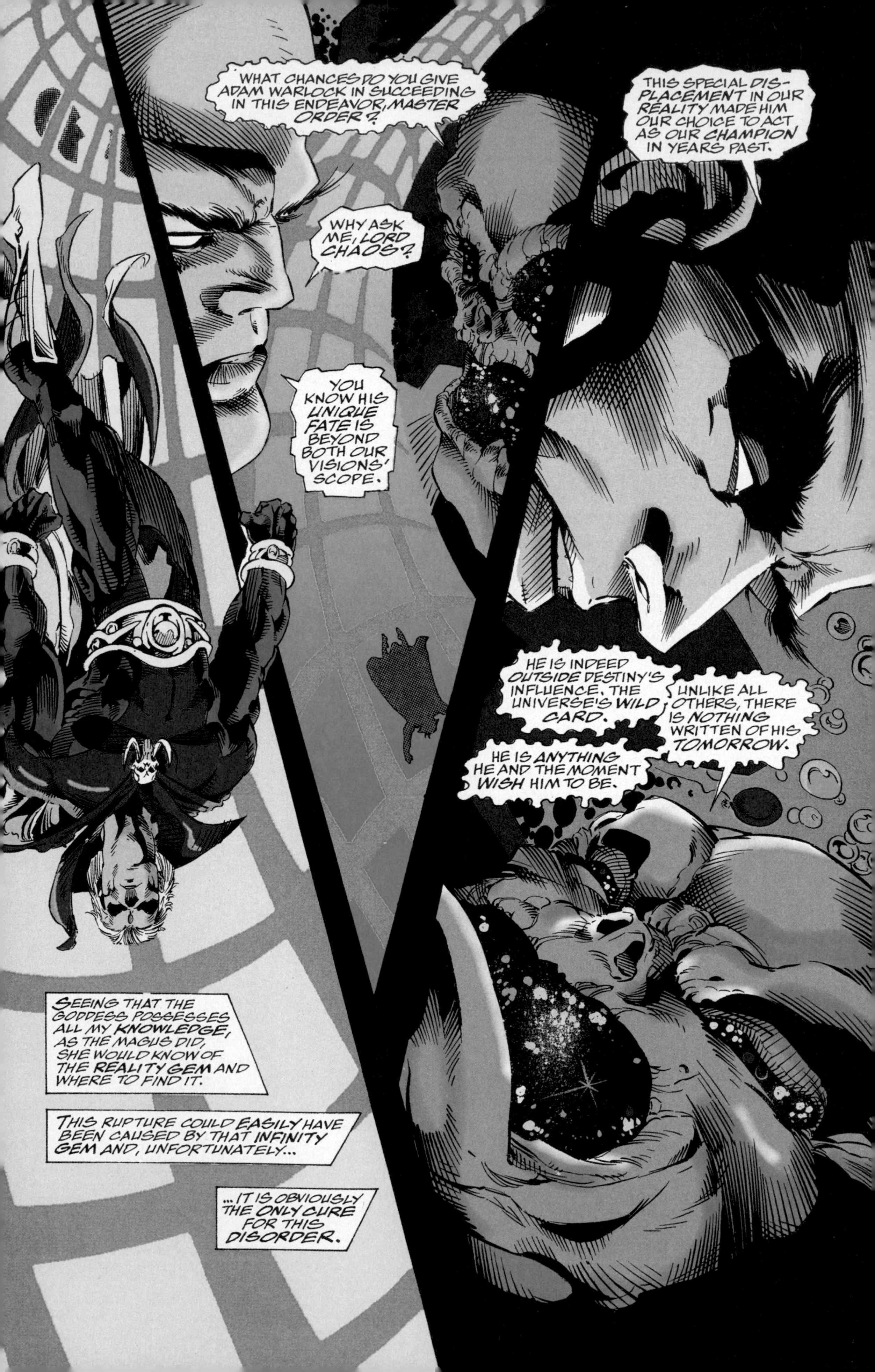
WHAT CHANCES DO YOU GIVE ADAM WARLOCK IN SUCCEEDING IN THIS ENDEAVOR, MASTER ORDER ?
WHY ASK ME, LORD CHAOS ?
YOU KNOW HIS UNIQUE FATE IS BEYOND BOTH OUR VISIONS' SCOPE.
THIS SPECIAL DISPLACEMENT IN OUR REALITY MADE HIM OUR CHOICE TO ACT AS OUR CHAMPION IN YEARS PAST.
HE IS INDEED OUTSIDE DESTINY'S INFLUENCE, THE UNIVERSE'S WILD CARD.
UNLIKE ALL OTHERS, THERE IS NOTHING WRITTEN OF HIS TOMORROW.
HE IS ANYTHING HE AND THE MOMENT WISH HIM TO BE.
SEEING THAT THE GODDESS POSSESSES ALL MY KNOWLEDGE, AS THE MAGUS DID, SHE WOULD KNOW OF THE REALITY GEM AND WHERE TO FIND IT.
THIS RUPTURE COULD EASILY HAVE BEEN CAUSED BY THAT INFINITY GEM AND, UNFORTUNATELY...
...IT IS OBVIOUSLY THE ONLY CURE FOR THIS DISORDER.

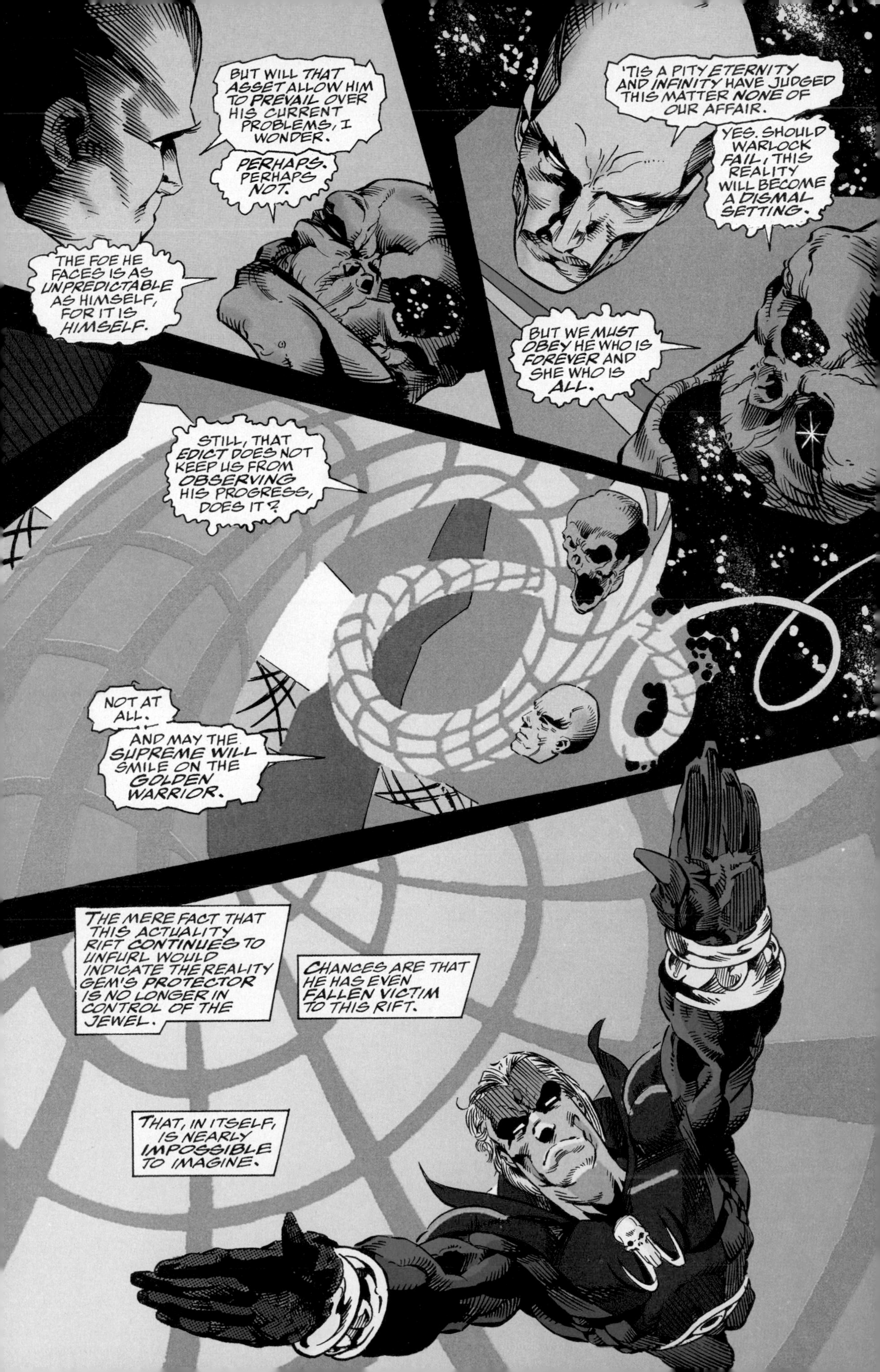
BUT WILL THAT ASSET ALLOW HIM TO PREVAIL OVER HIS CURRENT PROBLEMS, I WONDER.
PERHAPS. PERHAPS NOT.
THE FOE HE FACES IS AS UNPREDICTABLE AS HIMSELF, FOR IT IS HIMSELF.
'TIS A PITY ETERNITY AND INFINITY HAVE JUDGED THIS MATTER NONE OF OUR AFFAIR.
YES. SHOULD WARLOCK FAIL, THIS REALITY WILL BECOME A DISMAL SETTING.
BUT WE MUST OBEY HE WHO IS FOREVER AND SHE WHO IS ALL.
STILL, THAT EDICT DOES NOT KEEP US FROM OBSERVING HIS PROGRESS, DOES IT?
NOT AT ALL.
AND MAY THE SUPREME WILL SMILE ON THE GOLDEN WARRIOR.
THE MERE FACT THAT THIS ACTUALITY RIFT CONTINUES TO UNFURL WOULD INDICATE THE REALITY GEM'S PROTECTOR IS NO LONGER IN CONTROL OF THE JEWEL.
CHANCES ARE THAT HE HAS EVEN FALLEN VICTIM TO THIS RIFT.
THAT, IN ITSELF, IS NEARLY IMPOSSIBLE TO IMAGINE.

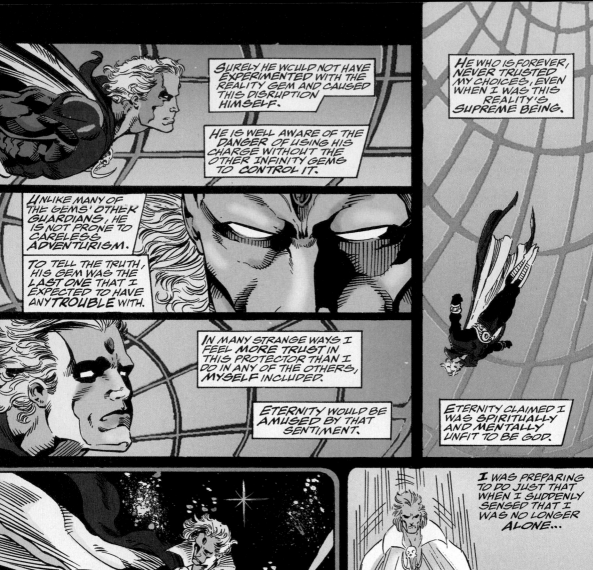

SURELY HE WOULD NOT HAVE EXPERIMENTED WITH THE REALITY GEM AND CAUSED THIS DISRUPTION HIMSELF.

HE IS WELL AWARE OF THE DANGER OF USING HIS CHARGE WITHOUT THE OTHER INFINITY GEMS TO CONTROL IT.

UNLIKE MANY OF THE GEMS' OTHER GUARDIANS, HE IS NOT PRONE TO CARELESS ADVENTURISM.

TO TELL THE TRUTH, HIS GEM WAS THE LAST ONE THAT I EXPECTED TO HAVE ANY TROUBLE WITH.

IN MANY STRANGE WAYS I FEEL MORE TRUST IN THIS PROTECTOR THAN I DO IN ANY OF THE OTHERS, MYSELF INCLUDED.

ETERNITY WOULD BE AMUSED BY THAT SENTIMENT.

HE WHO IS FOREVER, NEVER TRUSTED MY CHOICES, EVEN WHEN I WAS THIS REALITY'S SUPREME BEING.

ETERNITY CLAIMED I WAS SPIRITUALLY AND MENTALLY UNFIT TO BE GOD.

I WAS CALLED TO JUDGMENT BY THE LIVING TRIBUNAL, THE SERVANT OF THE ONE WHO IS ABOVE EVEN GODS.

THE VERDICT WENT AGAINST ME AND I WAS ORDERED TO DIVEST MYSELF OF FIVE OF SIX INFINITY GEMS IN MY CARE.

I WAS PREPARING TO DO JUST THAT WHEN I SUDDENLY SENSED THAT I WAS NO LONGER ALONE...

SHOW YOUR-SELF--

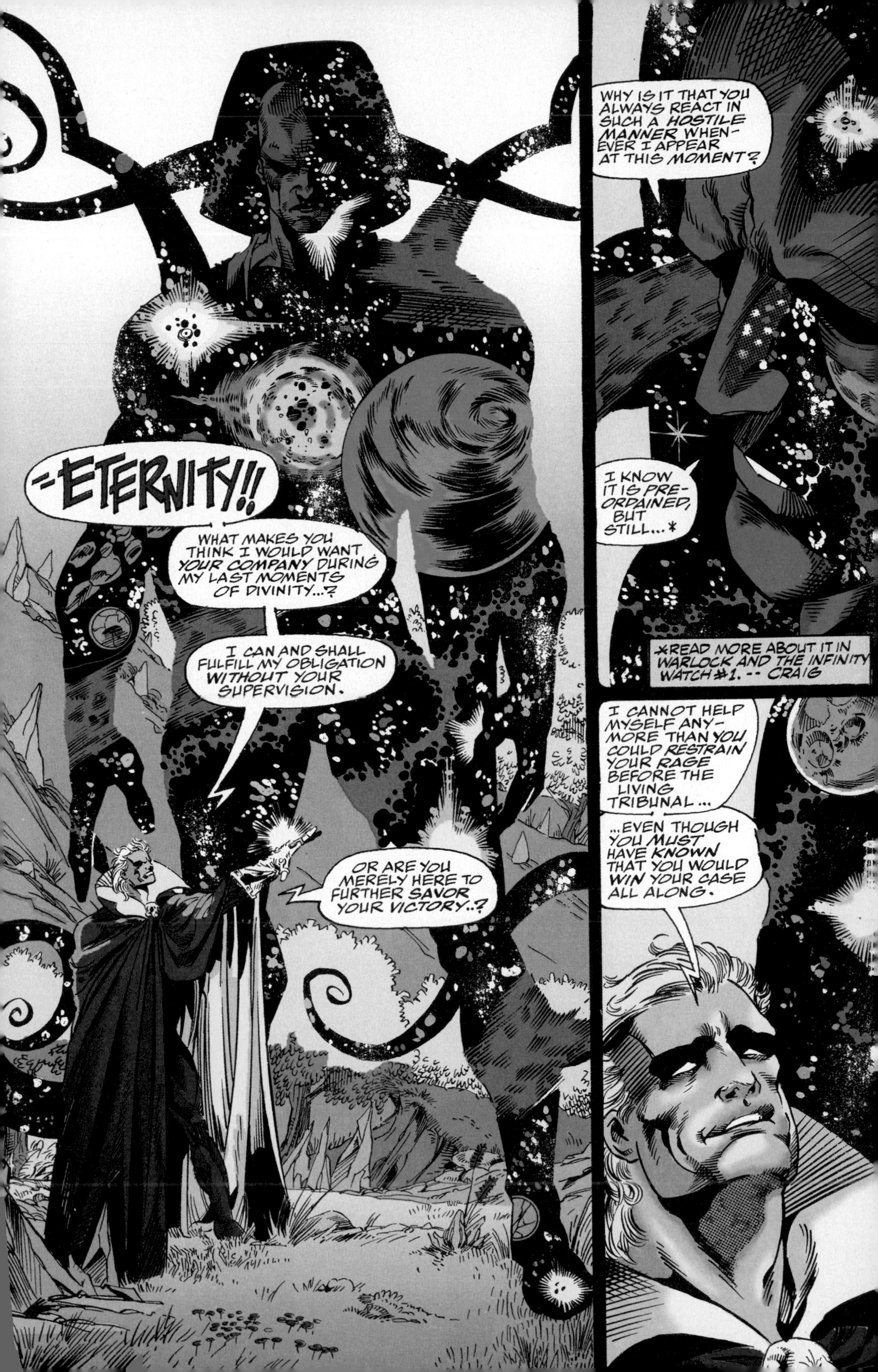

-ETERNITY!!
WHAT MAKES YOU THINK I WOULD WANT YOUR COMPANY DURING MY LAST MOMENTS OF DIVINITY...?
I CAN AND SHALL FULFILL MY OBLIGATION WITHOUT YOUR SUPERVISION.
OR ARE YOU MERELY HERE TO FURTHER SAVOR YOUR VICTORY..?
WHY IS IT THAT YOU ALWAYS REACT IN SUCH A HOSTILE MANNER WHEN-EVER I APPEAR AT THIS MOMENT?
I KNOW IT IS PRE-ORDAINED, BUT STILL...*
*READ MORE ABOUT IT IN WARLOCK AND THE INFINITY WATCH #1. -- CRAIG
I CANNOT HELP MYSELF ANY-MORE THAN YOU COULD RESTRAIN YOUR RAGE BEFORE THE LIVING TRIBUNAL...
...EVEN THOUGH YOU MUST HAVE KNOWN THAT YOU WOULD WIN YOUR CASE ALL ALONG.

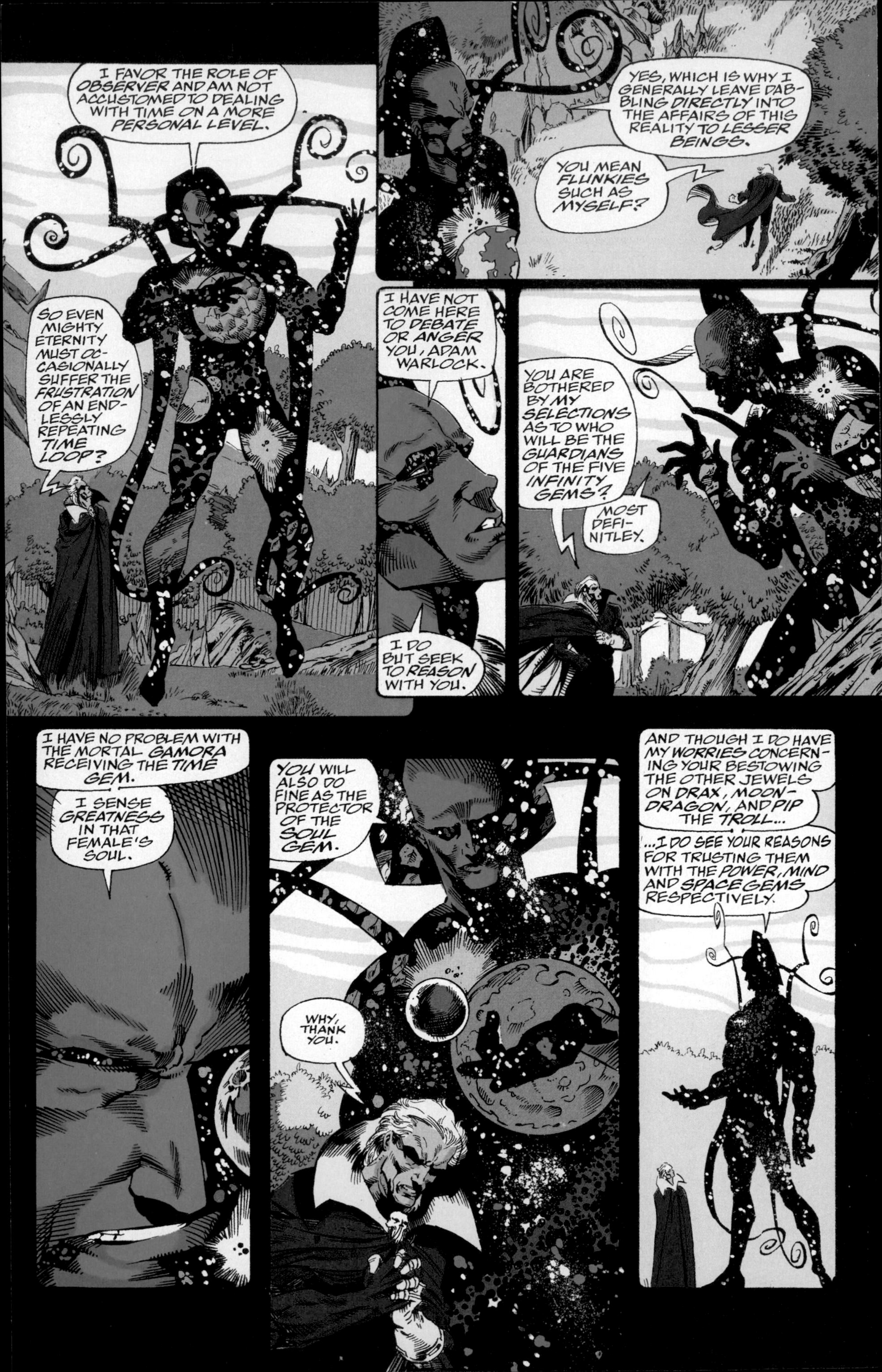
I FAVOR THE ROLE OF OBSERVER AND AM NOT ACCUSTOMED TO DEALING WITH TIME ON A MORE PERSONAL LEVEL.
SO EVEN MIGHTY ETERNITY MUST OCCASIONALLY SUFFER THE FRUSTRATION OF AN ENDLESSLY REPEATING TIME LOOP?
YES, WHICH IS WHY I GENERALLY LEAVE DABBLING DIRECTLY INTO THE AFFAIRS OF THIS REALITY TO LESSER BEINGS.
YOU MEAN FLUNKIES SUCH AS MYSELF?
I HAVE NOT COME HERE TO DEBATE OR ANGER YOU, ADAM WARLOCK.
I DO BUT SEEK TO REASON WITH YOU.
YOU ARE BOTHERED BY MY SELECTIONS AS TO WHO WILL BE THE GUARDIANS OF THE FIVE INFINITY GEMS?
MOST DEFINITLEY.
I HAVE NO PROBLEM WITH THE MORTAL GAMORA RECEIVING THE TIME GEM.
I SENSE GREATNESS IN THAT FEMALE'S SOUL.
YOU WILL ALSO DO FINE AS THE PROTECTOR OF THE SOUL GEM.
WHY, THANK YOU.
AND THOUGH I DO HAVE MY WORRIES CONCERNING YOUR BESTOWING THE OTHER JEWELS ON DRAX, MOONDRAGON, AND PIP THE TROLL...
...I DO SEE YOUR REASONS FOR TRUSTING THEM WITH THE POWER, MIND AND SPACE GEMS RESPECTIVELY.

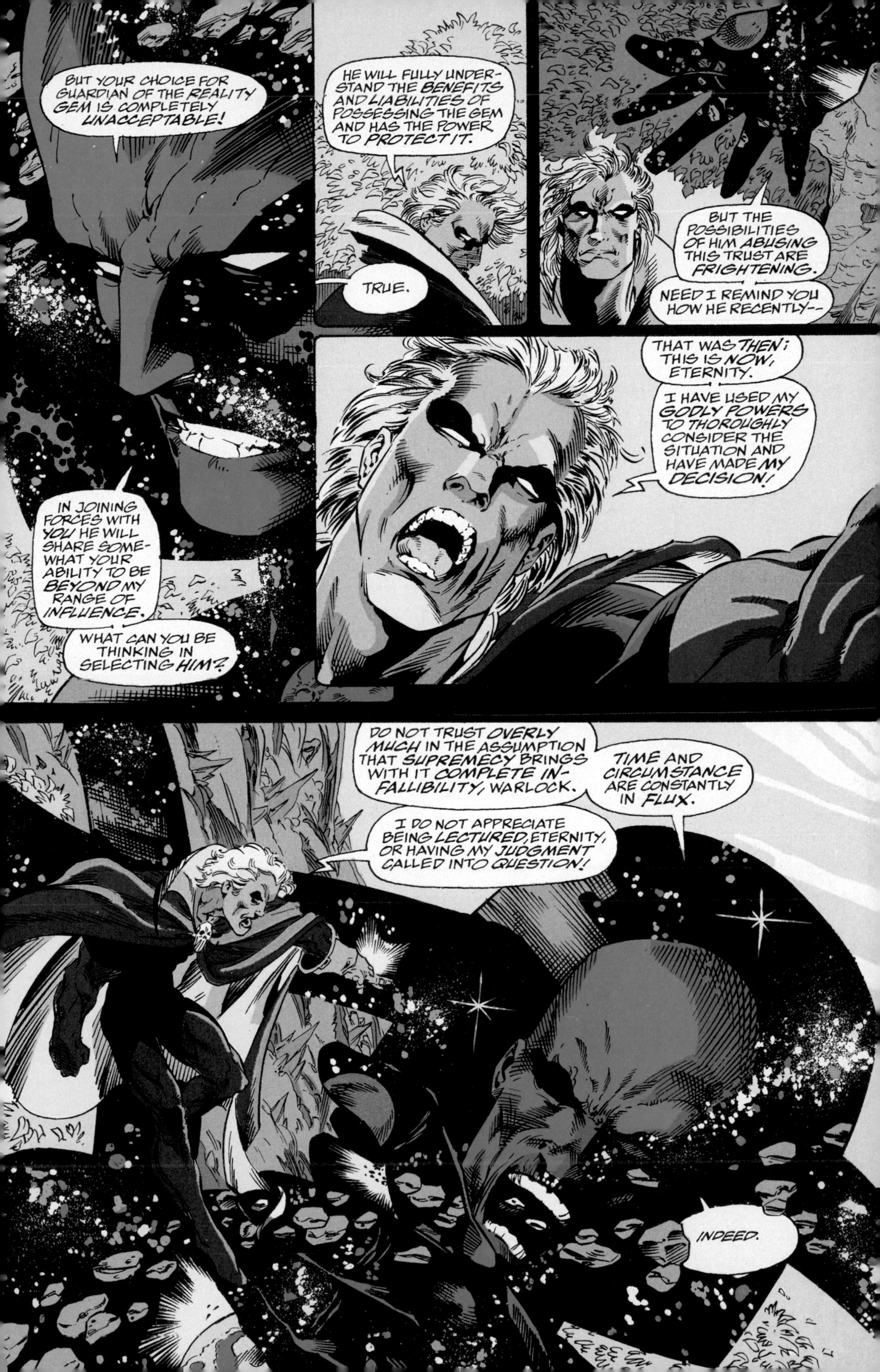
BUT YOUR CHOICE FOR GUARDIAN OF THE REALITY GEM IS COMPLETELY UNACCEPTABLE!
HE WILL FULLY UNDERSTAND THE BENEFITS AND LIABILITIES OF POSSESSING THE GEM AND HAS THE POWER TO PROTECT IT.
TRUE.
BUT THE POSSIBILITIES OF HIM ABUSING THIS TRUST ARE FRIGHTENING.
NEED I REMIND YOU HOW HE RECENTLY--
IN JOINING FORCES WITH YOU HE WILL SHARE SOME-WHAT YOUR ABILITY TO BE BEYOND MY RANGE OF INFLUENCE.
WHAT CAN YOU BE THINKING IN SELECTING HIM?
THAT WAS THEN; THIS IS NOW, ETERNITY.
I HAVE USED MY GODLY POWERS TO THOROUGHLY CONSIDER THE SITUATION AND HAVE MADE MY DECISION!
DO NOT TRUST OVERLY MUCH IN THE ASSUMPTION THAT SUPREMECY BRINGS WITH IT COMPLETE IN-FALLIBILITY, WARLOCK.
TIME AND CIRCUMSTANCE ARE CONSTANTLY IN FLUX.
I DO NOT APPRECIATE BEING LECTURED, ETERNITY, OR HAVING MY JUDGMENT CALLED INTO QUESTION!
INDEED.

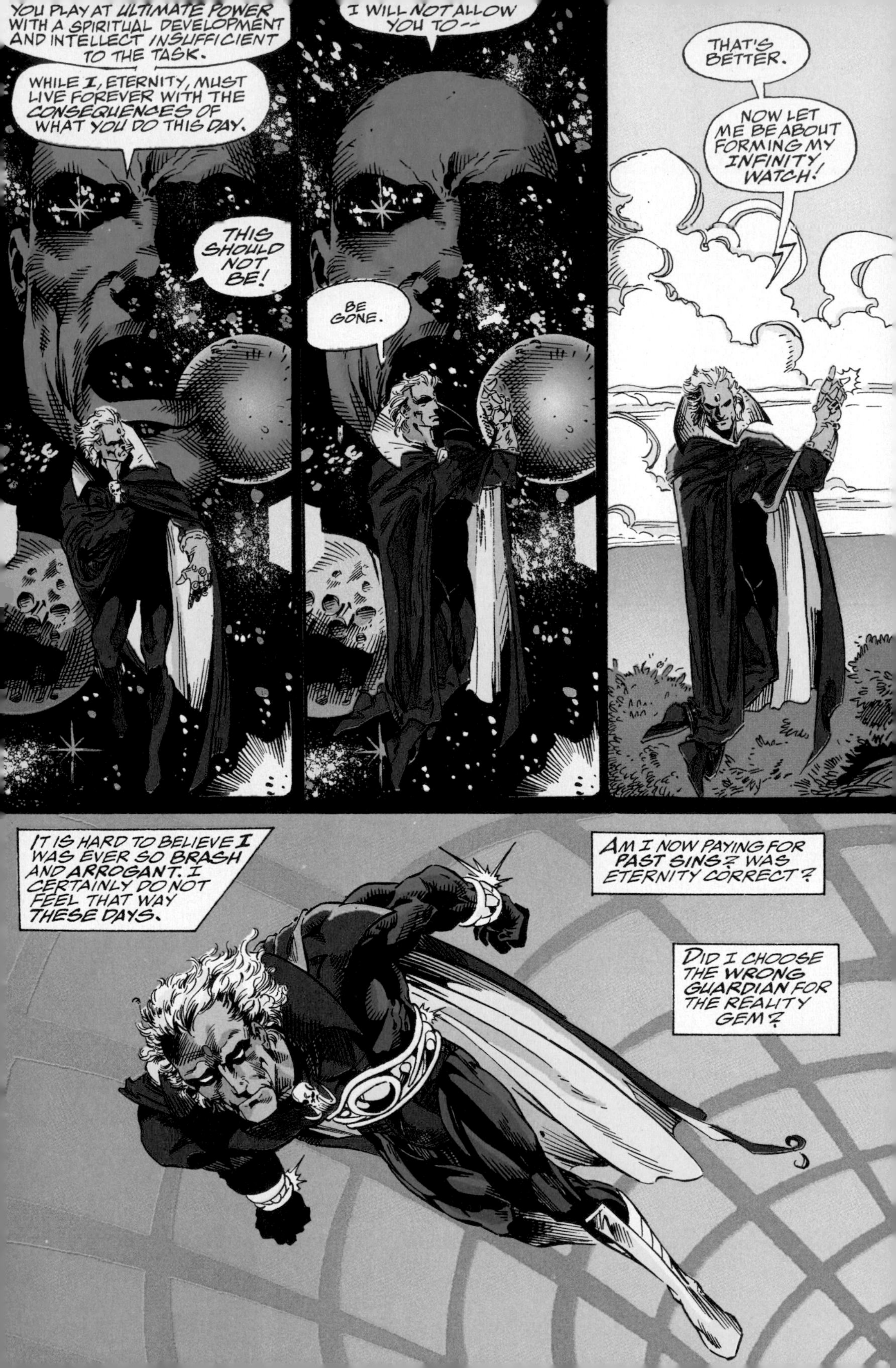
YOU PLAY AT ULTIMATE POWER WITH A SPIRITUAL DEVELOPMENT AND INTELLECT INSUFFICIENT TO THE TASK.
WHILE I, ETERNITY, MUST LIVE FOREVER WITH THE CONSEQUENCES OF WHAT YOU DO THIS DAY.
THIS SHOULD NOT BE!
I WILL NOT ALLOW YOU TO--
BE GONE.
THAT'S BETTER.
NOW LET ME BE ABOUT FORMING MY INFINITY WATCH!
IT IS HARD TO BELIEVE I WAS EVER SO BRASH AND ARROGANT. I CERTAINLY DO NOT FEEL THAT WAY THESE DAYS.
AM I NOW PAYING FOR PAST SINS? WAS ETERNITY CORRECT?
DID I CHOOSE THE WRONG GUARDIAN FOR THE REALITY GEM?

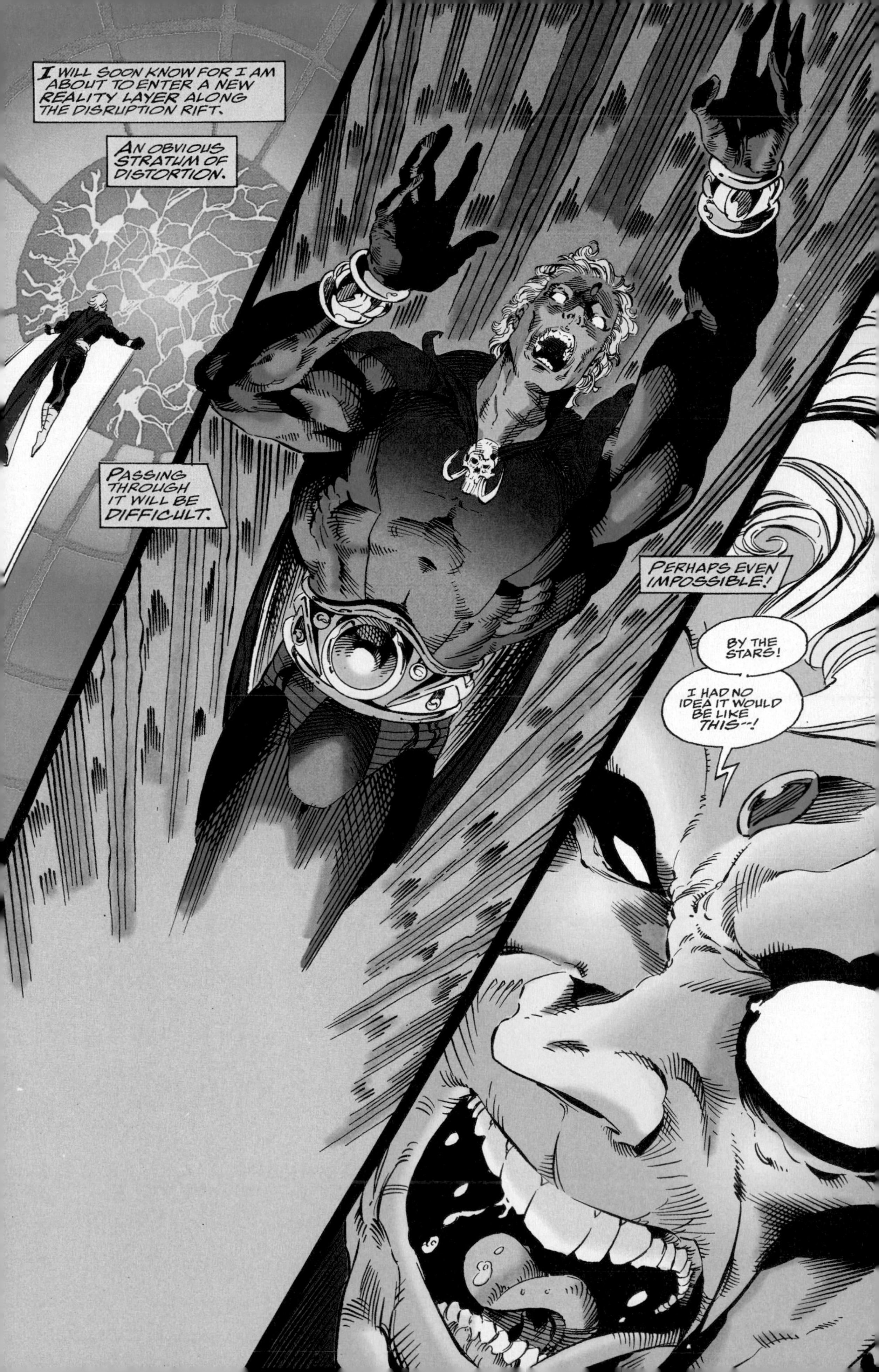

I WILL SOON KNOW FOR I AM ABOUT TO ENTER A NEW REALITY LAYER ALONG THE DISRUPTION RIFT.
AN OBVIOUS STRATUM OF DISTORTION.
PASSING THROUGH IT WILL BE DIFFICULT.
PERHAPS EVEN IMPOSSIBLE!
BY THE STARS!
I HAD NO IDEA IT WOULD BE LIKE THIS--!

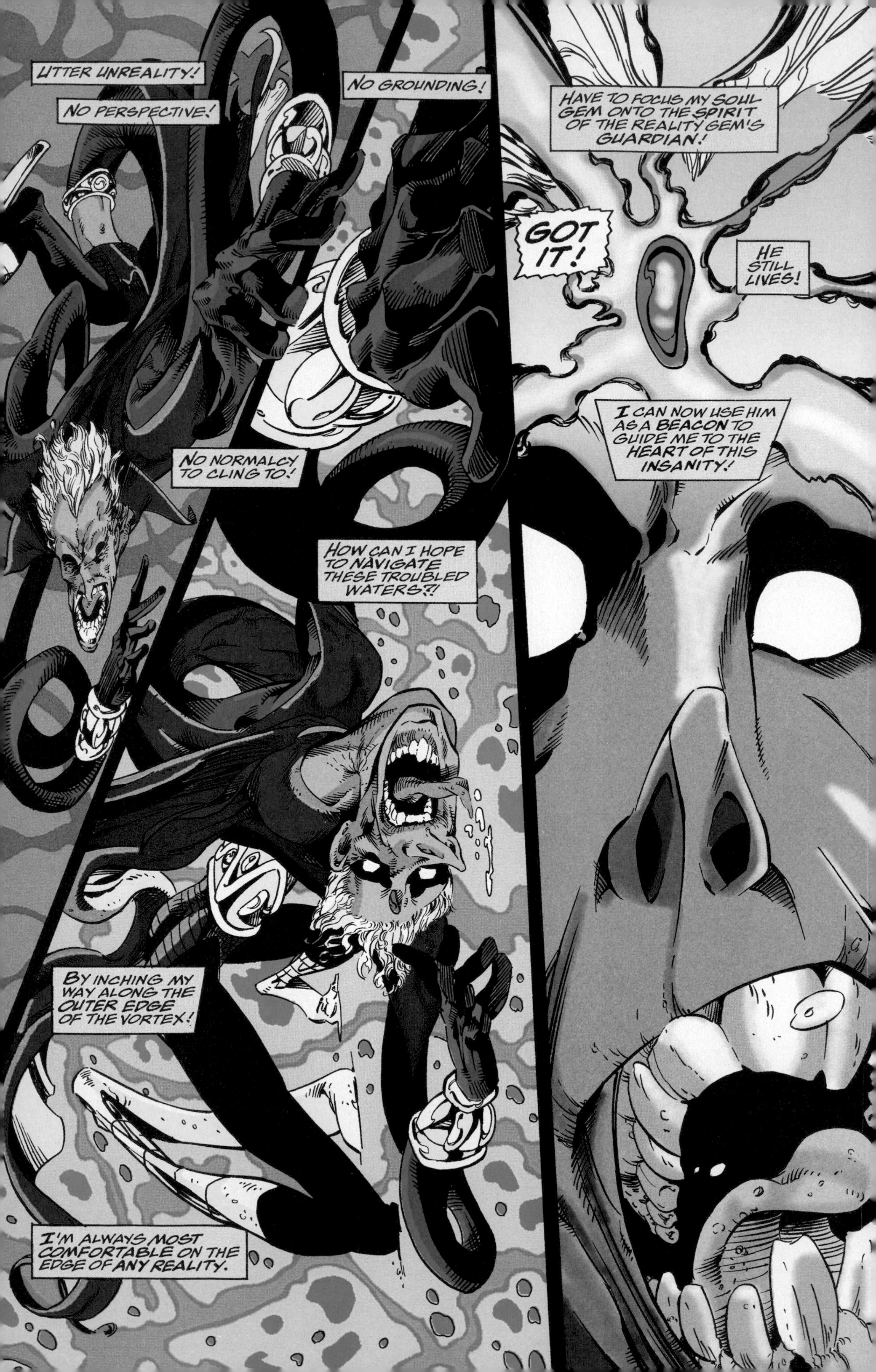
UTTER UNREALITY!
NO PERSPECTIVE!
NO GROUNDING!
NO NORMALCY TO CLING TO!
HOW CAN I HOPE TO NAVIGATE THESE TROUBLED WATERS?!
BY INCHING MY WAY ALONG THE OUTER EDGE OF THE VORTEX!
I'M ALWAYS MOST COMFORTABLE ON THE EDGE OF ANY REALITY.
HAVE TO FOCUS MY SOUL GEM ONTO THE SPIRIT OF THE REALITY GEM'S GUARDIAN!
GOT IT!
HE STILL LIVES!
I CAN NOW USE HIM AS A BEACON TO GUIDE ME TO THE HEART OF THIS INSANITY!

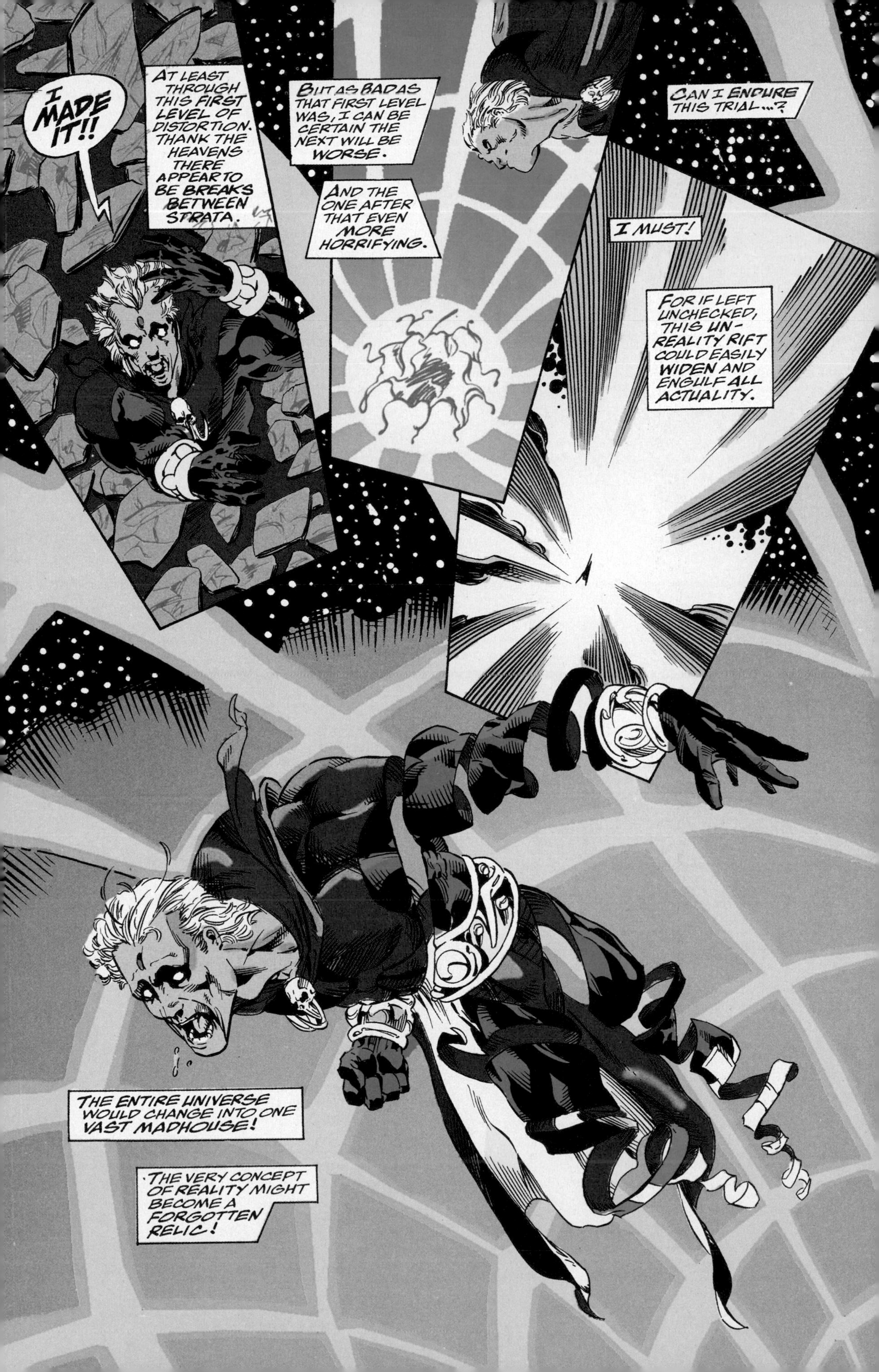
I MADE IT!!
AT LEAST THROUGH THIS FIRST LEVEL OF DISTORTION. THANK THE HEAVENS THERE APPEAR TO BE BREAKS BETWEEN STRATA.
BUT AS BAD AS THAT FIRST LEVEL WAS, I CAN BE CERTAIN THE NEXT WILL BE WORSE.
AND THE ONE AFTER THAT EVEN MORE HORRIFYING.
CAN I ENDURE THIS TRIAL...?
I MUST!
FOR IF LEFT UNCHECKED, THIS UN-REALITY RIFT COULD EASILY WIDEN AND ENGULF ALL ACTUALITY.
THE ENTIRE UNIVERSE WOULD CHANGE INTO ONE VAST MADHOUSE!
THE VERY CONCEPT OF REALITY MIGHT BECOME A FORGOTTEN RELIC!

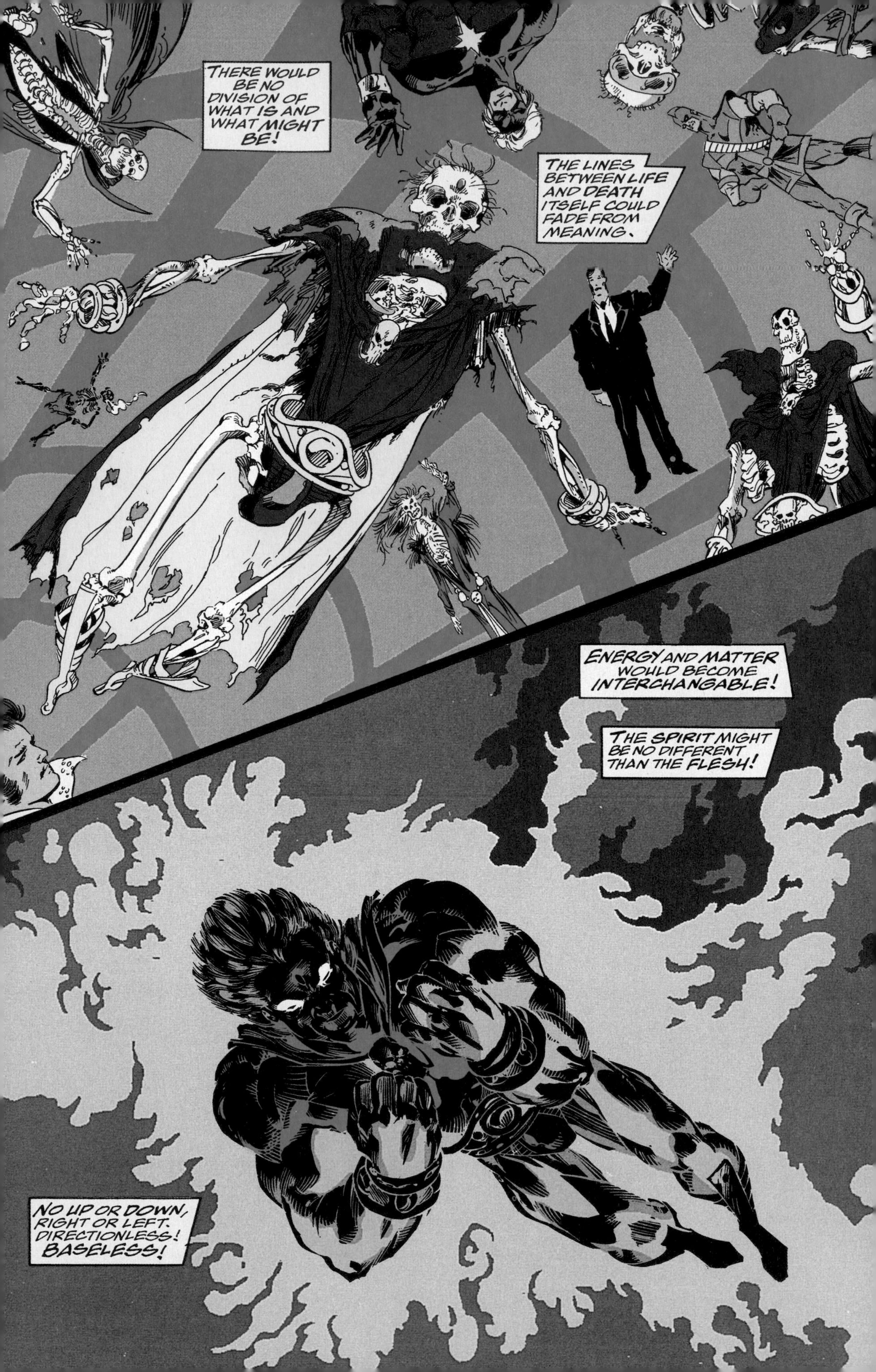
THERE WOULD BE NO DIVISION OF WHAT IS AND WHAT MIGHT BE!
THE LINES BETWEEN LIFE AND DEATH ITSELF COULD FADE FROM MEANING.
ENERGY AND MATTER WOULD BECOME INTERCHANGABLE!
THE SPIRIT MIGHT BE NO DIFFERENT THAN THE FLESH!
NO UP OR DOWN, RIGHT OR LEFT. DIRECTIONLESS! BASELESS!

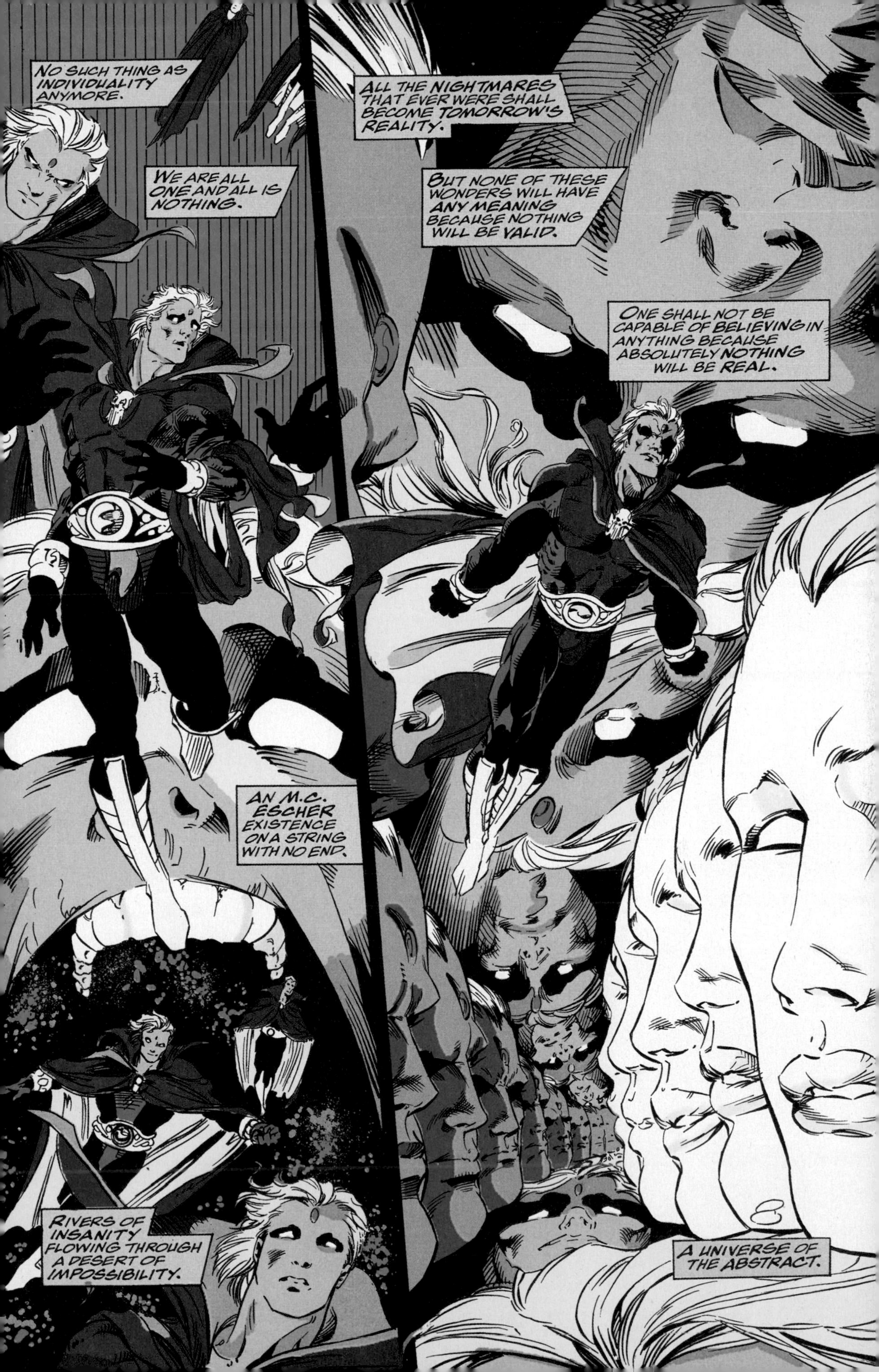
NO SUCH THING AS INDIVIDUALITY ANYMORE.
WE ARE ALL ONE AND ALL IS NOTHING.
AN M.C. ESCHER EXISTENCE ON A STRING WITH NO END.
RIVERS OF INSANITY FLOWING THROUGH A DESERT OF IMPOSSIBILITY.
ALL THE NIGHTMARES THAT EVER WERE SHALL BECOME TOMORROW'S REALITY.
BUT NONE OF THESE WONDERS WILL HAVE ANY MEANING BECAUSE NOTHING WILL BE VALID.
ONE SHALL NOT BE CAPABLE OF BELIEVING IN ANYTHING BECAUSE ABSOLUTELY NOTHING WILL BE REAL.
A UNIVERSE OF THE ABSTRACT.

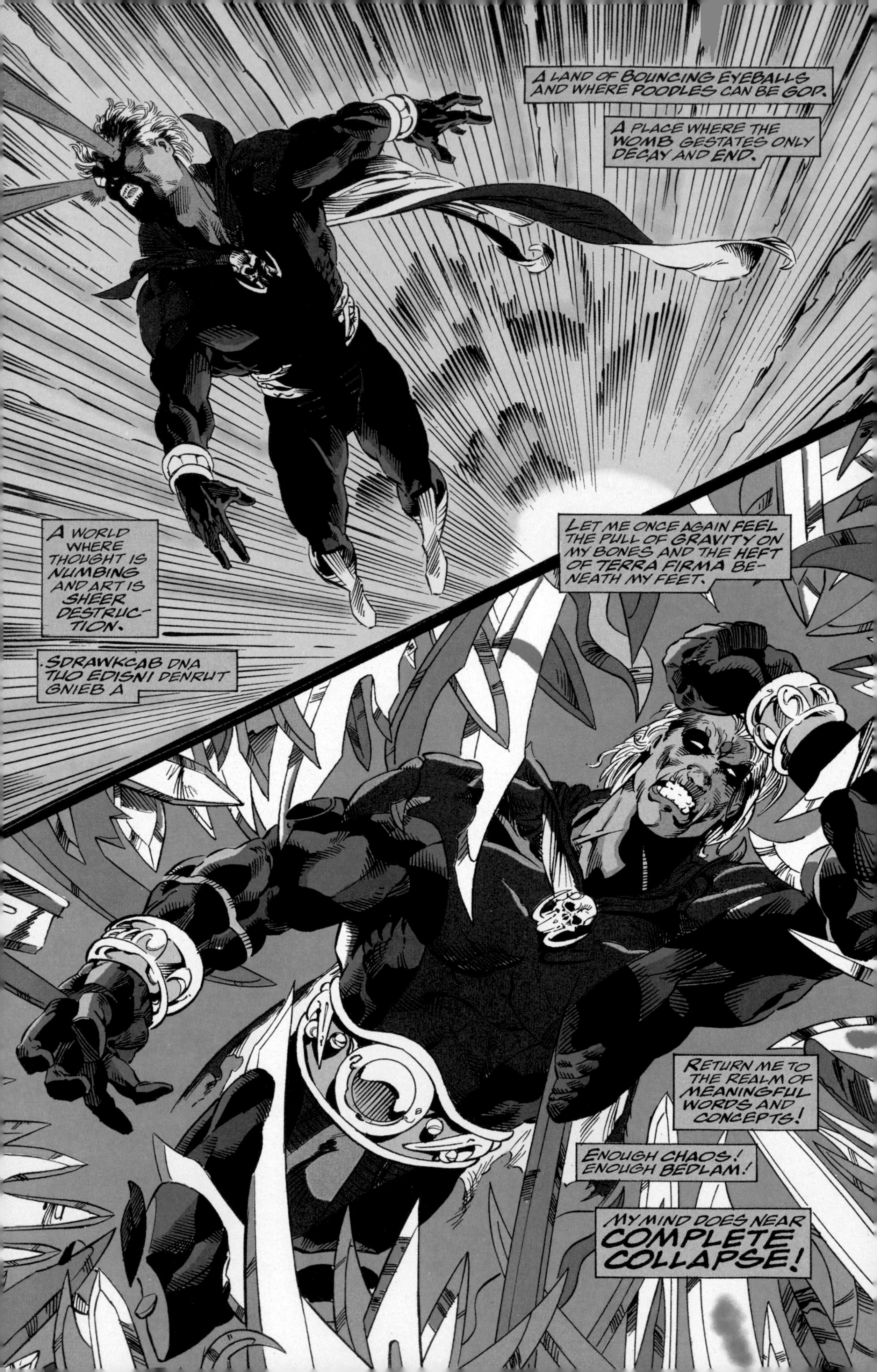
A LAND OF BOUNCING EYEBALLS AND WHERE POODLES CAN BE GOD.
A PLACE WHERE THE WOMB GESTATES ONLY DECAY AND END.
A WORLD WHERE THOUGHT IS NUMBING AND ART IS SHEER DESTRUCTION.
.SDRAWKCAB DNA TUO EDISNI DENRUT GNIEB A
LET ME ONCE AGAIN FEEL THE PULL OF GRAVITY ON MY BONES AND THE HEFT OF TERRA FIRMA BENEATH MY FEET.
RETURN ME TO THE REALM OF MEANINGFUL WORDS AND CONCEPTS!
ENOUGH CHAOS! ENOUGH BEDLAM!
MY MIND DOES NEAR COMPLETE COLLAPSE!

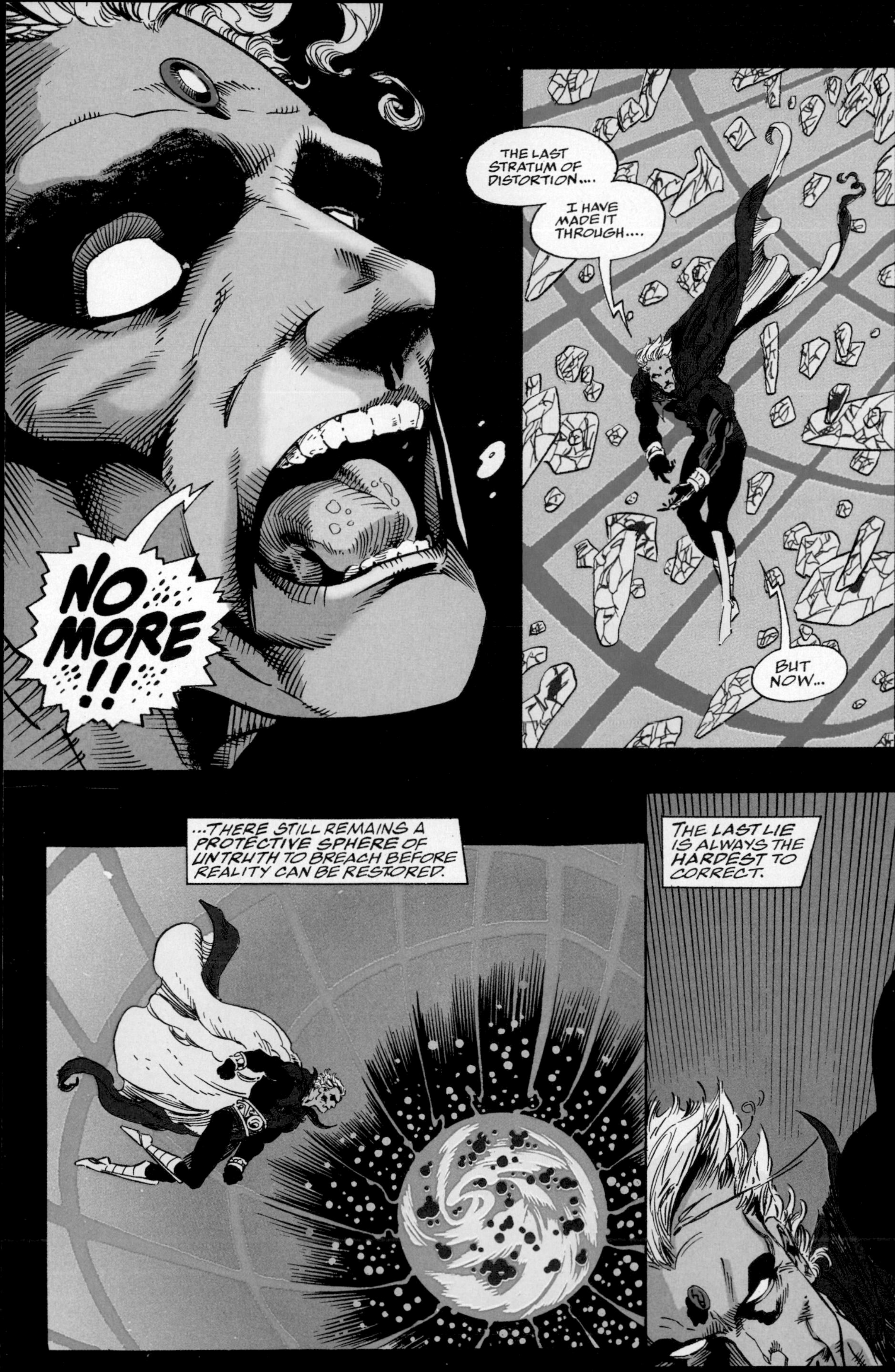
NO MORE!!
THE LAST STRATUM OF DISTORTION....
I HAVE MADE IT THROUGH....
BUT NOW...
...THERE STILL REMAINS A PROTECTIVE SPHERE OF UNTRUTH TO BREACH BEFORE REALITY CAN BE RESTORED.
THE LAST LIE IS ALWAYS THE HARDEST TO CORRECT.

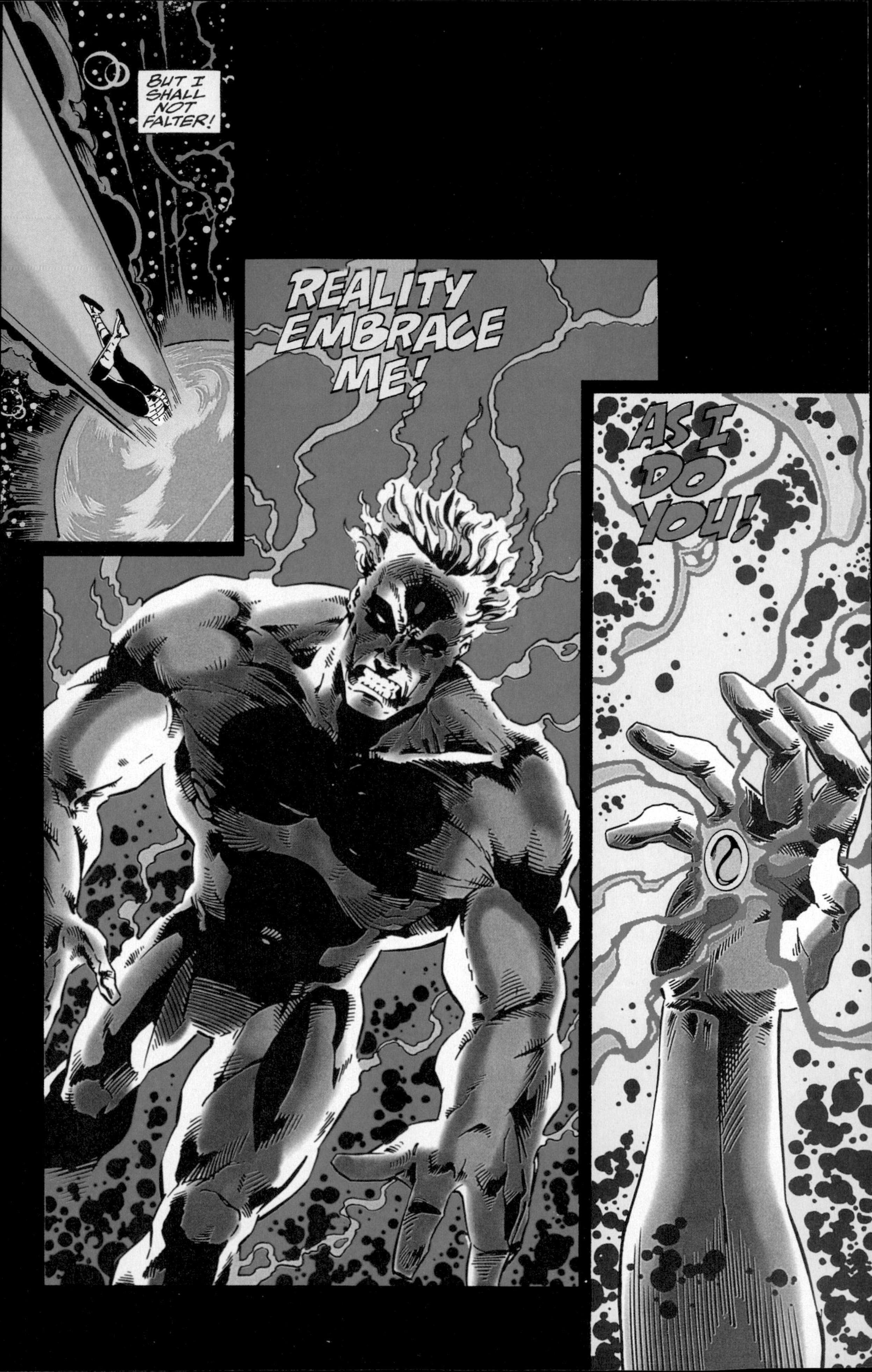
BUT I SHALL NOT FALTER!
REALITY EMBRACE ME!
AS I DO YOU!

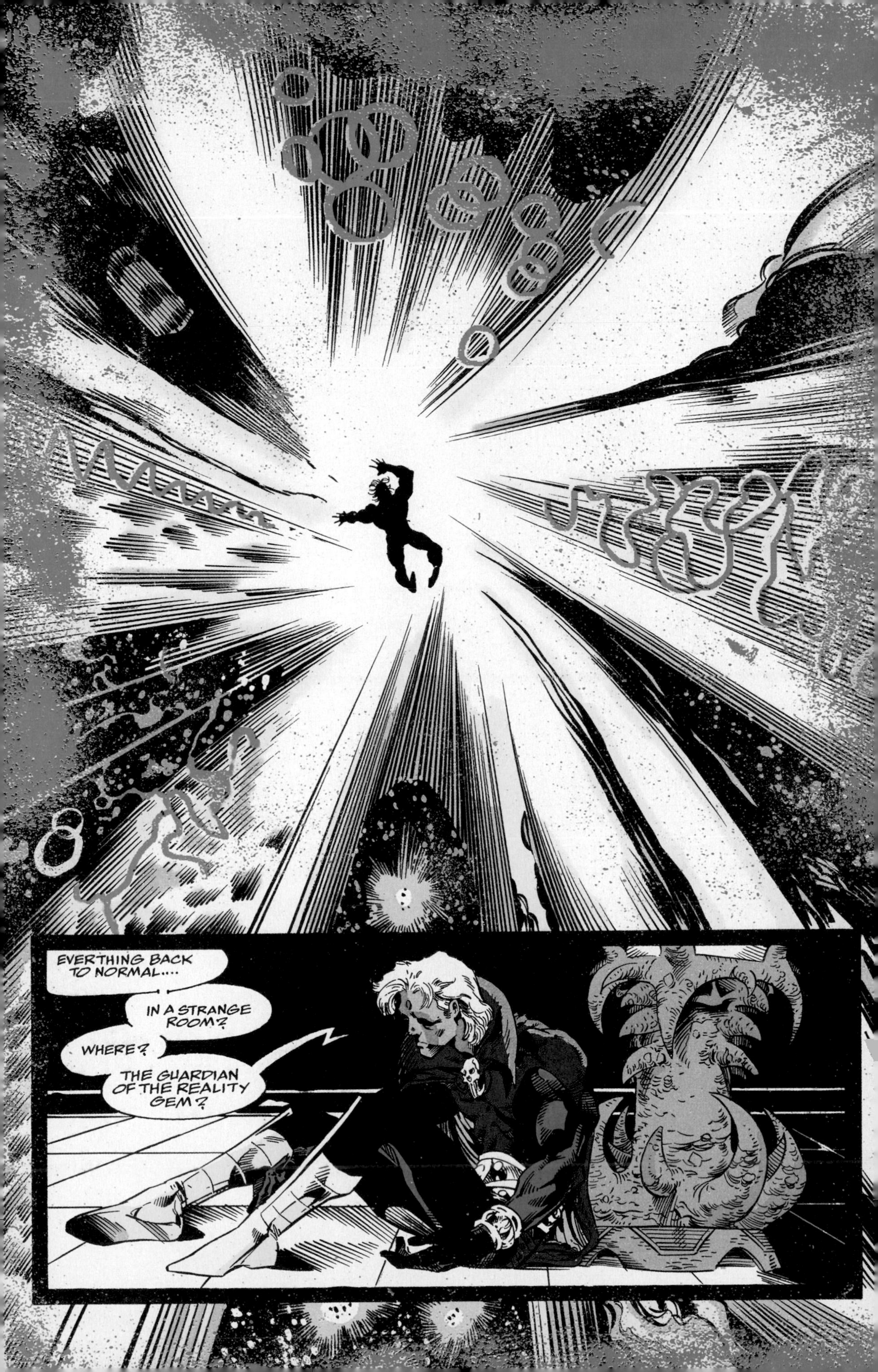
EVERTHING BACK TO NORMAL....
IN A STRANGE ROOM?
WHERE?
THE GUARDIAN OF THE REALITY GEM?

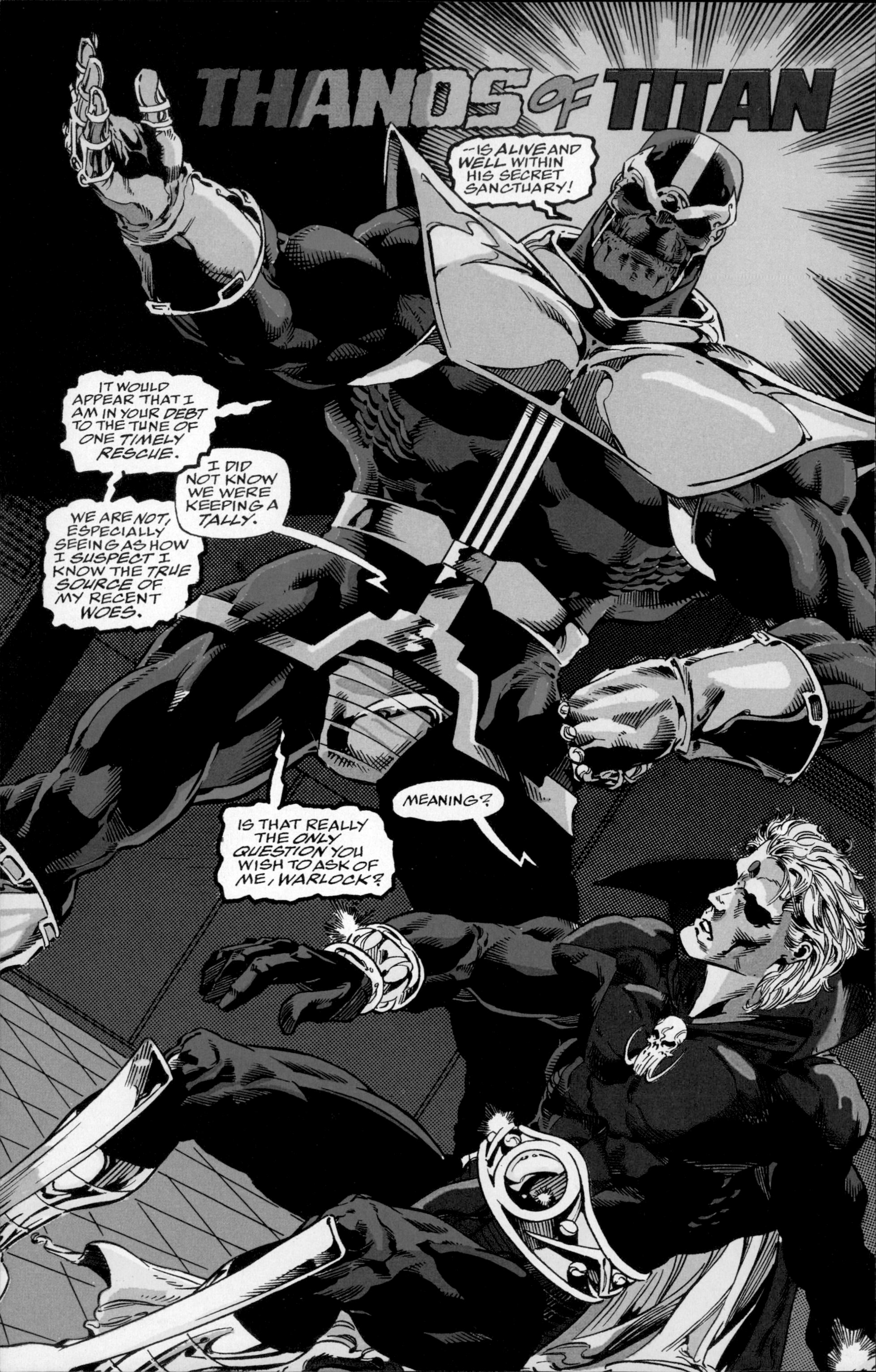
THANOS OF TITAN
--IS ALIVE AND WELL WITHIN HIS SECRET SANCTUARY!
IT WOULD APPEAR THAT I AM IN YOUR DEBT TO THE TUNE OF ONE TIMELY RESCUE.
I DID NOT KNOW WE WERE KEEPING A TALLY.
WE ARE NOT, ESPECIALLY SEEING AS HOW I SUSPECT I KNOW THE TRUE SOURCE OF MY RECENT WOES.
MEANING?
IS THAT REALLY THE ONLY QUESTION YOU WISH TO ASK OF ME, WARLOCK?

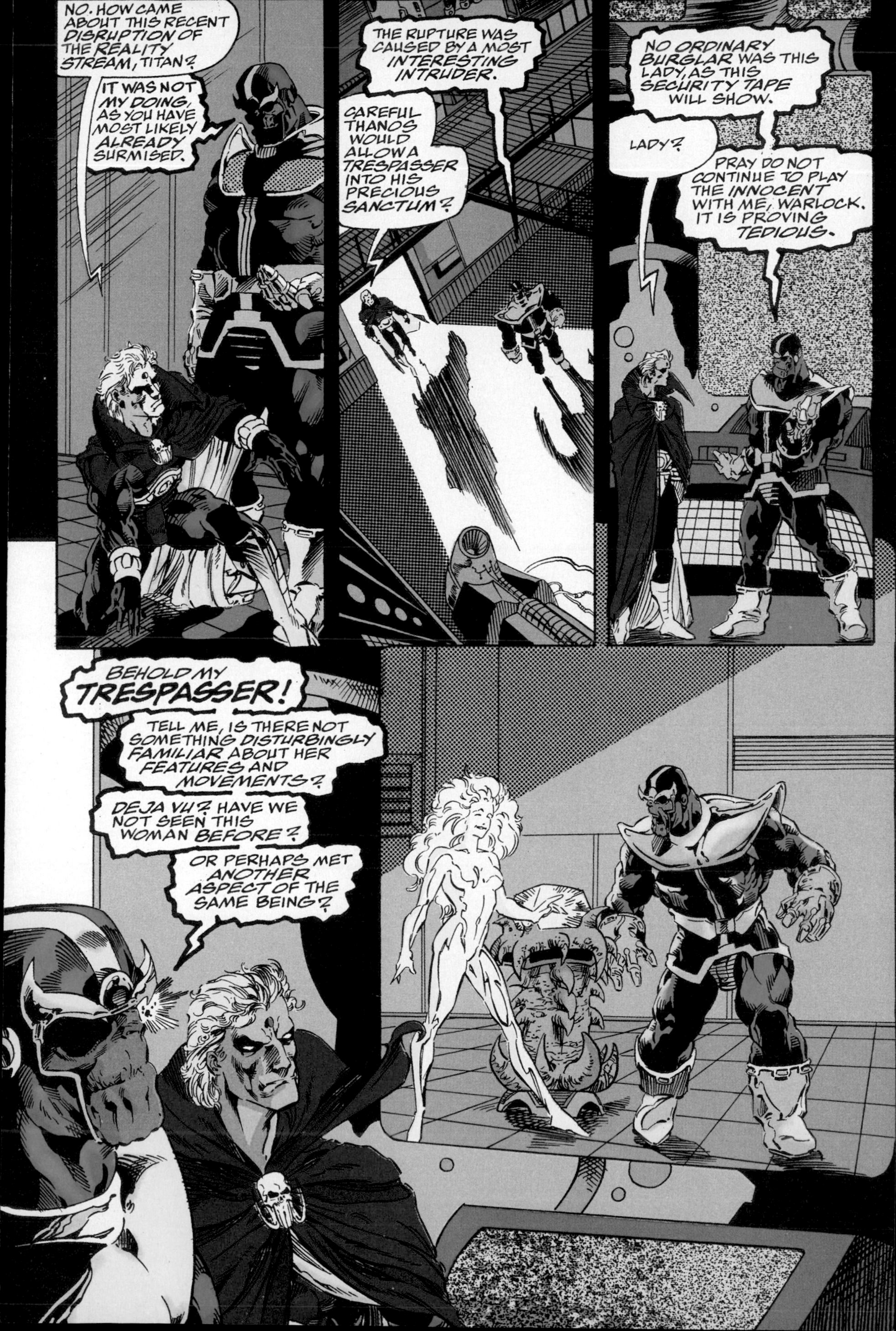
NO. HOW CAME ABOUT THIS RECENT DISRUPTION OF THE REALITY STREAM, TITAN?
IT WAS NOT MY DOING, AS YOU HAVE MOST LIKELY ALREADY SURMISED.
THE RUPTURE WAS CAUSED BY A MOST INTERESTING INTRUDER.
CAREFUL THANOS WOULD ALLOW A TRESPASSER INTO HIS PRECIOUS SANCTUM?
NO ORDINARY BURGLAR WAS THIS LADY, AS THIS SECURITY TAPE WILL SHOW.
LADY?
PRAY DO NOT CONTINUE TO PLAY THE INNOCENT WITH ME, WARLOCK. IT IS PROVING TEDIOUS.
BEHOLD MY TRESPASSER!
TELL ME, IS THERE NOT SOMETHING DISTURBINGLY FAMILIAR ABOUT HER FEATURES AND MOVEMENTS?
DEJA VU? HAVE WE NOT SEEN THIS WOMAN BEFORE?
OR PERHAPS MET ANOTHER ASPECT OF THE SAME BEING?

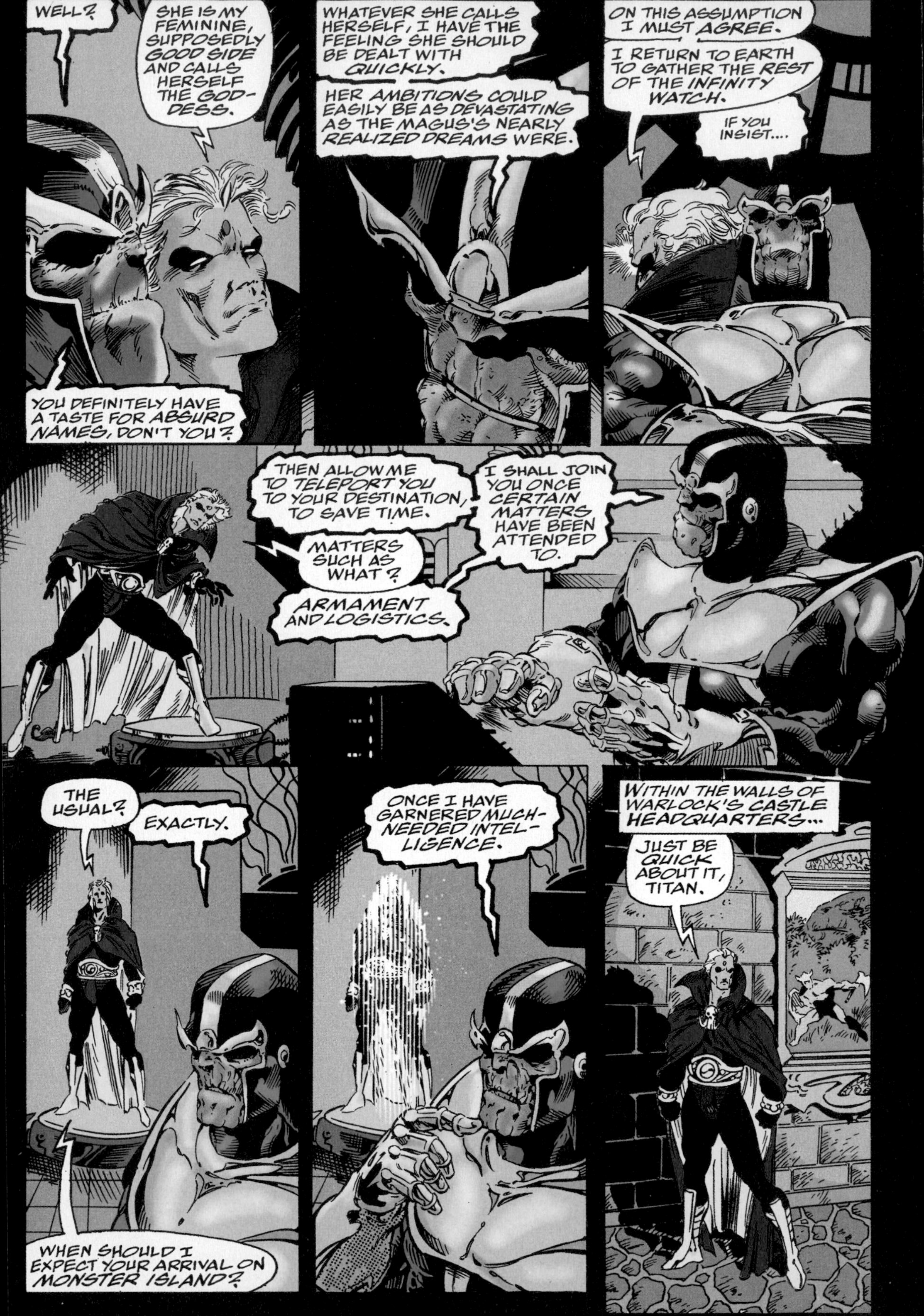

WELL?
SHE IS MY FEMININE, SUPPOSEDLY GOOD SIDE AND CALLS HERSELF THE GOD-DESS.
YOU DEFINITELY HAVE A TASTE FOR ABSURD NAMES, DON'T YOU?
WHATEVER SHE CALLS HERSELF, I HAVE THE FEELING SHE SHOULD BE DEALT WITH QUICKLY.
HER AMBITIONS COULD EASILY BE AS DEVASTATING AS THE MAGUS'S NEARLY REALIZED DREAMS WERE.
ON THIS ASSUMPTION I MUST AGREE.
I RETURN TO EARTH TO GATHER THE REST OF THE INFINITY WATCH.
IF YOU INSIST....
THEN ALLOW ME TO TELEPORT YOU TO YOUR DESTINATION, TO SAVE TIME.
I SHALL JOIN YOU ONCE CERTAIN MATTERS HAVE BEEN ATTENDED TO.
MATTERS SUCH AS WHAT?
ARMAMENT AND LOGISTICS.
THE USUAL?
EXACTLY.
WHEN SHOULD I EXPECT YOUR ARRIVAL ON MONSTER ISLAND?
ONCE I HAVE GARNERED MUCH-NEEDED INTEL-LIGENCE.
WITHIN THE WALLS OF WARLOCK'S CASTLE HEADQUARTERS...
JUST BE QUICK ABOUT IT, TITAN.

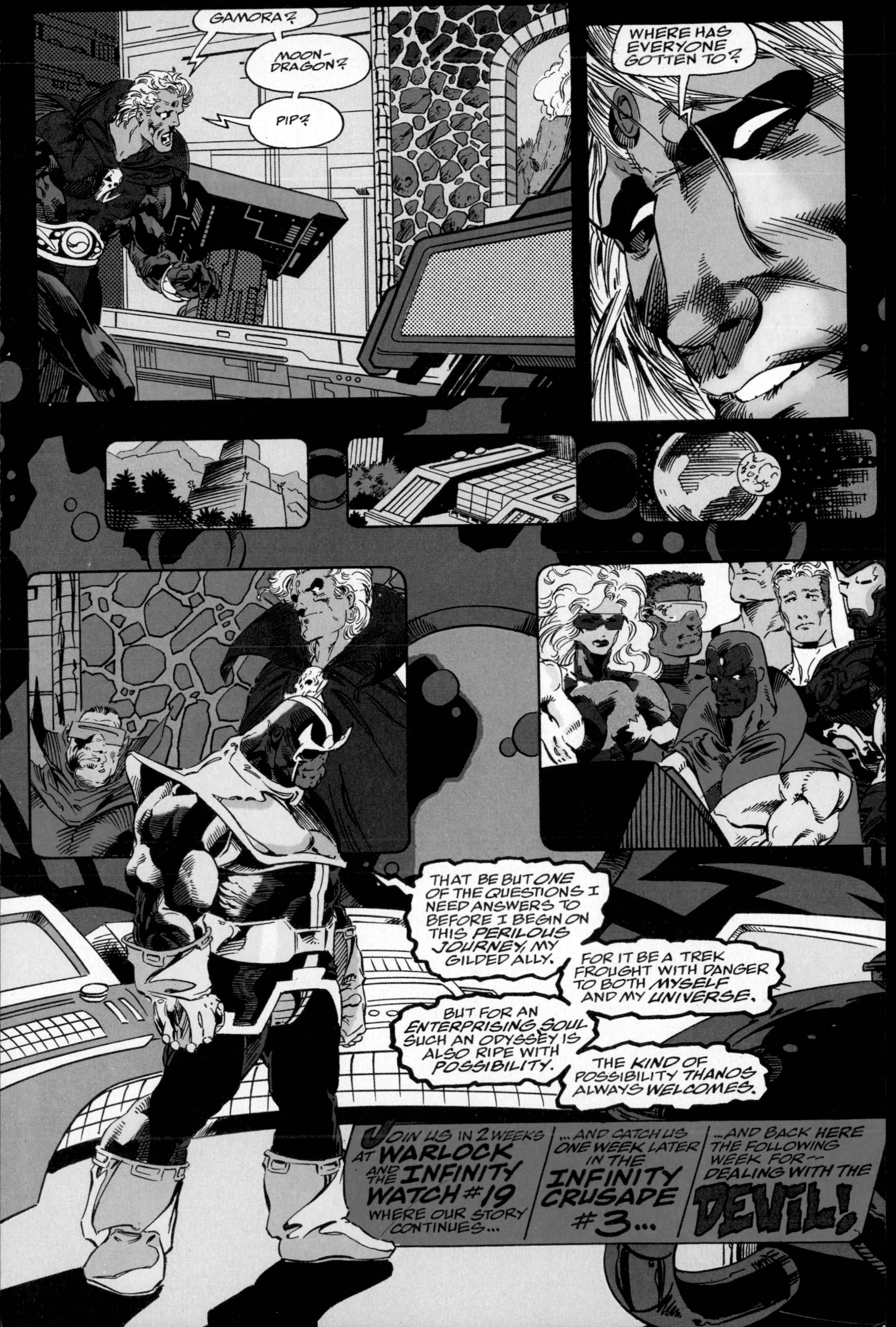
GAMORA?
MOON-DRAGON?
PIP?
WHERE HAS EVERYONE GOTTEN TO?
THAT BE BUT ONE OF THE QUESTIONS I NEED ANSWERS TO BEFORE I BEGIN ON THIS PERILOUS JOURNEY, MY GILDED ALLY.
FOR IT BE A TREK FROUGHT WITH DANGER TO BOTH MYSELF AND MY UNIVERSE.
BUT FOR AN ENTERPRISING SOUL SUCH AN ODYSSEY IS ALSO RIPE WITH POSSIBILITY.
THE KIND OF POSSIBILITY THANOS ALWAYS WELCOMES.
JOIN US IN 2 WEEKS AT WARLOCK AND THE INFINITY WATCH #19 WHERE OUR STORY CONTINUES...
...AND CATCH US ONE WEEK LATER IN THE INFINITY CRUSADE #3...
...AND BACK HERE THE FOLLOWING WEEK FOR-- DEALING WITH THE DEVIL!

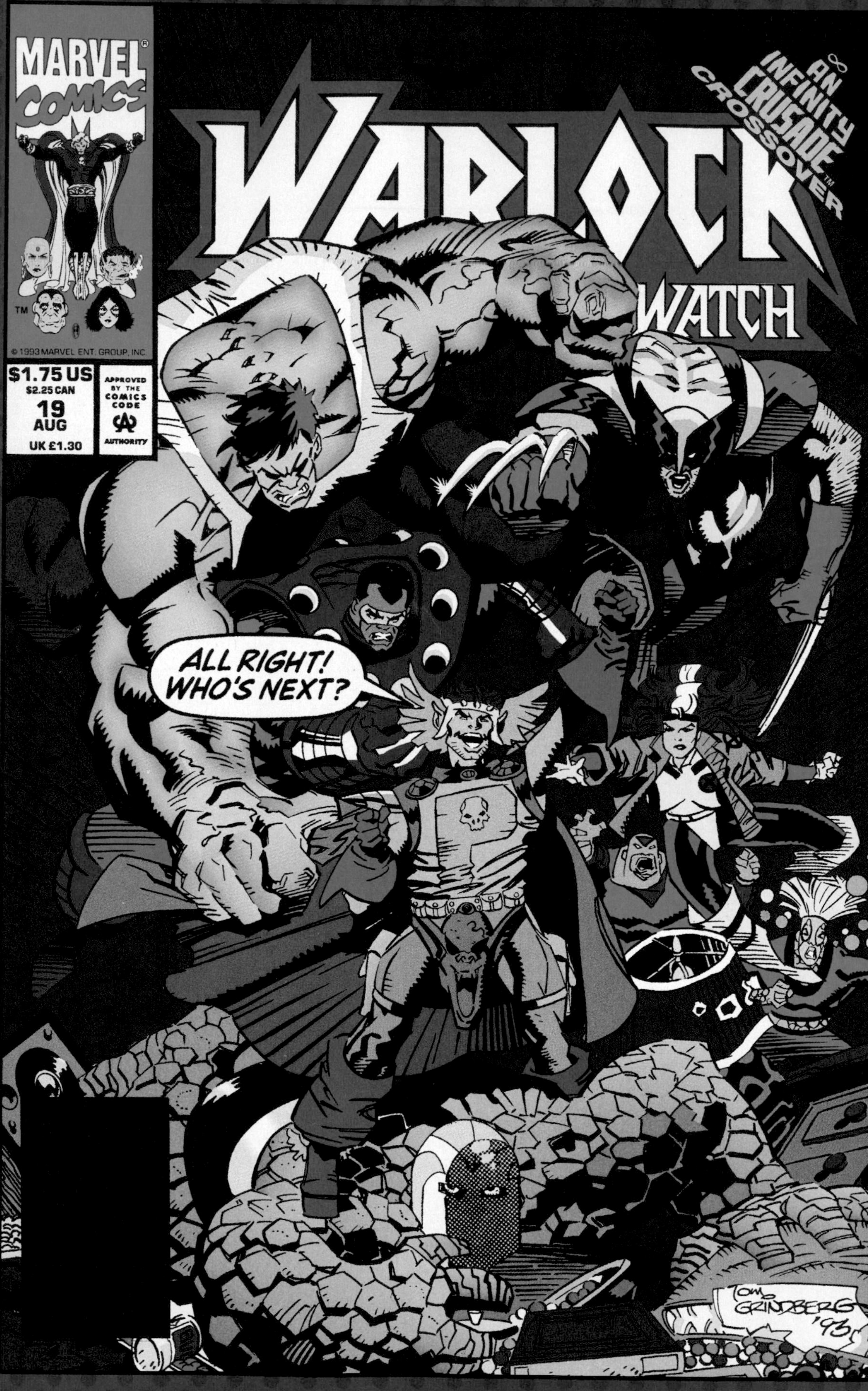

MARVEL COMICS
WARLOCK
WATCH
AN INFINITY CRUSADE CROSSOVER
© 1993 MARVEL ENT. GROUP, INC.
$1.75 US
$2.25 CAN
19
AUG
UK £1.30
APPROVED BY THE COMICS CODE AUTHORITY
ALL RIGHT! WHO'S NEXT?
TOM GRINDBERG '93

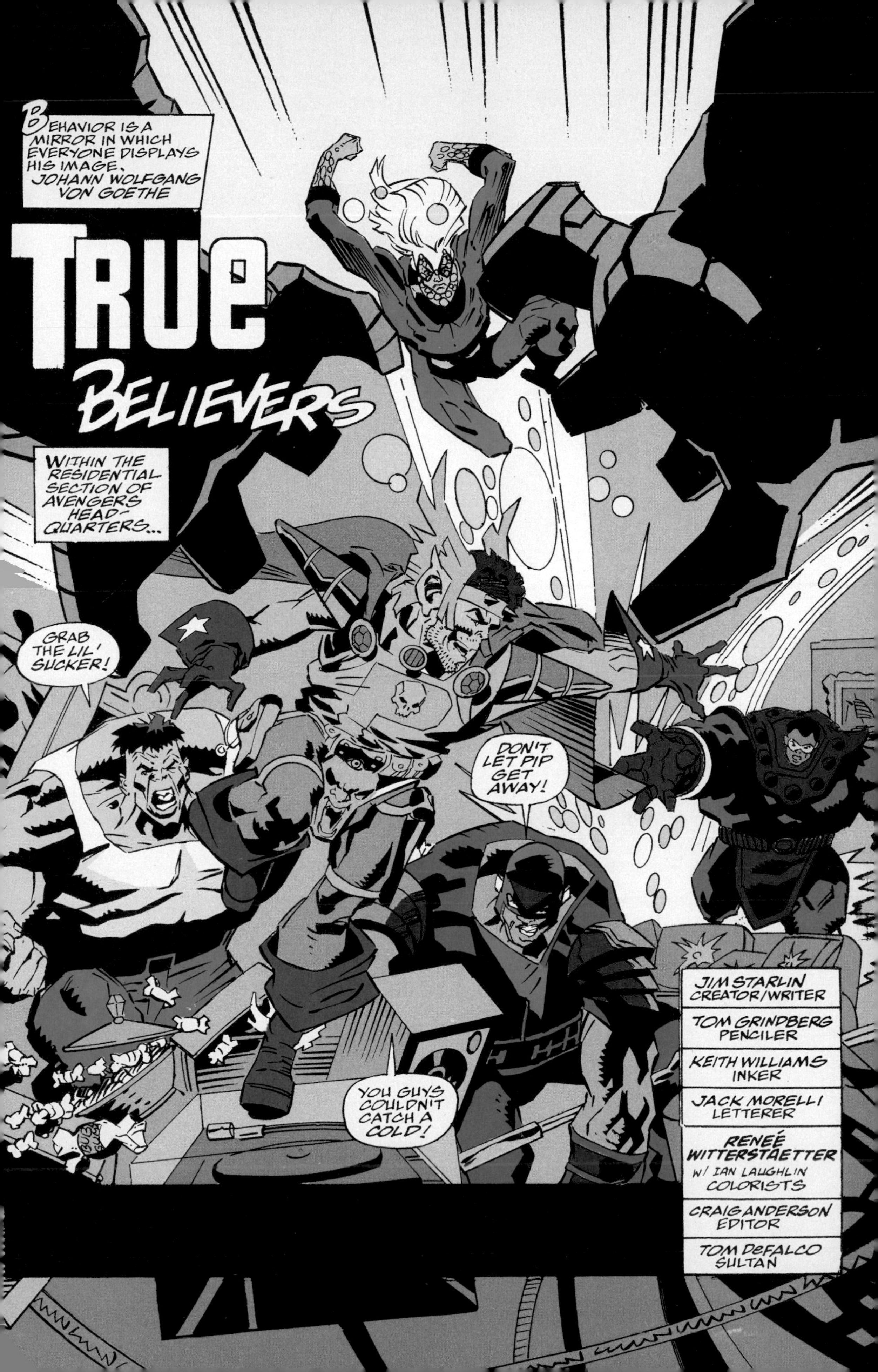

BEHAVIOR IS A MIRROR IN WHICH EVERYONE DISPLAYS HIS IMAGE. JOHANN WOLFGANG VON GOETHE
TRUE BELIEVERS
WITHIN THE RESIDENTIAL SECTION OF AVENGERS HEAD-QUARTERS...
GRAB THE LIL' SUCKER!
DON'T LET PIP GET AWAY!
YOU GUYS COULDN'T CATCH A COLD!
JIM STARLIN CREATOR/WRITER
TOM GRINDBERG PENCILER
KEITH WILLIAMS INKER
JACK MORELLI LETTERER
RENEÉ WITTERSTAETTER W/ IAN LAUGHLIN COLORISTS
CRAIG ANDERSON EDITOR
TOM DEFALCO SULTAN

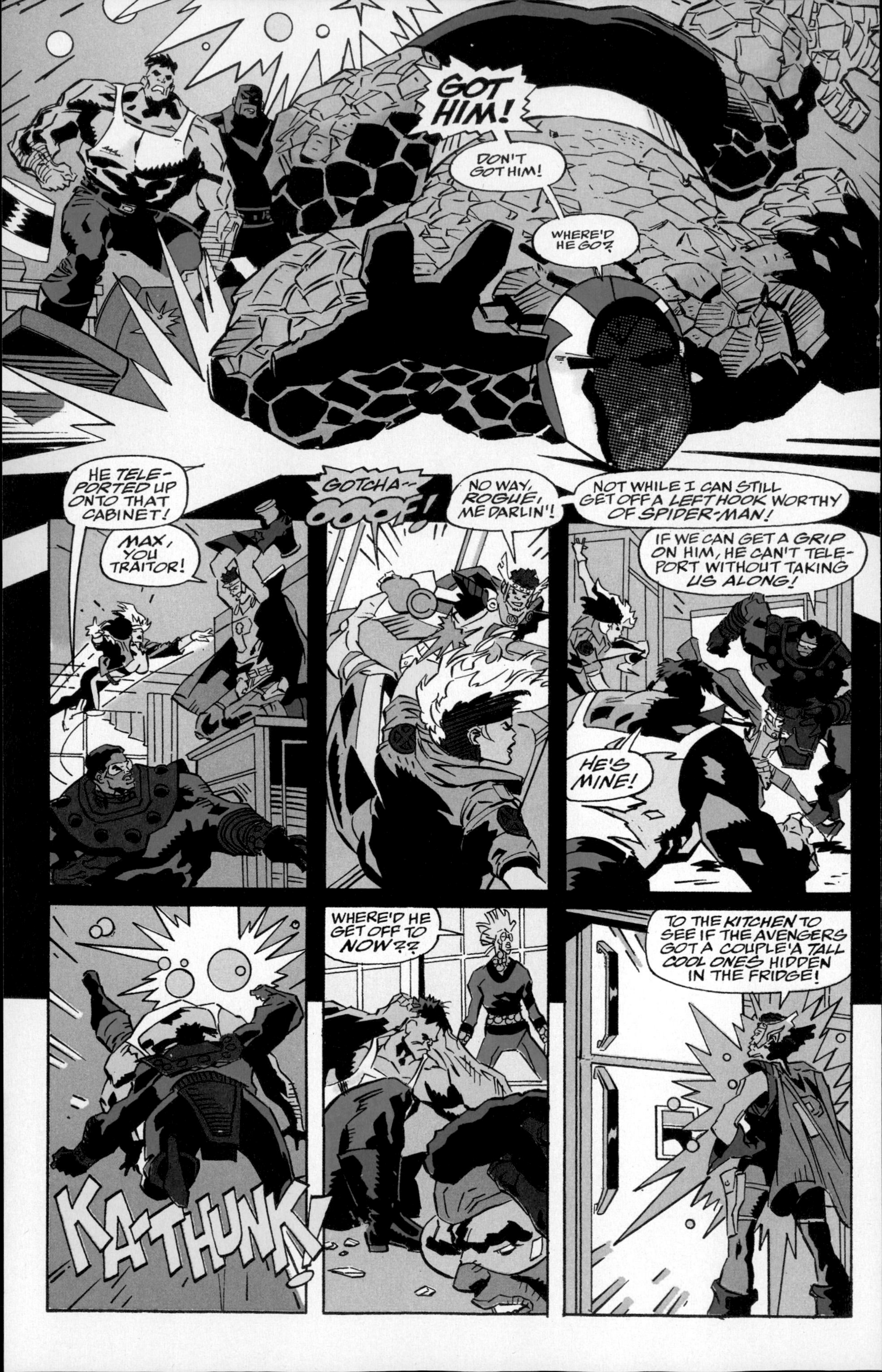
GOT HIM!
DON'T GOT HIM!
WHERE'D HE GO?
HE TELEPORTED UP ONTO THAT CABINET!
MAX, YOU TRAITOR!
GOTCHA--
OOOF!
NO WAY, ROGUE, ME DARLIN'!
NOT WHILE I CAN STILL GET OFF A LEFT HOOK WORTHY OF SPIDER-MAN!
IF WE CAN GET A GRIP ON HIM, HE CAN'T TELEPORT WITHOUT TAKING US ALONG!
HE'S MINE!
KA-THUNK!
WHERE'D HE GET OFF TO NOW??
TO THE KITCHEN TO SEE IF THE AVENGERS GOT A COUPLE'A TALL COOL ONES HIDDEN IN THE FRIDGE!

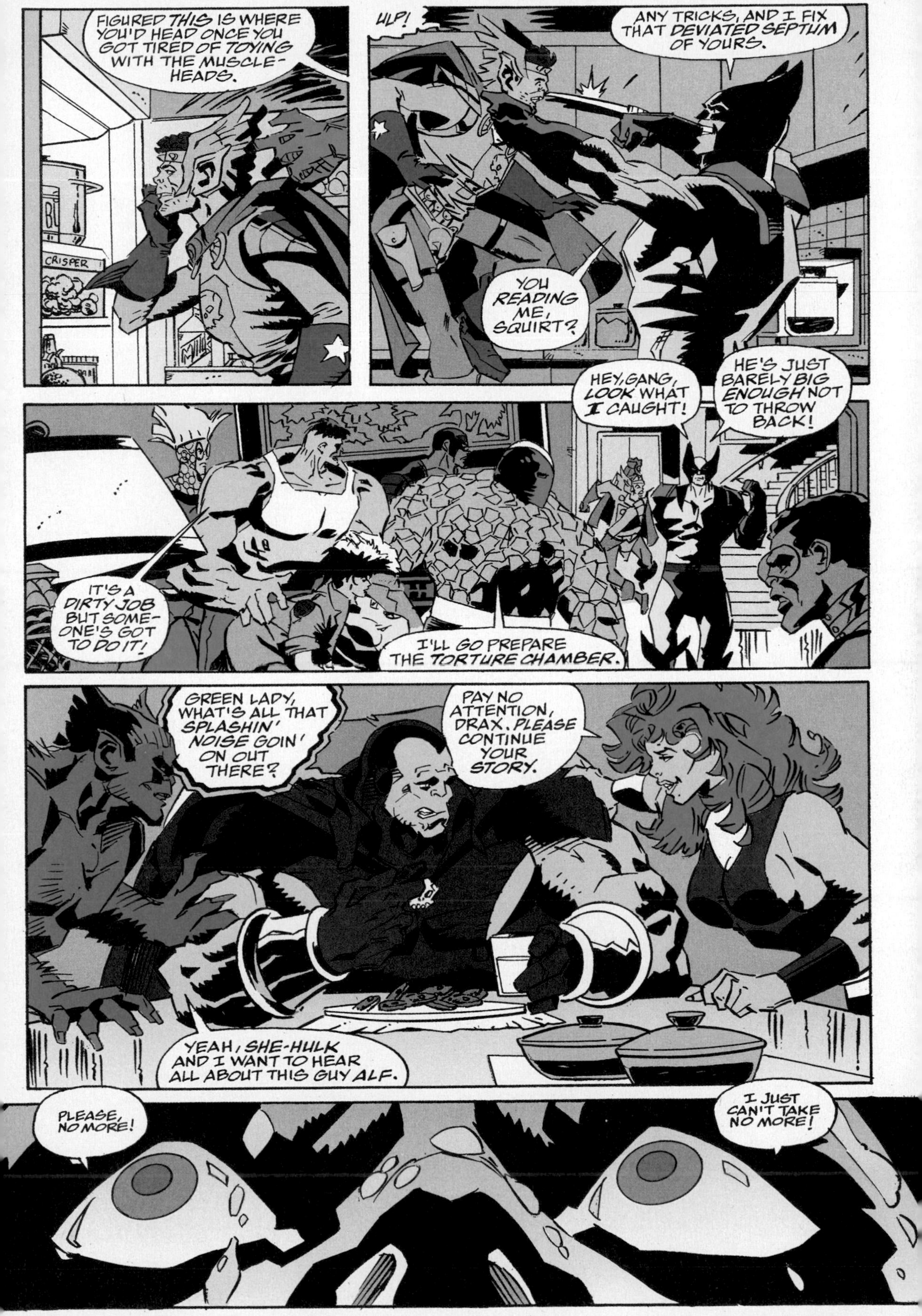
FIGURED THIS IS WHERE YOU'D HEAD ONCE YOU GOT TIRED OF TOYING WITH THE MUSCLE-HEADS.
CRISPER
ULP!
ANY TRICKS, AND I FIX THAT DEVIATED SEPTUM OF YOURS.
YOU READING ME, SQUIRT?
HEY, GANG, LOOK WHAT I CAUGHT!
HE'S JUST BARELY BIG ENOUGH NOT TO THROW BACK!
IT'S A DIRTY JOB BUT SOMEONE'S GOT TO DO IT!
I'LL GO PREPARE THE TORTURE CHAMBER.
GREEN LADY, WHAT'S ALL THAT SPLASHIN' NOISE GOIN' ON OUT THERE?
PAY NO ATTENTION, DRAX. PLEASE CONTINUE YOUR STORY.
YEAH, SHE-HULK AND I WANT TO HEAR ALL ABOUT THIS GUY ALF.
PLEASE, NO MORE!
I JUST CAN'T TAKE NO MORE!

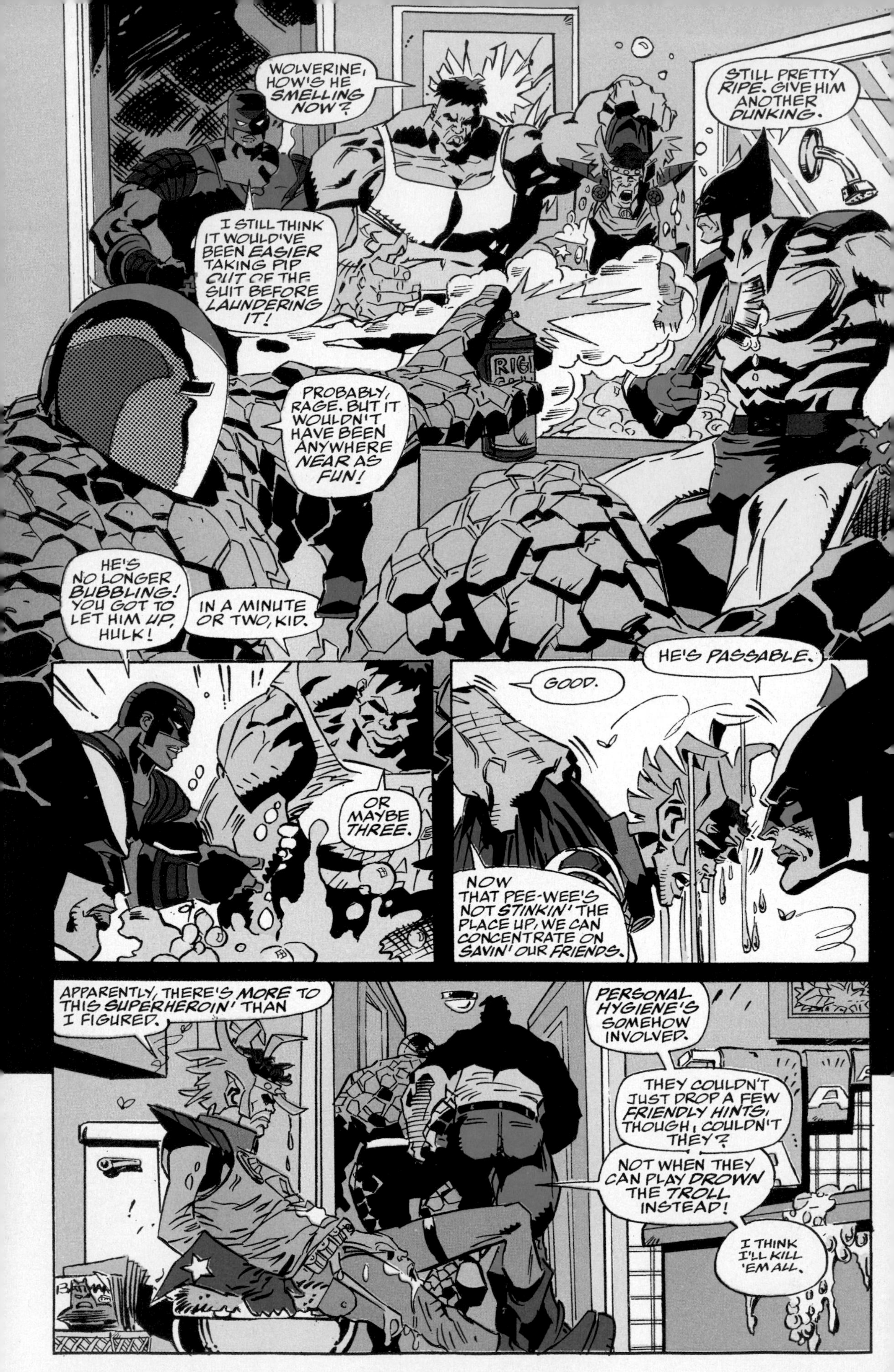
WOLVERINE, HOW'S HE SMELLING NOW?
STILL PRETTY RIPE. GIVE HIM ANOTHER DUNKING.
I STILL THINK IT WOULD'VE BEEN EASIER TAKING PIP OUT OF THE SUIT BEFORE LAUNDERING IT!
PROBABLY, RAGE. BUT IT WOULDN'T HAVE BEEN ANYWHERE NEAR AS FUN!
HE'S NO LONGER BUBBLING! YOU GOT TO LET HIM UP, HULK!
IN A MINUTE OR TWO, KID.
OR MAYBE THREE.
HE'S PASSABLE.
GOOD.
NOW THAT PEE-WEE'S NOT STINKIN' THE PLACE UP, WE CAN CONCENTRATE ON SAVIN' OUR FRIENDS.
APPARENTLY, THERE'S MORE TO THIS SUPERHEROIN' THAN I FIGURED.
PERSONAL HYGIENE'S SOMEHOW INVOLVED.
THEY COULDN'T JUST DROP A FEW FRIENDLY HINTS, THOUGH, COULDN'T THEY?
NOT WHEN THEY CAN PLAY DROWN THE TROLL INSTEAD!
I THINK I'LL KILL 'EM ALL.

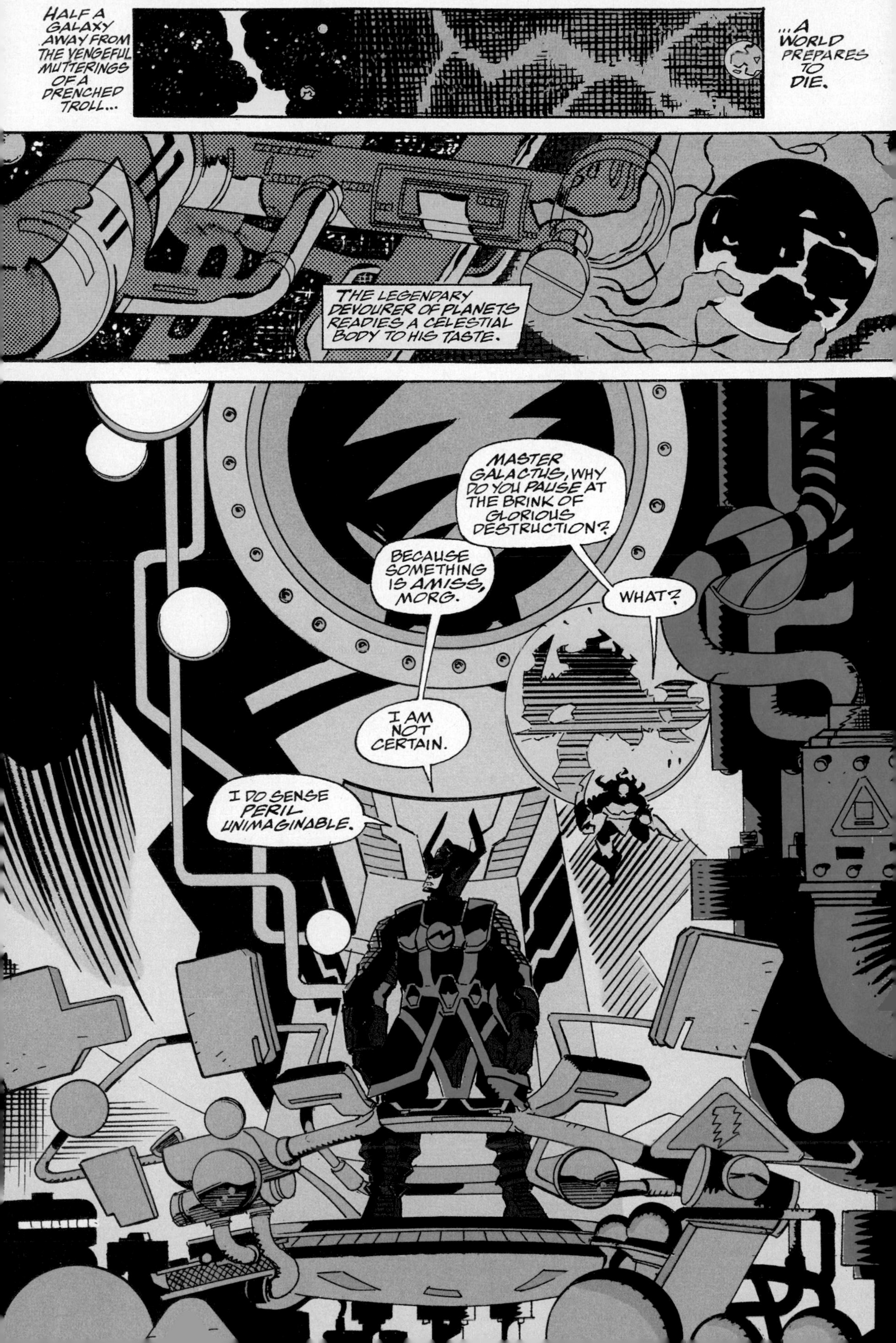
HALF A GALAXY AWAY FROM THE VENGEFUL MUTTERINGS OF A DRENCHED TROLL...
...A WORLD PREPARES TO DIE.
THE LEGENDARY DEVOURER OF PLANETS READIES A CELESTIAL BODY TO HIS TASTE.
MASTER GALACTUS, WHY DO YOU PAUSE AT THE BRINK OF GLORIOUS DESTRUCTION?
BECAUSE SOMETHING IS AMISS, MORG.
WHAT?
I AM NOT CERTAIN.
I DO SENSE PERIL UNIMAGINABLE.

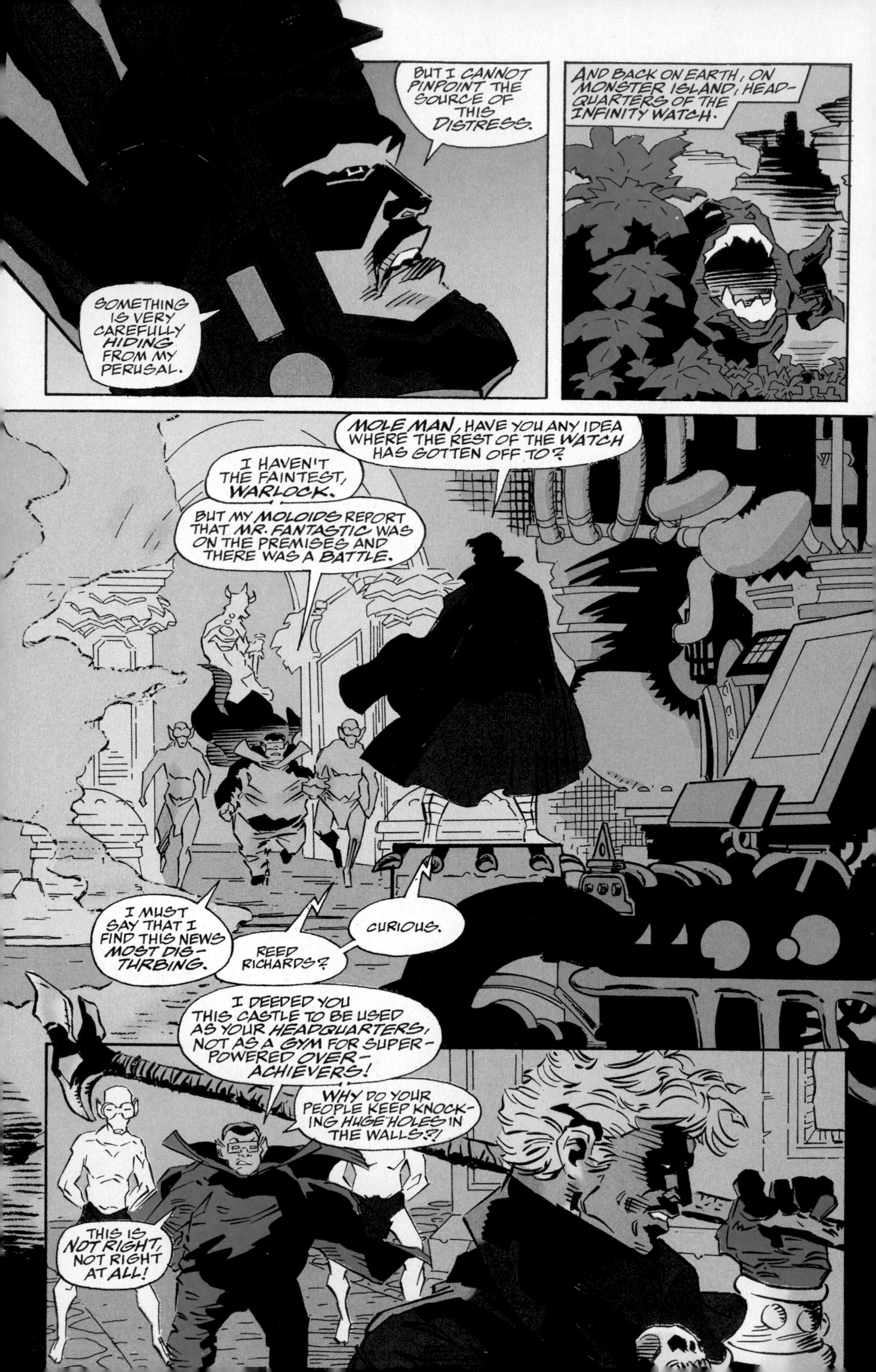
BUT I CANNOT PINPOINT THE SOURCE OF THIS DISTRESS.
SOMETHING IS VERY CAREFULLY HIDING FROM MY PERUSAL.
AND BACK ON EARTH, ON MONSTER ISLAND, HEAD-QUARTERS OF THE INFINITY WATCH.
MOLE MAN, HAVE YOU ANY IDEA WHERE THE REST OF THE WATCH HAS GOTTEN OFF TO?
I HAVEN'T THE FAINTEST, WARLOCK.
BUT MY MOLOIDS REPORT THAT MR. FANTASTIC WAS ON THE PREMISES AND THERE WAS A BATTLE.
I MUST SAY THAT I FIND THIS NEWS MOST DIS-TURBING.
REED RICHARDS?
CURIOUS.
I DEEDED YOU THIS CASTLE TO BE USED AS YOUR HEADQUARTERS, NOT AS A GYM FOR SUPER-POWERED OVER-ACHIEVERS!
WHY DO YOUR PEOPLE KEEP KNOCK-ING HUGE HOLES IN THE WALLS?!
THIS IS NOT RIGHT, NOT RIGHT AT ALL!

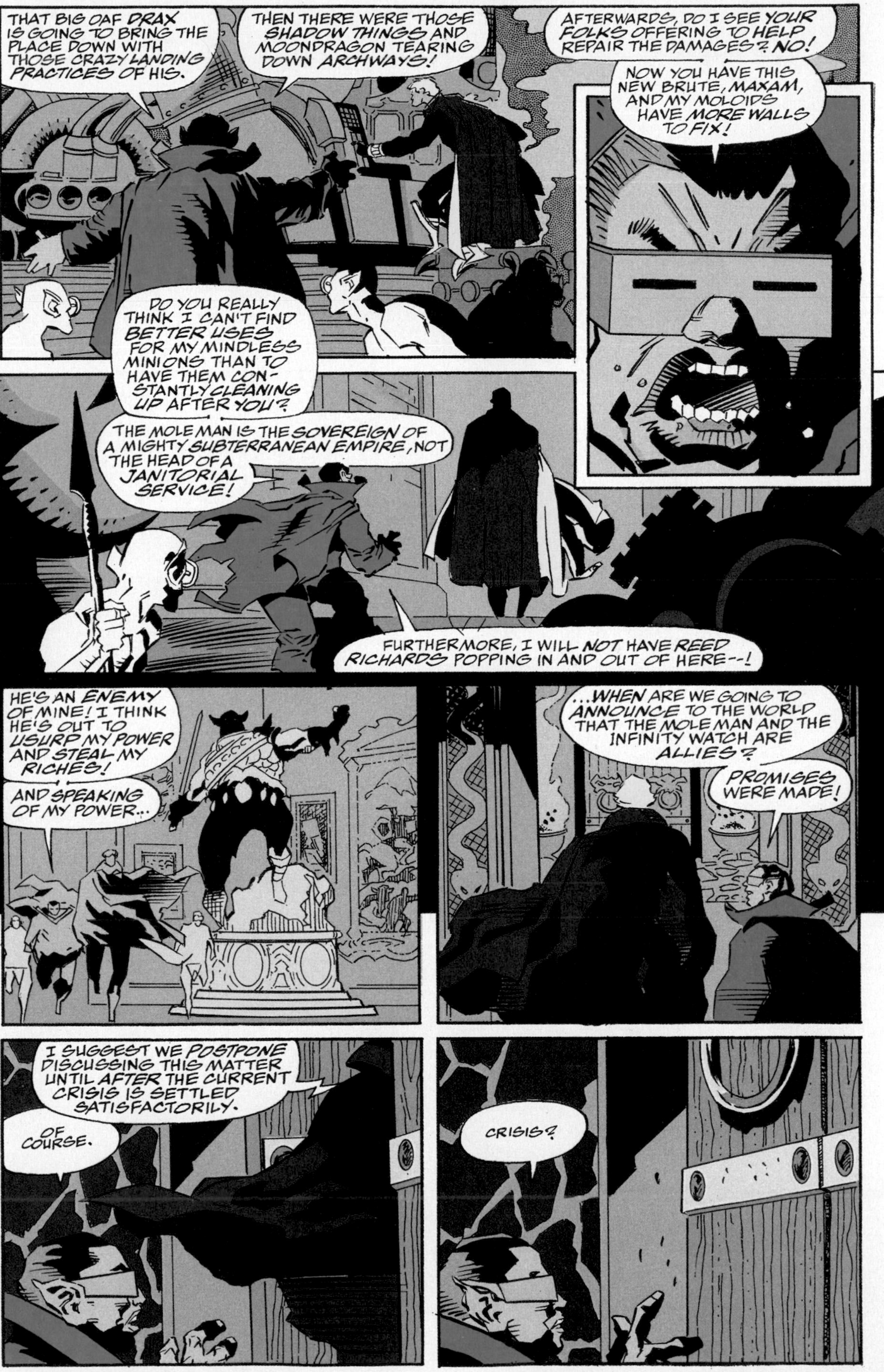
THAT BIG OAF DRAX IS GOING TO BRING THE PLACE DOWN WITH THOSE CRAZY LANDING PRACTICES OF HIS.
THEN THERE WERE THOSE SHADOW THINGS AND MOONDRAGON TEARING DOWN ARCHWAYS!
AFTERWARDS, DO I SEE YOUR FOLKS OFFERING TO HELP REPAIR THE DAMAGES? NO!
NOW YOU HAVE THIS NEW BRUTE, MAXAM, AND MY MOLOIDS HAVE MORE WALLS TO FIX!
DO YOU REALLY THINK I CAN'T FIND BETTER USES FOR MY MINDLESS MINIONS THAN TO HAVE THEM CONSTANTLY CLEANING UP AFTER YOU?
THE MOLE MAN IS THE SOVEREIGN OF A MIGHTY SUBTERRANEAN EMPIRE, NOT THE HEAD OF A JANITORIAL SERVICE!
FURTHERMORE, I WILL NOT HAVE REED RICHARDS POPPING IN AND OUT OF HERE--!
HE'S AN ENEMY OF MINE! I THINK HE'S OUT TO USURP MY POWER AND STEAL MY RICHES!
AND SPEAKING OF MY POWER...
...WHEN ARE WE GOING TO ANNOUNCE TO THE WORLD THAT THE MOLE MAN AND THE INFINITY WATCH ARE ALLIES?
PROMISES WERE MADE!
I SUGGEST WE POSTPONE DISCUSSING THIS MATTER UNTIL AFTER THE CURRENT CRISIS IS SETTLED SATISFACTORILY.
OF COURSE.
CRISIS?

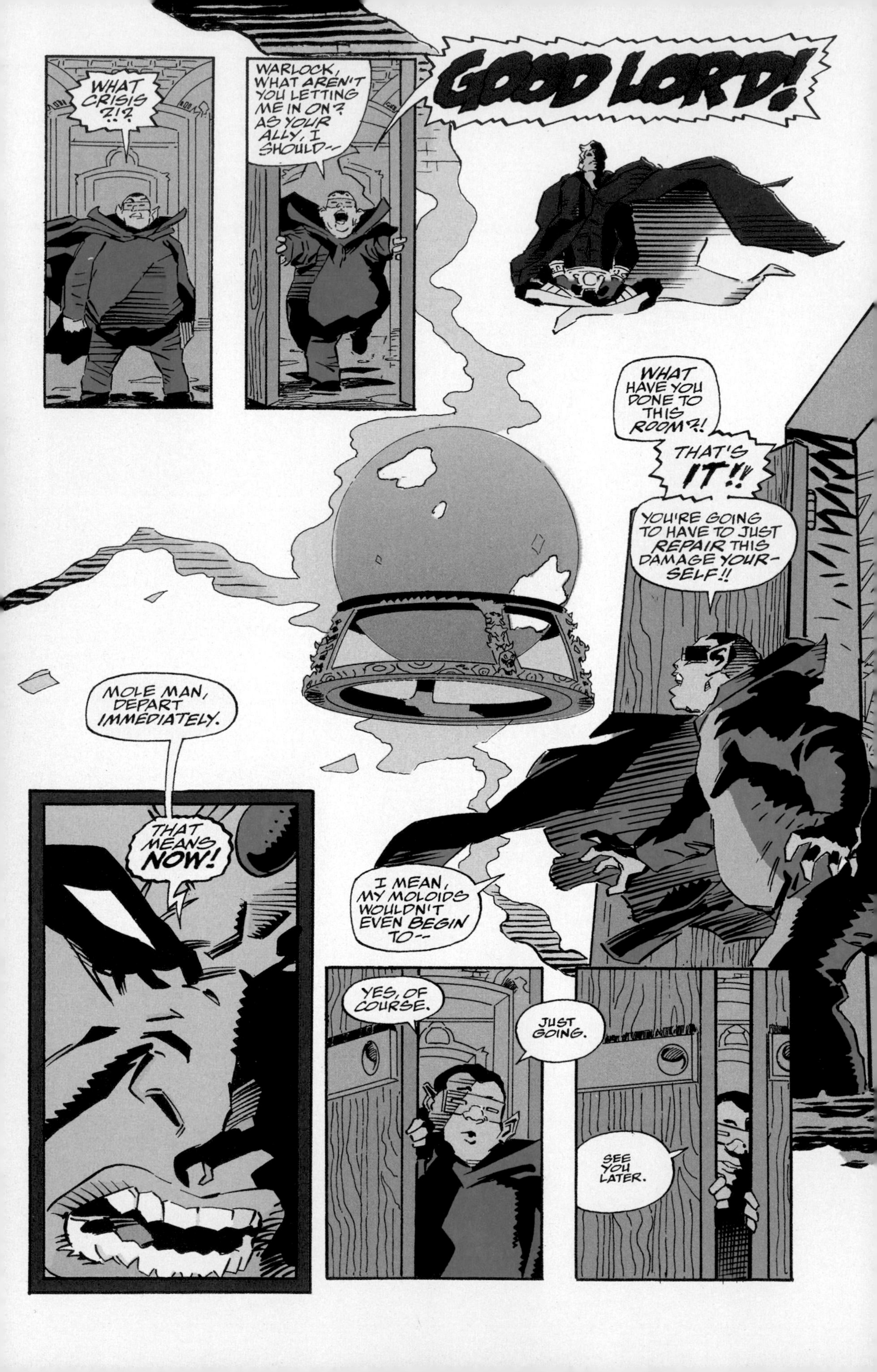
WHAT CRISIS ?!?
WARLOCK, WHAT AREN'T YOU LETTING ME IN ON? AS YOUR ALLY, I SHOULD--
GOOD LORD!
WHAT HAVE YOU DONE TO THIS ROOM?!
THAT'S IT!!
YOU'RE GOING TO HAVE TO JUST REPAIR THIS DAMAGE YOURSELF!!
MOLE MAN, DEPART IMMEDIATELY.
THAT MEANS NOW!
I MEAN, MY MOLOIDS WOULDN'T EVEN BEGIN TO--
YES, OF COURSE.
JUST GOING.
SEE YOU LATER.

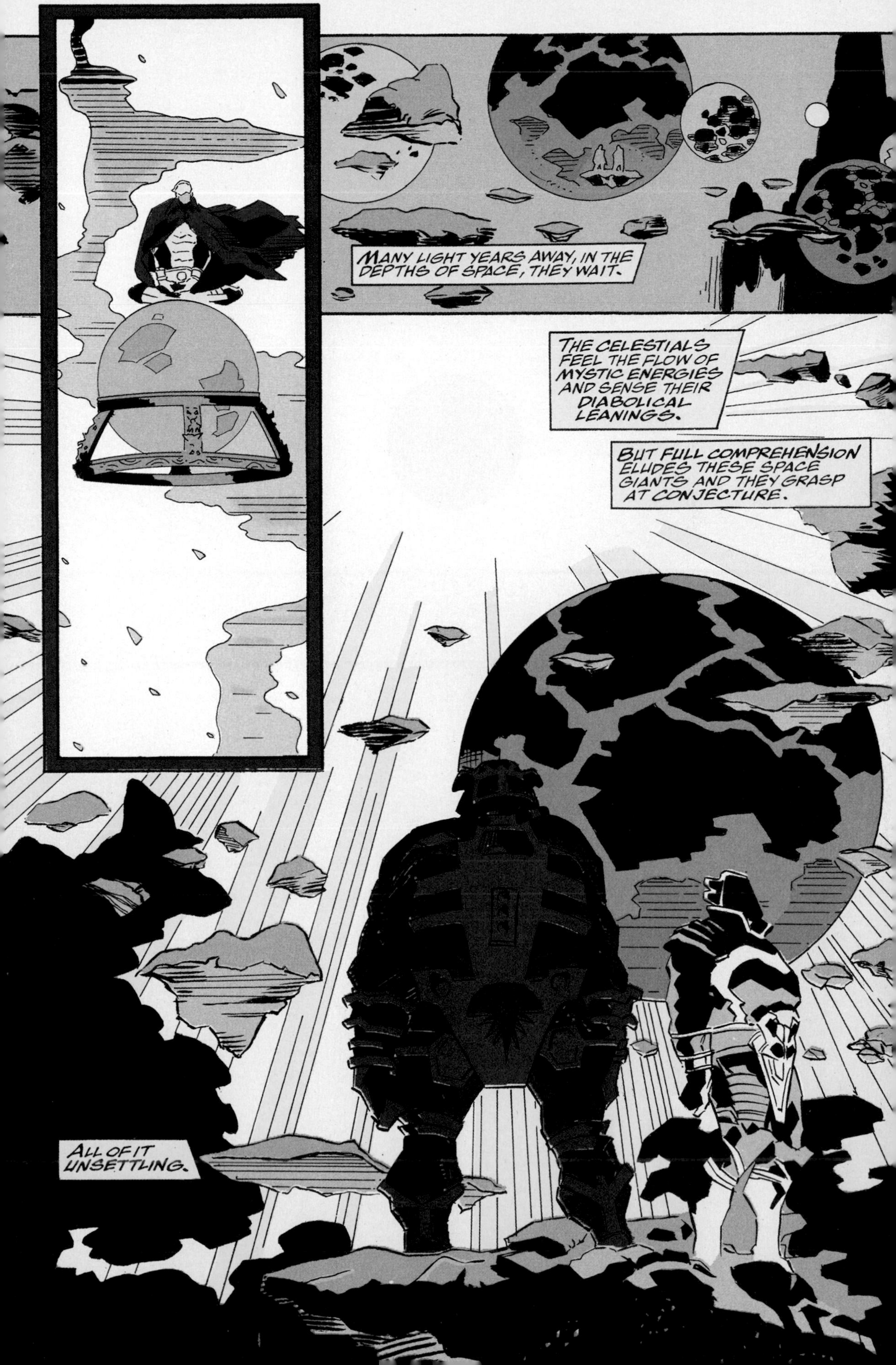
MANY LIGHT YEARS AWAY, IN THE DEPTHS OF SPACE, THEY WAIT.
THE CELESTIALS FEEL THE FLOW OF MYSTIC ENERGIES AND SENSE THEIR DIABOLICAL LEANINGS.
BUT FULL COMPREHENSION ELUDES THESE SPACE GIANTS AND THEY GRASP AT CONJECTURE.
ALL OF IT UNSETTLING.

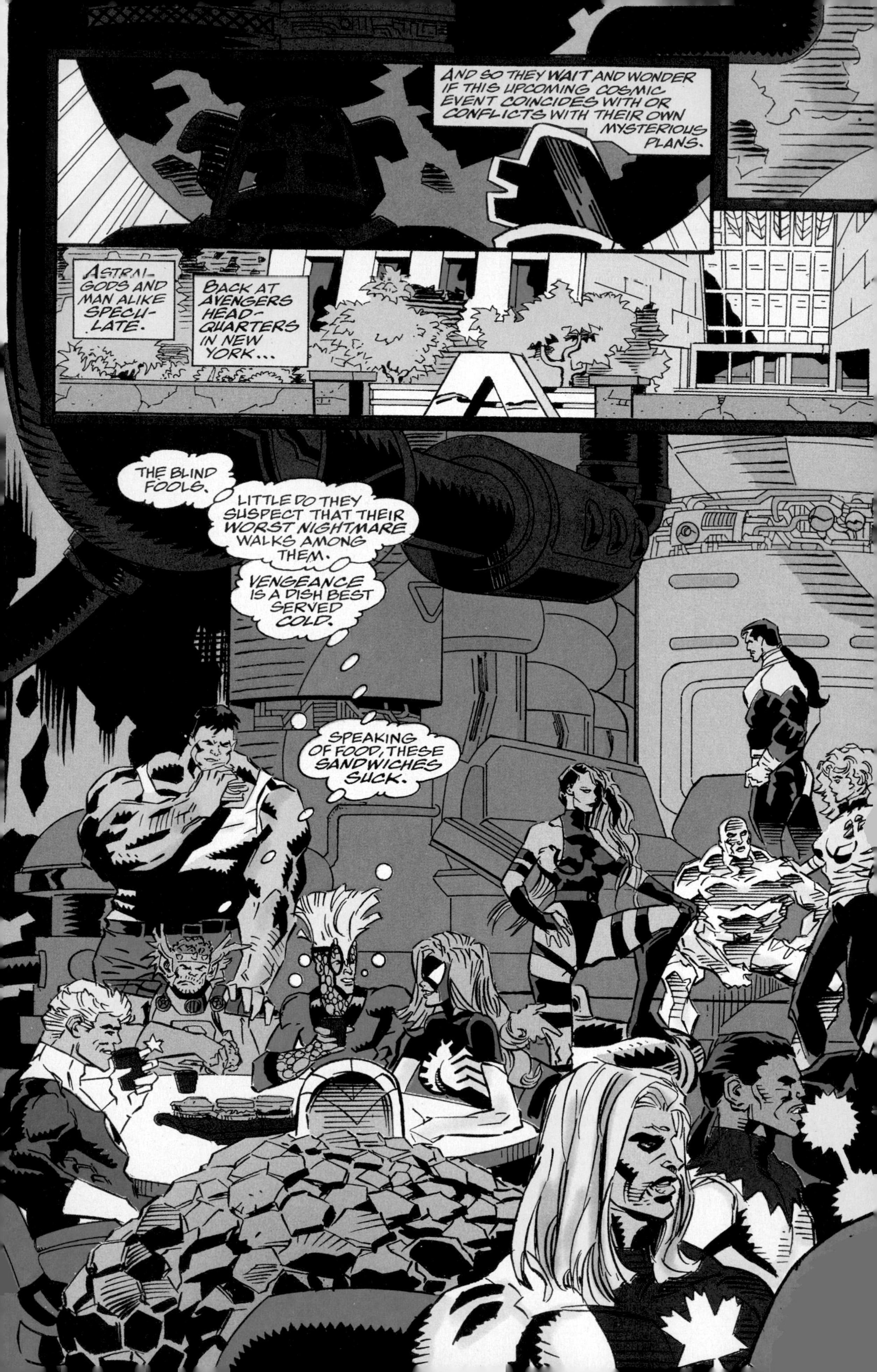
AND SO THEY WAIT AND WONDER IF THIS UPCOMING COSMIC EVENT COINCIDES WITH OR CONFLICTS WITH THEIR OWN MYSTERIOUS PLANS.
ASTRAL GODS AND MAN ALIKE SPECULATE.
BACK AT AVENGERS HEADQUARTERS IN NEW YORK...
THE BLIND FOOLS.
LITTLE DO THEY SUSPECT THAT THEIR WORST NIGHTMARE WALKS AMONG THEM.
VENGEANCE IS A DISH BEST SERVED COLD.
SPEAKING OF FOOD, THESE SANDWICHES SUCK.

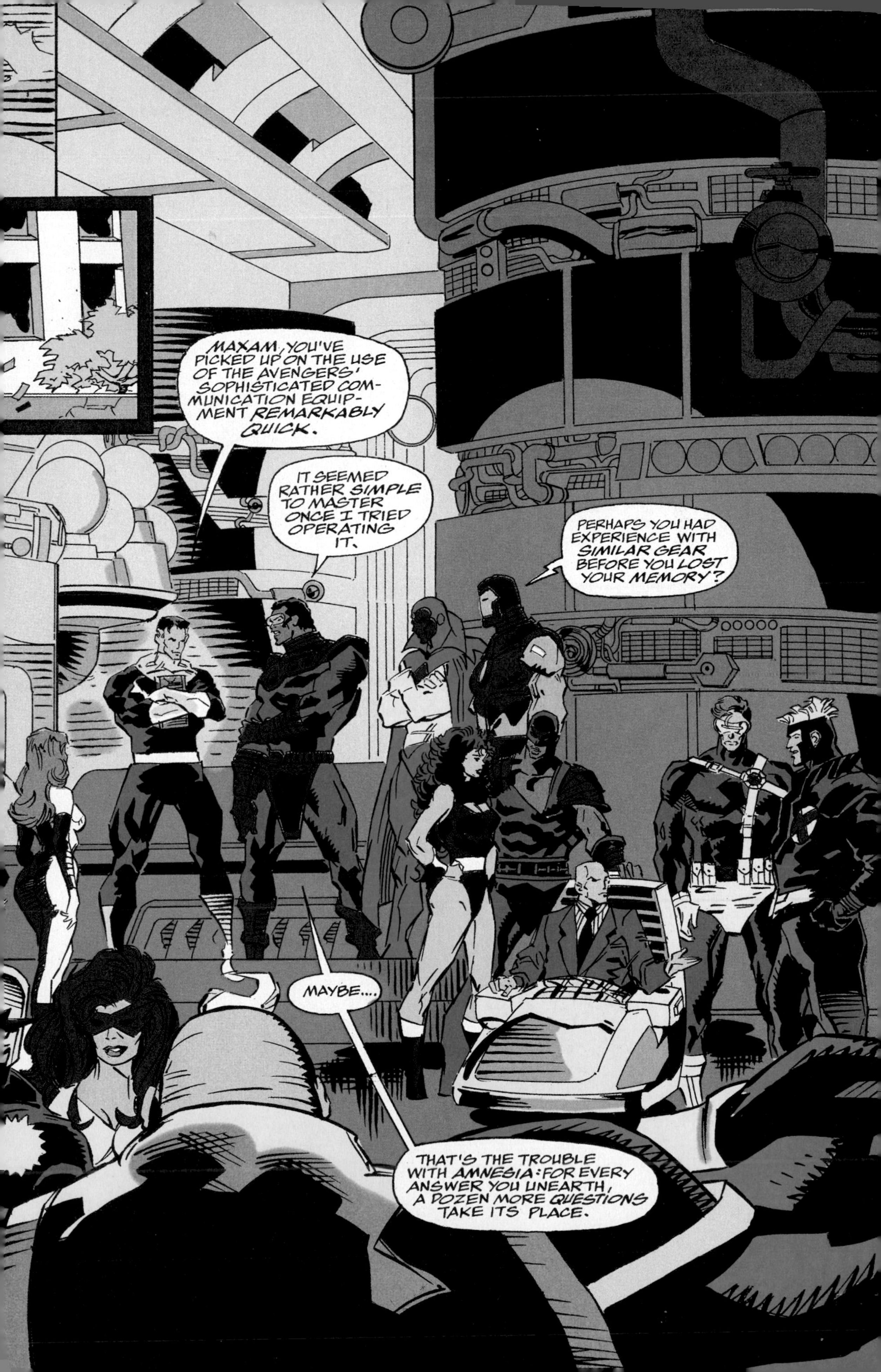
MAXAM, YOU'VE PICKED UP ON THE USE OF THE AVENGERS' SOPHISTICATED COM-MUNICATION EQUIP-MENT REMARKABLY QUICK.
IT SEEMED RATHER SIMPLE TO MASTER ONCE I TRIED OPERATING IT.
PERHAPS YOU HAD EXPERIENCE WITH SIMILAR GEAR BEFORE YOU LOST YOUR MEMORY?
MAYBE....
THAT'S THE TROUBLE WITH AMNESIA: FOR EVERY ANSWER YOU UNEARTH, A DOZEN MORE QUESTIONS TAKE ITS PLACE.

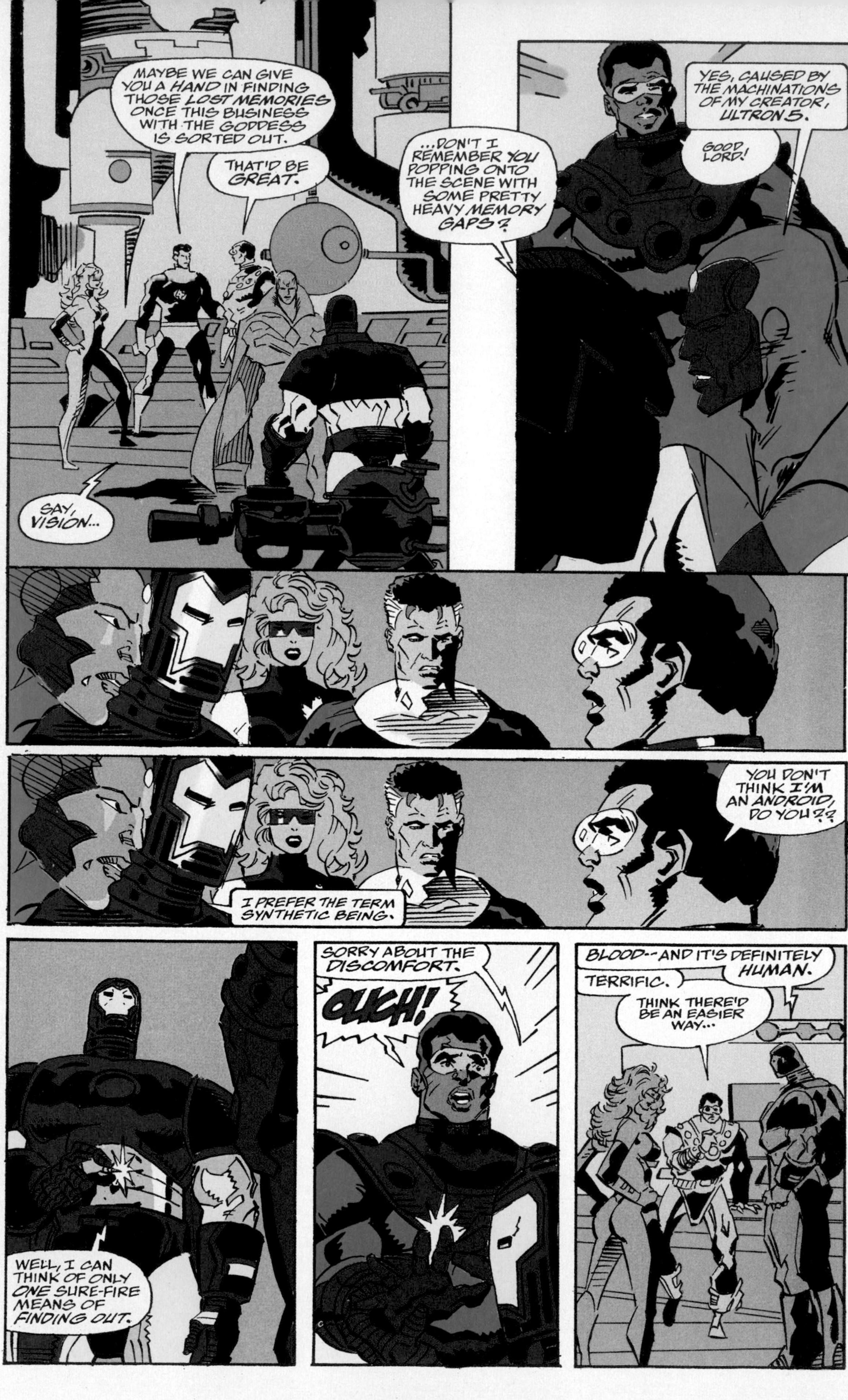
MAYBE WE CAN GIVE YOU A HAND IN FINDING THOSE LOST MEMORIES ONCE THIS BUSINESS WITH THE GODDESS IS SORTED OUT.
THAT'D BE GREAT.
SAY, VISION...
...DON'T I REMEMBER YOU POPPING ONTO THE SCENE WITH SOME PRETTY HEAVY MEMORY GAPS?
YES, CAUSED BY THE MACHINATIONS OF MY CREATOR, ULTRON 5.
GOOD LORD!
YOU DON'T THINK I'M AN ANDROID, DO YOU??
I PREFER THE TERM SYNTHETIC BEING.
WELL, I CAN THINK OF ONLY ONE SURE-FIRE MEANS OF FINDING OUT.
SORRY ABOUT THE DISCOMFORT.
OUCH!
BLOOD--AND IT'S DEFINITELY HUMAN.
TERRIFIC.
THINK THERE'D BE AN EASIER WAY...

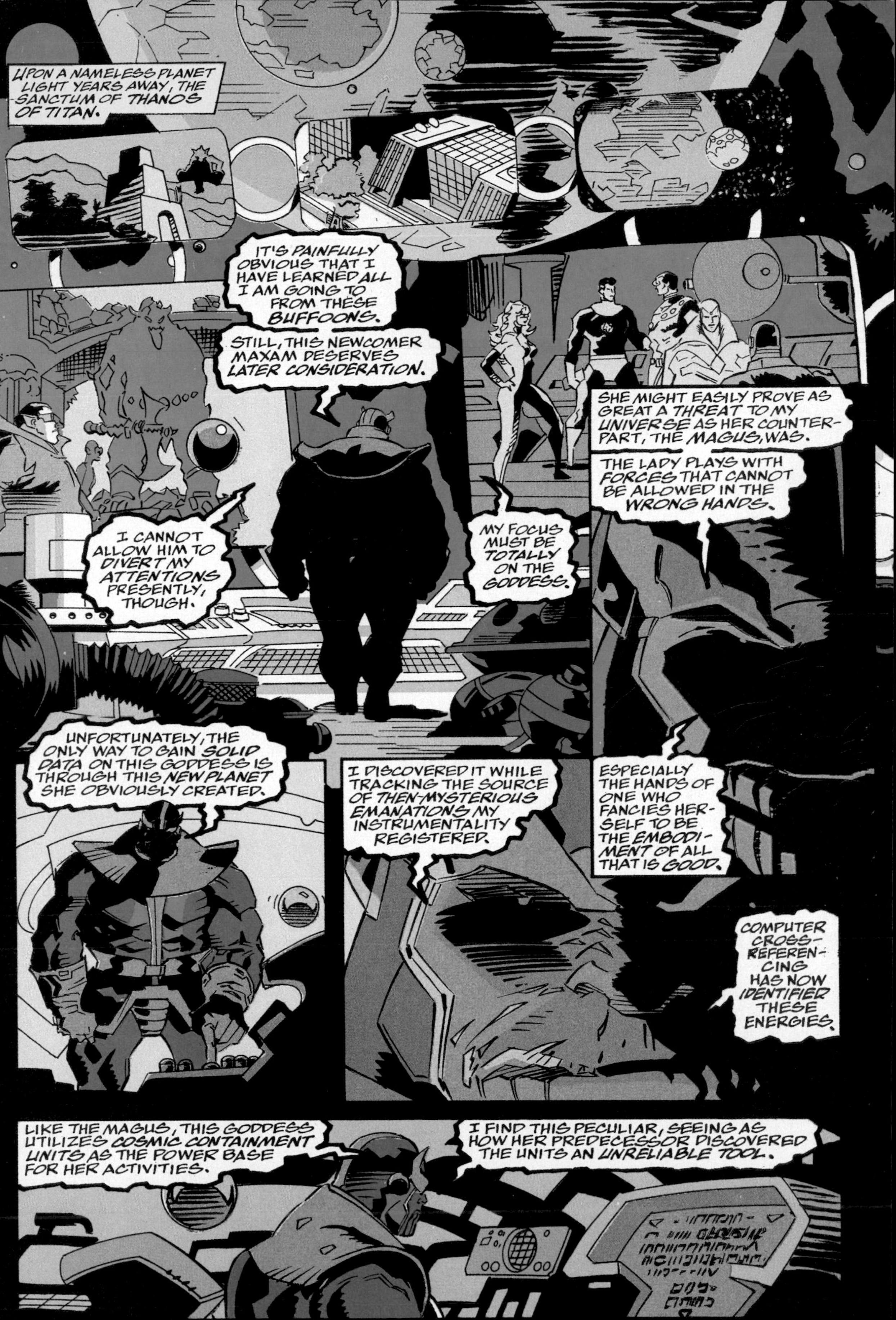
UPON A NAMELESS PLANET LIGHT YEARS AWAY, THE SANCTUM OF THANOS OF TITAN.
IT'S PAINFULLY OBVIOUS THAT I HAVE LEARNED ALL I AM GOING TO FROM THESE BUFFOONS.
STILL, THIS NEWCOMER MAXAM DESERVES LATER CONSIDERATION.
I CANNOT ALLOW HIM TO DIVERT MY ATTENTIONS PRESENTLY, THOUGH.
MY FOCUS MUST BE TOTALLY ON THE GODDESS.
SHE MIGHT EASILY PROVE AS GREAT A THREAT TO MY UNIVERSE AS HER COUNTER-PART, THE MAGUS, WAS.
THE LADY PLAYS WITH FORCES THAT CANNOT BE ALLOWED IN THE WRONG HANDS.
UNFORTUNATELY, THE ONLY WAY TO GAIN SOLID DATA ON THIS GODDESS IS THROUGH THIS NEW PLANET SHE OBVIOUSLY CREATED.
I DISCOVERED IT WHILE TRACKING THE SOURCE OF THEN-MYSTERIOUS EMANATIONS MY INSTRUMENTALITY REGISTERED.
ESPECIALLY THE HANDS OF ONE WHO FANCIES HER-SELF TO BE THE EMBODI-MENT OF ALL THAT IS GOOD.
COMPUTER CROSS-REFEREN-CING HAS NOW IDENTIFIED THESE ENERGIES.
LIKE THE MAGUS, THIS GODDESS UTILIZES COSMIC CONTAINMENT UNITS AS THE POWER BASE FOR HER ACTIVITIES.
I FIND THIS PECULIAR, SEEING AS HOW HER PREDECESSOR DISCOVERED THE UNITS AN UNRELIABLE TOOL.

THE GODDESS MUST BE AWARE OF THE LIMITS OF THE UNITS' USEFULNESS.

MANY HAVE PREVIOUSLY TRIED TO GAIN UNIVERSAL DOMINATION WITH THEM AND FAILED.

YET ONE MUST ASSUME THAT WARLOCK'S FEMININE SELF SHARES HIS SKILL AS A SCHEMER.

THE GODDESS WOULD NEVER PURSUE A TACTIC THAT WAS SO PREDESTINED TO FAILURE.

THUS, THE ONLY LOGICAL CONCLUSION I CAN REACH ON THIS MATTER IS THAT I AM MISSING THE POINT OF IT.

OBVIOUSLY I CANNOT PROPERLY FATHOM THE GODDESS'S INTENTIONS WITH THE MEAGER INTELLIGENCE--

--CURRENTLY AT MY DISPOSAL.

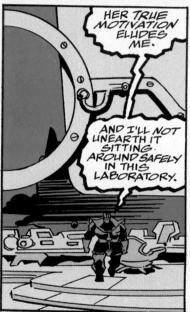

HER TRUE MOTIVATION ELUDES ME.

AND I'LL NOT UNEARTH IT SITTING AROUND SAFELY IN THIS LABORATORY.

NONE OF MY SPY PROBES HAVE BEEN ABLE TO PENETRATE HER PLANETARY DEFENSES.

SOMETHING IS HAPPENING ON THAT MUDBALL THE GODDESS DOES NOT WANT THE REST OF THE GALAXY TO WITNESS.

HOW CAN I POSSIBLY RESIST SUCH A CHALLENGE..?

I CAN'T.

INTELLECTUAL CURIOSITY WILL YET BE THE DOWNFALL OF ME.

HAVE ALL PREPARATIONS FOR MY DEPARTURE BEEN COMPLETED..?

Yes, sir.

CONTINUE TO MONITOR COM-FREQUENCY BC-7.

I HAVE MY SUSPICIONS THAT HEAVY-DUTY ARMAMENT MAY BE NEEDED IN THIS ENGAGEMENT.

HAVE STORAGE UNIT #D-666 POWERED UP AND READY FOR DELIVERY.

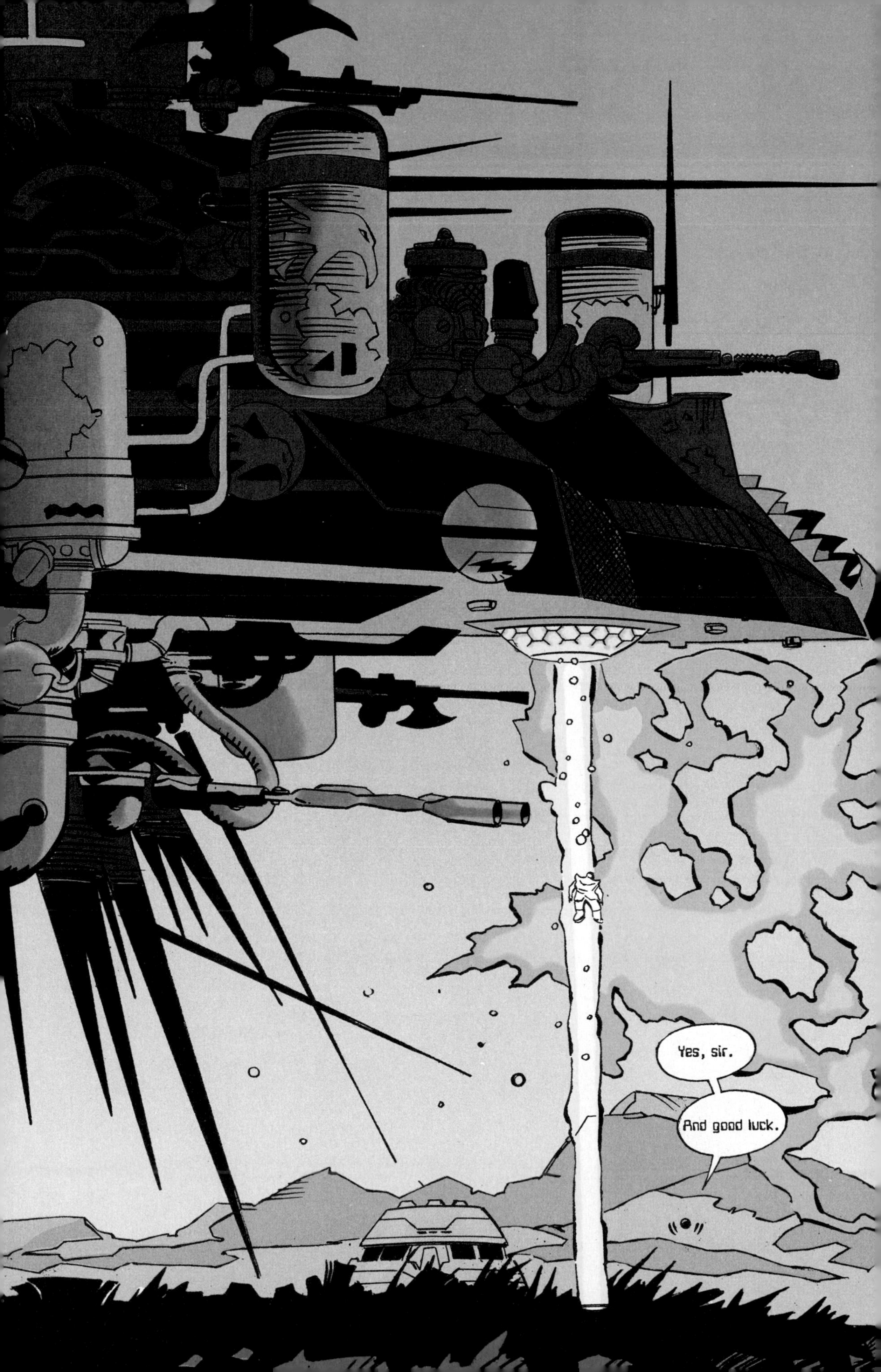
Yes, sir.
And good luck.

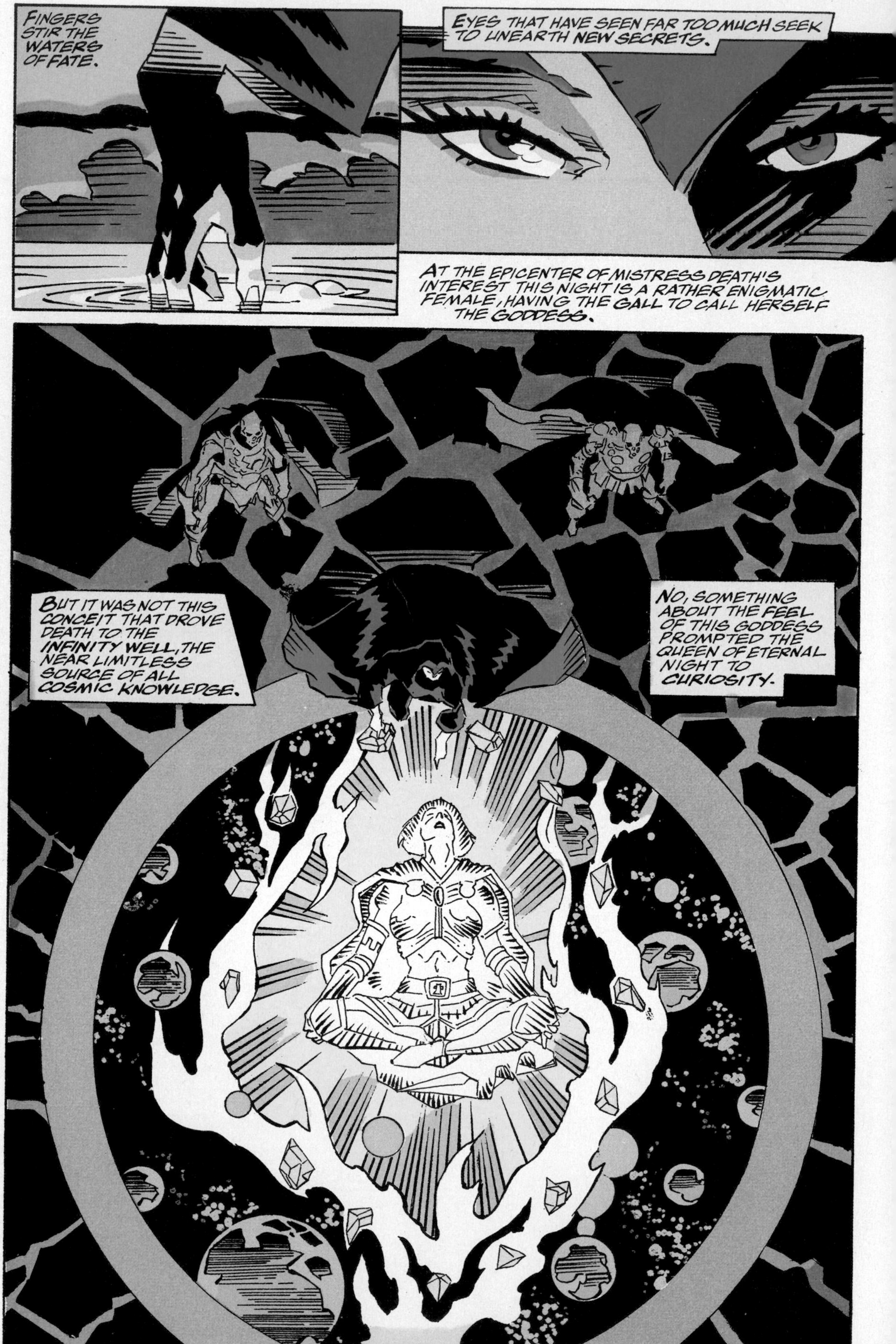
FINGERS STIR THE WATERS OF FATE.
EYES THAT HAVE SEEN FAR TOO MUCH SEEK TO UNEARTH NEW SECRETS.
AT THE EPICENTER OF MISTRESS DEATH'S INTEREST THIS NIGHT IS A RATHER ENIGMATIC FEMALE, HAVING THE GALL TO CALL HERSELF THE GODDESS.
BUT IT WAS NOT THIS CONCEIT THAT DROVE DEATH TO THE INFINITY WELL, THE NEAR LIMITLESS SOURCE OF ALL COSMIC KNOWLEDGE.
NO, SOMETHING ABOUT THE FEEL OF THIS GODDESS PROMPTED THE QUEEN OF ETERNAL NIGHT TO CURIOSITY.

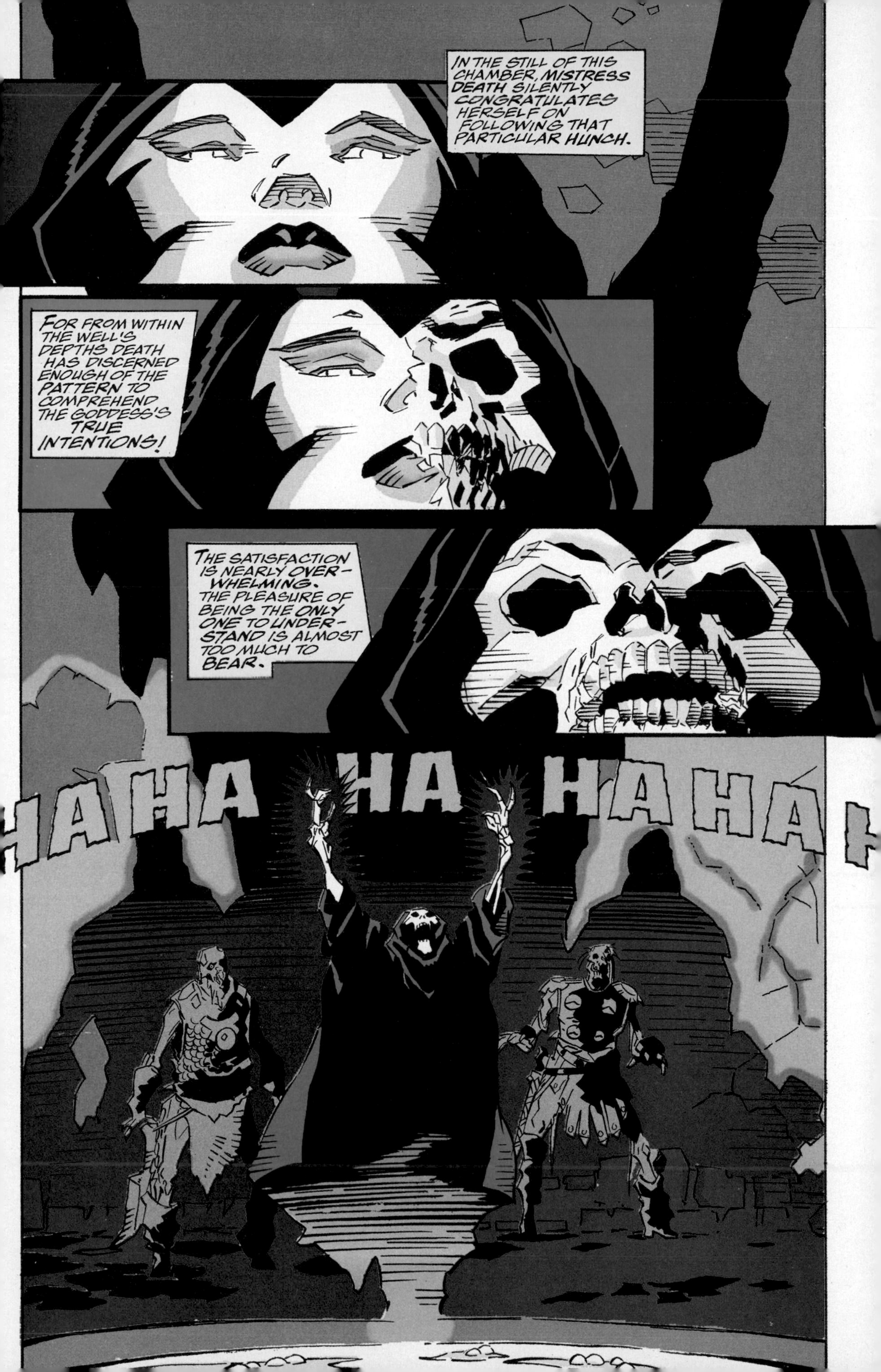
IN THE STILL OF THIS CHAMBER, MISTRESS DEATH SILENTLY CONGRATULATES HERSELF ON FOLLOWING THAT PARTICULAR HUNCH.
FOR FROM WITHIN THE WELL'S DEPTHS DEATH HAS DISCERNED ENOUGH OF THE PATTERN TO COMPREHEND THE GODDESS'S TRUE INTENTIONS!
THE SATISFACTION IS NEARLY OVER-WHELMING. THE PLEASURE OF BEING THE ONLY ONE TO UNDER-STAND IS ALMOST TOO MUCH TO BEAR.
HAHA HA HAHAHA

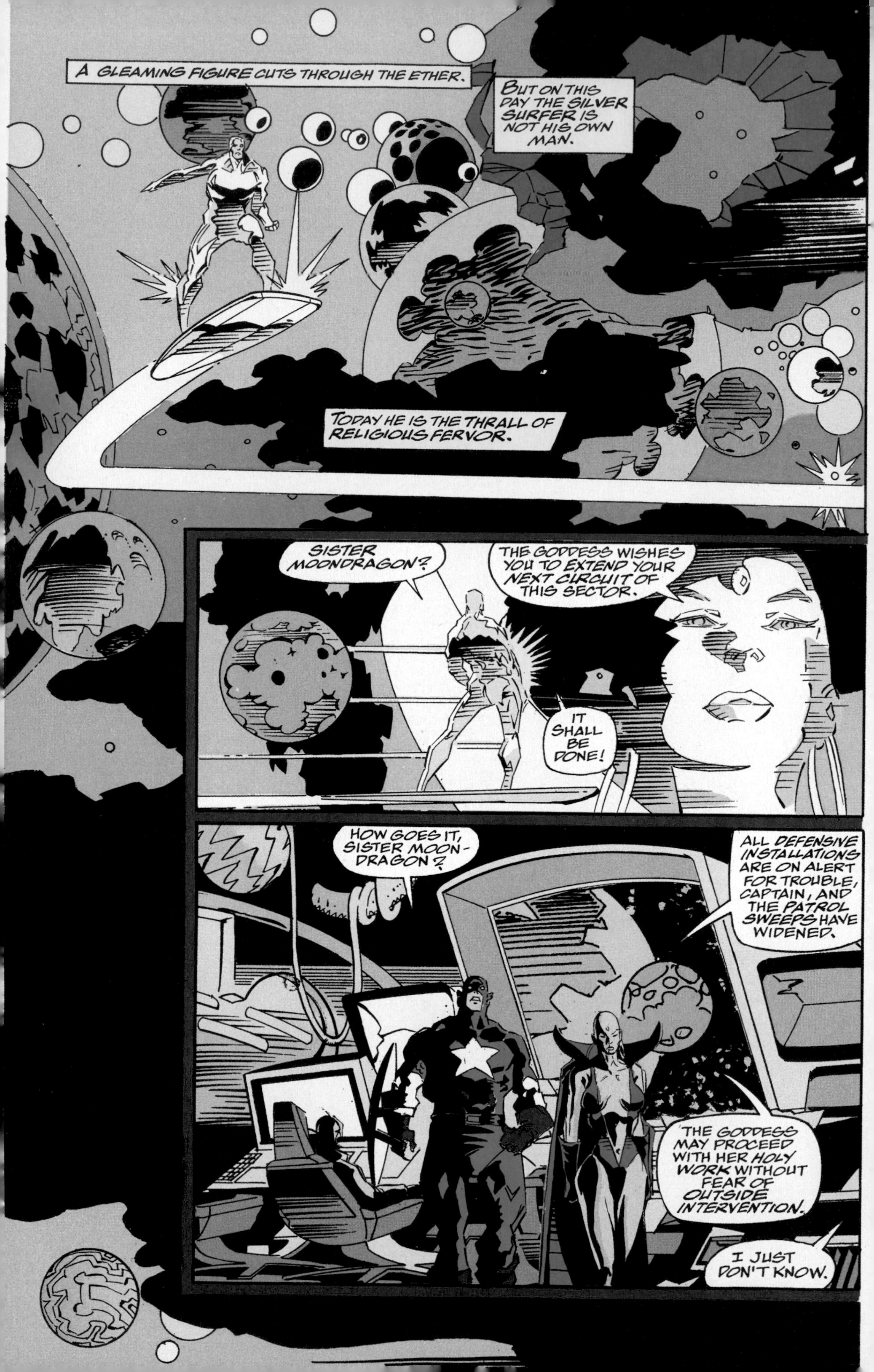
A GLEAMING FIGURE CUTS THROUGH THE ETHER.
BUT ON THIS DAY THE SILVER SURFER IS NOT HIS OWN MAN.
TODAY HE IS THE THRALL OF RELIGIOUS FERVOR.
SISTER MOONDRAGON?
THE GODDESS WISHES YOU TO EXTEND YOUR NEXT CIRCUIT OF THIS SECTOR.
IT SHALL BE DONE!
HOW GOES IT, SISTER MOON-DRAGON?
ALL DEFENSIVE INSTALLATIONS ARE ON ALERT FOR TROUBLE, CAPTAIN, AND THE PATROL SWEEPS HAVE WIDENED.
THE GODDESS MAY PROCEED WITH HER HOLY WORK WITHOUT FEAR OF OUTSIDE INTERVENTION.
I JUST DON'T KNOW.

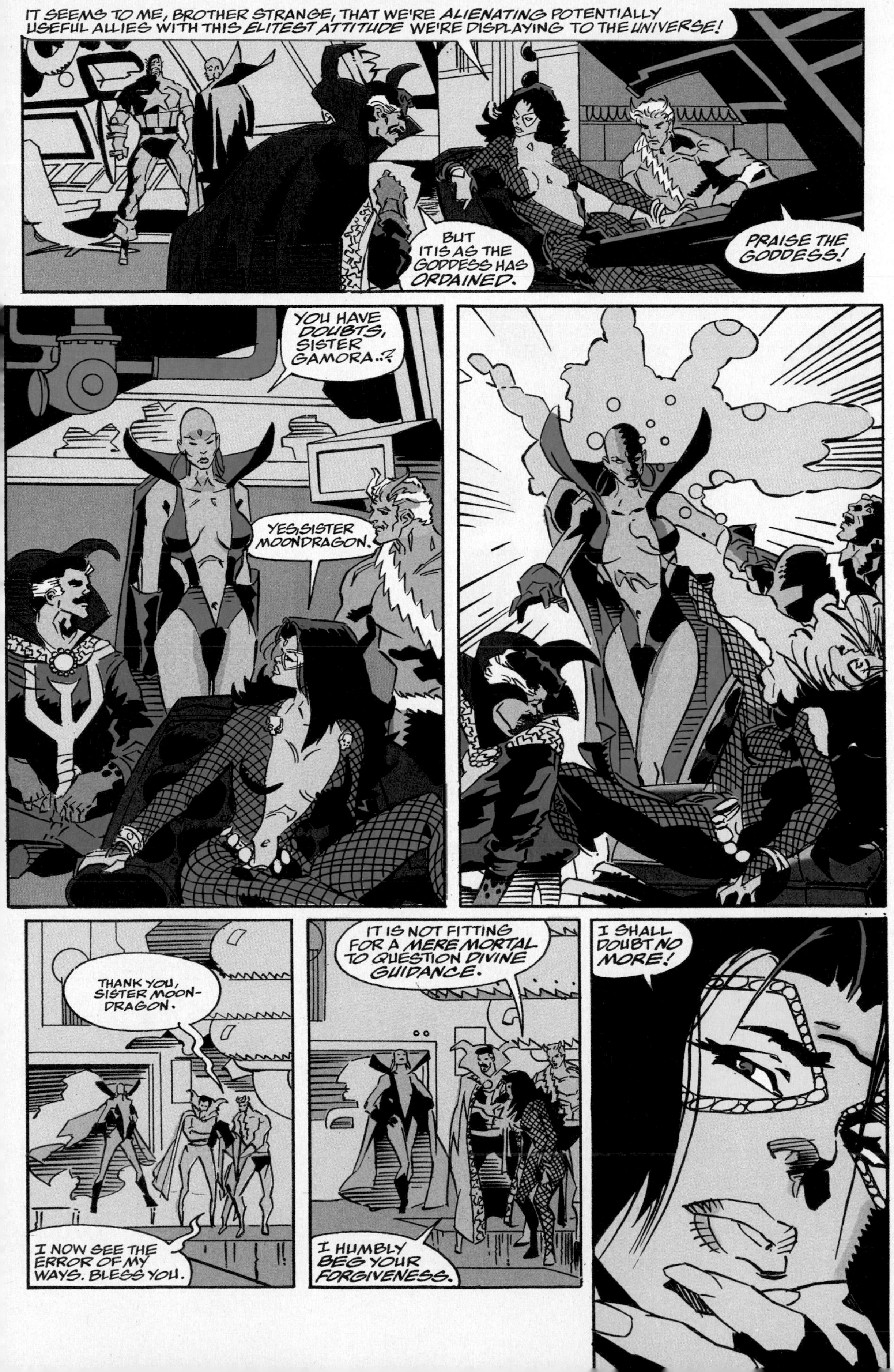
IT SEEMS TO ME, BROTHER STRANGE, THAT WE'RE ALIENATING POTENTIALLY USEFUL ALLIES WITH THIS ELITEST ATTITUDE WE'RE DISPLAYING TO THE UNIVERSE!
BUT IT IS AS THE GODDESS HAS ORDAINED.
PRAISE THE GODDESS!
YOU HAVE DOUBTS, SISTER GAMORA..?
YES, SISTER MOONDRAGON.
THANK YOU, SISTER MOON-DRAGON.
I NOW SEE THE ERROR OF MY WAYS. BLESS YOU.
IT IS NOT FITTING FOR A MERE MORTAL TO QUESTION DIVINE GUIDANCE.
I HUMBLY BEG YOUR FORGIVENESS.
I SHALL DOUBT NO MORE!

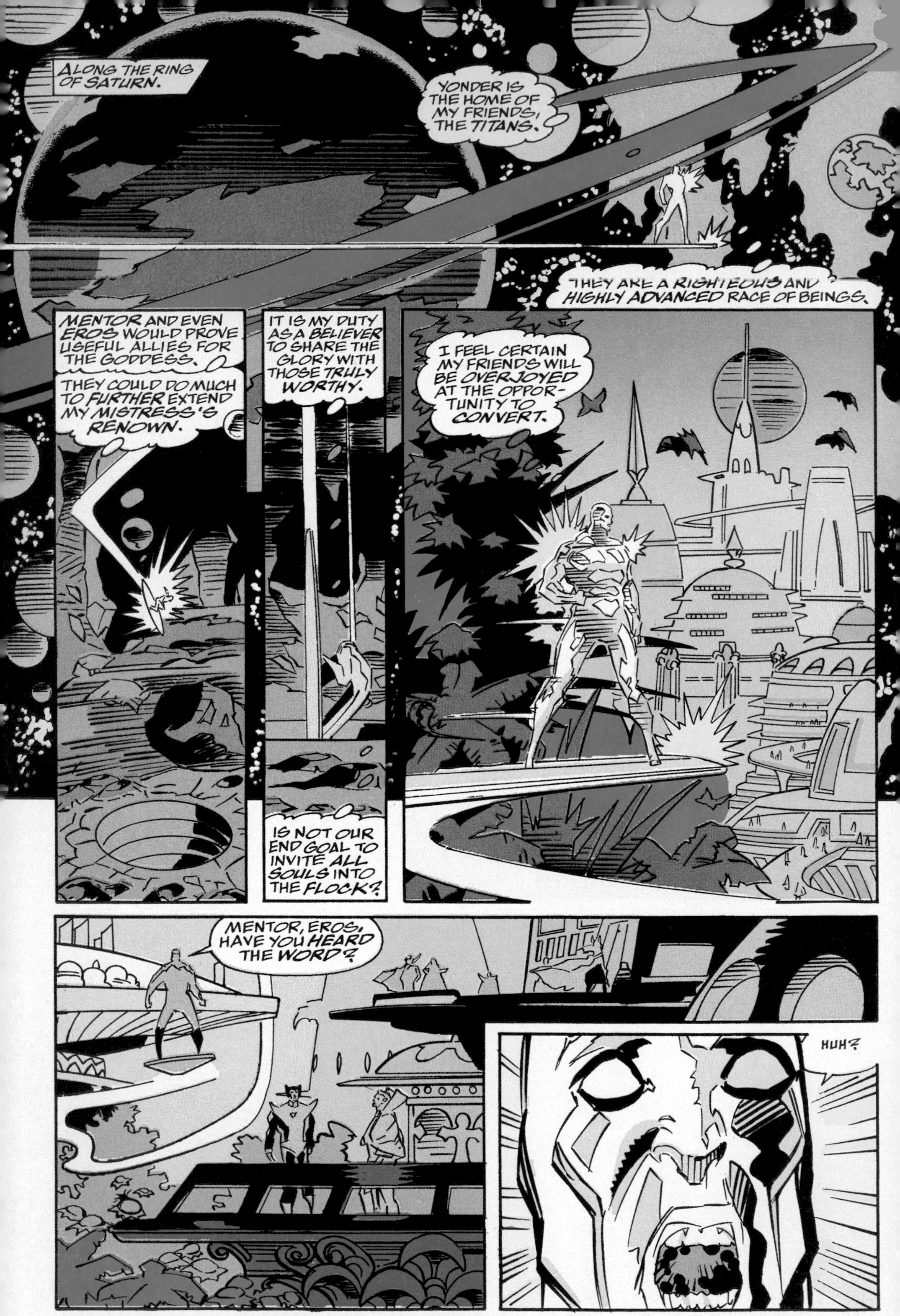
ALONG THE RING OF SATURN.
YONDER IS THE HOME OF MY FRIENDS, THE TITANS.
THEY ARE A RIGHTEOUS AND HIGHLY ADVANCED RACE OF BEINGS.
MENTOR AND EVEN EROS WOULD PROVE USEFUL ALLIES FOR THE GODDESS.
THEY COULD DO MUCH TO FURTHER EXTEND MY MISTRESS'S RENOWN.
IT IS MY DUTY AS A BELIEVER TO SHARE THE GLORY WITH THOSE TRULY WORTHY.
IS NOT OUR END GOAL TO INVITE ALL SOULS INTO THE FLOCK?
I FEEL CERTAIN MY FRIENDS WILL BE OVERJOYED AT THE OPPORTUNITY TO CONVERT.
MENTOR, EROS, HAVE YOU HEARD THE WORD?
HUH?

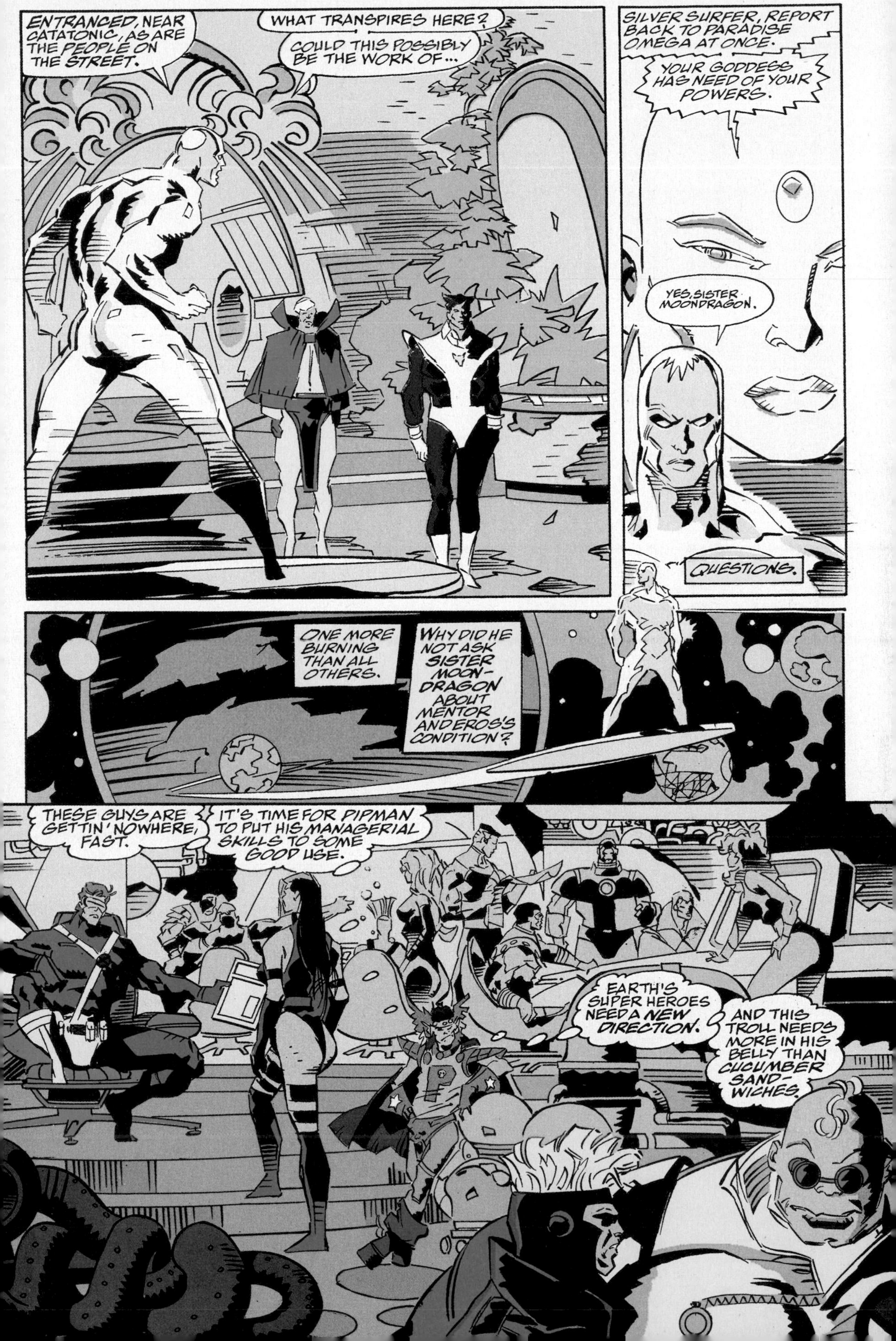
ENTRANCED, NEAR CATATONIC, AS ARE THE PEOPLE ON THE STREET.
WHAT TRANSPIRES HERE?
COULD THIS POSSIBLY BE THE WORK OF...
SILVER SURFER, REPORT BACK TO PARADISE OMEGA AT ONCE.
YOUR GODDESS HAS NEED OF YOUR POWERS.
YES, SISTER MOONDRAGON.
QUESTIONS.
ONE MORE BURNING THAN ALL OTHERS.
WHY DID HE NOT ASK SISTER MOON-DRAGON ABOUT MENTOR ANDEROS'S CONDITION?
THESE GUYS ARE GETTIN' NOWHERE, FAST.
IT'S TIME FOR PIPMAN TO PUT HIS MANAGERIAL SKILLS TO SOME GOOD USE.
EARTH'S SUPER HEROES NEED A NEW DIRECTION.
AND THIS TROLL NEEDS MORE IN HIS BELLY THAN CUCUMBER SAND-WICHES.

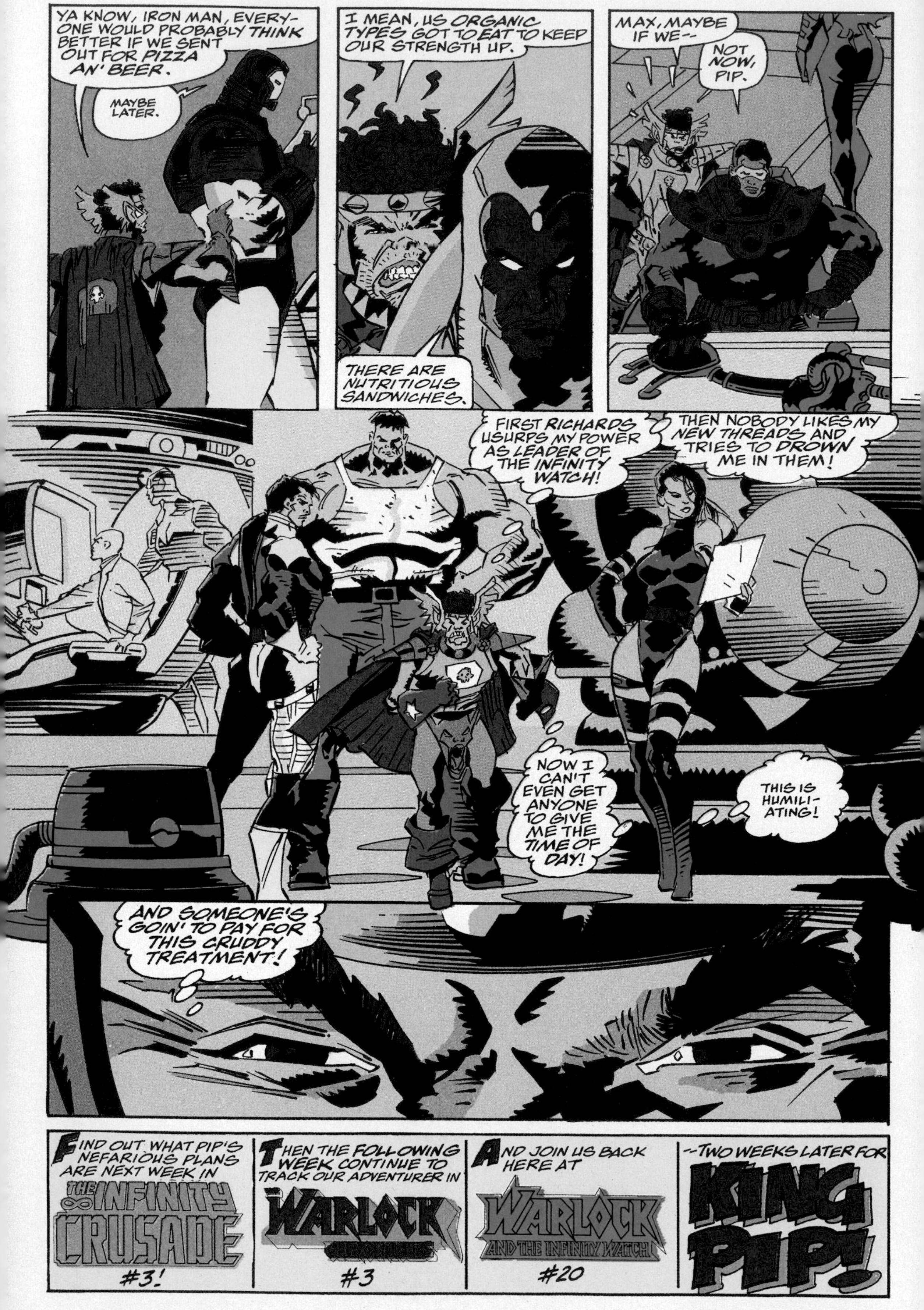
YA KNOW, IRON MAN, EVERYONE WOULD PROBABLY THINK BETTER IF WE SENT OUT FOR PIZZA AN' BEER.
MAYBE LATER.
I MEAN, US ORGANIC TYPES GOT TO EAT TO KEEP OUR STRENGTH UP.
THERE ARE NUTRITIOUS SANDWICHES.
MAX, MAYBE IF WE--
NOT NOW, PIP.
FIRST RICHARDS USURPS MY POWER AS LEADER OF THE INFINITY WATCH!
THEN NOBODY LIKES MY NEW THREADS AND TRIES TO DROWN ME IN THEM!
NOW I CAN'T EVEN GET ANYONE TO GIVE ME THE TIME OF DAY!
THIS IS HUMILIATING!
AND SOMEONE'S GOIN' TO PAY FOR THIS CRUDDY TREATMENT!
FIND OUT WHAT PIP'S NEFARIOUS PLANS ARE NEXT WEEK IN
THE INFINITY CRUSADE
#3!
THEN THE FOLLOWING WEEK CONTINUE TO TRACK OUR ADVENTURER IN
WARLOCK CHRONICLES
#3
AND JOIN US BACK HERE AT
WARLOCK AND THE INFINITY WATCH
#20
--TWO WEEKS LATER FOR
KING PIP!

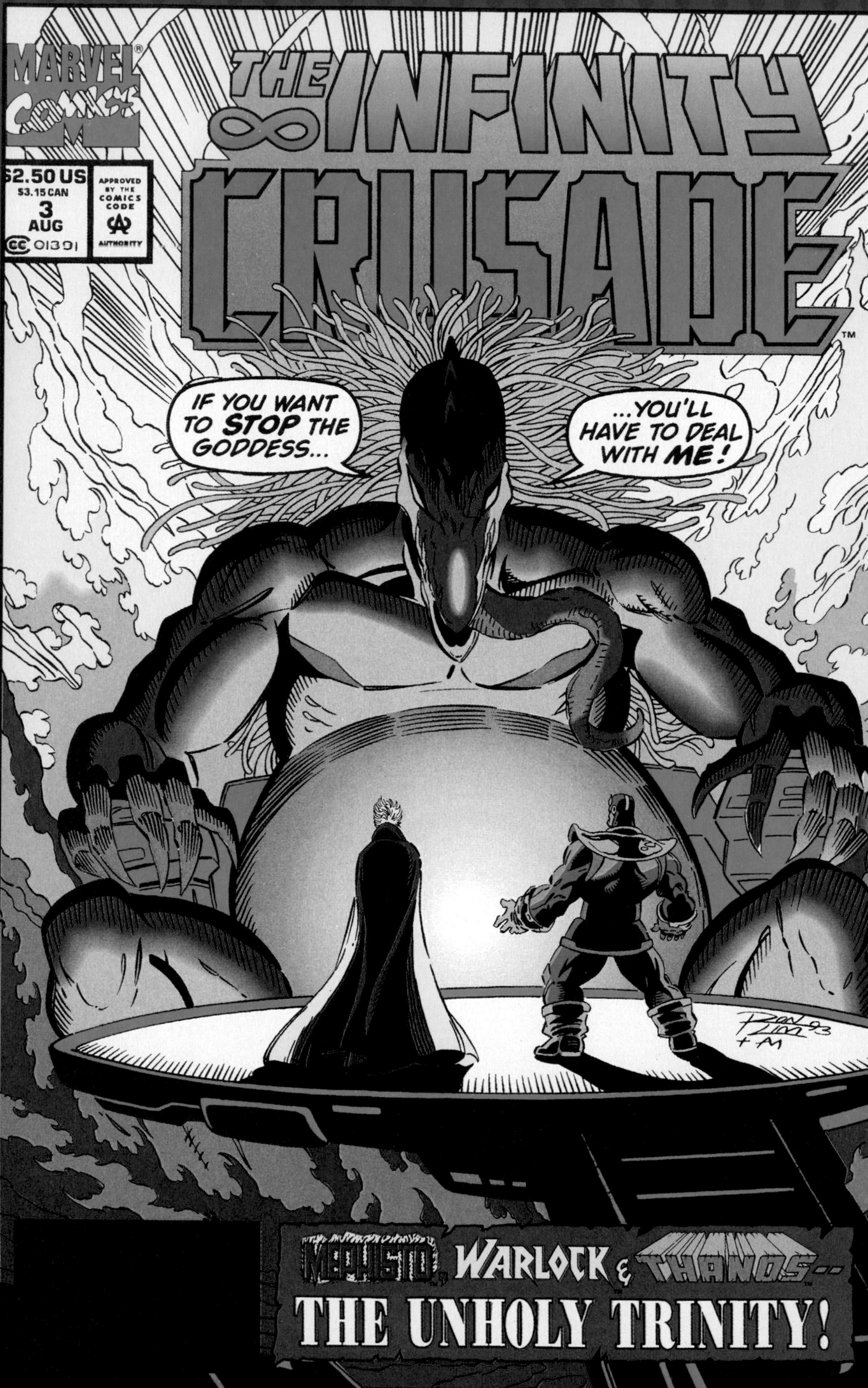
MARVEL COMICS
THE INFINITY CRUSADE
$2.50 US
$3.15 CAN
3
AUG
APPROVED BY THE COMICS CODE AUTHORITY
IF YOU WANT TO STOP THE GODDESS...
...YOU'LL HAVE TO DEAL WITH ME!
MEPHISTO, WARLOCK & THANOS--
THE UNHOLY TRINITY!

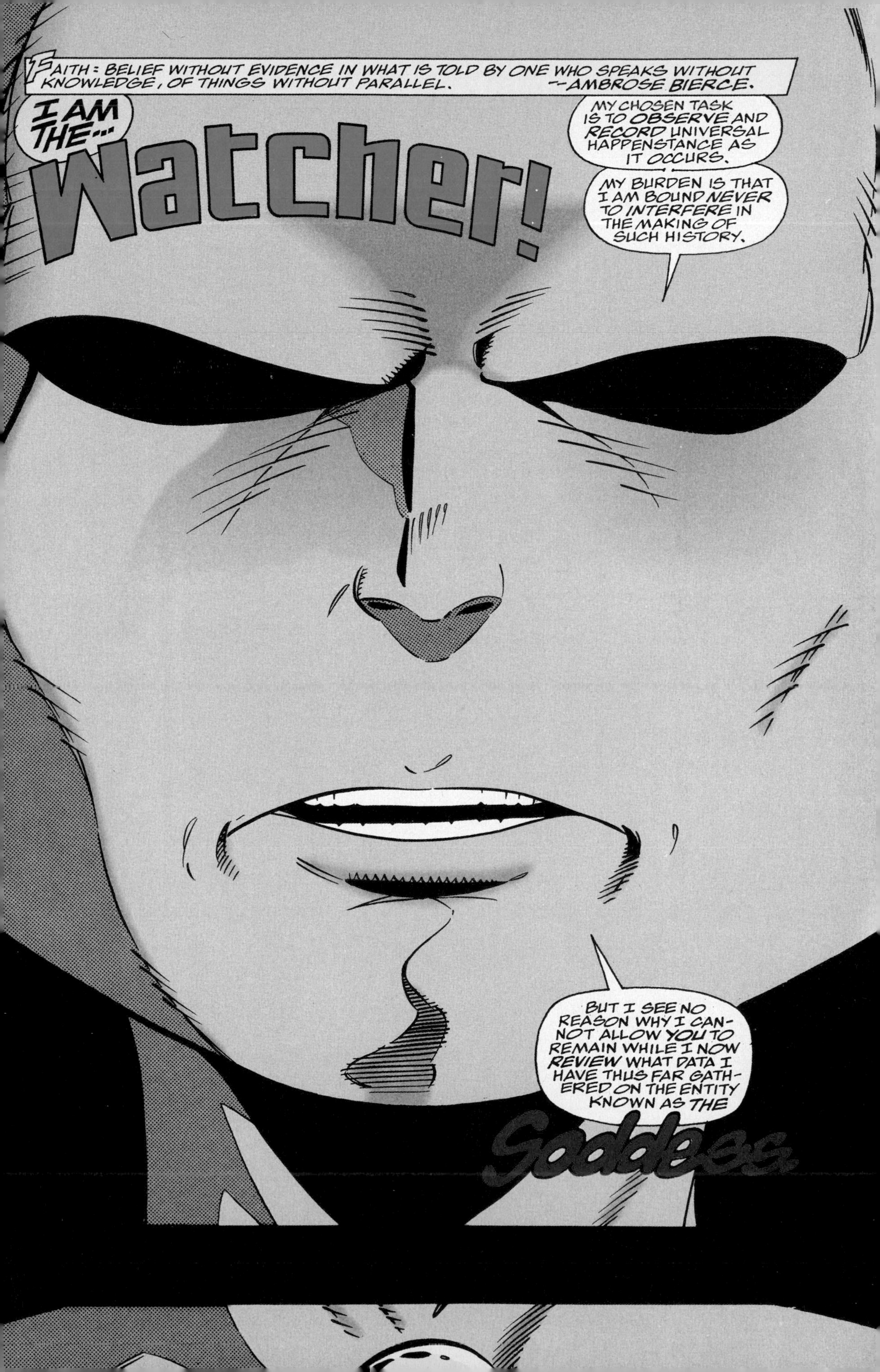
FAITH: BELIEF WITHOUT EVIDENCE IN WHAT IS TOLD BY ONE WHO SPEAKS WITHOUT KNOWLEDGE, OF THINGS WITHOUT PARALLEL. --AMBROSE BIERCE.
I AM THE...
Watcher!
MY CHOSEN TASK IS TO OBSERVE AND RECORD UNIVERSAL HAPPENSTANCE AS IT OCCURS.
MY BURDEN IS THAT I AM BOUND NEVER TO INTERFERE IN THE MAKING OF SUCH HISTORY.
BUT I SEE NO REASON WHY I CANNOT ALLOW YOU TO REMAIN WHILE I NOW REVIEW WHAT DATA I HAVE THUS FAR GATHERED ON THE ENTITY KNOWN AS THE
Goddess.

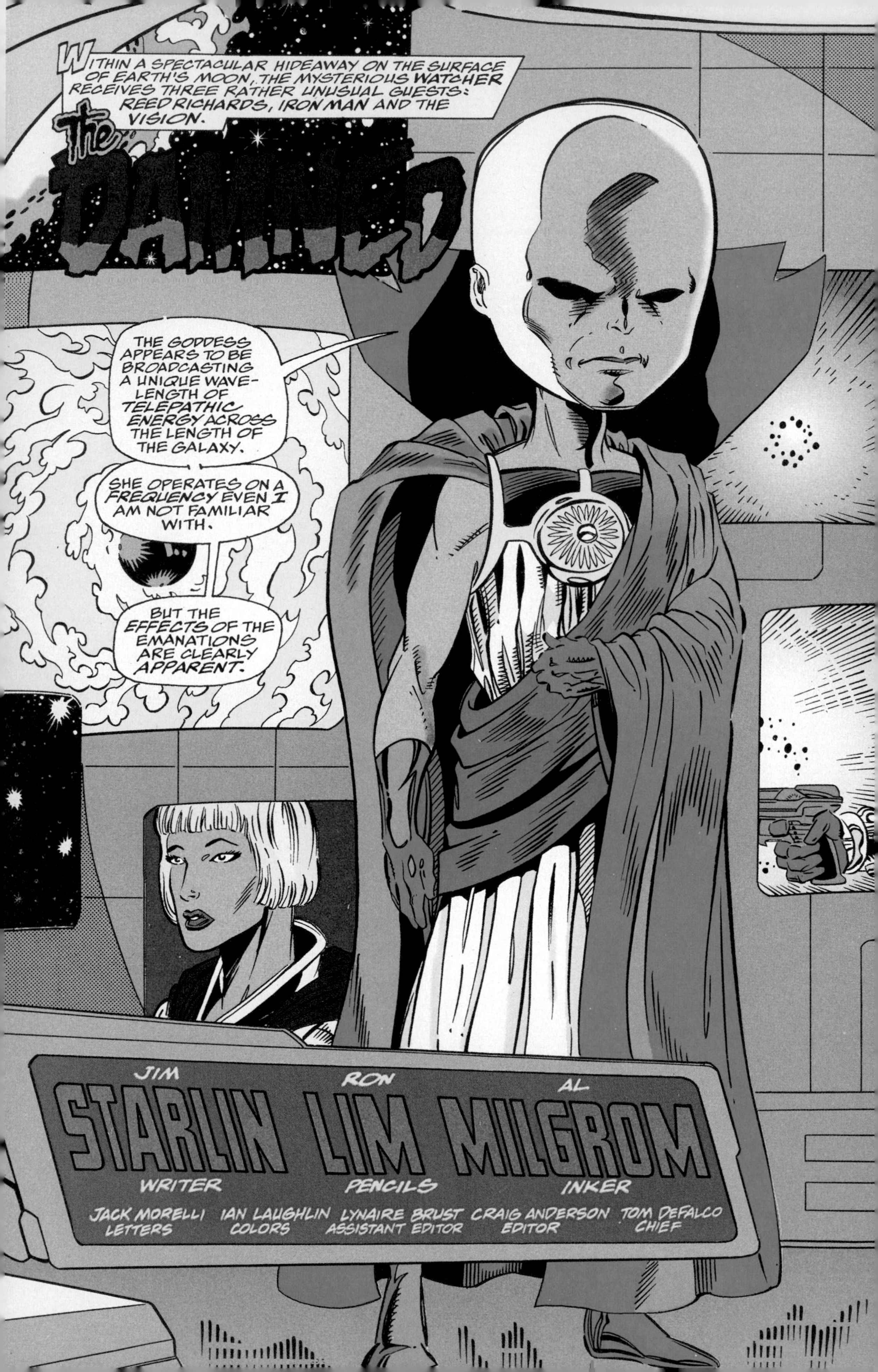

WITHIN A SPECTACULAR HIDEAWAY ON THE SURFACE OF EARTH'S MOON, THE MYSTERIOUS WATCHER RECEIVES THREE RATHER UNUSUAL GUESTS: REED RICHARDS, IRON MAN AND THE VISION.
THE DAMNED
THE GODDESS APPEARS TO BE BROADCASTING A UNIQUE WAVE-LENGTH OF TELEPATHIC ENERGY ACROSS THE LENGTH OF THE GALAXY.
SHE OPERATES ON A FREQUENCY EVEN I AM NOT FAMILIAR WITH.
BUT THE EFFECTS OF THE EMANATIONS ARE CLEARLY APPARENT.
JIM STARLIN WRITER
RON LIM PENCILS
AL MILGROM INKER
JACK MORELLI LETTERS
IAN LAUGHLIN COLORS
LYNAIRE BRUST ASSISTANT EDITOR
CRAIG ANDERSON EDITOR
TOM DeFALCO CHIEF

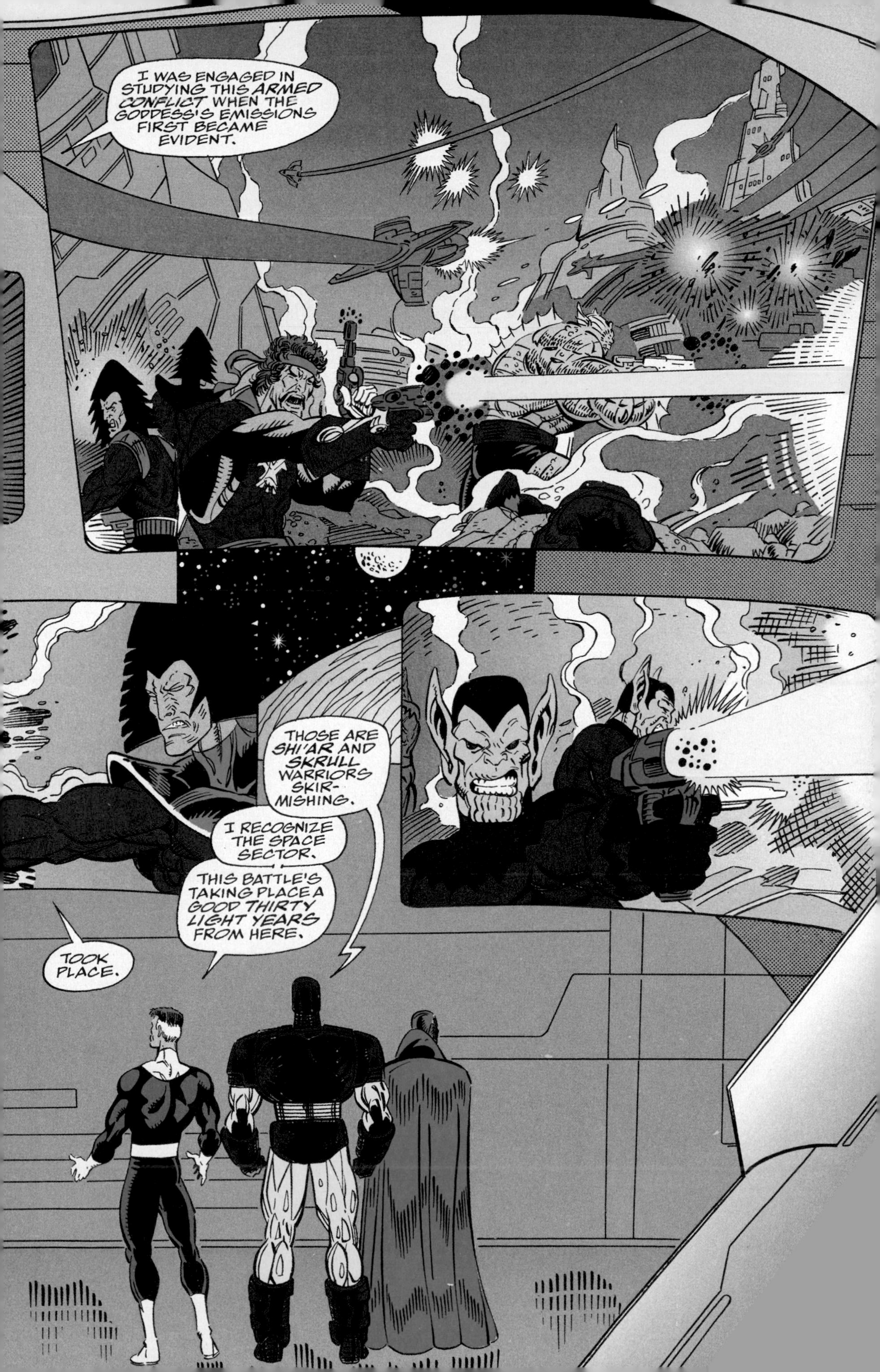
I WAS ENGAGED IN STUDYING THIS ARMED CONFLICT WHEN THE GODDESS'S EMISSIONS FIRST BECAME EVIDENT.
THOSE ARE SHI'AR AND SKRULL WARRIORS SKIR-MISHING.
I RECOGNIZE THE SPACE SECTOR.
THIS BATTLE'S TAKING PLACE A GOOD THIRTY LIGHT YEARS FROM HERE.
TOOK PLACE.

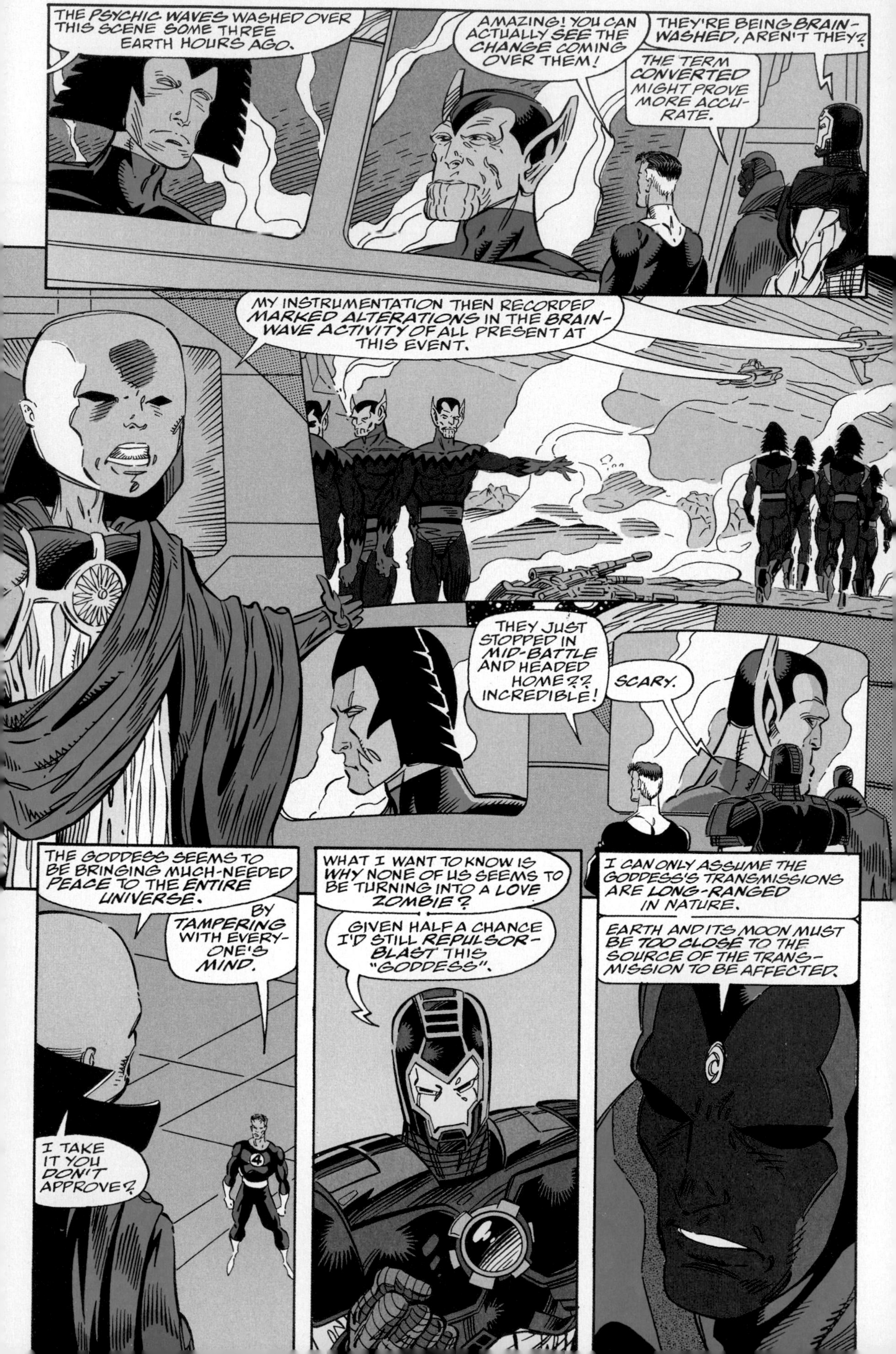
THE PSYCHIC WAVES WASHED OVER THIS SCENE SOME THREE EARTH HOURS AGO.
AMAZING! YOU CAN ACTUALLY SEE THE CHANGE COMING OVER THEM!
THEY'RE BEING BRAIN-WASHED, AREN'T THEY?
THE TERM CONVERTED MIGHT PROVE MORE ACCU-RATE.
MY INSTRUMENTATION THEN RECORDED MARKED ALTERATIONS IN THE BRAIN-WAVE ACTIVITY OF ALL PRESENT AT THIS EVENT.
THEY JUST STOPPED IN MID-BATTLE AND HEADED HOME?? INCREDIBLE!
SCARY.
THE GODDESS SEEMS TO BE BRINGING MUCH-NEEDED PEACE TO THE ENTIRE UNIVERSE.
BY TAMPERING WITH EVERY-ONE'S MIND.
I TAKE IT YOU DON'T APPROVE?
WHAT I WANT TO KNOW IS WHY NONE OF US SEEMS TO BE TURNING INTO A LOVE ZOMBIE?
GIVEN HALF A CHANCE I'D STILL REPULSOR-BLAST THIS "GODDESS".
I CAN ONLY ASSUME THE GODDESS'S TRANSMISSIONS ARE LONG-RANGED IN NATURE.
EARTH AND ITS MOON MUST BE TOO CLOSE TO THE SOURCE OF THE TRANS-MISSION TO BE AFFECTED.

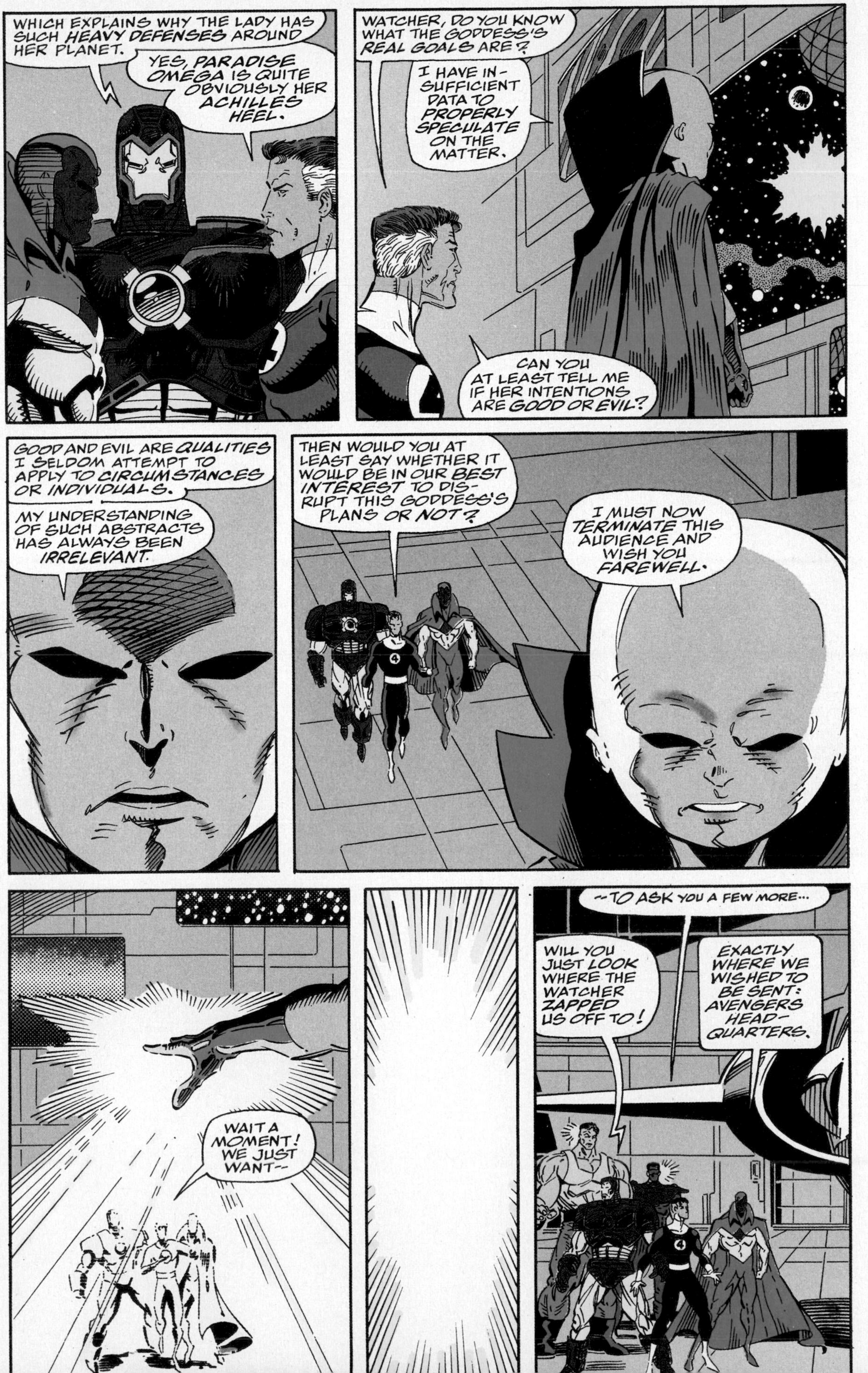
WHICH EXPLAINS WHY THE LADY HAS SUCH HEAVY DEFENSES AROUND HER PLANET.
YES, PARADISE OMEGA IS QUITE OBVIOUSLY HER ACHILLES HEEL.
WATCHER, DO YOU KNOW WHAT THE GODDESS'S REAL GOALS ARE?
I HAVE INSUFFICIENT DATA TO PROPERLY SPECULATE ON THE MATTER.
CAN YOU AT LEAST TELL ME IF HER INTENTIONS ARE GOOD OR EVIL?
GOOD AND EVIL ARE QUALITIES I SELDOM ATTEMPT TO APPLY TO CIRCUMSTANCES OR INDIVIDUALS.
MY UNDERSTANDING OF SUCH ABSTRACTS HAS ALWAYS BEEN IRRELEVANT.
THEN WOULD YOU AT LEAST SAY WHETHER IT WOULD BE IN OUR BEST INTEREST TO DISRUPT THIS GODDESS'S PLANS OR NOT?
I MUST NOW TERMINATE THIS AUDIENCE AND WISH YOU FAREWELL.
WAIT A MOMENT! WE JUST WANT--
--TO ASK YOU A FEW MORE...
WILL YOU JUST LOOK WHERE THE WATCHER ZAPPED US OFF TO!
EXACTLY WHERE WE WISHED TO BE SENT: AVENGERS HEADQUARTERS.

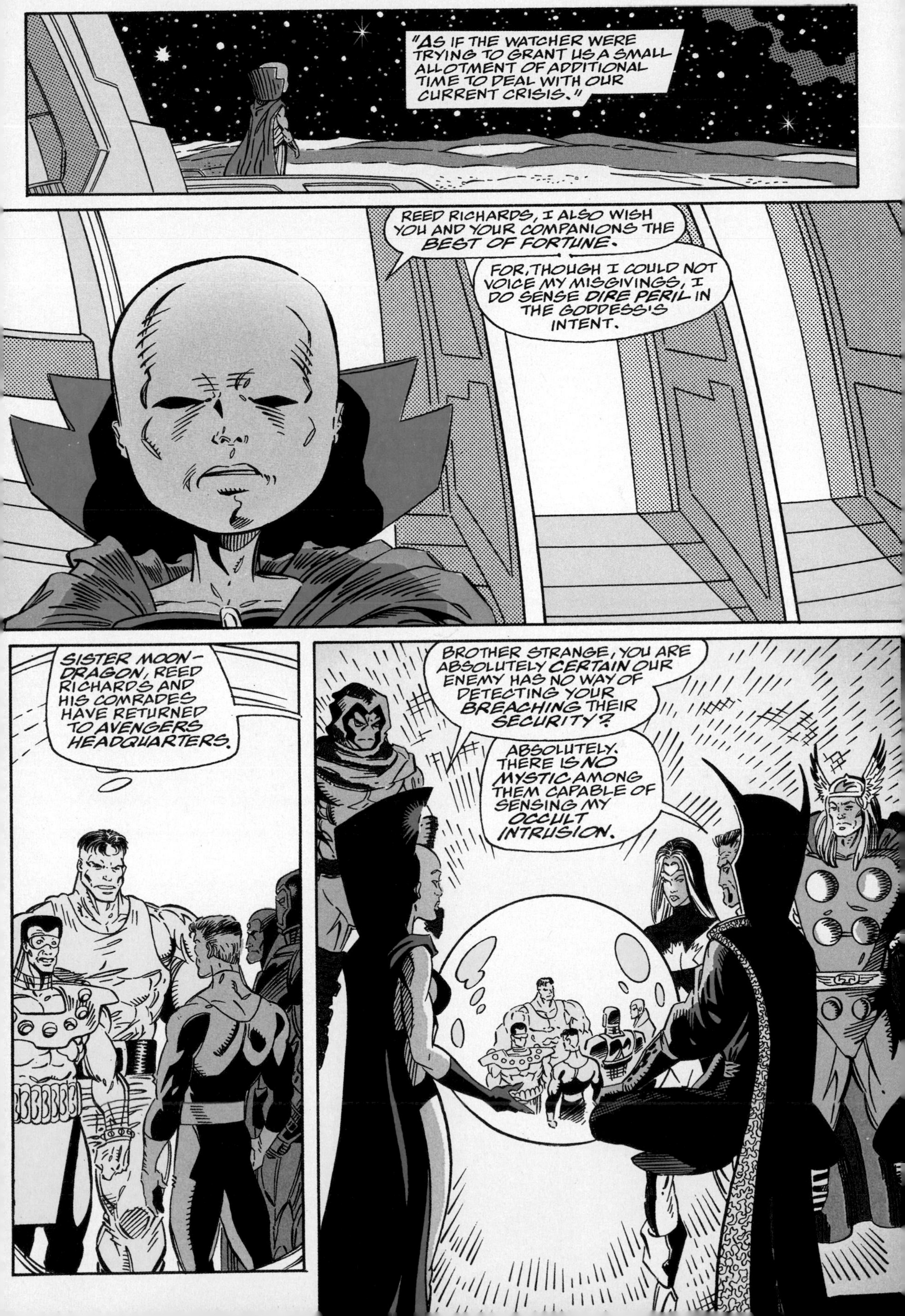
"AS IF THE WATCHER WERE TRYING TO GRANT US A SMALL ALLOTMENT OF ADDITIONAL TIME TO DEAL WITH OUR CURRENT CRISIS."
REED RICHARDS, I ALSO WISH YOU AND YOUR COMPANIONS THE BEST OF FORTUNE.
FOR, THOUGH I COULD NOT VOICE MY MISGIVINGS, I DO SENSE DIRE PERIL IN THE GODDESS'S INTENT.
SISTER MOON-DRAGON, REED RICHARDS AND HIS COMRADES HAVE RETURNED TO AVENGERS HEADQUARTERS.
BROTHER STRANGE, YOU ARE ABSOLUTELY CERTAIN OUR ENEMY HAS NO WAY OF DETECTING YOUR BREACHING THEIR SECURITY?
ABSOLUTELY. THERE IS NO MYSTIC AMONG THEM CAPABLE OF SENSING MY OCCULT INTRUSION.

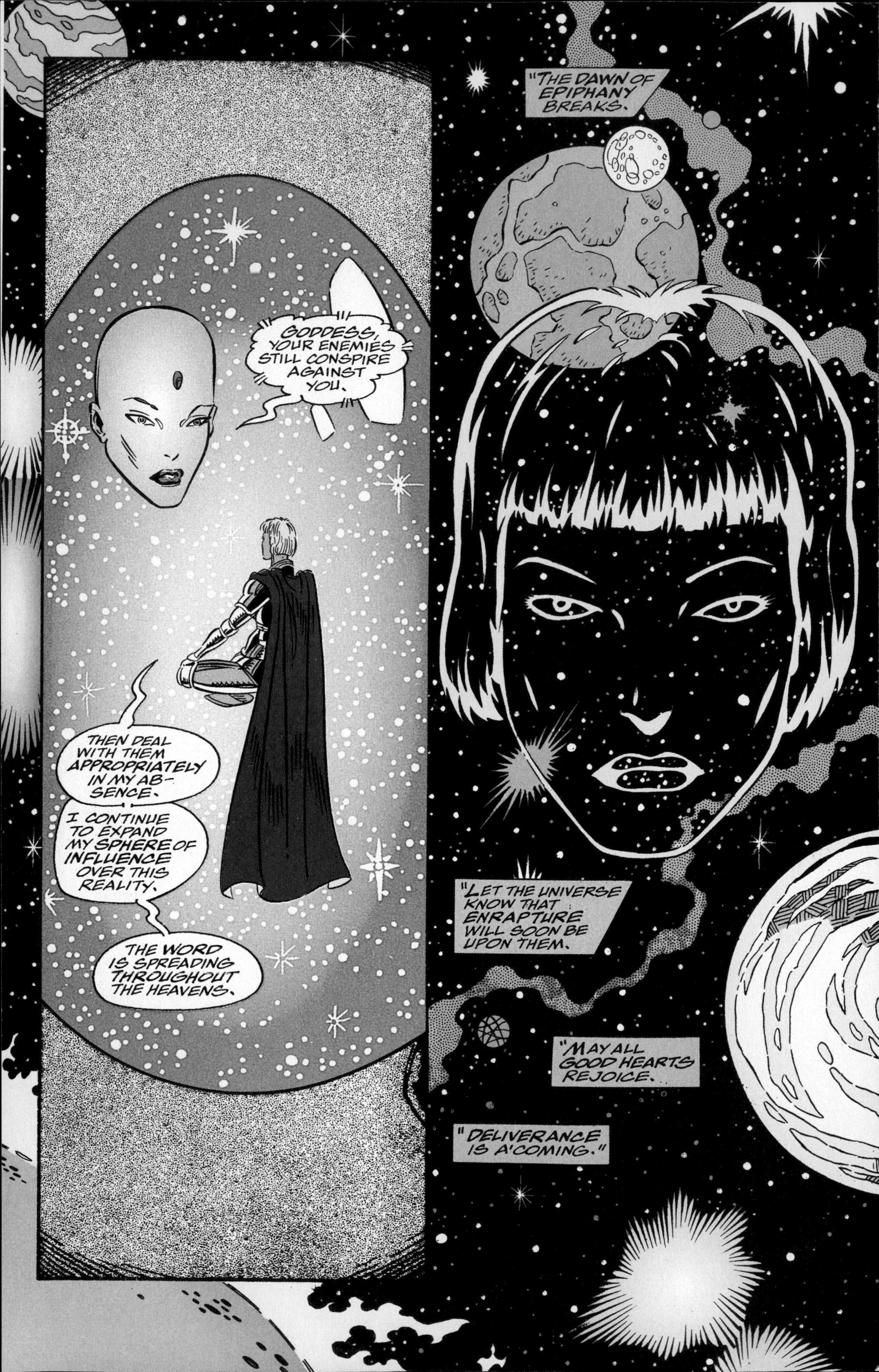
GODDESS, YOUR ENEMIES STILL CONSPIRE AGAINST YOU.
THEN DEAL WITH THEM APPROPRIATELY IN MY AB-SENCE.
I CONTINUE TO EXPAND MY SPHERE OF INFLUENCE OVER THIS REALITY.
THE WORD IS SPREADING THROUGHOUT THE HEAVENS.
"THE DAWN OF EPIPHANY BREAKS.
"LET THE UNIVERSE KNOW THAT ENRAPTURE WILL SOON BE UPON THEM.
"MAY ALL GOOD HEARTS REJOICE.
"DELIVERANCE IS A'COMING."

UPON THE THRONE WORLD OF THE SHI'AR EMPIRE...

THE STARJAMMERS HEPZIBAH AND RAZA.

COMMUNICATIONS HAS LOST ALL CONTACT WITH THE FOURTH BATTALION.

BAD NEWS. WHAT DO YOU SUPPOSE...

...HAPPENED?

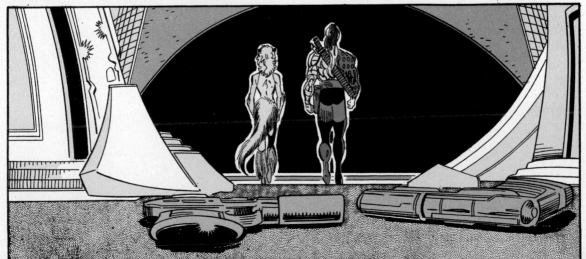

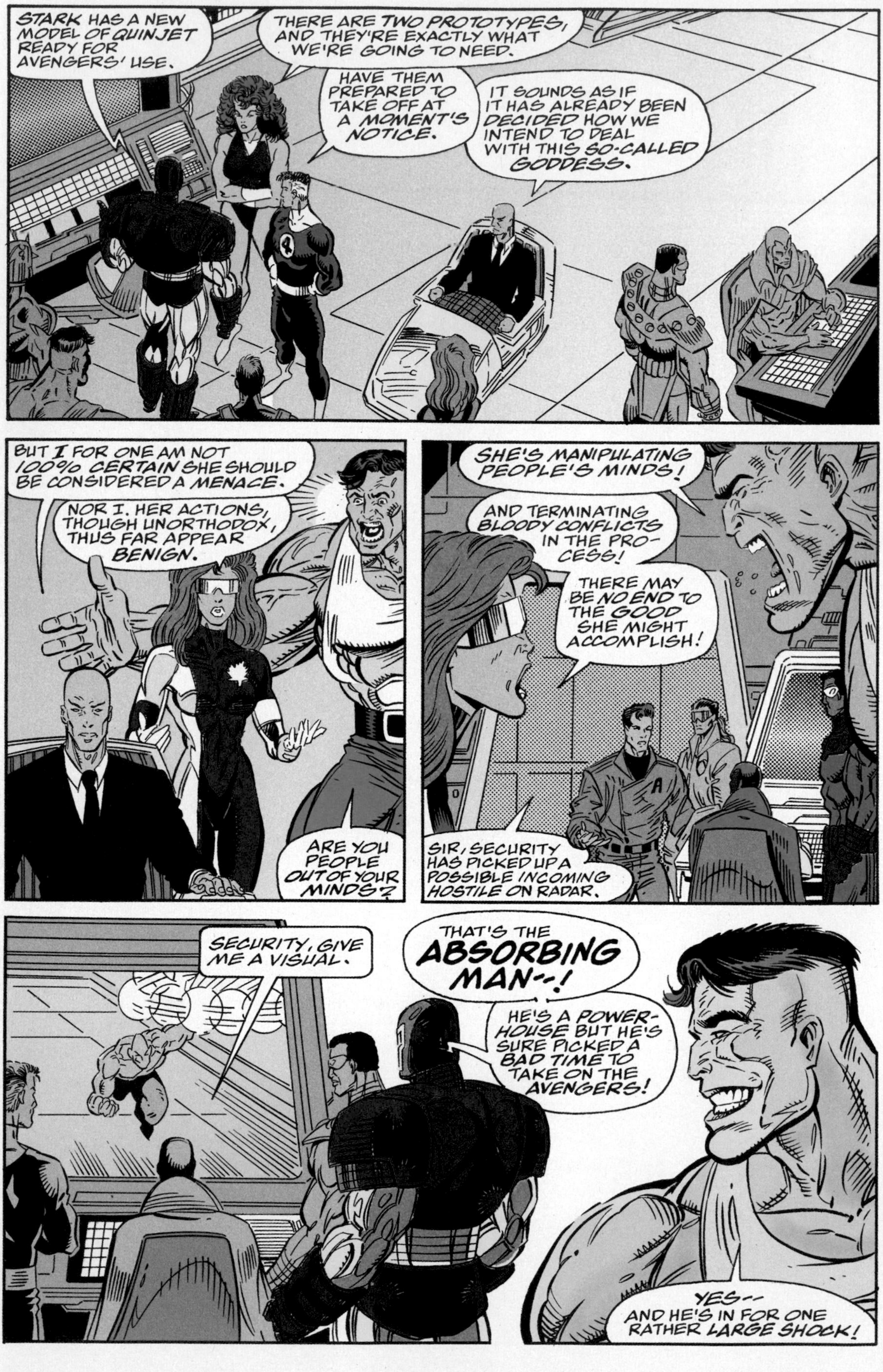
STARK HAS A NEW MODEL OF QUINJET READY FOR AVENGERS' USE.
THERE ARE TWO PROTOTYPES, AND THEY'RE EXACTLY WHAT WE'RE GOING TO NEED.
HAVE THEM PREPARED TO TAKE OFF AT A MOMENT'S NOTICE.
IT SOUNDS AS IF IT HAS ALREADY BEEN DECIDED HOW WE INTEND TO DEAL WITH THIS SO-CALLED GODDESS.
BUT I FOR ONE AM NOT 100% CERTAIN SHE SHOULD BE CONSIDERED A MENACE.
NOR I. HER ACTIONS, THOUGH UNORTHODOX, THUS FAR APPEAR BENIGN.
ARE YOU PEOPLE OUT OF YOUR MINDS?
SHE'S MANIPULATING PEOPLE'S MINDS!
AND TERMINATING BLOODY CONFLICTS IN THE PROCESS!
THERE MAY BE NO END TO THE GOOD SHE MIGHT ACCOMPLISH!
SIR, SECURITY HAS PICKED UP A POSSIBLE INCOMING HOSTILE ON RADAR.
SECURITY, GIVE ME A VISUAL.
THAT'S THE ABSORBING MAN--!
HE'S A POWERHOUSE BUT HE'S SURE PICKED A BAD TIME TO TAKE ON THE AVENGERS!
YES-- AND HE'S IN FOR ONE RATHER LARGE SHOCK!

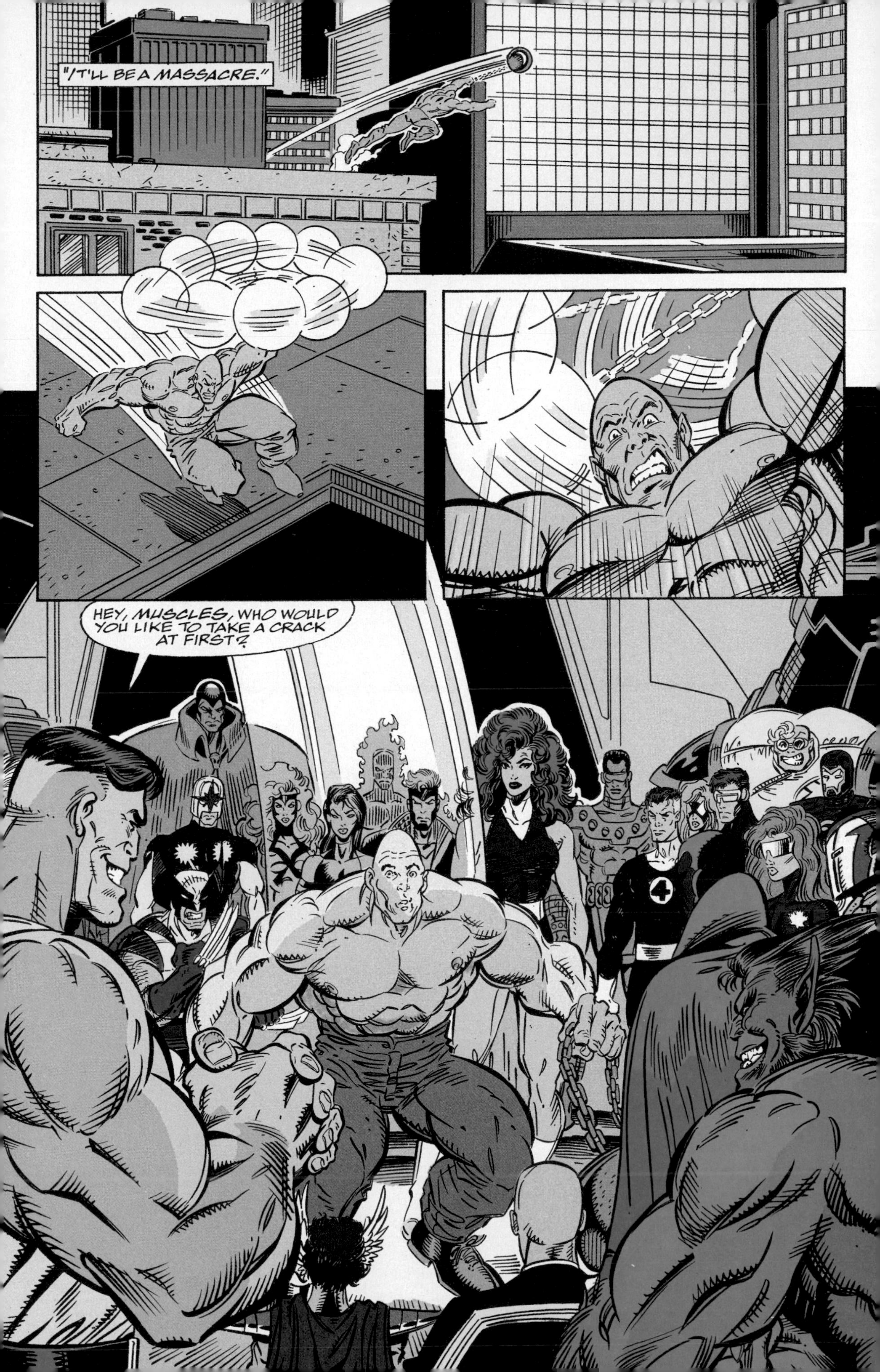
"I'LL BE A MASSACRE."
HEY, MUSCLES, WHO WOULD YOU LIKE TO TAKE A CRACK AT FIRST?

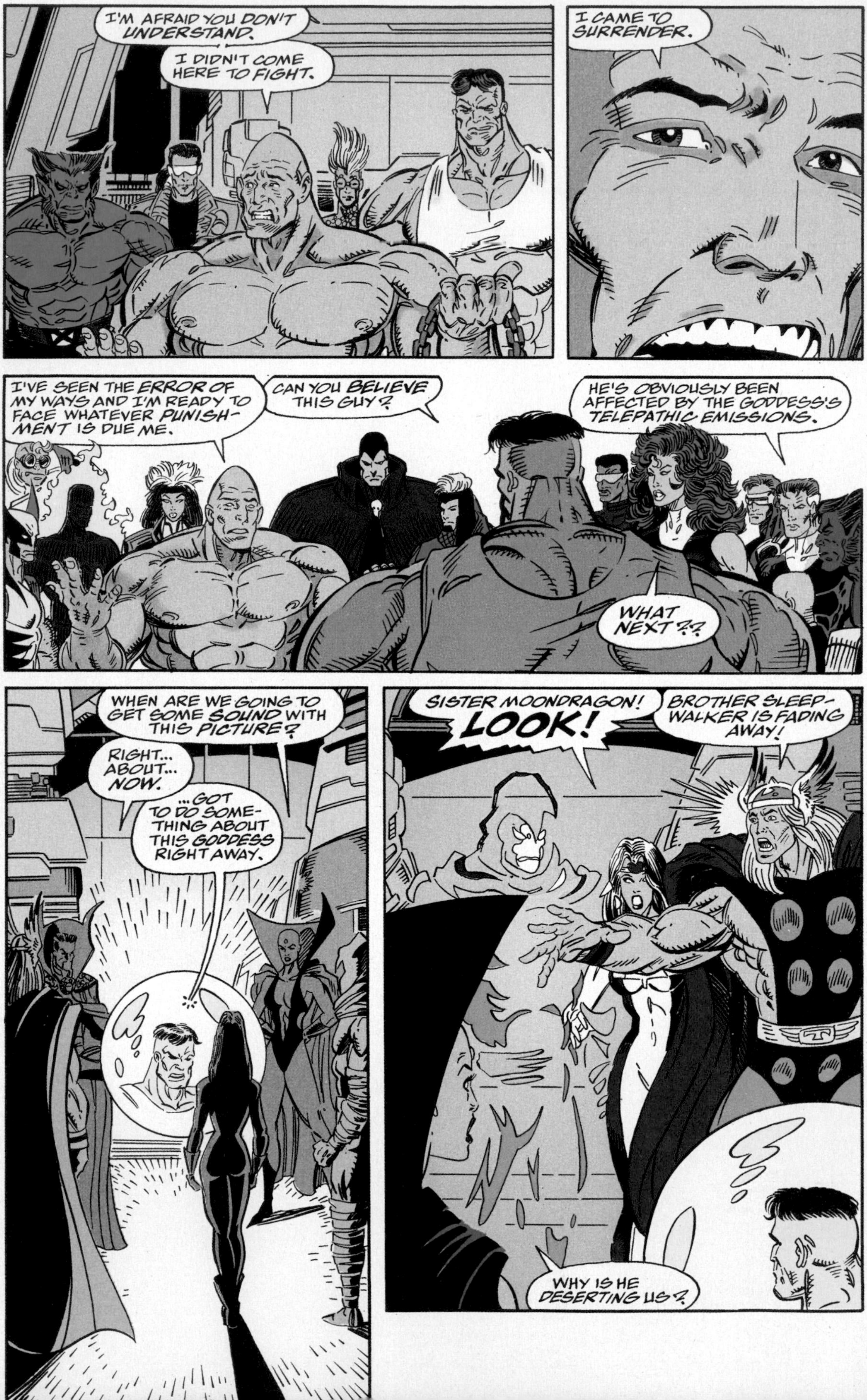
I'M AFRAID YOU DON'T UNDERSTAND.
I DIDN'T COME HERE TO FIGHT.
I CAME TO SURRENDER.
I'VE SEEN THE ERROR OF MY WAYS AND I'M READY TO FACE WHATEVER PUNISHMENT IS DUE ME.
CAN YOU BELIEVE THIS GUY?
HE'S OBVIOUSLY BEEN AFFECTED BY THE GODDESS'S TELEPATHIC EMISSIONS.
WHAT NEXT??
WHEN ARE WE GOING TO GET SOME SOUND WITH THIS PICTURE?
RIGHT... ABOUT... NOW.
...GOT TO DO SOMETHING ABOUT THIS GODDESS RIGHT AWAY.
SISTER MOONDRAGON! LOOK!
BROTHER SLEEPWALKER IS FADING AWAY!
WHY IS HE DESERTING US?

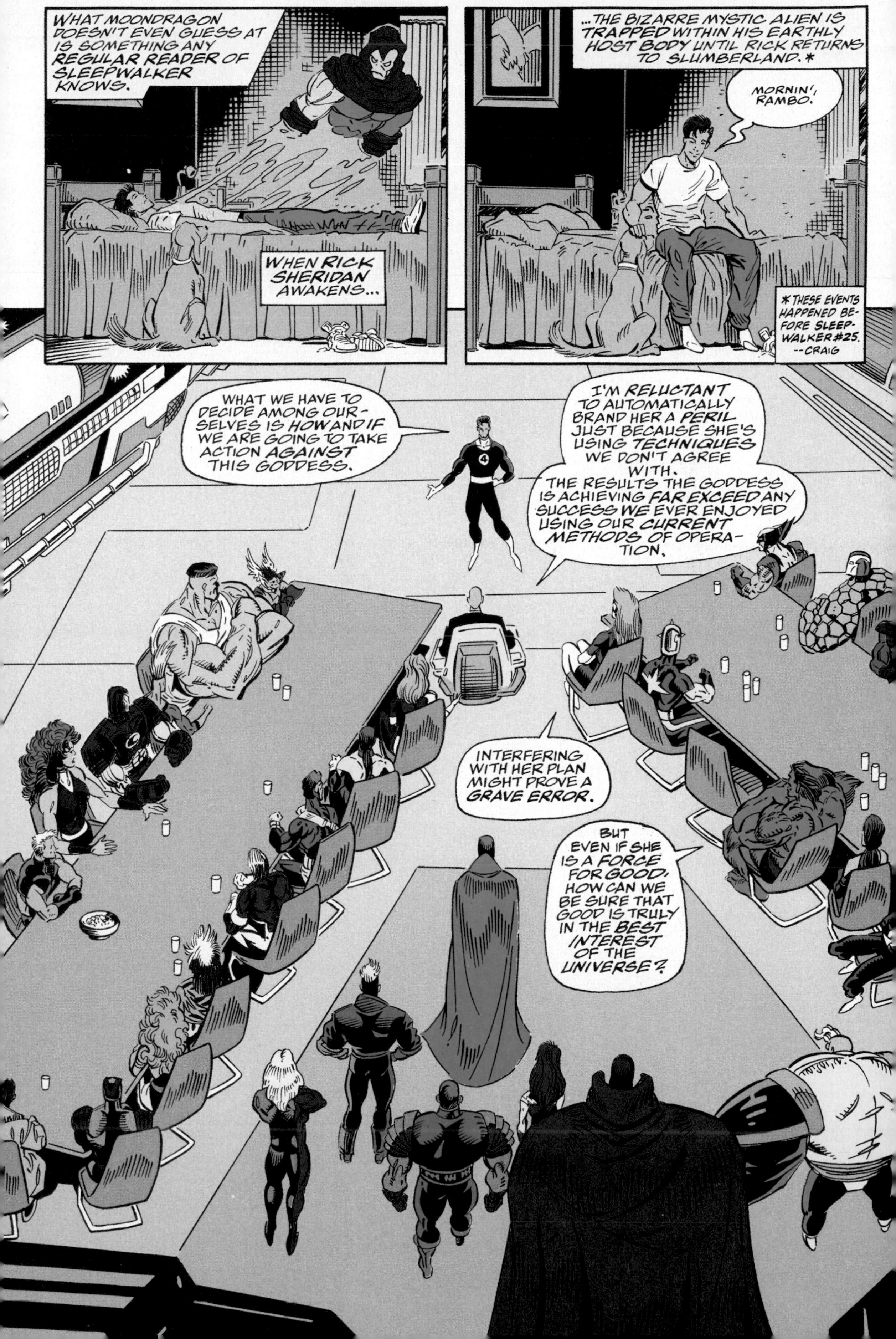

WHAT MOONDRAGON DOESN'T EVEN GUESS AT IS SOMETHING ANY REGULAR READER OF SLEEPWALKER KNOWS.
WHEN RICK SHERIDAN AWAKENS...
...THE BIZARRE MYSTIC ALIEN IS TRAPPED WITHIN HIS EARTHLY HOST BODY UNTIL RICK RETURNS TO SLUMBERLAND.*
MORNIN', RAMBO.
*THESE EVENTS HAPPENED BEFORE SLEEPWALKER #25. --CRAIG
WHAT WE HAVE TO DECIDE AMONG OURSELVES IS HOW AND IF WE ARE GOING TO TAKE ACTION AGAINST THIS GODDESS.
I'M RELUCTANT TO AUTOMATICALLY BRAND HER A PERIL JUST BECAUSE SHE'S USING TECHNIQUES WE DON'T AGREE WITH.
THE RESULTS THE GODDESS IS ACHIEVING FAR EXCEED ANY SUCCESS WE EVER ENJOYED USING OUR CURRENT METHODS OF OPERATION.
INTERFERING WITH HER PLAN MIGHT PROVE A GRAVE ERROR.
BUT EVEN IF SHE IS A FORCE FOR GOOD, HOW CAN WE BE SURE THAT GOOD IS TRULY IN THE BEST INTEREST OF THE UNIVERSE?

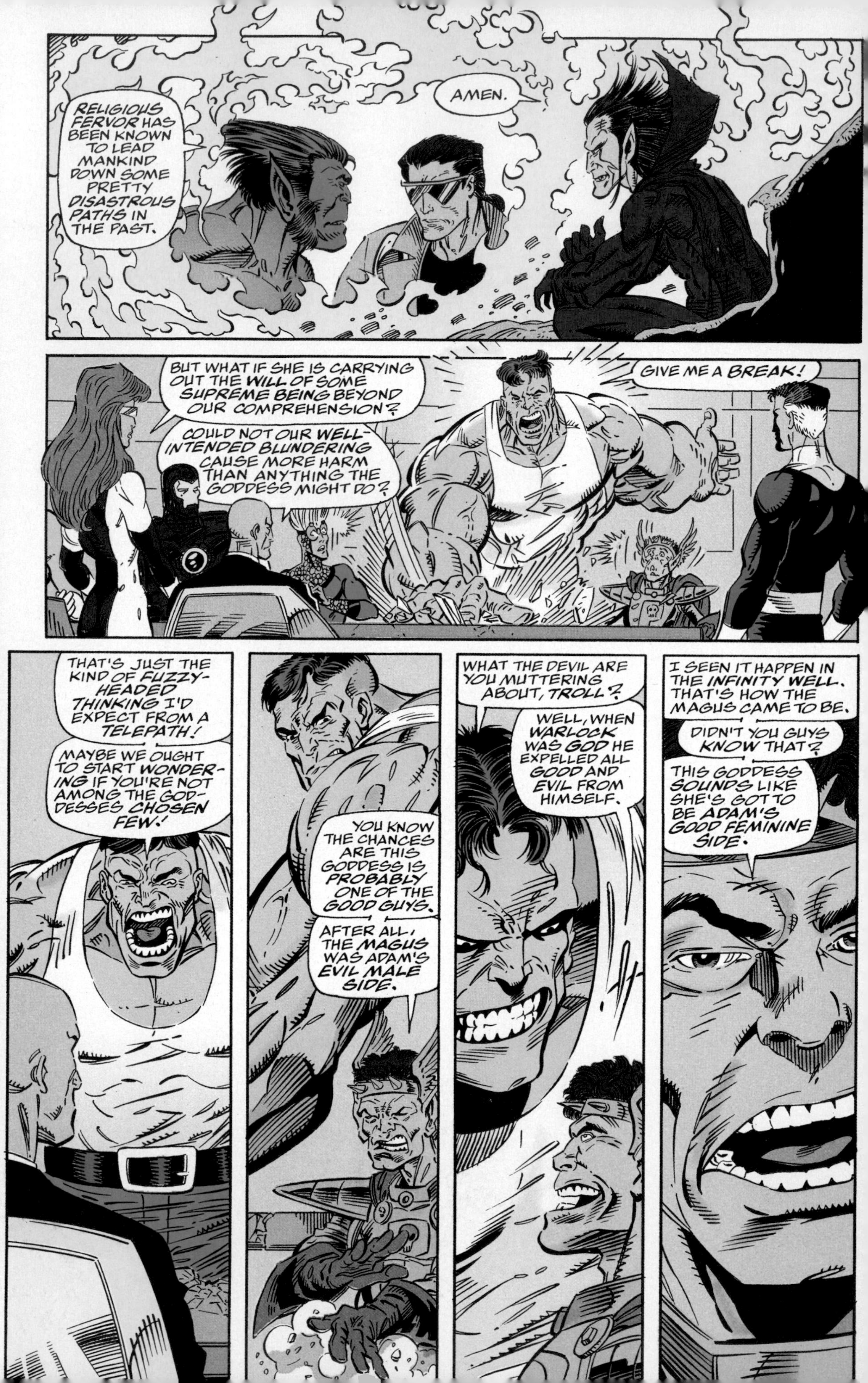
RELIGIOUS FERVOR HAS BEEN KNOWN TO LEAD MANKIND DOWN SOME PRETTY DISASTROUS PATHS IN THE PAST.
AMEN.
BUT WHAT IF SHE IS CARRYING OUT THE WILL OF SOME SUPREME BEING BEYOND OUR COMPREHENSION?
COULD NOT OUR WELL-INTENDED BLUNDERING CAUSE MORE HARM THAN ANYTHING THE GODDESS MIGHT DO?
GIVE ME A BREAK!
THAT'S JUST THE KIND OF FUZZY-HEADED THINKING I'D EXPECT FROM A TELEPATH!
MAYBE WE OUGHT TO START WONDERING IF YOU'RE NOT AMONG THE GODDESSES CHOSEN FEW!
YOU KNOW THE CHANCES ARE THIS GODDESS IS PROBABLY ONE OF THE GOOD GUYS.
AFTER ALL, THE MAGUS WAS ADAM'S EVIL MALE SIDE.
WHAT THE DEVIL ARE YOU MUTTERING ABOUT, TROLL?
WELL, WHEN WARLOCK WAS GOD HE EXPELLED ALL GOOD AND EVIL FROM HIMSELF.
I SEEN IT HAPPEN IN THE INFINITY WELL. THAT'S HOW THE MAGUS CAME TO BE.
DIDN'T YOU GUYS KNOW THAT?
THIS GODDESS SOUNDS LIKE SHE'S GOT TO BE ADAM'S GOOD FEMININE SIDE.

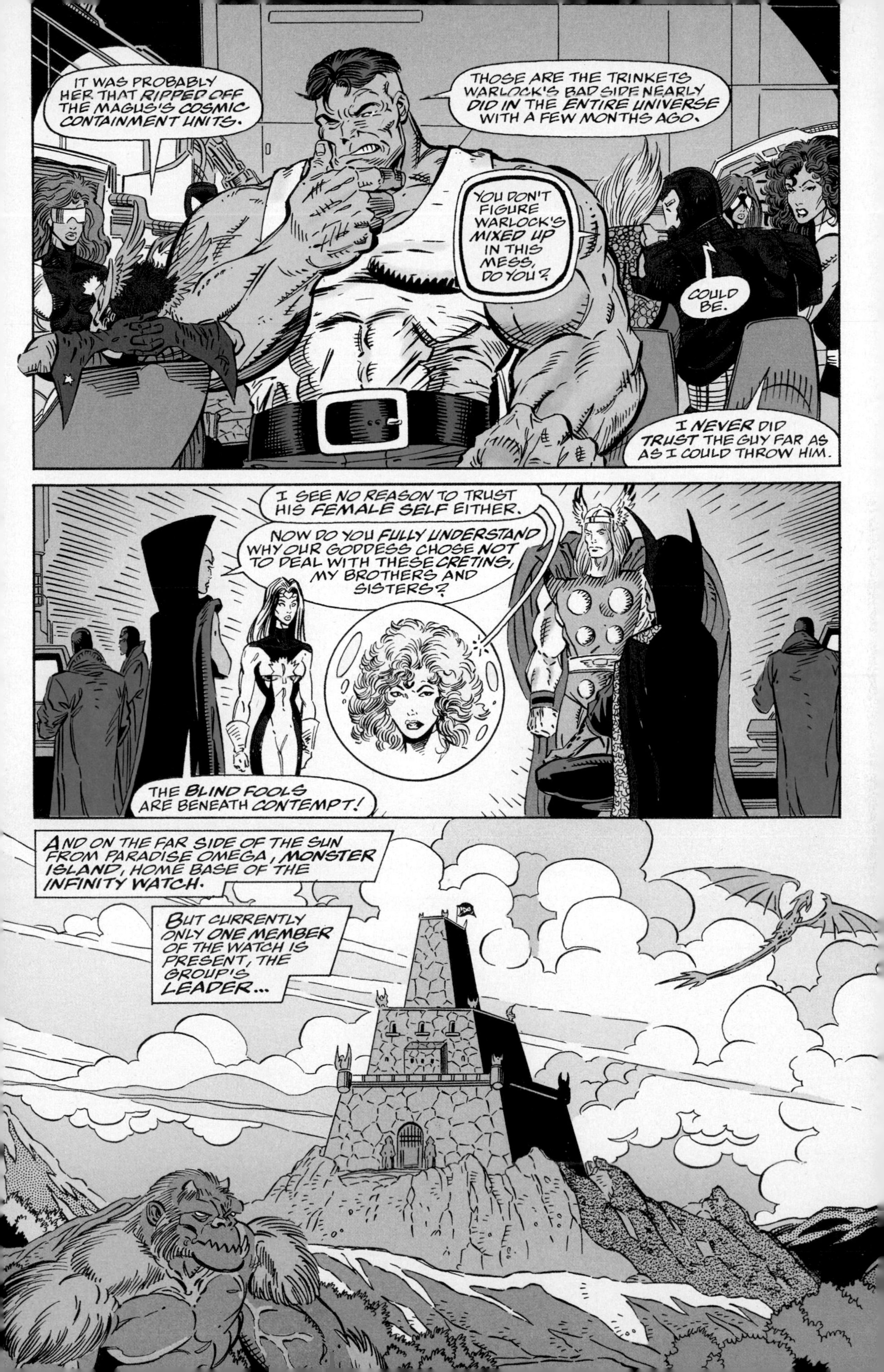
IT WAS PROBABLY HER THAT RIPPED OFF THE MAGUS'S COSMIC CONTAINMENT UNITS.
THOSE ARE THE TRINKETS WARLOCK'S BAD SIDE NEARLY DID IN THE ENTIRE UNIVERSE WITH A FEW MONTHS AGO.
YOU DON'T FIGURE WARLOCK'S MIXED UP IN THIS MESS, DO YOU?
COULD BE.
I NEVER DID TRUST THE GUY FAR AS AS I COULD THROW HIM.
I SEE NO REASON TO TRUST HIS FEMALE SELF EITHER.
NOW DO YOU FULLY UNDERSTAND WHY OUR GODDESS CHOSE NOT TO DEAL WITH THESE CRETINS, MY BROTHERS AND SISTERS?
THE BLIND FOOLS ARE BENEATH CONTEMPT!
AND ON THE FAR SIDE OF THE SUN FROM PARADISE OMEGA, MONSTER ISLAND, HOME BASE OF THE INFINITY WATCH.
BUT CURRENTLY ONLY ONE MEMBER OF THE WATCH IS PRESENT, THE GROUP'S LEADER...

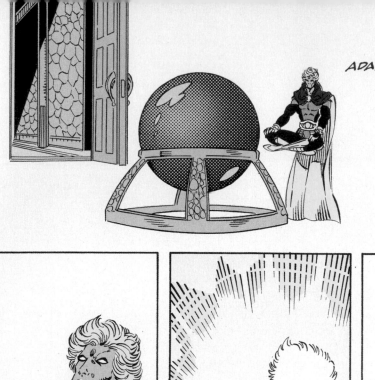

ADAM WARLOCK.

HE SEEKS ANSWERS WITHIN THE *VOID* THAT WAS ONCE HIS PRIVATE CHAMBERS.

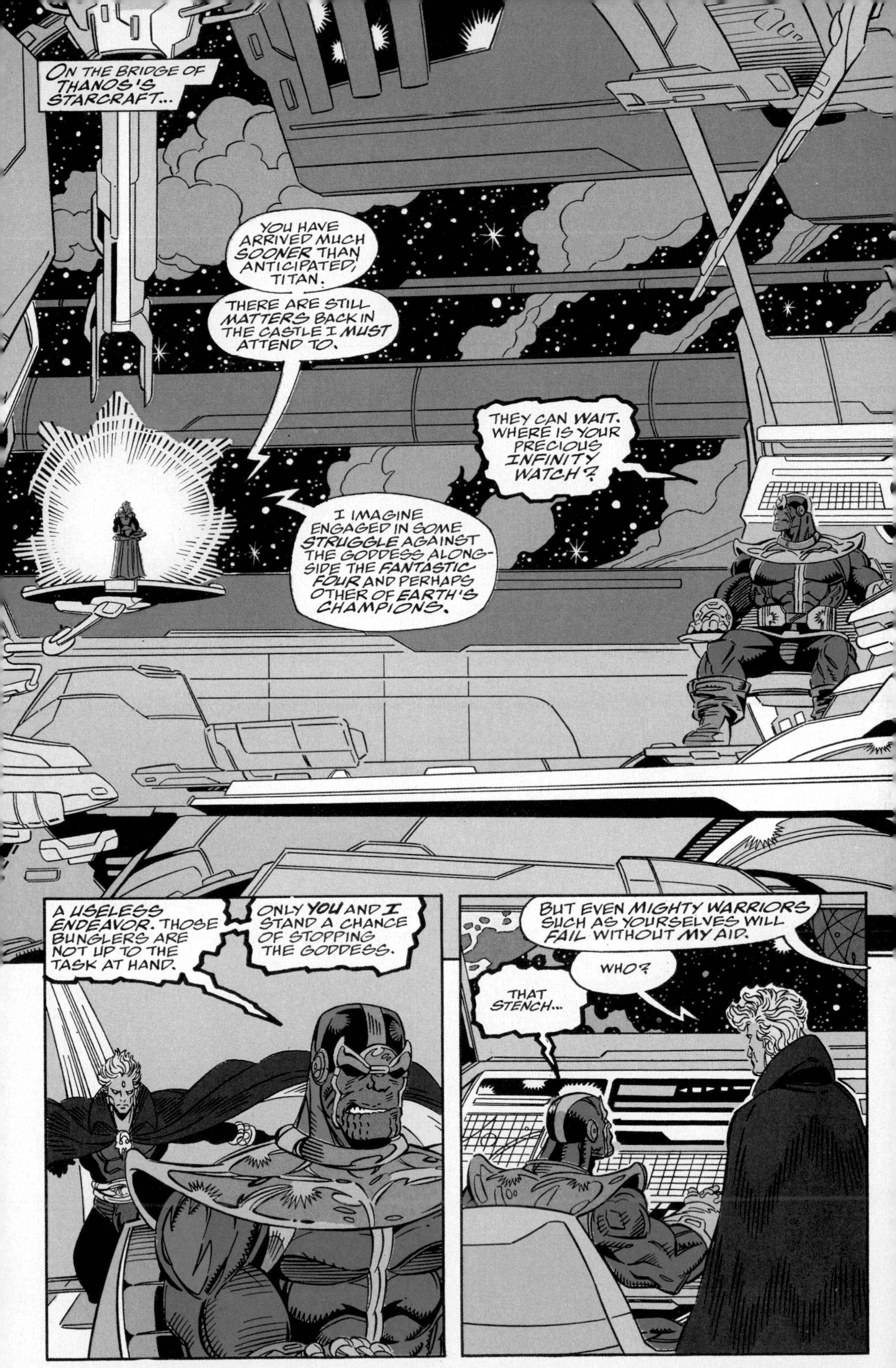
ON THE BRIDGE OF THANOS'S STARCRAFT...
YOU HAVE ARRIVED MUCH SOONER THAN ANTICIPATED, TITAN.
THERE ARE STILL MATTERS BACK IN THE CASTLE I MUST ATTEND TO.
THEY CAN WAIT. WHERE IS YOUR PRECIOUS INFINITY WATCH?
I IMAGINE ENGAGED IN SOME STRUGGLE AGAINST THE GODDESS ALONG-SIDE THE FANTASTIC FOUR AND PERHAPS OTHER OF EARTH'S CHAMPIONS.
A USELESS ENDEAVOR. THOSE BUNGLERS ARE NOT UP TO THE TASK AT HAND.
ONLY YOU AND I STAND A CHANCE OF STOPPING THE GODDESS.
BUT EVEN MIGHTY WARRIORS SUCH AS YOURSELVES WILL FAIL WITHOUT MY AID.
WHO?
THAT STENCH...

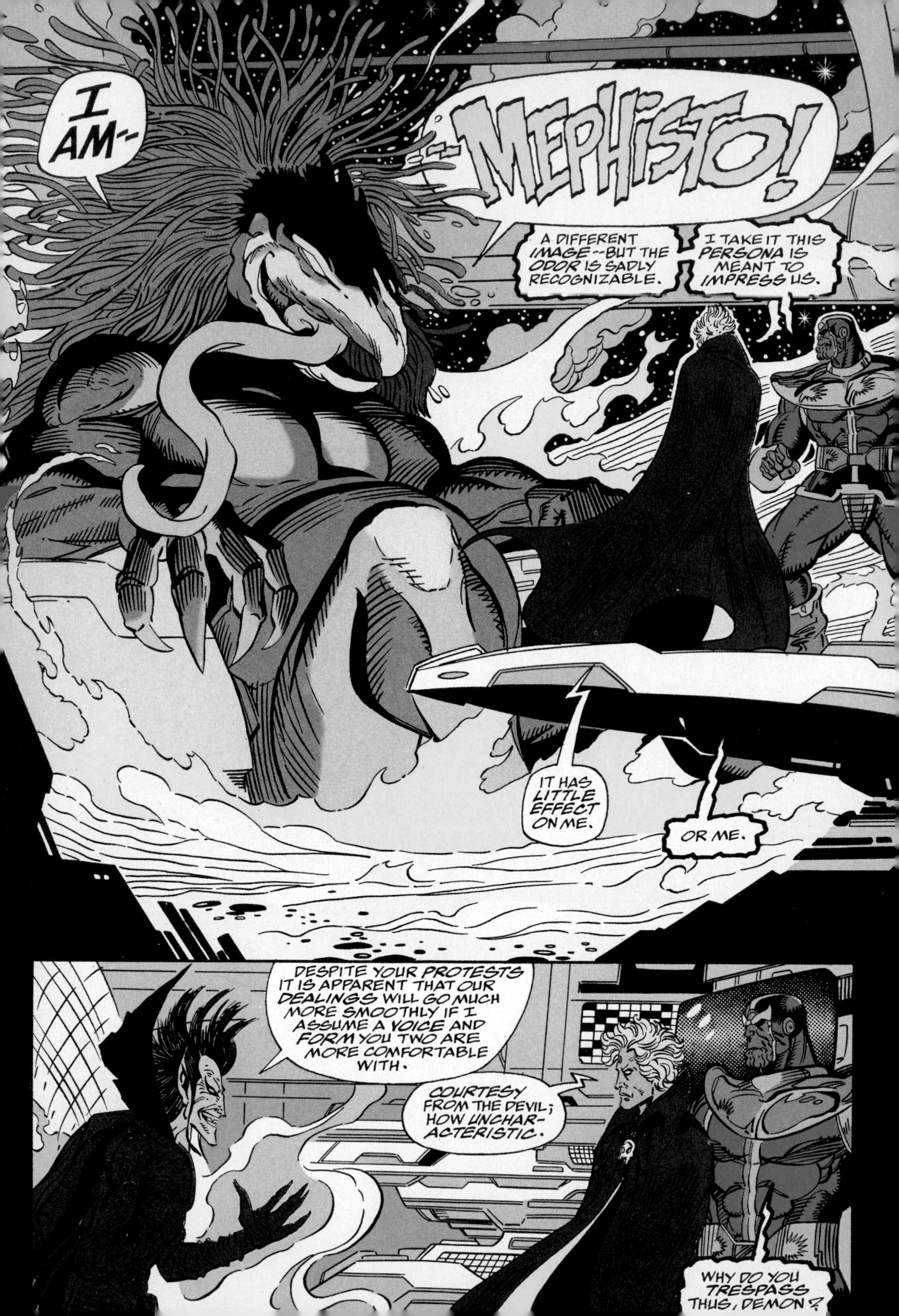
I AM--
--MEPHISTO!
A DIFFERENT IMAGE--BUT THE ODOR IS SADLY RECOGNIZABLE.
I TAKE IT THIS PERSONA IS MEANT TO IMPRESS US.
IT HAS LITTLE EFFECT ON ME.
OR ME.
DESPITE YOUR PROTESTS IT IS APPARENT THAT OUR DEALINGS WILL GO MUCH MORE SMOOTHLY IF I ASSUME A VOICE AND FORM YOU TWO ARE MORE COMFORTABLE WITH.
COURTESY FROM THE DEVIL; HOW UNCHAR-ACTERISTIC.
WHY DO YOU TRESPASS THUS, DEMON?

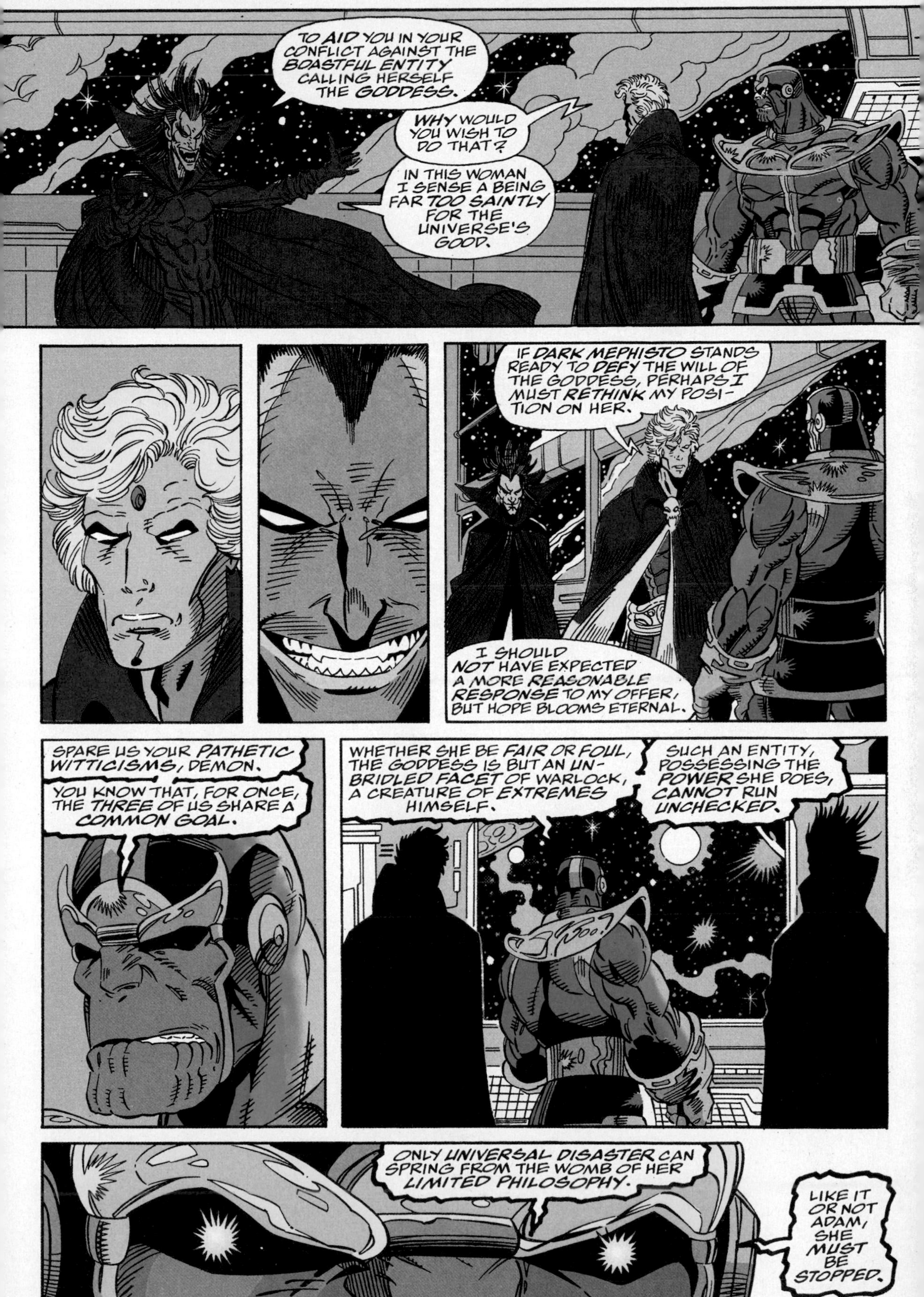
TO AID YOU IN YOUR CONFLICT AGAINST THE BOASTFUL ENTITY CALLING HERSELF THE GODDESS.
WHY WOULD YOU WISH TO DO THAT?
IN THIS WOMAN I SENSE A BEING FAR TOO SAINTLY FOR THE UNIVERSE'S GOOD.
IF DARK MEPHISTO STANDS READY TO DEFY THE WILL OF THE GODDESS, PERHAPS I MUST RETHINK MY POSITION ON HER.
I SHOULD NOT HAVE EXPECTED A MORE REASONABLE RESPONSE TO MY OFFER, BUT HOPE BLOOMS ETERNAL.
SPARE US YOUR PATHETIC WITTICISMS, DEMON.
YOU KNOW THAT, FOR ONCE, THE THREE OF US SHARE A COMMON GOAL.
WHETHER SHE BE FAIR OR FOUL, THE GODDESS IS BUT AN UNBRIDLED FACET OF WARLOCK, A CREATURE OF EXTREMES HIMSELF.
SUCH AN ENTITY, POSSESSING THE POWER SHE DOES, CANNOT RUN UNCHECKED.
ONLY UNIVERSAL DISASTER CAN SPRING FROM THE WOMB OF HER LIMITED PHILOSOPHY.
LIKE IT OR NOT ADAM, SHE MUST BE STOPPED.

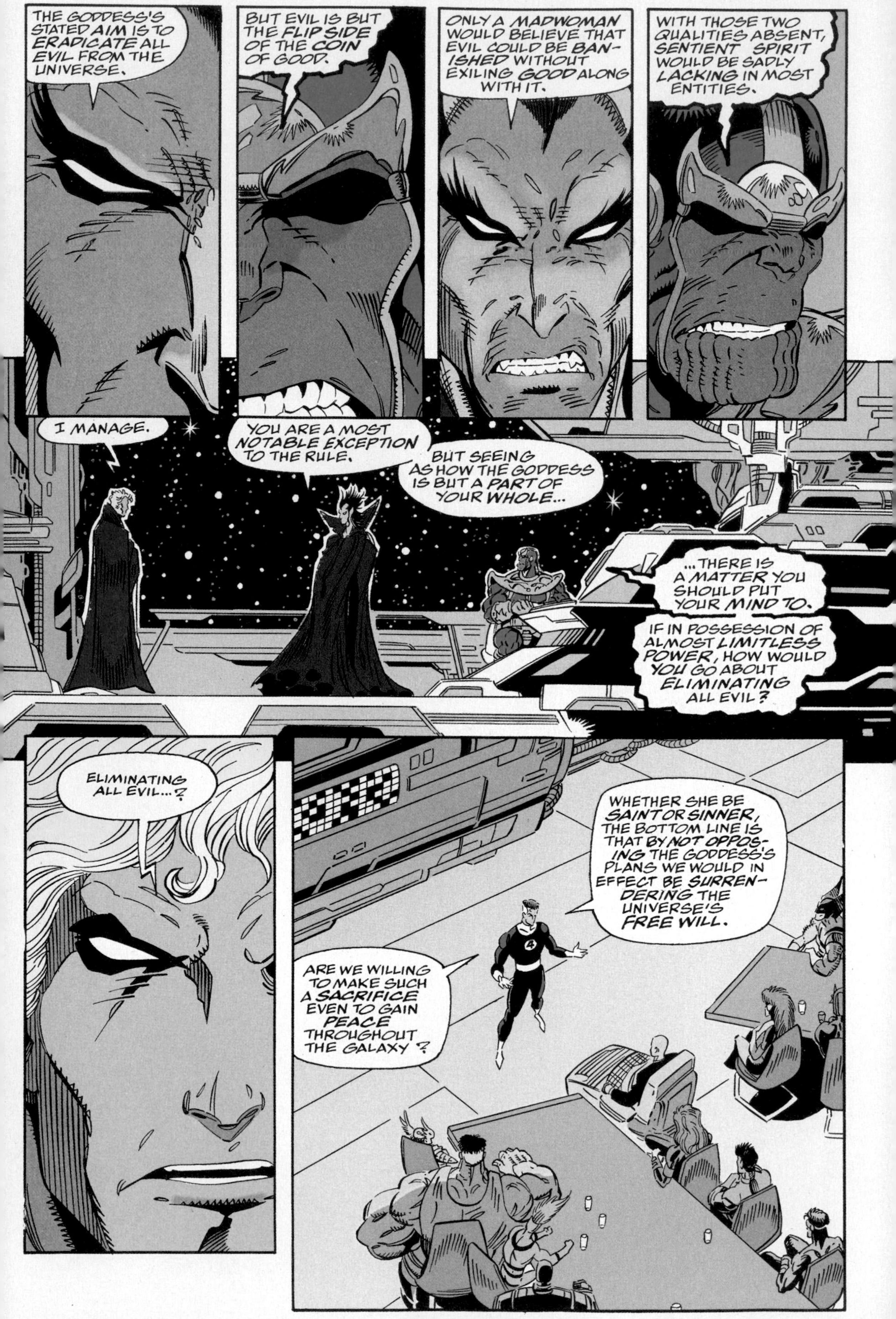
THE GODDESS'S STATED AIM IS TO ERADICATE ALL EVIL FROM THE UNIVERSE.
BUT EVIL IS BUT THE FLIP SIDE OF THE COIN OF GOOD.
ONLY A MADWOMAN WOULD BELIEVE THAT EVIL COULD BE BANISHED WITHOUT EXILING GOOD ALONG WITH IT.
WITH THOSE TWO QUALITIES ABSENT, SENTIENT SPIRIT WOULD BE SADLY LACKING IN MOST ENTITIES.
I MANAGE.
YOU ARE A MOST NOTABLE EXCEPTION TO THE RULE.
BUT SEEING AS HOW THE GODDESS IS BUT A PART OF YOUR WHOLE...
...THERE IS A MATTER YOU SHOULD PUT YOUR MIND TO.
IF IN POSSESSION OF ALMOST LIMITLESS POWER, HOW WOULD YOU GO ABOUT ELIMINATING ALL EVIL?
ELIMINATING ALL EVIL...?
WHETHER SHE BE SAINT OR SINNER, THE BOTTOM LINE IS THAT BY NOT OPPOSING THE GODDESS'S PLANS WE WOULD IN EFFECT BE SURRENDERING THE UNIVERSE'S FREE WILL.
ARE WE WILLING TO MAKE SUCH A SACRIFICE EVEN TO GAIN PEACE THROUGHOUT THE GALAXY?

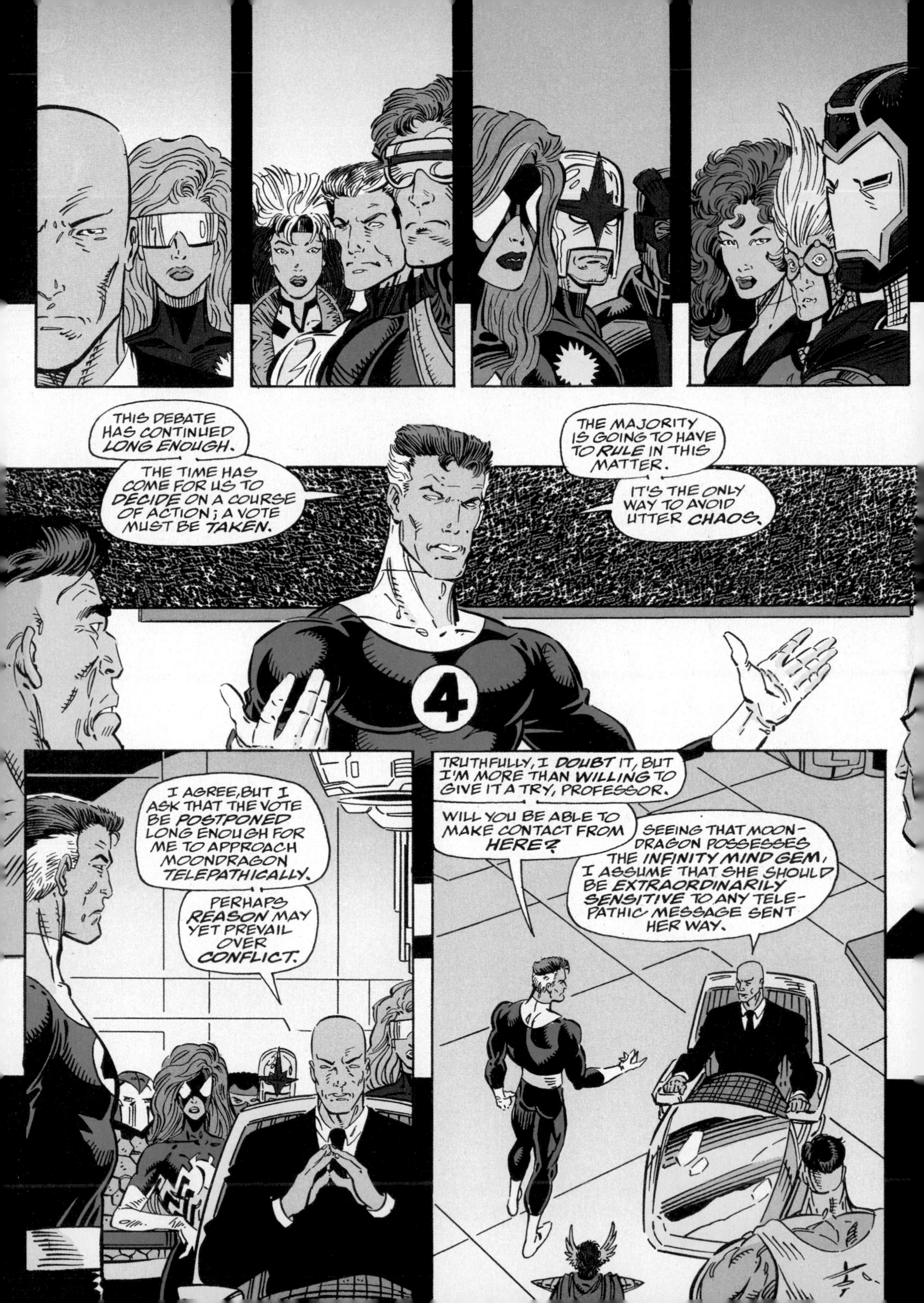
THIS DEBATE HAS CONTINUED LONG ENOUGH.
THE TIME HAS COME FOR US TO DECIDE ON A COURSE OF ACTION; A VOTE MUST BE TAKEN.
THE MAJORITY IS GOING TO HAVE TO RULE IN THIS MATTER.
IT'S THE ONLY WAY TO AVOID UTTER CHAOS.
I AGREE, BUT I ASK THAT THE VOTE BE POSTPONED LONG ENOUGH FOR ME TO APPROACH MOONDRAGON TELEPATHICALLY.
PERHAPS REASON MAY YET PREVAIL OVER CONFLICT.
TRUTHFULLY, I DOUBT IT, BUT I'M MORE THAN WILLING TO GIVE IT A TRY, PROFESSOR.
WILL YOU BE ABLE TO MAKE CONTACT FROM HERE?
SEEING THAT MOONDRAGON POSSESSES THE INFINITY MIND GEM, I ASSUME THAT SHE SHOULD BE EXTRAORDINARILY SENSITIVE TO ANY TELEPATHIC MESSAGE SENT HER WAY.

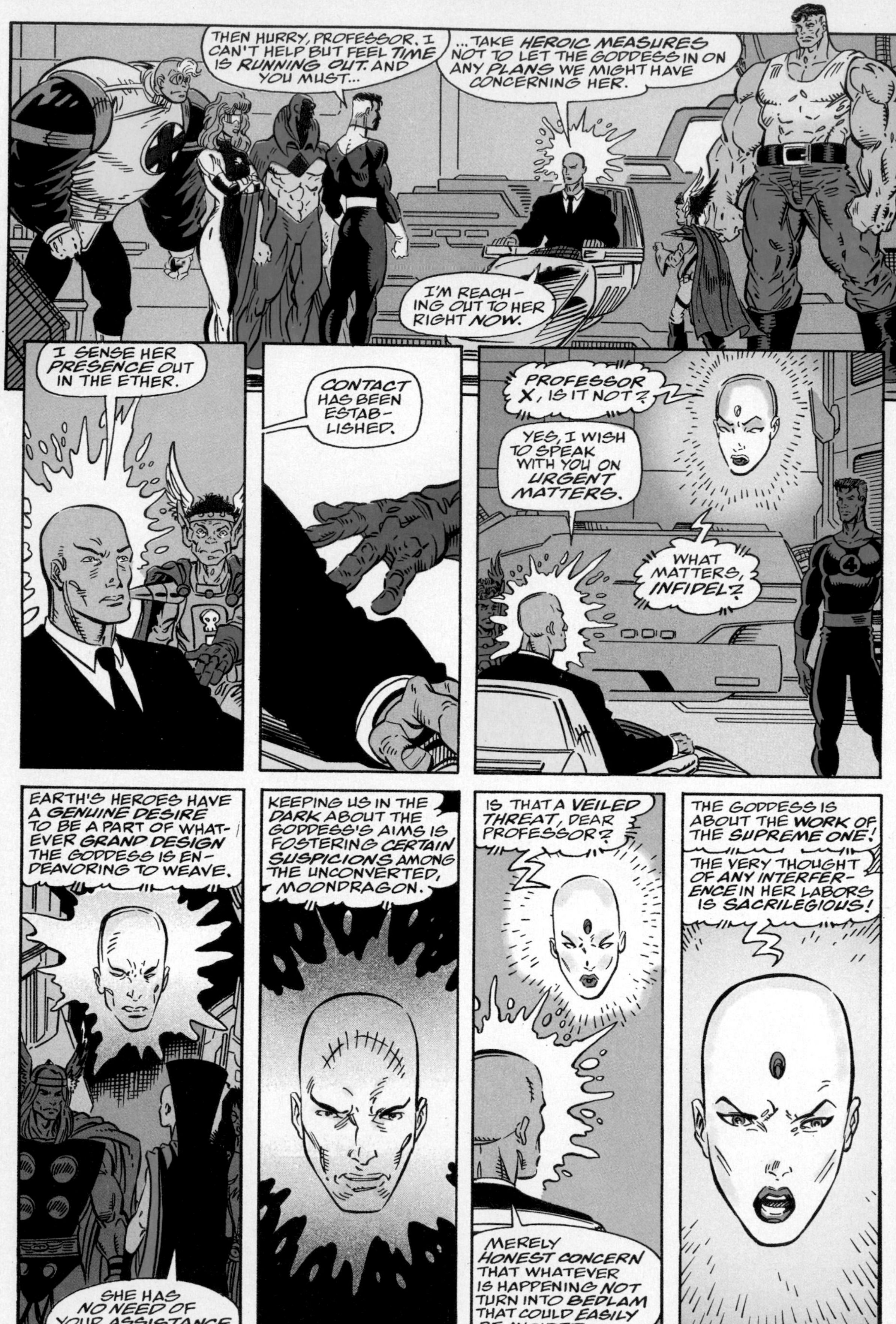

THEN HURRY, PROFESSOR. I CAN'T HELP BUT FEEL TIME IS RUNNING OUT. AND YOU MUST...
...TAKE HEROIC MEASURES NOT TO LET THE GODDESS IN ON ANY PLANS WE MIGHT HAVE CONCERNING HER.
I'M REACHING OUT TO HER RIGHT NOW.
I SENSE HER PRESENCE OUT IN THE ETHER.
CONTACT HAS BEEN ESTABLISHED.
PROFESSOR X, IS IT NOT?
YES, I WISH TO SPEAK WITH YOU ON URGENT MATTERS.
WHAT MATTERS, INFIDEL?
EARTH'S HEROES HAVE A GENUINE DESIRE TO BE A PART OF WHATEVER GRAND DESIGN THE GODDESS IS ENDEAVORING TO WEAVE.
SHE HAS NO NEED OF YOUR ASSISTANCE.
KEEPING US IN THE DARK ABOUT THE GODDESS'S AIMS IS FOSTERING CERTAIN SUSPICIONS AMONG THE UNCONVERTED, MOONDRAGON.
IS THAT A VEILED THREAT, DEAR PROFESSOR?
MERELY HONEST CONCERN THAT WHATEVER IS HAPPENING NOT TURN INTO BEDLAM THAT COULD EASILY BE AVOIDED.
THE GODDESS IS ABOUT THE WORK OF THE SUPREME ONE!
THE VERY THOUGHT OF ANY INTERFERENCE IN HER LABORS IS SACRILEGIOUS!

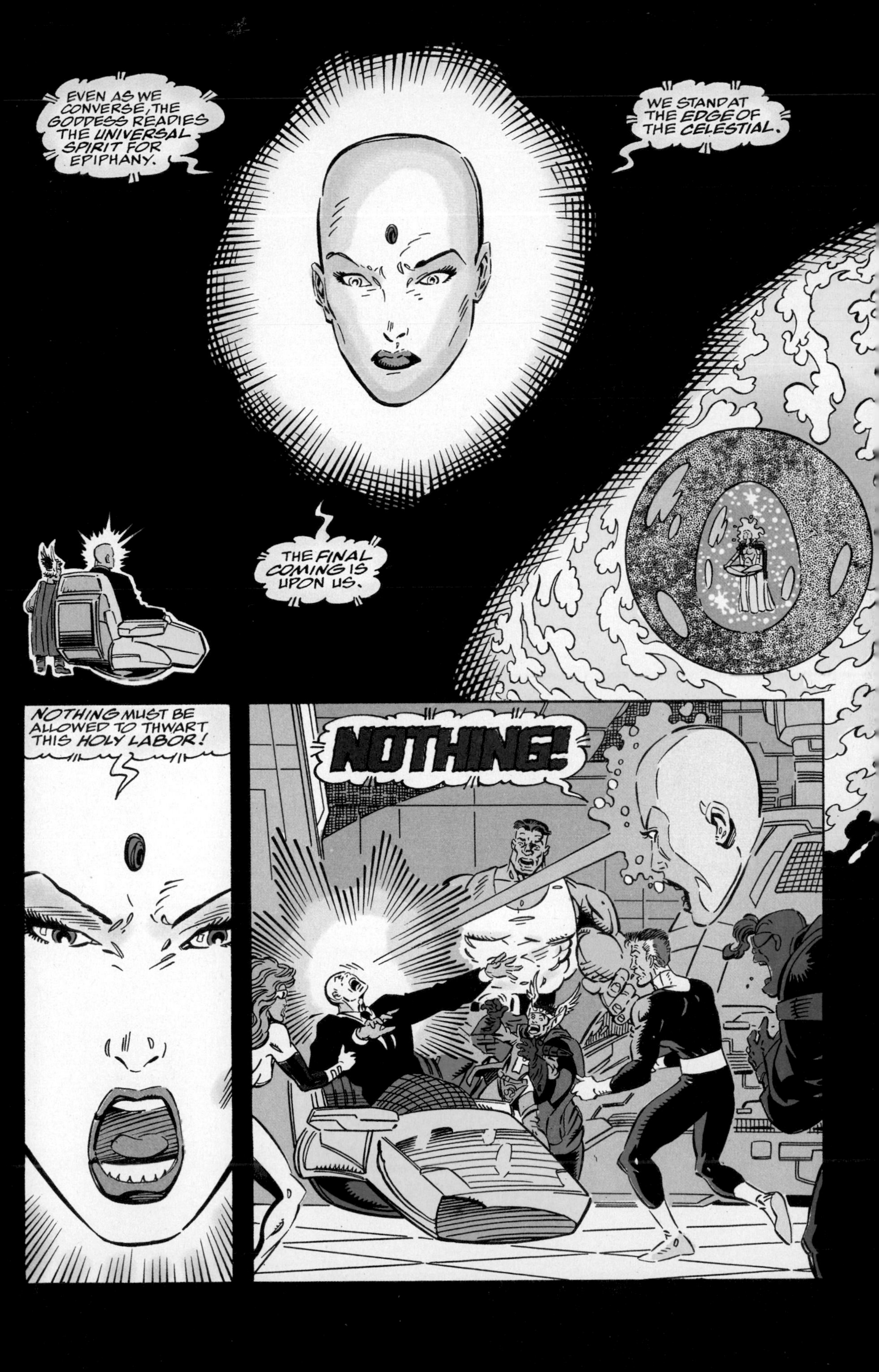
EVEN AS WE CONVERSE, THE GODDESS READIES THE UNIVERSAL SPIRIT FOR EPIPHANY.
WE STAND AT THE EDGE OF THE CELESTIAL.
THE FINAL COMING IS UPON US.
NOTHING MUST BE ALLOWED TO THWART THIS HOLY LABOR!
NOTHING!

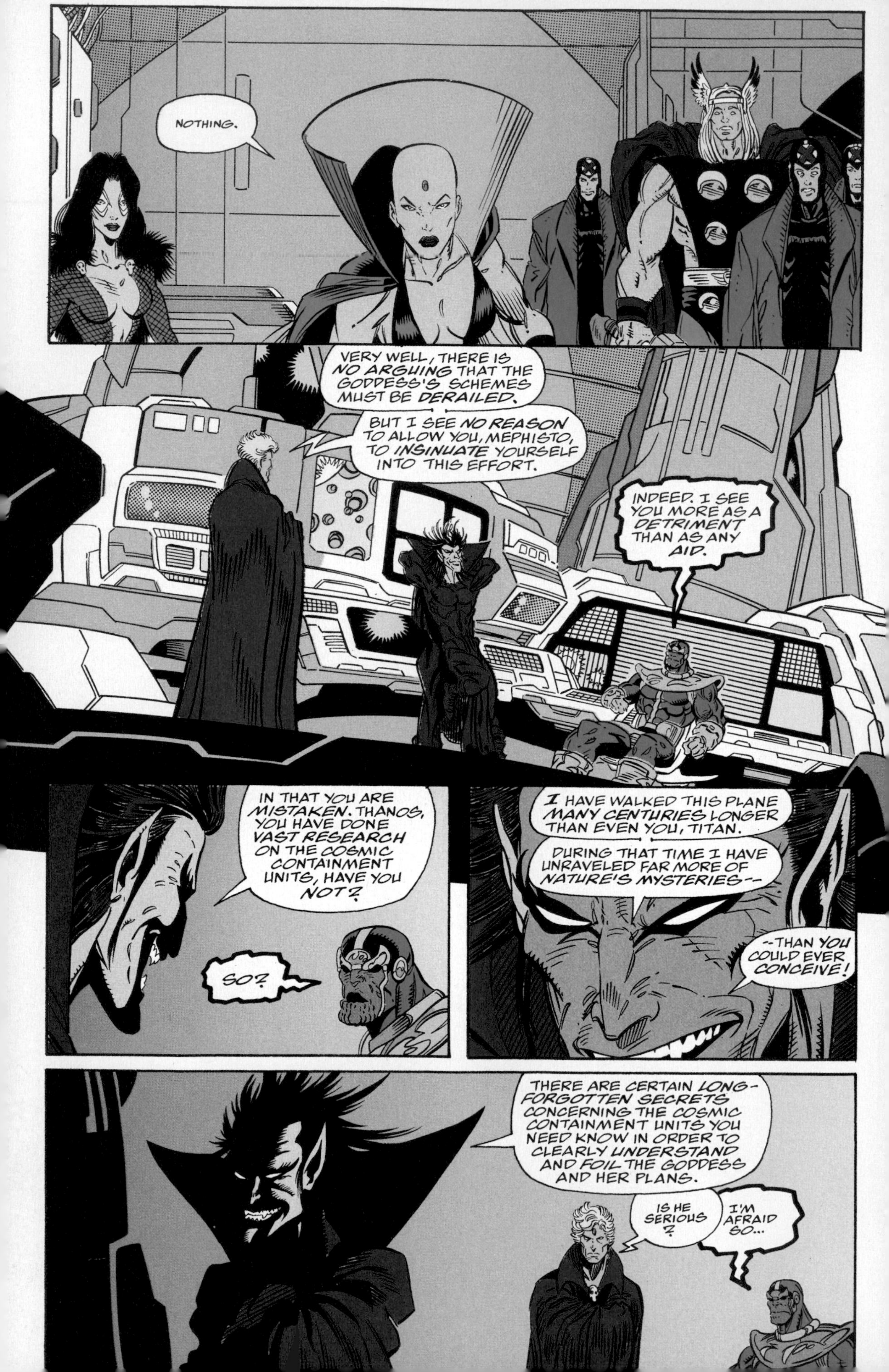
NOTHING.
VERY WELL, THERE IS NO ARGUING THAT THE GODDESS'S SCHEMES MUST BE DERAILED.
BUT I SEE NO REASON TO ALLOW YOU, MEPHISTO, TO INSINUATE YOURSELF INTO THIS EFFORT.
INDEED. I SEE YOU MORE AS A DETRIMENT THAN AS ANY AID.
IN THAT YOU ARE MISTAKEN. THANOS, YOU HAVE DONE VAST RESEARCH ON THE COSMIC CONTAINMENT UNITS, HAVE YOU NOT?
SO?
I HAVE WALKED THIS PLANE MANY CENTURIES LONGER THAN EVEN YOU, TITAN.
DURING THAT TIME I HAVE UNRAVELED FAR MORE OF NATURE'S MYSTERIES--
--THAN YOU COULD EVER CONCEIVE!
THERE ARE CERTAIN LONG-FORGOTTEN SECRETS CONCERNING THE COSMIC CONTAINMENT UNITS YOU NEED KNOW IN ORDER TO CLEARLY UNDERSTAND AND FOIL THE GODDESS AND HER PLANS.
IS HE SERIOUS?
I'M AFRAID SO...

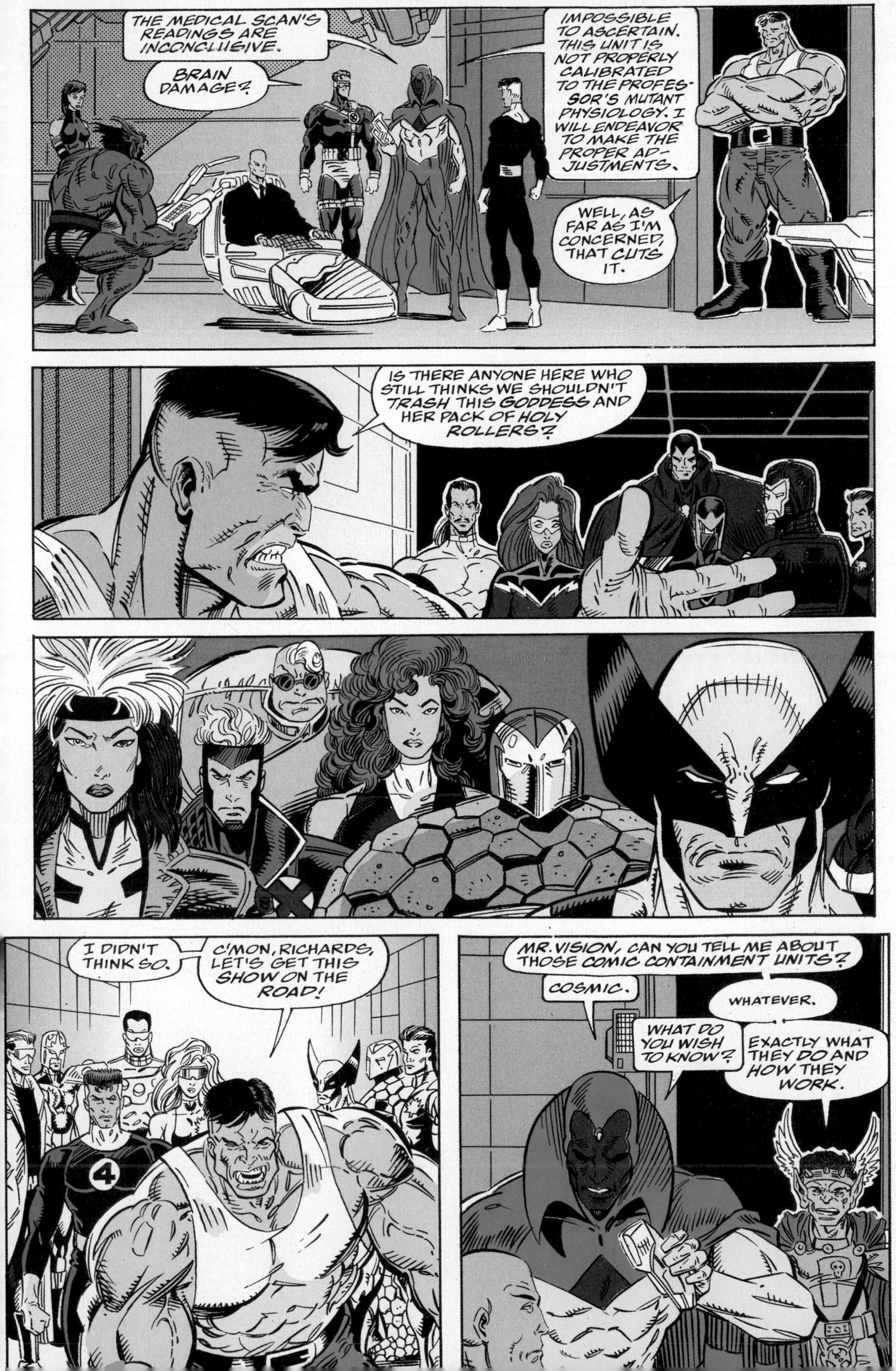
THE MEDICAL SCAN'S READINGS ARE INCONCLUSIVE.
BRAIN DAMAGE?
IMPOSSIBLE TO ASCERTAIN. THIS UNIT IS NOT PROPERLY CALIBRATED TO THE PROFESSOR'S MUTANT PHYSIOLOGY. I WILL ENDEAVOR TO MAKE THE PROPER ADJUSTMENTS.
WELL, AS FAR AS I'M CONCERNED, THAT CUTS IT.
IS THERE ANYONE HERE WHO STILL THINKS WE SHOULDN'T TRASH THIS GODDESS AND HER PACK OF HOLY ROLLERS?
I DIDN'T THINK SO.
C'MON, RICHARDS, LET'S GET THIS SHOW ON THE ROAD!
MR. VISION, CAN YOU TELL ME ABOUT THOSE COMIC CONTAINMENT UNITS?
COSMIC.
WHATEVER.
WHAT DO YOU WISH TO KNOW?
EXACTLY WHAT THEY DO AND HOW THEY WORK.

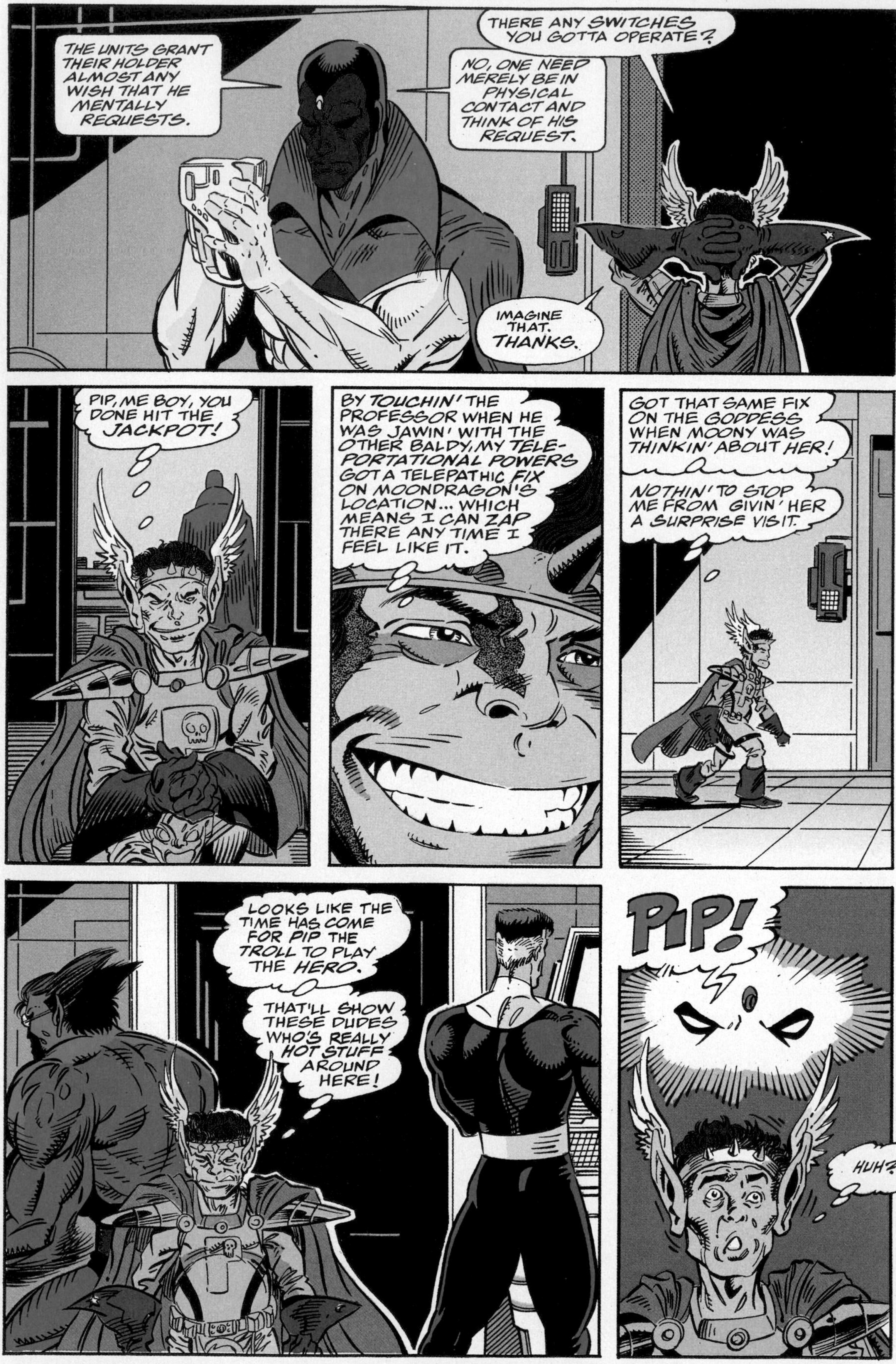
THE UNITS GRANT THEIR HOLDER ALMOST ANY WISH THAT HE MENTALLY REQUESTS.
THERE ANY SWITCHES YOU GOTTA OPERATE?
NO, ONE NEED MERELY BE IN PHYSICAL CONTACT AND THINK OF HIS REQUEST.
IMAGINE THAT. THANKS.
PIP, ME BOY, YOU DONE HIT THE JACKPOT!
BY TOUCHIN' THE PROFESSOR WHEN HE WAS JAWIN' WITH THE OTHER BALDY, MY TELE-PORTATIONAL POWERS GOT A TELEPATHIC FIX ON MOONDRAGON'S LOCATION... WHICH MEANS I CAN ZAP THERE ANY TIME I FEEL LIKE IT.
GOT THAT SAME FIX ON THE GODDESS WHEN MOONY WAS THINKIN' ABOUT HER!
NOTHIN' TO STOP ME FROM GIVIN' HER A SURPRISE VISIT.
LOOKS LIKE THE TIME HAS COME FOR PIP THE TROLL TO PLAY THE HERO.
THAT'LL SHOW THESE DUDES WHO'S REALLY HOT STUFF AROUND HERE!
PIP!
HUH?

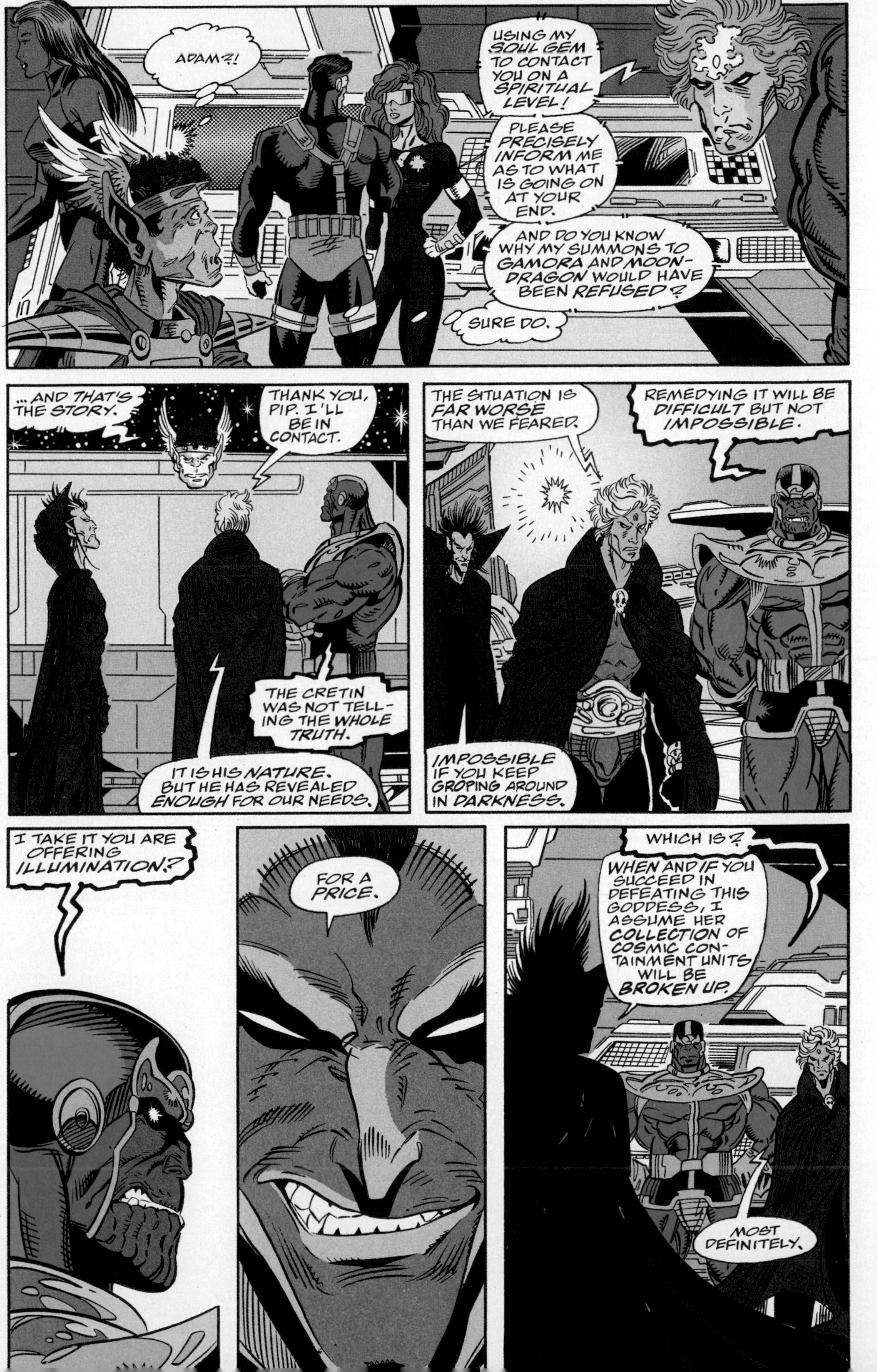
ADAM?!
USING MY SOUL GEM TO CONTACT YOU ON A SPIRITUAL LEVEL!
PLEASE PRECISELY INFORM ME AS TO WHAT IS GOING ON AT YOUR END.
AND DO YOU KNOW WHY MY SUMMONS TO GAMORA AND MOON-DRAGON WOULD HAVE BEEN REFUSED?
SURE DO.
...AND THAT'S THE STORY.
THANK YOU, PIP. I'LL BE IN CONTACT.
THE CRETIN WAS NOT TELLING THE WHOLE TRUTH.
IT IS HIS NATURE. BUT HE HAS REVEALED ENOUGH FOR OUR NEEDS.
THE SITUATION IS FAR WORSE THAN WE FEARED.
REMEDYING IT WILL BE DIFFICULT BUT NOT IMPOSSIBLE.
IMPOSSIBLE IF YOU KEEP GROPING AROUND IN DARKNESS.
I TAKE IT YOU ARE OFFERING ILLUMINATION?
FOR A PRICE.
WHICH IS?
WHEN AND IF YOU SUCCEED IN DEFEATING THIS GODDESS, I ASSUME HER COLLECTION OF COSMIC CONTAINMENT UNITS WILL BE BROKEN UP.
MOST DEFINITELY.

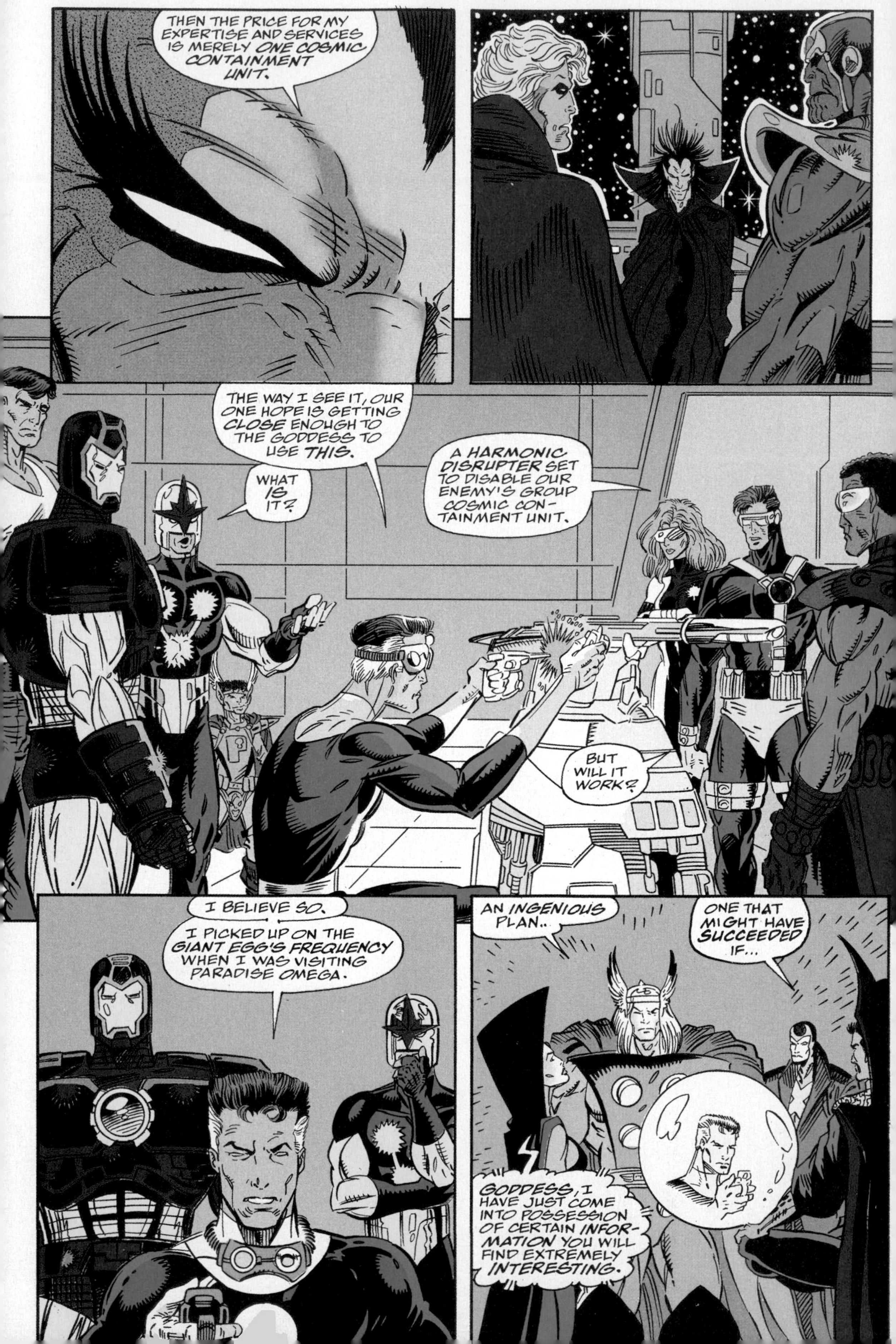
THEN THE PRICE FOR MY EXPERTISE AND SERVICES IS MERELY ONE COSMIC CONTAINMENT UNIT.
THE WAY I SEE IT, OUR ONE HOPE IS GETTING CLOSE ENOUGH TO THE GODDESS TO USE THIS.
WHAT IS IT?
A HARMONIC DISRUPTER SET TO DISABLE OUR ENEMY'S GROUP COSMIC CONTAINMENT UNIT.
BUT WILL IT WORK?
I BELIEVE SO.
I PICKED UP ON THE GIANT EGG'S FREQUENCY WHEN I WAS VISITING PARADISE OMEGA.
AN INGENIOUS PLAN..
ONE THAT MIGHT HAVE SUCCEEDED IF...
GODDESS, I HAVE JUST COME INTO POSSESSION OF CERTAIN INFORMATION YOU WILL FIND EXTREMELY INTERESTING.

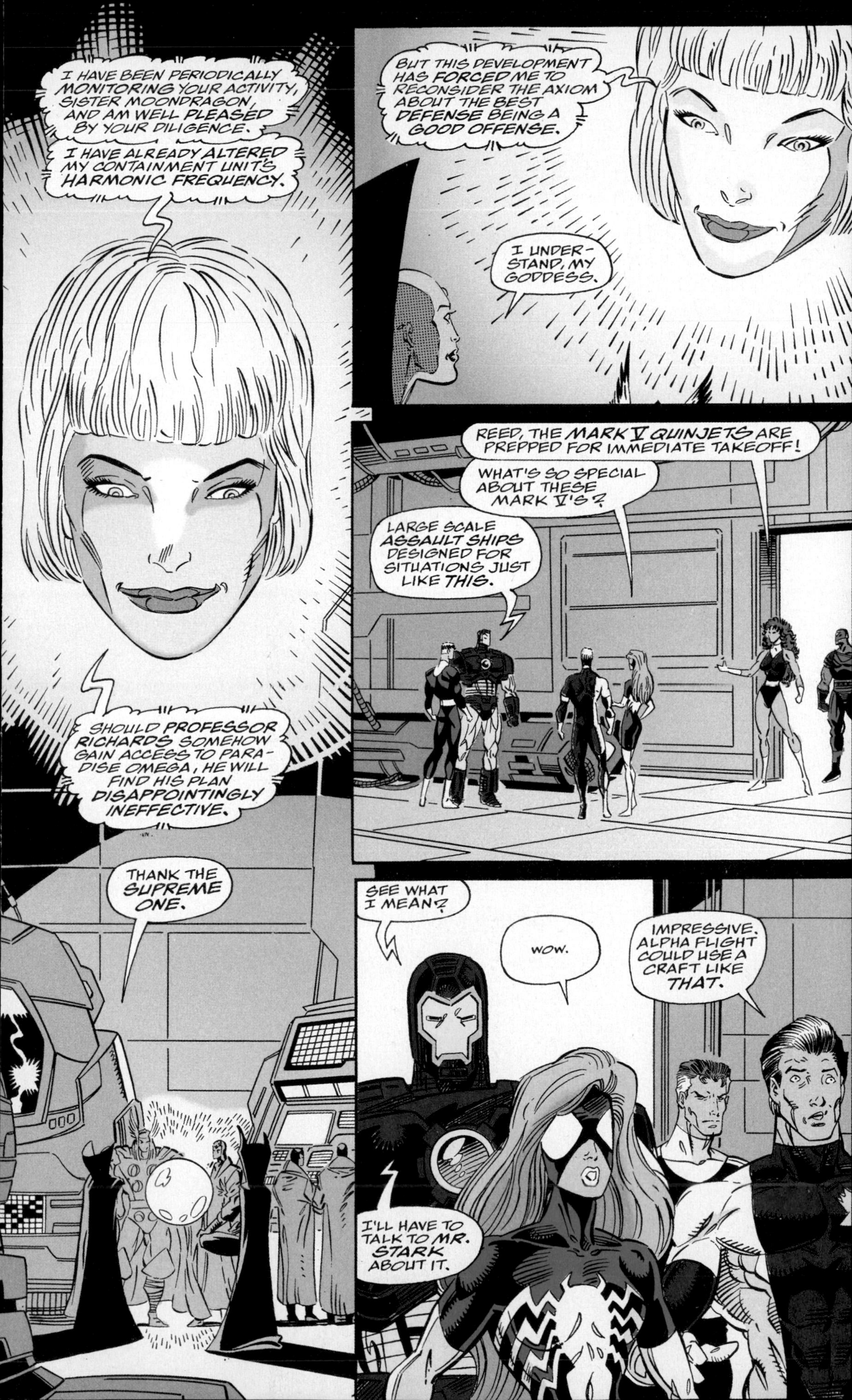
I HAVE BEEN PERIODICALLY MONITORING YOUR ACTIVITY, SISTER MOONDRAGON, AND AM WELL PLEASED BY YOUR DILIGENCE.
I HAVE ALREADY ALTERED MY CONTAINMENT UNIT'S HARMONIC FREQUENCY.
BUT THIS DEVELOPMENT HAS FORCED ME TO RECONSIDER THE AXIOM ABOUT THE BEST DEFENSE BEING A GOOD OFFENSE.
I UNDER-STAND, MY GODDESS.
SHOULD PROFESSOR RICHARDS SOMEHOW GAIN ACCESS TO PARA-DISE OMEGA, HE WILL FIND HIS PLAN DISAPPOINTINGLY INEFFECTIVE.
THANK THE SUPREME ONE.
REED, THE MARK V QUINJETS ARE PREPPED FOR IMMEDIATE TAKEOFF!
WHAT'S SO SPECIAL ABOUT THESE MARK V'S?
LARGE SCALE ASSAULT SHIPS DESIGNED FOR SITUATIONS JUST LIKE THIS.
SEE WHAT I MEAN?
WOW.
IMPRESSIVE. ALPHA FLIGHT COULD USE A CRAFT LIKE THAT.
I'LL HAVE TO TALK TO MR. STARK ABOUT IT.

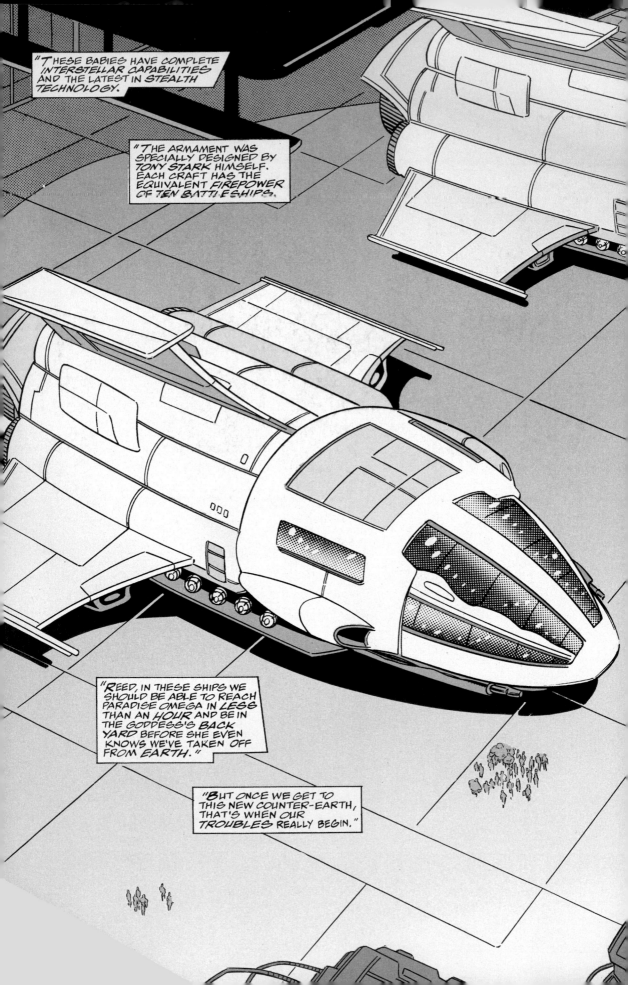

"THESE BABIES HAVE COMPLETE INTERSTELLAR CAPABILITIES AND THE LATEST IN STEALTH TECHNOLOGY.

"THE ARMAMENT WAS SPECIALLY DESIGNED BY TONY STARK HIMSELF. EACH CRAFT HAS THE EQUIVALENT FIREPOWER OF TEN BATTLESHIPS.

"REED, IN THESE SHIPS WE SHOULD BE ABLE TO REACH PARADISE OMEGA IN LESS THAN AN HOUR AND BE IN THE GODDESS'S BACK YARD BEFORE SHE EVEN KNOWS WE'VE TAKEN OFF FROM EARTH."

"BUT ONCE WE GET TO THIS NEW COUNTER-EARTH, THAT'S WHEN OUR TROUBLES REALLY BEGIN."

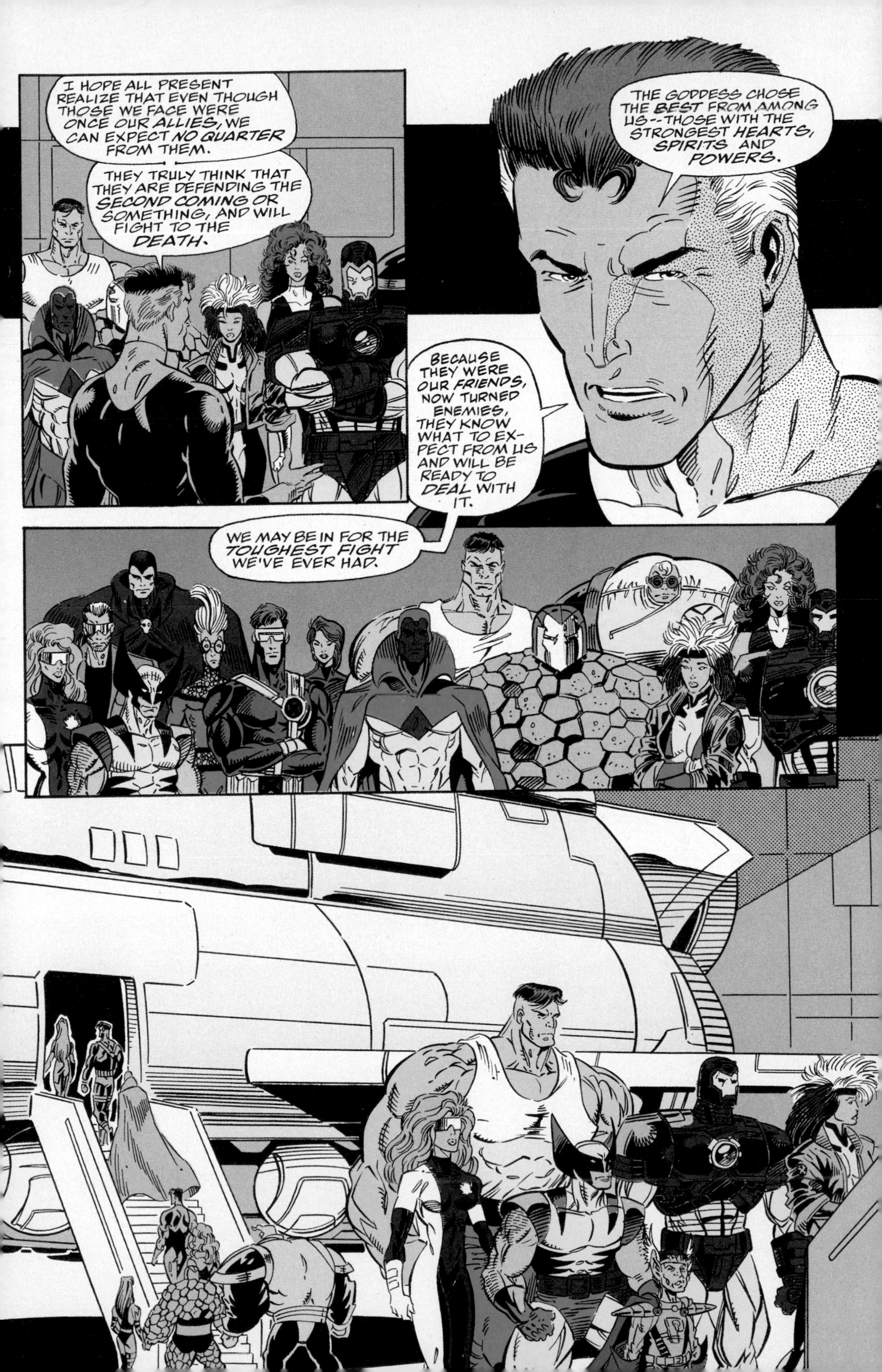
I HOPE ALL PRESENT REALIZE THAT EVEN THOUGH THOSE WE FACE WERE ONCE OUR ALLIES, WE CAN EXPECT NO QUARTER FROM THEM.
THEY TRULY THINK THAT THEY ARE DEFENDING THE SECOND COMING OR SOMETHING, AND WILL FIGHT TO THE DEATH.
THE GODDESS CHOSE THE BEST FROM AMONG US--THOSE WITH THE STRONGEST HEARTS, SPIRITS AND POWERS.
BECAUSE THEY WERE OUR FRIENDS, NOW TURNED ENEMIES, THEY KNOW WHAT TO EXPECT FROM US AND WILL BE READY TO DEAL WITH IT.
WE MAY BE IN FOR THE TOUGHEST FIGHT WE'VE EVER HAD.

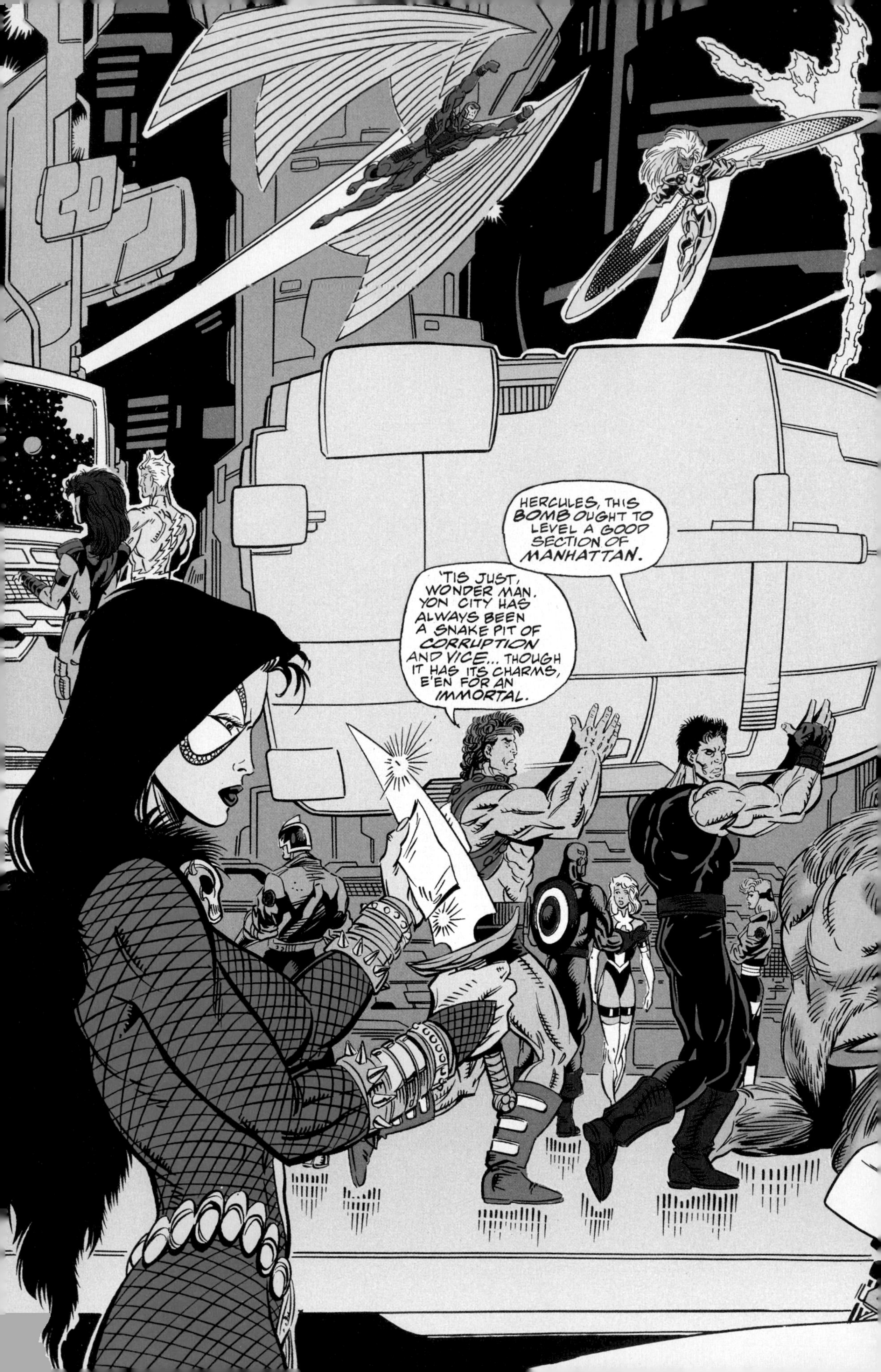
HERCULES, THIS BOMB OUGHT TO LEVEL A GOOD SECTION OF MANHATTAN.
'TIS JUST, WONDER MAN. YON CITY HAS ALWAYS BEEN A SNAKE PIT OF CORRUPTION AND VICE... THOUGH IT HAS ITS CHARMS, E'EN FOR AN IMMORTAL.

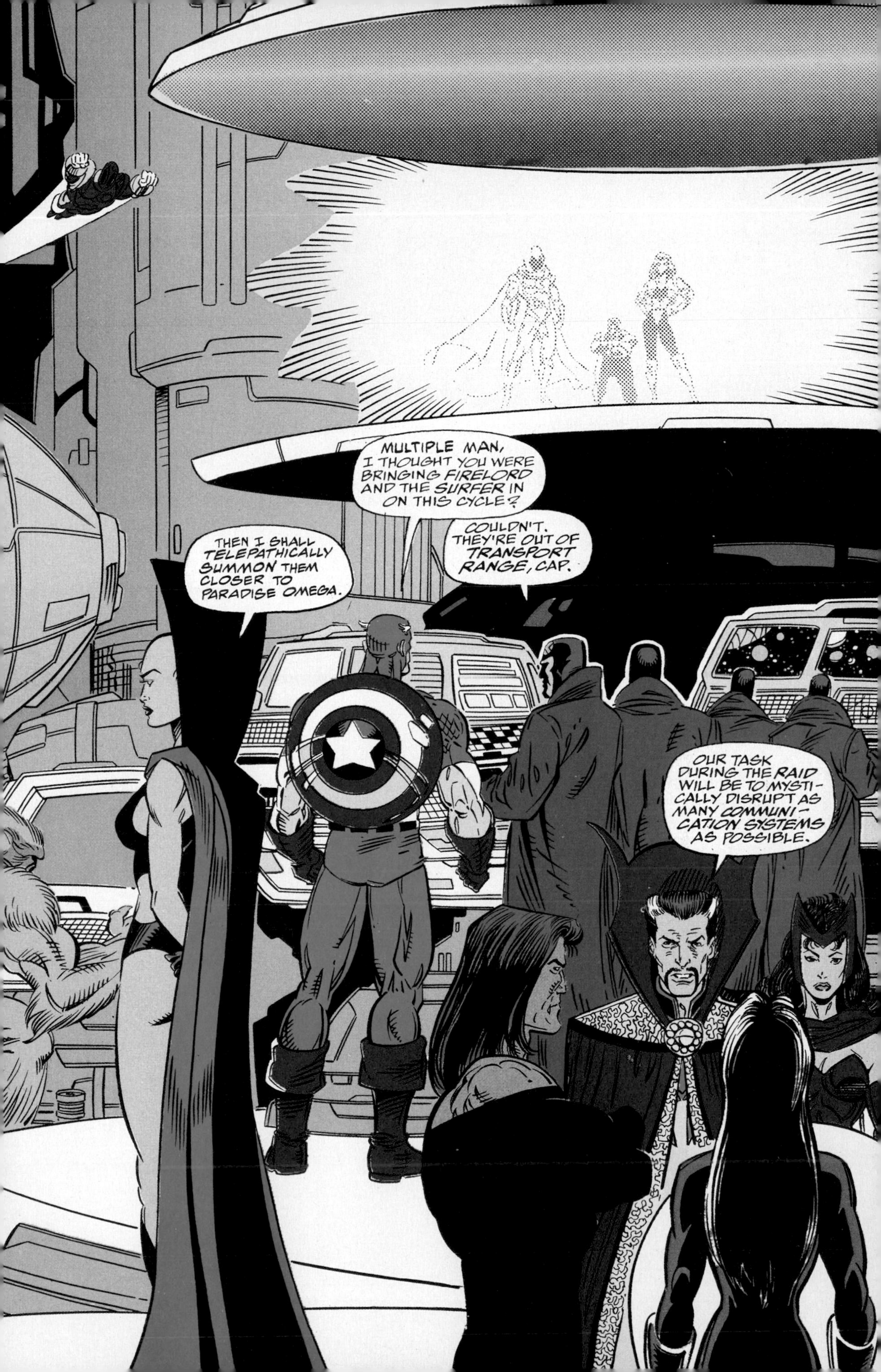
MULTIPLE MAN, I THOUGHT YOU WERE BRINGING FIRELORD AND THE SURFER IN ON THIS CYCLE?
COULDN'T. THEY'RE OUT OF TRANSPORT RANGE, CAP.
THEN I SHALL TELEPATHICALLY SUMMON THEM CLOSER TO PARADISE OMEGA.
OUR TASK DURING THE RAID WILL BE TO MYSTICALLY DISRUPT AS MANY COMMUNICATION SYSTEMS AS POSSIBLE.

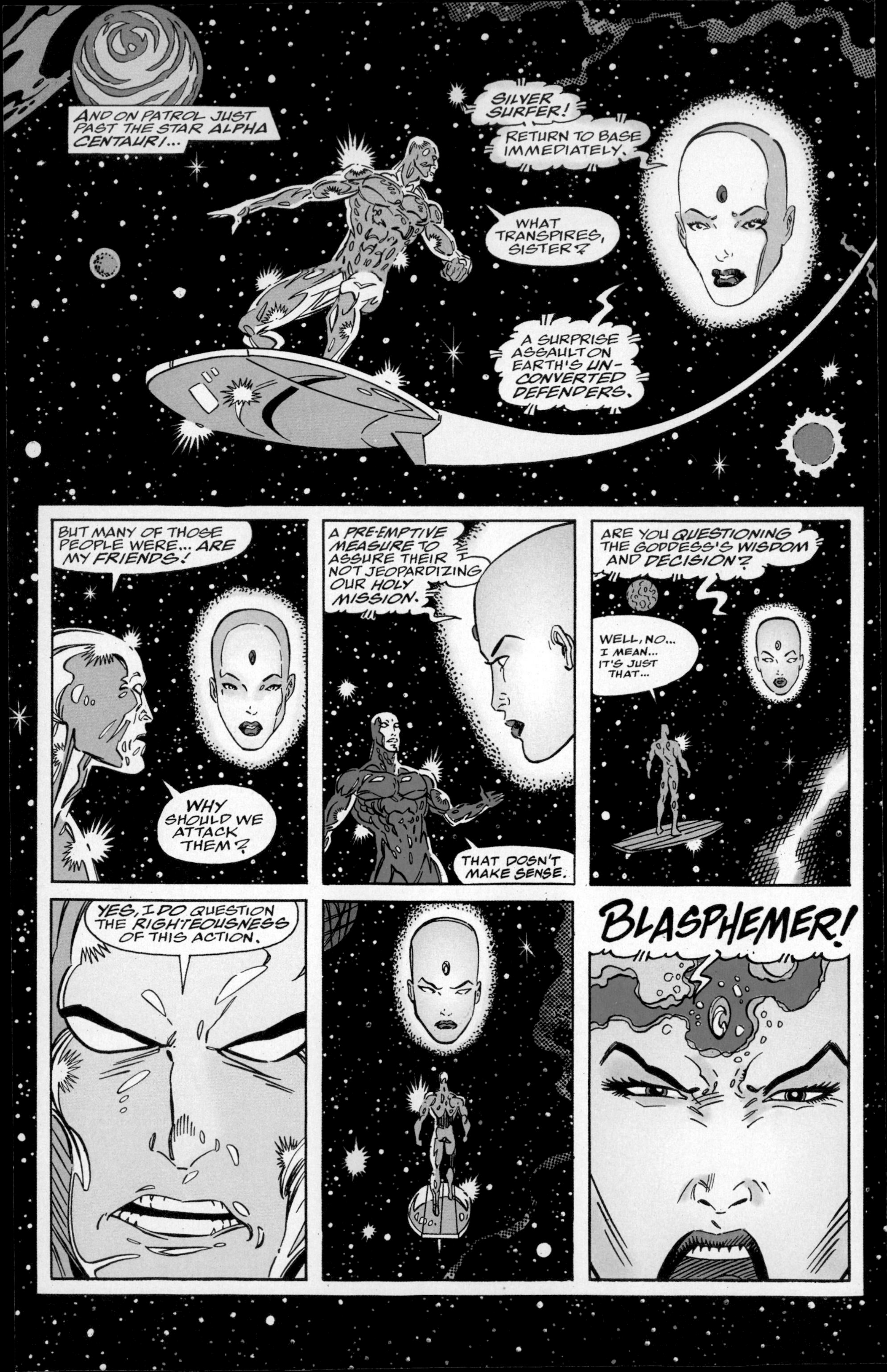

AND ON PATROL JUST PAST THE STAR ALPHA CENTAURI...
SILVER SURFER!
RETURN TO BASE IMMEDIATELY.
WHAT TRANSPIRES, SISTER?
A SURPRISE ASSAULT ON EARTH'S UN-CONVERTED DEFENDERS.
BUT MANY OF THOSE PEOPLE WERE... ARE MY FRIENDS!
WHY SHOULD WE ATTACK THEM?
A PRE-EMPTIVE MEASURE TO ASSURE THEIR NOT JEOPARDIZING OUR HOLY MISSION.
THAT DOSN'T MAKE SENSE.
ARE YOU QUESTIONING THE GODDESS'S WISDOM AND DECISION?
WELL, NO... I MEAN... IT'S JUST THAT...
YES, I DO QUESTION THE RIGHTEOUSNESS OF THIS ACTION.
BLASPHEMER!

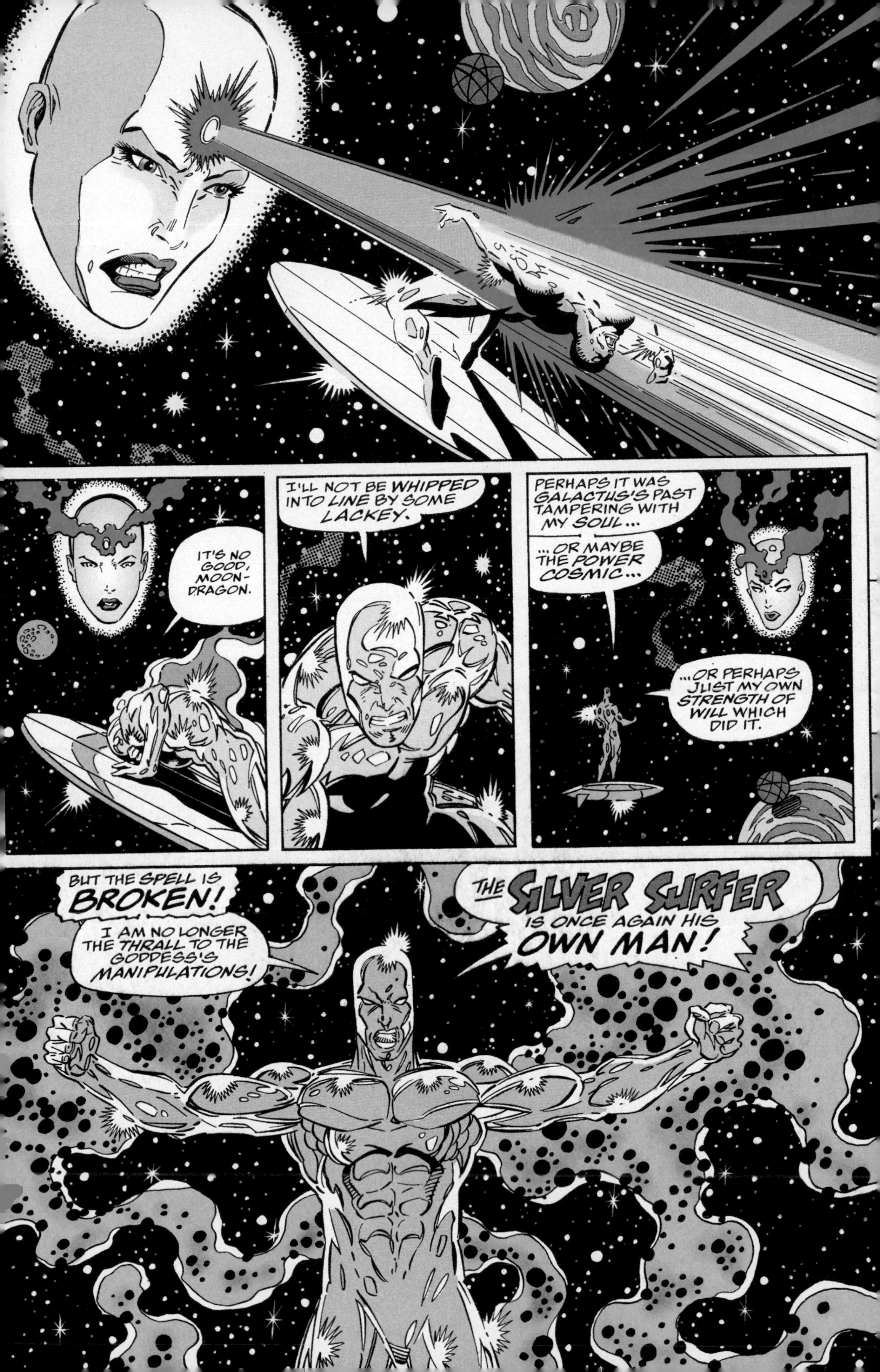

IT'S NO GOOD, MOON-DRAGON.
I'LL NOT BE WHIPPED INTO LINE BY SOME LACKEY.
PERHAPS IT WAS GALACTUS'S PAST TAMPERING WITH MY SOUL...
...OR MAYBE THE POWER COSMIC...
...OR PERHAPS JUST MY OWN STRENGTH OF WILL WHICH DID IT.
BUT THE SPELL IS BROKEN!
I AM NO LONGER THE THRALL TO THE GODDESS'S MANIPULATIONS!
THE SILVER SURFER IS ONCE AGAIN HIS OWN MAN!

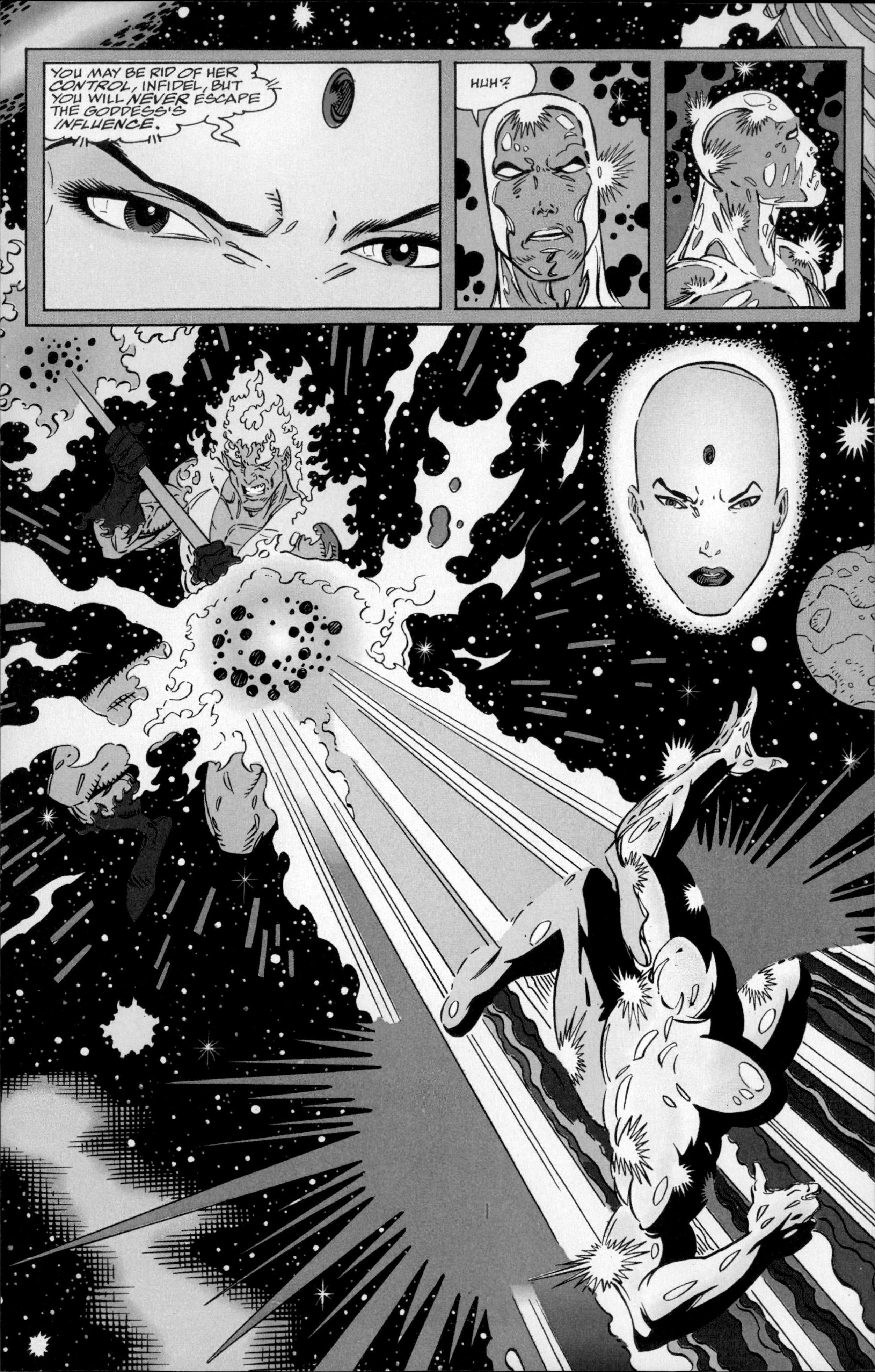
YOU MAY BE RID OF HER CONTROL, INFIDEL, BUT YOU WILL NEVER ESCAPE THE GODDESS'S INFLUENCE.
HUH?

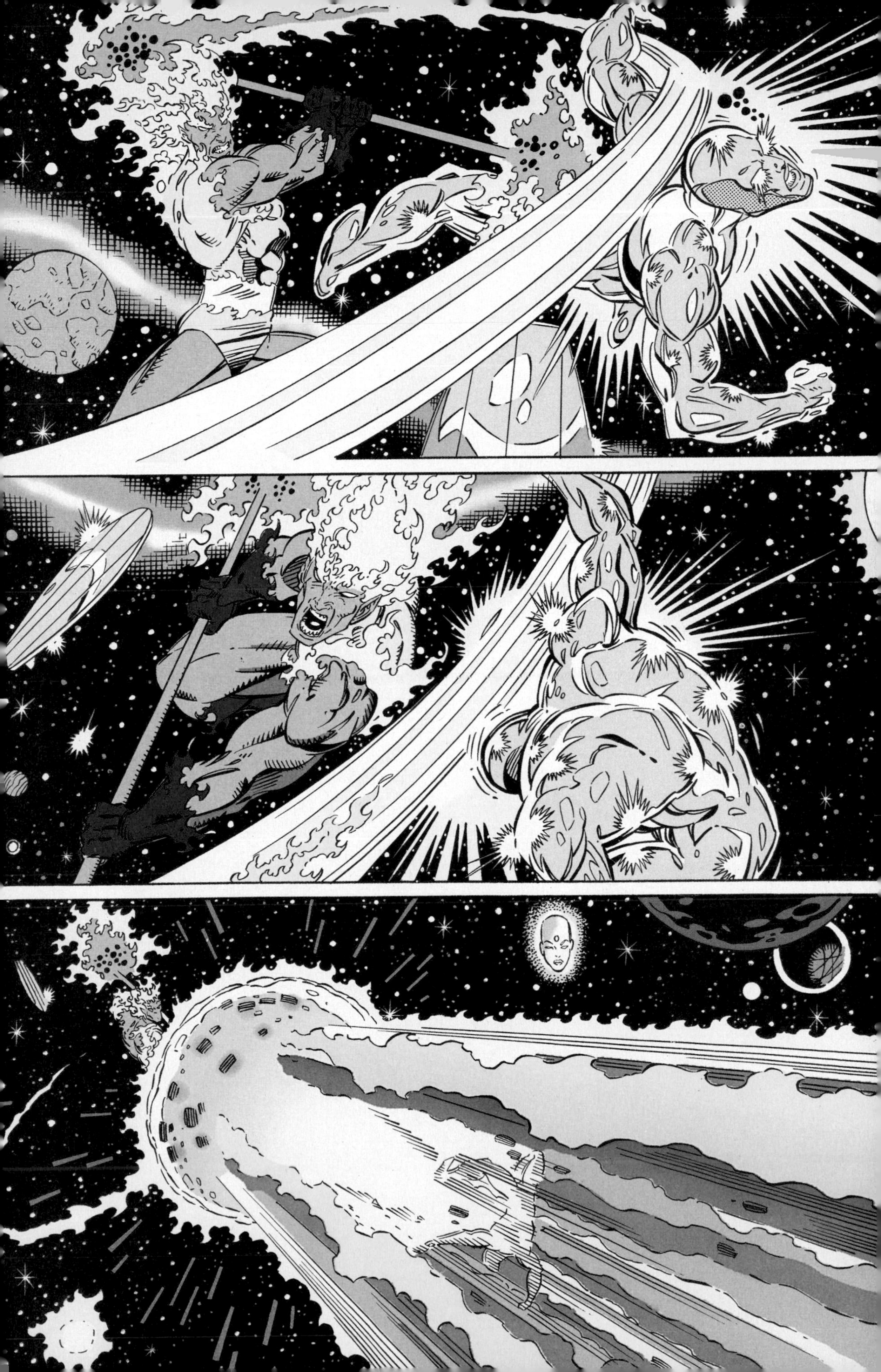

TO DENY ONE'S CELESTIAL DESTINY IS TO COURT DESTRUCTION.

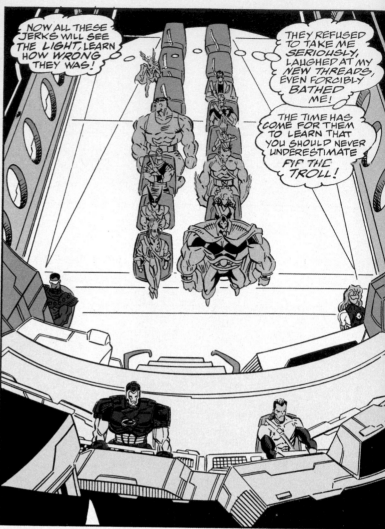

NOW ALL THESE JERKS WILL SEE THE *LIGHT,* LEARN HOW *WRONG* THEY WAS!

THEY REFUSED TO TAKE ME *SERIOUSLY,* LAUGHED AT MY *NEW THREADS,* EVEN FORCIBLY *BATHED* ME!

THE TIME HAS COME FOR THEM TO LEARN THAT YOU SHOULD NEVER UNDERESTIMATE *PIP THE TROLL!*

THAT *IRON MAN* THINKS HE'S GOT IT ALL UNDER CONTROL WITH HIS *BRAINS* AND *GIZMOS.*

BUT IN THE END THEY WON'T HELP HIM NONE AGAINST THE *GODDESS!*

THAT WALKIN' MUSCLE, THE *HULK,* THINKS HE CAN JUST POUND ANY *PROBLEM* INTO A *SOLUTION.*

WRONG.

NOT EVEN CLEVER OL' *MAXAM* IS GOIN' TO BE ABLE TO PULL OUR FAT OUTTA THE FIRE THIS TIME.

NONE OF THESE *YAHOOS* CAN DO *SQUAT* AGAINST THE GODDESS!

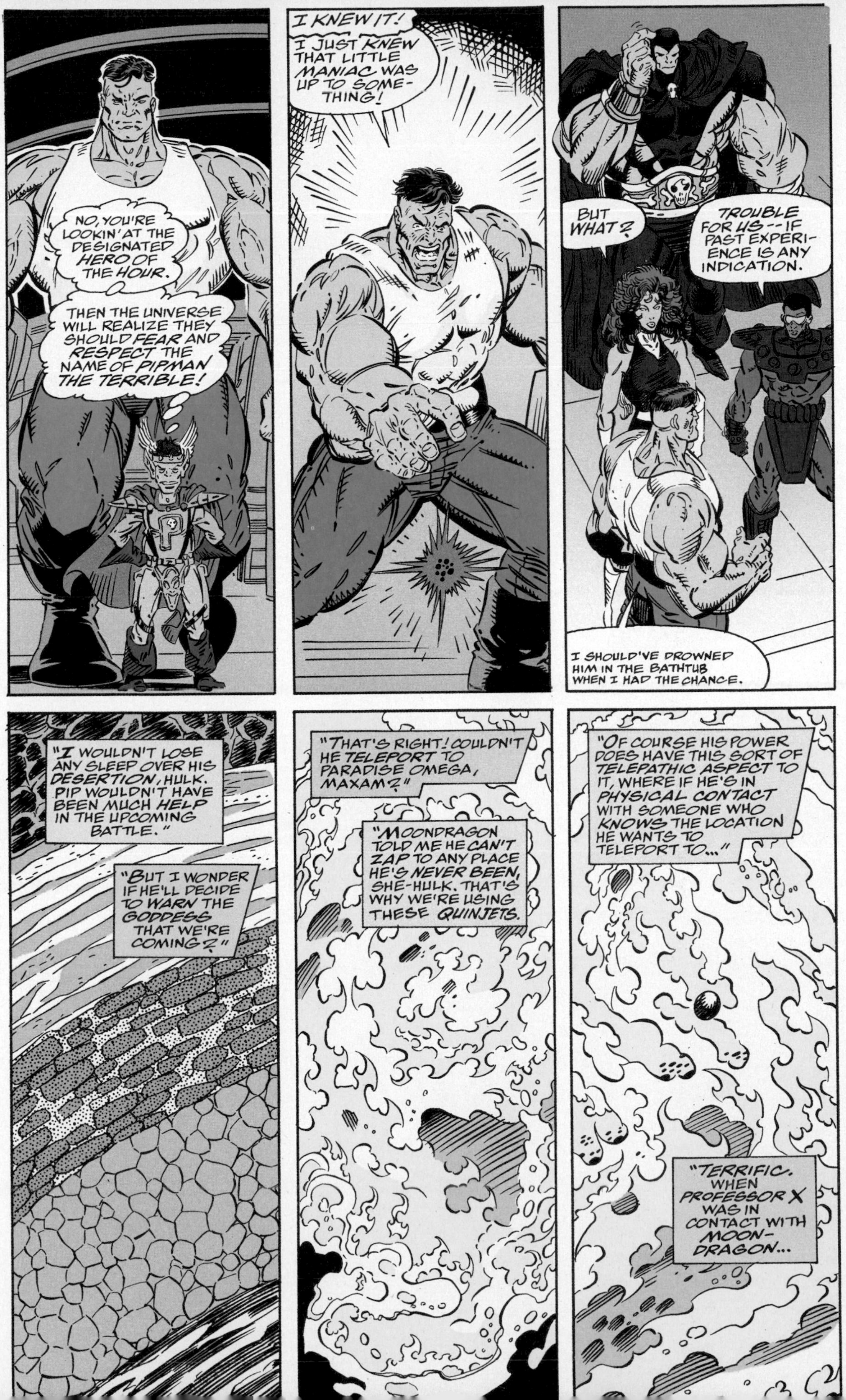
NO, YOU'RE LOOKIN' AT THE DESIGNATED HERO OF THE HOUR.
THEN THE UNIVERSE WILL REALIZE THEY SHOULD FEAR AND RESPECT THE NAME OF PIPMAN THE TERRIBLE!
I KNEW IT! I JUST KNEW THAT LITTLE MANIAC WAS UP TO SOME-THING!
BUT WHAT?
TROUBLE FOR US--IF PAST EXPERIENCE IS ANY INDICATION.
I SHOULD'VE DROWNED HIM IN THE BATHTUB WHEN I HAD THE CHANCE.
"I WOULDN'T LOSE ANY SLEEP OVER HIS DESERTION, HULK. PIP WOULDN'T HAVE BEEN MUCH HELP IN THE UPCOMING BATTLE."
"BUT I WONDER IF HE'LL DECIDE TO WARN THE GODDESS THAT WE'RE COMING?"
"THAT'S RIGHT! COULDN'T HE TELEPORT TO PARADISE OMEGA, MAXAM?"
"MOONDRAGON TOLD ME HE CAN'T ZAP TO ANY PLACE HE'S NEVER BEEN, SHE-HULK. THAT'S WHY WE'RE USING THESE QUINJETS.
"OF COURSE HIS POWER DOES HAVE THIS SORT OF TELEPATHIC ASPECT TO IT, WHERE IF HE'S IN PHYSICAL CONTACT WITH SOMEONE WHO KNOWS THE LOCATION HE WANTS TO TELEPORT TO..."
"TERRIFIC. WHEN PROFESSOR X WAS IN CONTACT WITH MOON-DRAGON...

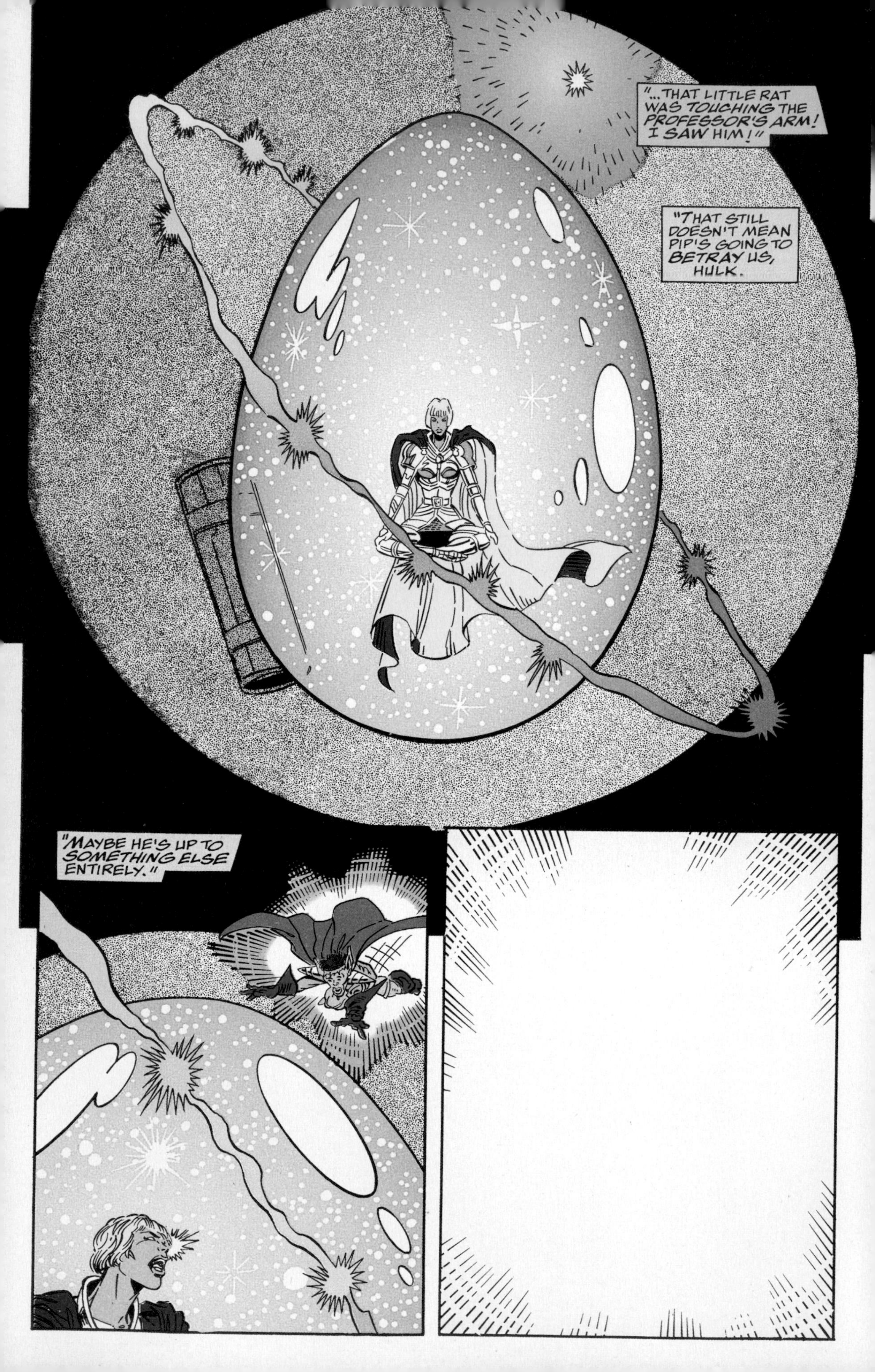
"...THAT LITTLE RAT WAS TOUCHING THE PROFESSOR'S ARM! I SAW HIM!"
"THAT STILL DOESN'T MEAN PIP'S GOING TO BETRAY US, HULK.
"MAYBE HE'S UP TO SOMETHING ELSE ENTIRELY."

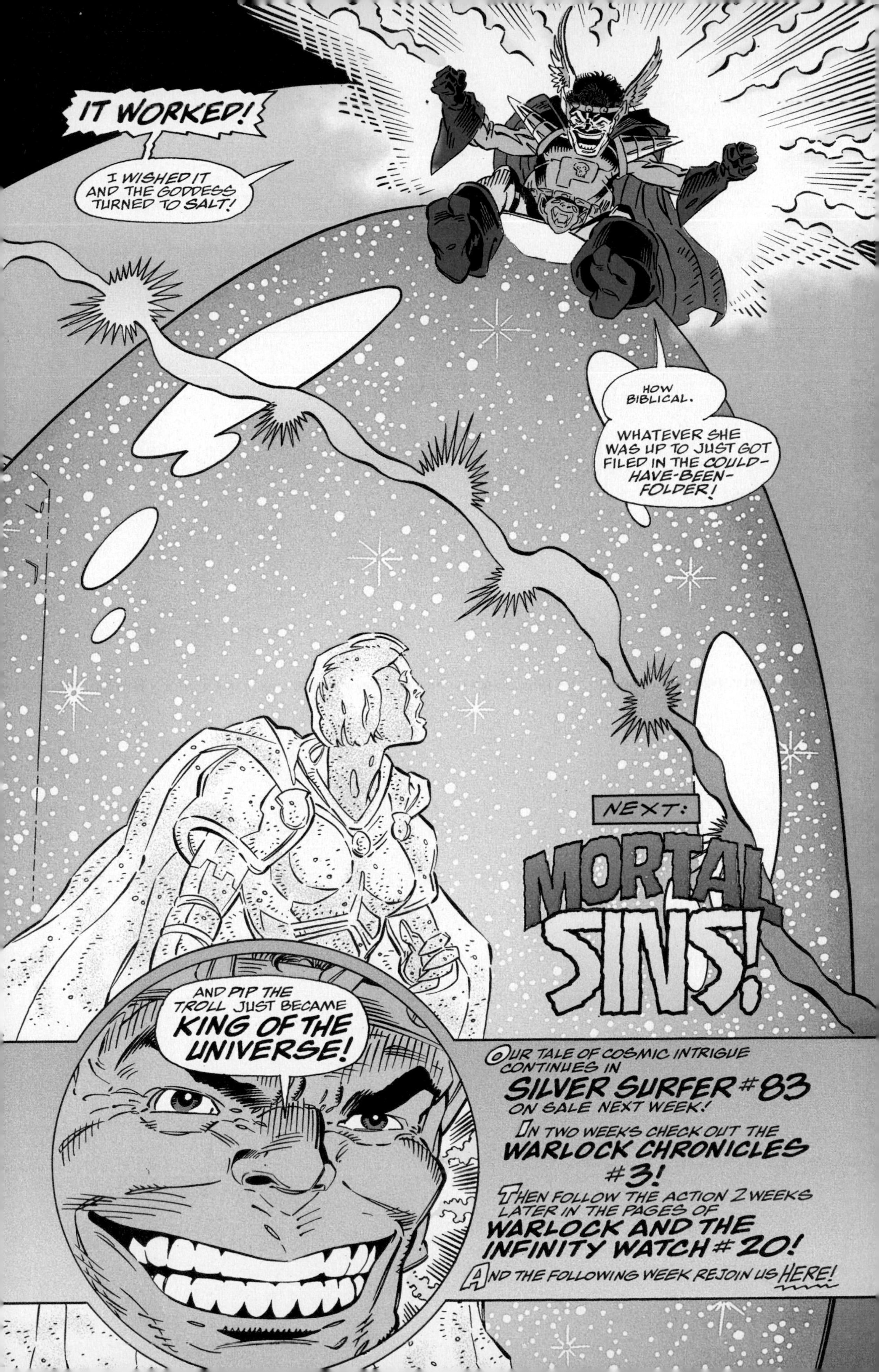
IT WORKED!
I WISHED IT AND THE GODDESS TURNED TO SALT!
HOW BIBLICAL.
WHATEVER SHE WAS UP TO JUST GOT FILED IN THE COULD-HAVE-BEEN-FOLDER!
NEXT:
MORTAL SINS!
AND PIP THE TROLL JUST BECAME KING OF THE UNIVERSE!
OUR TALE OF COSMIC INTRIGUE CONTINUES IN
SILVER SURFER #83
ON SALE NEXT WEEK!
IN TWO WEEKS CHECK OUT THE
WARLOCK CHRONICLES #3!
THEN FOLLOW THE ACTION 2 WEEKS LATER IN THE PAGES OF
WARLOCK AND THE INFINITY WATCH #20!
AND THE FOLLOWING WEEK REJOIN US HERE!

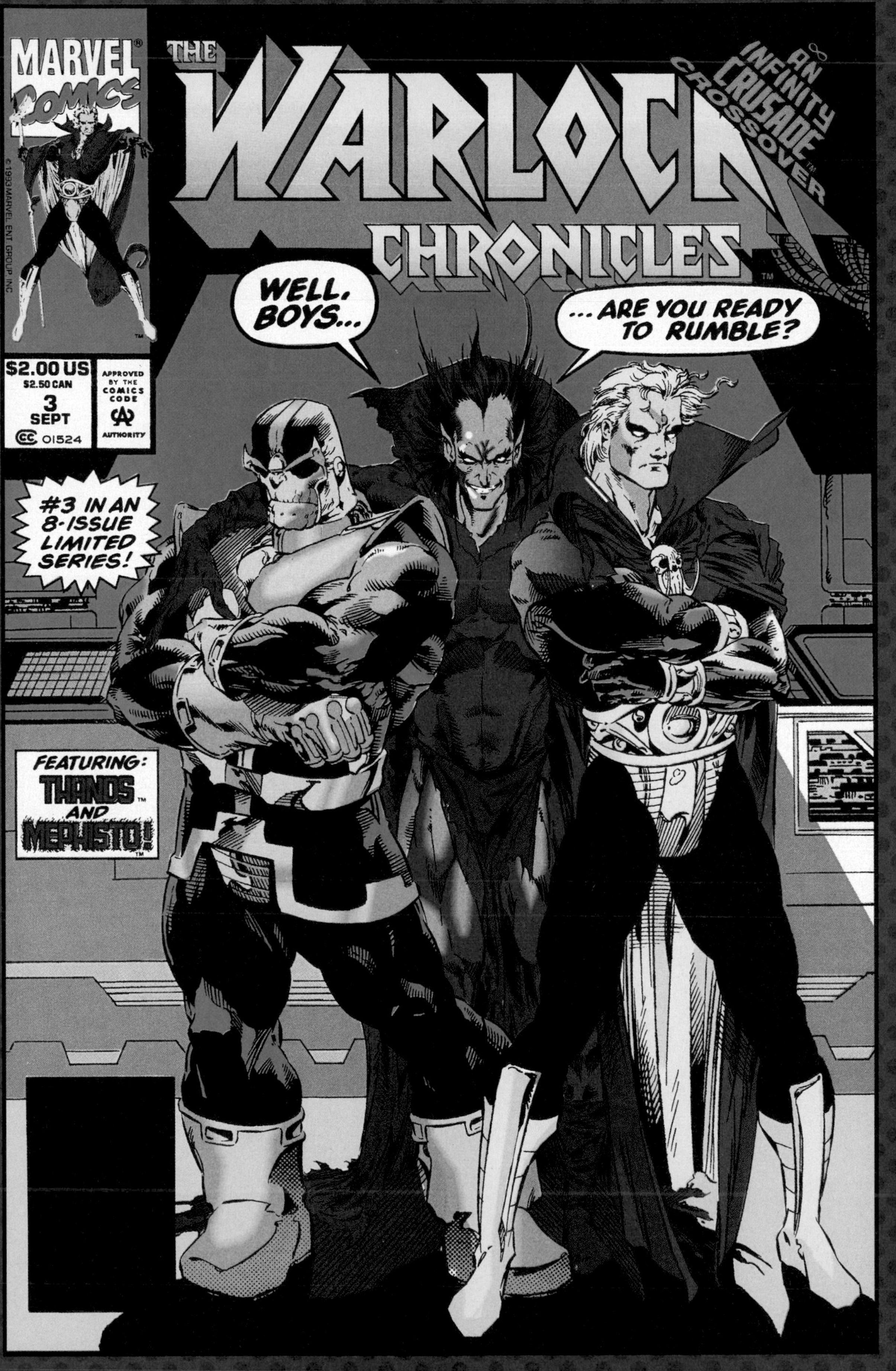
MARVEL COMICS
THE WARLOCK CHRONICLES
AN INFINITY CRUSADE CROSSOVER
© 1993 MARVEL ENT. GROUP INC.
$2.00 US
$2.50 CAN
3
SEPT
01524
APPROVED BY THE COMICS CODE AUTHORITY
WELL, BOYS...
...ARE YOU READY TO RUMBLE?
#3 IN AN 8-ISSUE LIMITED SERIES!
FEATURING: THANOS AND MEPHISTO!

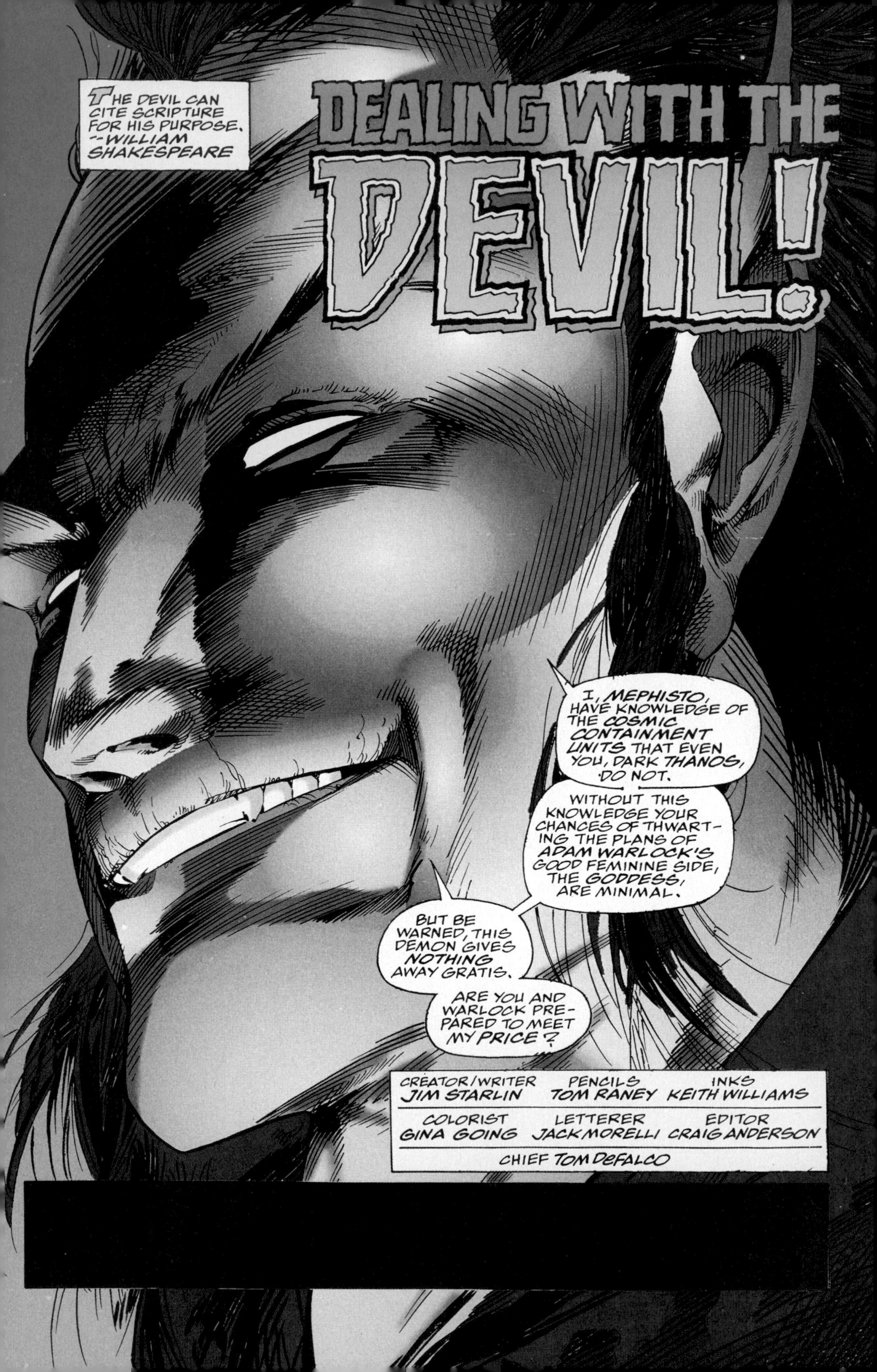
THE DEVIL CAN CITE SCRIPTURE FOR HIS PURPOSE. --WILLIAM SHAKESPEARE
DEALING WITH THE DEVIL!
I, MEPHISTO, HAVE KNOWLEDGE OF THE COSMIC CONTAINMENT UNITS THAT EVEN YOU, DARK THANOS, DO NOT.
WITHOUT THIS KNOWLEDGE YOUR CHANCES OF THWARTING THE PLANS OF ADAM WARLOCK'S GOOD FEMININE SIDE, THE GODDESS, ARE MINIMAL.
BUT BE WARNED, THIS DEMON GIVES NOTHING AWAY GRATIS.
ARE YOU AND WARLOCK PREPARED TO MEET MY PRICE?
CREATOR/WRITER JIM STARLIN
PENCILS TOM RANEY
INKS KEITH WILLIAMS
COLORIST GINA GOING
LETTERER JACK MORELLI
EDITOR CRAIG ANDERSON
CHIEF TOM DeFALCO

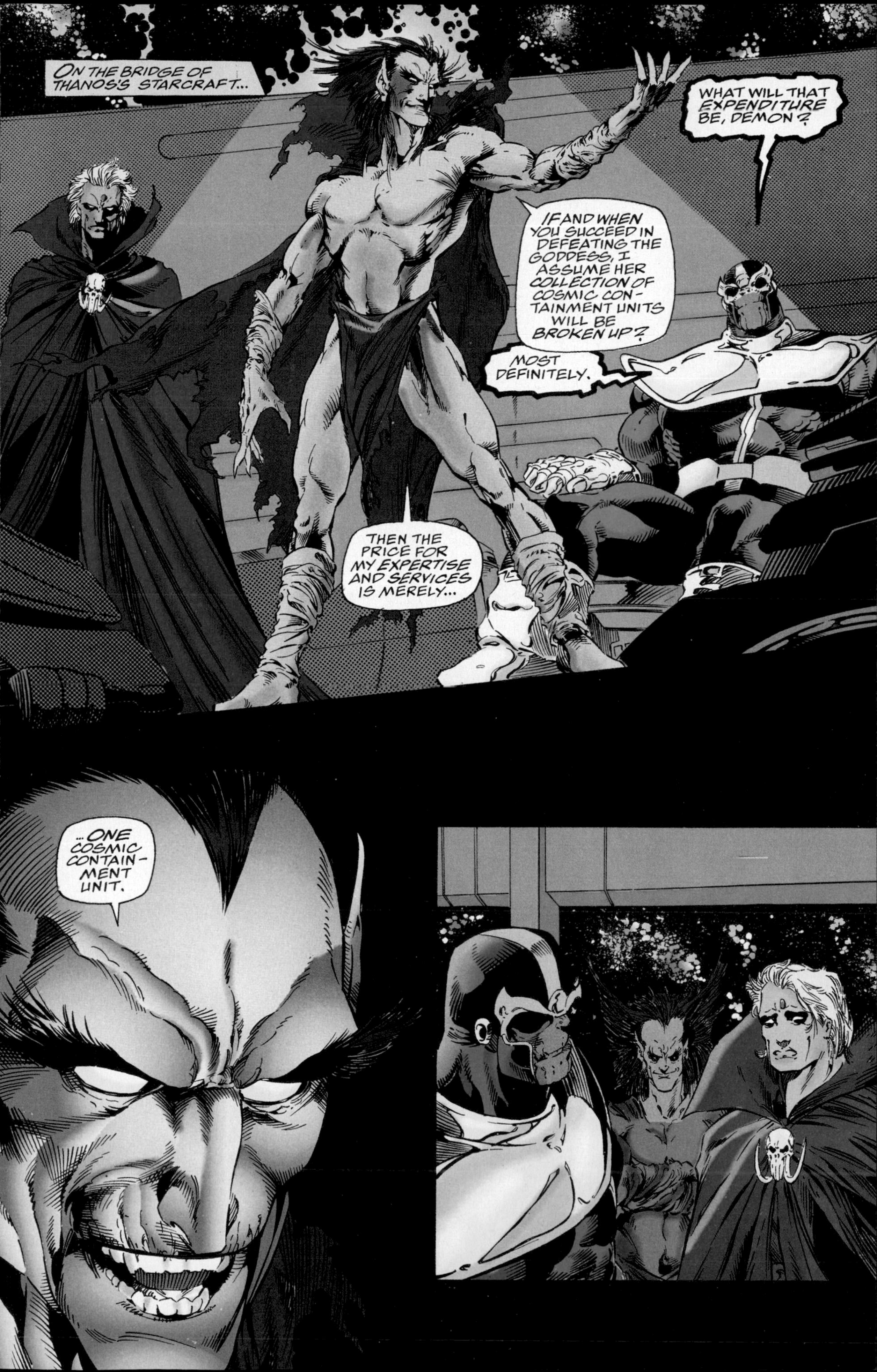
ON THE BRIDGE OF THANOS'S STARCRAFT...
WHAT WILL THAT EXPENDITURE BE, DEMON?
IF AND WHEN YOU SUCCEED IN DEFEATING THE GODDESS, I ASSUME HER COLLECTION OF COSMIC CONTAINMENT UNITS WILL BE BROKEN UP?
MOST DEFINITELY.
THEN THE PRICE FOR MY EXPERTISE AND SERVICES IS MERELY...
...ONE COSMIC CONTAINMENT UNIT.

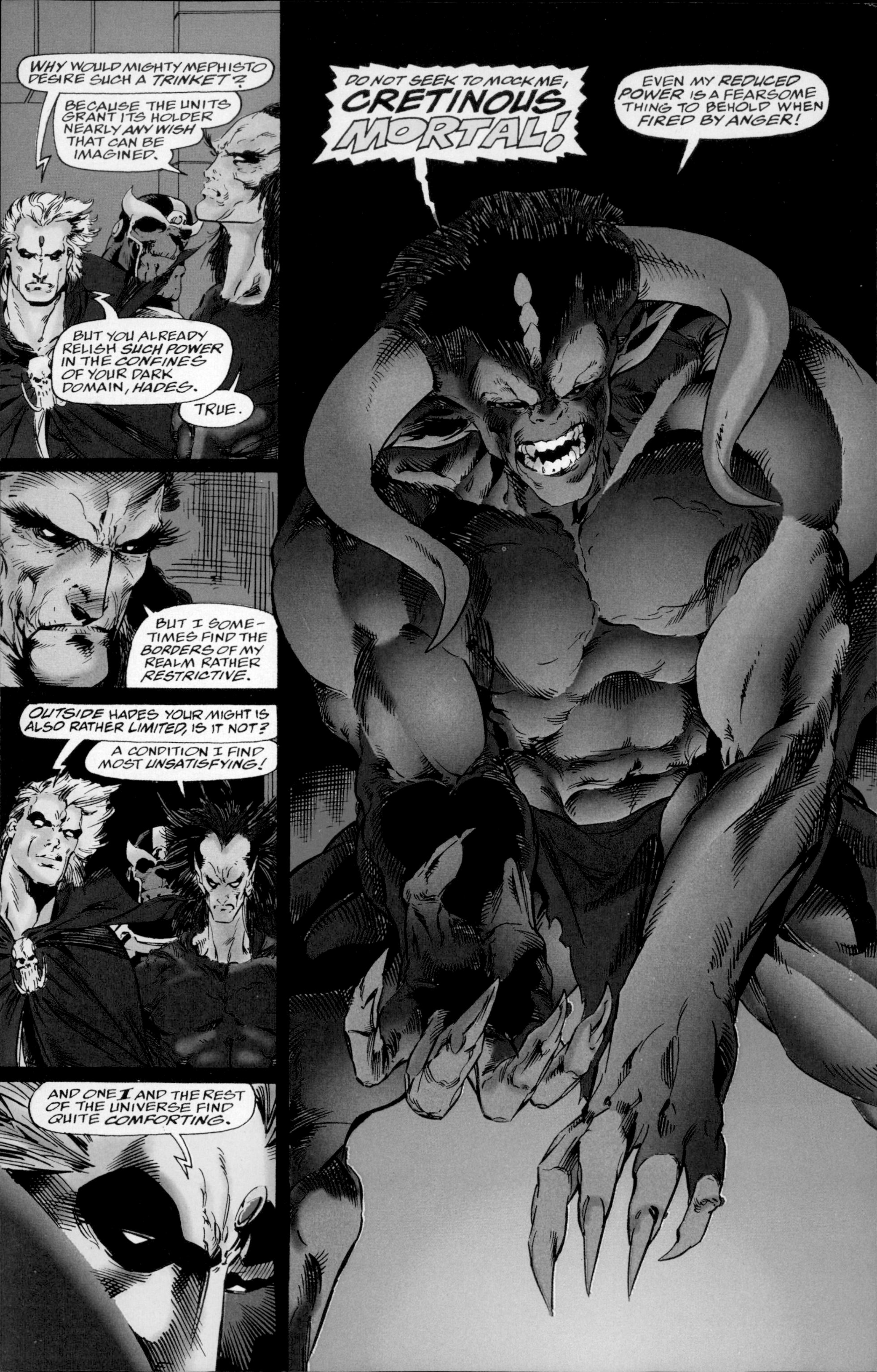
WHY WOULD MIGHTY MEPHISTO DESIRE SUCH A TRINKET?
BECAUSE THE UNITS GRANT ITS HOLDER NEARLY ANY WISH THAT CAN BE IMAGINED.
BUT YOU ALREADY RELISH SUCH POWER IN THE CONFINES OF YOUR DARK DOMAIN, HADES.
TRUE.
BUT I SOMETIMES FIND THE BORDERS OF MY REALM RATHER RESTRICTIVE.
OUTSIDE HADES YOUR MIGHT IS ALSO RATHER LIMITED, IS IT NOT?
A CONDITION I FIND MOST UNSATISFYING!
AND ONE I AND THE REST OF THE UNIVERSE FIND QUITE COMFORTING.
DO NOT SEEK TO MOCK ME, CRETINOUS MORTAL!
EVEN MY REDUCED POWER IS A FEARSOME THING TO BEHOLD WHEN FIRED BY ANGER!

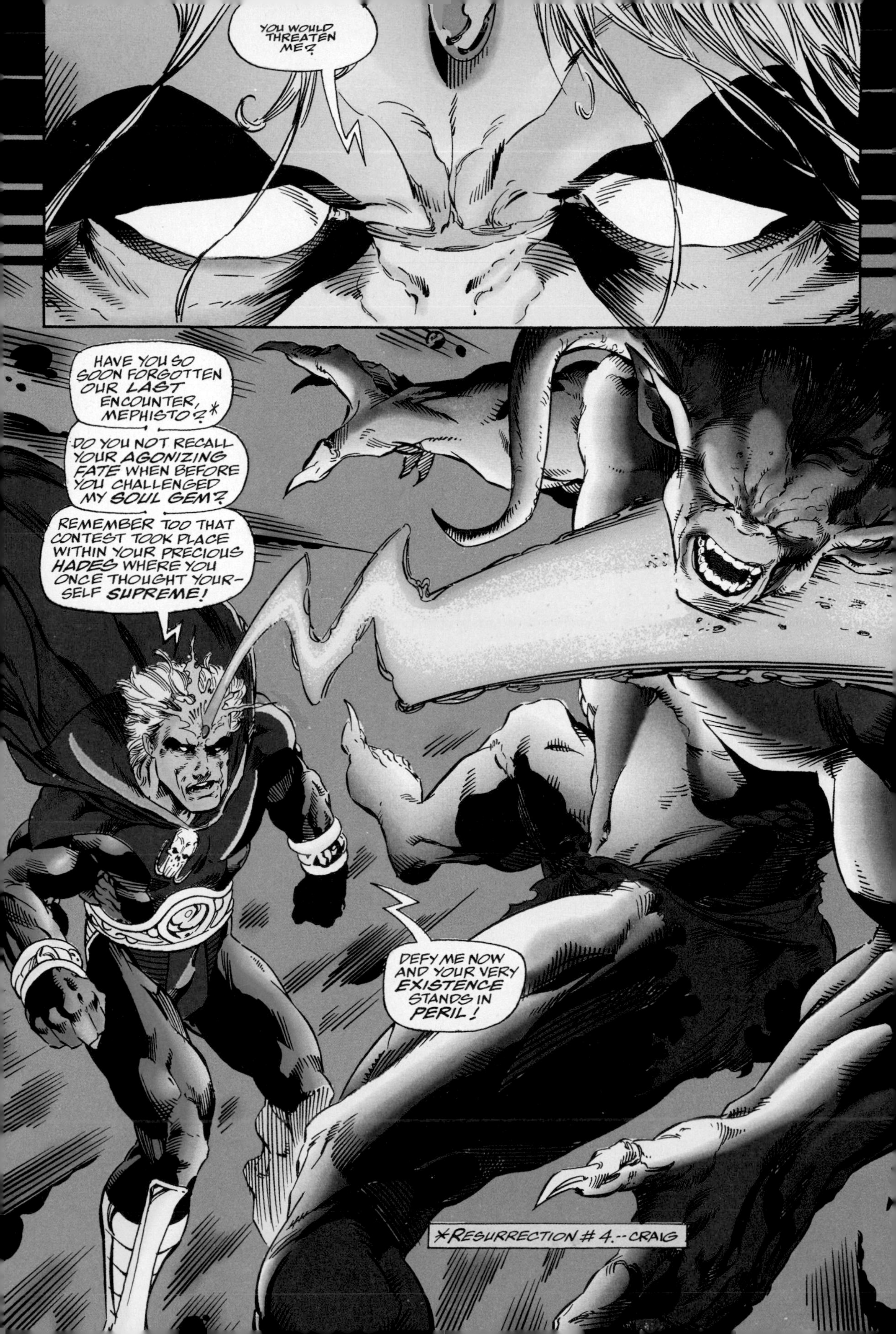
YOU WOULD THREATEN ME?
HAVE YOU SO SOON FORGOTTEN OUR LAST ENCOUNTER, MEPHISTO?*
DO YOU NOT RECALL YOUR AGONIZING FATE WHEN BEFORE YOU CHALLENGED MY SOUL GEM?
REMEMBER TOO THAT CONTEST TOOK PLACE WITHIN YOUR PRECIOUS HADES WHERE YOU ONCE THOUGHT YOURSELF SUPREME!
DEFY ME NOW AND YOUR VERY EXISTENCE STANDS IN PERIL!
*RESURRECTION #4.--CRAIG

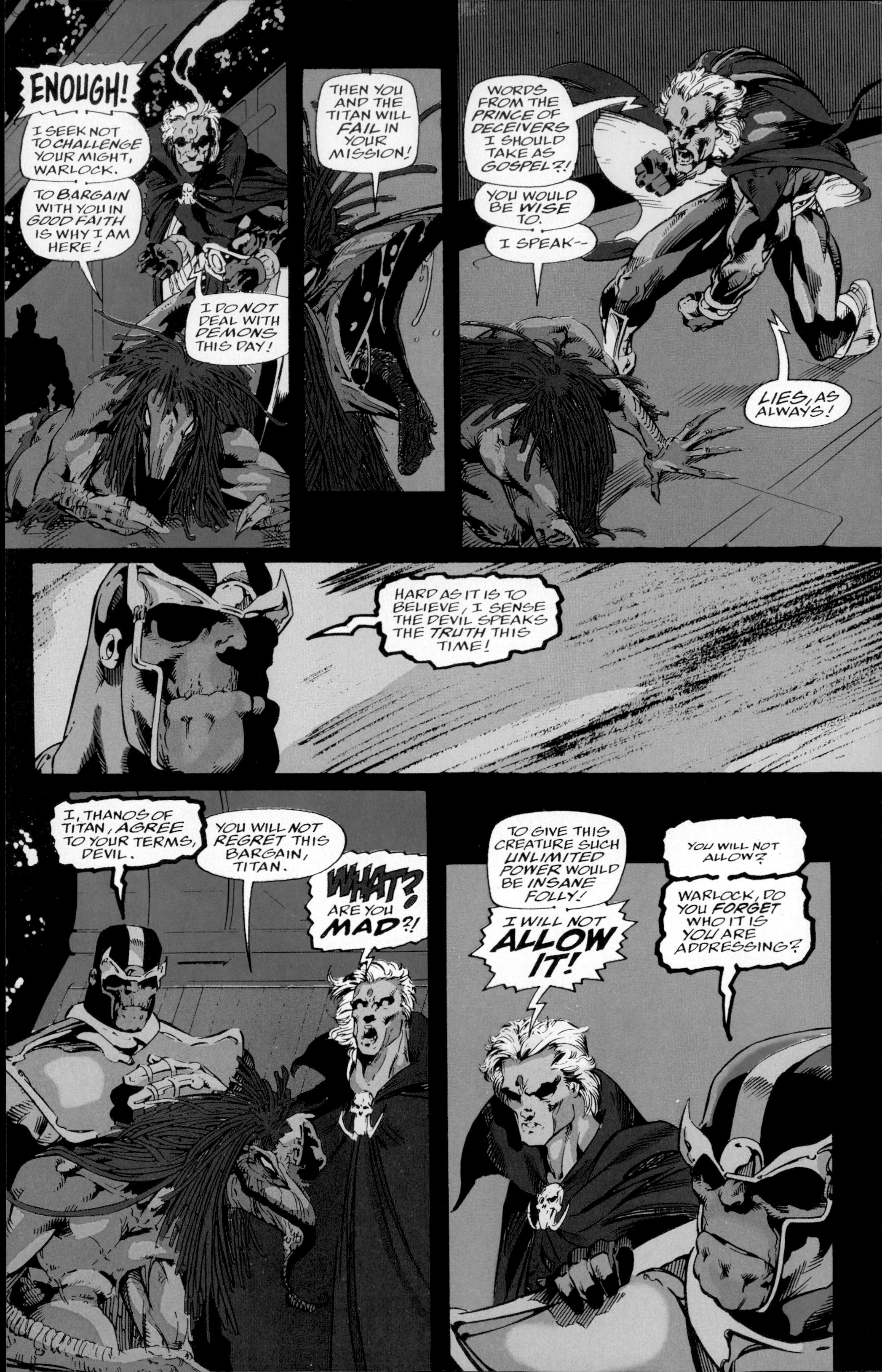

ENOUGH!
I SEEK NOT TO CHALLENGE YOUR MIGHT, WARLOCK.
TO BARGAIN WITH YOU IN GOOD FAITH IS WHY I AM HERE!
I DO NOT DEAL WITH DEMONS THIS DAY!
THEN YOU AND THE TITAN WILL FAIL IN YOUR MISSION!
WORDS FROM THE PRINCE OF DECEIVERS I SHOULD TAKE AS GOSPEL?!
YOU WOULD BE WISE TO.
I SPEAK--
LIES, AS ALWAYS!
HARD AS IT IS TO BELIEVE, I SENSE THE DEVIL SPEAKS THE TRUTH THIS TIME!
I, THANOS OF TITAN, AGREE TO YOUR TERMS, DEVIL.
YOU WILL NOT REGRET THIS BARGAIN, TITAN.
WHAT? ARE YOU MAD?!
TO GIVE THIS CREATURE SUCH UNLIMITED POWER WOULD BE INSANE FOLLY!
I WILL NOT ALLOW IT!
YOU WILL NOT ALLOW?
WARLOCK, DO YOU FORGET WHO IT IS YOU ARE ADDRESSING?

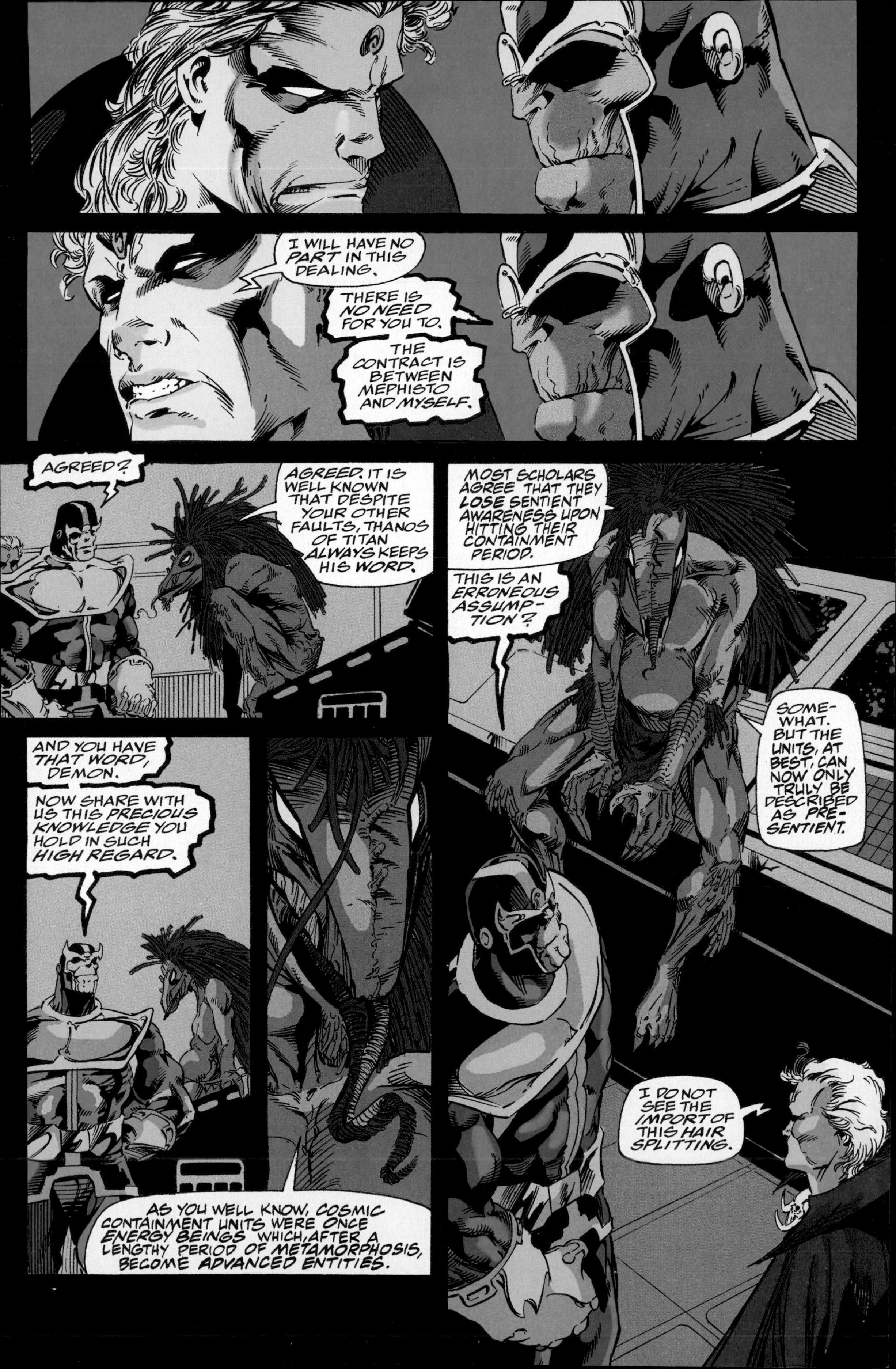
I WILL HAVE NO PART IN THIS DEALING.
THERE IS NO NEED FOR YOU TO.
THE CONTRACT IS BETWEEN MEPHISTO AND MYSELF.
AGREED?
AGREED. IT IS WELL KNOWN THAT DESPITE YOUR OTHER FAULTS, THANOS OF TITAN ALWAYS KEEPS HIS WORD.
MOST SCHOLARS AGREE THAT THEY LOSE SENTIENT AWARENESS UPON HITTING THEIR CONTAINMENT PERIOD.
THIS IS AN ERRONEOUS ASSUMPTION?
SOME-WHAT. BUT THE UNITS, AT BEST, CAN NOW ONLY TRULY BE DESCRIBED AS PRE-SENTIENT.
AND YOU HAVE THAT WORD, DEMON.
NOW SHARE WITH US THIS PRECIOUS KNOWLEDGE YOU HOLD IN SUCH HIGH REGARD.
AS YOU WELL KNOW, COSMIC CONTAINMENT UNITS WERE ONCE ENERGY BEINGS WHICH, AFTER A LENGTHY PERIOD OF METAMORPHOSIS, BECOME ADVANCED ENTITIES.
I DO NOT SEE THE IMPORT OF THIS HAIR SPLITTING.

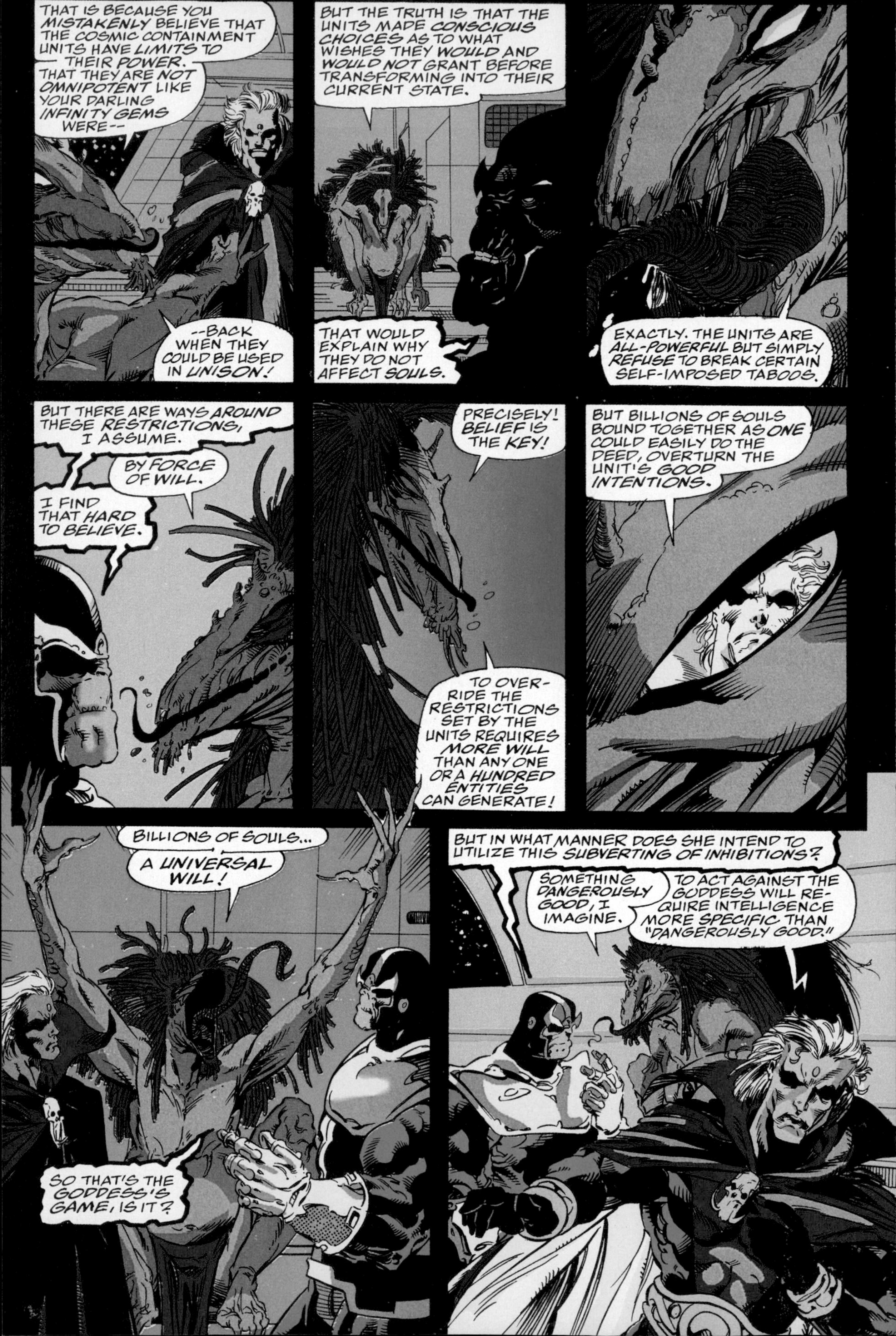

THAT IS BECAUSE YOU MISTAKENLY BELIEVE THAT THE COSMIC CONTAINMENT UNITS HAVE LIMITS TO THEIR POWER. THAT THEY ARE NOT OMNIPOTENT LIKE YOUR DARLING INFINITY GEMS WERE--
--BACK WHEN THEY COULD BE USED IN UNISON!
BUT THE TRUTH IS THAT THE UNITS MADE CONSCIOUS CHOICES AS TO WHAT WISHES THEY WOULD AND WOULD NOT GRANT BEFORE TRANSFORMING INTO THEIR CURRENT STATE.
THAT WOULD EXPLAIN WHY THEY DO NOT AFFECT SOULS.
EXACTLY. THE UNITS ARE ALL-POWERFUL BUT SIMPLY REFUSE TO BREAK CERTAIN SELF-IMPOSED TABOOS.
BUT THERE ARE WAYS AROUND THESE RESTRICTIONS, I ASSUME.
BY FORCE OF WILL.
I FIND THAT HARD TO BELIEVE.
PRECISELY! BELIEF IS THE KEY!
TO OVER-RIDE THE RESTRICTIONS SET BY THE UNITS REQUIRES MORE WILL THAN ANY ONE OR A HUNDRED ENTITIES CAN GENERATE!
BUT BILLIONS OF SOULS BOUND TOGETHER AS ONE COULD EASILY DO THE DEED, OVERTURN THE UNIT'S GOOD INTENTIONS.
BILLIONS OF SOULS...
A UNIVERSAL WILL!
SO THAT'S THE GODDESS'S GAME, IS IT?
BUT IN WHAT MANNER DOES SHE INTEND TO UTILIZE THIS SUBVERTING OF INHIBITIONS?
SOMETHING DANGEROUSLY GOOD, I IMAGINE.
TO ACT AGAINST THE GODDESS WILL RE-QUIRE INTELLIGENCE MORE SPECIFIC THAN "DANGEROUSLY GOOD."

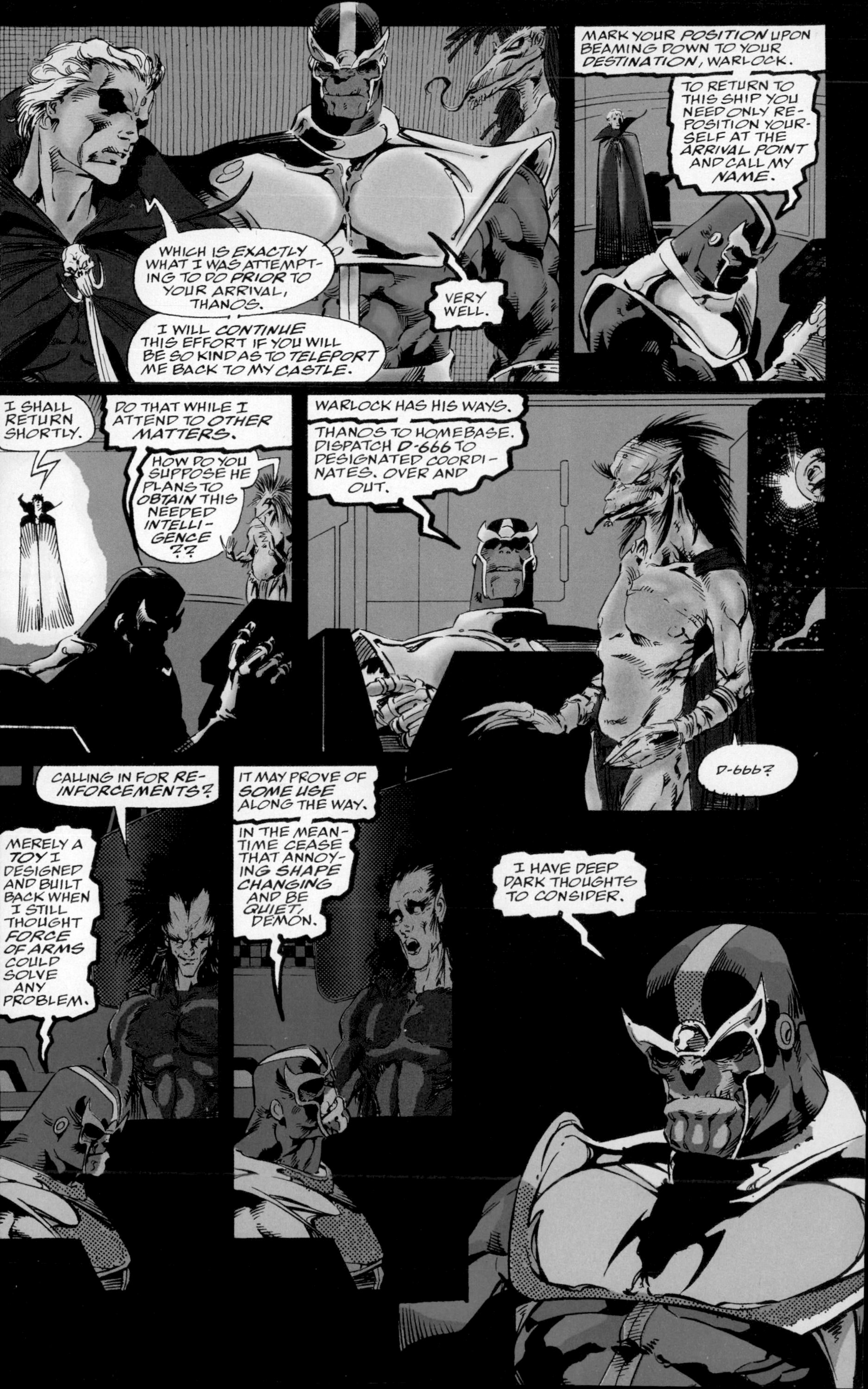
WHICH IS EXACTLY WHAT I WAS ATTEMPTING TO DO PRIOR TO YOUR ARRIVAL, THANOS.
I WILL CONTINUE THIS EFFORT IF YOU WILL BE SO KIND AS TO TELEPORT ME BACK TO MY CASTLE.
VERY WELL.
MARK YOUR POSITION UPON BEAMING DOWN TO YOUR DESTINATION, WARLOCK.
TO RETURN TO THIS SHIP YOU NEED ONLY REPOSITION YOURSELF AT THE ARRIVAL POINT AND CALL MY NAME.
I SHALL RETURN SHORTLY.
DO THAT WHILE I ATTEND TO OTHER MATTERS.
HOW DO YOU SUPPOSE HE PLANS TO OBTAIN THIS NEEDED INTELLIGENCE ??
WARLOCK HAS HIS WAYS.
THANOS TO HOMEBASE. DISPATCH D-666 TO DESIGNATED COORDINATES. OVER AND OUT.
D-666?
CALLING IN FOR REINFORCEMENTS?
MERELY A TOY I DESIGNED AND BUILT BACK WHEN I STILL THOUGHT FORCE OF ARMS COULD SOLVE ANY PROBLEM.
IT MAY PROVE OF SOME USE ALONG THE WAY.
IN THE MEANTIME CEASE THAT ANNOYING SHAPE CHANGING AND BE QUIET, DEMON.
I HAVE DEEP DARK THOUGHTS TO CONSIDER.

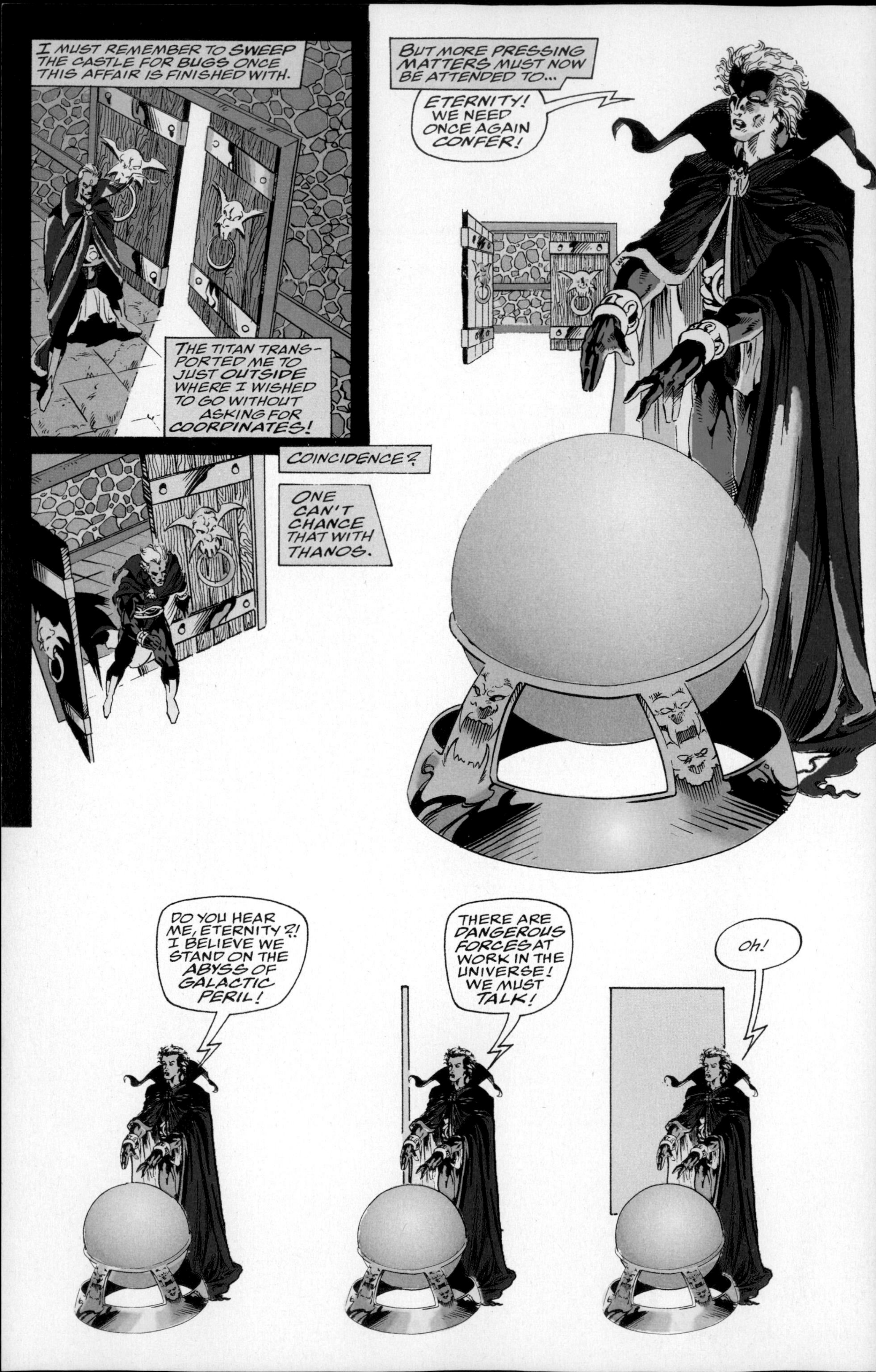

I MUST REMEMBER TO SWEEP THE CASTLE FOR BUGS ONCE THIS AFFAIR IS FINISHED WITH.
THE TITAN TRANSPORTED ME TO JUST OUTSIDE WHERE I WISHED TO GO WITHOUT ASKING FOR COORDINATES!
COINCIDENCE?
ONE CAN'T CHANCE THAT WITH THANOS.
BUT MORE PRESSING MATTERS MUST NOW BE ATTENDED TO...
ETERNITY! WE NEED ONCE AGAIN CONFER!
DO YOU HEAR ME, ETERNITY?! I BELIEVE WE STAND ON THE ABYSS OF GALACTIC PERIL!
THERE ARE DANGEROUS FORCES AT WORK IN THE UNIVERSE! WE MUST TALK!
Oh!

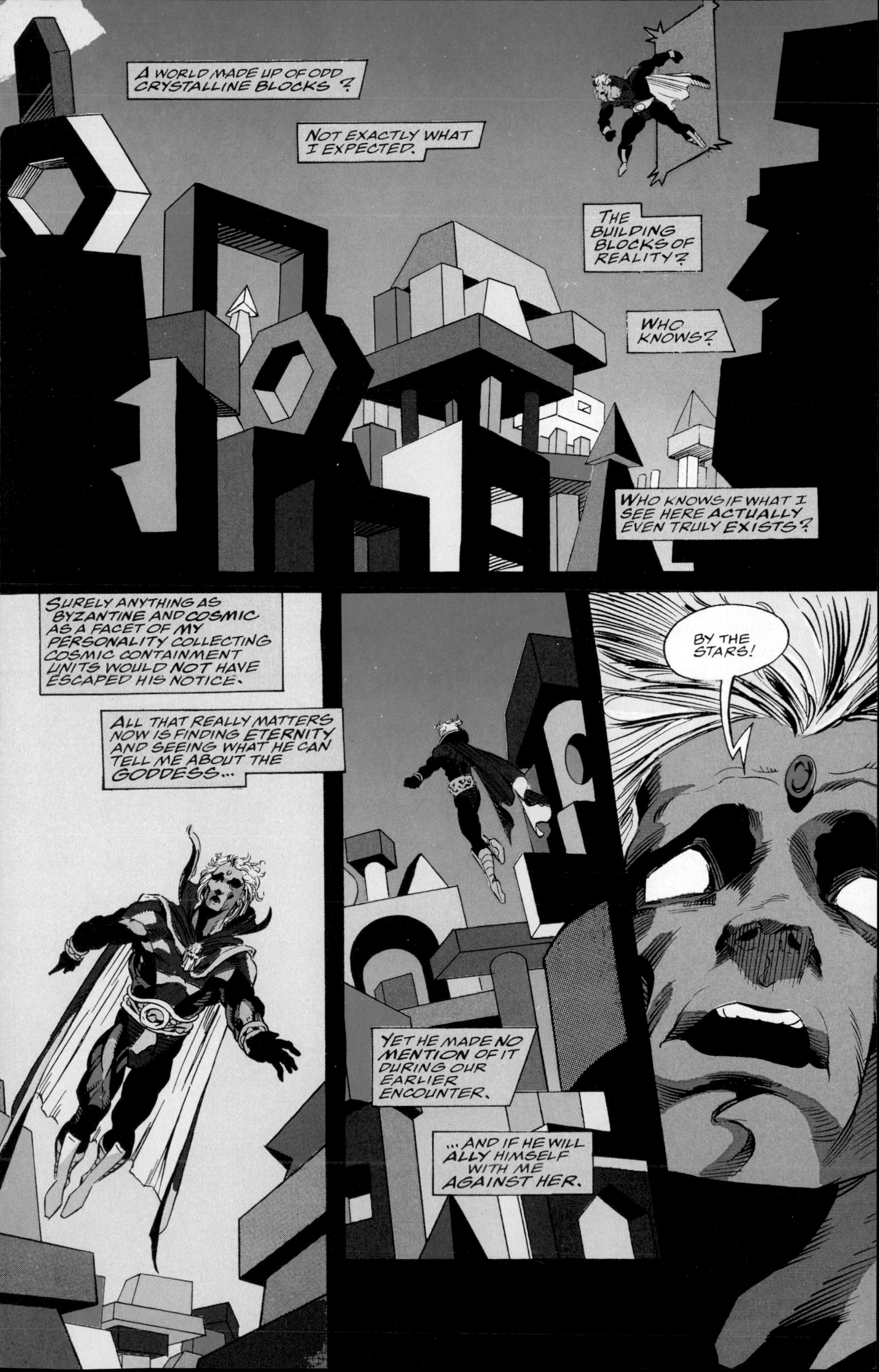
A WORLD MADE UP OF ODD CRYSTALLINE BLOCKS?
NOT EXACTLY WHAT I EXPECTED.
THE BUILDING BLOCKS OF REALITY?
WHO KNOWS?
WHO KNOWS IF WHAT I SEE HERE ACTUALLY EVEN TRULY EXISTS?
SURELY ANYTHING AS BYZANTINE AND COSMIC AS A FACET OF MY PERSONALITY COLLECTING COSMIC CONTAINMENT UNITS WOULD NOT HAVE ESCAPED HIS NOTICE.
ALL THAT REALLY MATTERS NOW IS FINDING ETERNITY AND SEEING WHAT HE CAN TELL ME ABOUT THE GODDESS...
YET HE MADE NO MENTION OF IT DURING OUR EARLIER ENCOUNTER.
...AND IF HE WILL ALLY HIMSELF WITH ME AGAINST HER.
BY THE STARS!

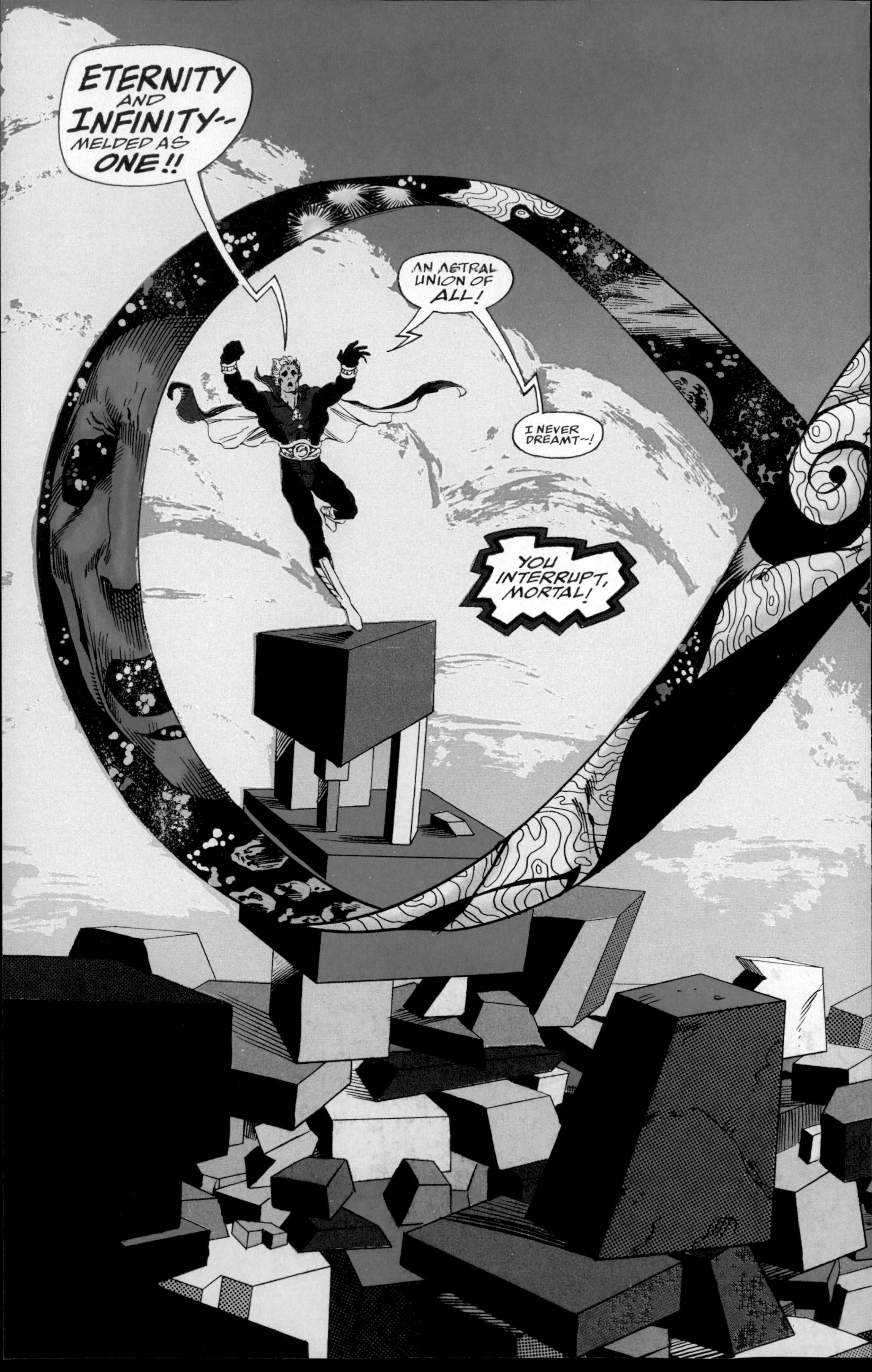
ETERNITY AND INFINITY-- MELDED AS ONE!!
AN ASTRAL UNION OF ALL!
I NEVER DREAMT--!
YOU INTERRUPT, MORTAL!

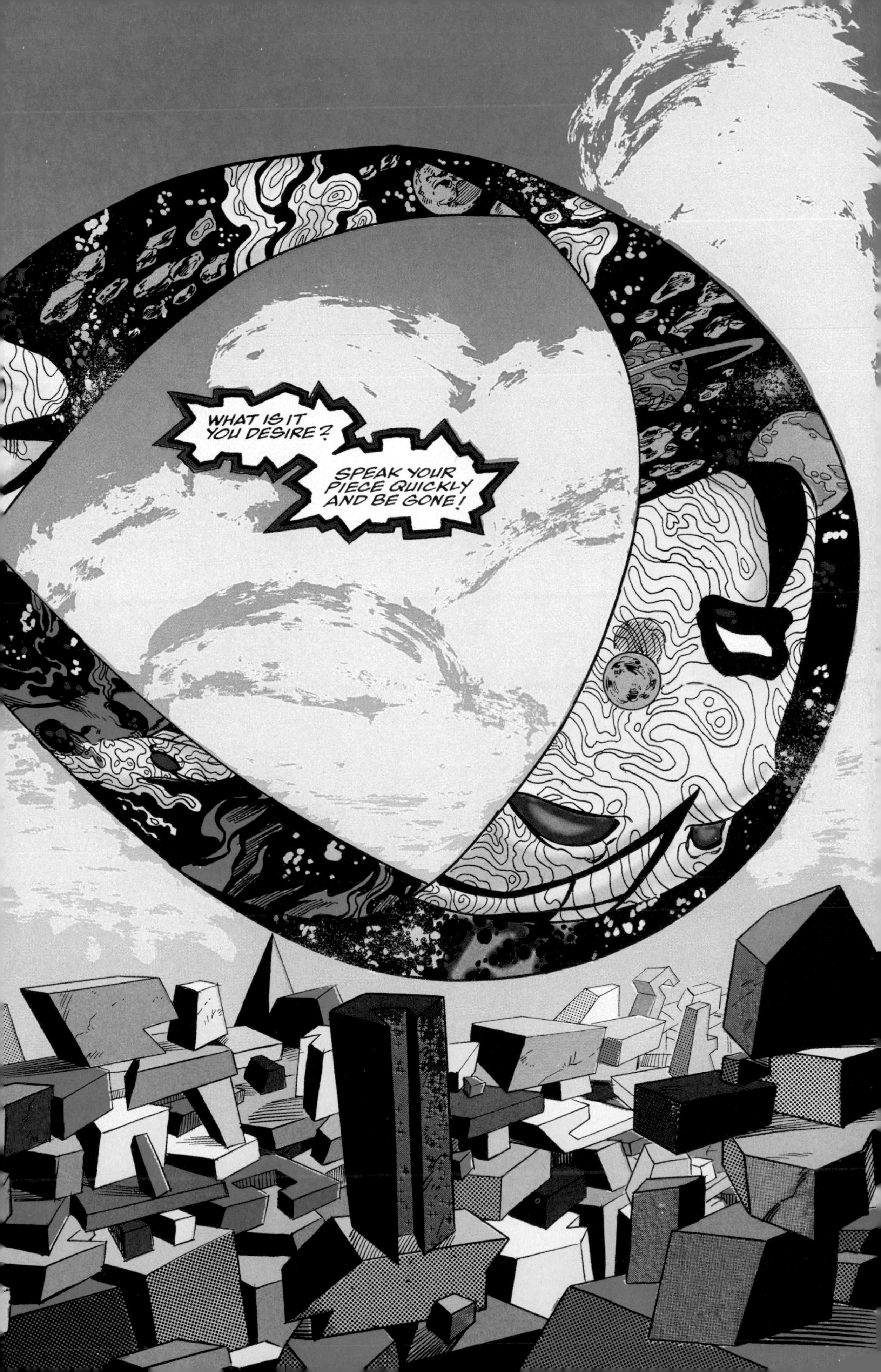
WHAT IS IT YOU DESIRE?
SPEAK YOUR PIECE QUICKLY AND BE GONE!

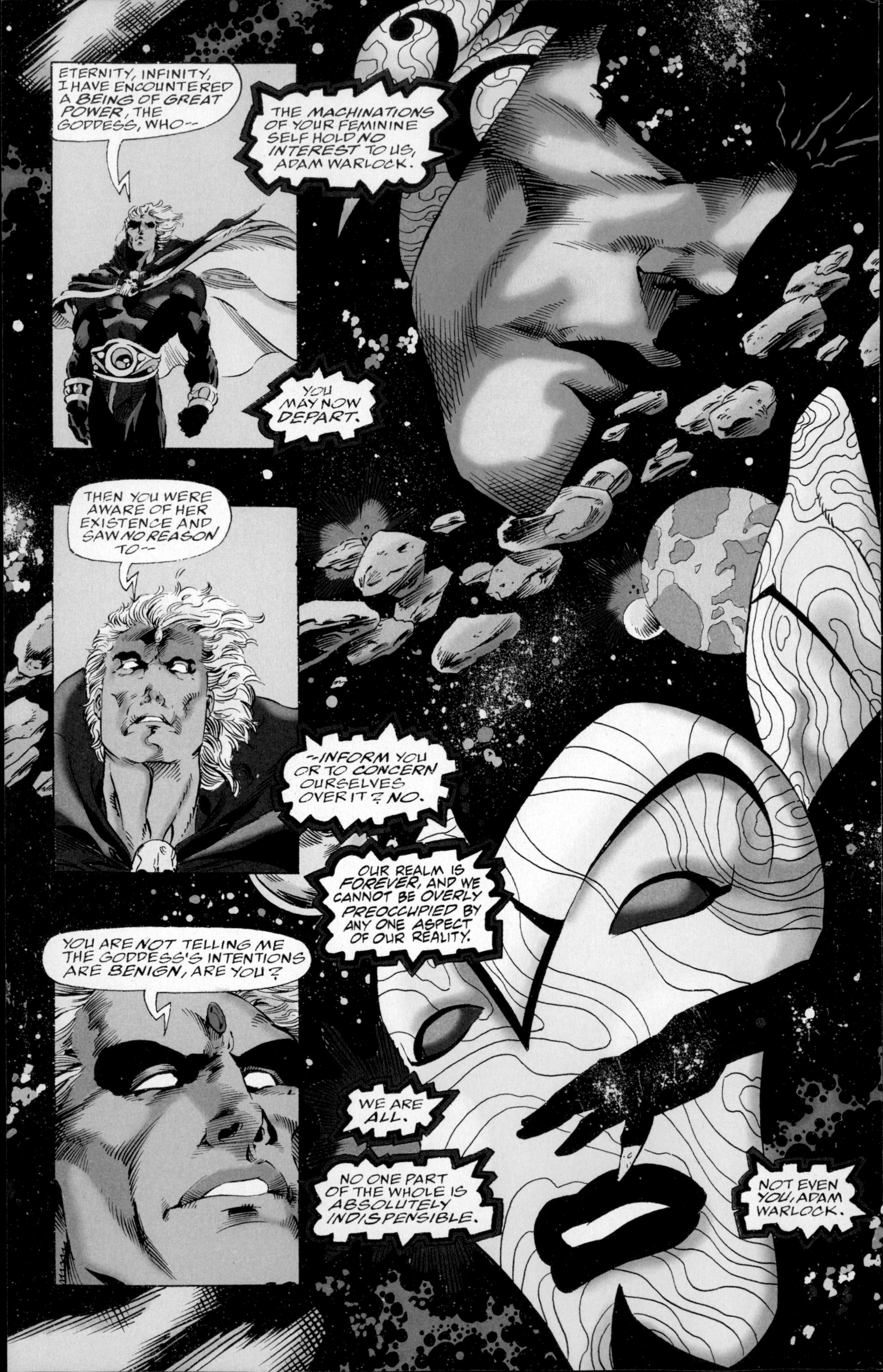
ETERNITY, INFINITY, I HAVE ENCOUNTERED A BEING OF GREAT POWER, THE GODDESS, WHO--
THE MACHINATIONS OF YOUR FEMININE SELF HOLD NO INTEREST TO US, ADAM WARLOCK.
YOU MAY NOW DEPART.
THEN YOU WERE AWARE OF HER EXISTENCE AND SAW NO REASON TO--
--INFORM YOU OR TO CONCERN OURSELVES OVER IT? NO.
OUR REALM IS FOREVER, AND WE CANNOT BE OVERLY PREOCCUPIED BY ANY ONE ASPECT OF OUR REALITY.
YOU ARE NOT TELLING ME THE GODDESS'S INTENTIONS ARE BENIGN, ARE YOU?
WE ARE ALL.
NO ONE PART OF THE WHOLE IS ABSOLUTELY INDISPENSIBLE.
NOT EVEN YOU, ADAM WARLOCK.

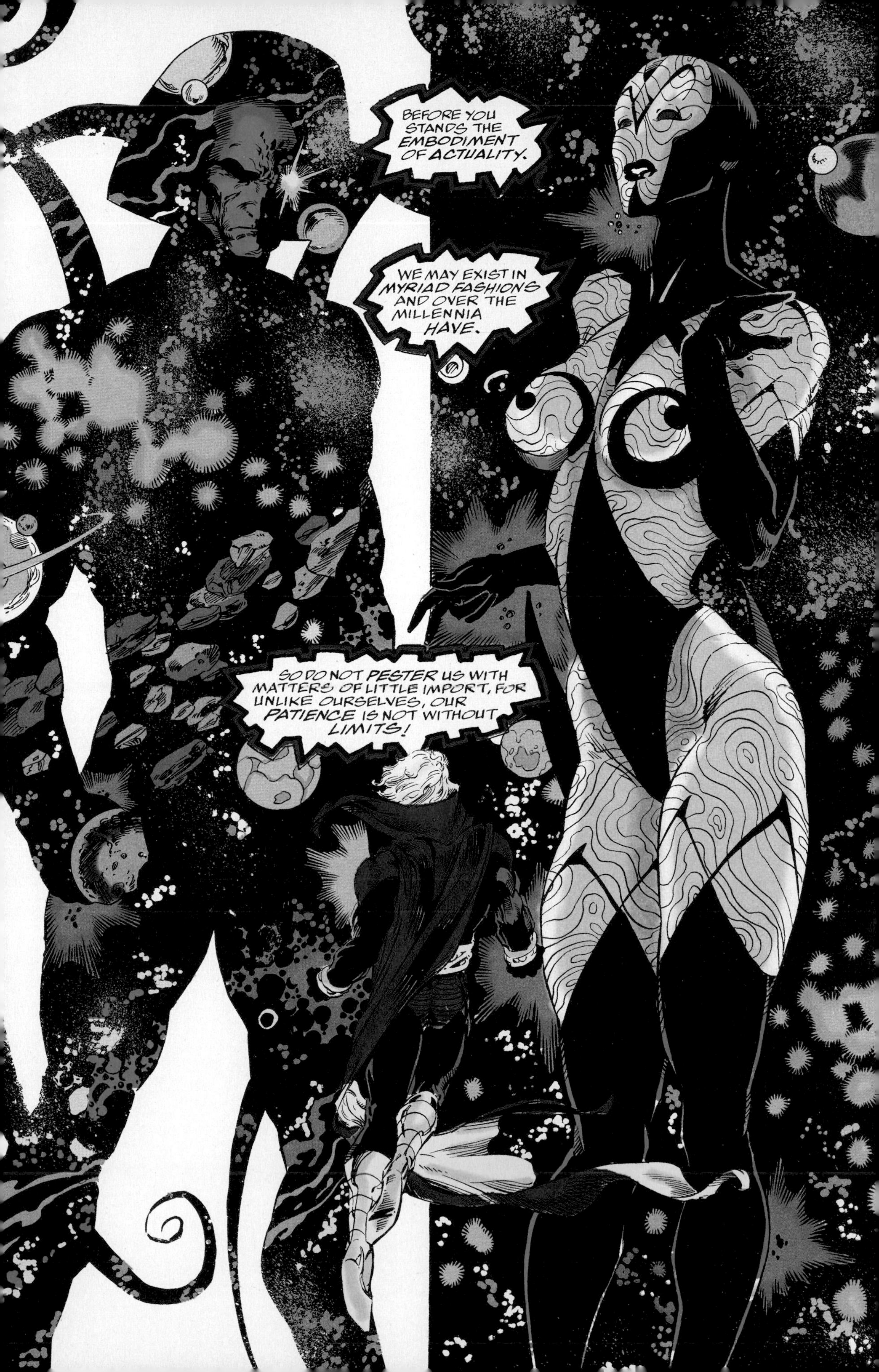
BEFORE YOU STANDS THE EMBODIMENT OF ACTUALITY.
WE MAY EXIST IN MYRIAD FASHIONS AND OVER THE MILLENNIA HAVE.
SO DO NOT PESTER US WITH MATTERS OF LITTLE IMPORT, FOR UNLIKE OURSELVES, OUR PATIENCE IS NOT WITHOUT LIMITS!

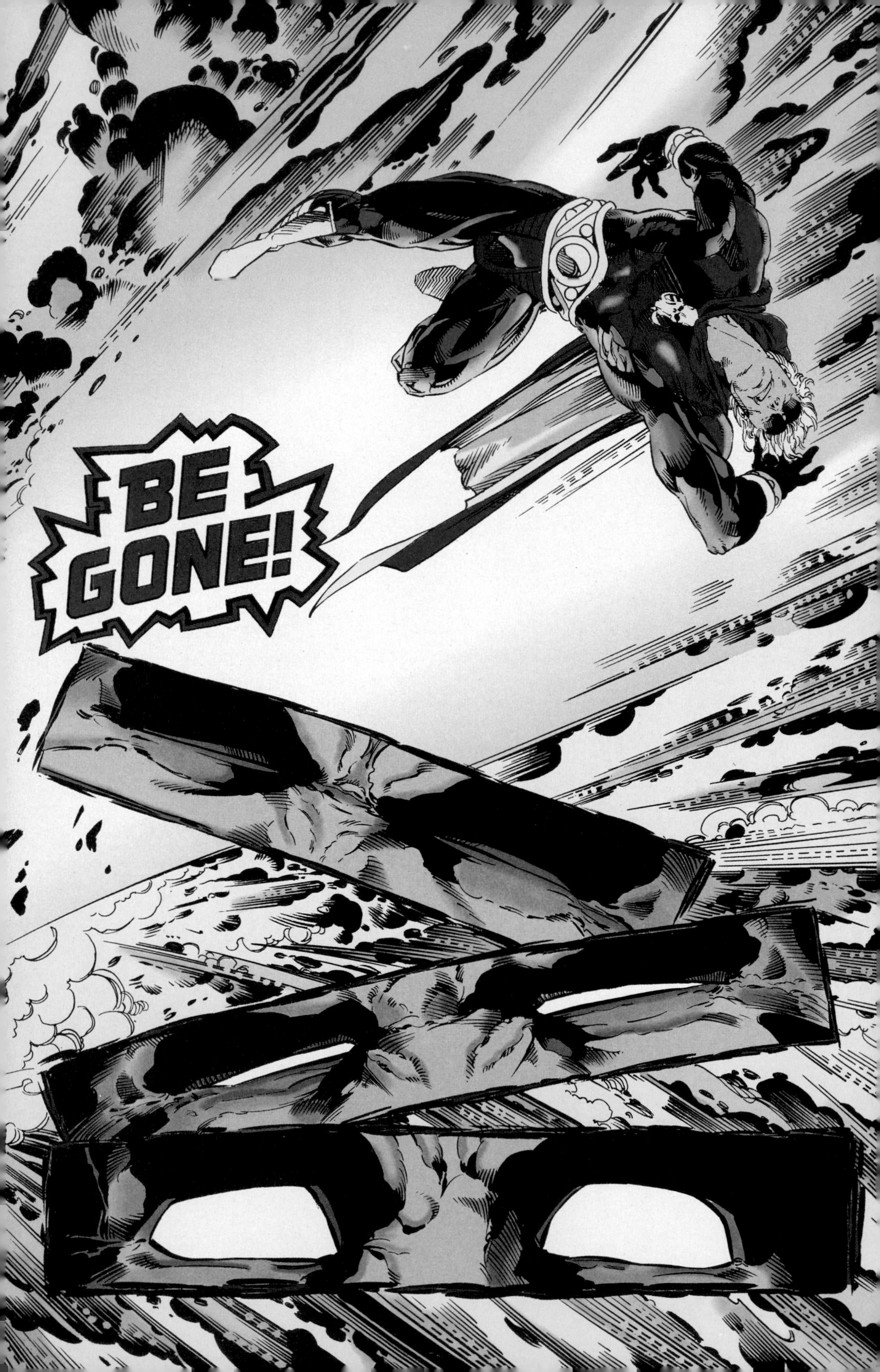
BE GONE!

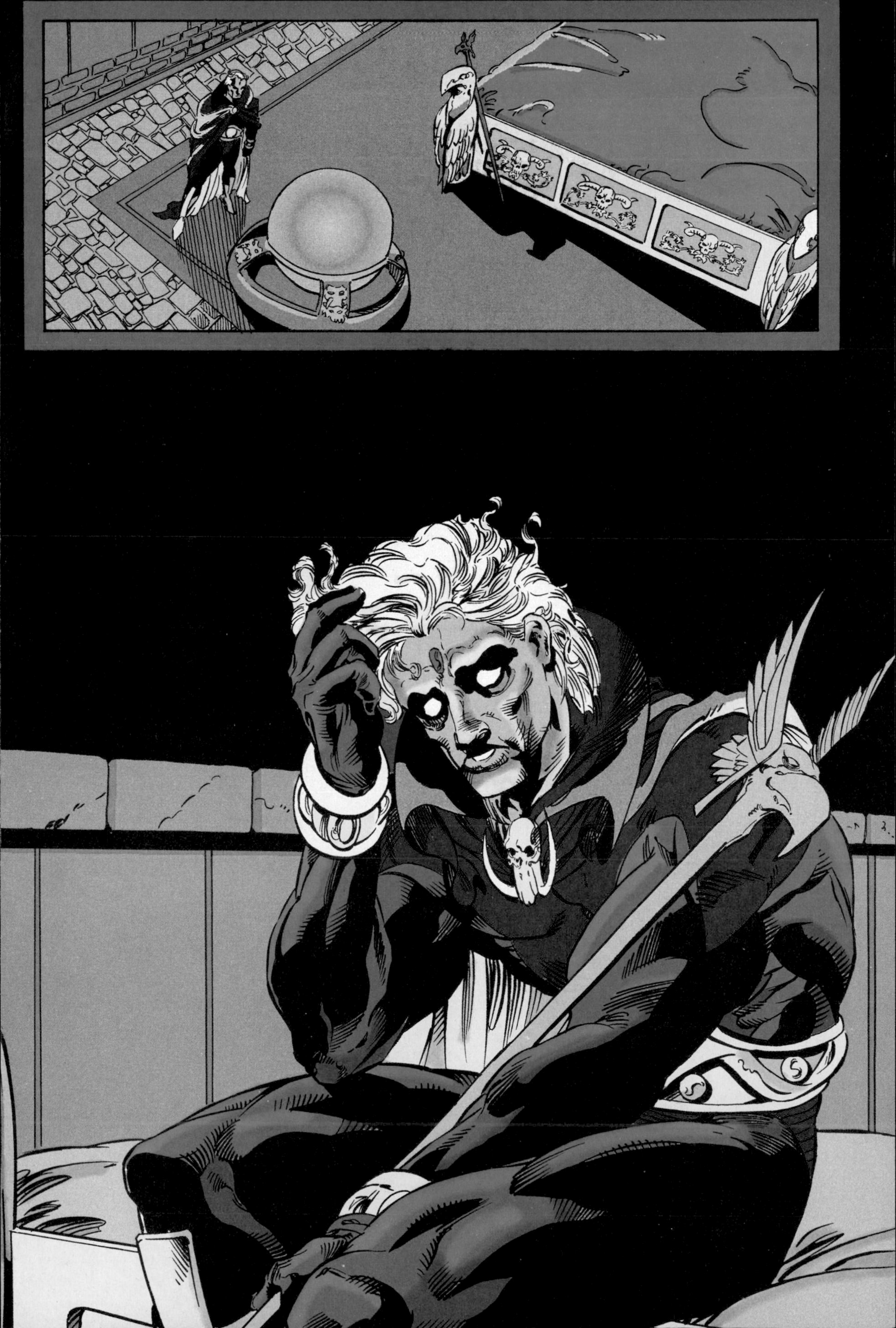

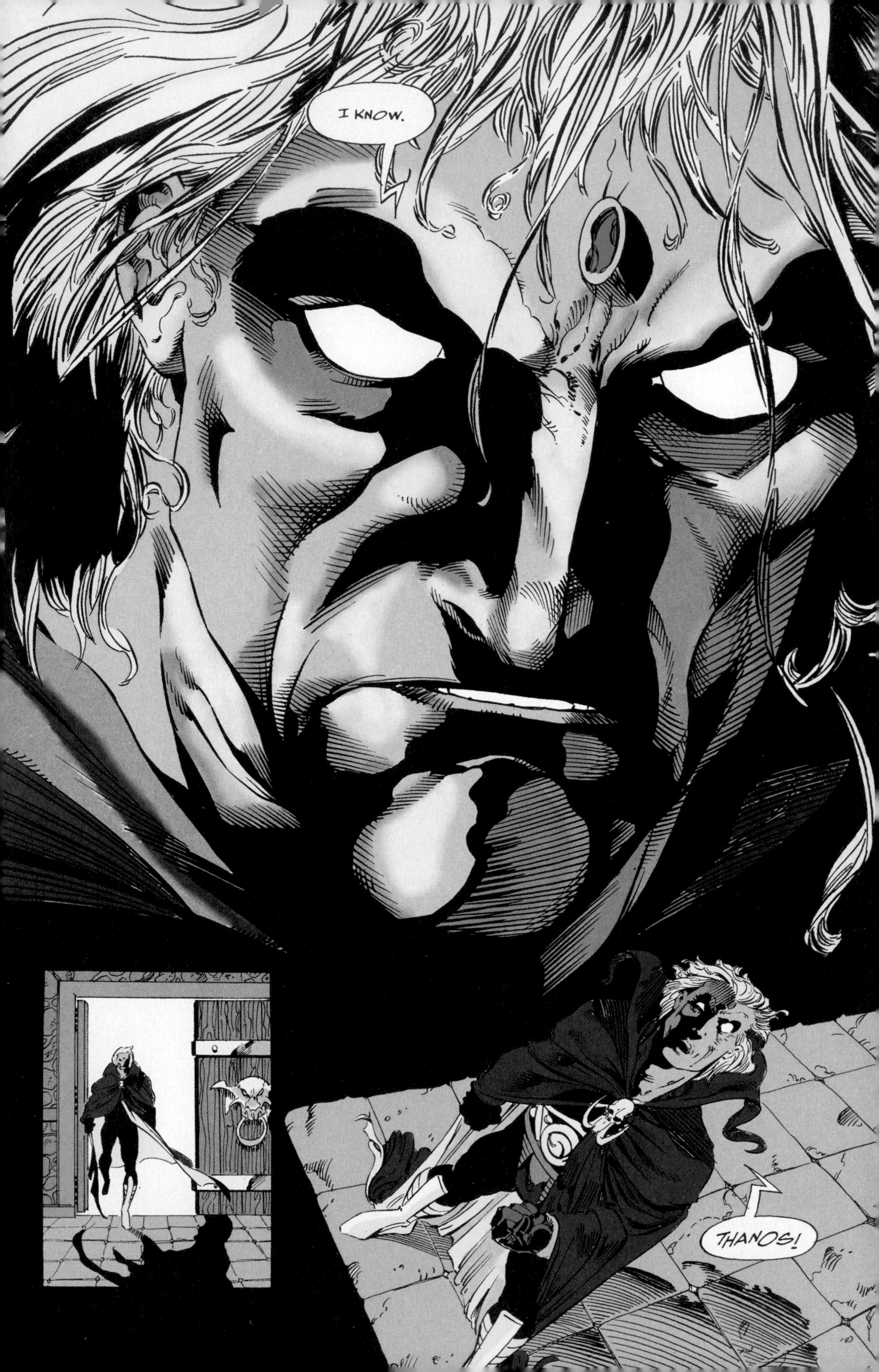
I KNOW.
THANOS!

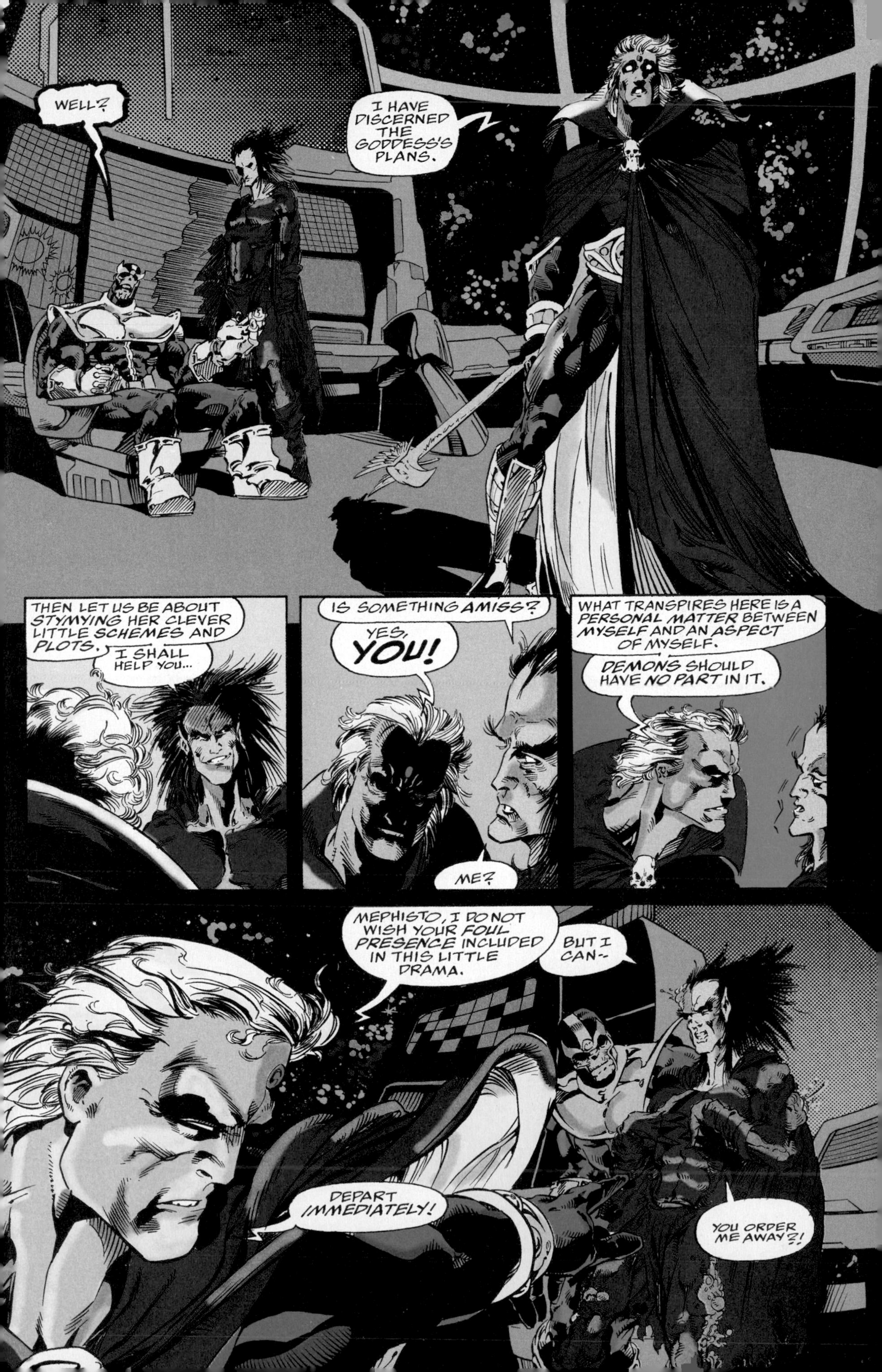
WELL?
I HAVE DISCERNED THE GODDESS'S PLANS.
THEN LET US BE ABOUT STYMYING HER CLEVER LITTLE SCHEMES AND PLOTS.
I SHALL HELP YOU...
IS SOMETHING AMISS?
YES, YOU!
ME?
WHAT TRANSPIRES HERE IS A PERSONAL MATTER BETWEEN MYSELF AND AN ASPECT OF MYSELF.
DEMONS SHOULD HAVE NO PART IN IT.
MEPHISTO, I DO NOT WISH YOUR FOUL PRESENCE INCLUDED IN THIS LITTLE DRAMA.
BUT I CAN--
DEPART IMMEDIATELY!
YOU ORDER ME AWAY?!

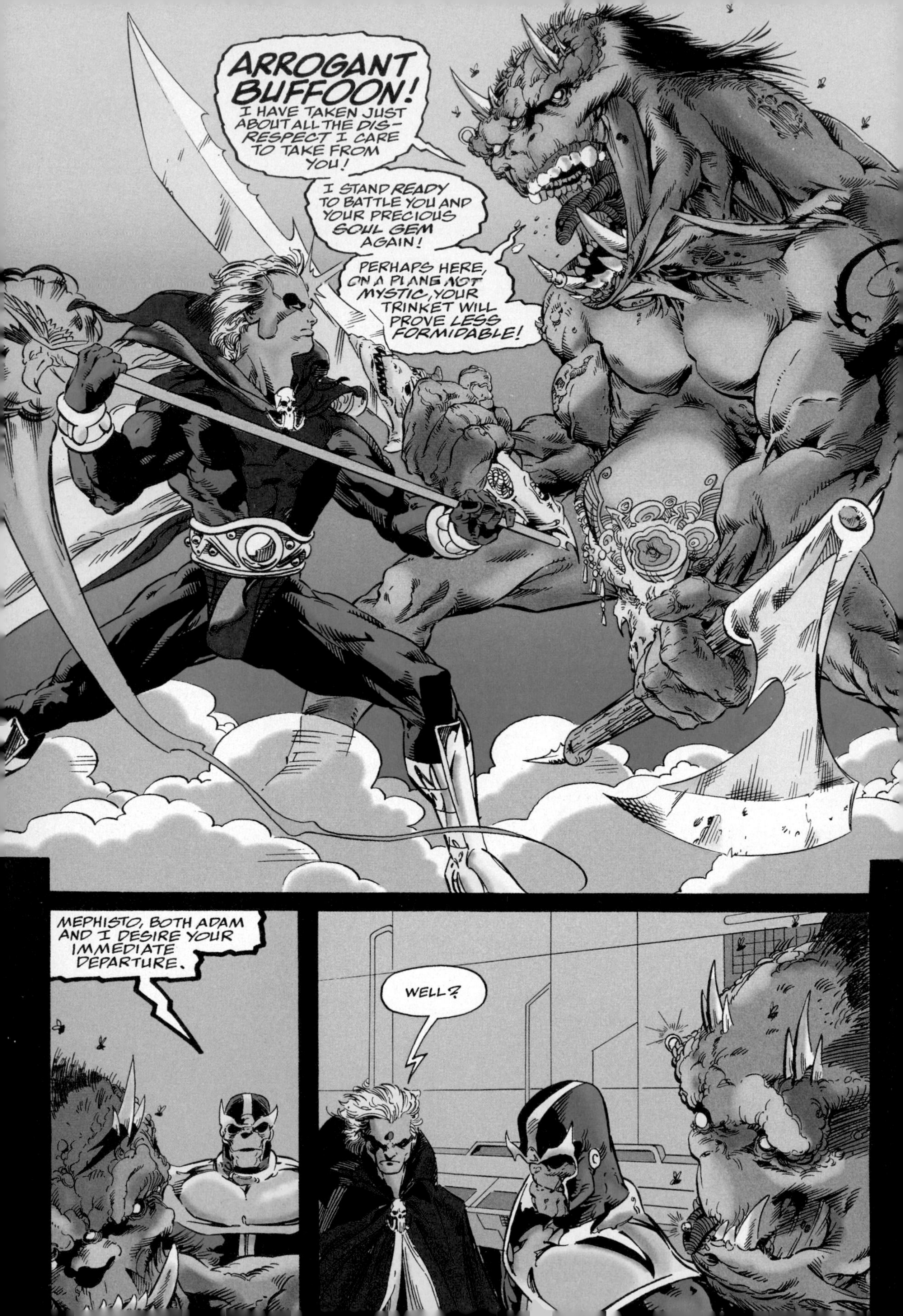
ARROGANT BUFFOON! I HAVE TAKEN JUST ABOUT ALL THE DIS-RESPECT I CARE TO TAKE FROM YOU!
I STAND READY TO BATTLE YOU AND YOUR PRECIOUS SOUL GEM AGAIN!
PERHAPS HERE, ON A PLANE NOT MYSTIC, YOUR TRINKET WILL PROVE LESS FORMIDABLE!
MEPHISTO, BOTH ADAM AND I DESIRE YOUR IMMEDIATE DEPARTURE.
WELL?

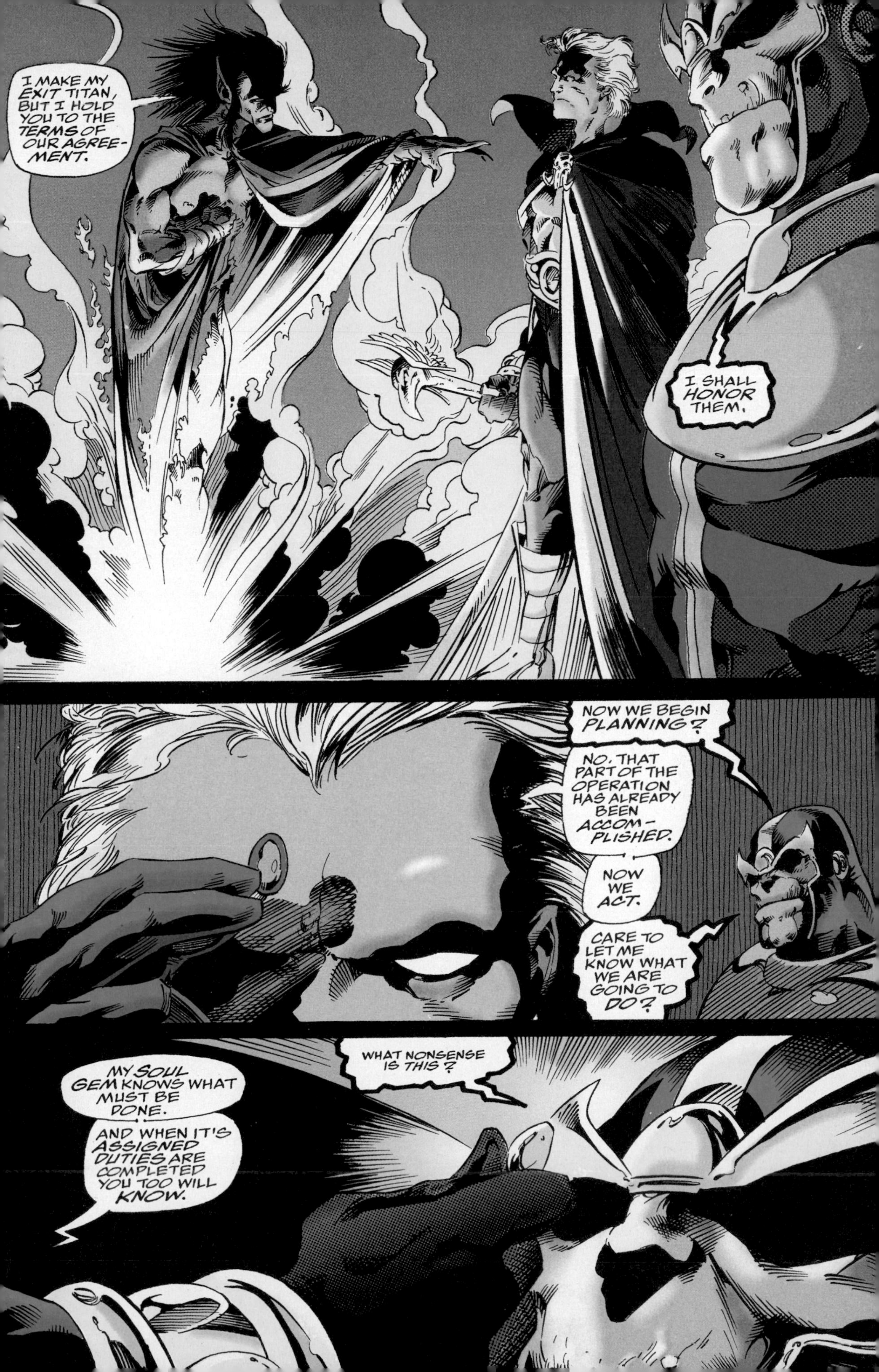
I MAKE MY EXIT TITAN, BUT I HOLD YOU TO THE TERMS OF OUR AGREE-MENT.
I SHALL HONOR THEM.
NOW WE BEGIN PLANNING?
NO. THAT PART OF THE OPERATION HAS ALREADY BEEN ACCOM-PLISHED.
NOW WE ACT.
CARE TO LET ME KNOW WHAT WE ARE GOING TO DO?
WHAT NONSENSE IS THIS?
MY SOUL GEM KNOWS WHAT MUST BE DONE.
AND WHEN IT'S ASSIGNED DUTIES ARE COMPLETED YOU TOO WILL KNOW.

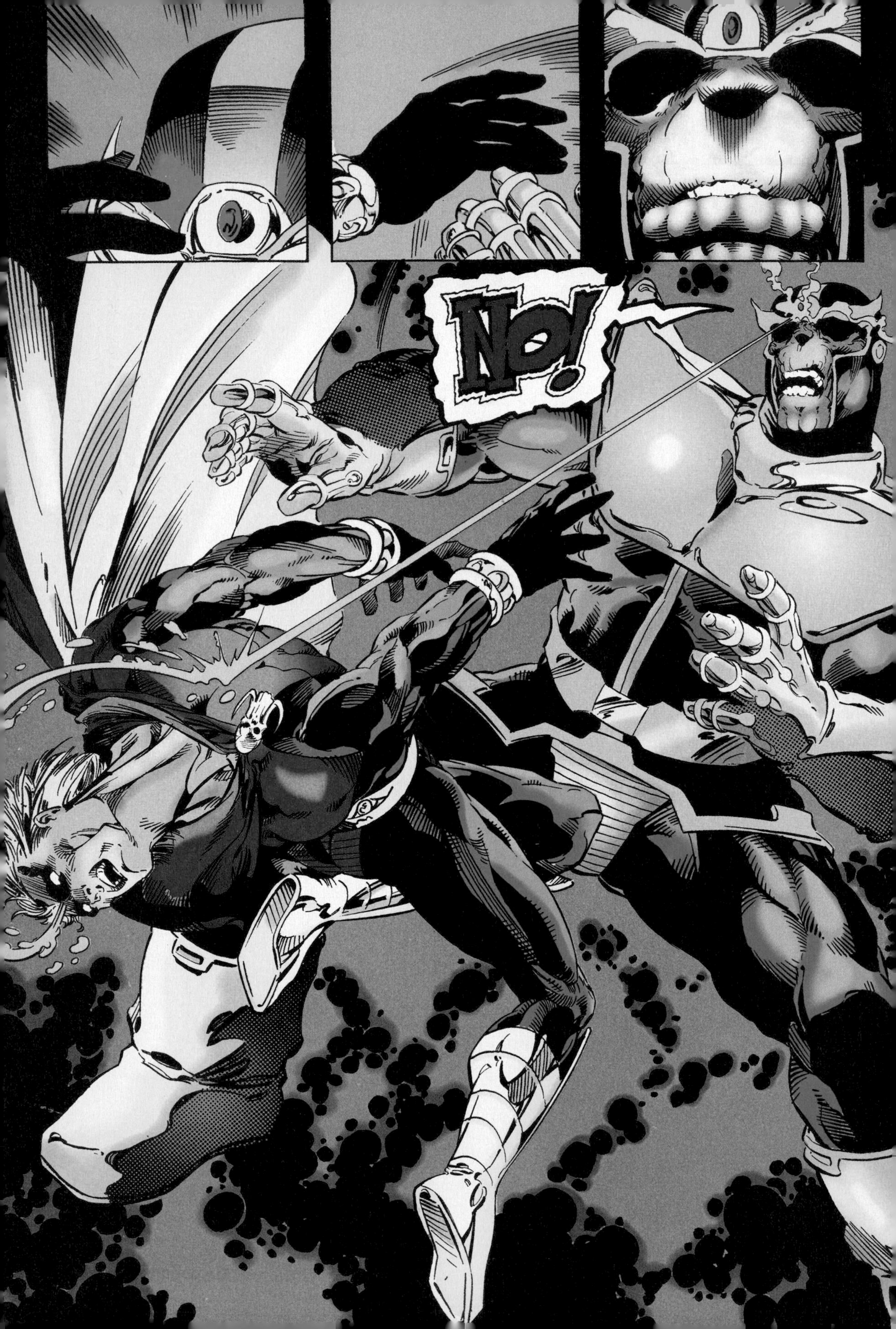
NO!

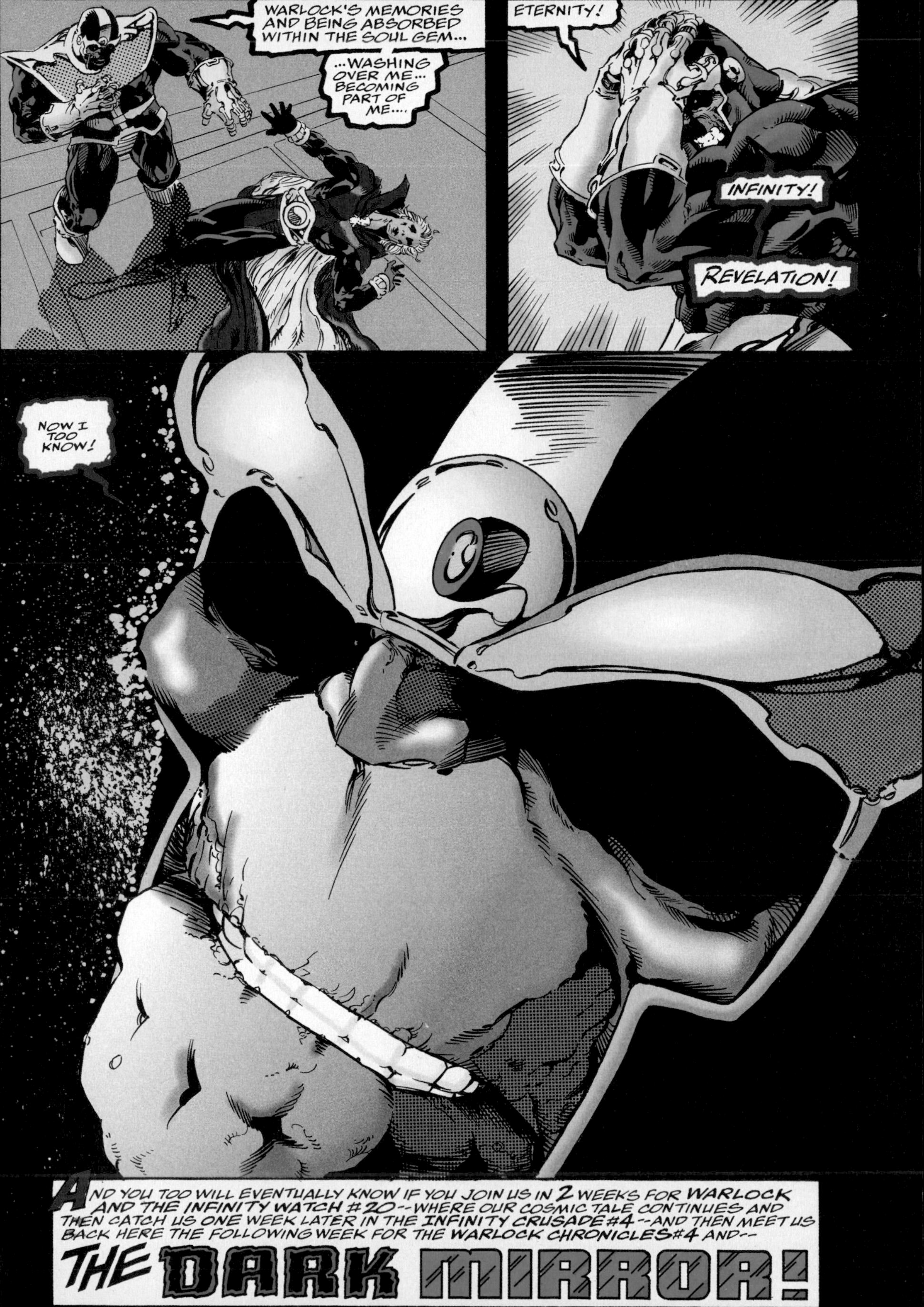

WARLOCK'S MEMORIES AND BEING ABSORBED WITHIN THE SOUL GEM...
...WASHING OVER ME... BECOMING PART OF ME....
ETERNITY!
INFINITY!
REVELATION!
NOW I TOO KNOW!
AND YOU TOO WILL EVENTUALLY KNOW IF YOU JOIN US IN 2 WEEKS FOR WARLOCK AND THE INFINITY WATCH #20--WHERE OUR COSMIC TALE CONTINUES AND THEN CATCH US ONE WEEK LATER IN THE INFINITY CRUSADE #4--AND THEN MEET US BACK HERE THE FOLLOWING WEEK FOR THE WARLOCK CHRONICLES #4 AND--
THE DARK MIRROR!